DEFEND

— THE —

VALLEY

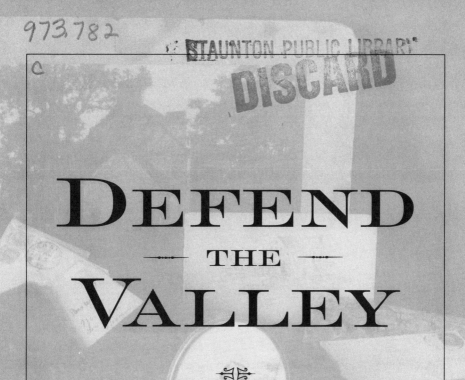

DEFEND
— THE —
VALLEY

A Shenandoah Family

in the Civil War

MARGARETTA BARTON COLT

ORION BOOKS • NEW YORK

For my family

Copyright © 1994 by Margaretta Barton Colt

Published by Orion Books, a division of Crown Publishers, Inc., 201 East 50th Street, New York, New York 10022. Member of the Crown Publishing Group.

Random House, Inc. New York, Toronto, London, Sydney, Auckland

ORION and colophon are trademarks of Crown Publishers, Inc.

Manufactured in the United States of America

Design by Cynthia Dunne

Library of Congress Cataloging-in-Publication Data
Colt, Margaretta Barton.
    Defend the valley : A Shenandoah family in the civil war / by Margaretta Barton
        Colt.—1st ed.
            p.   cm.
    Includes bibliographical references and index.
    1. Shenandoah River Valley (Va. and W. Va.)—History—Civil War, 1861–1865.
2. Barton family. 3. Jones family. 4. Winchester (Va.)—Biography.   I. Title.
F232.S5C63   1994
975.5'99103'0922—dc20
[B]   93-31529
                                                                                                          CIP

ISBN 0-517-59315-7
10 9 8 7 6 5 4 3 2 1
First Edition

Contents

Acknowledgments

This book would not exist without the generous and enthusiastic participation of Louise Barroll Barton, Eleanor Jackson Burleson, Edith Barton Sheerin, and Colin J. S. Thomas, Jr., who readily made available to me the numerous family documents in their possession, and offered their hospitality and friendship.

Louise Barroll Barton (Mrs. C. Marshall Barton, Jr.) provided the most important collection of letters and photographs and suggested leads toward others.

Ann Dudley Field Lalley made me aware of her grandfather Robert T. Barton's journals and gave me access to her cousins and her pictures.

Edith Barton Sheerin joined in the discovery process as new caches of family papers and artifacts came under her purview. She and her brother, the late Robert T. Barton III, gave early encouragement, and turned over their grandfather's rediscovered journals for my study.

Frances Whittle Jones has given me the benefit of her wisdom, perspective, and precise memory.

Colin J. S. Thomas, Jr. enlightened me on the role and practice of a nineteenth-century Virginia lawyer.

Elizabeth Crawford Engle became a friend through her old and my new love of Frederick County's history, and forwarded new clues as she came upon them.

Betty H. Stewart made me welcome at Springdale many times and provided me with Susan Davis Conrad's memoir, which was given to her by Louisa M. Crawford.

Catherine Seaman and Perkins Flippen helped identify Pharselia.

Randolph Barton III gave me his research assistance and his companionship.

Many other hitherto unknown cousins have offered their interest, encouragement, and concrete leads and suggestions. I would particularly like to thank Jane Catlett Ballard, Ann L. Barton Brown and Stuart E. Brown, Jr., Lucy C. Davis, T. Marshall Duer, Jr., Christopher Harrison, John T. Harrison, Jr., Bolling W. Haxall, C. Maury Jones, Jr., Jeffrey Brackett Potter, Trevor Potter, Charles W. Sheerin, Jr., Mary Taliaferro Steck, and Elizabeth C. Teviotdale.

The Handley Library Archives, Winchester, which include the collections of the Winchester-Frederick County Historical Society, have been of inestimable value; Rebecca Ebert's years of helpful guidance, research efforts, and faithful responses is deeply appreciated. I would also like to thank Eloise Strader, Elaine Walker Hall, and Robert K. Woltz of the historical society, and Cissy Shull, for arranging for me to work with the manuscript of Mary Greenhow Lee's diary; and Marianne L. Roos and Ben Ritter of the Handley Library. Diane B. Jacob, Archives, Virginia Military Institute, was another important and reliable source.

Additionally I am grateful to Gary W. Gallagher, Pennsylvania State University, for his belief and encouragement; Robert K. Krick, Fredericksburg and Spotsylvania National Military Park, for his prompt and full answers to both military and civilian questions; Stephen W. Sears for his advice and example; and Thomas W. Broadfoot for his early interest and help.

I am also indebted to the following people and institutions for their patience and thoroughness in answering a wide variety of questions:

Appomattox Court House National Military Park: Ron Wilson

Bar Association of Baltimore City: James F. Schneider

County Clerk's offices of Albemarle, Augusta, Fauquier, and Nelson counties

Enoch Pratt Free Library, Baltimore: Wesley L. Wilson, Jeff Korman, Maryland Room

Episcopal High School, Alexandria: Robert G. Watkin, Mary Kate Davis

Episcopal Diocese of Maryland, Archives: F. Garner Ranney

Fauquier County Historical Society: Mrs. L. G. Gold

Fort Delaware Society: Jocelyn Jamison

Frederick County Court House, Winchester, County Clerk's office

Historical Society of Frederick County, Frederick, Maryland: William G. Willman

Maryland State Archives, Annapolis: Kevin Swenson

Mt. Hebron Cemetery, Winchester: Linda M. Shade, Charlotte Kackley

Museum of the Confederacy, Richmond: Guy R. Swanson, Rebecca Ansell, Corinne Hudgins

National Archives and Records Service: William E. Lind, Michael Musick, Cindi Fox, Andrew L. Dyer, Military Reference Branch

New York Public Library: Robert Scott, Genealogy and Local History Room

New Market Battlefield Park: Frances Gerow

Trinity Episcopal Church, Staunton: Dorothy B. Stilley

U.S. Military History Research Collection, Carlisle Barracks, Pennsylvania: Michael J. Winey

University of Maryland: Richard J. Behles, Health Services Library

University of Virginia: Jeanne C. Pardee, Archives, Alderman Library

Virginia Historical Society: Janet Schwarz, Elizabeth M. Gushee

Valentine Museum, Richmond

Virginia State Library and Archives: Robert Clay, Mark Scala

Many others offered substantive help and suggestions. The following made unique and substantial contributions: Lionel Leventhal, Jeffrey Simpson, John Schwartz, and David Liebman. Also: Dr. A. J. Bollet, Fitzhugh Elder, John A. Hedrick, Ross Kimmel, and David Mark.

My colleagues at The Military Bookman, especially Jason Duberman, offered helpful leads, shared my excitement, and tolerated my aberrations and preoccupation. My agent, Julian Bach, believed in the project, and Peter St. John Ginna of Orion Books helped me find the book in the manuscript.

I especially wish to acknowledge the help of the late Michael A. Mullins, who was a moving force at many stages of this project. His encouragement, enthusiasm, lively interest, and ready research answers will always be remembered.

My thanks to my parents in this as in all else: Randolph Barton's family pictures and references, and his own memories of his grandfather and namesake were valuable, as was Ruth Dare Barton's discerning eye. I cannot quantify the contributions of my husband, Harris S. Colt, who provided sustained and sustaining belief, unstinting interest, military research, editorial aid, and cheerful tolerance of the disarrangement of our life.

Preface

My grandfather, as excited as I had ever seen him, arrived with a package of slim books one day when I was about ten. The books were copies of his father Randolph Barton's Civil War *Recollections,* and their arrival provided my first inkling of those who came before my beloved grandparents. Growing up in Delaware, I knew little of the war and when I asked grandparents to "sit and talk"—which meant I wanted to listen—it was more likely to be stories of their own experiences. My grandfather, Charles Marshall Barton, was fond of talking about his travels, confining his Civil War remarks to a few phrases such as his father's being one of "six brothers in the Confederate Army," a few stories about his grandmother, known as Funny Fannie, and references to his grandfather David W. Barton, an eminent lawyer who had "lost everything in the war." Never heard anything about any sisters, as my father was later to say.

By the time Granddad died, some thirteen years later, I had read his father's book at least once. So when from his desk came an ancient photograph, labelled Springdale, I knew what it was—the Barton family's home of several generations. The image—of a handsome porticoed stone house, people carefully disposed upon the porch and grass—had deteriorated in such a way that the house appeared to be emerging, like *Brigadoon,* from the mists of time. It gave shape to and enhanced the family legend, evoking an almost mythic, lost world that had no ties to present reality or geography.

But of course I knew that the Barton family had lived in Virginia, in Winchester, somewhere in the Shenandoah Valley. Perhaps ten years later, an

Some of the Barton family at Springdale in July 1873, shortly before the house was sold. Bolling Barton is seated on the ground at left, with nephew Stuart Baldwin at his right. Randolph Barton is in front of the porch column. Their wives, Ella and Agnes, and nieces, Fan and Madge Marshall, are with Mrs. David W. Barton on the porch. At right is "Uncle Isaac, former slave." (Randolph Barton)

aimless Sunday in Washington, a beautiful October day, and a borrowed Volkswagen took me over the Blue Ridge to the lovely, tranquil old town. Pleasant, wandering sightseeing, with no particular goal; but my browsing over the map discovered a pinpoint called Bartonsville south of town on the Valley Turnpike. Well, I thought, that must mean something, and decided to have a look. In the golden light of late afternoon, where the road drops down to the Opequon Creek, I came to a tatty bus shelter, not even a "wide place in the road," marked BARTONSVILLE, and pulled over to get the feel of it. I turned my head to survey the scene, and there across the road—the myth, in sturdy limestone reality— Springdale! I was too astonished to cross the road and knock on the door. Perhaps fifteen years elapsed before I passed that way again.

By then I had embarked on the modest project of reprinting the little privately printed book Granddad had been so excited about: his father's very personal reminiscence of his four years of service with the Stonewall Brigade, a tale of many battles, wounds recuperated from in hospitable houses (always with lovely young ladies in attendance), encounters with Jackson and Lee, a few daring deeds, and some narrow escapes. It did not say much about his large family, even his soldier brothers, and certainly not much about any sisters, but by then I knew there had been four. What had happened to all of them in the war, when Winchester was repeatedly in the midst of the action?

I was determined, too, to have a try at finding the two wartime *carte de visite* photos of Randolph Barton which were reproduced in the original book. (These little novelty photos, so popular with soldiers on both sides, measure only about two and a half by four inches—easy to lose in the shuffle of several generations, no matter how reverential.) It did not seem likely that other evidence might exist, aside from a somewhat suspect body of "family legend."

To begin, I wrote to Randolph Barton's descendants in Baltimore. The first heard from was my aunt Louise Barton who knew nothing about the photos, but told me that a cache of family letters had been found in my uncle's desk. They appeared to be of Civil War vintage, and the first one she read was from Mrs. Robert E. Lee, "regretting she couldn't come to the wedding." This was beyond anything I might have imagined. A few weeks later she called again to say that a cousin Dudley Lalley wanted to talk to me about publishing the mem-oir of *her* grandfather, Robert Barton, Randolph's next older brother. Having already read Robert's stirring account of his first battle, I knew how well he wrote. I went to Baltimore to see Dudley and Louise, and collected what they so generously and unhesitatingly offered—from Louise over seventy letters of the war period and some old photos, and from Dudley the transcript of her grandfather's journal. Robert's memoir recounted how the family at home had endured enemy occupation, privation, and disease—a story I could only have hoped to reconstruct in its general outlines.

Elated by these discoveries, I was compelled to keep looking for more. A be-nign network carried me along a chain of family connections to other unheard-of cousins and other groups of documents. Links and friendships were established in the present which reflected the closer bonds of earlier generations.

Not all my introductions were proper Southern ones, nor were all my research methods the standard historical ones; some entailed virtual detective work, and others came from sheer serendipity and luck.

As I immersed myself in the documents, my perspective about the family and their story broadened as their closeness—geographical, social, and emo-tional—became apparent. It was a prominent, well-to-do, and numerous fam-ily. When war came, the six Barton brothers, brother-in-law Tom Marshall, uncles Frank and Bev Jones, and three cousins saw active service, most in the legendary Stonewall Brigade. The sum of writers grew until I had testimony from nine of the ten young Bartons, both parents, Grandmother Jones, three aunts and uncles, a brother-in-law, three of the Bartons' grandchildren, a couple of cousins, and two slaves. In addition to the two memoirs, two battle accounts, and a wartime diary, there were well over 200 letters by family members. The most vital documents were the letters, which dovetailed so that I was able to trace the family through the war years. As I had been caught up in the momentum of the hunt for documents, the search for their significance drove me on. I was moved by an insatiable curiosity and a sense of responsibility to people whose lives it might be possible to reconstruct. It was wonderful to turn up a new trove which shed light on testimony found months before, and thrilling to see an image of a person whose words I was familiar with. Sometimes a startling resemblance to the living or the dead leapt out of a daguerreotype. My growing knowledge of the context of the letters increased my understanding of how this family's relationships were woven into the dense fabric of the community.

After a while, I became so saturated with the writers' words and stories as to feel almost possessed by them. It seemed as if they roused me at night, and at those strange times or even on waking some mornings, connections and pieces of the puzzles came together felicitously and naturally, as they did not do in daylight hours. New people came into focus through their own distinctive words. Some characters came across the years vividly in their own writing and as portrayed by others: assertive Mat; brother David, serious and humorous; Robert, dependable and sensitive; the loving and perceptive grandmother; the wisdom and forbearance of David Barton expressed in the measured cadence of his language; the flightiness and wit of Funny Fannie; Rannie, optimistic, perhaps headstrong, fearless, a bit brash; sister Fan, sweet and playful; Strother's wit, a certain flair, and elegant penmanship. Other characters frustrated my attempts to know them better; they remain shadowy and mysterious, their personalities muffled, their paths all but obliterated.

For a while it seemed that almost no one remained in Winchester to help me chart my course. It was strange and a bit poignant that a family which had had such a presence there in the not too distant past had gone completely. All that remained of these firm fixtures of the community were a few passing references in local lore, some of which were as factually shaky as the family legend. Eventually I was to meet, through an author's query in the *New York Times,* the last of the family still living in Winchester. This was the beginning of a precious friendship, only part of which was the exchange of information, speculation, and gossip on generations past. Miss Frances Jones, as old as this century, is a primary source. She had known Randolph, Robert, and others who figured in the story.

My explorations became geographical as well as archival and genealogical. Someone resident for thirty years in New York does not expect to visit her own physical past, let alone that of her ancestors. But gradually, and long after the almost miraculous apparition of Springdale, I came to realize that the past could be found—and became bold and occasionally downright brazen—in looking for it. In some of these quests I was fortunate to have the company and guidance of Miss Frances Jones, and Mrs. Elizabeth Engle, a local historian whose grandparents were Barton neighbors. With them, I drove around Winchester and the northern Valley, looking for old houses, farms, and places I might not have learned of otherwise, such as Robert's escape route from occupied Winchester through a hidden valley in the Massanutten Mountain.

Many buildings, roads, and even battlefields in this story retain much of their nineteenth-century aspect. But some of my discoveries were tinged with melancholy—family graveyards choked and disarranged by weeds or used as trash dumps; the standing ruin of Frank Jones's cherished home, alone on its lovely hillside. The Bartons' Winchester house was demolished over forty years ago. At the Joneses' deserted Vaucluse, once famous for its fabulous spring and its hillside garden, Grandmother Jones's beloved flowers are long since overgrown in a tangle of brush, and the weedy marsh, once a lake, is fed by a spring whose waters are now, it is said, polluted by pesticides. On the Winchester battlefields, the search for troop positions is often in the midst of housing developments. The Kernstown battlefield is traversed by a bypass, from which at present one can at least see the terrain. Industrial "parks" threaten to overwhelm Cedar Creek, the remaining visible battlefield in the county. Even now, Winchester's late-twentieth-century sprawl of car dealerships and malls is about to encroach on Springdale. Springdale, right on the Pike, has been embattled before. It was constantly in the line of advances and retreats, with soldiers dying on the lawn and Yankees riding up on the porch, searching it for Rebels, or using it as headquarters, snipers taking position under the lilacs. Its present beauty and tranquility belie the devastation of the war years. Opequon Creek, scene of camp fires along its banks and soldiers washing in its waters, flows on beside the house.

Springdale in particular is a silent witness to this story, but luck and circumstances have provided human narrators. The rich testimony of Randolph Barton's book became only a piece of a still incomplete mosaic. I wanted to tell this family's story, but the writers have done it for themselves; all they needed was exposure. Their words are, for the most part, simple and unassuming. In their straightforward language there is eloquence and beauty, humor, a sense of their values, responsibilities to each other and themselves, and the obligations that came with privilege. When they suffered and lost so much and so many, they took strength from their family ties, their religion, and their sure sense of themselves.

It is highly unusual to find a family's chronicle of a crucial period in their own words. It is a story that parallels that of many families in this time and place—families who gave a full measure of devotion and, through our cruelest war, endured, survived, and started again.

THE BARTON AND JONES FAMILY

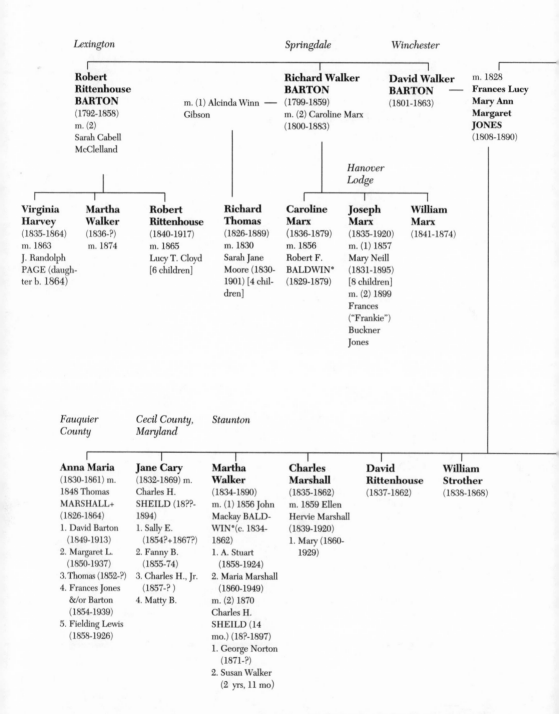

Lexington

Springdale *Winchester*

Robert Rittenhouse BARTON (1792-1858) m. (2) Sarah Cabell McClelland

m. (1) Alcinda Winn Gibson

Richard Walker BARTON (1799-1859) m. (2) Caroline Marx (1800-1883)

David Walker BARTON (1801-1863)

m. 1828 — **Frances Lucy Mary Ann Margaret JONES** (1808-1890)

Hanover Lodge

Virginia Harvey (1835-1864) m. 1863 J. Randolph PAGE (daughter b. 1864)

Martha Walker (1836-?) m. 1874

Robert Rittenhouse (1840-1917) m. 1865 Lucy T. Cloyd [6 children]

Richard Thomas (1826-1889) m. 1830 Sarah Jane Moore (1830-1901) [4 children]

Caroline Marx (1836-1879) m. 1856 Robert F. BALDWIN° (1829-1879)

Joseph Marx (1835-1920) m. (1) 1857 Mary Neill (1831-1895) [8 children] m. (2) 1899 Frances ("Frankie") Buckner Jones

William Marx (1841-1874)

Fauquier County *Cecil County, Maryland* *Staunton*

Anna Maria (1830-1861) m. 1848 Thomas MARSHALL+ (1826-1864)
1. David Barton (1849-1913)
2. Margaret L. (1850-1937)
3. Thomas (1852-?)
4. Frances Jones &/or Barton (1854-1939)
5. Fielding Lewis (1858-1926)

Jane Cary (1832-1869) m. Charles H. SHEILD (18??-1894)
1. Sally E. (1854?+1867?)
2. Fanny B. (1855-74)
3. Charles H., Jr. (1857-?)
4. Matty B.

Martha Walker (1834-1890) m. (1) 1856 John Mackay BALDWIN° (c. 1834-1862)
1. A. Stuart (1858-1924)
2. Maria Marshall (1860-1949)
m. (2) 1870 Charles H. SHEILD (14 mo.) (18?-1897)
1. George Norton (1871-?)
2. Susan Walker (2 yrs, 11 mo)

Charles Marshall (1835-1862) m. 1859 Ellen Hervie Marshall (1839-1920)
1. Mary (1860-1929)

David Rittenhouse (1837-1862)

William Strother (1838-1868)

°Brothers: Robert F., John M., Cornelius Baldwin

Vaucluse

m. (1) 1806 **Anna Maria Marshall** (1783-1823) — **William Strother JONES** (1783-1845) — m. (2) 1825 **Ann Cary Randolph** (1794-1877)

Fauquier County

James Fitzgerald JONES
(1820-1866)
m. 1845 Anna (Nannie) Marshall+ (1823-1880)
[7 children]

Charles Marshall JONES
(1806-1847)
m. 1838 Theresa Stringer
1. Anna Marshall (1841-1867) m. Cornelius BALDWIN°(1840-1916)
   1. Marshall (1867-?)
   2. Charles Marshall (1843-1893)

William Strother JONES
(1817-1893)
m. (2) 1850 Mary Eliza Barton (1823-1868)
1. Thomas Barton (1851-1929)
2. & 3. Names unknown
4. Ann Cary R. (1854-1902)
5. Francis Howard (1856-1906)
6. William Strother (1857-1925)
7. & 8. Frederick B. & twin (1860-1921)
9. Susan Catherine (1861-1931)
10. Charles Marshall Barton (1863-1884)
11. girl (1868)
(#s 2, 3, 8, 11 all lived less than a month)

Francis Buckner JONES
(1826-1862)
m. 1853 Susan Peyton Clark (1828-1907)
1. Louisa Peyton (1855-1939)
2. William Randolph (1857-1927)
3. Ann Cary R. (1860-1944)
4. Frances B. "Frankie" (1862-1940)

Beverley Randolph JONES
(1832-1912)
m. 1854 Rebecca "Bec" Tidball (1834?-
1. Lucy Bolling (1855-1939)
2. Alexander T. (1857-1928)
3. Ann Cary R. (1859-1907)
4. Edward McG. (1861-1927)
5. Elizabeth H. (1869-1947)
6. Susan M. (1866-1928)
7. Beverley R. (1875-1913)
8. Mary Strother (1872-1962)

Frances Jones
(1840-1864)

Robert Thomas
(1842-1917)
m. (1) Katherine Knight (1845-1887)
m. (2) 1890 Gertrude W. Baker (1871-1963)
1. Robert Thomas Jr.
2. Gertrude W.

Randolph Jones
(1844-1921)
m. 1869 Agnes Kirkland (1849-1936)
1. Robert R.
2. Randolph
3. Charles Marshall
4. Agnes P.
5. Carlyle
6. Katherine K.
7. David Walker
8. Bolling W.
9. Alexander K.

Bolling Walker
(1845-1924)
m. 1872 Ella J. Gibson (18?-1879/80)

+Marshall sister and brother

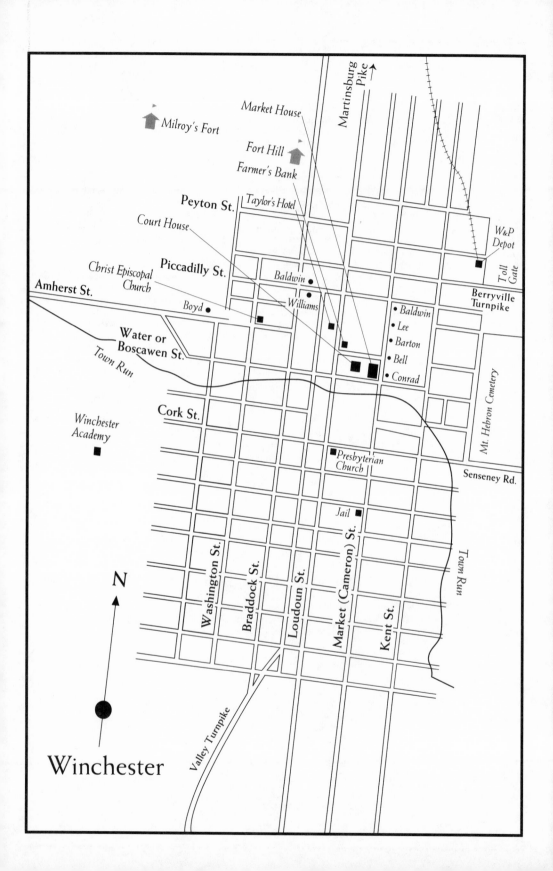

Milroy's Fort

Market House

Fort Hill

Farmer's Bank

Peyton St.

Taylor's Hotel

Court House

Piccadilly St.

Christ Episcopal
Church

Baldwin

Amherst St.

Boyd

Williams

• Baldwin
• Lee
• Barton
• Bell
• Conrad

**Water or
Boscawen St.**

Town Run

Berryville
Turnpike

W&P
Depot

Toll
Gate

Mt. Hebron Cemetery

Cork St.

Winchester
Academy

Presbyterian
Church

Senseney Rd.

Jail

N

Washington St.

Braddock St.

Loudoun St.

Market (Cameron) St.

Kent St.

Town Run

Valley Turnpike

Martinsburg Pike

Winchester

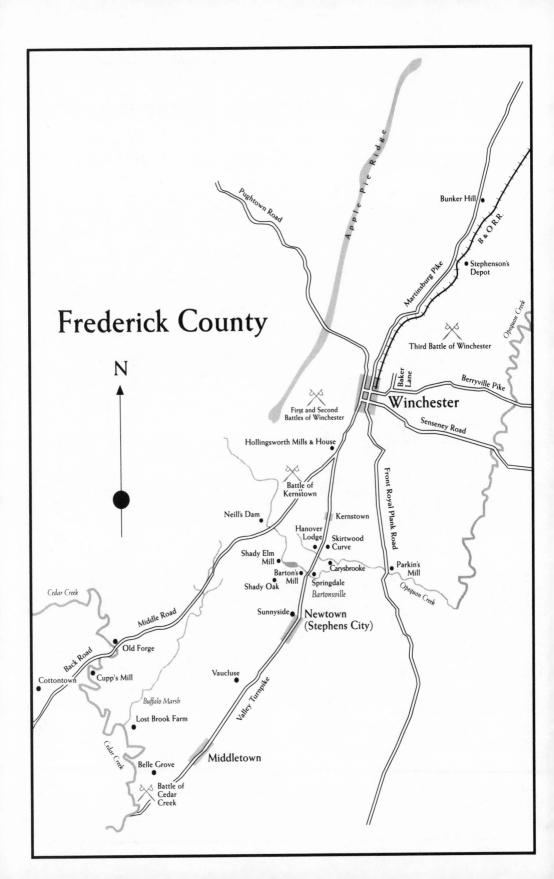

Frederick County

N

Pughtown Road

Apple Pie Ridge

Bunker Hill

B & O.R.R.

Martinsburg Pike

Stephenson's
Depot

Third Battle of Winchester

Baker
Lane

Berryville Pike

Opequon Creek

Winchester

First and Second
Battles of Winchester

Senseney Road

Hollingsworth Mills & House

Front Royal Plank Road

Battle of
Kernstown

Neill's Dam

Kernstown

Hanover
Lodge

Skirtwood
Curve

Shady Elm
Mill

Carysbrooke

Parkin's
Mill

Barton's
Mill

Cedar Creek

Shady Oak

Springdale
Bartonsville

Opequon Creek

Sunnyside

Newtown
(Stephens City)

Middle Road

Old Forge

Back Road

Vaucluse

Cottontown

Cupp's Mill

Valley Turnpike

Buffalo Marsh

Lost Brook Farm

Cedar Creek

Belle Grove

Middletown

Battle of
Cedar
Creek

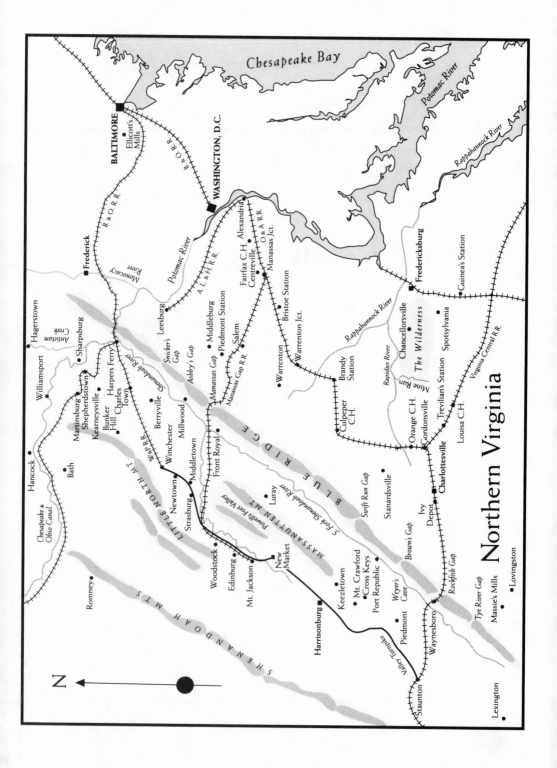

Chesapeake Bay

Potomac River

Rappahannock River

BALTIMORE

Ellicott's Mills

B & O R R

WASHINGTON, D.C.

Frederick

Monocacy River

Potomac River

A. L. & H. R. R.

Leesburg

Fairfax C.H.
Alexandria
Centreville
Manassas Jct.

O & A R.R.

Middleburg
Piedmont Station

Snicker's
Gap

Ashby's
Gap

Salem

Manassas Gap

Manassas Gap R.R.

Warrenton

Bristoe Station

Warrenton Jct.

Fredericksburg

Guinea's Station

Rappahannock River

Chancellorsville

Spotsylvania

The Wilderness

Mine Run

Brandy
Station

Culpeper
C.H.

Rapidan River

Trevilian's Station

Louisa C.H.

Virginia Central R.R.

Hagerstown

Williamsport

Antietam Creek

Sharpsburg

Shepherdstown

Harpers Ferry

Bunker
Hill

Kearneysville

Martinsburg

Charles
Town

Berryville

W. & P. R. R.

Winchester

Millwood

Shenandoah River

BLUE RIDGE

Orange C.H.

Gordonsville

Charlottesville

Hancock

Bath

LITTLE NORTH MT.

Newtown

Middletown

Strasburg

Front Royal

Powell's Fort Valley

Luray

S. Fork Shenandoah River

MASSANUTTEN MT.

Swift Run Gap

Stanardsville

Brown's Gap

Ivy
Depot

Chesapeake &
Ohio Canal

Romney

SHENANDOAH MTS.

Woodstock

Edinburg

Mt. Jackson

New
Market

Keezletown

Mt. Crawford
Cross Keys
Port Republic

Weyer's
Cave

Piedmont

Rockfish Gap

Tye River Gap

Massie's Mills

Lovingston

Harrisonburg

Valley Turnpike

Waynesboro

Staunton

Lexington

N

Northern Virginia

Among us we might write quite a readable book and call it

"The Adventures of six soldier brothers"

ROBERT T. BARTON TO RANDOLPH J. BARTON, MAY 26, 1897

After all this time I suppose you will think I ought to have forgotten these little incidents; and so I had, but as I write the memory of those long ago times comes back to me fresh and bright—full of sweetness and full of sadness—and on the tide there seems to float these trifling things. . . . I tell them to you so that you may know my life and its incidents, great and small, just as the current ran on.

ROBERT T. BARTON, 1893

Introduction

Robert T. Barton, a lawyer of Winchester, Virginia, began to write a very pri-
vate reminiscence not long after he became a father. He was almost fifty.

To my son Robert T. Barton.

This is Thursday November 3, 1892, and I will be fifty years old on the 24th
day of this month. I have sometimes regretted that I had not kept a Journal or
diary of the events of my life, and at the times when this feeling had possession
of me I determined that I would amend my neglect, at least to the extent of
keeping a diary from that time on. But up to the last two or three years of my
life when disposed to put my resolve into operation, I have been deterred by
the sentiment "cui bono?" I had no child or prospect of children. My precious
wife and I were nearly of the same age.[1] It was not probable that she would long
survive me should I die before her, and at her death there would be no one to
whom my past life would be of interest enough to justify the labour involved in
writing up the events of the years gone by or in keeping a narrative of the days
as they pass.

But how different is all this now. You came into the world between 4 and 5
o'clock in the morning of October 15 1891 and hence on this day you are one
year and nineteen days old. Every moment of your little life has been a joy to
me, even when I was undergoing the agony of apprehension during your
extreme illness in July last when you came so near dying of pneumonia. I only

1

then realized how very dear to me you were, and how a father's heart could go out to even such a little baby boy as you. During this year of your life, in the prospect and hope that I may live long enough to see you grown up and to make you love me, and that you may long survive me; and also in the natural expectation that your sweet young mother may live many years after my death; and feeling that to both of you my past life will be interesting and that I may preserve enough of the events of the days yet to come to entertain and possibly to instruct you, I have this day begun to put my oft-considered resolution into execution and with these pages I begin the narrative of my past life.

Robert T. Barton, c. 1895.
(Edith Barton Sheerin)

This narrative of my life I have written for my son Robert T. Barton, to be read by him after my death. To my wife, Gertrude W. Barton I commit it, asking her to keep it until such time as Robert is able to comprehend and take an interest in it. In her goodness and discretion in this and all other matters I have unbounded confidence.

The above was written before the birth of my sweet daughter Gertrude W. Barton Jr. I intend all that is written in this and in subsequent volumes as much for her as for my dear boy: hoping that both of my dear children may bear me in loving remembrance.

R.T. Barton, March 26, 1900

Unbeknownst to Robert, his younger brother Randolph Barton, a lawyer of Baltimore, began to record his memories of the Civil War when he was fifty-one, sometime in 1895.

I find myself rapidly approaching the completion of the fifty-third year of my life, and although a kind Providence has blessed me with almost unexampled good health, and I have all the reasons man may ever have to expect reasonable prolongation of my life, I am warned that if I wish to leave my children anything

Randolph Barton, c. 1898.
(Randolph Barton)

by which to identify me other than the memory of my great devotion to them, it is time that I was placing something on record to which in after years they may turn, with the hope that when they do turn to it, they will be reminded of the infinite pleasure it gave me to dwell upon the reminiscences I here record, and will reflect that the respectful patience with which they listened to my oft-told tales was but a part of the family discipline which tended to make their youthful days at Vaucluse the period of their lives when they learned how charitably and kindly through life they may treat the foibles of others.[2]

I am aware of the fact that nothing has occurred in my life or may occur, which makes it differ much from the lives of millions who have come and gone and been forgotten, and will come and go and be forgotten, unless it was that I belong to the generation upon whose heads fell the awful scourge of civil war. I have observed that no event among men is so lasting in its impressions as that which involves heroic action, that no opportunity is so great to bring out all that is great and good among men as that which involves awful danger. And so I have often thought that as in the dispensation of Providence this country was to be the scene of horrors hardly equalled in the history of man, I could congratulate myself upon having witnessed the rise and progress of the great civil disturbance and upon having gone through it all as an active participant, and emerged safely with a record, while not distinguished, at least creditable.

And so I have thought that in years to come it might be of interest to my children to leave from my own pen a sketch what I saw and did in the years 1860–1865. It may be that some of them may inherit my fondness for military affairs, or that some of my descendants may want to know exactly what part I took in the war between the States, and as I know no one who can give the account as accurately as I can—certainly of no one who will be as much interested in giving it as I am—I have determined to commit to writing these memories.

These recollections are written for the exclusive benefit of my immediate family and my most partial and considerate friends. I could not give a fair narrative of my experiences without being, in many cases, quite personal and so there I have taken the liberty of introducing the names of relatives, and particularly of my friends of the gentler sex, I trust to their pardon for so doing when they consider the narrowness of the circle to which I limit the perusal of what I have written.

Randolph Barton April 24, 1897 (Revised 1913)

THE VALLEY AT PEACE

The world into which Robert and Randolph Barton were born in the 1840s had been discovered for them by their grandfather Richard Peters Barton. Born in Lancaster, Pennsylvania, in 1763, one of the younger children of an immigrant Church of England clergyman who would not cease to pray for his king, Richard perforce made his own way in the world. In the mid-1780s, he was drawn to the milder climate of Petersburg, Virginia, where in about 1790 he took to wife Martha Walker of Kingston, of an old but not monied Virginia family. After some years in Dinwiddie County, he and his young family decided to try their fortunes in the west. Richard settled six miles south of the busy little town of Winchester, first paying taxes in Frederick County in 1799. It appears that at first he rented Shady Oak farm and what was a little later known as the Carlile farm, near the small milling community on Opequon Creek. In several years he was able to buy the fine house and farm, Springdale, slightly to the east on the main road. There the youngest of the Bartons' eight children, David Walker Barton, was born.[3]

Robert and Randolph's world was shaped by David Walker Barton, their father. Educated at Yale where he was graduated Phi Beta Kappa in the class of 1821, he returned to Winchester and read law. Until his marriage, he would walk or ride from Springdale to town. In 1823 he came to the bar and went into practice in Winchester, later attending the law classes of Judge Henry St. George Tucker. In about 1833, Barton formed a partnership with Philip Williams, an established lawyer from Woodstock. This was, by all accounts, a most successful and harmonious relationship that lasted until dissolved by death, the two partners complementing each other's talents. Williams was an exceptional litigator; Barton's reticent nature lent itself to the scholarly trust and chancery part of the business. The firm of Barton and Williams made a fine reputation and, in the growing economy of the Valley, small fortunes for the partners.

The broad Shenandoah Valley offered ample opportunity for all comers. It is watered by innumerable springs, many of the mineral ones believed to have healing powers. Fast-falling streams feed two forks of the unnavigable river, which flows north into the Potomac. Rich limestone soil supported verdant grasslands, and later rolling fields of grain. The Valley was a breadbasket for the early Republic, and in retrospect it seems inevitable that a local boy would have invented the reaper. Cattle thrived on rich pastures as had the buffalo, and sheep on the poorer ones and in the hills.

The northern part of the Valley had been initially settled in the early eighteenth-century by Palatine Germans, then Quakers, who moved south from central Pennsylvania along the Indian trails and natural highways of the mountain valleys. Dutch, Scotch-Irish, Welsh, and a few English filtered down from the New York vicinity. There was little migration over the Blue Ridge from eastern Virginia until after the Revolution. Some settlers built log houses (many still existing), which were often later faced with clapboard or plaster. The Germans built handsome and enduring houses (like Springdale) of the local bluish limestone, and stone mills that took advantage of the many streams. At first the mills were to process the local grain into flour (or alcohol), but by 1860 Frederick County listed ten woolen mills, producing a coarse durable workmanly fabric. The land was heavily cultivated, but the major crops were not the labor-intensive tobacco and cotton of the stereotypical South, and the farms were smaller holdings, usually of a size to be worked by a family and perhaps a hired man or two. (There appear to have been plenty of "day laborers" as well as transient farmhands available for seasonal work.) These were farmers, gentleman farmers perhaps, who may have received a classical eduction from a tutor or at one of the new boarding schools like the Episcopal High School, and might even have attended the university or faraway Yale or Princeton.

Slavery existed, but few were the slaveholders who owned more than several slaves, and their primarily domestic employment was perhaps a more humane variable of the "peculiar institution." To the families whose story is told here, the relationship was an intimate one with lifelong retainers, and the people they referred to as "servants" were an integral part of their lives.

In town the men were merchants and lawyers and bankers and doctors, but many did not confine themselves to a single occupation. They may have styled themselves for a census taker as "coppersmith," "schoolteacher," "miller," or "attorney," but they turn up as preachers, merchants, town officials, or developers of turnpike and gaslight and telegraph and fire companies or the town's water system or the railroad. Within the growing economy of this region at this

Looking south on Loudoun Street in Winchester, from an 1845 travel book. At right is the Taylor Hotel, where the stages stopped. (Library of Congress)

time, it was not unusual for a man to have an active participation in what would be thought of today as several careers.

Winchester was a flourishing market town with a population by 1860 of about 4,400, in 701 families. Of these, just over 3,000 were white; of the remainder, the 708 slaves outnumbered 655 free blacks. It was the county seat of Frederick County and the commercial center of the northern Valley. By this time, it boasted paved and leveled streets, an imposing courthouse, a handsome market house, a jail, a Masonic Hall, lyceum, two newspapers, at least two banks, several fire companies, and over fifty stores, not to mention a dozen churches, one large hotel, and more than a few taverns. Gaslight was introduced in 1855. There were a number of schools for both boys and girls, and a new medical college had just opened its doors. Trade depended on grain, livestock, and its by-products (such as tanned hides, tallow, soap), and to a certain extent the remnants of the fur trade and a little tobacco. By 1855, numerous resorts had developed in the Valley, at the various mineral springs. Large hotels, surrounded by cottages, drew visitors from the North and South, who would take a cure in the midst of an active social whirl. (One of the sights to see on the way was Weyer's Cave, near Port Republic.) Many travelers passed through Winchester because of its transportation network. Winchester's roads, as good as could be had in the country, fostered its commercial importance. It was the hub of an excellent network of nine roads and turnpikes—mostly privately built toll roads—connecting it with eastern Virginia through the Blue Ridge passes, south or north within the Valley by the macadamized Valley Turnpike—something of a marvel, equivalent for its time to Roman roads or autobahns. On the westward pikes, wagon trains—"land schooners"—regularly set off for Tennessee or Ohio. The town's only railroad link went north, to the Potomac at Harpers Ferry about thirty miles away, where it met the B.&O. Railroad. This railroad, the tracks running into the depot near the center of town by the large grain warehouses, was emblematic of the Valley's mainstay of commerce and of its connections with Maryland and the North. Baltimore, only a hundred miles away, was Winchester's "city" both before and after the war. It was Winchester's major market for its cattle and flour, and many people had business ties and relatives. Baltimore was then the third largest city in the country and an important port of immigration, import-export, and other business. To travel from Winchester to Norfolk or Richmond or farther south, it was common to take ship from Baltimore. Washington, seventy-odd miles away and a bit raw and unsophisticated with its still-unfinished Capitol, had less to offer. Richmond, about 140 miles, required a more uncomfortable or roundabout trip. Indeed Richmond and tidewater Virginia were a different mentality, a world away.

Due to the Valley's pattern of settlement, there was more of a religious mix (Quaker, Presbyterian, Lutheran, Mennonite, Amish) than in eastern Virginia, where the Church of England prevailed. After the Church of England was disestablished by the American Revolution, it languished in Virginia until its revival in the early nineteenth century, sparked in part by Bishop William

Though the wagons belong to the Union Army, the busy traffic in this 1864 view of the Market House in Winchester resembled the commercial traffic of prewar times. The sketch is by Union artist James E. Taylor. (Western Reserve Historical Society)

Meade and other dynamic churchmen. The regenerated Protestant Episcopal Church took on an evangelical character that manifests itself in many of the letters to follow. It was a pious era; it would be hard to overstate and indeed it is difficult for the late twentieth century to grasp the preoccupation with God and the hereafter. Teenage boys wrote to each other at length of their souls and their conversions; from camp, a cavalry officer wrote his young brother-in-law a letter entirely devoted to a discourse on the nature of the Trinity, only belatedly inquiring about the family at home; and most members of these families were convinced and comforted by the belief that their dear young men killed in battle would, if they had joined the church, be among the ranks of the blessed. The stern Presbyterian zeal of Stonewall Jackson came to pervade the Army of Northern Virginia, but the seed of his faith fell upon fertile ground. While it might be too strong to say these men believed that theirs was a crusade, they did think of themselves as Christian soldiers in a just cause. How many were buried with the simple epitaph "a soldier of Christ."

THE VALLEY AT WAR

Although there was only one vote for Lincoln in Frederick County, probably most of the people in 1860 would have described themselves as Unionists. But the issue became not the Union, certainly not (in the Valley) slavery, but states' rights and the encroachment of federal authority. By the time battle was joined in 1861, most of the people were secessionists. They rallied to support the new country, buying Confederate bonds, contributing silver to be melted down for the purchase of munitions. A broad spectrum of feelings, loyalties, and beliefs continued to coexist, from a staunchly Unionist family who abhorred abolition and abolitionists, through slaveowners who welcomed the end of slavery, and a Quaker teacher who provided Sheridan with military information, to militant Southerners who refused to walk under the Stars and Stripes at the door of the hospital where their own soldiers awaited their ministrations.

Frederick County's natural blessings and position made it a rich resource for the South. It became mandatory for the Confederacy to hold this region that not only was bountifully productive of the sinews of war—wheat, beef, leather, horses, cloth—but also was strategically placed and shielded by the Blue Ridge so that a Confederate Army in Winchester and the northern Valley would always threaten not only Washington but also Maryland and Pennsylvania. Winchester is north of Washington, almost as far north as Baltimore, and within striking distance of both; it is closer to Gettysburg than to Staunton.

The fine roads radiating from Winchester made this more feasible, and were sufficiently well built to hold up even under four years of marching armies.

Conversely, it was crucial for the North to block the northern end of the Shenandoah to obviate the threat to their capital, and to protect both the Potomac River (with its parallel C.&O. canal artery) and the vital rail link, through Harpers Ferry, with the west. During the early part of the war, the Union ignored the Valley. Federal strategists were concerned about protecting their own capital and obsessed with taking Richmond. Their focus on the symbolic, industrial, and commercial center of the Confederacy was valid, but shortsighted. When they first moved into the Valley in March 1862 (having been delayed by their own overestimates of Confederate strength), it was more a defense tactic than an invasion. Nevertheless the ordeal of Winchester began. From this time until the end of the war, the town was in enemy hands over half the time.

It did not become apparent to Northern strategists until about 1864 that they must deny to the Confederacy the bounty of the Shenandoah. They had seen that the natural pathway south in the Valley would carry a Federal army west, away from Richmond, but eventually they realized that if they could attain Staunton with its railroad east, they could sever that valuable connection and flank the Confederate capital.

Winchester's war story may be unique: closer to the North than to the South in sentiments and economy—but Virginian, and determined to defend their state. No other town of its size experienced so much action in four years. Elsewhere there were larger and more significant battles, but the county's immutable strategic significance and its equally vulnerable character made it a scene of conflict from the summer of 1861 through the fall of 1864. From the first summer of the war to the last winter, Winchester knew the occupation or threatening proximity of one army or the other. And whether friend or foe, an army's attendant drain on resources, general wear and tear, and strain on the environment and health took the same toll.

Frederick County was the locus of five significant battles (three fought through Winchester), and the focus of innumerable skirmishes and raids. Always desirable, never defensible, it suffered dozens of actions in four years of war. There were seven Federal occupations, and control of the town changed thirteen times. It was between the lines for about a fifth of the war, and these were possibly the most dangerous periods. By one count, military action occurred in the Winchester vicinity on 138 days, and on an additional 27 in places south along the Valley Turnpike to Middletown. Local historians say

Winchester "changed hands" over seventy times, but this is misleading as the
great majority of these engagements were cavalry forays and did not result in a
new occupation or even change of control.[4] Nevertheless it should not diminish
the fact that there were over seventy occasions of real physical danger for the
people, and the stress and anxiety that each raid might endanger the town, their
homes, or their soldier boys—always so close—and that a new force might hold
sway over their lives by the end of that day. Federal forces threatened many times
to destroy the town by fire, and in part they did succeed, if only accidentally.

The civilians' stress takes on a different dimension when it is comprehended
that the sound of artillery carried over great distances, and almost any large
Virginia battle was known to be taking place because it could be heard. It might
not be known for days who was bearing the brunt of the fighting, who was
winning, losing, or dying, just that it was happening. Sometimes a week or two
would pass before reliable news was received at home.

Frederick County was populous and fervent enough to raise and then to
replenish several regiments. The Valley provided one of the most famous units
in military history—the Stonewall Brigade. It is a matter of record that on the
Bartons' block in Winchester there were twenty young men, all of whom
enlisted as soon as they could in the Confederate Army and served as long as
they were alive and able. This group was from the six (of seven) households who
had sons of the right age: three Baldwins, two Burwells, six Bartons, two
Hollidays, two Bells, and five Conrads. This could probably be replicated
throughout the town and perhaps the state. At the university, 515 of the 530
students from the South enlisted.

For four years the Army of Northern Virginia fought on and for their home
ground as no other Americans have ever had to do. Upon secession, northern
Virginia immediately became the frontier, the front line, and very soon the continuing battleground of the war in the east. From the first the troops were of
the community, going to war with friends, brothers, cousins, classmates, neighbors, fighting in and for their own land near their own homes—fed on the
morning before or after battle by their mothers, sweethearts, wives, or their
cousins' or friends' mothers or sisters. Foraging for themselves or their horses
from friendly farms, if not their own. Fighting over their own fields or retreating through woods where they had hunted and fished in more innocent years,
leaving camp unofficially to get a new horse or for harvest—or fretting if they
didn't. "Flanking out to see the girls," creeping home through enemy lines to
take good news or bad, for a brief time with dear ones, perhaps getting for the
first time in months a meal better than bread and bacon, and a night's sleep in a

bed and under a roof, or perhaps not. Being nursed and comforted by someone they knew, if they were fortunate. Seeing their friends fight and sometimes die. Burying or being buried by friends or brothers, at times on family or familiar burying grounds within miles or less of where they fell.

The home people ran to watch battles from rooftops or nearby hills, heedless of their own danger and exhilarated that they might soon be liberated, but terrified of the price that might be paid. They sent their young men off to war clad in homemade uniforms, armed with beaten biscuits in linen napkins. They knit socks for them (however ineptly), bandaged them with strips of their linen sheets or tablecloths, carried countless baskets of food and clothes past piles of amputated limbs, into the makeshift hospitals, nursed them in their debilitating illnesses or with their grievous wounds, took them—friends or strangers—into their homes to convalesce. When the lines changed, if necessary they hid them under the bed or in the wardrobe, smuggled letters (or even boots) out to them in hoop skirts, bonnets, and shoes, purloined and hoarded Yankee supplies. If their soldiers were captured, they visited them at the jail or behind the courthouse fence, or traveled through the lines to do so if they could arrange it. And when their army returned in triumph, feasted the living within their slender means, and buried the dead sometimes from their parents' houses.

Even the children were enlisted to help take baskets to the hospitals, to carry messages, to eavesdrop on the occupying forces, to take "nice things" to the wounded lying "under the trees in Grandma's orchard." Some young boys, inevitably, ran away to join the army, successfully lying about their age or, when discovered, being sent home to fight another day.

The troops' continuity with their community, sustained by its moral support, and motivated by their knowledge of its hardships, danger, and subjugation, inspired the soldiers more than all the biscuits and socks that were forthcoming.

Within the army, associations and command were often familial, not unlike, it has been remarked, those of a clan, and indeed it was not uncommon for younger to serve elder brothers as their lieutenants or for command to pass within a family as in a clan. Frequently several members of a family served in the same unit, where they could maintain or even strengthen those ties in this new framework, interwoven, bonded, with those of other family groups. Young men who had played together, schooled together (or with each other's brothers), now fought together—if they were lucky—throughout the war. Courage was expected. They fought side by side, almost always on open ground in sight of each other. Their heroism might be attributable to peer pressure, the knowledge that many of their friends would see and judge their actions, but there was undoubtedly a measure of the romantic ideal that imbued many in the South. Their loyalty to their unit cannot be determined by rates of attendance or desertion—many "informal" leaves were taken, the men returning after some business at home had been tended to or with the prospect of a new campaign.

HARDSHIP AND DISEASE

These farm or country or even town boys were used to the outdoors and to physical work—long walks to school or the fields, or to go hunting. Horses and riding were part of their lives (as they were not for many Northern city-dwellers). They traveled light, confident that their victories would replenish supplies, and indeed the Confederate Army in Virginia was more consistently fed and clothed and armed by captured Union stores than it was or could be by its own quartermasters. A big win might mean new boots all around and a feast including ginger cookies, canned lobster, or other exotica from the Union commissary.

The Southerners were hardy, but they were inadequately clad and fed, exposed to all weather, sleeping on wet ground—perhaps in tents but these were sometimes lost to capture or far away in a wagon bogged down in the mud. (Winters were severe, and after the terrible experience of the Bath-Romney Campaign, armies generally went into winter quarters and were better sheltered.) Water and food supplies were usually insufficient and often contaminated. Diet and nutrition were not understood and even if they had been, the deficiencies could not have been supplied. Daily rations were a half pound of flour or bread and a half pound of meat, usually fatty bacon, with occasional infusions of vinegar, peas or beans or rice, and a quota of salt and sugar not always met. Real coffee was soon a thing of the past, and burnt rye a better-than-nothing substitute. Foraging along the way helped. Almost anything was cooked with flour and fried with bacon fat by the inexperienced and heavy hand of men learning to cook. The utensils were pots, frying pans, or spiders, owned by the individuals and carried in the wagons. If the wagons did not arrive, neither did dinner. If the wagons were late, food was undercooked. The stodgy end product would clog the stomach. Despite this, constipation was unusual, diarrhea the norm. The "Tennessee quick step," produced by a variety of enteric infections and vitamin deficiencies, was the army's most common complaint.

The effect of a serious wound or amputation on a system already weakened by disease or malnutrition could be fatal. The massed infantry tactics of the time did not take into account the advances in weaponry and repeatedly produced huge numbers of casualties in proportion to the number of combatants. The lacerating wounds made by the new weapons could only be treated by amputation, and this occurred with great frequency, often under terrible conditions on the battlefield, hasty, dirty, and sometimes without benefit of chloroform or ether. But the major killer in the war was disease, not the enemy, and the worst of these were typhoid and dysentery. Diphtheria, scarlet fever, scurvy—often suggestively called debilitas—all played their part in the army and the community. Measles, mumps, whooping cough, those childhood diseases so threatening to adults because they could predispose the victim to the dreaded consumption, were often contracted by soldiers from rural areas who had never been exposed. The "seasoning" of troops meant sickness more than company drill. Thousands of enlistees came down with a serious illness within weeks of joining the army. Typhoid was primarily a disease afflicting the army, especially in the first years of the war. Disease did not take sides, but did accompany large numbers. The presence of an army made for bad health conditions in the community; where the army was encamped, typhoid and other diseases relating to bad sanitation spread to the local population. Winchester had several epidemics.

Stress was a factor, too. One diarist wrote, "Death is doing its work with unusual rapidity, in quiet homes, as well as on the battlefield." Whether the town was occupied or not, the people must have suffered from general malnutrition, which accelerated existing maladies, activated others, and foreordained others. The stress and malnutrition that were constants both in Winchester and in the army eroded healthy constitutions and often hastened the end of those already "delicate," frail, or just plain elderly. Many—soldiers and civilians—who survived the war were never truly well or strong again, and fell victim to early deaths in childbirth or from consumption, or their general weak health made them prey to any passing disease.

Randolph Barton must have had a very healthy constitution, surviving not only five wounds, at least two of which were serious, but also a debilitating four months as a prisoner of war. Apparently he did not at any time suffer from consumption, which afflicted many in his family. He appears to have been quite run down and probably malnourished early in 1863, but possibly his health was re-built during his long recuperation from his Chancellorsville wound in Staunton with a wealthy family. After that, as an officer, he was more able to buy food (as the troops usually could not) and was more likely to be entertained by local citizens. He was extremely fortunate in spending most of his convalescent periods not in hospitals (where he would have been prey to infection and disease) but in private homes, and in this his brothers were lucky, too. Strother Barton was out of action all of the summer of 1862, recovering from typhoid fever, with a family near Staunton. Frank Jones may well have been suffering from malnutrition, which brought on the chronic diarrhea mentioned as weakening him so much he could not survive an amputation. Robert Barton may have had pulmonary problems before 1862, but the physical ordeal of the Valley Campaign surely brought on consumption. Cousin Willie was hospitalized several times, and possibly he had lingering afflictions that resulted in his untimely death.

The practice of medicine in the mid-nineteenth century seems closer to the era of witchcraft than to the present. There was no understanding of the nature of infection or the transmission of disease. Antisepsis was only another rumor, and the dirty hands of a physician were often death-dealing. Communicable diseases, once started, could spread through and decimate a family or community. It was not uncommon to lose several children within weeks as scarlet fever or diphtheria or whooping cough ran through a single household. Consumption was easily communicated within a family—even the well-to-do had several children (to say nothing of visitors) sharing rooms. The disease could be latent indefinitely, and become active in times of stress, malnutrition, hardship, and other bad health conditions. If the sufferer survived, the disease might perhaps subside for years or decades.

There were no real remedies for most of these—quinine for fevers, calomel, morphine, paregoric, laudanum, mustard plasters for coughs, whisky for anything and everything. Often these medicines were misused and added to the suffering.

All these shortcomings were accentuated by the conditions of war and the prohibition by the Federal government on sending medicines to the Confederacy. Even if medical facilities had existed in proportion to the community, the unimaginable numbers of the sick and wounded would have been overwhelming. More than once, the town of Winchester had to receive numbers of wounded that were larger than its total prewar population. For long periods during the war, churches, public buildings, hotels, and schools made crude shift as repositories for the wounded—hospital would be too grand a term. The peacetime town had had plenty of doctors (almost as many as lawyers), but all but a few of the older ones had gone with the army. Extraordinary efforts were made by the women of Winchester to nurse and to comfort and to gather provisions of all sorts for their wounded. The townspeople took as many as they could into their homes to recuperate. And, only too aware of the horrible uncertainties in the aftermath of battle, they worked to compile lists of the wounded and the dead for dissemination to North and South.

OCCUPATION

When the Federal forces first came to Winchester in March 1862, U.S. Secretary of War Stanton made haste to visit. A lady sourly remarked to her diary that the devil was viewing his new province. Stanton did not linger, and reported on his return, in an oft-quoted remark, that "the men are all in the army and the women are the devil." Thus the antagonists defined each other; the lines were early drawn by those of extreme sentiments on each side. Federal occupations tended to transform Unionists into Rebels; one pious lady confessed to her diary that it would be easier to love her enemies if they were at a distance. Some Yankees arrived in Winchester expecting a civil reception if they bore the proper introductions. They were quickly and rudely disabused of this notion, and instead were constantly and repeatedly bemused and insulted by the calculated affronts and outspokenly hostile language of many of the women. Other citizens, more devious, formed what might be termed the resistance movement in the Valley, taking every opportunity (and developing more) to pass information through the lines, to smuggle and hoard food, medical and clothing supplies from the North, and to collect money from Confederate sympathizers in the North. One clever lady managed to obtain and hide 600 pounds of sugar in one maneuver. She also spoke of this time as "the day of women's power," when the remaining men, the older town leaders, seemed tentative, timid, and conciliatory in their direct dealings with the Federals and were afraid to attempt any clandestine activities.[5]

The town became somewhat depopulated. Many men not yet in the army were now either motivated to join, forced to do so because of the recent conscription legislation, or impelled to escape the same at the hands of the Federals. Many families who could afford to leave, or had another place to go, left town to avoid being under Yankee rule. Blacks, free and slave, began to "run off," prompted by wild Yankee stories of what the Rebels would do to them when they returned; there were pitiful stories of children overrun by Banks's retreating army and of scores who at that time drowned trying to cross the Shenandoah. During Winchester's first occupation, young girls were sent away to protect them from the barbarian invaders. While there was plenty of pilferage, trespassing, and annoyance to contend with, and the restrictions of a military occupation, it was deemed safe enough for the girls to return in a few months. Many women whose husbands were with the army bravely remained, with their children, to protect their homes. Those who stayed often found themselves and their friends behaving like fishwives, giving "such a scoring as is not often heard from a lady."[6] Would they ever be "refined ladies" again, even some of the young women found that "mild and ladylike" language was inadequate for certain occasions and resorted to a little profanity in referring to the conquerors.[7] They took on the Yankees to contest the refusal of a pass through the lines for one of their number to go home, to win dispensation for feed for the milk cow, or intercession when their house was eyed by an officer for his lady or for use as a hospital, or protection when the unruly soldiery was burning fences or stealing chickens. The practice of billeting Federal officers in private houses was a bitter pill, sometimes a necessary evil. The loss of privacy could be preferable to having no protectors in residence, but it was galling when there were so many unoccupied houses in town.

The composition of the Northern army anticipated the future mixture of America while the Confederacy reflected the American past. It was significant for the Valley people that many of the invaders were doubly alien—not only Yankees but foreigners, immigrants. Another of the many difficulties of the Federal occupations was that the rules kept changing, or different rules were applied at the same time by different generals whose commands might overlap. Arrests were made randomly; often these led nowhere but nevertheless could be terrifying. A nighttime knock on the door or noises around the house might be drunken soldiers trying to get in to rob the household or an authorized search for some sort of contraband. Sometimes the Yankees employed spies, both white and black, to report suspicious conduct on the part of "secesh" citizens; entrapment by someone wearing Confederate uniform was a favorite device, and the Jessie Scouts always wore gray for this reason. In 1863, General Milroy brought in professional detectives to find out who was smuggling letters to the Rebels.

The volume of mail that managed to pass through the lines and then find its way to its destination is difficult to determine. Those entrusted with carrying mail took the task seriously, knowing how precious it was. Occasionally an alert provost marshal managed to intercept and burn a batch of letters coming in or going out of town. A substantial amount of mail must have eluded Federal sleuths; even during the last Federal occupation, there is mention of "sacks" of mail being taken out of town nightly.

Daily life depending on local trade and traffic to supply basic needs—food and firewood—was disrupted as early as March 1862 and did not really return to normal until after the war. It became a struggle to round up the necessities for another day; when a supply of goods was obtained legitimately or otherwise, it was necessary to conceal any excess against possible search and confiscation. There could no longer be a regular market, and food shortages were chronic. The usual labor force (black and white) had been depleted: some slaves had gone with their masters to the army and others had fled. The young and able white farm workers had joined the army. At times the farmers were forbidden to plant, sometimes they simply gave up because of the destruction caused by the passage of armies. No wonder that when they had something to offer they charged exorbitant prices in gold. Inflation was rampant by fall 1862, but often it did not even matter, there was nothing to buy anyway. Remake and makeshift became the order of the day and ingenuity was maximized—old hats and dresses were restyled, and it was discovered that burning rye made a passable substitute for coffee, and sorghum syrup for sugar. In addition, there were calculated attempts by Federal commanders to exact submission by starvation. On several occasions, food and other necessities could not be brought in to town or made available except to those who had taken the oath of allegiance to the United States. (Other prohibitions, on marriage and any kind of business transactions, were rumored.) The economy of the region on a larger scale was entirely disrupted, since the crux of it was also agricultural. By late 1864, the nadir was reached and the citizens were compelled to ask occupying Federal forces for rations to ward off starvation.

Rumor and false news made the situation both better and worse. The expectations of foreign alliance (the French fleet that had not arrived, the English recognition of the Confederacy), the agonies of suspense and the wealth of misinformation on who lived and died in battle, the fictitious victories and defeats, the punitive measures to be enacted by the Yankees—all caused hope, illusion, fear, disappointment.

At first the troops of both sides had a degree of idealism. As the war went on, not only were the armies made up increasingly of resentful conscripts, but the original troops became battle-hardened, and more cynical toward civilians, whom they viewed as indifferent to their physical hardships, privations, and sufferings while reaping profits from the war. Theft, looting, vandalism, and destruction became more common by 1864. As the Confederacy became weaker, it relied more on guerrilla warfare; this in turn provoked some extreme reactions, with threats of worse, from the Federals. The once noble conflict turned to terror and a war of attrition.

From the sorry perspective of the late twentieth century, the outrage of the people of Winchester toward their occupying forces seems extreme. Amidst the anger, frustration, and vituperation given vent by the citizens in the confessionals of their diaries, to each other, and in public, it is hard to discern what they had expected this war to be. It is as if they did not think the Yankees would fight, that a Northern army would ever come to Virginia; surely they did not expect Yankees to be "gentlemen."

The secessionists were wont to call the Yankees "Goths" or "Vandals," but the militantly defiant ones among them went unmolested for long periods before being, at worst, exiled—sent through the lines. It is true that the invaders stole everything from onions in the field and rusks from the oven to the family silver; that they destroyed, at first randomly and later by design, all the necessities of commerce and farming; that they seized civilian leaders in a few instances and held them hostage and in prison. Some few citizens were treated roughly, but there are really no records of atrocities committed upon civilians, certainly not on women and children. It is said that each time Federal forces had to retreat from Winchester in the wake of a Confederate victory, they were fired on by the townspeople, who joined in the fray, taking potshots from their windows and doors. But even when the Federals were back within the week, as in June 1862, they did not seek retribution. And despite their many threats over the years to burn Winchester, the Federals never put it to the torch. And at the same time, the upright citizens were doing everything they could think of to give aid and comfort to the Rebels.

By the winter of 1864–65, there were only murmurs from the Valley. The people must have felt beaten, if not cowed, and were certainly impoverished and near starvation. They were occupied, almost smothered by Sheridan's enormous army whose camps spread south from Winchester through Kernstown and Bartonsville almost to Cedar Creek. The sheer numbers and resources marshalled by the North crushed almost all resistance. Guerrilla groups, darting out of the mountain valleys, inflicted only the merest stings, and could accomplish nothing. Little was left to the people; even their privacy was lost to the widespread occupation of private homes by Federal officers. Finally, late in the winter, the large armies withdrew from the Valley to concentrate on Richmond, leaving an occupying force.

AFTERMATH

The magnanimity of Grant and the spirit of Appomattox lasted little more than a week. In the wake of Lincoln's assassination, the North's attitude hardened. The Southern states were not welcomed back into the Union, but were under military government. Confederates and their states had to serve a hard penance before they could resume citizenship or statehood. Not for the Shenandoah or anywhere in the South the generosity of a Marshall Plan.

The Valley soldiers came home to a wasteland—no trees, no fences, no barns, no mills. One Scottish visitor compared it to a moor. Lucky were those who had managed to extricate a horse from the war—there were few to be had at home. Livestock had been almost all stolen or slaughtered, farm equipment destroyed. Many villages and towns were battle-scarred and partially burned, and there was hardly a whole window in the northern Valley. Winchester and the towns along the Valley Turnpike had suffered the most severely. But it was spring, and there was peace in time to put in a crop, although the workforce, black and white, had been decimated. For many there was barely seed money for farms or new enterprises. It would be a long time before Winchester could regain its former commercial position. Great stretches of railroad and all rolling stock had been destroyed; most of the warehouses in town had been burned. Store inventories had been looted. Banks had failed. A great many people had invested their all—what was not in the ravaged land—in Confederate money and bonds. There was no remaining capital to fuel new enterprises.

Some Confederates emerged from occupation or returned from the war to rebuild the devastated community. Some left and began new lives elsewhere; others held on as long as they could to the old farm or the old way until, defeated by new economic realities, they were forced to change. Of those who stayed, some became pillars of their communities as their fathers had been before them. Others, their health ruined by wartime conditions, disease, or wounds, led limited lives and perhaps died untimely deaths. Like many others, the Barton/Jones family lost one third of its adult members in the war period and the years immediately following.

The world Robert and Randolph had known was changed forever. In this blighted economy, just so much farming and lawyering could be done. Randolph and Bolling Barton, as younger sons, left the farming to Strother and the lawyering to Robert and set off to seek their fortunes. Bolling was sponsored by their father's cousin Bolling Haxall, who enabled him to pursue his education in Europe. Randolph, after some period of preparation back at home, joined what amounted to a Valley exodus to Baltimore.

THE DOCUMENTS

Randolph Jones Barton began writing his reminiscences in 1895. With his albeit brief VMI education, he was interested in military history in general, and his war experiences naturally intensified it. He was active in Confederate veterans organizations, contributed articles to the publication of that name, and corresponded with other veterans, as well as with historians of the war. The

Recollections has the patchy quality of a collection of anecdotes or a scrap-book—old newspaper clippings interspersed with his own writing, readings from other books incorporated with his opinion of them, excerpts from his correspondence with other veterans. Clearly it was the pastime of the busy lawyer who would return occasionally to his manuscript and add another episode, or read someone else's account and think of a rebuttal or relevant story of his own. He did not set out to describe the war in Virginia or even give a linear account of his own service. The book was intended for his offspring, who were familiar with many of the references. A satisfactory draft was completed by 1897 and, after some review if not revision, it was finally published, in a very small private printing, in 1913. Randolph's sons reprinted the book in an edition of seventy-eight copies, adding an appendix of memorial services and tributes (and changing the frontispiece), for their grandchildren in 1949.

Robert Thomas Barton's memoir supplies to a great degree the information about the family's war, which is missing in Randolph's account. Robert's army service was curtailed by ill health, so he spent much of the war in the Valley in reach of, or with, his family. He described how the family endured enemy occupation, privation, and disease and included his parents' story and that of their many relatives. It was a large but close-knit family that eventually sent six brothers, a brother-in-law, two uncles, and three cousins to active service in the Confederate Army.

Robert began writing his memoir in late 1892, and released a flood of memories, writing the story of his life up to the 1893 present in just four months. Apparently he never went back to alter a word or fill in the few factual gaps he had left open in his ledger, but continued it as a journal off and on for the rest of his life. Written in secrecy in his office, Robert's ledgers were found there by his son after his death in 1917. The journal and other papers that Robert had saved from the war years have come down in his family. Robert was active in the local Turner Ashby Camp of the Confederate Veterans. He wrote about the war on several occasions, contributing an unattributed memoir of Col. Thomas Marshall to James B. Avirett's compilation, Ashby and his Compeers, and a series of three articles on his experiences at Port Republic to a Winchester paper. A memoir of the First Battle of Winchester, which may have been written for a talk for the Turner Ashby Camp, was never published.

The third son to survive the war period, Bolling, was childless, and probably for this reason, as well as his feeling that his part had been minor, left no record of his experiences. He wrote a memoir of the Battle of New Market for VMI, which, aside from a brief published quote, has not survived. His part in telling

To My Son Robert T. Barton—

    This is Thursday November 3- 1892, and I will be fifty years old on the 24- day of this month— I have sometimes regretted that I had not kept a journal or diary of the events of my life, and at all the times when this feeling had passed over me I determined that I would amend my neglect, at least to the extent of keeping a diary from that time on— But up to the last two or three years of my life when disposed to put my resolve into operation I have been detained by the sentiment "cui bono"? I have no children or prospect of children— My precious wife and I were nearly of the same age— It was not probable that she would long survive me. Should I die before her, and at her death there would be no one to whom my past life would be of interest enough to justify the labour involved in writing up the events of the years gone by or in keeping a narrative of the days as they pass—

    But how different is all this now— You came into the world between 4 and 5- o'clock on the morning of October 15- 1891 and hence on this day you are one year and nineteen days old— Every moment of your little life has been a joy to me, even when I was undergoing

A page from Robert T. Barton's journal. (Edith Barton Sheerin)

this story was as the recipient and preserver of the letters written to him when he was at VMI for the school year 1862–63. Bolling must have taken the letters, neatly grouped by date of receipt, home to Springdale in the summer of 1863. Almost nothing survives from his second year at the institute, and it can be speculated that the letters that he had received and saved that year were lost in the chaos of Hunter's attack in June 1864. The existing letters apparently were taken by Bolling to Randolph's at some later date, either when Bolling lived with the Randolph Bartons at Vaucluse in Maryland or perhaps when he lent them to Randolph to help in the writing of his Recollections. The letters and some belonging to Randolph were kept by his daughters, and then dispersed among several grandchildren.

The Barton boys' step-grandmother, Ann Cary Randolph Jones, wrote long, loving letters, replete with family and local news. Many of those sent to her Florida cousins were saved. The "Harriet" addressed in some of the letters— Harriet Parkhill—eventually sent them back to Winchester, to her cousin, Mrs. Jones's grandson Alexander Tidball Jones. His only child, Frances McNeece Whittle Jones, recently gave them to the Handley Library in Winchester.

The weekly letters of the Barton boys' uncle, Francis B. Jones, were saved and treasured by his wife and mother (Ann C. R. Jones), and they and other family letters remained in his family, as did his diary of the Valley Campaign until very recently. The diary is now in the Winchester-Frederick County Historical Society, with some other papers of the Jones and Clark families, including Peyton Clark's brief diary.

The wartime diary of Mary Greenhow Lee is a voluminous document of which the transcript runs almost a thousand pages. This noteworthy account by the Bartons' next-door neighbor, which was secreted under a parlor floorboard along with the Stars and Bars when the Yankees were in town, has come to rest in the collections of the Winchester-Frederick County Historical Society.

Neither Robert nor Randolph professed to write anything but their own very personal and understandably opinionated accounts of what befell them in the great civil conflict. Robert hoped his children would be able to arrive at balanced views.

[MEMOIR OF ROBERT BARTON]

I shall not write you a history of the Civil War. That you may read in numberless books, many of which are very false; but I will have to trust you to find out the truth for yourself. No doubt, if my life shall be spared until you grow to be a big boy, I will be able to point you to the books from which you can get the fairest impression of what actually occurred. I will only tell you of the part I took, which indeed was but an humble part compared with the experiences of my brothers and the other young men of my age.

Randolph led off with his unreconstructed opinions.

[MEMOIR OF ROBERT BARTON]

At this distant day my mature and deliberate judgement is that the pure and unadulterated desire to preserve the Union was a remote and uninfluential incentive on the part of the North. Hatred of the South and hatred of slavery were the animating causes. Thousands of the Northmen were honest patriots, and towards them I entertain, as I always have done, feelings of the profoundest respect, but to the masses of the North I feel that the South was the victim of simple diabolical ill-will.

As I write the foregoing I am unconscious of any animating cause driving me to the conclusions I have reached but the influence of pure reason, the deductions of more than thirty years of study of the subject, the observation of the relations between the sections ever since the war, and as impartial a view as I can take. To say that I have no vindictive feelings would be insincere. I would not burn all Northmen at the stake, but if I had autocratic power I would levy upon the sordid Yankees the largest tribute the world has ever known. I would transplant from the rich Northern cities billions of the wealth grown with the blood and destruction of the South. I would work retributive justice and restore to the South by pensions or otherwise the wealth of which it was robbed by Sheridan and Grant and the invading armies of the North. I would then reunite the Union with stronger ties than ever, and then I would die content.

In 1897, Randolph sent his manuscript to Robert for his comments. Robert responded with interest, approval, and nostalgia, musing, "Among us we might write quite a readable book and call it 'The Adventures of six soldier brothers.'" The sum of these papers is larger. The many writers of this book tell of trials and tribulations, innocent amusements, faith, death, grief, and fortitude. Their story was fragmented and scattered with them in their own diaspora, but the documents that have come together here are a portrait of a Virginia family in the Civil War.

I

The Valley at Peace

THE FAMILY

By 1855, David Barton must have felt he was truly blessed. As the youngest son of a well-to-do farmer who had settled near Winchester, Virginia, in the 1790s, he had been well educated but not particularly endowed with inherited substance. He had become a lawyer in the days when lawyers were respected and looked up to as leaders of their communities. By 1855, he had built a fine personal and professional reputation in his chosen field, and had accumulated what was, for those times, a small fortune. He lived in town, but had put much of his wealth into the rich farmlands of Frederick County, focusing his interest on the imme-diate vicinity of his childhood home, Springdale.

In his domestic life, he enjoyed the then almost unheard-of good fortune in having had and raised to maturity ten healthy children with one wife. He had married the only daughter of a neighboring gentleman farmer, William Strother Jones. The families were old acquaintances, but from all accounts this was a love match, although Fannie brought a dowry to the marriage. Ties with both their families and more distant relations were geographically close and socially frequent: dinner after church, children going to the family farms on weekends or in summer, young men coming to spend their Sundays in town. Sometimes there were more extended visits to relatives in Fauquier County or even distant Norfolk, possibly occasional trips to Baltimore "in the cars" (the railroad was still a bit of a novelty for the older generation).

David and Fannie lived on Market Street in town, in a house they enlarged to accommodate their growing family, servants, and slaves. In 1855, the ten

The Barton house on Market Street. (Ann L. Barton Brown)

children ranged in age from twenty-five to ten; the household also included
Fannie Barton's niece Anna Jones (daughter Fan's age). By then the eldest
daughters were married, Maria to a man particularly dear to her father. Tom
Marshall was a cousin, so Maria may have known him before he came to town
after attending the University of Virginia. The young couple had lived nearby
for the first years of their marriage. The second daughter, Jane, married a minister whom she had doubtless met when she was visiting Maria and Tom after
they had moved to Fauquier County. Grandchildren were arriving. Third daughter Martha was soon to marry a young doctor whose family lived around the corner on Piccadilly Street. It was too early perhaps to tell what his own sons'
strengths would be. The eldest, Marshall, was at the Virginia Military Institute,
for a practical education. David, the second boy, was starting at the University
of Virginia; bookish and serious, he seemed meant to become a clergyman. The
five younger children and Anna were all of school age, Strother at the Episcopal High School in Alexandria, where his two elder brothers had preceded him,
and the others—Fanny, Robert, Randolph, and Bolling—at schools in Winchester.[1] It was far too early even to imagine that two of the younger sons
would become, like their father, eminent lawyers in their own time.

As it happened, two of the elder sons shared their father's love of the land
and the beautiful farms he had acquired with them in mind, south of Winchester along the Valley Turnpike near the farm where he was born—a place often

then and still sometimes called Bartonsville. It was not really a town, just a collection of houses around two mills—one near the turnpike milling wheat, the second, upstream, a woolen factory. It centered where the Valley Turnpike crossed Opequon Creek, on the beautiful house named Springdale. This house, where David Barton had grown up, was already fifty years old when his father bought it early in the century. All of David Barton's family felt the tie to Springdale although none of them had lived there.

Their family house in Winchester fronted on the street now called Cameron, but its lot, as did its neighbors', ran deep, back to the next street (Kent), providing space for the stables and carriage house, the pig sty, coops for birds, laundry house and other outbuildings, for vegetable garden and fruit trees.[2] It was near the center of the thriving town, just around the corner from the county courthouse and David's law office and about four blocks from the Episcopal church, where David was a vestryman. Along the street were similar houses and similar families with whom the Barton children were to play, smoke a first illicit cigar, "knit a quilt," marry, go to school, and go to war.

Next door one house north lived Mr. and Mrs. Hugh H. Lee and his two spinster sisters; their four motherless Burwell nephews and nieces living with them corresponded in age from Barton's fourth child to his ninth. Mr. Lee's law office was in an annex to the house. The Burwell girls and young Fanny and cousin Anna were back and forth constantly. Beyond the Lee household, at the corner of Piccadilly Street, was one Baldwin family, whose two younger boys Johnny and Lud were particular friends of the three youngest Bartons. Along Piccadilly, one block west, was Mrs. Eichelberger's school, where some of the Barton children went in their early years. One block farther west was another Baldwin family, cousins of the first—the oldest boy, Robert, was going to marry cousin Cary Barton, and the second, John, was engaged to marry Martha Barton; a third, Cornelius (Strother's age), later courted cousin Anna. All the Baldwin men seemed to be doctors, which was doubtless a little confusing. Across Piccadilly from those Baldwins, the family of Philip Williams, Barton's law partner, included two sons the ages of Robby and Rannie Barton.[3] Robby and Johnny Williams later suffered being sent away to school together. Philip Williams's oldest son, by his first wife, was a doctor in Baltimore. His sister Eleanor was married to Rev. A. H. H. Boyd, minister of the Loudoun Street Presbyterian Church. The Boyds lived over on Amherst Street in Gen. Daniel Morgan's old house, on the other side of town near the Winchester Academy on Cork Street. Of the three boys, Holmes was the oldest, about Strother's age.

On the other side of the Bartons lived Fred Holliday, Maria's contemporary;

both his father and his brother were doctors, but Fred, a promising young law-yer, was already Commonwealth Attorney and had political aspirations. South of the Bartons on Market a few doors was the Conrad family, which included nine children. Powell and Marshall Barton were friends, although a couple of years separated them. Daniel Conrad, already a doctor and away in the navy, was as far removed as if he were of another generation. Holmes Conrad and next door north of him, Bob Bell, were Fanny Barton's age, enough older to look like "the big boys" to Robby and Rannie. Bob's father had a dry goods and book store over on Loudoun at Boscawen; Bob's brother was clerking in the store, but Bob wanted to be a farmer. Across from Mr. Bell's store was the Farmer's Bank, and over it lived the Sherrard family. Mr. Sherrard was an officer of the bank. Joe was about David's age, but a friend of Strother's, too. Lizzie was of an age with Fanny and Anna. The other girls, older, were friendly with Maria and Jane and Susan Clark.

The ruins of the old frontier fort, on Fort Hill near the corner of Peyton and Loudoun streets, must have been a good place for the boys to reenact Indian sieges or Revolutionary battles. The Clark family lived over on the east side of Fort Hill. Susan had married the Barton boys' young uncle Frank Jones, which made it necessary to view Sue in another light than as just one of Maria's friends. (The Joneses lived at Carysbrooke, about a mile from Bartonsville; Frank's younger brother Bev had married one of the Tidball girls and had a farm farther down the Opequon.) Sue's younger brother Frank Clark and David Barton talked about sharing rooms at the university when Frank followed Dave to Charlottesville in a few years. Sue's oldest brother Peyton taught some of the Barton boys at the Winchester Academy.[4] Another brother Will had fin-ished Yale and gone into law practice with his father. Young Julia was about Fanny Barton's age. The Clark house was right next to Mr. Clark's grain ware-houses, near where the railroad came into town. Mr. Clark had his finger in a lot of pies, including the railroad, the telegraph company, and the academy.

The Barton family was accustomed to visiting their relatives in the country, either David Barton's family at Springdale or Fannie Barton's family at Vaucluse. The Valley Turnpike ran right past Springdale, about six miles south of Winchester; it was another mile to Newtown (now Stephens City), and about three miles farther to the turn to the long Vaucluse lane. The Jones family had been at Vaucluse for over seventy years, and Mrs. Barton's grandfather had built the house on the hill from which the great spring emerged. Her mother had died leaving four living children, and her father remarried two years later and had two more sons who reached maturity.[5] Mrs. Barton's father had been dead for ten years, but the ever growing household of her brother William Strother Jones embraced their beloved stepmother of thirty years, Ann C. R. Jones, and Fannie and Strother's nephew Marshall Jones, Anna's brother. Strother and his second wife, Mary, had been married only five years; by now they had had four children, but had lost two. Fannie and Strother's older brother was dead, and they had taken his two children into their families.[6] Their younger brother James had married one of Tom Marshall's sisters and lived in Fauquier County. Their two half brothers Frank and Bev were recently married and farming not far from Bartonsville.

The families visited back and forth, and for the younger boys it added to the pleasures of being at Springdale to have the companionship of cousin Willie Barton, about Robby's age, and the nearby Davis children, and at Vaucluse, cousin Marshall, Rannie's age. Charlie Davis and Bolly were contemporaries, Susie a little older. Together they spent long summer sojourns or weekends hunting and fishing, picking watercress in the streams or berries in the woods. Until recently, the boys' sister Maria and Tom Marshall had lived at Shady Oak, up the hill from the millpond and the Shady Elm factory near Bartonsville. (A few years after Tom and Maria left Shady Oak, cousin Joe Barton, Willie's older brother, rented it until he could buy his own farm.) When the boys were at Springdale, they could easily rove to Uncle Frank's, to Brother Tom's and a little farther to the Davises' and beyond to Vaucluse. The young Marshalls and Joneses became very friendly when they lived two miles apart.

In 1855, Springdale was owned by David's next-older brother Richard, who had taken it over from their parents. As his second wife he married Caroline Marx of Richmond in 1833, and it was some time later that Springdale was given its fashionable Greek Revival portico to face the new Valley Turnpike.[7] They had three children together—Joe, Cary, and Willie—adding to two children from Richard's first marriage. Not content, it seemed, with his life as a gentleman farmer, Richard was ambitious—politically and financially. Politically perhaps he was frustrated; five terms in the State Assembly and one in Congress in the early 1840s was the limit of his achievements. It may have been after that that he turned to financial schemes—speculation in land and grain—which proved to be the undoing not only of Richard, who conveniently died before the full disaster displayed itself, but also of David and their brother Robert (who lived in Lexington), who had guaranteed him and who honorably proceeded to try to make the debts good.[8] Richard's greed and bad judgment would have ruined David Barton even if there had not been a Civil War.

The first cracks in the foundation of David Barton's prosperity and happiness opened in 1856 with Richard's financial failure. Robby Barton remembered well "that distressing event and what a change it made in my father's theretofore most happy life, and how it changed the circumstances of his family. . . . This failure occurred in 1856 when I was fourteen years old. The family continued to live at the old house. . . . We never lacked for comforts and the sons and daughters were carefully educated, but that debt seemed a constant burden on my father and weighed down his naturally gay and happy temperament."

Both Robby and Rannie regretted their father's aversion to being daguerreotyped, but he was still a clear, strong presence to them. Full six feet high (without his boots, Rannie added), broad shoulders, "his head well and gracefully set upon them. He wore no beard whatever, his face, as was the custom with his generation, being always clean shaven. . . . His face was, except when intent upon his business, always sunny, open and handsome," wrote Rannie. For as long as they could remember, their father had had white hair, "as white as it could possibly be, with not infrequently a dab of black ink in it, where he had mechanically wiped his quill pen. I never knew him to use a steel pen," Robby affectionately recalled.

They both remarked how he ran, rather than walked, up stairs—two steps at a time, Rannie said—"a trick which I have myself inherited," confessed Robby, continuing:

> He was fond of exercise, consisting mostly of walking over his farms. I never knew him to hunt, altho he was very fond of fishing.
>
> My father inherited all along the line of his ancestry a devotion to natural history. He never tired of observing, talking, and reading about the natures and dispositions of animals, especially of dogs. He was fond also of plants and fruits and all that, in an amateur way, related to botany. . . .
>
> He was devoted to books, especially books of travel and biography and I have often seen him moved to tears while quietly reading to himself, altho he was not a demonstrative man.
>
> He took a decided interest in geology. When a student at Yale, he walked over the New England States and made quite a collection of stones. Many years afterwards, when I was quite a well grown boy, a mysterious and very heavy box came to him by freight, which when opened proved to be the collection of stones which he had left at Yale. It was afterwards deposited in what was known as the "dark garret" at the old house on Market Street, and for aught I know may be there now.

Rannie summed up:

> *He was concentrated in his business, but when at home was always*
> *the life of the house, and particularly was he always happy at his gen-*
> *erous and hospitable table.*
>
> *He was very democratic in his manner, and for everyone, rich or*
> *poor, high or low, he had a kind word. Many times have I seen him in*
> *the late afternoons in the summer, walking up and down the pavement*
> *in front of our house on Market Street, and to every passerby he would*
> *have some kind and pleasant word. He was entirely domestic, distin-*
> *guished by his industry, energy, punctuality and excellence and faithful-*
> *ness as a lawyer and business man.*

Robby Barton was the eighth of ten children, so that his eldest sisters and brothers were almost grown up by the time the younger ones first became conscious of them. Robby's eldest sister Maria married when he was six and she was eighteen; she married Tom Marshall, who had come to Winchester to read law with her father, but then decided he preferred to be a farmer. They lived near Bartonsville for the next five or six years. Around the time the young Marshalls moved to Fauquier County (about thirty miles away, east of the Blue Ridge), sister Jane met and married a man who was the Marshalls' pastor there—Charles Sheild. Three years later, in 1856, the third sister Martha married Dr. John M. Baldwin, a Winchester neighbor, and they moved to Staunton.[9] The older boys began going away to school in the early 1850s. With large families whose birth dates spanned fifteen or twenty years, it was natural that neighboring cousins might know each other better than brothers and sisters. Robby began his story with his first memories.

[MEMOIR OF ROBERT T. BARTON]

My earliest recollection of myself is that I was a rather undersized and weak child with a freckled face and light brown hair. I grew up, however, to be almost five feet and ten inches high and to weigh at the date of this writing 154 pounds. I was not especially delicate as a child, altho I could not stand fatigue very well and lacked the wind to compete in races with the other boys. As a result I did not excel in manly sports altho I was a fairly good shot with a gun and was fond of fishing.

I was affectionate and warm hearted but very sensitive and easily provoked to anger—indeed given sometimes to ungovernable fits of rage which the impotence of my weak body served only to increase. I was very devoted to reading and from the overheard remarks of my parents and elders I thought I was considered very bright, and thus my vanity was flattered and my native conceit stimulated. I remember that I was always very energetic and methodical in all that I undertook and I was very ambitious always to succeed and to excel. I had considerable fluency of expression, and many more words than I had ideas. I came afterwards to learn how much better it is to reverse those precession and to let your words be much fewer than your ideas. In the debating societies to which I belonged I was rather a leader and I believe I enjoyed all the places of honour in such associations, which small boys usually prize. . . . I was a constant reader of boys histories and of Sir Walter Scott's novels. Some books of travel too I remember reading with interest.

My recreation consisted mainly in going to Vaucluse and Springdale on friday afternoons and remaining there fishing and hunting until Sunday morning when I would come back to town with one or the other of the families when they came to church. Quite frequently I would walk out on friday afternoon to Vaucluse or to Springdale, which, as I look back on them now, seem to have been quite long walks for such a little boy.[10] Generally too we boys carried our guns. Swimming and fishing in the mill pond at Springdale were always of great delight, and I never pass the old pond now in the railroad train without recalling those sweet days of my childhood. My usual companions were my brother Rannie and my cousin Willie Barton, who died some years ago. Later my cousin Marshall Jones accompanied us.[11]

Vaucluse was a second home to the Barton children; their Grandmother Jones had lovingly managed to integrate her husband's first family with her own. Another step-grandson, Strother Jones, remembered her as "the best and most affectionate of mothers, stepmothers, and grandmothers . . . a tall & dignified Randolph, a refined lady of the old school, who never used the back of her chair and never raised her voice in anger. She had the courage of a lion, & feared only her God."[12] Robby remembered her as his "dear, good grandmother . . . up into my manhood years."

[Memoir of Robert T. Barton]

At home, I lived as children usually do. I studied my lessons at night in the dining room or the room called the library, not infrequently nodding over my books. My father was generally busy in the sitting room and was impatient of the noise and interruption of his many boys. He was affectionate however and in most respects indulgent. He had built for me a hennery with a large enclosure, giving up a part of his beloved garden at the Market Street house for that purpose. He also had me a pigeon house arranged, and both were objects of great pleasure to me.

The fresh eggs and young chickens and squabs my father would buy from me at market rates, altho he furnished all the food for my chickens and pigeons. The proceeds of these sales constituted my main supply of pocket money, which was principally invested in powder and shot for my hunts, or in the purchase of the numerous things which make up a boy's equipment.

Rannie, red-haired and mischievous, was close enough in age to Robby to provide plenty of fraternal conflict.

I had to take my brother Rannie in as a partner in the hennery, and as he disliked the drudgery of it very much, our partnership was the source of not a few fights and quarrels. In the fights, Rannie, altho the younger, being much the larger and stronger boy, would have been the victor but for the fact that my temper and pugnacity supplied, to some extent, the place of strength.

Rannie was a great tease and dearly loved to provoke me to anger, but as a rule first provided himself with a safe way of escape.

On Saturday nights my two brothers Marshall and Strother, who were farming in the country, usually came home to spend Sunday.[13] My cousin Joseph Barton before his marriage often came, as did also my uncles Frank and Beverl[e]y R. Jones before their marriages.[14] When at home on Sunday morning I regarded it as a Special feast. We were allowed to sleep later: an unusually good breakfast was provided: we generally had a large and merry company: and the absence of business cares for the day gave my father's genial and interesting nature full play, while my mother was always witty and bright.

Mrs. Barton was noted for her wit and had for years been known as "Funny Fannie." (It was said that she had turned down a suitor named Mr. Finney on the grounds that she would not become Funny Fannie Finney.) Robby related, "Her maiden name was Fannie Lucy Mary Ann Margaret Jones, but she never used all these names altho her children in frolicsome moods often gave them to her.[15] In my recollection she always signed herself Fannie L. Barton." He remembered her "naturally buoyant disposition" and the "sense of humour and power of quick repartee," which never left her.

Oak Hill, the Marshall family seat in Fauquier County, as it appeared during the Civil War. The fashionable Greek Revival wing (left) was added to the original colonial house. (Virginia Historical Society)

My sisters Fannie and Martha were very bright, and the pretty young children of my sister Maria who was married to Col. Thomas Marshall were frequent visitors at our house and added very much to my pleasure.[16] To Col. Marshall I was especially devoted, and his kindness and affection to me never abated, but grew with advancing years and the sad experiences which befell us both. . . .

I recall vividly the marriage of my sister Maria in 1848 to Col. Thomas Marshall. That same summer when I was 6 years old my father and mother took my sister Martha and myself in the family carriage with the pair of white horses (Billy and John) so well remembered by me, and our coloured man John as driver, to my father's farm in the glades of Hampshire County, now West Virginia. My brother Marshall and Powell Conrad, an older brother of Major Holmes Conrad, accompanied us on horse back.[17] It is strange how vividly the impressions of that trip were made upon my young imagination and how long they remained there. . . .

A large part of my summers from 1851 or 1852 to 1860 were spent at "Oak

Hill" in Fauquier Co, whither my brother in law, Col. Thos. Marshall had moved after his purchase of that place.[18] Prior to that time he had lived at "Shady Oak," a farm not far from Springdale which he had purchased from my father and which he resold to him when he bought the "Oak Hill" farm.[19] If you look into the history of the Marshall family, you will recognize this place as an old family seat. Near it and a part of the original "Oak Hill" farm is "Woodside," where my uncle James F. Jones lived. He married Nannie Marshall a sister of Col. Thos. Marshall and she owned the place. Other members of the Marshall family and connections had their estates in that neighbourhood, and the same connections clustered thick in other neighbourhoods of Fauquier Co.[20]

These people were all well born and cultivated, but by habit and association not disposed to thrift. They were exceedingly hospitable and kept open house to all who came. A large army of negro slaves rendered housekeeping possible under such circumstances, but it was most extravagant, and as people of that kind were not much given to keeping careful balance sheets, they ran in debt. . . . No more attractive way of living ever existed than that which prevailed in the Country houses of Virginia in the ante-war slavery days. In point of material civilization and comforts, the people were much behind the present age, and even then behind our northern neighbours; but in social pleasures, hospitality, purity of life and religious sentiments, no community of people ever excelled those old Virginians. Their slaves were members of these families and the relations between them and their masters was only second to that of the children themselves. They were well fed and cared for and most kindly treated. Personal chastisement was administered, it is true, but in those days that was also the punishment usually meted out to the children. A refractory slave who could not be subdued by punishment would be sold, and this was often a sad sight. But then such partings were no more than those frequently occurring among the masters, between parents and children. That there were abuses of the system is true, for as there are bad parents, so there would be bad masters. Straightened circumstances sometimes also caused a master to sell his slaves and this became necessary frequently at the death of the master, either to provide funds with which to pay debts, or for division among the members of the family, of the estate. As a rule however purchasers for slaves could be found in the neighbourhood and such sales were always made, if possible, unless the slave was sold because of his base or unmanageable disposition. In divisions of estates too the slaves were commonly divided without a sale, or if sold were bought in by members of the family. The system, on the whole, was better for the slaves than it was for the masters and I am glad that it has been abolished. You may be

taught to believe that it was a bad and wicked institution. I, who lived under it
and understood it, tell you that no more admirable and virtuous people ever
lived than the slave owners, and there was nothing wicked about the institution
except its abuses, and abuses abound in any human institution.

*Susie and Charlie Davis grew up at Sunnyside, a farm on the northern edge of
Newtown. Among their playmates was Willie Barton at Springdale, only a mile
away. Susie was a year or two younger than Willie and his cousin Robby. She
had clear, fond memories of Springdale in the 1850s.*

[MEMOIR OF SUSAN DAVIS CONRAD]

. . . The atmosphere, point of view, entourage of the time in Virginia to
which my first recollections go back, sixty-nine years ago, are absolutely
indescribable. As different from life here now as if lived on another planet. Its
dignity, its peace, freedom from the mad rush for amusement, constant diversion, so general now. When the ladies not only read their Bibles every day but
[led] Morning and Evening Exercises; looked after the manners and morals not
only of their, usually, numerous, children, but manners and morals and religious teaching of all the small darkies on the place, besides having all the
garments the colored people of all ages wore cut out and made under their
supervision; they had no time for committee meetings or bridge parties. This
quiet sway touched many souls. . . . In my childhood and girlhood I had really
three houses—Vaucluse, the fascinating home of the Strother Joneses . . .
Springdale and, a mile away, my own Sunnyside.[21] The closest intimacy existed
between the three families. In my knowledge of Springdale it was successively
owned by two brothers. First Mr. Richard [W.] Barton, and about 1860, Mr.
David Barton. Mrs. Richard Barton was from a fine old Jewish family of Richmond; highly cultivated, witty, of much distinction of bearing, though a small
person; a grande dame. She was very lovely to me. . . .

Her youngest son [Willie], near my age, my brother [Charlie] and I played
almost daily—coasting on the many hills of Springdale, playing in the mill and
sharing many of the charms of the mill dam. The Sunnyside woods were our
happy hunting grounds, as soon as lessons were over, full of endless delights.
Forty acres of beautiful woodland, cut down in '64 by Sheridan's 6th Corps to
build winter quarters. Springdale was famous as a wheat farm, and there and at
our place, harvest was a time of joy. We went with the women at four o'clock to
take the men their "four o'clock piece." The pies seemed ambrosia to us. We

followed the cradlers swinging their cradles in perfect rhythm, and delighted in their singing—wonderful mellow voices and quaint African hymns. The binders followed, tying up the bundles and then the [man] who formed the shocks. Sometimes we found a treasure-trove in the wheat stubble, partridges' nests— once twenty eggs in one nest. They were delicious to eat; and our consciences were calmed by the assurance of the harvesters that the birds never came back to a nest touched by human contact; the sheltering wheat gone too. The sight of the tall yellow wheat just at harvest, while at sunset waves of fireflies rose and fell in it on those Springdale fields west of the road, was never to be forgotten.

The house was plainly furnished; no rugs or hangings, simple furniture, but the routine of life was one of simple elegance and great comfort. Mrs. Barton had brought from Richmond some highly trained servants. Charles, the gardener, whose fine vegetable beds were screened by a huge lilac hedge from a little formal garden opposite the back porch; Aunt Bella, the tall cook, whose delicious food was cooked by an immense open fireplace in the kitchen in the south wing. A crane hung in the chimney and Dutch ovens of many sizes were on the broad hearth. They were on feet for the hot coals to be piled below, and had lids with a rim to hold the coals. A huge "Tri-Kitchen" [spit] for roasting meats; many saddles of mutton were cooked. Sarah, the head maid, was in charge of the handed teas for which the house was famous. She came first, in the parlour in the winter, on the front porch in summer, with her large array of plates, dainty napkins and wonderful food: rolls light as feathers, buttered corn batter cakes baked the size of a small plate, cut twice across making triangles, thin as wafers, buttered hot from the griddle and eaten like the rolls with the fingers; dried beef like nothing ever seen now, shaved thin as paper, as tender as chicken, a deep crimson color and delicious taste, the tenderloin of beef smoked in their own smokehouse. This was varied by delicious thin ham; wonderful butter-sponge cakes or fragrant gingerbread baked in small cups. Sarah was followed by another maid with a tray holding cups of tea and coffee and rich cream and sugar. Managing plates and cups was a little difficult but it was done. We children sat on the porch steps, the floor our table.[22]

After the Marshall family moved to Fauquier County, Maria missed the constant and close associations with her own family, particularly Susan, Mrs. Frank B. Jones (her uncle's wife). The Marshalls and the Joneses were about the same age and were good friends, as well as being neighbors and relatives. Maria's sister Jane Cary Sheild, who lived nearby, and their Grandmother Jones had been with her at Oak Hill for the advent of her fourth baby in June

1854, and Mrs. Jones's departure prompted a plaintive letter to Susan. Maria felt "perfectly overwhelmed with my cares," the heat, her husband's absence in the harvest field, and her lack of success with the turkeys and ducks.[23] In short, she was a bit homesick and wanted Susan to come: "would begging do any good," Maria wrote.

The Joneses did visit their many family connections in Fauquier County. An undated letter from Frank written from his stepbrother James F. Jones's home to his mother at Vaucluse suggests the tenor of such visits.

[LETTER OF FRANK B. JONES TO ANN C. R. JONES]

Woodside Thursday morn-[24]

My dearest Mother,

Knowing your anxiety to hear from us, I write by today's mail. We had a very comfortable, indeed pleasant ride down, reached Brother James just before dark, did not suffer at all from cold. Sister Nannie and all are well, with the exception of little Randolph, he looks very delicate, but Aunt Lucinda insists that he is improving. We are only staying in the house with fifteen children, fourteen of them under eleven, I wonder Sister Nannie is not *quite entirely crazed.* . . . Maria and Tom [Marshall] came over yesterday, and are expected today to dine. All are much disappointed that you did not come with us. I am very glad we came, and trust we will have as pleasant a trip back as down. The baby recognized your daguerreotype yesterday, and kissed it—most affectionately.[25] . . . excuse this, I have written with the baby in my arms. Mammy is well, but is at her breakfast—love to all

Your devoted child

F.B. Jones

Frank's farm and young family made for a full life, but both local tradition and his VMI background impelled him to participate in the militia. He continued to fulfill this duty, but it had evidently palled after a few years. He wrote to Susan, "I received a very polite letter from Col [Lewis F.] Moore asking me to take part in the military parade of yesterday & join the military at supper, but I feel too old now for such occasions and I politely declined going, I expect a scold from William who wrote to me saying I must not fail to come."[26]

During this time, Frank's eldest nephew Marshall Barton was receiving a military education also. After early schooling at Winchester Academy, Robby and Rannie's elder brothers all attended the Episcopal High School in Alexandria, as

had their brother-in-law Tom Marshall and their uncle Frank Jones. Marshall Barton continued his education at the Virginia Military Institute. He was clearly tired of school and finding his classes pointless when, in the fall of his final year, he wrote to his cousin Joseph Barton. Marshall was yearning to be elsewhere especially when Joe forwarded his lady love's letter to him at the institute.

[LETTER OF C. MARSHALL BARTON TO JOSEPH M. BARTON]

V.M.I. Sept 28th, 1855

Dear Joe

In the eloquent language of one of my roommates, *Thank God* friday night has come again. You cant imagine with what deep interest I count the days as they come & go. I have a calendar on my wardrobe door & the first thing after my return from reveille in the morning is to scratch off the preceeding day & generally I find my way back into bed pretty near as fast as I have to get out of it, although in direct opposition to the regulations of the V.M.I. But from many years, I may say of practice, I have become cute enough to dodge Spex, Gil——— & the other *grand rascals*.[27]

I can assure you that I am heartily sick of the military, studies & everything else connected with the V.M.I. I don't think I will touch a gun, book, or anything that bears any resemblance to them for some time after I leave here, that is if I ever do get away.

I have been here so long that I feel as if I had been living here all my life, and the idea of leaving it, perhaps never to return, seems almost impossible to believe.

I find the studies this year a great deal more interesting than they have been heretofore, with the exception of one single one, which so counterbalances the rest as to throw all the good part into the shade. We commenced studying engineering this year. I find the military engineering quite interesting.[28] I hope I may find civil equally so as it is the only thing I care about knowing anything about. The study I referred to just now was Optics, which from being so very difficult & taught by such a *hell of a fool*, whose name is Jackson, has suggested the following lines,

The V.M.I., Oh what a spot,
In winter cold, in summer hot.
Great Lord Almighty, what a wonder
Major Jackson, Hell & Thunder.[29]

I am afraid I have digressed too far to refer to the reception of your letter which I can assure you was the most welcome one I have received for a long time. I'll *swear* I am almost ashamed send off a letter like this full of erasures, mistakes, etc., but I know that you will excuse me when I tell you that I have four room-mates in a very exciting discussion, cursing and ripping so that I can hardly hear myself. In such a fuss as this I can hardly compose myself sufficiently to refer to that *sweet note* that has been ringing in my ears ever since its reception. Oh, how much I wished to be back at least for a day or two. It brought on quite a relapse and I felt like leaving the V.M.I. immediately. I felt nearly reconciled to stay this year out but for three or four days I have not been able to open a book, I can't account for the reason. You asked me to burn up your letter. Of course you did not include that part of it & even if you did, I don't think I would grant your request. I carry it in my left pocket and have nearly worn it out already. I think I must send soon after an original copy. . . . Write soon. Give love to all enquiring friends.

I remain your

Affectionate cousin,

C.M. Barton

David R. Barton, their second brother, chose the University of Virginia, where he entered in the fall of 1856, and his "ticket," or course of study, was "literary": math, natural philosophy, moral philosophy, Latin, and Greek. His friends knew he was seriously considering the ministry, but he evidently enjoyed the lighter moments of university life. Toward the end of the first year he wrote his friend Frank Clark.

[LETTER OF DAVID R. BARTON TO FRANK P. CLARK]

University of Va. April 18th/57

Dear Frank,[30]

Although your letter was only received a few days ago nevertheless I will not let a good opportunity for dropping a few lines to you pass by unheeded. . . .

You evidently from the tone of your letters, seem to be "struck." Not by any particular & (*in that case*) fortunate young lady; but by the female sex in general. Take care; "there is many a slip between the cup and the lip." You will be caught napping by some of them yet. I dont mean to say that the captivating charms of a lovely black or blue eyed lass should be in all cases resisted. For I myself feel that "I" am thus inclined; that is to say *not* to *resist them*. But for a student a small degree of caution is not only necessary but even indispensable. I know that the charming lovely "critter", as the Dutch man said when he took up a pig, "is not only pretty but useful." But you know there is a place & time for everything. Of course I don't give you the above advice for fear that you will cut me out of all hopes of getting myself a "wife" ("a dear") in Winchester. In what do I want with any of your Shepherstown or Winchester girls when the prettiest girl in Culpepper county sends her ——— love & ——— to me? You might pick out the most beautiful features of all your girls & mould & proportion them and the girl thus formed couldnt hold a patching to—the-prettiest-girl-in-Culpepper-county-of-Virginia, so renowed for its beautiful lasses. Frank, dont grow jealous, but be content with your lot and hope for a better day to come. . . .

You must give my best love to Bob [Baldwin] and ask him in my name to write to me. I have engaged a room on Carr Hill for next year my reasons for getting a room there are several and good. 1st the crowd there is always composed of gentlemen, although some few are generally dissipated. 2ndly the rooms are good. 3rdly the fare is better than at any other place and I really suffer so much now from the Dyspepsia that I must have my food well cooked, & lastly I could not get a room on the lawn.[31] The room I expect to get is considered by a good many as one of the best up there; and all things considered I think that we are quite well arranged for next year. You speak of taking a ticket, which I think you will regret having taken. So far as I am concerned, I would prefer your taking that ticket; for roommates are always to try and take the same but take my word for it you will regret it. I shall not take such a ticket of course, but I expect, or rather hope, to get through on Math, and if I get through on Math & morral I should only take Ancient & Modern & would think that I were taking a large ticket, although I shall have studied Latin quite well one year under the professor here. However, exercise your own judgement. Such a thing has been done here once or twice, as to graduate on all three. . . . It getting rather late so I think I will close. Please if you can spare time write to me soon, whether there is any news or not. I will send you a catalogue as soon as they come out.

yr very true friend

David R. Barton

After two years at the university, David took a year off as a private tutor in the J. T. B. Dorsey family in Ellicott's Mills, near Baltimore.[32] It is impossible to know whether he was taking stock of himself with regard to future pursuits, or whether his father's financial problems, which developed in 1856, made it nec-

essary for him to earn his own way. In any case, he appears to have spent this time debating between being a teacher or a minister. He determined to keep a journal of his time in Maryland, but as many such resolutions do, it petered out after a month or so. Nevertheless, the diary recorded another side of David: conscientious, serious, prayerful. He spent his free time reading history and religious tracts and trying to "cultivate humility and charity." "Every week I resolve to do better and how very far short of my hopes and duties do I fall!"[33] By the next spring, David had evidently come to some decision and hoped to take advantage of his father's return trip from Norfolk (probably by ship to Baltimore) to discuss it with him. David W. Barton had likely gone to see his sister-in-law's family there about his brother's unfinished business: Richard had died in March, deeply in debt. Caroline Barton's family, the Marxes, had lent Richard money, too.[34] While David W. Barton was away, two of his young sons (Bolling, thirteen, and Robby, sixteen) wrote him about matters at home, including the local elections, the vegetable patch in the back garden, the country farms, and marauders in the smoke house.

[LETTER OF ROBERT T. BARTON TO DAVID W. BARTON]

Winchester, May 18th 1859

Dear Father

I write at Ma's request enclosing a letter to you from brother David, asking you to stop on your way home, at Mr. Dorsey's which she earnestly requests you to do and tells me to beg you, if you only stay a day longer from home, not to omit paying him a visit, for Mr. & Mrs. Dorsey will no doubt be very glad to see you.

I suppose you have heard through some of our letter writing, of the accident to our smoke-house; the rogues entered through the roof of the ash house and took every peice of bacon except one, which one, I suppose, they did not see, both on account of its smalness and also on account of the retired position in which it hung; I did every thing I could, to find out the theives, and to get the constables interested in finding *them* out, (for there was certainly more than one) but I was unsuccesful; I however have some very well grounded suspicions, that it was Dr Baldwins servant William, who having heard of them, came over to day and denied it entirely, but that signifies nothing.[35]. . .

Brothers Marshall & Strother came in to night and report, the corn coming up finely and every thing on the farm coming on as well as could be wished. Mr. Goggin is to speak here on fryday next and Ran says the chance for Mr. Botelers election is very good, I hope you will be back in time to vote for him.[36] . . . All unite with me in love to you, and hope that you will have a pleasant trip. I remain your affectionate son.

Robert T. Barton

It can be surmised his father did stop in Baltimore to see David and approved whatever plans and conclusions the young man had formulated. David left his teaching post and returned to the university in the fall of 1859, having decided, according to one friend, to take orders, and remained there until the spring of 1861.[37]

The third brother, Strother, spent two years at the Episcopal High School, finishing in June 1858. He may have had no desire for further education, or possibly his father could not then afford it with the younger boys still in school. In any case Strother took over Lost Brook, his father's fine farm of over 860 acres, fourteen miles south of Winchester near Buffalo Marsh and Cedar Creek. Although Richard Barton had transferred Springdale to his brother David in 1858 as part of his colossal indebtedness, it seems that he continued to live there until his death in March 1859.[38] Richard was buried in the family cemetery on the grounds. His widow Caroline and young Willie probably left Springdale then, going to live with Joe and his family at Hanover Lodge, just a mile down the turnpike. Marshall Barton was living at Springdale and running that farm for his father by the summer of 1859. (Mail from the VMI caught up with him even though they had his name wrong.) He could now not only contemplate but also plan marriage, and on September 27 he married his second cousin Ellen Hervie Marshall, of Fauquier County.

Robby Barton's life also changed dramatically in the fall of 1859. At sixteen, he had completed his studies at the Winchester Academy, and was sent away to school—not to Episcopal High School, where so many of his family had gone, but to a school near Charlottesville with a friend from home.

[MEMOIR OF ROBERT T. BARTON]

In the fall of 1859 I went with John J. Williams and Hugh McGuire to "Bloomfield," a school in Albemarle Co. Va. about five miles from the University of Virginia. . . .[39]

My father and Mr. Philip Williams were law partners and intimate friends and were about the same age. It was natural therefore that John J. Williams who is about six months older than I am, should also have been my intimate friend.

We had been schoolmates, in the same classes since 1851 and when in 1859 we went to boarding school together we were room mates and with the exception of a single study towards the end of our term at Bloomfield we remained in the same classes. . . .

I vividly recall my trip to Bloomfield in the fall of 1859. I had never been far away from home and had never seen a city, so that my timidity and sadness at leaving home were much alleviated by the excitement of the trip. . . . There was no railroad from Winchester directly to Washington and none at all up the Valley. Our choice of routes therefore lay between a stage ride to River Station (now Riverton) in Warren Co. Va., where we would have reached the Manassas Gap Railroad, and a stage ride to Leesburg in Loudon Co. Va., where we would take the S. L. & H. Railroad (now the W.&0.) to Alexandria. We might have gone, as I afterwards frequently did, by rail to Harpers Ferry, and thence by B.&0. Railroad to the Relay Station and from there to Washington. For some reason, which I do not recall, the Leesburg route was selected. I remember the ride a beautiful September morning on top of one of the old-fashioned stages with four fine horses through the beautiful Country, by Berryville, Snickers Ferry, Snickers Gap, over the Mountain, and by the pretty road to Leesburg. Then by the massive and rather slow railroad coach to Alexandria where we stopped at the "Mansion House." I remember how wide open my eyes and mind were to all new impressions: the jokes and fun we boys had on the stage; the decidedly novel and unusual experience of a railroad ride; the comparatively busy sight of Alexandria's streets, my first impression of anything like a city. Then the good dinner at the hotel and my desire to exhaust the bill of fare. After dinner we took the Steamboat for Washington. I had never ridden on a Steamboat, nor indeed had I ever seen one. I am quite sure that my subsequent experience in crossing the ocean in a great ship was not near so wonderful or awe-inspiring to me as that voyage from Alexandria to Washington. Then the sight of Washington itself: the Capitol and the White House and all the wonders of the great city! Do not think that Washington then was to compare with Washington now, but still it was amazing to my rustic and inexperienced eyes. The Capitol was not nearly finished and great piles of stone and rubbish lay around it. The dome was incomplete and the Statue of Liberty was still in the Rotunda waiting to be lifted to its place. The frescoes of the halls and rooms was just being put on and scaffolding filled the great building. The grounds were comparatively quite rude and primitive. A high paling fence enclosed the whole space, and the walks were the ordinary dirt and gravel of a country home.

There were of course, no street cars, but omnibuses instead ran in the principal streets just as they do now in London and Paris.

Pennsylvania Avenue, now such a beautiful street, presented then a very different aspect. It was macadamized like a turnpike, and rows of tall poplar trees grew up each side of the street. The houses too have greatly improved since then. Ours must have been a curious looking procession as we walked up towards the Capitol. At one time, I remember falling behind the rest of the party and hearing the remarks of the hackmen and others standing along the pavement. As the boys strode on with their rustic clothes and linen dusters, I heard one hackman say, "The Kildees seem to have come to town." I was much amused and we all had a hearty laugh over it. . . .

The next day we went on to Gordonsville and thence to Ivy Depot in Albemarle Co. by rail. I remember well my arrival at "Bloomfield," the cheerless and comfortless appearance of our room which was shared by John Williams and myself: how we sought to improve it by putting up calico curtains, and placing on the shelves the little things we had brought from home. Then later we had a rag carpet on a part of the floor. These things helped us a good deal, but the pains of homesickness which I suffered there—who can tell it but he who has suffered the like?

I was not long in getting acquainted with the large crowd of boys, some of whom I learned to like and some to dislike. To the majority of them I was entirely indifferent. We had capital teachers, the discipline of the school was good and kindly; the fare was healthy clean and of attractive quality and variety. Then too, we had such strong young appetites. On Saturdays we frequently went hunting and as a consequence on Sunday morning we had game breakfasts, which the principal permitted to be cooked for us and sent to the table at which the hunters sat. Of course, we shared our game with the other members of our mess. . . .

Robby was lucky to have some relatives down the road, who provided a counterpoint to school routine and the beginning of long friendships.

One of the pleasantest recreations of my school life was my visits to my cousins the Colstons at their home called Hill-and-Dale about a mile and a half from the School.[40] I would sometimes go there on Saturday or even friday afternoon and stay until Sunday. Then I went to Church with the family in their carriage and walked back to the school with the boys. I was much envied by the other boys, altho many of them also were invited from time to time to that hospitable house. Bettie, Annie and Jeanie were the three girls and all of them pretty and sweet. I was quite in love with Bettie but feeling that at least two of the boys were preferred by her I kept myself in bounds. Several of the other boys addressed her however and I believe she was engaged to all of them. . . .

At Xmas of the year 1859 I was permitted by my parents to come home for the holidays. I remember that the question was in doubt for some time, as my father could not well afford, in his then great difficulties, the expense of so many boys and so many things to do for each of them. I remember too how I longed for and feared to receive the letter that would determine the question of my coming, and the exultant joy with which when the letter came, I found that I was to go home for the holidays. It is hard for parents to understand how much such an indulgence is to a homesick boy, and I recall that of this and many other matters I used to say that if I ever had a son I would try to put myself in his place. It yet remains, my little boy, to be seen whether I can fulfill my promise.

Well Xmas came at last and John Williams and I started together for home. We went by what was known then as the Virginia Central Railroad (now the C.&0.) to Staunton. Then about 3 o'clock P.M. we took the Stage at the Virginia Hotel for Winchester, where we arrived the next morning about 9 o'clock. I well remember that long night ride and all of its incidents: the stage at times crowded; the close atmosphere and then the cold as it became necessary to let in some fresh air; the sick baby that was especially unpleasant; the intervals of sleep and wakefulness; the stoppages to receive and deliver the mail and to change horses. Then as morning came and we reached familiar ground: Middletown, the Vaucluse lane, Springdale, and then Winchester—how my heart bounded at the sight. Then the sweet home coming—my father's "Why, my boy" and my mother's warm embrace. These and the sweet sense of being home again come back to me after all these long years like a breath from Heaven.

My recollection is that I went back by the same route, but with very different feelings from those experienced at my home coming. Still the school had its pleasures. I was glad to meet my friends among the boys once more, and to exchange experiences with them about the joys of home and Christmas. It is a great mistake for older people to think that boys have no real troubles. This surely is not true, but I have lived long enough to be quite sure that the joys of boys are freer from alloy or the apprehensions of trouble in the future than ever comes to the grown up man. Still there is no joy in boyhood equal to the love of a man for his sweetheart, his wife, and his child.

Shortly after my return to school early in January 1860 I began to feel quite badly and this indisposition increased until a case of what is called "walking typhoid fever" developed itself. I tried hard to keep up with my lessons, but was

Martha W. Barton in a pastel portrait done about the time of her marriage to John M. Baldwin. (Martha Barton Ballard)

so sick that I had to give it up at last. Then letters from home directed me to leave school and go to Staunton. This I did and I was under the charge there of Dr. John M. Baldwin, who had married my sister Martha. They had their rooms in a stone house close to the Virginia Hotel and took their meals at the hotel. I stayed there for about two weeks, but not improving it was thought best for me to go to Winchester. I went home by the Stage, but in the course of about four weeks I was well enough to return to school. I had been absent about four weeks and besides had lost about two weeks by illness before I left school. This was a great loss to me, but by hard study on my return I caught up to my classes and got through my final examinations quite creditably.

I failed to mention the intense excitement caused among the boys by the John Brown raid, and the effect especially upon us near whose homes that great outrage was perpetrated. We were all wild with excitement, but the speedy capture of John Brown and his hanging relieved the great apprehensions which we felt at the first alarm.

John Brown's raid took place October 16. Marshall Barton's friend Powell Conrad was on his way to Leesburg on legal business when he heard of Brown's attempt, and hastily joined his militia unit at Harpers Ferry. A few days later he wrote his younger brother Holmes.

[LETTER OF POWELL CONRAD TO HOLMES CONRAD]

Everything is quiet now at the Ferry. The Prisoners are to be tried by Virginia courts for murder & if they escape, by the U. S. Courts for treason, old Brown is like to get well of his wounds—but only to stretch a halter. If he gets off before a jury on the ground of insanity, he stands a good chance of lynching, indeed they are compelled to guard the Charlestown jail every night, strongly, to prevent lynching now.

We have had a very exciting time of it and there is still some excitement. We were advised by wire that two of the insurgents had escaped in this direction. Two men with a mule team and a wagon passed through here [Winchester] on Monday evening,[41] answering the description. On Wednesday two parties started in pursuit, Strother Jones heading one & Sheriff Correll the other. They have not yet been heard from.[42]

After Brown's conviction and sentencing, Virginia was on a virtual war alert as there were real fears that abolitionists would attempt to free him. One Sunday at the Marshall family church near Oak Hill, the Reverend Mr. Sheild's service was interrupted by a messenger sent by Turner Ashby to rally members of the local militia to prevent an anticipated jailbreak. James F. Jones, Tom Marshall, and one of his brothers were among those who responded, and rode with three troops of cavalry through the night to Charlestown—to find "there was no occasion for us to be there."[43] Rannie Barton, still at home in Winchester and attending the academy, felt a keen interest in the proceedings.

["REMINISCENCES" OF RANDOLPH BARTON]

With John Brown condemned and awaiting execution I have shaken hands and talked. He had on his table the Bible and the Baltimore Sun—the consolations of a future life, and the misery of the present in sharp contrast. He had been tried on the charges, I suppose, of an endeavor to cause an insurrection among the slaves, and murder, no doubt, as lives were lost at Harper's Ferry. He had been fairly tried, Judge [Richard] Parker, of Winchester, Virginia, whose law class I attended in 1865-6, presiding, a man of eminent judicial qualities and unimpeachable fairness. He had been convicted, sentenced to death by hanging, and was waiting execution. There was great curiosity to see him and I among others (I was then in my fifteenth year) was stirred by the prevailing desire. My father at first refused to let me go to Charlestown, where Brown was imprisoned, some twenty miles distant by railway, but upon second thought said, "It is an historical occasion, you may go." Visitors were admitted to the jail in groups of five or six. As we entered his room, which was clean, bright and sunny and although limited as to furniture, was very comfortable, he arose from his chair and received us with dignity and composure. Under such circumstances conversation is, of course, limited to common-place topics, such as his health, the weather, etc. He was well near six feet tall, slender, well clad, very dignified, speaking in a measured and easy way with a well modulated voice.

After a visit of some ten minutes we bade him good-morning, shaking hands with him as we parted. It was not the handshake of forgiveness but that of humanity.[44]

Robby Barton appears to have shared his father's views on John Brown, and politics in general, with a different perspective due to his years. The polarizing beliefs on states' rights and slavery issues, soon to split the country, fractured the 1860 elections into a contest between four parties. Robby supported the Democratic candidates, Breckinridge and Lane. His father and brothers were for the diehard Whigs of the Constitutional Union ticket, Bell and Everett.

[MEMOIR OF ROBERT T. BARTON]

You will read about all this in history, and when you do I hope you will learn the truth about it and not the falsehoods taught by Northern historians and magazine writers. The only element of the hero in John Brown was his mad fanaticism on the subject of slavery. All the rest was wicked hate. There was neither wisdom nor patriotism in any of that band or in its Northern supporters. They richly deserved the felons fate which, after fair trials the law awarded to them. The rise of the Republican Party out of the cry for the abolition of slavery was the most conspicuous political feature of that year. Of course there was no Abolitionist or Republican among the boys, but they were sharply divided between Union boys and Secessionists; between Whigs and Democrats, and the sub-divisions of Democrats, which served to destroy the power of that party at the general election of the next year.

As my father was, so was I, an old line Whig and a Unionist. But in my society debates, I learned a good deal of the story of the Constitution and thinking that the Whig party offered no protection to the South from the oppressions of the Abolitionists, and that its tendencies were too much towards the old idea of Federalism, I gave up my boyish predilections and after the nominations, I announced myself for Breckinridge & Lane. I remember the anger of my brothers and associates, nearly all of whom were for Bell and Everett the Whig candidates. I remember too the mixed sentiments of my father. He was for Bell & Everett and, of course, thought that I should be of that persuasion also, but he approved my independent views and my expression of them. In that day the boys would put short poles and flags on the Chimneys. My Whig Associates, to crowd me out, "preempted" the two front chimneys of our Market Street house and insisted that I should not occupy either of the other chimneys, but my father interfered in this, and I was permitted to put up my Breckinridge & Lane flag on a back chimney. I remember how I sought to overwhelm my associates with my arguments in favor of the Democratic platform, but I remember how, in turn, I was always silenced by the indignant cry that "Papa" was a Whig and hence the Whigs must be right.

I came home from school in the month of June 1860. Shortly after my return I became a member of the Episcopal Church and was confirmed by Bishop Meade.[45]

As usual I spent a portion of the summer [with the Marshalls] at Oak Hill. It was only made eventful, so far as I remember, by the hot discussions of politics, the threat of certain of the states that they would secede in case of Mr. Lincoln's election, and the intense anxiety which the situation created in the minds of those who while they loved the Union, were yet determined that the rights of the Southern States should be preserved. I was not then eighteen years of age, but I remember how keenly I shared the anxiety continually expressed on that subject by men like my father. I often discussed politics with him, and he did not differ very widely from me when I urged that the only hope of the Country was in the election of John C. Breckinridge to the Presidency. Yet he threw away his vote on Bell.

In the fall I returned to Bloomfield and pursued my studies as zealously as the excited condition of the Country, in which the school boys and teachers all shared, would permit. I had not entirely recovered from my illness of the preceding winter, and altho not actually sick, I was extremely weak and delicate.

During both of my years at Bloomfield, my brother David was a student at the University. Bloomfield was only about five miles distant, and he often walked down there on Sunday mornings, returning that afternoon, and sometimes I went down either by the train or on foot and spent Saturday night with my brother. Politics was as rife among the Students as in any other body of men. Mr. Holcombe, the Professor of Law, was an original Secessionist. He once spoke to the Bloomfield boys on that subject. He was a fine speaker, well versed in Constitutional Law and of pleasing and attractive manner.[46] I also heard Mr. Yancey of Alabama, the great apostle of Secession, speak at Charlottesville, to an audience largely made up of University students.[47] The little band of Unionists, to which I belonged, hotly contested the views of the Secession boys, many of whom were from the States of the far South, and we received for our pains the ignominious epithet of Submissionists. We conceded the right of revolution, that is, the right of any people to change or overthrow its government when it became tyrannical and too grievous to be borne, but we denied the Constitutional right of any State to secede. To this view I earnestly

adhered during the war and since its end for a number of years, but as I have
grown older and read fully on the subject and reflected about it since it has
become only an abstract question, I no longer doubt it, and I often wonder that
I was ever misled by what seems to me now to have been the sophistry of those
who denied the right of secession.

About a month or two after the beginning of the session I heard from home
of the removal from Fauquier of my sister Jane, who was married to Rev. C. H.
Sheild and who had for some years had charge of the Episcopal Church near
Oak Hill, to Cecil County Md., where her husband went that fall to take charge
of St. Stephen's Church in that County.[48] How little did I think then what an
important influence that move was to have upon a very large part of my life.

*The Sheilds and their children had been living at Piedmont near Jane's sister
Maria and Tom Marshall, and the parting must have been painful for both
sisters—even more so for Jane, as she must have known by that time that Maria
was very ill. Consumption, perhaps early contracted, was doubtless accelerated
by the toll of having six children in ten years.[49] Maria worsened only a few
months later. Back at the university, in February 1861, David recorded a last
entry in his little notebook.*

[DIARY OF DAVID R. BARTON]

. . . To day I received intelligence of the death of my dear Sister Maria B.
Marshall, who died on the 11th inst. . . . Oh God, may this event, the first death
in my immediate family, direct me more constantly to thee! Protect those children thou hast rendered motherless, through Christ our Lord.

*A lady of Charleston, South Carolina, with ties to Winchester and the Bartons,
wrote an extraordinary letter to Mrs. Barton, combining her sense of personal
loss with her presentiments of imminent national catastrophe.*

[LETTER OF ROSA ACELIE TOGNO TO FANNIE L. BARTON]

25 Feb. 1861

My dear Friend,

I cannot attempt at this time to write you words of consolation, but of the
heartfelt sympathy that I have for you in sorrowing! Dear Maria was willing to

go, & now enjoys happiness that we know not of. & while you miss her affectionate & gentle intercourse, while you weep for her absence, lift up yr soul & see her gain! Those little ones now so sad, & who will miss her good example & care, are in the keeping of a loving Father—& he is a pious good man. May God have mercy on that little household, & soften to them the severity of the stroke. I think of those children constantly & I know Mr. Marshall will mourn in truth & sincerity that gentle unselfish, quiet spirit, that has ministered so faithfully to his happiness. He was devoted to Maria & I feel satisfied he will do all that is right with the children. They, poor little things, will soon be comforted; childhood sorrows lay as lightly on their hearts as dew drops on flowers. They will cheer up, & be joyful again while you will be the most enduring Mourner! A good child is such a joy, such a blessing as I think of your sorrow I gaze on my *only two*. I think you are deserving of *the all* of sympathy! would that I could be with you! I think I appreciate Maria as you did, & that I knew all the sweet innocence & purity of her heart. I am so glad I ran over to see her in the summer, & that I was with her even for those few days! I hope you bear up with your sorrow, & that you are able to speak of comfort & resignation to Mr. Barton & to those poor little motherless children! . . .

We are in a state of political excitement bordering on phrenzy. How it will end no one can tell. But the 4th is at hand & a few days makes clear our position.[50] Better certain misery, than than this unsettled, unsatisfactory excitement. Today———war & bloodshed troops & powder. Tomorrow ruin & flight from a shell'd city! Time, the great revealer will set us in our true light; before many days too! I fear the worst, & am not as sanguine as to the *immediate* happiness & prospect of the country. I am a kind of philosopher in my corner, & history is to me a great teacher, It tells me of republics reaching the acme of power, glory, wealth, & civilization—of the insidious effect of vice, of pride, of arrogance! The citizens of the United States considered themselves the Lords of Creation—equal almost to God—& this, like other before it, must have a fall! what brings more ruin, sorrow, disaster than civil war? People laugh at my solemn view of our prospects, but I have a conviction that the chastisement for pride & ungodliness is upon us, & pray we may lament & pray that it deal no heavy blows!

The fort, Fort Sumter, is still before in defiance of all our threats & fretful anger, the Stars & Stripes wave over it—& woe to us, the day it is substituted by the Palmetto! So far as I am concerned, being no politician, having no sons, I can but suffer by my purse, & it is a ruinous season. Provisions bringing fabulous prices—coal $17 & $18 per ton & servants wages 17 & $18 per month—you can imagine the rest!

I cannot tell what change a regular engagement commenced in the harbor will bring for the inhabitants of the city. This we anticipate certain for the present week. The preparations are terrific & three or four days I fear make us "see light." There is a determined spirit of revenge—of hatred—of exasperation that can bring no good. Maryland & Virginia too are shuffling, & unreliable, & I think against us [*illegible*] not in spirit *with* us. Little did I dream when I came home in fine spirits, with every corner of the house engaged, & all things so bright & prosperous that I would find myself in such a mess in a few weeks.

Remember me I repeat it, affectionately to Mr. Barton & the girls to Mat, Jane, all the family, & accept the love of my Girls. They speak of you daily with great affection & are in excellent health.

And now my dear Mrs. Barton receive the assurance of my heartfelt sympathy, & affectionate & grateful regard.

R. Acelie Togno[51]

Robby's particular memories of Maria and summers with her family must have grieved him especially, despite the twelve-year age difference, as Oak Hill clearly was a second home to him.

[MEMOIR OF ROBERT T. BARTON]

. . . After [Maria's] death her children continued to live with my parents, and after events changed the conditions of things so that they never did return to "Oak Hill." Col. Marshall himself only visited his old home from time to time, but remained most of the time at Winchester, until he entered the Confederate Army in the early summer of 1861.

Lincoln was elected and the extreme Southern States passed ordinances of Secession. In Virginia, a convention was elected, composed of a large majority of Union men. That Convention earnestly set itself to preserve the Union and peace and to act as the arbiter between the extremes of both sections. It would eventually have succeeded and I confidently believe that the ordinance of secession would have been repealed and the Union preserved without a war, had Mr. Lincoln and Mr. Seward kept their promises, and acted with frankness and consideration. All of this, my boy, is history, and you can read it for yourself.

The advocates of the two views are very far apart and their statements of fact are very contradicting. I give you only the impression I had at the time and which my reading of history confirms. That was surely the impression of the Union men of Virginia, but they were also very bitter in their feelings towards the "fire-eaters" of the South, classing them with the abolitionists of the North.

As State after State seceded and it looked more and more like war, Military companies were formed all over the State, and the school boys followed the example. The teachers were members of the Company. Mr. Brown [one of the principals] himself was a private in the ranks and some of the boys were officers.[52] I remember being greatly amused when at a drill Mr. Brown undertook to rebuke one of the boys for some dereliction during the day, and the boy being a sergeant shut Mr. Brown up with the stern order "No talking in ranks, Private Brown." Mr. Brown enjoyed the joke as much as the rest of us.

Finally the crisis came. Lincoln called on the States for troops to coerce the South and this being the question upon which Virginia drew the line, the convention passed the ordinance of secession and prepared for war. Many of the boys had already gone home, and this climax of political affairs rendered further study almost an impossibility. I entreated to be allowed to go home and finally my request was unwillingly granted.

My sister Fannie had gone on a visit of some length to my sister Jane in Cecil Co. Md. She was as sweet and gentle as she was bright and attractive the purest, best and most unselfish person I ever knew. She would frequently write to me and often mentioned in terms of enthusiasm a young girl whom she had met in Cecil and whose name was Katie Knight.

Rannie Barton opened his reminiscence not with his childhood but with his first intimation of war.

[MEMOIR OF RANDOLPH BARTON]

I was born on the 24th of April, 1844, and so in 1859, in which year I locate the incident which first turned my thoughts to the dread possibilities of war, I was only fifteen years of age. I remember in that year driving a carriage in which my mother and cousin, Richard Barton, were seated, from Winchester to Springdale.[53] The conversation which was going on behind me was upon the political condition of the country; and I recall my mother's remark, "that if they (the Yankees) ever waged war upon the South she would send six sons into the Southern army; to see three of them sacrificed and three exposed to all the perils of battle. And yet I never but once saw her flinch from the stern duty of pressing us on to perform our part. In the summer of 1864, when our army was pressing General Crook down the Valley towards Winchester, I stopped at Springdale, and when I arose to go on, she yearningly entreated me to stay a while longer. I did not stay, however, but went on, and on the outskirts of Winchester, within an hour, a ball from a Yankee skirmisher struck the ground immediately beneath my horse.

The incident I have related of my mother's resolution was the first impression I had of what might come. Whether it influenced my parents in their conclusion to send me to the Virginia Military Institute or not, I do not know; but thither I went in July, 1860, and entered as a cadet. There for one year I had the advantage of a military training, an experience which radically changed my entire disposition, and the benefits of which I have always felt. Major T. J. Jackson was there as a professor—modest, taciturn, obscure, the butt of the cadets, and while respected by all—faculty, cadets and citizens—was regarded as a quiet, harmless eccentric, who would one day die and quickly pass into oblivion. His star was just below the horizon; within a year it began to rise. It reached its zenith at Chancellorsville in May, 1863, and now, after thirty-four years, it shines with undiminished glory. As long as men live and admire fortitude, virtue, resolution, modesty, the bravery of an Agamemon [sic], and the military skill of a Lee or a Napoleon, so long will the name of "Stonewall" Jackson stand pre-eminent.

Rannie's memories of his year at the Virginia Military Institute were, understandably, mixed. Much later, he recalled for the cadets of 1912:

[ADDRESS OF RANDOLPH BARTON]

. . . If my arrival had been only a week ago my recollection would not be more vivid of what occurred, or of my first impressions. Of course I reported at once to General Smith in his office, the basement of his private residence. I recall his cordial and encouraging reception, and the chill creeps over me now that crept over me then, when he passed slowly but distinctly from the graciousness of a host, to the bluntness of the military man. In ten minutes I had orders

The Virginia Military Institute's new barracks, built in 1851. (Virginia Military Institute Archives)

from him which left not a trace of uncertainty as to what he expected me to do, and I left his office to report at the camp.

My course took me in the neighborhood of the "guard" tree.[54] The day was bright, the sun was hot, the grass was green, I was green, I wanted to take my bearings, the shade was inviting, and I loitered for a moment near the tree. Several cadets lying upon the ground invited me to sit down, which I considered very polite. One cadet, who at the moment seemed to me to be taking a good deal upon himself, pointedly and briefly told me to move on, as it was against the rules for me to hang around the tree. Those lying upon the ground urged me to remain, not to mind that fellow, that he was simply putting on airs &c &c. I yielded to their blandishments, and in two minutes I was informed that I was under arrest. I did not know exactly what that meant, but I instinctively felt it was something horrible. I had never been "under" anything of the kind before, and whatever it was it became very crushing. My head swam, I had a vague consciousness of innocence, but the misery of the lost soul is joy to what I felt. I wanted to go home. I will not pursue the subject. I will not tell of the pitying looks given to me, as between two armed men, I was marched to my tent—the visits of condolence from strangers—of the prospective court martial—of death. If any one coming to me had said, fifty-two years from this time you will be jocosely telling your experience to a most polite and patient audience, in one of the halls on these grounds, I would have said "behold the dreamer cometh. . . ."[55]

In later years Rannie was fond of reminiscing about his professor, Thomas J. Jackson.

[ADDRESS OF RANDOLPH BARTON]

. . . Of the members of the Faculty, the man who impressed me most was one who in manner and appearance was least impressive. This man we knew as Major Jackson. . . . When I first saw him in July 1860, he was in his thirty-seventh year. Look around you and note some one of that age, and you will not regard him as an old man, not even a matured man, certainly not as having reached the zenith of his manhood. And yet even then we called him—not to his face—"Old Jack". Although he had graduated at West Point and had had the benefit of the fine physical training of that great school, nature had made him clumsy, you might say, in his gait and ungainly in his postures. He walked awkwardly. He stood with a stoop. But there his physical unattractiveness ended. His eye was as steady as a star. His countenance was open, honest and firm. He was mysterious, not intentionally so, but by nature taciturn, he thought and observed and prepared day by day for any event he might have to face on earth, or in the great hereafter. He knew nothing but duty. No matter if his position was humble and obscure, by comparison, he was still faultless in the discharge of every obligation. As a teacher he taught to the best of his ability. As a profound believer in the doctrines and practices of Christianity, he was without a flaw. In his attendance at the Institute he was as regular as the rising of the sun. In his attendance at the Presbyterian church he was the soul of punctuality and reverential attention.

We boys saw all this day after day. And yet we made fun of him. Not disrespectful or malicious fun, but if any joke on any member of the Faculty was to be planned, "Old Jack" by natural course of action was the victim. He had large feet, and the artists in the class to which I belonged, always decorated the black board in his lecture room with the outlines of a colossal foot. . . . I have seen an audacious cadet lockstep with him as he walked away from the barracks. All of this he feigned not to see. That he knew it was going on I am convinced. But he controlled himself; he contained himself. I think sometimes that it was pathetic to see how he endured these evidences of disrespect. His time had not come. He was preparing himself for something, he knew not what. His preparation was prayer and meditation. Somewhere I believe it is recorded, that he would at home express his fears that he was doing no good, that his life was a failure.

How little did he know what was in store for him. How little did he know that the boyish pranks were only irrepressible playfulness. . . .[56]

Rannie was at the institute during the elections. In his memoir he recalled the perceptions of oncoming war.

[MEMOIR OF RANDOLPH BARTON]

As the autumn elections of 1860 came on, with the election of Lincoln, the war spirit rose. Our studies were not much interrupted until the spring of 1861, when events tending to a violent disruption of the Government followed one another in quick succession. We drilled and recited as usual, Major Jackson being our master incidentally in both exercises—not altogether so, but occasionally. I recall with interest the fact that the class in declamation once recited to him. To all appearances and in the experience of all, he was as unfitted for the purpose of criticizing a speech as he was for playing a fiddle; but it happened that the professor to whom the duty ordinarily fell was ill on the particular occasion I refer to, and Major Jackson took his place. The class assembled, sitting in a horse-shoe curve around him. One by one the trembling cadets made their little speeches, and while the speakers were thus engaged in front of him, the mischievous cadets at the heels of the curve were bombarding each other with paper balls over his head. He neither saw nor heard them, or pretended not to. His gaze was riveted upon the boy in front, and I had the satisfaction of being one of five to receive from him a commendatory remark at the close of the exercises. I have frequently thought since that the judgment of his contemporaries as to his unfitness in that line [teaching], was vindicated. Physically he was ungraceful. His face was calm and pleasant, perhaps handsome; but he was a crouching lion.

In my life I have never known two men who in every walk were more illustrious exemplars than General Lee and General Jackson. With my dying breath I will pray that my boys will imitate them in all things.

I remember in June, or perhaps May, 1861, after what was nearly a bloody fracas between the cadets and the still Union-loving citizens of that sturdy little Scotch-Presbyterian town of Lexington, the cadets in great excitement called a corps meeting and the faculty was urged to address them upon the condition of the country.[57] General Smith, the Superintendent, always ready with a speech, led off—others followed. Major Jackson sat modest and unmoved. Why the cadets should have pressingly urged him by vehement calls to speak I do not know. He had won, so tradition said, a reputation most creditable, in the Mexican War; but it had almost passed into the realms of the legend. Many years of peace had worn it out. It was remembered by old men, but to the youthful cadets it had a far-away sound, which placed it on the borders of the unauthentic. And yet some mysterious intuition told them that this silent, steady, retiring man had something about him which would blaze out if opportunity brought him in the right contact. And so he was vigorously called upon. General Smith, when Major Jackson sat immovable, spoke to him and asked him why he did not say something. And then, slowly rising, he turned impressively to the throng of youthful faces, and slowly, but sharply, said: "Gentlemen, I am a man of few words; when the time for fighting comes I draw the sword and throw away the scabbard."[58]

History tells the rest of his story. Soon afterwards he marched the corps, probably two hundred and fifty strong, to Richmond.[59] To my great mortification and chagrin, with perhaps fifty others, I was left in charge of the barracks and arsenal. I have always attributed this to the spite of some few cadets. I was closely attentive to my duties. While at Lexington, notwithstanding the excessive rigidness of the rules, when the most trivial disorder or irregularity in dress, condition of one's room, arms and accoutrements, unpunctuality at the fifteen or twenty roll calls a day, were noted and marked as a demerit (200 of which in a year caused disgraceful expulsion) I never received a mark which stood. I escaped all demerits and I did it by intense obedience to the rules. I felt I was at the school to learn; to learn its discipline; and from being a wild, harum-scarum, frolicsome boy, I became at once a disciplined soldier. This was enough to arouse the prejudice of my fellow-cadets and, with the half dozen others in the corps who made it a point thus to be punctilious in the discharge of military duties, I became unpopular. I would follow exactly the same course if I was called upon to go over my cadet life. It is no guarantee of the future how a boy performs in school, but as I know I so conducted myself from a laudable ambition mainly (not altogether, as I will presently confess), I would do it again. The confession is this: Holmes Conrad of Winchester, considerably my senior, was just such a boy at home as I was—wild and disorderly, hating books and loving snow balls and the sport of breaking window panes. He was sent to the Virginia Military Institute, and with incredible swiftness was sent home.[60] When it was rumored among my friends that I was going, it reached his ears, and I learned afterwards that he was intensely amused at the idea, and said that I would be back within three weeks. Some kind friend reported this to me, and rather than come back after that I would have died. Holmes Conrad went with credit through the war. His natural ability afterwards soon made him an excellent lawyer. Fortunate circumstances brought him to the attention of President Cleveland. He was appointed Assistant Solicitor-General of the United States; a short while ago the Solicitor-General resigned and, as I write (February 14, 1897), he fills that position, with ability. He succeeded in spite of his demerits, but General Lee, the Johnstons and many other illustrious men preferred the other course.

The place of the departed corps was measurably filled with young men from the University of Virginia and elsewhere, who sped to Lexington to learn the rudiments of military tactics. . . .

II

The Valley at War

APRIL–JULY 1861

HARPERS FERRY

FIRST BATTLE OF MANASSAS

Frank Jones arrived at Harpers Ferry on April 18 with the first Virginia units. With his VMI education and later militia experience, he was immediately appointed Assistant Adjutant General to Brig. Gen. J. H. Carson, in command of the Virginia militia. As was everyone, he was quickly caught up in the almost frenzied zeal of the first days, but was overburdened with staff work as an infant army struggled to become organized. He had no idea how long he would be away and disliked the fact that his wife and three small children were without him at Carysbrooke. Having grown up in town, Sue knew little about the farm and the spring planting was behind schedule. All in all, Frank thought the family would be better off with his mother at Vaucluse, or in town with Sue's father.

[LETTER OF FRANK B. JONES TO SUSAN C. JONES]

Harpers Ferry 23 April 1861

Dearest Sue

This is the first spare moment that I have had since I have been here, and now I have no time to go into detail, I think you had better go to Vaucluse until I can tell you something more about my movements. Do you believe that I know of nothing that is going on I feel as if I had been in a tread mill & that in a

*Susan and Frank Jones about the time of
their marriage in 1853.*
(Eleanor J. Burleson)

prison ever since I have been here. I inspected at a Battalion Inspection this morning from 700 to 1000 guns & my hands are bruised & swollen so that I could not write but much better now I want white gloves badly, can you send me 4 pair by some certain individual who will deliver it. Do all you can to superintend my affairs at home, I have met with many friends who meet me cordially & have made *one or two* that I am especially pleased with, I hold an office whose duties are new to me & being ignorant & exceedingly engaged by orders & inquiries from every body I am greatly engaged. Although I am in an executive officer I am not able to say the exact no. of men on duty here, indeed it is only known exactly at Division Head Quaters, There are over 800 men in my Brigade, the very flower of Virginia too, the very first are here in the ranks I noticed several myself at the Inspection of one of the Regiments. I do not know whether to prosecute my application at Richmond or not, I greatly prefer my present position but how long I shall hold it, *time alone* can tell. The gentlemen here in the ranks, I say *gentlemen* are working at the lowest & hardest kind of service [smear] there is but *one heart & one mind devoted to one great cause.*

Bev is sick, broken down, & is going home just the morning I want to send this letter by him but where & how to find him I do not know.[1] How am I to have my clothes washed? I have written to you several times by different persons but have not heard from you except a few pencil lines that I found amidst a no. of papers on one of the public writing desks in my office. Is not this Revolution awful? Did you ever hear of such an enemy, *burn & run*, coward, they can never conquer the Southern spirit.[2] . . . I have been two hours in trying to write this *much, so constantly* have I been interrupted, but of this do not speak, I see no prospect of any attack here, in the course of time things might change but you need not now be afraid of any danger to myself, Sue can you tell me about my oats & home affairs, our garden & the grapes. . . .

Kiss my sweet children &
believe me yours always
Frank B. Jones

Mother will go & stay with you for a while at Carysbrooke to have the garden finished—I want two needles & some black & white thread. . . .

Tom Marshall had left his children with the Bartons and joined the Virginia militia at the Ferry on April 17. Powell Conrad was there, and both were under Frank Jones's command, by April 25, when Powell wrote his mother, "Everything here looks like war, there are more than 2,000 troops & more expected. . . . The Duty is pretty hard, the discipline strict. Every train is stopped & generally examined." That night, about 2:00 a.m., the Virginia forces, having received information that troops would be on the train to Washington, were ordered to proceed to the armory yards and stop the train. Tom Marshall, in charge of the operation, confided to Powell that "the reason for the alarm was partly . . . to see how the men would behave," and that their real purpose was to arrest Union Gen. W. S. Harney, one of the heroes of recent Indian wars. Powell accompanied Tom in searching the train for Harney, who was identified, in the light of an oil lamp unscrewed from the ceiling of a car, by his "military air" despite his civilian dress. Powell, writing in detail to his father, said that what impressed him "in the conduct of Capt. Marshall was his modest courage, & his perfect coolness under high excitement."[3] Frank did not mention the episode in his letters. A few days later, on April 30, Col. T. J. Jackson had come from the VMI to assume command of the Virginia militia at Harpers Ferry.

[LETTER OF FRANK B. JONES TO ANN C. R. JONES]

Harpers Ferry Sunday night
12 th May 1861,

I commence another Sunday letter my very dear mother, you do not know how I have tried to write to you for 10 days, my duties instead of decreasing, increase, but I am becoming better acquainted & more apt I think. Col. Jackson has ordered me now to attend every day at the G Mtg, it will require a walk or ride of a mile to the Parade ground & a mile back, it will be good exercise, I dont object, I am here to serve and if I can be useful I am satisfied.

13rd May

I had written the above my dearest Mother when I was interrupted and I have not been able to write another line since and I have missed the chance of the morning mail, it is now arriving, and alarms have great been given & our troops are moving in large bodies in two directions but I am sure it is a false alarm, and now as I write an officer has just appeared & informs me it is so, a heavy rain is falling & our troops poor fellows are out in it.

My position here is very prominent, I only fear I cannot sustain myself, the duties are exceedingly heavy but of this say nothing, I am sure I have so far gained friends & reputation, I speak to you as I would speak to myself, Army officers are now reporting to me for orders every day and I feel quite out of place, I do not know when or whether I shall at all receive an appointment as Adjutant General, I know that Col Jackson has written a very strong letter in my favour but it [is] a post which I fear I may fail in if appointed. Our force is being enlarged now greatly and as they come in my duties increase.

I think of you often & all the time my very dear Mother but you do not know how difficult it is for me to write a letter, I was cheered with letters from your self & Sue & Bev to day & my bundles, my boots were too large & I had to send them back. I want my linen coats badly, I can wear them in my office, and white pantaloons must be got for me & brown linen, but not yet I will write for these but send my coats. I hardly know how to give any directions about home my mind is so occupied that I cannot think now, I wrote to Bev to have Berry & the jumping steer sent to Catlett, please tell Sue that no fields must be grazed on the home place but the one below the barn—& the old Bald field. Has the water gate been fixed on the road, have it done at once. Let the Catlett lot *alone* be grazed on the Catlett farm, *and the lot in front of the house,* Old Dicks must take the two *calves out of the timothy field,* If he could sell that calf I *bought of him I wish he would for* I cannot raise the money to pay him & if any calf needs better pasture he had better be brought up home.[4] I want the timothy field to be cut for hay, Bev writes me he has taken some hay & wants corn, he must get it elsewhere if possible as I have not a grain to spare, Bev must pay Sherman the money for the flour & tell Sherman I want him to finish them but how I can pay him I do not know, or when, let him understand. . . . let the cedar hedge be finished, I think Sue had better not have the walks made, the difficulty of haying is so great. I have lost I may say all hope of peace, how can it be! & what is the use of adding to a spot that may soon be a barracks for soldiers. . . .

O for one look at my farm & its affairs, but leave here now I cannot, *no one* I may say can get away, I do not think we will have an attack at present and every day is our gain, we have fine army officers reporting here all the time & [with] some time at drill we can fortify ourselves against the world. I have a number of friends here and it is very pleasant to meet them, but I would not give one look at dear little Ran for a week with them all.[5] You would have been pleased dear Mother if you could have seen us at Service yesterday, we had a Methodist sermon in one of the Quarters & 150 present, singing & joining in the service with a devotion that was delightful to see. We had a sermon on moral courage and it was a good one.

Bev must stay at home by all means, I am sorry for Bev but I could not by any means take him in my office I wanted men who I could rely upon in many ways and Tom [Marshall] & Frank suit me admirably, intelligent, active & willing for any amount of labour.[6] I have the use of another assistant who has been very important to me, an old clerk in the Armory department here for 25 years. Tell Bev & all good citizens to frown upon such men as Conrad & Marshall, not to think of such a thing as voting for them, able men indeed![7] Who would vote for men lost to Patriotism, honour & all that men hold dear! *Here are* we from a stern sense of Duty, with an enemy in front, & they *enemies in our rear* even in our own homes. I have not words to express my indignation. . . . My sheep are not to be sheared yet, it is so important for me to be there, that if such a thing is possible I will Delay it. Good night my dear good Mother take care of my wife & my children

Yours &c
Francis B. Jones

Tell Kitten I was very "sankfull" for the candy[8]

I want the key to my trunk, it is a great trouble to get it open, my washing costs me a great deal

I owe you $2, & I do not know how to pay you, if we were to get paid for our service I might do better

In mid-April David Barton had left the university to rush to Harpers Ferry with the Southern Guards. The university militia unit included his friends Jim Garnett and Randolph Fairfax. They traveled north through the Valley by train to Strasburg, then marched eighteen miles to Winchester, pausing long enough for supper, many of them at the Bartons', before taking another train on to the Ferry.[9] The Guards returned to the university in about two weeks but the distracted doodling in his notebook around May 11 showed that David was mentally many miles from academe.[10] Cousin Willie Barton had joined Capt. William L. Clark, Jr.'s, Winchester Rifles on April 18 (although he was sick for

most of May), and Strother Barton joined the same volunteer company May 1
and was at Harpers Ferry by May 11. As Virginia rallied all available talent to
its defense, an attempt was made to reach VMI alumni and enlist their efforts.
The institute's mailing list still had Marshall Barton's name wrong, and the
Winchester postmaster finally approached the senior Barton in town, who of
course identified the intended recipient as his eldest son. Barton wrote Colonel
Smith in Richmond where the latter had gone to help organize the war effort.
Marshall had already left the farm at Springdale to help in raising a volunteer
company, and his postscript expressed a general situation with regard to recruiting: the men preferred to join a regiment being raised locally by a known
commander.

[LETTER OF DAVID W. BARTON TO COL. FRANCIS H. SMITH, WITH
POSTSCRIPT OF C. MARSHALL BARTON]

Col. Francis H. Smith

Winchester
May 15 1861

My Dear Sir

Our Postmaster *to day* & not before, handed to me a Letter directed to
Leut. *E. M.* Barton Winchester Va, for which he said he had been unable after
a more than a weeks detention to find an owner.

Thinking it probable it may have been designed for my son Charles M.
Barton at the instance of the post master I broke the seal & found a Letter of
instructions to *E. M.* Barton to open a recruiting station at Woodstock & intimating that a commission as 1st Leut. in the regular army would be sent to him.
The Letter was signed by Col. R. H. Chilton Virginia Forces & is evidently
authentic & official: My son happened to be in town engaged in forming a volunteer Rifle company of which F. W. Holladay has been chosen Captain & my
son 2nd Leutenant.[11] This places him in some thing of a Dilemma from which
I am sure your kind offices may relieve him; if not will gladly accept the same
position in the other service. As Col. Chilton is (I believe) in Richmond will you
do me the favour to confer with him & shew him this Letter explaining the mis-
carriage of his communication; & the additional favor to see that my son obtains
one or the other of the proferred commissions if you should deem him worthy.

Very truly yours
D.W. Barton

P.S. I have thought it necessary to add a few lines to what my Father has
already said, to thank you for your influence in the appointment I have just

received & at the same time to express a doubt whether I would not be more service in a volunteer company. Persons seem very reluctant, & in fact do not recruit atall, whereas at the same time they are rapidly filling up, & forming new *volunteer companies.* I speak for this portion of the *state,* but I suppose it is universally the *case.* I had no idea of entering the *Army* permanently untill the receipt of this, but am perfectly willing to leave it to your discretion as to the importance of accepting the position & will without hesitation abide by your decision. I have requested Col. Chilton to be so kind as to confer with you upon the subject, & if you think proper, directly upon the receipt of my commission I will open a Rendezvous at Woodstock & obey the other instructions given.

Believe me to be your's most sincerely

Chas. M. Barton

Marshall continued to recruit and drill new soldiers, and as spring turned to summer, he turned his VMI engineering training to work on rebuilding the colonial fortifications around Winchester. On Jackson's staff at the Ferry, Frank Jones was heavily involved in staff work—everything from writing the VMI for rockets to answering requests for shoes.[12] *In the midst of a sea of paperwork, he wrote faithfully to his wife and other members of his family. His quarters were at Bolivar Heights, overlooking the spectacular confluence of the Shenandoah and Potomac rivers. Tom Marshall had arrived at the Ferry on April 17 and was serving as a volunteer aide on Jackson's staff, and the two old friends were able to see something of each other.*

[LETTER OF FRANK B. JONES TO SUSAN C. JONES]

Harpers Ferry 23 May 1861.

Your letter Dear Sue was received today & received with much pleasure. You did not sent me any clean cloathes, I write in great hurry, my dear wife you spoke of coming down here, do not do so, you wouldnt be paid for your trouble and & would say be*tween you &* I it would not be proper for you to come to headQuarters, as to seeing me in the morning it is impossible, unless you chose to be exposed to the face of a constant number who are in my office and in the army you would have to go home. A Dress Parade is the only thing worth seeing & that takes place at sunset and to see one you have to see a good many other things that I would prefer my wife not seeing.

I send a bundle of cloathes, I reckon you had better employ Sherman &

Newcome to shear the sheep & get Bev to see to it.[13] I wrote to Meade to send me my paper, but I wish you would send me the Richmond Dispatch, Col Jackson made a request that I would read the papers for an hour each day, I want the Richmond paper badly & know you will not forget to sent it to me as it is an important paper in my office, here we see nothing but the [Baltimore] Sun & that does not give me the Richmond news (proclamations) which is necessary for me to see.[14] Sherman would be a good hand to shear the sheep, charge them not to cut them, I think it probable that I may be at home next week.

Gen Johnson [Joseph E. Johnston] is here who superseeds Col Jackson, Col J will probably be ordered to another portion of the state, I cannot believe it possible that I will be retained in so important an office although I am certain that I have given complete satisfaction so far to the Col, he has without my suggesting it written twice to the Governor urging my appointment, I only heard this by accident. The life in the line is perfectly horrid, do not say so before sister F[annie] or Mrs. Barton but I assure you that of a private in the ranks is desperate, they have by no means the shelter of my own cattle, there are hundreds of men out, exposed to all kinds of weather with nothing but a blanket, night & day.[15] I deeply lament Marshall Barton's position, a Lieutenant, but his time will be very hard, I cannot understand the good luck that has given me my present position, I fare with the commanding officer & have many comforts, though I miss my house, my dear home, & all its comforts sadly, I wrap up in my blanket sometimes at 11 & sometimes at 12 or after at night; in the morning I cut stale bread of a weeks cooking, brown sugar in tea & sometimes no butter, I am willing however to do & suffer in the cause though the circumstances must be [ ] pressing to make me take a position of Captain or lower.

Do send me at early convenience a hair brush & my cloathes, let them go through Mr. Clark so that if I come home as I think it more than probably I will immediately inform him so as to stop them, if I stay I want them.[16] . . . kiss sweet little Kitten for the candy & tell Ran he must learn how to ride his colt before I come . . . excuse my hurry, Frank [Clark] goes up tomorrow I believe. Will [Clark] you know is detached from the command with his whole Regiment.[17] Gen Johns[t]on is a brother I think of Peter C. Johnson, tell mother, he has a fine head & has the reputation in the Army of a gallant officer. He called at my office yesterday. Be careful about my sheep.

yours my dear Sue

Francis B. Jones

AAG

[LETTER OF FRANK B. JONES TO ANN C. R. JONES]

Bolivar June 3d 1861

I sat down to write to you to night my dear Mother, I wrote to Sue this morning to let her know that I had sent a bundle to Miss Eliza, I felt quite concerned when Frank [Clark] came in & told me that my sheep were not yet sheared. . . .

I then rode out in the country on a high hill where the Engineers are planting heavy batteries, I had a pleasant ride, witnessed the drill of the 1st Infantry where I have many friends, they are encamped near the battery as a support to it. Tom Marshall was with me & from this high hill we enjoyed the green fields & lovely prospect & we mourned over what may be soon a desolate scene. I could see my own mountains that I love so dearly I mean the Fi[r]st Mountains that we see from Vaucluse, I felt as if I had seen more of home than I have done since I have been here, a cloud was passing over the location I imagined Carysbrooke to be & I could see the rain descending.

After viewing the beautiful scenery I rode down in the encampment where I found Wm Clark & Strother Barton, they both look remarkably well.[18] They have undergone a great deal of hardship & they fatten under it. I then rode back along the banks of the Shenandoah. You have no idea of the beauty of the scenes along the Potomac & Shenandoah. The high hills just above the Potomac are grand indeed & the view from there surpasses description. . . . Sues reason for not shearing the sheep was a good one but it is very late.

4th June

It is raining this morning & unless my sheep have been early secured in the shelter it will prevent them being sheared to day, I fear Bev takes little interest in my affairs, he never writes & I hear he does not often go to Carysbrooke. . . . I am much at a loss what to do, I feel so much obliged to you for your kindness in staying with Sue. There are families from Alexandria & other exposed places who would be glad to board in the county, and I have been thinking if Sue could get some family to live with her, it would give mutual protection & she could hire servants to assist her.[19] Then I have thought if W. S. J. could secure me the services of some worthy & respectable man who could live at Carysbrooke he might afford sufficient security for Sue.[20] No farming can possibly be done with any profit whilst I am away, that is a certain fact, but the negroes must be taken care of & the farm too, could I hire out one of them I would, if I could go home for a week or ten days I might make some arrangement, can not some of my friends do it for me? . . .

I am sorry there is no horse but Sue agreed that I had best not buy one under the circumstances, and I knew as long as you were with her your carriage was always at her service, that she need not fear to drive Billy with Austin, if Billy is of no use he had better be put up at auction & sold, had I a good horse it would be probably impressed. . . . There are over 100 teams (waggons & horses) now at this place, impressed against the will of the owners . . . so had I good horses or a good horse there would be no security that I could keep it.

. . . we have a large force here & you would be pleased to see what a fine material there is, I would not have believed it possible there could be such absence of profanity, of intemperance, & of general wickedness. I attended service on Sunday in the Alabama Cav, it was excessively hot, out in the sun the men were setting down on the ground whilst the minister (a methodist) gave us a good sermon in which he defended our action, taking passages from the bible in proof of the righteousness of our cause, at the conclusion he sang the Doxology & every man rose to his feet as if an order had been given, I was surprised to see such manners, rough looking men they were from Alabama. I would not have supposed they knew enough of forms in the church or had the reverence to rise as they did. . . .

I often think of the Randolphs in Washington & I feel deeply for the noble spirited Marylanders who are subjected by the force of arms to submit to such despotism.[21] A little more time however & Va. cannon will be heard from the heights at Arlington, the intruders will be driven from Maryland & the war will be carried into their border, I have every faith in the impetuosity of our troops, you may depend we are not going to stand still & return fire for fire, close quarters & cold steel is to be the war cry and the Yankees are bound to give way, they cannot stand the steel. I look with great interest at our force at or near Alexandria & suppose an action will take place there soon but Alexandria is of no account at present. I would have satisfaction however in knowing that Arlington was not in their possession & for this reason I would like to have them driven from Alexandria. . . . Tell Sue to be very careful about sending me my [Richmond] "Dispatch" it is my only mode of knowing many orders from HdQrs which is necessary for me to know. I receive a number of written & printed ones by mail, but still I do not get them all.[22] I have my Winchester paper sent direct & would do so with the Dispatch but I expect any moment to have orders to go some where else I have no idea how long I will be in one place. . . .

Have you read Pres. Davis proclamation for a day of fasting & prayer it is an admirable thing, non but a Christian could have written it, I liked Bishop Meade's very much O! we have a noble cause & I trust in Providence, we are going to have fearful times but it will all end well. I can not get a pair of pistols any where, indeed there is no manufactory in the South. I want you to tell Brother Strother that if he will trust me with my grandfathers pistols I will take good care of them & I will not disgrace them. Tom [Marshall] sends his best love to you.

Do tell Sue not to allow any book of tactics to go out of *my house to any body who ever it may be,* when she sends my bundle down let her send me a copy of the "Militia Law", the *3d Vol* of *Scotts Tactic's,* let her take a memorandum of this, but she must not send this bundle down *until I write for it* & then she must have every thing ready.[23] Thank her for her minute letter about the rails, fencing &c. I know every thing will go right when she is at home. . . . Tell me whether Ran obeys her implicitly, I hear he has a puppy, dear little fellow how I would like to see him with his dog. . . .

I have never said any thing to you about Col. Jackson, he is a member of the Presbyterian church, one of the most conscientious men I know, pious, determined and brave. I like him very much, very fair very polite, he has very little to say, but I have a vast deal of confidence in him, he was 2nd Lieut at Vera Cruz just from West Point, at Mexico he was a Major so rapid was his promotion & all his honors are on the battle field, so modest you would never know he had won his epaulets. . . .

I reckon you will be amused at my long letter but I have been trying to write to you every since I have been here and this is the first spare moment. I have now more time than I ever had but still have a great deal to do. Col Jackson is at the head of 8 Regts all the Va Force but we are now so much better organized & my work is much less. Good night my dear Mother, make Sue go with you whenever you go & please *exercise contraul over my* children, make them obey you, at once & implicitly. I received a kind letter from dear brother Strother today.

yours my very dear Mother

Frank B. Jones

I wish you would have my shirt collars taken off & made narrower & tell Sue to send me another night shirt I have had only one since I have been here, Frank Clark goes up this morning & I will get him to take this letter

yours FBJ   June 5 1861

Winchester, about twenty-five miles southwest of Harpers Ferry, was afire with secessionist sentiments as soon as Lincoln made known his plan to invade the South, although many there had been staunchly Unionist up to that point, and many others were to maintain their Northern sympathies throughout the con-

flict. *The young men wanted to be off to whip the Yankees once and for all, and the girls would not look at anyone not in some kind of uniform. David W. Barton, with six sons between twenty-five and fifteen, could not have been in a more anguished position. Marshall had left the farm and was recruiting. David had returned to the university but left before school closed to join the Rockbridge Artillery, June 27. Strother had been elected Lieutenant of Company F, 2nd Virginia Infantry, and was at Harpers Ferry. Mr. Barton was, with difficulty, insisting on his younger boys finishing the school year. He wrote again to his old acquaintance Colonel Smith of the VMI for advice.*

[LETTER OF DAVID W. BARTON TO COL. FRANCIS H. SMITH]

Winchester
June 5/61

Dear Col.

The military fever is so rife among our young men that parents are sorely put to it to know how to restrain or govern their sons. I have five sons old enough (or who fancy they are) for military duty. Marshall you know. He is commissioned in the regular army & the three next in the order of age are in the ranks, or getting ready to be there. The fifth is Randolph at the Va Military Institute & from a Letter received from him this morning I fear it will be difficult to repress his ardour; for he shows great eagerness for active service. I do not know what to do with him without exerting an authority which I never deem it prudent to overstrain. In the present excited state of the country—a condition of things more apt to continue than to abate—it seems vain to expect attention to any regular course of studies, & besides such is the utter derangement of pecuniary matters, that I shall be obliged to withdraw him from the Institute at the close of the current year (July). Can you suggest any science such as drill master or other such employment in the military line in which he could be usefully engaged? I do not know what proficiency he has made or what he is fit for but of this you will be very competent to judge. If I take him home at the close of the session it is almost certain he will go into the ranks as a volunteer & I am not prepared to consent to this.

Can you relieve me by a suggestion & thereby add to the many obligations under which I am already resting?

Very truly yours
D.W. Barton

Col. F.H. Smith

Frank Jones, captive to his convictions and sense of duty, remained at Harpers Ferry despite the conflict and confusion between commands. Both Frank and Tom Marshall were disturbed that their staff positions had not been confirmed by commissions in the Confederate Army since the militia units had been incorporated into the regular army June 8. Frank was worried about Tom, too.

[LETTER OF FRANK B. JONES]

Poor Tom is very much depressed, I feel very uneasy about him, he gives way a good deal & nothing but exciting news keeps him up. . . . [He] mourns over his absence from his children. . . .[24]

Frank must have received some assurances in early June that his position on Jackson's staff would be regularized, because he took steps to find a servant to attend to his personal needs, his equipment, and his horse, asking that Sue hire him a servant in town or arrange to send the slave William Braxton from Vaucluse. He had been using one of his farm horses but decided to switch to his young riding horse, Guy Darnell, the family's favorite. His mother wrote seeking to allay his concerns about Sue, alone at Carysbrooke running the farm; she added her assurance of her own willingness to help. At the moment Mrs. Jones had conflicting loyalties, as her younger son Bev's wife, Rebecca, was having a baby, in their new house downstream from Carysbrooke. Perhaps in return for taking their mother away from Sue's, Bev finally saw to the sheepshearing Frank had been fretting about.

[LETTER OF ANN C. R. JONES TO FRANK B. JONES]

June 10th 1861

Your letter of the 5th reached me on the 7th my dearest Child, it was *most* welcome, & I offer you my grateful thanks for its length, & interest. My heart turns to you often. . . . You may hear from Sue, before this reaches you, & will know that another duty has called me from her side . . . dear Rebecca could look to no one but me. A few hours after I received your letter I came here, rode behind Bev & owing to Bev's ignorance & his unwillingness to leave Sue alone, I should have delayed my trip till morning but for Sues prompt decision, & entire forgetfulness of self, *urging* me to leave her. I was thoroughly uneasy, & anxious. . . . Bec was so sick yesterday, Sunday, Bev went for the Dr, & she is much better to day. . . . He is attending to your Sheep shearing, was at Carysbrooke all day Saturday, & has been there from early this morning, the work will go on to the end, unless another rain should come. His own sheep have not been sheared yet, & will not be untill yours are done. I heard him say your Cattle were looking very well, & he was going to see them again after the Shearing was over.

Mr. Clark was with Sue on Saturday night & last night she staid at Joseph [Barton]s, William Braxton took her to Church yesterday, she dined in town & intended coming here to stay all night, Bev was so anxious, & so was she, but I feared for her to try it, under the circumstances, and advised her not, in consequence she stopped at Josephs.[25] . . .

The Dr. found Bec much better. She calls her little Boy Edward, but it is so expressly like Bev, you would feel inclined to call it so, it is really Funny to see a little thing so much like a big one but I have no Idea of its remaining so. . . .[26] You cannot think how comfortable the new house is, as far as it goes, after a long sojourn too in that miserable kitchen.[27]

I am so glad Tom [Marshall] & yourself had such a pleasant ride, & hope it was of service to you, I wish I could have seen such wild & beautiful views as you were looking at. I need not tell you *how* glad I should be to see you once more, & how ardently I wish the command should go forth, that Israel should not go up against Judah. I have a great pleasure in believing that war is *forced* upon the South, that the proceedings of the North were unbearable, & that the stand we take is right, & I truly believe we shall be successful.

Your "Precious children" are well, happy & good, dear little creature it is amusing to see Rans pleasure at being able to say three words. Rebecca requests me to give you her love, she *enjoys* the change in her dwelling poor Child! & I am too, too thankful she is in it *now*. . . . my best love to Tom, God Bless you my own Precious Boy, Your fondly devoted Mother

A.C.R. Jones

I rejoice to hear of the modesty in your Camp. God Grant there may be a higher feeling.

I can hear nothing from my Washington relations [the Innes Randolphs] except Lucy's absense from the place but I do not know where she is.

David W. Barton had not only the concern of his sons' decisions to interrupt their education but also very real financial problems should they be willing to return to their schools. His law practice virtually evaporated in the uncertainty of impending conflict, and his farms were bereft of men to supervise the work, as even the overseers had been called to the army. Marshall had left the

Springdale farm, and it seems that the house was closed, his wife Ellen and the baby returning to her family in Fauquier County. Strother had forsaken the Lost Brook farm for the 2nd Virginia. Mr. Barton's brother-in-law Frank Jones had written in the hopes that Robby, home from school in early May, could look after Carysbrooke. Their father hoped that both Robby and Rannie would be willing and able to help with the Barton farms.[28]

The army was at Camp Stevens near Winchester, and Frank was at home briefly in late June and until July 3. The last night at home he made his will, pessimistically beginning "I leave in the morning perhaps never to return."[29] The conscientious Frank had already seen enough to know how poorly prepared the Confederacy was to wage any sustained war. His family joys and responsibilities made his military duties heavy for him. In contrast, carefree young fellows like Rannie Barton were counting the days until they could go into action. In early July Rannie returned to Winchester. He had been champing at the bit until the institute closed on July 2—not, as usual, for its summer holidays but until there was a more certain future. All of the faculty had gone into the army and the institute did not reopen until the following January. Since the cadets, even those of only a year, had more military discipline than other volunteers, they were detailed to train raw recruits throughout the army.

[MEMOIR OF RANDOLPH BARTON]

In July, 1861, the school entirely closed and I went to Winchester. There I learned that I had been appointed Sergeant Major of the regiment Colonel Arthur C. Cummings, of Abingdon, Va., was forming.[30] I entered upon my duties at once, drilling the raw companies from Woodstock, Tom's Brook and other points in the Valley to the great disgust of the company officers and to the extreme exhaustion of the clumsy countrymen in the ranks. Young and agile as I was, and impressed as I had been at Lexington with the importance of quick movements of the limbs and body, I sought to educate the raw recruits to the same degree I had been educated. I met with partial success, and somewhat prepared them, or better fitted them for the stirring events they were soon to experience. . . .

In the commands around me were the flower of the youth of Virginia . . . all inspired by the spirit of their forefathers to drive back an invasion which originated in a fanatical spirit, and was conducted with an infernal disregard of pledges and rights.

*Robby Barton, to his parents' apprehension, was as caught up in the war fever
as the others, and his generally frail health did not seem, to him, a proper reason not to join the army. But his father's need of help in his office and with the
farms, in the absence of his other boys, prevailed for a while.*

[MEMOIR OF ROBERT T. BARTON]

I came home I think in May 1861, filled with the idea of entering the army
at once. My parents and friends earnestly opposed it as it was evident to them
that my health would not permit me to stand the fatigue of the service. Then
again my brothers Marshall, David, Strother and Randolph were already in
active service. The same was true of my brother in law Col. Thos. Marshall, and
my other brother in law, Dr. John M. Baldwin of Staunton, was in service as a
surgeon. My mother's brothers Frank and Beverl[e]y Jones were in the field
and my other uncle Strother was acting as a Quartermaster.[31] In view of all this,
of my health, and of my father's need for my services I was for a while restrained from entering the army, and I tried to content myself with helping my
father to take care of his property. This aid was particularly needed as my
brother Marshall had left the Springdale farm and my brother Strother the Lost
Brook farm with all the slaves, stock and crops to be cared for at that busy season. Then too the movements of troops, sometimes quartered on the farms; the
impressment of wagons, teams and slaves; the seizure of stock & c. for the
needs of the army, required constant care and protection.

But the atmosphere was too much ablaze with excitement to permit a boy of
eighteen to be contented with such employment. I saw my comrades all turned
into soldiers with their pretty uniforms, and the eyes of the girls wholly over-
looked any young man who did not at once rush to the front and become "a
bold soldier boy." My parents finally yielded to my insistence and I enlisted as a
private in Co. F. 2nd Va. Regiment of Infantry.

I went at once to join my company, the army under Jackson having then just
evacuated Harpers Ferry and was slowly moving back to Winchester along the
Martinsburg turnpike.[32] I reached the Command about sixteen miles from
Winchester and took my place in the ranks and marched back along the dusty
turnpike through the heat of that May day reaching camp about five miles
from Winchester utterly broken down and worn out. I will never forget that
night in the dewey clover field, on the hard ground, with a single blanket and no
supper. Nor shall I forget the desperate gaze which I cast upon the self cooked

breakfast of flour, water, and fat bacon which formed my breakfast. That day we marched to a lot this side of the Fair Grounds close to Winchester, and pitched our tents. I had a chance to get home then and, by comparison to fully under-stand the hardships of a soldier's life to a delicate and pampered boy; but I had no idea of giving it up.

In a few days we were ordered on the march and having heard of Gen. [Robert] Patterson's approach with the Federal Army, to Martinsburg, we were jolly over the idea of a real battle. We marched to Martinsburg and destroyed the B. & 0. car shops and railroad there, and then continued our march down near the Potomac where we went into camp. We were so near the river that we fre-quently had the long roll beaten and marched rapidly in the direction of the enemy. I do not remember how many days this lasted, but each day of hard marching and camp fare with the night exposure, guard duty, & c., told upon me until I was worn out and reduced to skin and bone. At last I was ordered back to Winchester by the Surgeon, and I confess I came home shame faced and depressed. What added to my misery was that a few days after I left the army it had a real skirmish near Falling Waters with the enemy.[33] This was the first real fighting in this part of the State or by the army to which I belonged. The army had been much enlarged and Gen. Jos. E. Johnston had assumed command, Gen. Jackson then with the rank of Colonel, commanding a brigade to which the 2d [Virginia] regiment belonged and which afterwards was known as the "Stonewall Brigade.". . .

After the skirmish at Falling Waters, the war fever broke out in me again, and expecting another battle near Darksville where Johnston's army was in line of battle with the enemy in his immediate front, I procured a rifle, and mount-ing my horse rode to Darksville and arranged there to be allowed to take my place in the ranks of my old Company in case of a fight. Not a few others from Winchester and the Country about did the same. Later in the war this was not permitted.

I stayed at Gen. Jackson's headqtrs and saw a good deal of him. I remember a bright comet was visible in the sky and the superstitious speculated about it as to what the omen was. One night I recall I slept in a grave yard and found that the most comfortable place to sleep was between two graves and rolled up in my blanket.

When it was determined [July 11] that the army was to fall back again to Winchester I preceded it on my horse. I remained then at home, altho I was every day in the camp, hoping that I might be able to rejoin the command. I helped my father with writing & c. in his law office, and also about the care of his farms.

One day I remember that Mr. James M. Mason, who had been the U.S. Senator from Virginia and whose home stood on the hill just in front of where the fine home of Mr. A. R. Pendleton now stands, came to my father's and asked me to write a letter at his dictation.[34] I was somewhat awed when I found that it was addressed to Jefferson Davis, President of the United States. I have forgotten what the subject of the letter was, but remember that I was admonished not to tell what it was.

In a few weeks the movements of the Federal Army in front of Washington led to the famous march of Johnston's army from Winchester to Manassas. We did not understand the movement, but believed a great battle was to be fought and many tears were shed in Winchester when the boys from town marched away with their commands. I rode some miles out of town with the boys and at last bid them farewell sorrowfully, obeying the positive commands of my parents, but ashamed that I could not be with them in the fight, altho I knew that I had not the physical strength to make the march.

This was the first Union advance on the Confederate capital of Richmond, which was to be their unvarying objective. Each side anticipated a decisive battle that would end the war. The Northern invasion prompted an urgent call to support the small Confederate army near Fairfax. The Rebel forces at

Woodside, near Piedmont Station. (M. B. Colt)

Winchester responded immediately, setting out for Manassas Gap to take the
train east—a revolutionary movement in warfare.

Three of Robby's brothers, cousin Willie, brother-in-law Tom Marshall,
and uncles Frank and Bev Jones were on their way with their various regiments
to Manassas. Capt. James Power Smith recalled stopping, with a dozen other
soldiers of the Rockbridge Artillery, at the James Joneses' for breakfast on
July 19—at Bev Jones's instigation, it can be surmised.[35] *Woodside, the Joneses'*
house, was just up the road from Piedmont Station, where the army massed for
infantry units to go by train to Manassas Junction, near Bull Run. The Stone-
wall Brigade was about to receive its baptism of fire. The following account is an
amalgam of Rannie's memories, taken from his book and from a speech deliv-
ered to veterans of the Stonewall Brigade in 1900.[36]

[FROM THE RECOLLECTIONS]

. . . Our command reached Manassas Junction on the 20th of July, in the
morning, I think. We marched during the day to the right of the [army's] line,
and the next day we marched and counter-marched, halted and rushed as the
changing localities of the conflict, so far as our commanders could anticipate,
seemed to require. My dinner was made from blackberries, for being outside of
the ranks (as Sergeant Major) I could pick them as we passed over the fields.

[FROM THE SPEECH]

It is a long stretch from June, 1900, back to July, 1861—nearly forty years.
Men now in the vigor of life were then unborn. Boys then are tottering old men
are now. But from the memory some things are ineffaceable. Does any man
who was in that battle with our brigade forget when and how we spent the preceding night? Do you not remember that on the Saturday night just before the
greatest Sunday of our lives we slept in and about the pine coppices near
Mitchell's Ford, toward the right of our general line of battle? Does any one
forget the solemn feelings with which we then realized that we were on the eve
of some terrible event? We knew that on the 18th. near where we slept, the first
collision of any magnitude had occurred, and blood had been shed. If any of us
hoped that, after all, battle—real bloody battle—would be averted, the thought
by that time had vanished. We almost smelled the battlefield—that most horrid
of odors, especially when it arises from the living or the dead or dying pine
trees. To me there is something inexpressibly melancholy even at this day at the

smell of a pine woods. We always find them in poor countries. Nearly all of our great battles were fought on poor land; and thus pine woods and blood, blood and pine trees, are to me inseperably connected. Who of us fresh from the garden spot of Virginia, the beautiful Valley, but did not contrast what we had left with our dismal and sandy surroundings? and as quiet settled down upon our bivouac, what man was so hardened not to ask himself: "What has the morrow in store for me?" It was not alone the question, "Will I be killed?" but, "Will I have the nerve to stand and unfalteringly face death? Will the sun of tomorrow sink with my record that of a brave soldier or that of a coward? How will my comrades behave? How will my company, my regiment, my brigade, behave? Are our officers trustworthy? Is our scarcely known brigadier general, Jackson, the man to direct us in the awful emergency?" And as these harrowing thoughts crossed and recrossed our minds and drove sleep from our eyes, how lovingly we turned to all the endearments of home. Will we ever see home again— father, mother, sisters, little ones? I tell you, gentlemen, these ante-battle meditations are unnerving. Do you think you could stand them again? And yet think of the brave souls who did stand them, and who resolutely braced to do their duty the next day, come what might, and who fell into their last earthly sleep. . . .

Picket-firing and the early rising sun awoke us the next day and our movement soon began. You remember that the battle, proposed by Gen. Beauregard, was to be fought mainly on the line of Bull Run, the left of our line being the stone bridge and the right extending some six miles down the run as it leisurely flowed to the south.[37] A possible crossing of the run and a grand left wheel of our entire line was contemplated, indeed was feebly begun, when the unexpected movement of the enemy completely changed the plans of our commanders. McDowell, instead of marching boldly to the run and by a frontal attack sweeping across the stone bridge and the various little farm fords we were guarding, sent Gen. Sherman—then commanding a brigade, the subsequent famous William T. Sherman, who marched through Georgia—to keep the Confederate forces at the bridge engaged, while with some twenty thousand men he turned off to the right between Centreville and the stone bridge, and by a circuitous route reached the head waters of the run about Sudley Springs, when, crossing, he came in strong array down upon the left flank of the Confederate army, and at exact angles with it.

Now, gentlemen, you know what that means. On the morning of July 21, 1861, we knew instinctively that an attack on the flank was something ugly. An attack in the rear was something sinful. By sunset that day we were postgraduates in the whole subject. I have no respect for a soldier who has not the most abject respect for a flank attack. Such a man is a fool or a knave, or probably both. And so when the feeble skirmishing along our front, and the telltale columns of dust raised off to the front of our left flank, told Gens. Johnston and Beauregard to look out for squalls, a rapid movement began from the right of line toward the left, now in great danger of being rolled up and back, and the formation of a new line at right angles to the stream and facing the approaching host. Several causes saved our army from being crushed before the new conditions could be prepared for. [Union Brig. Gen. Irvin] McDowell's circuit was longer than he had anticipated; the day was hotter; his men broke down. And after he had completed his preparations and was fiercely forcing the fighting, the gameness of [Col. Nathan G.] Evans, who threw his command away from the bridge to meet this new advance, retarded him some fateful hours. But it was an exceedingly close call, and you all must remember how through the dust and heat we hurried across open fields, making for the direction of the heavy firing. My impression is that the brigade reached its line of battle near the Henry House about one o'clock. The gallant Rockbridge Battery, with its little guns and caissons on the rear of the wheels of ordinary farm wagons, had been boldly replying shot for shot to the grand discharges of Griffin and Rickett's regular army Federal batteries. We were quietly formed in line, the Fifth (Col. [Kenton] Harper) on the extreme right, a portion of it in the pines; then the Fourth (Col. Preston); then the Twenty-Seventh (Col. [John] Echols); then the Second (Col. Allen); the last three regiments more in the open; and then the Thirty-Third, with its eight companies under Col. Cummings, on the left, and quite well screened in the edge of the thicket of pine and scrub oak.[38]

[FROM THE *RECOLLECTIONS*]

As we approached our position we heard for the first time the horrid screaming of hostile shells going over our heads, high up in the air, but not so high as not to be dangerous. I recall now with some amusement the intense gravity and astonishment written upon the faces of the men as these dangerous missiles from the batteries of Ricketts and Griffin went hurtling over us; but I recall no signs of timidity. The men kept in their ranks, obeyed orders and moved into position on the left of the Second Virginia, of which brother Strother, my cousin, Willie Barton, and all my Winchester friends were members, with steadiness and resolution. My brother David was in the Rockbridge Battery, which was being supported by our brigade. My uncle, Frank Jones, and my brother-in-law, Thomas Marshall, were on Jackson's staff. I felt the solemnity of the moment, but I recall no disposition whatever to turn and run. On the other hand, a sense of pride, a desire to emulate the action of the best men on the field, possessed me, as it did, I believe, all of our command, except the Adjutant of our regiment.[39] I think I went into that action with less trepidation than into any subsequent one. Inexperience, doubtless, had much to do with it, but again I attribute much of the nerve that sustained me to my year at Lexington. I felt on the field that the orders of our officers were supreme; that come what might, they must be obeyed, and discipline told on me from first to last. . . . after taking our position on the left of the brigade, we laid upon the ground listening to the musketry and cannonading going on to our right, or rather somewhat in front of our right, from the Confederate forces, which was being vigorously responded to by the Yankees. The "Henry House" was in front of our brigade, over the hill, the upper part of the house visible, and the "Robinson House" was to the right of that a few hundred yards. Occasional shells would explode over our regiment and the solemn wonderment written on the faces of the men as they would crane their heads around to look out for falling branches, was almost amusing. I was near the left flank of the regiment, a few steps in the rear, where, upon the formation of the regiment in line of battle, I belonged. Doubtless I wished I was at home, but I had to stick.

[FROM THE SPEECH]

In September, 1896, I revisited the very spot on which the line of our brigade was formed. . . . I believe I stood almost upon the exact spot upon which I stood in 1861. Of all the battle fields in Virginia, this one has undergone the least change. Standing where I did, just on the edge of the woods, and then advancing as our line had advanced in 1861, I noted the thin wiry grass barely covering the slaty [sic], poor land; the washing of the hill side; the occasional little pine bushes; the tops of the Henry and Robertson Houses, developing more and more as in 1896 I charged safely up the slope over which in 1861 our men had gone with a rush in the face of a pitiless storm of bullets. I was absolutely alone; my companions had remained in the woods or in the carriage on the Sudley Mills Road, and here I was in fancy repeating after an interval of thirty-five years the action of which I believe I am prouder than of any in my life—charge upon the enemy's battery which gave immortality to the men, and to our leader and commander a place among the foremost captains of the world. I believe I even lowered my walking stick into a charge of bayonets. I barely repressed the stirring yell. I did everything I could just once more to get the thrill of that heroic day.

Now gentlemen and comrades, do you not remember how long we lay on that line waiting for the advancing enemy? Do you not remember the order from Gen. Jackson "to hold our fire until the enemy got within fifty yards?" And did not Tom McGraw, of the Thirty-Third, who had been afraid that the fight would be over before he could get a crack at the bluecoats, when the order was read and Casler asked him how he liked it, reply: "That was closer quarters than I anticipated."

I do not know what occurred along the line to the right of the Thirty-Third while we were waiting and the shells were exploding in the treetops over our heads, but I do recall that some amusing incidents occurred near me. Old Maj. Nelson (as he was called), of the artillery, simply did not understand what danger was. The falling boughs cut by the spiteful shells gave him no more concern that if squirrels were throwing acorns at him. He came into the battle clad partly as a civilian and partly as a soldier. He moved up and down on horseback in the rear of our line, and part of his gear was a very high old black hat, a cross between a stovepipe and a silk dress hat. It was, as you may imagine, somewhat incongruous under the circumstances. The men were silently lying on the ground awaiting the order to charge. It was a very solemn scene. At that moment a most sepulchral voice rose from the ranks: "Good Lord, what have I done that the devil should come after me? Good Lord, what have I done that the devil should come after me?" All who heard it supposed that some poor fellow had been mortally wounded, and, strange selection though it might be, was uttering his dying exclamation. All looked at him, when, still repeating his solemn protest, he pointed through the woods, and there, riding toward us with utter unconcern, was Old Maj. Nelson with his wondrous hat.[40] . . .

Now, what I am proud of is the conduct of the brigade during the two or three hours immediately preceding its famous charge. We all know that nothing was so trying as to lie inactive under a heavy shell fire, knowing that it preceded an advance. And yet this was exactly what our brigade was subject to, and this it stood unflinchingly. We knew that the enemy in great numbers was advancing. We knew that the gallant men of Evans and Bee, on the far side from us on Warrenton turnpike, had been overcome, and were coming back in utter disorder and tumult.[41] We knew that the tide was running strongly against us, and we knew that if we did not turn it the day was gone. But our line, as in double ranks with ready guns it crouched upon the ground, was silent, was serene, was confident. Gen. Jackson slowly, coolly, and apparently unconcernedly moved along our front. [He was accompanied by two staff officers, Frank Jones and Tom Marshall.]⁴² Our officers, field and line, stood at their posts, simply telling the men to keep ready and to keep cool. Truly, as one looked along that line of 2,600 men he saw a stone wall. It was just then that Bee, overwhelmed by his inability to stem the disorder of his men, rode back to Jackson and despairingly cried that he was being beaten back. Jackson said: "We will give them the bayonet." This was worth a thousand men to Bee, and, his brave spirit rising to the occasion, he turned, and rushing toward his retreating men, cried with almost his last: "Look at Jackson's Brigade; it stands like a stone wall! Rally on the Virginians!" This version of what Bee said is that given by Brig. Gen. (later Bishop) Capers of South Carolina, Bee's native state. I have often wondered what prompted Bee to use this happy metaphor, and I have long ago concluded that Gen. Bee, fresh from the Valley of Virginia, with its long line of limestone fences securely and rigidly guarding the fertile fields, suddenly saw in the inflexible line of our men crouching for the spring the resemblance to those massive walls, and eloquently used the simile to tell his men upon what they could rally. How strange it is, that with so little premeditation, with so sudden an impulse, this dying hero stamped a name upon the men and leader that will last with the ages, and will ever be associated with his own most glorious end!

. . . just at the time Gen. Bee fell our right was in great confusion. Indeed, beyond the Fifth Regiment to the right we had at that moment little or nothing that was stable. To our left, the left of the Thirty-Third, reinforcements were being hurried with all speed, but barely in time to meet the surging masses of the enemy then athwart the Sudley Mills road, and in a line covering the Henry and Robertson houses, eagerly advancing to overwhelm us. Griffin's and Rickett's splendid batteries were being rushed up the Sudley Mills Road, had turned into the Henry farm at the farm gateway and were fast preparing to deploy on the ridge in front of us, and not over two hundred yards from us.

Still our brigade obeyed the order: "Wait until the enemy is within fifty yards." We were with five minutes' time of the crash of shrapnel from a dozen cannons and the hail of bullets from five thousand muskets and still our men held their line. Still they crouched, and still they obeyed the order to hold their fire. This was the last, as it was a splendid, picture that Bee beheld. No wonder the idea of a stone wall impressed itself upon his imagination. A few moments more and the cloud of skirmishers from the enemy had insinuated itself into the edge of the woods on the left of the Thirty-Third and behind the banks of the sunken Sudley road, and were trying the staunchness of that battalion of eight companies. Restlessness began to show itself on the left of our regiment (the

Thirty-Third). Bullets and exploding shells began to exhaust the grim patience
of our inexperienced boys. The main line of the enemy was advancing up the
hill on the side separated from us by its crest.

[FROM THE *RECOLLECTIONS*]

Colonel Cummings and Lieutenant-Colonel Lee were in front of our regiment, perhaps a hundred yards, stooping down, and finally standing to get a view
over the crest of the hill that rose gently before us for a little over one hundred
yards.[43] The musketry kept up on our right, and then Colonels Cummings and
Lee were seen to rise and bending down to come back with somewhat quickened
steps to the regiment. I remember as Colonel Cummings drew near he called
out, "Boys, they are coming; now wait until they get close before you fire."

Almost immediately several pieces of artillery, their horses in front, made
their appearance on the hill in front of us, curving as if going into battery, and
at the same time I descried the spear point and upper portion of a United States
flag as it rose in the hands of its bearer over the hill; then I saw the bearer and
the heads of the men composing the line of battle to the right and left of him.
At the sight several of our men rose from the ranks, leveled their muskets at the
line, and, although I called out, "Do not fire yet!" it was of no use; they fired,
and then the shrill cry of Colonel Cummings was heard, "Charge!" and away the
regiment went, firing as they ran into the ranks of the enemy and particularly at
the battery towards which our line rapidly approached. Although bearing a non-
commissioned officer's sword, I had obtained a cartridge box, belted it on, and
had in some way secured a flint-lock musket, with which one of our companies
was armed. This gun, after two futile efforts, I fired at a man on horse-back in
the battery, one of the drivers, I think. I got near enough to the battery to see
that it was thoroughly disabled, horses and men falling and our line driving
ahead, when I felt the sting of a bullet tearing a piece from my side, just under
my cartridge box, which I had pulled well around on the right and front of my
waist. I called out that I was wounded to my uncle, Frank Jones, who helped me
up on his horse and carried me to the rear.

I think it can be demonstrated that the victory of First Manassas is traceable
to Colonel Cummings. . . . Jackson had, within the half hour before, passed
along his brigade the order not to fire until the enemy was within thirty feet,
and then charge. So Colonel Cummings writes to me, under date of September
20, 1896. But, says Colonel Cummings, the shells of the enemy had caused
some confusion "with the left company of my regiment," or rather his command

of eight companies, and when Griffin's Battery showed itself on the hill in front of us, and occasional shots began to fall among us from the enemy moving towards our left to flank us, when the tumult of the broken ranks of Bee and [Col. Francis S.] Bartow was threatening the steadiness of our right, and the enemy with exultant shouts was pressing on, Colonel Cummings, like a flash, thought if those guns get into battery and pour one discharge of grape and cannister into the ranks of his raw recruits, the day is gone; and then it was with splendid discretion he took the responsibility of changing his orders, with the changed conditions, as Grouchy should have done at Waterloo, and charged the enemy.

The suddenness of our attack: the boldness of it, for our men went over and past the battery, the disabling of the guns, all checked the advancing line. It was immediately followed up by the remainder of the brigade charging, and the troops on our left poured in. The tide of battle turned when it dashed against the farmer boys of the Thirty-third Virginia. It was the first resistance it had met. The enemy came upon the point of a spear, one small regiment of undisciplined boys and men, not a month from the plough and the mechanics shop. The point broadened as to the right and left assistance poured in, until it became a sharp blade against which the enemy could not and dared not rush; but the Thirty-third led the van of the movement that first arrested McDowell's victorious line, and from that moment the scene changed, and from the brink of disaster our army turned to a great victory. Colonel Cummings changed the life of McDowell by his order, "Charge!" He may have changed the history of the war. The battle pivoted upon his nerve. It was the turning point in tremendous events.

. . . Instead of the Confederate Army flying as a mob to the Rappahannock, the Yankee Army fled as a mob to Washington. . . . The Thirty-third turned the tide, and Colonel Cummings' timely order let loose the Thirty-third at the very crisis of the battle. . . . I distinctly claim that with the order and because of the order came the first check McDowell sustained. That other troops immensely aided in forcing back the Yankee line, when thus checked, I freely admit. But our regiment called the halt in the victorious advance of the enemy. I dwell upon the circumstance because of the great interest it adds to the engagement to know that you belonged to the regiment that received and repelled the dangerous thrust of the enemy at the nice turning point of the day. I should think to Colonel Cummings the circumstance would be of extraordinary interest and that he would time and again reflect how little he thought when he braced himself to give the order to his regiment that he was making a long page in history.

The Thirty-third Regiment in that battle had only eight companies (ten being the complement). It took into the engagement four hundred and fifty men, and lost forty-three killed and one hundred and forty wounded. . . .

My brother, Strother being wounded in the same battle, together we went back to Winchester. Captain William L. Clark was also wounded, and so three wounded soldiers enjoyed the luxurious comforts of my father's house. We were "heroes," and although I suffered a great deal from the soreness of my wound, I tasted the real advantages of being creditably and mildly disabled.

While convalescing from my wound, I frequently rode around the town with my brother, Charles Marshall, then a Lieutenant in the Provisional Army of the Confederate States, who was assigned to the duty of locating fortifications on the surrounding hills.

Frank Jones, on Jackson's staff, remained encamped with the army not far from the battlefield. He communicated his safety to his family immediately following the battle, but evidently the news was not received. A few days later, he was able to send full accounts home to his family with his visiting brother-in-law.

[LETTER OF FRANK B. JONES TO SUSAN C. JONES]

Thursday July 25 1861.

Dear Sue, I take a moment to write you a line by Peyton who is here, he goes off today. I was sorry to learn that you did not receive my telegraphic dispatch sent to the office on sunday night. I wrote however on monday morning. I was so glad to see Brother Strother on tuesday, he left a coat with me which will supply to some extent my oil cloth & Havelock which I lost on the field of battle. Brother James is here & he promises to send me an oil cloth to wrap my blanket in which will be of great comfort to me, also his horse, he will send to me, my colt [Guy Darnell] is a good deal fagged, poor fellow he gave way twice under me during the battle, but caught against a Pine which supported him.[44]

O Sue we have had such a splendid victory; just think of our taking all the Artillery except, they say, two pieces. I witnessed the full retreat & saw none in route, four of our Regiments charged bayonets. In the Charge of Col Cummings I was, and there Randolph behaved so well, there were I do not think more than two hundred men who went into the charge, they met the fire of the New York Zouaves and a regiment of infantry, 46 men were killed at once, & over 112 wounded, here it was that the gallant W. F. Lee was wounded, poor fellow, I mourn over his fate so much![45] He is not dead yet, but I fear it is impossible for him to recover, 158 killed & wounded in our charge of about two hundred was enormous, it was the hottest part of the fight. Our Brigade has covered itself with honor, it stood for 4½ hours in the most galling fire, when Providence sent a panic amongst them & the vast horde moved off in the most rapid style, leaving the ground where they fought & their path of flight covered with dead. Then came Col Cummings's Stuart & Radford with their Regts of Cavalry in hot pursuit, and drove them beyond the Ct House of Fairfax Co.[46]

I want to hear very much from you. By a late Ordnance an overseer cannot be taken away in the Militia, Padgett can therefore remain & attend to my business, let him know, how are they getting on at home?[47] I feel as if I had been away for time & times without number. . . .

I supposed when I wrote last that we would move at once upon Washington but why this delay I do not know. May God prosper our cause and take care of our many friends in the Army. Saw young Powell brought from the field, poor fellow, he died as McGuire took him from the horse.[48] Gen Bee was killed, Col Bartow, & Col Thomas of Maryland also, his son is not dead, but his case is very doubtful, he is shot through the lungs.[49] Poor Peyton Harrison I mourn over his untimely fate, he married Miss Hunter of Martinsburg who you knew very well, her brother Adjt Hunter pursued & shot the Zouave who killed young Holmes [A.] Conrad.[50] Let me hear from you & the dear little ones. Best love to mother, sister Mary & Aunt Kitty & all the servants.[51]

Yours my Darling

Francis B. Jones

[LETTER OF FRANK B. JONES TO ANN C. R. JONES]

Camp near Manassa[52] July 27th 1861

I have been wanting to write to you My dear Mother for a long time, but many are the interruptions and impediments in the way. Camp life has no conveniences you know of any kind. It is now nearly two weeks since I left you all, I have only heard of you all through Brother Strother, but I suppose Sue has written, the mails are irregular. On the night of the battle I sent a telegraph message by an officer to the Junction to be sent up to W.S.J. but it never reached him. . . .

I left Winchester as you may imagine with a sad and heavy heart. I did not think that Gen [Robert] Patterson would leave the Valley, & I supposed he would in all probability occupy Winchester and levy upon my property. . . . there was great dissatisfaction amongst those who came from the Valley. We reached Paris about 12 o'clock on the night of thursday, and layed down in the woods on the other side of town, early in the morning we came to Piedmont and from that depot to Manassa. Gen. Jackson then reported his command to Gen Beauregard and he ordered the Brigade out about four miles from the Junction, where we are encamped, but expect to move into Fairfax Co near Centreville this evening if a suitable encamping ground can be selected, On Friday night we came to this place as I have said after getting out of the cars, I was nearly broke down, and layed myself under a little Pine where I slept until morning, early saturday we were ordered to the right of our line of entrenchments where we lay all day in a pine thicket and also the following night. When I layed down at night, I hoped for a quiet sabbath, although I knew the battle was impending, yet I thought in this age of christianity the blessed sabbath would not be chosen for such a scene as we had.

At day light however I heard Gen Jackson call for all his staff, he had just received a dispatch ordering two of his Regiments to support Gen Longstreet who was momentarily expecting the attack, soon the booming of one or two heavy cannon commenced, it was only a feint however on the part of the Enemy in hopes of drawing our forces to that point, whilst in fact the whole column was moving rapidly 4 or 5 miles up the Bull Run to the left of our entrenchments. But Gen Beauregard was as smart as they were and our Brigade was immediately put in motion. Gen Bee was on the extreme left outside of our entrenchments, he engaged them and fought with great loss. We arrived on the ground about 11 o'clock in the day and found Gen Bee in full retreat. Gen Jackson immediately placed his Brigade in the line of battle and opened upon them with his Artillery. The Yankees fought far better than I expected, and kept up for 4½ to 5 hours a constant roar of cannon and musketry. Under Gen Jackson's command were for the time being nearly all the battalions, which he placed on an elevated position.

The enemy advanced by degrees on these Battalions bringing up their own Artillery, finally our battery of 6 or 8 pieces approached very near our left, where Col. Cummings was posted, he immediately gave the order to charge bayonet. I happened to ride up to the rear to his Regt just before, and there I witnessed the most awful scene of the day. Only about two hundred of his Regt had the courage to go into the charge, and of those poor fellows 158 were killed & wounded. Tom [Marshall] had his horse killed under him, & Col Thomas was also killed here. I was burnt on the side of the neck by a bullet which grazed me. We were on horseback and of course aimed at. The Regt was fired at by the Zouaves on one side, & the 69th New York Regt on the other, it was a deadly cross fire, the battery however was taken, but the men were forced to retreat, then the General ordered Col Preston to charge, which he did with his whole Regt, it was from all accounts a *splendid charge* I did not see it, but it was very successful, some reinforcements came up, and in about half an hour the retreat of the enemy commenced, then came our cavalry pursuing them, & cutting them all to pieces, although Alexandria was thirty miles off yet the Enemy ran the whole distance by 10 o'clock that night, rushed to the warves & crowded the boats for Washington, perfectly panic stricken. The Authorities it is said forbid the boats returning and drew up the "draw" over the Long Bridge to prevent the stream of men from crossing, the road was strewed with the dead & dying, with guns, & blankets & accoutrements of all descriptions.

Thus has the Lord of Host's fought on our side, and given us a glorious victory, over a force nearly three times our number, and a victory gained too not behind entrenchments, but in the open field. May God have mercy on us all, and spare our country yet, it seems to be concluded on all sides that this was the greatest battle ever fought on the Continent, whether we consider the numbers, the intensity of the fight or it's many other circumstances attending it. Gen Jackson tells me no battle in Mexico equalled it, and such a route [sic], & such a capture of Cannon & munitions of War was hardly ever heard of before. I have talked with many of the wounded, and they unanimously tell me they were deceived & drawn into this by the wickedness & folly of their rulers. They seem thankful for any kindness & promise never to come again to Virginia for such purposes. I have seen many of the killed, & those belonging to the New York Zouaves are the most horrid looking wretches you can imagine. Late as last thursday I rode over the Battle Field, and still large numbers of the dead laid unburied. (I mean the dead of the enemy). Dear Bev escaped without a scratch, whilst the battle raged I often thought of him, & wondered how he fared, but the God to whom I had commended him, spared him in that awful day, and to His name be all the Praise. Tomorrow I have made arrangements with Col Pendleton to hold Divine Service in our encampment.

Frank's letter returned to farming concerns the next day, and he sent it up to Winchester with Peyton Clark.

III

August–December 1861

ON THE POTOMAC AND BACK IN THE VALLEY

Robby Barton undoubtedly would have preferred to be with his brothers and friends in action. But the First Battle of Manassas began to change everyone's idea of what the war would be.

[MEMOIR OF ROBERT T. BARTON]

The Sunday that followed—the 21st day of July 1861—was a lovely bright day, but oppressive in its dreadful silence after the departure of the army and more oppressive still in the brooding apprehensions that seemed to hover like a cloud over the town.

The houses and hospitals were full of sick and some had died here, far away from their homes in the South.[1] A Federal army was not far off or rather, was supposed to be not far to the north of us and Winchester was protected by a small body of untrained militia.

We had begun to realize what war was, and when in the afternoon of that Sunday we could hear the faint distant boom of the guns, our hearts beat for the boys in such danger, and we went about the house stepping lightly and speaking low.

I think it was the next morning early that we heard rumours of the great battle: that David was safe, but Strother and Randolph both wounded. Then came news of this one and that one who had fallen. Burgess, whom I knew so well, and Powell and Harrison and the two Conrads from Martinsburg who had breakfasted at the house the morning that the army left.[2] Those two boys were all that were left of their father's family. I saw the rough farm wagon that brought them back in rough boxes piled on each other, while the blood ran out of the seams of the boxes through the straw in the bed of the wagon.

In the midst of all this woe there was a shout of triumph that we had met the enemy and had utterly routed them: that in one great battle we had won our independence, and now the war would soon be over. My wounded brothers came home, and I remember how I envied them, the fame they had won, and now the war was over and I had not seen a battle.

Strother's wound was in the knee and looked quite serious, but it healed at last. Rannie's was in the side, was slight, and healed rapidly. Both returned to camp as soon as they were fit for duty.[3] Besides our own boys other wounded were brought to the house, and the hands of all were full with these and the many sick of the army. The Federal army to the north of us had disappeared, and our militia command was as proud as if it had driven those Yankees away.

I was offered an easy position with the militia, but I declined that hoping soon to get into the volunteer army again. . . . I spent most of my time in my father's office helping him and studying law as far as my excited state of mind would permit me to study at all.

The Stonewall Brigade was at Camp Harman, and Jackson's staff at the Utterbach farm. Frank was enthusiastic: "a very delightful place for encamping, good water & fine breezes & a house near by where the owner has kindly offer me to sleep on the floor in the parlour, I availed myself of his invitation last night."[4] David Barton was sharing a mess with Holmes Boyd, Johnny Williams, and Bev Jones from Winchester, and university friends like Jim Garnett.[5] Robby went down for a visit a few days after the fight.

[MEMOIR OF ROBERT T. BARTON]

. . . My brother David having escaped without a wound did not come home and as he was in need of many things I joined a party of young men anxious to see the battle field and their friends in camp and drove with them to the neighbourhood of Manassas where the army was in camp. Of course, we filled the wagon with eatables, clothing, & c.

We found the Stonewall brigade in quite a pretty camp and the tents of the General and Staff in the yard of a gentleman's house. Among the other things carried down by me was a pair of boots which Gen. Jackson had written up to have sent down to him. We had been amazed at their great size, but when I gave them to the general, he sat on a log and tried them on, but finding them much too small, he asked me to carry them back, which I did. I stayed at Headquarters and found the General and staff very genial and kind. In the battle Gen. Jackson had had one of his fingers wounded and was obliged to hold it up nearly all the time. This became a habit which I often noticed in him afterwards. At this time it prevented him from holding his paper while he wrote and as the wind blew it about he asked me one day to hold the sheet. I, of course, complied but he wrote so slowly that my fingers became cramped, perceiving which, he made me get him four rocks which he placed on the corners of the paper in lieu of my fingers. I was amused lately in reading the life of Jackson by his wife, to recognize from the date and other incidents that very letter as one written to Mrs. Jackson.[6] This, of course, I did not know at the time.

The battle field interested me very much, but it was full of horrors with its only partially buried dead decaying in the hot sun: its broken wagons, artillery, dead horses, and debris generally. This was all very shocking at the time, but I saw so much worse afterwards that it almost faded from my mind. . . .

Bev Jones had gone home sick for about two weeks in August and his brother, Frank, was suffering from "exceeding debility" when he wrote Susan on August 27. He attributed his ailments to overwork, heat, and:

[LETTER OF FRANK B. JONES TO SUSAN C. JONES]

. . . horrid water in Prince William [County] which came near to disabling our whole Brigade, added to my sickness I have been compelled to work all day long. I work as hard as I used to do in H Ferry. I never gave up except for parts of Days when I was obliged to do so, then I had no place to go where I could be quiet & take rest. I have longed for your kind & soothing hand & for something delicate to eat. I go to sleep at night upon the hard floor, for which indeed I am thankful rather than to sleep out. . . . Do not speak of my complaints as I had rather do & suffer in this cause without complaining and I mention it more to show you that I have not been able to write to you. I am writing now whilst I allow papers to accumulate upon me.[7]

With cooler weather and wearing his flannels again, Frank felt better.[8] There were said to be 4,000 sick soldiers at the Junction. Already in Virginia, shortages and inflated prices were beginning to affect civilian life, as were the usual diseases, exacerbated by an enlarged and dislocated population, both of soldiers and refugees. Bev's illness was brief: he was back with the brigade by August 22, and was camped not far from Frank. Still serving on Jackson's staff, Frank was finding camp life tedious and unproductive when he answered a letter from his young sister-in-law Julia Clark.

[LETTER OF FRANK B. JONES TO JULIA CLARK]

> HdQrs 1st Brigade
> 4th Sept 1861

   . . . It has been a long time since I saw you and then you recollect only for a few moments in my office at Harpers Ferry, I was standing on Jeffersons rock when you ladies moved off in the cars & I was very much amused at the incessant waving of handkerchiefs, it presented at the distance . . . a singular & amusing sight. The soldiers cheered you enough I suppose for a life time. It is very seldom a lady is seen in this part of the world, we see nothing but men & hear nothing but the everlasting drum & fife which I wish I could never hear again, I would not give one day spent at home with my little boy Ran for a thousand such as I spend here, should we live to see Peace again, how we will appreciate its many blessings! I suppose all the beaux have left town, and you young ladies must be left quite desolate, parties I suppose have been give up entirely. . . . Winchester must look sad with the many cases of sickness there, how I would like to be there once more & to see you all again. Will the day every come when we will be gathered again around our common fireside? Write to me dear Julia though I have treated you so badly & believe in the kind affection of

> your brother Frank
> Francis B. Jones

Sue was managing well at Carysbrooke, aided by Frank's weekly instructions and advice, and Frank had gained confidence in her abilities. But she evidently complained about his letters—too much farming and not enough sentiment— especially as they marked their eighth anniversary August 31. Frank responded: "You allude to our wedding day, surely it is not necessary for me to say how happy you have made me, & how good you have been to me, so true is all this that in these sad days of trial I cannot allow my thoughts to run back & dwell upon the pleasures of the past. . . ."[9]

   James Jones had recently been to camp, trading back his own horse for the

recovered Guy Darnell who, Frank had written the children, had been "recruit-
ing at Uncle James's" for a few weeks (Frank thought he still did not look well). [10]
Since James and Tom Marshall had been selling the Oak Hill cattle, Frank now
had in mind to sell his cattle to the army. In the midst of a letter ranging from
farming to daguerreotypes, Frank touched on a notorious episode in which
General Jackson had denied furlough to an officer whose wife was dying.

[LETTER OF FRANK B. JONES TO SUSAN C. JONES]

> HdQrs 1st Brigade
> Camp near Centreville
> 6th September 1861

Your letter of the 3d instant my dearest Sue is at hand. I understand the hay
acct & the money matter perfectly and have to render you much praise for your
wonderful business qualities, I hardly know where you excel most, in the home
or in the field. You have had so much hay cut & sold & done so many other
splendid things that Tom Marshall declares that I had best abdicate in your
favour and let you manage hereafter.[11]. . .

Tell Kitten & Ran they must write me a letter & tell me all about the horse
whether he is fast or slow, what is his colour &c &c & tell Ran he must tell Pa
how many leg's Ma's horse has, My dear children! what would I give to have one
hours talk with them! O how I mourn over this life, it is so distasteful, so horrible in all its features and yet I have many blessings for which I am thankful.

You send me a commission as Major in the Light Infantry, "it never rains but
it pours" [Gov. John] Letcher has noticed me at last, but he comes too late, I
had rather be an adjt Gen with a commission from Pres Davis than a Major in
the line, unless he would allow me with that rank & pay to retain my present
position. . . . Keith is staying at the [Manassas] Junction but I never see him,
indeed there is neither time nor place to see any body. The Junction is the most
terrible place you can well imagine, it is crowded all the time, *the place is,* for
there are no houses except one or two, seathing mass [of] soldiers, & tents, &
cars & boxes & all sorts & manners of discomfort in every shape.

Tell Mother I am very glad to hear she has fixed my book & I wish she would
cut out Gen Jacksons official report when it appears & paste it in for me, I suppose it will appear before long.[12] Sometimes I cant make out words in your letters but I reckon you write so as to pay me for my bad writing. I want you to
send me some of that money that you are afraid to keep, I am now entirely out
of money, having given to day my last 25 cents to change to pay for a letter to

Louisa ("Kitten") and Rannie Jones, in the photograph made for their father in September 1861. (Eleanor J. Burleson)

Brother Strother.[13] By the way if Frank [Clark] is willing to give a clerkship to Bev, it is a great matter for him, it will be a very difficult matter for him to get a discharge, but I will do the best I can to effect the object. I wrote to W.S.J. & also to Frank how to proceed about it, a clerkship is worth $720 a year, & if Frank is continued in Winchester Bev could live at home with little or no expense.[14]. . .

I have just heard that Mrs Harper the wife of Col Harper is dead, Col [Kenton] Harper of the 5th Regt of our Brigade, a telegram informed him a week ago of her illness & expected death, yet he was refused leave of absence to go & see her, he then tendered his resignation & the acceptance of his resignation & the telegram announcing her death came together.[15] When you get sick my Darling I am coming to see you, you may depend on that. . . . Write to me soon, tell me what the hands have done & *are now doing.* Give much love to mother, & make Kitten & Ran write to me & tell me something about your likeness & theirs I want an ambrotype or *a good picture*, not a dauguereotype . . . good bye my darling make the children obey you without a word, train them for Heaven & may we all meet there is my humble prayer,

yours always
Francis B Jones

The fall of 1861 was frustrating and confusing for the Rebel army in Virginia. The troops were eager to attack Washington to follow up on their stunning victory at Manassas and strike a blow that would end the war and win independence. But the army seemed mired in inaction. In this context it did not seem as if Colonel Harper's request to visit his dying wife of thirty years were unreasonable. Yet Jackson required total devotion to the cause.

Frank's mother, again at Carysbrooke with Sue, had sent her news, and urged him to look up his Randolph cousins from Washington, who had joined the army after the battle. Frank was at a loss to describe the size and confusion of the vast army encampment, but he was clear on the state of the mails when he had to reiterate a request for money.

[Letter of Frank B. Jones to Susan C. Jones]

Camp near Centreville
7th Sept 1861.

My dear Mother,

Your letter of the 4th reached me tonight, I judge you had not received my last to you when this was written, you say you wrote to Bev & my self. I have not heard of that letter and Brother Strother says he has written to me I have not received that either, I wrote to Sue to send me 15$. I wish she would send me 20$ as soon as she received this. It is a great satisfaction for me to know that you are with Sue, but I fear at times it is a great task, you must want to go to Vaucluse sometimes. I have no idea where to find Cousin Innes [Randolph's] sons.[16] We are here in a wilderness of human beings and I have many friends prominent in the service that I have not seen at all. . . .

You ask me about the movements of the Army, I am like old Uncle Jim "I dont know nothing" our Pickets are fighting every day, & we are losing men every day, & this may bring on a general fight, but it is hard to say, the Enemy are falling back by degrees, slowly, but it may be a trap to draw us in. Our Brigade is 12 miles in the rear of the most advanced forces. From Munsons hill, we see the dome of the Capitol & in it can be seen men & women with glasses looking upon us to see what they can, I heard the booming of cannon for some time the other morning, our Pickets were playing across the river & dislodged a position the Army held above Georgetown, a large force will move in a few days below Dumfries on the Potomac. Our scouts run in very close to Alexandria, they (the Enemy) are entrenching at the [Episcopal Theological] Seminary & just in front of the Fairfax house just this side of the Seminary and indeed from there all the way up to Arlington with a force of 30,000 men they are guarding the approaches. Please cut out of the papers what you think valuable & paste them so I may know they are of your selection. . . .

Love to all & write to me soon & believe always in my sincere love

yours & c   Francis B. Jones

By the time Frank wrote on September 19, the army had moved camp again. As before, Frank revealed by his lack of preparedness for the new season his

dashed hopes of being by then at home. He wrote to Sue for his greatcoat, blankets, and the like; his frequent requests for money and supplies met with her
objections—or at least queries—until he finally wrote, in some exasperation,
"the Army furnishes an officer nothing but his horse feed."17

[LETTER OF FRANK B. JONES TO SUSAN C. JONES]

> Camp near Fairfax C.H.
> 19th Sept 1861

I cannot thank you too much my very dear Sue for your long & interesting
letter which came to hand this morning. . . . The weather is getting cool or
rather the nights & I would like to have two good warm blankets or a large,
thick *comfort* the one I took with me is an excellent one, I lay down on half of it
& cover with the other half but it is not enough now. I make my servant build
me a large fire in front of my tent & the heat & smoke together blows in the
tent & helps to dry & warm it but it goes out in the night. I sleep on a *stretcher*
which one of the Surgeons lent to me, and it is quite comfortable as I can do no
better.

Our encampment is not as pleasant to me as the other, I have no house to
put my head in when it rains, and the water to drink is by no means as plentiful,
the water through this county is very delightful, but the springs are small
though numerous. The immense body of troops which are encamped here
require a great deal of water and we are obliged to husband the little wet
weather streams between the hills by damming them up. You have no idea of
the immense scale upon which every thing is carried on, the whole country for
miles & miles is filled with *white* tents & to feed & water so large a force is no
small matter. You must write to me at Fairfax C.H. now. We are 12 miles from
the Junction and only about ¾ of a mile to the C. H. which by the way is an
interesting village, it is now filled with troops, wagons, soldiers, & dashing
troopers who are riding at full speed. One sad feature that meets your eye at
every encampment are the hillocks of new graves, many are the deaths; To hear
the muffled drums & the soldiers last salute at the grave are constant & common occurrances.18

By making inquiry at Mr Boyds or Mr Williams or Sister Fannies you could
hear of a waggon which would bring me down the things I write for, they had
best be put in a box, Mr. Philip Meade comes down once a week in a waggon &
he would bring me anything, if you could send it down to him, is my great coat
a nice warm one, I charged Denny about making it warm & putting a long cape

on it.[19] [Dr.] Hunter McGuire went home to day sick & I fear he may have a spell of typhoid, he is a very talented man & a first rate fellow. . . .

I inclose a blank check that you can fill, send me 10 or 15 dollars, I am again out of money entirely, I received the 20$ safely, you say I did not acknowledge it, *did you want a receipt?* A young officer of Longstreets Brigade called to see me a few days ago and in the course of conversation he bragged a good deal of his wifes management on his farm, I told him that my wife was managing every thing so well at home that I had been advised by a friend to abdicate & hereafter to allow her to manage for me, & had I known that you wanted a receipt for your remittances to me I could have out bragged him all to pieces. . . .

Tell Marshall Barton that I am going to try & have him elected 1st Lt in your brothers company, I am clear for getting him in the same fix I am in.[20] Mr. [F. W. M.] Holliday wrote to me that he would accept the position, I sent word to the Co to day. Allen's Regt [2nd Virginia] is 10 or 12 miles in the advance lines with 5 days rations, they will return Saturday I reckon, another of our regts Col Preston's [4th Virginia] goes down to-morrow. . . .

Frank, like his mother a faithful correspondent, wrote her when she returned to Vaucluse. He knew she would understand his outrage at the Yankees' entrenching on the grounds of his alma mater, the Episcopal High School.

[LETTER OF FRANK B. JONES TO ANN C. R. JONES]

Camp near Fairfax C.H.
21st Sept 1861, Saturday night

I do not know whether I can finish a letter to you to night my dearest Mother, but I can begin one, I am sitting down in my own tent with a very indifferent fixture for a table to write upon, the night is Dark & gloomy, & raining hard, I have a big fire in front of my tent doors but the rain blows in so that I had to put down the doors & with the help of two of Aunt Kittys pins I have succeeded in shutting up myself right securely from the weather. Tom [Marshall] suggested that it would be better if we had two straps sewed on & tie the wall's together, and I said Aunt Kitty could do it, but I reckon it is most too far for her to come down & try her handiwork on my tent.

I am thankful to say that I am perfectly well, though my friends tell me I am getting grey, I have no means of seeing myself so I cant tell how it is. For a

month or more, after the battle of the 21st I was very unwell, & with every prudence in eating I got no better. The Surgeons advised wearing flannel, I came
off from home with my one flannel shirt expecting to get my trunk soon, but we
moved so hurriedly from Winchester that I did not & could not have carried it
with me, soon after the battle I took my flannel off as I had no change, the life I
led sleeping out in the open air & such constant exposure without flannel was
too much for my system, as soon as my trunk came I put my flannel on, and in
two or three days I was a new man, & have never been sick since. Tell Sue I
have my great coat, it is a very nice one & it will do for me to cover at night as
well to wear in the day, I sleep on a stretcher & my servant builds me a fire &
spreads my blanket on my lowly couch every night.

Two days ago or rather it was yesterday I rode down into the advanced lines,
& was highly delighted with my trip, you know our grand army is in full sight of
the Enemy, Munson & Masons hill's [near Alexandria] have lately been captured from the Enemy & they drive nearer, & into their entrenchments. Col
Stuart the officer in command, a dashing Cavalry officer, I know very well, he
received me with his usual politeness & shewed me all the points of interest, he
sits on the top of the hill all day in full view of the Enemy & near enough for a
minie ball to take him at any time.[21] The hill has been trenched and a good deal
of work has been done of a temporary character, I could not see Arlington
House for the trees & forest this side, but the flag is distinguishable, and in full

Episcopal Theological Seminary, near Alexandria. (Edith Barton Sheerin)

sight was the lofty dome of what was once our beloved Capitol, from Arlington all the way down to Hunting Creek below Alexandria are immense fortifications & with a glass I could see the Yankees with their coats off working away with spades & picks, in full sight are the blue waters of that noble river with now & then a white sail appearing or the smoke stack of a steamer.[22] You can see the tall spire of the [Episcopal] Seminary building and a large U.S. flag waiving over Fort Albany or Ellsworth just this side of the Seminary, this is an immense earthwork where they have mounted heavy guns, how dare the vandals to occupy those grounds I love so well; where is the [Episcopal] High School? I could not see it; just then Col Stuarts glass was handed to me & to my delight the roof of the seminary & the chimneys came in view, & to the left old Howard with its long roof, & its *cupola's* where I have so often studied my Virgil & spent so many pleasant hours became distinctly visible, from each one a U.S. flag was waiving, how long, O how long will the enemies of our country be allowed to tread upon our soil & desecrate our holy places![23]

Whilst I stood there a white handkerchief was raised by the Pickets a little to my right & soon 4 or 5 of the enemy & 4 or 5 of our men went over to the middle ground between & there held a short conference. Col Stuart sent his adjutant to know what it meant but I came away soon after & did not learn the cause of the parley, our pickets & their pickets are about the same distance from each other as that oak tree is from my house which stands in front & just above the Opequon, they get behind trees & creep up a little closer for sure aims & let fly the minie balls at each other, one of our men was killed to day, he belonged to Allens Regiment. Our Camp is 10 or so miles from Munsons Hill but our Regts go down according to detail & stay five days at a time, we have two Regts there now, Allens & Prestons, Allens will be back to-morrow.

I rode over to Masons hill which is the beautiful residence of Murray Mason a brother of James M. Mason, this hill they are fortifying & it is sad to see the desolation of war in that sweet & quiet house. The view from this point is similar to that of Munson & is a high elevation. The wind has changed to the N west & it has turned colder, I dread living in these whited sepulchres all winter, I tell you the cold wind drives in at a great rate. Well it is getting late & I am beginning to think whether I am going to sleep warm or cold to night, my great coat will help the cause, good night!

In October, Sue was closing Carysbrooke and planning to spend the winter at her father's house on Fort Hill in Winchester, as Frank had suggested. Frank,

*by now resigned to wintering with the army in Fairfax County, was relieved to
have his family in town, but at the same time worried about illness there; he was
worried, too, about his brother Bev's feckless ways.*

[LETTER OF FRANK B. JONES TO SUSAN C. JONES]

> Camp near Fairfax Ct House
> 4th October 1861

. . . how sad it is to lose the society of my children at a time when I feel they
most need my care, so young & so impressible, now is the time to train them
properly, "As the twig is bent so is the tree inclined", watch their principles
closely & make them honest & scrupulously truthful. I am glad to hear that you
anticipate so much pleasure in living with your father & I want you to go when
you desire it, whilst the weather is pleasant however I would stay in the country. Be very careful about taking the children where they would be exposed to
scarlet fever, and when you are in town I would not let them go down street
unless under your care as they might come in contact with the disease somewhere, Do not consent to live with your father without paying board. . . .

We cannot agree upon peace until Maryland & Kentucky have come over
to us, and the day was never darker than it is at present for Kentucky.[24] I
long for our Army to cross over into Maryland & attack Washington there or cut
off her supplies; the sacrifice of life would be too great attacked from this point
& I believe it is not the policy of our Generals to attack her by the way of
Arlington. Our position is a very strange one. A few days ago we ran them into
their fortifications & took hill after hill bearing upon them, & now we retreat
from them in a precipitate manner, it is no doubt done to draw them out to an
open fight, but this I am sure McClellan will not do, for should he fail his Capitol is gone. . . .

I am much distressed about the condition Bev's family is left in. I will see
him this evening & have a talk with him, you must not let her [Rebecca] want
for any necessary that you can buy on credit, flour &c, &c and let me know so
that I can try & pay for it. Bev will probably send her some money before long,
his expenses amt to 5$ a month and he only gets 12$, I wonder nothing is done
towards getting him a *discharge*, I can do nothing here, Johnston would certainly defeat the application, & if he agreed to it, it has then to go before the
Secty of War, it is proper then that the application be made to him first &
directly & let some one present it who would use some influence in his favour.

Discharges are sometimes granted & a promotion is always acceeded to, & this looks like a promotion.[25]

I hope Padgett manages the servants well, & I hope they are house staying. I am surprised at what you told me of Tom, if they [the slaves] become disatisfied I am sure there will be trouble and I fear if they attempt escape they will effect it. I want the most vigorous measures taken & high rewards if any should attempt to go. One poor negro attempted to run our lines the other evening, endeavouring to make his way into the Federal lines when some of our men put a ball through him & he fell perfectly dead. If you have had no frost, & the corn is green let it stand, be very careful if cutting it too green, let me know how the young timothy looks in the corn. . . .

My colt has improved but the feed is inadequate for his necessities, I will make out with Guy Darnell until next spring unless we have many hard marches, which I do not now expect. . . . I want the corn pulled off in the shuck & hauled up in that way & the shucks put away for winter food, commence feeding the hogs as soon as [the overseer] can, & buy mill feed for them to make slop dont neglect this, let it be done at once. Make the children write to me, I look at their likenesses every day

> Yours my Darling
> Francis B. Jones

While fervently wishing to be at home, Frank was not optimistic about the future. On October 14, he wrote from Fairfax Court House to his brother-in-law Peyton Clark:

[LETTER OF FRANK B. JONES TO J. PEYTON CLARK]

Our policy is clearly to act on the defensive, and I never knew so well before that we are *obliged* to do it *because we are weak.* I have given up all hope of peace. A gloomy war, a long war, and a bloody one, you may depend upon it, is before us, and we may as well make up our minds to it.[26]

Frank was in need of physical and spiritual comfort. His young sister-in-law Julia Clark attempted to relieve the former by sending "her gutta percha piano cover which is lined inside with flannel . . . so large that I can wrap up in it . . ."; Frank was truly grateful. As for the latter, he wrote his mother requesting a small Bible; he had only a New Testament. He liked the camp in Fairfax and had time to wander near Fairfax Court House.[27]

"Shin plasters." (Ann Dudley Field Lalley)

[LETTER OF FRANK B. JONES TO ANN C. R. JONES]

. . . not far from our encampment there is a very interesting old building, a large brick church built in the Colonial times, I wish you could see this old antiquity, I have been there several times, there is an old grave yard around it but the graves are so old that you can hardly distinguish them, I noticed the name of Harrison upon a comparatively new one, the yard however has rapidly filled up with new graves, soldiers! & I was surprised in riding by the other day to see so many more new occupants put there in but a few days.[28] The church is built on the edge of a very dense forest on the main road leading from Fairfax Ct House towards the Station, I was very much impressed when I first was there it was a cloudy evening but as I entered the old door way (which is very much decayed) the sun shone out through the trees & the old window panes and fell upon the 1st Commandment "Thou shalt have" &c &c and made the old gilt letters glitter in the sun light, I halted, and I could not help thinking how many now passed away had sunday after sunday looked at those words and had still worshipped other Gods. The floor is paved & the pews are raised & have the old fashioned high backs, the old pulpit & the sounding board & the reading desk are all there, on one side the commandments, the creed & the Lords prayer are in large gilt letters, there is an old stove there which certainly came over [from England] with the brick, it is a very quaint old structure.

I am writing whilst several of my friends are in my tent talking about tactics & to my worry they are constantly putting questions to me for the purpose of stumping me on difficult movements, I have written so far through many difficulties, I have a pen so bad I can hardly make a letter with it, I commenced it yesterday & this day (11th Oct) is now gone & I have not finished.

This has been a gala Day with us Gen [P. G. T.] Beauregard, [J. E.] Johnston, [F. H.] Smith, Stewart [J. E. B. Stuart] & staff, Sir James Furguson and an Hon. M.P. of England a Mr Burke, reviewed our troops, it was a fine evening and every thing passed off handsomely.[29] . . .

We have had no battle yet, and I dont believe we are going to have one now at any rate, though every preparation is going on in expectancy. I dread the winter, it will no doubt be spent here in huts, we had better fight it and at once & be done with it. . . . I have no specie to pay my postage & the Fairfax P.M. is so fastidious he wont take a shin plaster.[30] Good night my dear mother, excuse a hurried line & believe me

yours &c &c
Francis B. Jones

A week later, the Confederate forces moved back to Centreville, to a stronger position on the Heights. Frank, awestruck, wrote to both his mother and Sue about the colossal movement of the army, "a countless host . . . a sight never to be forgotten."[31]

[LETTER OF FRANK B. JONES TO SUSAN C. JONES]

Camp near Centreville
7th Oct 1861

Dear Sue,

I wrote you on the 15th that we are striking tents to march back to Centreville, I write again to say that I am near this village & you can direct to me at Centreville P.O. for the present. The whole Army had moved back. I witnessed yesterday a sight that I never supposed I would see—the whole Army in motion, I can only describe it by referring you to the discriptions in the Bible of vast numbers, or to pictures that you have seen of moving armies. We struck our tents in the night & marched at 3 o'clock in the morning by the way of the Braddock road, I never saw anything to equal the immense train of waggons, the major road was so blocked that we were obliged to take the old Braddock road, the waggons were heavily loaded & such a time with balky horses & bad hills I never saw, we reached our camping ground by 3 o'clock in the evening.[32] Let me hear from you my dear Sue. I have not heard from you for I think near two weeks

Yours in haste
Frank B. Jones

Rannie, recovered from his Manassas wound, had rejoined the 33rd Virginia Infantry in Fairfax County in September. On October 7, Jackson had been promoted to Major General, and was soon put in charge of the newly created Valley District. On November 4, his old command, the five Valley regiments now known as the Stonewall Brigade, were paraded to bid him farewell. This was the occasion of Jackson's famous farewell address to his brigade. Happily, his old brigade was almost immediately assigned to him.

With Jackson's promotion, his staff resigned to allow him to restructure for his new responsibilities. Tom Marshall returned to Oak Hill for a few weeks, and in November raised a cavalry company, recruited in his neighborhood, which later became part of the 7th Virginia Cavalry under the command of his friend and neighbor Turner Ashby. Frank Jones had been appointed Major, 2nd Virginia Infantry, in August, but remained as A.A.G. with Jackson well into the fall.

The Stonewall Brigade returned to Frederick County in early November and was encamped near Winchester for the rest of the year. Since there were no major actions in Virginia that fall, the war did not seem very grim. There were expeditions against the B.&O. Railroad, and some thought was given to using Federal-supplied track to connect Winchester with Strasburg; Powell Conrad, as an army engineer, had surveyed the possibility of using the Valley Turnpike as a roadbed, and Frank Jones had worried that the tracks might run between his house and barn.[33] With so many of the troops near their homes, it was even at times somewhat festive. There were social gatherings with frugal collations, whose avowed purpose might be to knit for the soldiers—but more flirtations than socks were accomplished.

Nevertheless, the brigade was still an army, and one unused to discipline. Perhaps in the absence of immediate danger, soldiers are more inclined to get

into other kinds of trouble, and a notable and notorious incident had occurred on September 8. Two privates of the Virginia Rangers (later 12th Virginia Cavalry), James A. Miller and George W. Kerfoot, were accused of attempting to murder their captain. The ensuing court-martial took place in Winchester in late October, and David W. Barton defended Kerfoot. This was unusual because Barton did not as a rule litigate; conceivably Barton's taking the case was due to his shortage of work, as there was rarely a shortage of lawyers. The court-martial was presided over by Gen. Gilbert S. Meem, and George W. Ward was judge advocate. David Barton's final argument (thirteen closely written legal-size pages, tightly folded and obviously clenched in hand in court) demonstrated that Kerfoot was relatively uninvolved in the act, and that if anyone had incited it, Kennerly had done so in irresponsible jest. 34

[ARGUMENT FOR GEORGE W. KERFOOT, BY DAVID W. BARTON]

. . . The evening or the night preceding Mr. Kerfoot & Mr. Miller had been selected or detailed to go the next morning to the margin of the Potomack, some miles from camp, to watch & capture if they could a man named Tom Pitcher, suspected of holding improper communication with the enemy across the river. . . . About day break they set out on that excursion. . . . The next we hear of Miller & Kerfoot from witnesses whose evidence is properly before the court is from W. L. Kennerly a Lieutenant in Col. Ashby's command who met with them at Halltown & road with them on their return as far as the entrance or outside of their camp. . . . Mr. Kennerly—who is evidently a man of mind, but from his own account of himself evidently prone to make sport & run rags though incapable as I verily believe, of any design to create mischief or to instigate violence—unfortunately got into conversation with these men about their pay & the manner in which they were mustered into service—tantalized them with the small consolation that a special act of Congress might provide for their case & then added in the same vein of well dissembled irony, that "he would shoot any damned rascal who would muster him into service in that way.". . .

Kennerly is a man of shrewd bright mind, a man of authority in Ashby's command, skilled in the use of strong & specific phrase & it is not to be questioned that his words left their impression & unluckily a wrong one on the minds of these men in humbler positions than he, not half so well informed & naturally enough inclined to defer to his superior intelligence. Inflamed with Licquor as the three who took that ride together, confessedly were, it is not to be denied that Miller & Kerfoot—whose subsequent acts show that they took Kennerly to be in earnest—were excited by his taunts & suggestions & that before the conversation had ended they had been persuaded that they with the other men in the same command had been imposed upon & that Capt. Henderson was the man who practiced this imposition.

This Court will not understand me as intimating that Capt. Henderson had really done any wrong—far from it: nor as intimating that if he *had practiced* the imposition & done the wrong, it would have justified the violence which followed—far from it; for other & *proper* means of redress could have been found. I am only carrying out the narrative as drawn from the whole record testimony—in its natural & I think logical order.

Miller & Kerfoot *were* excited by the conversation—to what degree they were severally excited, & to what extent they might be driven to develop it in action, would depend on the temperament & disposition of the two men. Both may have felt aggrieved, as doubtless they did—& each may have resolved in his own way & at such time as he might deem most suitable & favourable to success, to seek redress. The rash high-tempered & impetuous man (Miller), allowed his sense of injury to master him at once & yielding to the impulse he sought the *first opportunity* to resent the real or imagined wrong. Nothing is more obvious than that it was under the immediate influence of that conversation with Kennerly, stimulated by his taunts, & jeers & inflamed with whiskey that Miller rushed into the camp, made his way direct to the lodging place of his victim & madly perpetrated the act which came so near depriving our cause & country of one of its most gallant champions. . . .

After separating from Kennerly as before related, Miller & Kerfoot proceeded to their camp close by. Miller talking loudly & highly excited rode up to the spot where he found Capt. Henderson distant from 120 to 150 yards from the gateway where he came in, & after angrily reproaching the Captain, shot him. So much for Miller.

The conduct of Mr. Kerfoot though very reprehensible & deserving punishment, is of a very different phaze & his guilt of a very different degree. . . . When Kerfoot came into camp what did he do? If conspiring with Miller to perpetrate some instant act of violence, his natural course of conduct would have been, like Miller to have been armed with loaded weapons—like Miller, to have remained on horseback—like him, to have *hurried* to the scene of action & committed at once the meditated act. His actual conduct lacks all these features of complicity. He rode leisurely into camp—entered into & kept up a conversation of some length with a man at the gate, quietly took his horse to his usual hitching place—fastened him with a halter instead of the bridle, requiring double the time to accomplish & doubling the time & labour of loosing him in case of sudden need—took off the saddle—& was still in conversation with Mr Boyer, when the report of Miller's rifle startled & interrupted them & with others in the camp—they both repaired toward the spot; Kerfoot evincing in his gate & movements no greater haste than all the rest. His gun & pistol were with him as he came in from the scout, for he had not yet been to his lodging—but both gun & pistol were without loads. Kennerly's evidence that he & Kerfoot fired off their pieces as they neared the camp with the evidence of another witness that there were 12 or 14 different reports would have been still incomplete, but for the testimony of Legg & Roberts that they examined the pieces—the one the pistol—the other the rifle of Kerfoot & found them empty. No interval of time & no opportunity of access to them had been afforded to Kerfoot to fire them off or draw the loads after the affray—if such a theory were even suggested. It is very true & I seek not to keep it out of sight, or to extenuate it, that Kerfoot hearing what Miller had done, did in his folly or madness *justify* the act, & thereby expose himself most wantonly & without the least necessity, to the suspicion of being an accomplice & accessory. . . .

I can very well understand and I think this court composed of practical & intelligent minds accustomed to scan over poor humanity in all its vicissitudes of trial & temptation, can understand as I do, that this man Kerfoot who had just spent the whole day with Miller in a long & wearisome ride, on an enterprise not free from danger & responsibility—their journey just ended—when he heard what Miller had done & saw that every man's hand was raised against him—some attempting to shoot him & others to drag him from his horse, should have found his sympathies drawn out instinctively & in spite of himself toward his forsaken & suffering comrade; & in the very consciousness of his impotency to help him in any other way against such fearful odds, should have given vent to *strong words* of defence & justification—all the stronger & the more extravagant because it was the only aid & comfort he could render.

If the use of such language in such a moment of sudden surprize & commotion is to be regarded in itself as *mutiny* & *insubordination* to be visited by penalty appropriate to such offenses, be it so. In that aspect of his case I cannot & will not attempt to excuse my client, or even to extenuate his conduct, except so far as it is just & proper to try & examine all human conduct, in the light of the particular circumstances & peculiar temptations to which the actor may have been exposed. If tried in *too hot* a furnace, I am afraid there is too small a proportion of fine gold in any human conduct to stand the fiery ordeal.

Barton made his case; he was eloquent enough to gain Kerfoot the relatively light sentence of one hundred days hard labor with ball and chain. Miller was judged guilty of attempted murder. The court's unanimous petition for pardon was denied, either by Jackson or Johnston or both. Julia Chase, a Winchester diarist of Union sympathies, coolly reported on November 26: "Today one of the soldiers from Jefferson County, a Mr. Miller, was shot. He attempted taking the life of his Captain, tho he did not succeed in killing him but deprived him of the use of his right arm forever, by shooting near that point. A petition was sent on to Richmond, but no reprieve was given him and his own Company shot him. He saw them put his shroud in the coffin, then being blindfolded was seated on his coffin and his life taken. He is said to have been rather an ill tempered, bad sort of a fellow, and this sentence was executed as an example to others."[35]

Although Jackson now commanded the Army of the Shenandoah with his new rank, he still counted on the Stonewall Brigade—"the First Brigade in the affections of [its] General"—for the most difficult tasks. In mid-December, he led them north to the Potomac, in an attempt to disrupt traffic on the important and well-defended C.&O. Canal, paralleling the Potomac. Repeated assaults on Dam Number Five and others took place during a cold and wintry week, in an arduous and relatively fruitless effort. The brigade returned to Winchester a few days before Christmas, where once again court-martials and discipline seemed to be the everyday substance of an army-in-waiting in winter. On returning to camp after Christmas, Frank Jones wrote to his mother (enclosing religious tracts for her and small Christmas gifts for the servants) that he was in command of his regiment while his superior officers attended to just such duties.[36]

IV

January—May 1862

The Stonewall Brigade began the new year with a new campaign, one that always seemed pointless to its veterans but that drove out Federal troops gathered in western Virginia and temporarily severed the valuable B.&O. Railroad. Most accounts of this foray sound like Valley Forge—extreme cold; not enough clothes, food or shelter. Years later, Rannie vividly remembered the severe conditions.

[MEMOIR OF RANDOLPH BARTON]

January 1, 1862, we started upon the Bath and Romney campaign, eventful only because of the bitter weather we encountered.

The morning of January 1, 1862, succeeding a warm, gentle rain, was spring-like in its mildness. The grass and limbs of the trees glistened and everything betokened one of those freaks in the weather which are not uncommon in the latitude of Virginia and Maryland. About eight o'clock we started on one of the northwesterly roads and by two o'clock we encountered a rapidly rising and bitter north wind. By sunset the thermometer had fallen nearly to zero. When the wagons came up we made all haste to erect some shelter for the night, and Neff, the Adjutant of the Thirty-third, and myself, by laying fence rails from the top of the span of fencing to the ground; and throwing over it an oil cloth or something of the kind, and under it some straw and our blankets, secured a delightful night's rest, which was not at all disturbed by a capital supper of fresh sausage and buckwheat cakes obtained at a nearby log cabin.[1] The expedition was most arduous and as far as we could see, useless. In spite of the high credit he had won at Manassas, Jackson's reputation for a while sank to low-water mark, on that expedition.

After a campaign of a month or more, going to Berk[e]ley Springs [Bath] and then to Romney, both now in West Virginia, we returned to Winchester, and went into winter quarters, our brigade going out on the "Pughtown" road about three miles from the town.[2] The name of the road has since been changed to the Gainesborough road—the original name apparently retarding improvements.

Contrary to his expectations, Frank Jones was campaigning in western Virginia rather than settled in winter quarters near Winchester.

[LETTER OF FRANK B. JONES TO SUSAN C. JONES]

Camp opposite Hancock
Monday evening Jany 6th 1862

I take the first opportunity my dearest Sue to let you hear from me, I am perfectly well although I have never in my life gone through as much suffering & as much exposure, as we have done on this trip, Wednesday night we slept on Sleepy Creek Mountain without our blankets & with nothing to eat, our wagons did not get up with us until late the next day, the next night thursday it was bitterly cold but Botts & myself put our blankets together & I rested delightfully, friday night after 8 o'clock we halted in a few miles of Bath & as it was snowing here pitched a tent & slept tolerably well, the next day saturday we entered Bath the Enemy firing upon us with Artillery, they made good their retreat however leaving in our hands some stores & two 12 pd guns, (cannon).[3] In Bath I craved permission of a widow lady; Botts & myself, to sleep on the floor by a stove, the next day.

Yesterday, the blessed Sabbath as it was, we were all day & all night under arms, standing or marching on the road to Hancock which is only five miles from Bath, so large is the train & so narrow the road that again our wagons could not get up & the hardest night I ever spent was last night, by a fire with no blankets & snowing most of the time, I eat my breakfast yesterday morning about sun rise & from that time till nearly 11 o'clock to day I could get not a single mouthful to eat, the road is blocked up in this narrow valley with men & wagons, the sight is only equalled by the march on the Braddock road, Capon bridge was *burnt* yesterday, we have lost some 5 or 6 killed & 15 wounded. The Enemy are across the river & occasionally a shot is exchanged with Artillery.

We are laying still today having marched back to within 3 miles of Bath & I have just pitched my tent. I have my stove up & both Botts & Hunter are with me each of us writing to our wives, I do not know (nor does Gen Garnett or any body else) what we came here for or when we are going & never was more at a loss, the condition of the roads is very bad not deep cut, but very slippery, the horses are not reigned, I have seen two wagons upset this morning just from my tent door & in the night whilst I was laying down I heard a wagon heavily loaded go over a high precipice, horses & all, it made a terrible crash, the horses strange to say were not killed.[4] I send this to Martinsburg would go on writing, but am obliged to close at once, my dear precious wife & children can any one tell how much I love them & how often I think of them? Love to all

yours &c &c

Francis B. Jones

send me my silk handkerchief

[LETTER OF FRANK B. JONES TO ANN C. R. JONES]

Romney   Jany 22 1862.

My dear Mother

I wrote to you about two weeks ago from Ungers X roads but do not know whether you have ever received it, I sent the letter by private hand & requested it should be left with brother David [W. Barton], I was much delighted to receive this morning a letter from Sue & one from Bev, a regular mail is now established between this point & Winchester, we have been here (Romney) a week yesterday.

On Monday week last the drum beat at ½ past 3 o'clock & we were ordered to strike tents & be ready to march by daylight, it was very cold & raw, by day light we were ready to move, each Regt train was to preceed the Regt, the roads were in horrid condition & constantly the *stalling* teams would keep us hours on the road standing still freezing & imprecating the cause of our delay, the distance to Romney was about 34 miles over mountains, mountain after mountain & we seemed to be ascending all the time except the descent to Capon river & the north river as it is called. We reached Romney in the evening of wednesday cold & wet for we had been exposed to a sleeting rain, it was strange to see the men encased in ice & icicles hanging from the visors of their caps, we made 14 miles that day but it was a very fatiguing one as the snow was so slippery that we could hardly get along.

Since we have been here the rain & snow has been falling all the time. We were for several days quartered in a large building but were afterwards turned out to make room for the sick & on the wet & saturated ground we pitched our tents a little distance from the house in which we were quartered, we found however a good deal of plank that the Yankees had collected on their camping grounds & this has kept us out of the mud but so great is the moisture that the planks are very wet & the ground gives under them, to day the rain has ceased to fall, but the clouds are dark & the mountains tops just the crest's are clothed in white the snow fell on the Pine trees but lower down the mountains where the rain fell it melted, I wish you could see it the contrast is very beautiful.

Each day since Saturday, except sunday we have been ordered to get ready to move towards Pattersons creek but the streams have been so high & the roads so bad it has been postponed, *yesterday* we were ordered to move at daylight this morning, & after I had gone to bed last night an order came countermanding the move. I fear you can hardly read this letter, the place, time & circumstances are all against me, I cannot help indulging the erant hope that the expedition has been entirely given up & when we move that we move towards Winchester.

Our Qr Master with his asst's has his HdQrs in a smoke house nearby, he belongs to my mess & in the smoke house we take our meals, my tent is some little distance from the building; my path to it lays across a large graveyard (the nice plank fencing of which has all been burnt up by the Yankees) and backwards & forwards each day I step upon & step over the hillocks of the young & of the old who lay buried there, once a sweet resting place, with here & there the remains of a flower or a shrub which some loving hand had planted but now trampled by stock & horses & run over by waggons. This is a strange life I am leading, ah! it is a sad one, & notwithstanding all I have seen & gone through, I am still startled with new developments of its horrors, I cannot be too grateful to a kind Providence that notwithstanding all the exposure of this ever to be remembered trip I have escaped sickness, I take good care of myself however, am careful not to undergo any unnecessary exposure and I really believe that I am this day in better health & more able to undergo fatigue than I ever was in my life. I feel great responsibility & a good deal of anxiety in having command of the Regt it is a new place to me, but I hope I will do well.

Love to sister Mary & all
& believe yours
Francis B. Jones.

At almost the same time, Frank's mother was writing to him, with word of Sue and the children and other family. She was preoccupied with the war and had little other news.

[LETTER OF ANN C. R. JONES TO FRANK B. JONES]

Monday night

Vaucluse   January 20th 1862

My own precious Child, I may venture to write now, that it *may* be, you are stationary. It has not heretofore occurred to me that a letter upon my part was to be thought of. How I long to hear from you, how I long to see you, but I must *wait*, you are in the Path of duty, & may God grant it to be the path of safety for this world, as well as the next. I am a poor weak Christian, but I am greatly supported, I *do try* to rest upon my Heavenly Father, & look to him for that help that he alone can give, your great exposure to the cold & wet, the fatigue you undergo & sometimes hunger too, are calculated humanly speaking to injure your health extremely, but I know with the kind protection of Heaven you can escape all harm & I pray God to grant us such a mighty blessing. . . .

Altho I am writing to Romney I feel no *security* that you are there altho you may have come back, I cannot help thinking that Gen Jackson may have marched you all in pursuit of the Yankees, I cannot hear what has been done, but I trust all is well with my dear ones, I am very anxious to hear from Ran & David & any relative I may have amongst the troops. . . .

I cannot think of any thing worth talking about, this war is still most absorbing I sorrow over the sick soldiers, & the bad weather, & by the time it is ended, if I live to see the war closed, I shall be well nigh in my dotage _ not so bad as that either, but the mind declining. God Bless you my darling (Ann Cary sends her love to you) I am with the truest affection

your devoted Mother

A C R Jones

I forgot to tell you of Nancys gratitude for the 50 cents, she made more courtesys than you ever imagined to have been perpetrated at one time, & begged her thanks might be sent to you. Kitty & Mary were also very thankful & would wish to be remembered to you if they knew I was writing.[5] Farewell yours ever

Aunt Kitty reciprocated by sending Frank eggs from Vaucluse when the 2nd Virginia returned to the Winchester vicinity. The regiment was at Camp

Zollicoffer by January 25. Jackson had left Gen. William W. Loring's brigade in Romney, in an extended and disagreeable position. (One of the units left in Bath and Romney was the 31st Virginia Infantry. Its colonel, Robert F. Baldwin, cousin Cary's husband, was captured there and sent to Fort Warren in Boston.) Loring's complaints, which did not go through military channels, reached Secretary of War J. P. Benjamin and rebounded in an order to Jackson to withdraw Loring. He complied and resigned because of this interference. Frank was distressed. When next he wrote to his mother, he declared, "Romney is evacuated, so is Bath, Genl Jackson has resigned I declare I believe the world is turned up side down."[6]

Jackson's resignation on the issue of General Loring's assignment was not accepted; his superior, Gen. Joseph E. Johnston, supported him and persuaded him not to resign. Nevertheless, Loring and his forces were reassigned south, and Jackson was to defend Winchester with greatly diminished numbers, although new forces were forming. When Tom Marshall took his children home to Oak Hill for a visit he recruited a cavalry company in his Fauquier County neighborhood.[7] As the army grew and reorganized, Tom was made Captain in the 7th Virginia Cavalry. Marshall Barton joined the Newtown Artillery on March 10 and became a first lieutenant. Robby Barton also had missed the Bath and Romney campaign, which surely would have killed him; he decided to reenlist in early March, and joined brother David in the Rockbridge Artillery.

[MEMOIR OF ROBERT T. BARTON]

After some time [the army] returned to Winchester and soon began to reorganize for the Spring campaign. Gen. Jackson spent the winter at Winchester and I used to see him very often.[8] . . .

The war fever, which had been hot upon us all the time flamed out again as the Spring approached and it began to look as if in the change of hostile lines the army would draw back from Winchester. I enlisted, therefore, in the Rockbridge battery, of which McLaughlin (afterwards Judge) was the captain, Captain Pendleton having been promoted.[9]

My first camp was in what was then a piece of woods on the hill beyond the Fair Grounds, along the Gainsbrough Turnpike. This was in March 1862. We manoeuvered about a few days, confronting the army of Gen. [Nathaniel P.] Banks which was approaching Winchester from the North. During this time the feelings of our people were mixtures of distress, apprehension and defiance. Even yet, they had not seen real war.

One afternoon the whole army was put in regular but rapid motion and passed through Winchester and encamped a few miles to the south. Banks' great army lay just north of Winchester, but it was believed and confidently hoped that we were to return in the night and make a night attack upon them. Such indeed had been Gen. Jackson's intention, but he was persuaded out of it by his chief officers. Jackson had not then acquired his great reputation and there was quite a difference of opinion about his fitness for command.

Even now I think about the failure to make the attack with infinite regret. We were fairly wild to try it and we believed we could whip Banks and save the town from his invasion. I now believe that if Jackson had been permitted to have his way and had led his men back that night we would have completely surprised Banks and have entirely routed his army. It would have been a splendid enterprise, and one of the most remarkable and successful in the history of war. After events showed how possible it was to have accomplished it, but the genius of Jackson which conceived the undertaking was stifled by the commonplace reasoning of his officers.[10]

Frank Jones may have had a brief furlough, or at least some time with his family, in February before the spring campaign began. Sue gave him a small blue leather diary when they parted.[11] The first event he recorded was the Confederate retreat from Winchester, in the face of Federal General Banks's vastly superior force advancing from Harpers Ferry.

[DIARY OF FRANK B. JONES]

This blank book my dear Sue gave to me to keep a memoranda in & I intend to write something in it every day or when anything worthy of note occurs.

On Tuesday the 11th March 1862 about one o'clock whilst we were laying in the Baldwin woods near Winchester I heard the *long roll* beat & quickly we were under arms, Col. [James W.] Allen & Botts both being absent I led the Regt., & by Gen. Garnett's order we were placed some distance in the advance, & took our positions at the edge of a wood near the line of the R.R. The enemy were advancing in large force on the Martinsburg turnpike & we confidently expected an engagement, but they did not come quite near enough, their scouts I saw plainly, & in rifle shot, but they concluded to wait until the morning when they could be joined by other columns coming up the Berryville road & down from the Bath road. Night coming on, Gen. Jackson withdrew his forces & we marched out with heavy hearts & bivouacked on the turnpike four miles from

Winchester. I laid down in a fence corner on the E. side of the turnpike, near a large locust tree. My heart is very sad, here in sight of my own deserted home [Carysbrooke]. I slept in the open air & am now a refugee from my wife & children & native land! When shall I see them again? God alone knows, but to Him, I trust it all, feeling sure that if I go to Him in trust & prayer He will not cast me off. . . .

Robby's health soon broke down as a result of the long marches and terrible weather after the army left Winchester.

[MEMOIR OF ROBERT T. BARTON]

Well we marched on and marched back and then on and back again, through wind and rain, cold snow and wet, without tents or other protection, sleeping on the wet ground in wet clothes and eating such food as we could get and cook, which was bad enough. A few weeks of this life drove me to the hospital and I was carried back to Staunton. There I stayed at the home of Dr. John M. Baldwin the husband of my sister, Martha. I got well but Dr. Baldwin was slowly dying. . . .

Robby could not go home to recuperate this time. Winchester had been occupied by Federal forces on March 12, Jackson retreating under the pressure of superior numbers. Many citizens had left town in fear of Yankee barbarisms— girls and women were sent south in the Valley to safe refuges. Some men who had not already joined the Southern forces were moved to do so; some whose constitutions were not strong enough for active service left to avoid Yankee conscription. Civilians who had reason to fear Yankee retaliation for their participation in the Confederate war effort also refugeed south in the Valley or to Richmond. It was Winchester's first real experience as a war zone, and the remaining population—largely women, children, and older men—found their lives drastically changed. Many who had thought themselves still Unionists realized they were Southerners, and some lukewarm Confederates became militant. Federal troops thronged the streets, either in military formation, or roving, sometimes invading houses looking for food, whisky, or the family silver. There was a large contingent of German immigrant troops, and the Valley people, despite the German background of many, came to equate them with the Hessian mercenaries of the American Revolution only eighty-five years before.

The occupying forces placed restrictions on all movements in and out of town, resulting in serious shortages of food, firewood, and other daily necessities. Soon, it was said, business could not be conducted or marriages solemnized by any who had not taken the oath of allegiance. Of course the Federals forbade any communication with Southern forces, but many letters—of greater or lesser military significance—were smuggled through the lines, as indeed were medicines and other goods from sympathetic friends in Baltimore or other points north. For the first time since war began, the people were able to communicate directly with relations and friends in the North, and even to visit. Supplies of many scarce items, from carpets to calico and coffee, could be replenished secretly. Some unionists were willing to help their secessionist neighbors (although others reported their suspicions). A black market of sorts established itself in town, as only those who had taken the oath could buy from the Yankee sutlers. Federal vigilance included searches both at picket lines and in private houses that had attracted suspicion—for commodities ranging from blankets to molasses—but tons of goods must have escaped them, some quantity eventually making its way to the Rebel army. The townspeople also had to contend with the dislocation and erosion of the remaining labor force, as runaway slaves from outlying farms fled to Winchester, and many of the town domestic slaves left their owners. Some were hired in town, some were sent north on the cars by abolitionists, but some wandered aimlessly or followed the army. Most of the churches remained open throughout the war, although some were taken over at times for use as hospitals or jails. The Episcopal church was adopted by the Yankees as their own, and some members who objected to worshiping in the presence of the enemy formed prayer groups that met in the members' homes, where they could pray for Jefferson Davis in private. Only a few doctors, older men, were left in town. Business was entirely disrupted. Banks had closed their doors and hidden or moved assets and operations when they knew the Yankees were coming, and the local government, at the urging of Messrs. Barton and Williams, had removed the county records, it was whispered, to caverns in the mountains near Luray. The Union Army took over a number of public buildings for their operations, and soon for hospitals. One was the building of the Winchester Academy, so Bolling and his friend Lud Baldwin were at loose ends, and for amusement and possible information eavesdropped on the Yankees on the street.[12]

Soon the people learned grimmer occupations. After the battle of Kernstown, March 23, the women turned to nursing—there were no other provisions for it—and the men went to the battlefield to identify and bury the dead. Experienced as they might be with serious disease, illness, and death, nothing had prepared them for the dreadful wounds and maimings of the battlefield.

Mary Greenhow Lee, Mrs. Hugh Holmes
Lee, about the time of the war. (Maryland
Historical Society microfilm, courtesy Hand-
ley Library Archives)

In her frustration at being unable to communicate with a dear friend, the Bartons' next-door neighbor, a forty-one-year-old widow, Mrs. Hugh H. Lee, began a journal in the form of a letter, which she kept almost daily for the duration of the war. From March 12, when she saw Mrs. Barton slam her front door at the sight of Yankee troops—who responded "there is a d——d Secessionist!"—she recorded the daily annoyances, difficulties of life, insults and outrages on both sides, strategems and devices, and incidents ranging from funny to heroic and horrifying, as well as the terrible losses sustained by all she knew.[13] Always there was the hope of the Confederate Army returning. Always there was the fear of the Yankees' oft-voiced threats to destroy the town if the Rebels came back, a threat bolstered by the very tangible menace embodied in the massive munitions storages right in the middle of town.

Rumor was always rampant, but the Bartons, and the Lee household next door, had been aware that Sister Mat's husband, John Baldwin, was very ill, indeed had for weeks been fearing the worst. Young Dr. Baldwin succumbed to consumption April 17, but the news took over a week to reach Winchester from Staunton.[14] Mrs. Lee recorded in her diary April 26:

[DIARY OF MARY GREENHOW LEE]

Yesterday was another cold, drizzling day, & very uneventful, till night; after tea Fannie [Barton] & Anna [Jones] came in, & were unusually bright & joyous, but before they had been here half an hour, Sukey came over in great distress for the girls, a messenger having come from Staunton, bringing letters announcing John Baldwin's death. Nettie & I went over & found Mrs. Barton in a great state of distress.[15] The letters had been brought by Stottlemeyer who was closeted with Mr. B. he had got through by wearing Yankee uniform &

William Strother Jones, c. 1850.
(Trevor Potter)

brought glorious news from York-town.[16] . . . How to communicate the news to Dr. & Mrs. Baldwin was the question. We sent Bolling [Barton] for Carey [Baldwin], who came immediately, without causing any surprise at home; then Mr. Barton, Carey, Nettie & I went around & Mr. Barton went in first, & told them, and as soon as we heard Mrs. Baldwin's shrieks we went in; at first she would not listen to any one, so violent were her self reproaches at not having gone to Staunton, but at last she became more quiet, & let me read Mattie's & Sallie's letters, & was comforted by them.[17] Mattie's fortitude & resignation are beautiful to hear of.[18]

In his diary, Frank made daily notes about the weather, campsites, the length of the arduous marches, and his difficulties in keeping a servant. His slave George had run off, not necessarily to find freedom but because the army life was so hard. Frank also wrote in his diary of the "majestic mountains" and "noble streams" in the Valley. Another pleasure was the frequency of his encounters with Brother Strother, who was "establishing a line of couriers across the mountain to Orange Court House," and Brother James, probably already working for the Confederate Nitre and Mining Bureau in the Valley.[19]

Frank took every chance he could to write home. He sent a letter north with his brother Bev, who with Rannie Barton had a short furlough and decided to try to reach the family at Vaucluse. Hearing that the two had been stymied short of Woodstock, Frank tried another carrier, who got through, to his mother and to Sue.

[LETTER OF FRANK B. JONES TO SUSAN C. JONES]

Camp near Mt Jackson
Wednesday, Mch 19th 1862

My dear Sue, I have found a man who lives near Newtown & he says he is going there to morrow, I embrace the opportunity at once of writing to you although I sent a letter yesterday but do not know whether it will ever reach you. . . . How sad, Oh how sad is this separation: & Reverse after reverse is meeting our arms. . . . Bev left here this morning to try & get through the lines to Vaucluse he and Randolph Barton, but I have just learned that he could not get further than Woodstock . . . how I wish I could hear from you & know some thing about the way the Yankees are treating you.[20] I wrote to beg you to have my books in the parlour removed & indeed all had better be packed up, I hear the negroes are running off in great numbers if mine go or if my loss is great in any way dont distress yourself in the least about it. I dont care, I can repair it, & you will help me as you have always done. My trust is in Providence & as the Yankees gain upon us, so determined is my purpose to resist to the uttermost, they cant subdue the army that is now organising if all will only hold true to each other. let me know if any of the citizens are countenancing them, & any news will be acceptable beyond measure.

Dont forget to write to Mrs Botts & tell her I shall take care of the Col he is in my tent as he has none of his own, he is very well. I am so sorry our Army committed such depredations at Spring dale, but the wagons were pushing ahead when a courier stopped them there with orders to take the fencing for cooking, they were obliged to have wood & could get nothing else. I laid out that night under a fence corner not far from Joseph Bartons lane, I rode down

Carysbrooke on a wintry day, c. 1885. (Eleanor J. Burleson)

home as I wanted to give some directions, sad was my visit & sorrowful to think I was fleeing away & taking my leave of all, as I rode through the upper field my sheep followed me, wanting salt I suppose. Dear little Kitten & Ran how are they & the sweet little baby that I was afraid to let out my heart to, tell Ran I have his ten cents which he insisted upon my taking, dear little fellow he did not know the sorrows of my heart when I took leave of him.[21] I have nothing new to write it is uncertain how long we will remain here, but I will try & write whenever I can find an opportunity

yours my dear Sue
Francis B. Jones

you heard how George treated me running off after I got so far from home that I *could not* get Tom or Austin[22]

Frank's diary records "cold & cheerless," sometimes snowy, marches north for the next few days; he took some comfort from brother Strother's having provided a new servant, Edmund. Jackson's instructions were to protect the northwestern flank of Virginia and to prevent Banks from leaving the Shenandoah to succor the new Federal Commander-in-Chief George B. McClellan at a then-anticipated thrust at Manassas. McClellan's master plan, as it happened, was to launch a great amphibious operation in order to attack Richmond up the Yorktown peninsula. Jackson, rightly believing that the Federals were redeploying from the Valley toward Manassas, decided to attack Winchester in order to hold them in the Valley. Union forces crossing the Blue Ridge heard the guns and turned back. The battle of Kernstown, on March 23, was fought within a mile of Frank's home, Carysbrooke, and largely on Joseph Barton's farm.

[DIARY OF FRANK B. JONES]

22nd March 1862

Took up the line of march in the direction of Winchester & camped on the Cedar Creek. 24 miles. Men very much fatigued & a large number of stragglers strayed from the Regiment.

23rd March 1862

Eventful day! heard that the Enemy were evacuating Winchester. Fatal mistake! Our little army pushed on but reaching the last field on SpringDale found that the enemy were in large force on the hills back of Kernstown. Regt. turned into the woods & I was ordered to take charge of a company thrown out in the advance as skirmishers. It was soon withdrawn however & I joined the Regt. The 2nd Regt. then with others took positions in the large wood back of Kernstown & rather beyond Jos. Barton's house. Soon after this Gen. Jackson ordered me to his side & I acted as his aide all day. This was about 2½ P.M. He ordered me to lead the Rockbridge Artillery & three Regts. of the Brigade across the open fields & take positions on the high & long ridge overlooking the back road. The Enemies batteries had full play upon us but they did little damage & we soon reached the cover of the woods. I was then ordered to bring up Capt. [James] Water's "West Augusta Guards" & Capt. [Joseph H.] Carpenter & Capt. [William B.] McLaughlin together did great execution.[23] Large forces were then seen turning our left & I was sent to Gen. Garnett with orders to bring up his brigade [Stonewall]. Lt. Col. [John M.] Patton & Lt. Col. [Alexander G.] Taliaferro with their Regts. were already there & soon the most terrific fire of musketry that can be imagined commenced & continued for one hour & 35 minutes, until nearly dark, when having exhausted the supply of ammunition we were ordered to retire. The men retired in good order as there was no panic & no running, although they were scattered. The Enemy did not pursue us & we bivouacked this side of Newtown. After assisting the other field officers in collecting the Regt., I rode on to Vaucluse & spent the balance of the night once more in my dear old home. O, sad work was this for the blessed Sabbath: may the Lord forgive our sins for they are many, & may Peace once more shine upon this distracted country.

Frank, because of his familiarity with the terrain, was detached to serve on Jackson's staff during the battle, and was commended for his "zeal and daring" in the general's after-action report.[24] Frank did not mention in his journal, although he soon was aware of, the capture of some Winchester boys, including Willie Barton and Frank's nephew Rannie, at Kernstown.

[MEMOIR OF RANDOLPH BARTON]

On the 23rd of March, 1862, we fought the battle of Kernstown. There my pistol was shot from my hand. Upon picking it up I found that the ball had so smashed the revolving portion as to render it useless. Upon the breaking of our lines late in the evening I was captured, carried to Winchester, lodged in jail, thence to Baltimore, where I was again lodged in a jail, in which I remained a week. While there looking out upon this fair city of Baltimore I often wondered, would I ever tread its streets a freeman? Fate had it in reserve for me to pass daily under its walls, a freeman, for twenty-nine years counting to this date. I often look at the entrance to the jail, recall my going in and going out, and wonder at the vicissitudes of life. . . .

Through the jail windows I could see pedestrians, vehicles and the horse cars turning up towards Charles Street. Many of the houses I looked upon then with unsatisfied curiosity as to their inmates have since been opened most hospitably to me. . . .

My capture at Kernstown was in this wise. The battle was fought upon ground and in a neighborhood in which I had time and again as a boy hunted and shot wild pigeons, doves and partridges. Neil's Dam was back of us, somewhat to the left, a very familiar spot.

Still to the southwest of the dam was what we all knew as the "Big Woods," on the edge of which I had hunted partridges on bright, crisp, October Saturdays with fine dogs, no responsibility, in the very vigor of youthful enjoyment. Upon the breaking of our line, falling in with Willie Barton, Robert Burwell, and one or two others, as we moved back, someone suggested that we should make for the Big Woods, follow it to the neighborhood of Vaucluse, my uncle's place, there get horses and escape down the Valley.[25] We never had experience in retreating and thought that the mass of our army would be followed and that we alone would escape.[26] We did not know then that the cavalry was placed upon the flanks of the enemy to pick up just such stragglers as we were. Sure enough we ran into the cavalry of the enemy. We had none at that point; and with the "Big Woods" in full view, probably not a half mile away, we were ordered to halt at the point of sabres and the muzzles of carbines. I had the mortification of surrendering my sword, a very pretty little dress sword, with which I had grown up. It had been purchased by my uncle Strother when a militia major, and for years had hung upon the walls of the "office" my grandmother's cottage at Vaucluse.[27] As a boy of ten I had time and again taken it down, strapped it on, and paraded around the yard with it, little thinking that I would wear it in actual war.

With about two hundred prisoners we struck across the fields towards Winchester, coming out at the turnpike about a mile south of the toll gate, and thence going on the turnpike to the town, where we lodged in jail. The Yankee officers politely invited me to go to their room, but I declined and spent a troubled night on the hard floor. My father and mother the next day visited me in the jail and we conversed through the bars.[28] That afternoon we were marched to the Winchester and Harper's Ferry depot, passing my home, the doors of which as I remember, being open, my father and mother, and others on the pavement, waving their handkerchiefs to us and encouraging us by their cheers. Miss Nett Lee rushed out with a cullender full of beaten biscuits and, the vessel being soon emptied by the prisoners, she waived it over her head, cheering most lustily. We were the first prisoners who had ever passed through Winchester, and the severities of the war had not yet come into practice. After that, for such an exhibition of sympathy, she would have been bayonetted on the spot.[29] We went to Baltimore in ordinary burden cars, reaching there about midday on the 25th of March, I think.

My first sight of Baltimore was upon my arrival at Camden Station, where we were greeted by a great crowd, which was somewhat variously demonstrative. Some were friendly, and some were hostile, but our guard protected us from any disagreeable collision.[30] Forming in columns of fours, we marched up Howard Street to Madison, and thence to the jail, the entrance then being on that street with a somewhat different arrangement from the present one. Robert Burwell and myself were assigned to adjoining cells on the second floor, north wing. While in the jail we received many kind attentions from persons in the City, some of whom we knew and many of whom were strangers.

Not often were we reduced to jail fare, but I know, if I never find out hereafter, what it is to be ordered to your cell, to hear the click of the cell-door lock, to look around at the stony, staring, comfortless room, and to have a tin plate with some mongrel victuals, and a tin cup with some warm decoction, thrust through a small opening at the bottom of the grated door. But we had one comfort, and that was a coarse, but very warm blanket. When, a week after our confinement, we were notified to be prepared to move, we made a roll of the clothing, etc., which had been supplied to us in Winchester and were ready and waiting for marching orders. While thus unoccupied, Burwell and myself thought, if we were going to a colder climate, the jail blankets would be very handy. After humbly asking for guidance, when the guard for a few moments was absent, we quietly inserted a blanket apiece in our own belongings, and, carefully concealing them, so as to prevent them from being injured by exposure, we left the building when the order to march was given. We felt more guilty going out than coming in, but we kept the blankets. I have never since then robbed my host.

Jackson's army was retreating south, covering thirty miles in three days. He had achieved his purpose: A portion of the previously detached Federal force returned to the Valley. But the cost was high. Confederate losses at Kernstown approximated 25 percent of the small force engaged, proportionately equivalent to the losses at Gettysburg.[31] *Frank spent the night after the battle at his family home, Vaucluse, about eight miles south of the battlefield.*

[DIARY OF FRANK B. JONES]

24th March 1862

Took leave this morning of my dear mother & looked perhaps for the last time on the sweet environs of my beloved home. Hastened to join the army which had Bivouacked on the turnpike. Found Edmund missing & I suppose he has now gone too. About 10 A.M. the Army commenced moving in the direction of Strasburg. Found my mare Peytonia very lame from the hard riding of yesterday, had one shoe put on in Middletown. Halted on the high hill just above & this side of Cedar Creek & set down to cook our dinner. The enemy however pressed on & just as I had taken a piece of bread & meat in my hand saw the cavalry galloping in, jumped up & had the Regt. formed directly, & the waggons were hurried off without taking time to put in quite a number of tents which had been taken out so as to get at the cooking utensils, my tent amongst the number. Soon I saw a battery put in position & the shells were bursting over us. The waggons just got out in time. The 2nd & 5th moved to the right & wound around amongst the hills, but our direction was seen & afforded a fine target for the Enemy, though they fell very near us, we escaped. The 27th was cut in two & 6 men were killed, or reported so, left of course on the field as there was no time to recover them. We moved on & bivouacked at the "Narrow Passage".

On the twenty-sixth, General Jackson, perceiving that the Union pursuit had slackened, ordered infantry north to support Col. Turner Ashby and his cavalry brigade along the pike near Narrow Passage, about three miles south of Woodstock. Skirmishing commenced on March 27, and continued through April 1.

Behind the Narrow Passage de-

General Jackson, sketched by one of his staff, A. R. Boteler, in July 1862.

(Alderman Library, University of Virginia)

fense line, the Confederate Army rested. There was time for stragglers to catch up, time to see who was among the missing, and time to write letters which might or might not reach their destinations. Some mail caught up with the army. From Winchester, Mrs. Lee began sending all the military information she could glean to Jackson's forces, and was scornful of the men who would not take the risk.

[LETTER OF FRANK B. JONES TO SUSAN C. JONES]

[not dated]

My darling Sue,

I have another opportunity & I hope this may reach you. Letters have been received this morning from Mrs Lee & from Mrs. McGill stating our loss of prisoners was 160, I trust it is not so large.[32] We have a number missing but they are coming in, I hope the Yankees dont think there was any panic amongst our troops, we all set down at Newtown & cooked our supper, and the next day we only went to Cedar Creek & cooked our dinner, Although the Rascals did shell us before we had time to eat it. . . . Gen. Jackson is determined to fight those following as soon as possible, we have a large number of noble fellows turning out & the spirit of the people is far better than in those border counties where we came from, every man woman & child is on the side of right & you may depend upon it whilst they can & will overrun our country by their numbers they cant put down the spirit of Old Virginia. . . .

I have no servant Edmund has gone too, I wish you would tell Tom or Austin if they would like to come to me, I wish they would try & work their way through by coming cross the fields as I have no one to feed my horse, he can come on & inquire for the 2nd Regt, if either one who comes dont like the life he can go back again at any time. . . . Fare well my Darling take care of yourself & believe me with love &c

always yours
Francis B. Jones

[on outside of folded letter]
Nothing heard from Ran or Willy Barton or Robt Burwell I fear they are taken prisoners

Frank found another chance to send a letter a few days later.

[LETTER OF FRANK B. JONES TO SUSAN C. JONES]

My dear Sue,

I have just learned of another opportunity to our neighbourhood & I have determined to avail myself of it, though I cannot hear from you it must be a pleasure for you to hear from me. We are at present laying in a woods near Mt Jackson, our tents have all been stored away & for the balance of the Campaign we will bivouack I suppose. For the last two days we have had a cold rain & our suffering has been great, I had my fly & it has kept me dry though my discomfort is very trying, I intend to get a very small A tent & strap it to my horse so that hereafter I shall be better off. Our men stand out in the rain & sleep in the wet, yet they are cheerful & hopeful beyond belief. Tom [Marshall] is standing by my fire, sends his love to you & all, & says David [Barton] & all are well. I received a letter from Joseph Barton written after the battle & wanting to know if Willy could get his furlough, said all were well, he is in Nelson Co.[33] . . .

To think this time last sunday I was so near you & yet could not get to see you, I think of you all the time my darling & I know how sad it must have been for you to hear the noise of the battle & not know whether I was dead or alive, God has again spared me & I humbly thank Him for all his mercies. The condition of our country & the disaffection amongst the negroes gives me great uneasiness as I cant hear from home, but I do hope if all the negroes go & every thing else you will not distress yourself upon my account or on yours, rely upon it that I have made up my mind to expect & look for these evils & that I trust by the blessing of God to repair them hereafter. I do want a servant badly & had written to you to try & get one of the boys to come up to me, it would be attended however with great difficulty, WSJ [Strother Jones] who is in New Market has sent me word that he had secured a servant for me & if you have said nothing to the boys about it, you had best say nothing until you hear again from me. . . . O when will these evil times be past & peace once more return. It is Sunday, but how little like Sunday to me,

> farewell my darling
> Francis B. Jones
> Mch 30th 1862

On April 1, a fresh Confederate defense line was established at Stony Creek, and General Garnett was dismissed as commander of the Stonewall Brigade. Garnett had retreated from the field at Kernstown without orders to do so, after his troops ran out of ammunition. Later it was learned that Jackson's displea-

sure also related to Garnett's troop positioning. Frank and the other officers were shocked.

[DIARY OF FRANK B. JONES]

2nd April

Sent for by Gen. Jackson & questioned by him closely in regard to orders, & c. passed on the battlefield. Heard this evening Gen. Garnett had been suspended from command. It fell like a thunderbolt on our Brigade & officers hastened to his tent to express our astonishment & sorrow to lose so valuable & so gallant an officer. Gen. [Charles S.] Winder assumed command of the 1st Brigade. Ordered out to oppose the enemy who were said to be coming through Edinburg. The bridge across Stony Creek however was burnt & there they halted. Withdrawn & bivouacked in woods near Mt. Jackson.

4th April 1862

Weather fine, quite warm. Tom Marshall of Happy Creek came out today & hired me a negro boy & bartered me for a trade for Guy Darnell.[34] . . . I felt sorry to part with Guy Darnell as he carried me through the battle of Manassas & as my children loved him but he was too small for my service & I had given him up as a riding horse. I rode Peytonia on the 23rd & she is I think a fine animal in many respects. . . .

5th April 1862

Cloudy & dull day. Rain in the night, but I had secured a tent yesterday & Botts & Hunter & myself slept in it & were well protected. Servant woke me early this morning to say that Peytonia had broken loose & could not be found. Got up & dressed & was just going to saddle my other horse when the servant brought her in, having found her in an adjoining Regt. . . .

Despite the dangers and confusions of the movements of two armies, there was still civilian traffic up and down the Valley, and before long Frank found someone else willing to take a letter through the lines. He had decided to sell his livestock since otherwise the Yankees would be likely to take it.

[LETTER OF FRANK B. JONES TO SUSAN C. JONES]

I have just heard My Darling Sue of an opportunity to Winchester & though I have no convenience for writing I will try to scrawl you something of myself. . . . I hear that the Yankees have taken my mules, some old horse had better be bought at once & my lame mare at the Catlett farm put together to get us some corn to support the negroes. . . . Have you hid the books &c, &c in the parlour, it is very important, Botts has had all his library destroyed. I think Kitten & you might get those mules back by representing to the Genl that it is only means of supporting the negroes by their work or hauling them a load of wood.[35] Dont distress yourself about any loss at home, I am prepared for the worse that can happen. . . .

Do not believe that we had more than 3000 men in the fight of Sunday, it was the most astounding battle, considering the odds against us, our men had marched 24 miles the day before & 18 the day of the fight, I tell you it was a gallant affair. Gen. Jackson has sent for me two or three times to question me about the battle, he told me he thought it was the hardest fight ever made on the Continent, Gen. J has arrested Gen. Garnett & deprived him of his command, we do not really know why, but Gen. Garnett acted with great gallantry on the 23d & our Brigade is astounded at the order & had it not been that our cause was too sacred to jeopardize there would have been considerable commotion made amongst us. When the charges are made out he will be tried by a Ct Martial. . . .

Keep a good heart my dear wife & pray that the war may soon end. All are well of our friends, Tom [Marshall] & David [Barton] & Marshall & Will & Frank I see often, WSJ has gone to Fredericksburg[36]

Yours &c &c
Francis B. Jones

April 7th 1862

[Col.] Allen is much complimented in the papers for his gallantry on the 23d

Jackson's action at Kernstown was having the desired effect in engaging Federal attention and forces at the expense of their major effort on the Yorktown peninsula. The Valley army was hearing news and rumors of what was happening there.

[DIARY OF FRANK B. JONES]

April 10, 1862   (Rudes Hill)

The clouds have broken away. Sunday was a lovely day. Botts & I wandered in the evening on the river bank & laid down on the ground & enjoying the bright sunshine & the lovely view of this lovely country. Monday morning, however, it was cold & cloudy, it soon commenced raining & for three days it has hailed & rained & snowed in the most unaccountable manner. Our encampment is worse than any barnyard for in many places there seems no bottom.

Our tent floors are deep in mud, but the sun is out & I hope there will be more comfort after a while. Tuesday morning was so cold & cheerless that I laid in bed a long while rather than expose myself to the bitter damp & cold. My heart was very sad. Our great discomfort & our cause weighed upon me. I turned to God in prayer, & whilst I was praying most earnestly that He would bless our army in the great battle I knew was impending in the West, Capt. S——— put his head in my tent & announced the report of a great victory near Pittsburg on the Tennessee river. . . .

This was glorious news! Today we have confirmation of it.[37] Sunday, flying rumors of Yorktown, but I think nothing has occurred of any moment. Today, it was said we had been defeated.[38] God, grant us success! The enemy were cheering yesterday at a great rate about something. Their force is said to be over 20,000. Ours is very small, but has been increased by the militia in the last few days. Every preparation is being made for another battle. How can we stand up against so great odds! Our army is left alone, Gen Johnston can't succor us & our only reinforcements must come from the people around us. We are looking daily for news from Fredericksburg & Yorktown & daily is the booming of the cannon heard in our midst.[39] O! These evil times! What would I give to have once more the domestic joys of my happy home!

April 11th, 1862

Rumors of the Yorktown fight untrue. The victory in the west confirmed. Our encampment is the most muddy place I ever was in, can scarcely get along without sinking deep in mud. Botts & myself rode to New Market today to get a supply of cooking utensils as we had determined to mess together. Our original mess being too large, we found great difficulty in getting anything. An oven could not be bought for love or money. In despair I heard of an old Irishman who had one, hunted him up on one of the back streets & found he had in his hog pen an oven which his wife had been using for the hogs.[40] Gave him two dollars for it & went on my way rejoicing.

[LETTER OF FRANK B. JONES TO SUSAN C. JONES]

Rhudes Hill   April 11th 1862

My Dear Sue, I received a note from Mrs [Caroline] Barton yesterday requesting me to try & get her passed through under a "flag of truce" I was almost certain she could not effect it but went to HdQrs to see.[41] I will ride to Mt Jackson this morning and will write you a line though it may be a very long time before you will get it, I have also written a letter to Peyton 10 days ago which she has. I am exceedingly anxious to have every thing sold at once that is in Danger of the Yankees even the milch cows had best go. They are killing every thing in this country even ewes with lambs by their sides & I am sure they will leave nothing of mine. . . . I hope my negroes remain firm. . . .

I do hope if you should have any reports of my being wounded or killed you will not give credence to it. Rumour says any thing, ask Mrs Barton to tell you what she has heard of Willy. One of our officers not in the battle heard that I was killed when he was coming up from Richmond. I only mention these things to caution you against believing rumours. The Yankee force is so heavy that I do not believe Jackson will give them a pitched battle so do not make yourself uneasy. You have heard of the great victory in the West, it is a Manassa defeat to the Enemy. We have lost Johnston & it is a severe [*illegible*] price [*illegible*].[42] Pray for the victory at Yorktown, if we lose it sad will it be. We have had a most terrible spell of weather, for three days & 3 nights a cold rain & snow & our discomfort has been great. I was pleased to hear that Gen Jackson had complimented me in his report, and so did Col Allen, but I desire no laurels in comparison to the approving smiles of my dear wife, and the love of my sweet children, & for Peace & all its blessings once more, but let us remain firm one to another & to the last resist the power of an enemy who is vindictive & cruel.

We hear of the noble conduct of the ladies of Winchester, & Mrs. Lee's letter has been read & admired by all in Camp.[43] Keep a stout heart & let them know that you are the wife of a Secession officer & that little Ran will one day be big enough to fight for his country. Do not distress yourself about any loss that I sustain but hear me about *removing every little thing from the house* (Carysbrooke) They are taking any & every thing from these poor people here, Beg Mrs. Lee to write again but to be *very very* careful how she does it, & say nothing about the strength of the enemy or any thing which would give Jackson important information as it would subject her to harm.

Yours &c &c

FBJ

Miserable weather and the Confederates' strong defensive position at Stony Creek had impeded Federal progress until April 17, when Union cavalry outflanked and surprised Ashby and pursued him over the unburned bridge at Mount Jackson, and began shelling Rude's Hill. The Confederates were forced to retreat to Swift Run Gap, an easily defensible position in the Blue Ridge, some twenty miles east of Harrisonburg. From there they could outflank a Union advance on Staunton and the coveted railroad to Richmond.

[DIARY OF FRANK B. JONES]

17th April 1862 (Thursday)

Heard the "long roll" beat at 5 A.M., heard the order to pack up immediately. Jumped up, dressed, had my tent struck, & baggage put in the waggon. The train was hurried off to the river & our whole force was drawn up to protect its retreat. Soon, the shells of the enemy were seen bursting in the air & so rapid was the march of the enemy that Col. Ashby failed to burn the bridge over the Shenandoah river. The Col. came near being killed, his white horse was shot in the lungs, but bore him off the field. He died after being led away a mile or two. Moved on & camped about 7 miles [sic] of Harrisonburg.

18th April Friday

Reveille at 2 o'clock A.M. Baggage moved out in half an hour. Troops drawn up in line & moved at about 4 o'clock towards Harrisonburg. Halted at various points. Sun was hot. Felt depressed & miserable. Had suffered the day before from a violent nervous headache.[44] Halted on the edge of Harrisonburg. Layed down under an apple tree & had a pleasant nap. Roused up by the drum, mounted my horse & moved off to a point 5 miles below Harrisonburg. Raining part of the way & just as we reached our ground to encamp a heavy shower fell. The men bivouacked on the wet ground. I was fortunate enough to get into a carpenter shop & slept comfortably on the dry floor.

In the next week, Frank logged four days of "searching" rain, some snow, much mud and cold, and a leaky tent—a "dull, stupid life."

[DIARY OF FRANK B. JONES]

25th April Friday   (Swift Run Gap)

Rained hard all night & some part of this morning. Cold & gloomy & camp is muddy & as unpleasant as possible. Frank Clark came to see me. Felt very sick in the night & have been so all day. Doctor M——— gave me some medicine & I am much better but very weak.[45] How I did wish for home, my dear wife, & my many comforts there. Brother Strother & brother James came into camp today & stayed two or three hours with me in my tent. I was delighted to see them. . . . They took their dinner & rode on in the evening to Stannardsville in Green Co. Heard today that the enemy was turning Gen. Johnston's flank & coming up the Rappahanock so as to land & attack Richmond in another direction. Fears are entertained of the necessity of evacuating Richmond consequent upon a defeat of Johnston. If so great a calamity befalls us, our army will be compelled to evacuate Virginia & thus the enemy will give us a heavy blow. Patience, energy & a determined spirit can however repair hopes & give us victory in the end. Hired Albert of J.F.J.[46]

27th April (Sunday)
(Camp Swift Run)

Roused us at 2 o'clk A.M. by the "Long Roll", baggage packed & sent off about two & a half miles in the Gap. Regt. under arms & waited orders until nearly sun down. Lovely day. Rev. Dr. Dabney preached at the camp of the 2nd Brigade, his subject, the uncertainty of life & too great stake against the chances.[47] . . . Noticed Gen. [William B.] Taliaferro & many friends present, Gen. Jackson stood with head uncovered through the whole exercises, whilst the soldiers formed a circle & sat upon the ground. . . . The Yankees attacked our Forage trains about one o'clk today & Capt. Baylor was very badly wounded in making a charge with his co. to defend them.[48] Orders came late to join our train & up through the mountains we marched. Found Albert had a good fire & a supper for us. . . .

28th April (Monday)

Rode into the mountains this morning to try & find some one to wash my clothes. The morning was lovely & I enjoyed the ride very much. The streams are so clear, so beautiful, tumbling over the rock, & dashing away into the secluded groves. How grand is nature. O! that sin had never clouded it all over! Found a young woman who after some persuasion said she would have them ready for me in the morning.

29th April (Tuesday)

Orders to move back to the other encampment. Heard that Gen. Ewell had come over & his army would probably follow. Today off to get my clothes & found the Regt. after it had gotten into the encampment. Order from Gen. Winder to report to him as F.O. Day [field officer of the day]. Took charge of three companies & posted them on the roads. Found the country very beautiful. The low ground on the Shenandoah was very fine. Felt very badly all day, but with a flask of whiskey which W.S.J. had given me I was enabled to ride & attend to duty.

The next day, Gen. Richard S. Ewell's division arrived from the Rappahannock to reinforce Jackson, providing the means to implement his bold plan. Federal General Banks was at Harrisonburg about thirty-five miles north of Staunton, but the more immediate threat was from the west, where Union Gen. Robert H. Milroy was pressing the small Confederate force under Gen. Edward Johnson at McDowell. Ewell's arrival freed Jackson to attack Milroy, but first he pretended to leave the Valley to go to the defense of Richmond. The deception began on April 30, when the Valley army left camp without greeting Ewell's troops, feinted Banks's pickets, and marched east over the Blue Ridge.

[DIARY OF FRANK B. JONES]

30th April (Wednesday)

Reveille at 1 & 1/2 A.M. Waggons packed & troops under arms & marched off & up the river. Reported to Gen. Winder at 3 A.M. to know if the pickets should be drawn in. He ordered me to return to Camp & await orders from Gen. Jackson. About 2 P.M. the Army moved back & out on the Port Republic road. Drew in the Pickets & joined my Regt. just at the mill on the river where poor Capt. Shands was killed yesterday.[49] The road runs along near the river & is the worst road I ever saw. We were kept standing about, marching a little distance & then halting. Soon it commenced raining & such mud & mire & stalled teams has rarely ever been seen. We halted soon after dark & found the boys had pitched my tent & had my little stove up & really I was quite comfortable, & by the morning my g[reat] coat was nearly dry. The poor soldiers are without tents & lay down tonight in the rain on the bare ground.

1st May 1862 (Thursday)

Reveille before dawn. Waggons packed & sent off up the river road. Clouds lowering & dark & gloomy, so like my disturbed mind. The horrors of this war are now seen by me more clearly than ever before, the almost certainty of the confiscation of my property & the heart rending future now stand prominent before me. Sad, sad as it all is I do not regret my course, duty to my country requires the sacrifice of all & I pray God I may be enabled to bear up well & trust all to Him. New Orleans has fallen, & the enemy press us on all sides.[50] Can we be subjugated? God forbid.

Troops commenced to move about 12 o'clock. The train is halting all the time. Rain commenced falling heavily, the road is dangerous on horseback. Regt. halted & I met with Tom [Marshall] & had a half hour chat with him. Troops moved on, found the road pioneers had made corduroy roads with rails, thus wheat fields & grass fields were thrown open. Soon night came on, men all scattered & wading in places up to the ankles & knees. Raining hard & so dark

I could pick my way with difficulty, never saw or could not imagine such a road. Rode on to the head of the Regt. Joined Allen & Botts & found the men so scattered that there was no organization of the Regt. Soon we saw a dim light in the mountains & far away over the tree tops. Pushed on, passed by Gen. Lewis['s house] & saw a light across the river in a house which I knew from the location to be on the farm formerly owned by my g[reat] grandfather.[51] About 3 miles more & we reached camp, & laid down & slept soundly.

2nd May (Thursday) (Friday)[52]

(Brown's Gap)

Waggons packed & troops under arms, but remained in camp all day. Rode down Botts & myself to the river to see the country. Rode on to call on Gen. Lewis, found the old gentleman not well, but he welcomed us kindly & seemed pleased at our calling.[53] It was a lovely evening, the sun lit up this beautiful valley. My G[reat] Grandfather's estate layed opposite to Gen. Lewis on the river & is a most magnificent stretch of land. Never did my eyes rest on so beautiful a prospect, the larger fields were green with wheat. What a country to fight for! What a country to die for if need be!

Jackson, having given Banks the impression that he had left for Richmond, reversed his direction and returned in secret to Staunton. A few days later, when the army was briefly near the town, Frank was able to go into town to call on friends and relatives. He especially wanted to see his newly widowed niece Martha Baldwin.

[DIARY OF FRANK B. JONES]

6th May (Tuesday)   (near Staunton)

Embarked at daylight this morning & came in within a mile or two of Staunton. Cooked two days' rations & are now ready to march. Rode in to see dear Mat. How sad to see one so young left so desolate. . . . Miss Sally ——— talked about my dear Sue . . . [I] felt quite at home seeing those I know so well.[54] What our destination is & where we are going & when, I know not.

Jackson's advance guard started west toward McDowell on the sixth, the Stonewall Brigade being a day behind in the march. The Confederates surprised and overwhelmed Milroy at McDowell and pursued him north to Franklin. Frank did not find time to write for a week. He resumed his diary during the rapid withdrawal from Franklin.

[DIARY OF FRANK B. JONES]

Tuesday, 13th May,[55] on the Head Waters of S. Branch Potomac. This has been an eventful week. There has been no time to make a note. On Wednesday last we marched through Staunton & bivouacked in the Mts. some distance this side of Staunton. W.S.J. joined me at night & stayed until the morning.[56] Thursday, 8th May the army moved on & found the enemy under Gen. Millroy at or near McDowell, a little village on the Bull Pasture river.[57] His advanced forces or pickets occupied the Shenandoah Mt. Pass, but retreated on our approach. Gen. Jackson was in front, the 1st Brigade brought up the rear. The enemy then made a stand in a fine position near McDowell on the Bull Pasture Mt. Gen. Jackson placed [Gen. Edward] Johnson on the top of a Mt. near to, which was partially cleared & remained there until so late in the day that not withstanding the nearness of the enemy, he concluded there would be no attack & ordered two Brigades back to their waggons, but he was mistaken, the enemy made a vigorous attack about 5 P.M. The 1st Brigade waggons were furthest off & the battle was nearly fought & won before the order reached us to come on & re enforce Johnson. Although we had had a long & dusty march & our men very much tired, they turned out with great eagerness & hurried off to the Battle field nearly 8 miles in advance. We reached the battlefield about 10½ P.M O, the dead! the dying! the screams of the wounded! I have never seen so much of it. I was deeply affected. The ascent to the top of the Mt was up a narrow, rocky path, part of which I could not ride. When we reached the top we were ordered to lie down & wait for further developments. Our men were hastily gathering up the poor wounded. The firing had ceased & stillness reigned. I laid down, resting my head on a log & fell into a profound sleep. I knew the importance of recuperating all I could to be ready for a renewal of the attack in the morning, but I had not been asleep long when I was awoke by the order to form the Regt. & march back to our waggons, nearly 8 miles distant. We reached them about 2½ & taking a cut of twisted wheat I laid down & slept until dawn when we were hastily roused up to march at once to the Battle field.

When we came up however there were no signs of the enemy. They had moved in the night, carrying off their dead & wounded, at least *many* of them. I saw a number of our own dead layed side by side. Poor fellows! shot in the head or breast. Whilst a detachment was digging their graves. We lost in killed from 50 to 60, &, I fear, a large number wounded, & very badly wounded, too. We hurried on to McDowell were we found a quantity of stores destroyed & others left, tents, & c., & c., some 30 dead & some few wounded. One poor man laying under a waggon (with a mortal wound) on the road side & apparently no one to hand him a cup of water, this was Friday. We encamped in the Mts. Saturday we moved on, taking the Franklin road, the enemy still fleeing. Just as we reached the S. Branch Potomac (there a little stream) we heard the enemy had made a stand. We hurried & made ready for battle & advanced slowly, but they made no stand & we bivouacked for the night on the S. Branch. Sunday we pushed on, our Brigade leading & came upon the enemy on a very strong position on a high hill overlooking the river. We halted, deployed & reassembled.

We drove the skirmishers back, losing one man killed, but the battery was in too strong a position & whenever a head could be seen through the bushes, they would open fire. The 2nd Regt. layed in the woods until about 9 P.M. & we then were ordered back to our waggons. The next morning Monday, we marched back to very near the battery & layed in the woods. I felt sick & very tired, having slept but little in the night, layed down on my great coat & fell asleep, but the loud report of a bursting shell partially aroused me, & then another shell, loud & long reverberating through these everlasting mts, thoroughly aroused me from my uncomfortable nap. About 1 P.M. we moved back to the waggons & taking up the retreat we came last night to this point on the S. Branch.

I have been much struck with the wild & mountain scenery. The Shenandoah Mt. Pass is grand indeed, you ascend to the very top of the mountain & from there you see as far as the eyes can reach, Mt. after Mt. in every variety of shape & grandeur whilst away down below a little valley & a stream with the winding road, winding around from Mt. to Mt. to desend the grade. After reaching this valley we asend the HdWtrs of the James to a point where the waters turn the other way & then we discerned the Hdwaters of the Potomac. The Mts. tower above us beautifully. Every now & then you will find a fresh & sparkling stream gushing out of the mt. side & running away into the larger streams of the Valley. . . .

Sunday 18th May near Stribbley's Springs

Beautiful morning, lovely sabbath & thanks to our God, a day of rest. O, how delightful it is to have a Sabbath of rest, last Sunday we were under fire of the enemy for several hours. Today we have had quiet & peace in this sweet little valley. Mr. Hopkins preached on the "wages of sin, etc." to an attentive congregation & distributed tracts afterwards to the men who were glad to get them. I have been very unwell & have been laying down nearly all day. Had a prayer meeting this evening. Gave $50. to Mr. Hopkins to buy testaments & tracts for the soldiers.[58]

V

May — June 1862

FIRST BATTLE OF WINCHESTER
BATTLE OF PORT REPUBLIC

The Union Army's retreat to Franklin in the west and the presence of Ewell's division to the east had made Banks's position vulnerable. He withdrew north to Strasburg. Jackson on the nineteenth began another bold stroke designed to threaten Banks and draw more Union troops into the Valley to the detriment of McClellan's thrust on Richmond. This time the instrument of deception was topographical: the Massanutten Mountain, splitting the Valley north to south. Ewell was ordered north up the Luray Valley behind the Massanutten shield, while Jackson marched up the Shenandoah to New Market. Jackson feinted at the apprehensive Banks at Strasburg and abruptly disappeared over the mountain ridge. Together with Ewell he struck the tender spot in Banks's side—Front Royal, a garrison of only 1,000 men. The Stonewall Brigade was in the rear of Jackson's march when Front Royal was overwhelmed.

After an arduous two weeks with the Rockbridge Artillery in March, Robby Barton had left the unit for a sick leave. He returned to duty in the first week of May, joining his brother David and his uncle Bev Jones (who had reenlisted May 7) and the rest of the family—brothers Marshall and Strother, Uncle Frank, and cousin Marshall Jones—in the Stonewall Brigade.

[MEMOIR OF ROBERT T. BARTON]

I joined the army again near Staunton on its way to the west and my first fight was the battle of McDowell.[1] Our command was really not actually engaged in that fight, but we were close up to the line of fire waiting to be called into action. I call it my first fight because we were almost if not quite in range of the enemy's fire and in the very thick of the dead and wounded as the lines advanced and as the wounded and dead were brought back——— The next morning we pressed on after the enemy and for several days in that narrow valley we were continually under the fire of the enemy, but suffered no casualties in our own command. Gen. Jackson several times had his bivouack close to our battery and I was struck with his sharing equally the discomforts and suffering of the men.

The following is Robby's separate account of events preceding the First Battle of Winchester, and the battle itself.[2]

[Battle account by Robert T. Barton]

The rapid and continuous march of the army through the mountainous country west and north-west of Staunton, before and after the battle of McDowell . . . all the time without tents and many days and nights in the cold rain without any sort of shelter except our blankets and oil cloths; separated frequently from the wagon trains and eating raw our fat bacon, at last brought our division, under the personal command of Jackson, back to Harrisonburg, where we got in touch with Gen. Ewell. The addition of Ewell's division brought our army up to the dignity of a corps, containing about 15,000 men of all branches, united now under the command of Jackson.

Hard as our work had been in the western counties, we were yet well equipped and clad, in fine spirits, and eager to press on to the lower valley. From Harrisonburg the army marched down the pike to New Market, resting there all night, but, as we had been doing for some time, leaving our bivouac at New Market about daybreak on the 22nd, and crossing the Massanutten Mountains towards dawn. Our battery, attached to the Stonewall Brigade, moved out near the head of the column. The rising sun greeted us as we reached the tip of the mountain, whence looking back down its western slope a long line of rifles on the winding road glistened in its rays. The army in the far off curves of the road looked like a great snake with a shining back, twisting along its sinuous path.

Obstacles to the march and crossing the river delayed our reaching Luray until after dark. We went on some miles further and then lay down along the Front Royal Road, wherever a company or regiment happened to stop, or else in the fields or roads adjoining.

I was on guard that night, and I remember what a struggle it was to keep awake through my two hours of duty, which alternated with four hours of sleep, wherever I could get a place to lie. That weary vigil, as many another had done, gave me, a sickly boy of nineteen, more time than I wanted to think of the lost comforts of home and of my parents and sisters in the hands of the enemy, but the hope that we were on the march to drive them out and capture our homes again revived my spirits and lessened my appreciation of the constant dangers and horrible discomforts of such a life.

Again, at daybreak, on the 23rd of May, the army resumed its march in the direction of Front Royal. It was a hot day and for the first half of it we moved very rapidly; later we had such frequent and long stops that we would break down the fences and take out our guns and caissons into the grass fields where the hungry, tired horses could eat the clover. The best two guns of our battery had been hurriedly ordered to push on to the front, and detachments of cavalry and regiments of infantry marched by us on the road. Gen. Jackson himself had gone to the front, and members of his staff and couriers galloped back and forth, their horses sweating and blowing from the hard riding.

We knew, of course, that they were fixing for a fight in front of us, and that orders for us to hurry on would soon come. Later, as we resumed the march, the boom of cannon and the lesser sound of distant volleys from rifles assured us that the ball had opened.

We hurried our pace, closing up our column of infantry and artillery, but it was night before we got to Front Royal and the fighting had ceased. Tired couriers carrying messages to the rear would stop long enough to tell us of the fight near Riverton, where the Confederate and Union Maryland regiments had encountered each other and had done their killing with a will; else that it was our own two guns whose booming we heard, and that our cavalry, swimming the river above the bridge had made the Federal infantry cross over and scurry up Guard's Hill, after setting fire to the bridge.

Our four guns found the other two in bivouac on a flat field, now built over as a part of the town of Front Royal. The men told us of the fight and how gallantly both Maryland regiments met in the hot encounter, of the effective part taken by our two guns, and then of the inevitable flight of the surprised little body of the enemy, and the plucky stand made by them until they could fire the bridge, which it gave our people much trouble to put out.

At day-light the next day, we were again on the road, moving through the site of the little battle of the day before, crossing the partly burned bridge and up Guard Hill. There we met an officer whom we knew, accompanying on horseback an ambulance in which he had the body of his younger brother who had just been killed, where the sound of a few cannon and some sharp volleys had come to us from about a mile away.

It turned out that General Jackson himself had pressed on ahead of us with a regiment of cavalry, and finding the Union Marylanders, who had fought the battle of the evening before, with some cavalry and artillery, well posted in an orchard commanding the road over which he intended his army to march towards Middletown, he had ordered the Confederate Cavalry to make a mounted charge upon the enemy's position and this they had successfully done, putting the Union Cavalry to flight and capturing their artillery and most of their infantry. But they did this at a serious loss, and strange to say, among the killed were five young cavalrymen of one company, who, two nights before, when we stopped at Luray, had together paid a visit to some pretty girls named Broadus, who lived in that town.[3]

We marched on, and turned to the left by the scene of the morning's fight near Cedarville, and thence on by the road towards Middletown. Some couriers came back to hasten our march, and again our two best guns left us and galloped on to the front, while we and the infantry went on at a trot. The army of Banks meanwhile remained within its heavy fortifications at Strasburg, believing Jackson to be still on his hunt for Milroy, and Ewell quiet at Harrisonburg. Fugitives from the Riverton fight had reached Strasburg in the night and, by morning, Banks, becoming convinced that something was wrong, but still insisting that the Riverton affair was a mere cavalry raid, had yielded at last to the importunities of his officers and had commenced a leisurely retirement from Strasburg towards Winchester, carrying with him long wagon trains loaded with great stores of supplies which he had accumulated at Strasburg.

The order to us to hurry was because we were needed to confront the advance of Banks' army at Middletown, or if a part of its long column should pass that point before we reached it, then to strike his column there. When a mile or more from Middletown, we heard again the boom of the big guns and as we got nearer we found a clover field filled with Cavalry prisoners with their fine horses and equipments, their own brand-new uniforms covered with Turnpike dust, which also stood thick upon their perspiring faces. We passed them with some good natured guying, which they returned in kind.

Then we learned that our quick moving guns and cavalry forces had struck the column of Banks just north of Middletown and cut it in two, the larger part, however, with its army stores, passing on towards Winchester, while the other part had turned back towards Strasburg.

When we arrived at Middletown, our column was turned to the left towards Strasburg, down the street on which the Episcopal Church stands, and we marched with our colors all uncovered, and the band of every regiment going at full blast, each probably playing a different tune.[4] Everything in Middletown turned out to greet us, men, women, girls, children, dogs, cats and chickens, and nobody corrected the frequently repeated mistakes when some pretty girl would take some young man for her brother. As soon as our march southward was stopped, and learning that the great body of the enemy had passed on towards Winchester, while the smaller part, which had turned back towards Strasburg, had by that time practically moved out of our reach, or at any rate was where we could get at them later, we countermarched and moved down the dusty pike towards Winchester. The road was strewn with guns, blankets, oil cloths, sutler's stores, cartridge boxes, and a long line of abandoned wagons stretched out for more than a mile towards Stephens City, then called Newtown. I remember that two men from our battery climbed into a sutler's wagon and knocked out the heads of some gingersnap barrels, pouring the contents on the dusty pike. We stuffed our mouths and haversacks with the tasty snaps, not having seen one since Virginia seceded.

We soon struck the rear guard of Banks' army and simultaneously it struck us. We found it well posted and a sharp exchange of artillery and rifles ensued. But from one point, and then from another, we drove the enemy either by flanking or direct attack. This, however, accomplished their purpose and gave the main body of Banks' army time to hurry on. They had to hurry because meantime Ewell was advancing on the Front Royal road, seriously threatening the flanks of Gen. Banks' retreating forces, and their only hope of safety lay in getting to a point at which they could meet the attack of both of our divisions, on their front.

The last stand of the rear guard was close to Stephens City and all the guns of our battery were engaged. We lost a man or two and some horses, but we pushed the enemy back and drove them hurriedly through the town. By this time it was near ten o'clock at night, and here again the people met us as they had done in Middletown, with the same uproarious and delighted greeting, illuminating their houses with bits of candles stuck in the inner sash, while the people broke out into the street. The same mistakes of kinship which occurred in Middletown were made again, but I recalled that afterwards, that while they gave me things to eat nobody kissed me, and I was not a bad looking lad then, as my photograph shows, although I was delicate and slender. I don't think I resented it at that time, as I would have done later, *or even now.* For a half mile we were beyond Stephens City the road was lighted by the still glowing coals of a burned wagon train, making it hot for us as we marched by on the other side of the road. Our necessarily slow march, and the long delays which had occurred, brought the head of the column close to Springdale near one o'clock in the morning while the army was stretched nearly as far back as Middletown. Our battery led the column, the only troops in front of us being Gen. Jackson, his staff and a company of cavalry. Those in front had gotten down to the bridge that crosses the Opequon [at Bartonsville], while we were close behind them coming down the hill. Just then the darkness was illuminated by a brilliant flash of fire, and bullets fell all around us, hitting our wheels and a few scraping the sides of the horses.[5] Naturally Gen. Jackson and his escort turned back, and we halted in the road, while the second regiment in our rear, led by my brother [Strother], who was an officer in Company F, and knew well the lay of the land, quickly climbed a stone fence and moved rapidly along through the [Springdale] barn yard and thence to the rear of the house, from which point of vantage they poured a volley into the enemy, lying flat behind the lilac hedge which screened the yard from the public road. There was a rush of the ambuscaders to get away, only leaving their dead and wounded on the ground.

Our column on the Turnpike at once advanced. As we went by the Springdale gate, seeing the overseer and his family standing in the yard, I tried to open it, that I might get a glass of milk or water, which I needed very much to help me in this long march which had continuously kept up since five o'clock in the morning, and it was then one o'clock the next morning.[6] Endeavoring to open the gate, I found it obstructed in some way, and looking down I discovered a dead Federal soldier with a bullet through his head, and his head against the gate. Later I found the hole made by the bullet, which had gone through a panel of the gate and had evidently been fired by one of Gen. Jackson's escort in return for the first volley from behind the lilacs. I made no further effort to get in but hurried on to join my slowly moving company.

The head of our column was now pushing itself close up to the whole force of the enemy in the darkness of the night, and we were obliged to move at a snail's place, for time and time again the night was lighted up by the flash of guns from one side of the road or the other, for at that time there were lots of woodland that came directly up to the pike. Moving at a snail's pace and halting, and then moving again and halting again, falling asleep at the halts and being suddenly wakened up when motion was resumed, we fairly staggered on, worn almost to exhaustion by the weariness of such a march. When we got a little beyond Kernstown, we turned a little to the left in a field and parked our guns, and as the column came up it formed in a sort of line of battle, the men falling down where they stood and going to sleep, for it was then near three o'clock in the morning. I remember how chilly and damp the dewy grass felt to me, but how soon my weariness overcame the thought of cold and I was fast asleep. The next thing I knew was a popping sound of something not far ahead of me, and, in my half asleep condition, I thought I was at home and that it was the Fourth of July and we boys were saluting the coming anniversary with the firing of Jackson Crackers. The sharp call of "Fall in men", repeated all along the line, awoke me to a vivid consciousness of the situation. It was a skirmish line just ahead of us opening up the battle that I taken for Jackson Crackers in my dream.

In a very few moments we were on the road, the infantry moving to the right and left and marching now in column and now abreast, trying to keep something of a line of battle.

Daylight had come, and with it the guns of the enemy from the hills back of what was then the Hollingsworth Mills, now the Hack place, were sending their screaming shells over our heads.[7] When we reached the toll gate our column halted and the men were directed to find shelter behind a stone house that then stood just to the right of the road as we approached the town.[8]

Our battery consisted of about 150 men of whom about 100 were college men and boys, like myself, from preparatory school. The other 50 were mainly sons of farmers, and laborers from the town of Lexington, where the battery had first been organized. In our mess of 10 were Bob Lee, the General's son, and Bob McKim, a fine young fellow, full of fun, from the City of Baltimore.[9] We were called "The Three Bobs." Feeling a little of the sense of safety which the stone house afforded, Bob McKim slapped me on the shoulder and said "I will breakfast with you this morning in Winchester" and I replied, "I will dine with you when we get to Baltimore."

As had been done during the preceding several days, our two best [Parrott] guns Sec. No. 1 of the battery, were sent forward at a run, and regiments of infantry passed us making to the right and left as mounted men delivered orders to their commanders. Soon the call to "fall in and mount caissons" came to us, and we ran out from behind the stone house to where the screaming shells seemed to come closer and closer down to the road, as if they were hunting for us and screaming in anger because they did not find us. All but I climbed quickly upon the caissons, I don't know why I did not do that also, unless it was because I thought we would move but a little before we should unlimber for action again. Here I made a mistake. The horses went off at once in a trot, and I had only time to catch hold of an iron seat-guard on a caisson, when the horses were lashed into a gallop. I hung on with both hands, swinging to and fro and only now and then touching the ground with my feet. The men on the seat could not pull me up, and to let go would mean that the plunging horses and the heavy pieces and caissons, which they drew, would crush me to death if I fell. But I did succeed in holding on, thanks perhaps to my light weight of about 115 pounds. I still had hold with both hands when the battery slowed up by the grave yard by the old mill wall just this side of the Hacks, then the Hollingworth house. When I let go there was hardly a patch of skin on the palms of my hands and the inside of my fingers. We did not stop, but hurried along the road leading up the hill, while the terrible noise of firing guns and bursting shells just above us drowned even the sound of voices close by. Behind us was a column of infantry, with two other batteries and their accompanying caissons intervening. As we mounted the hill the shells seemed to spit in our faces, as they threw all around us the ragged pieces which their explosions scattered right and left.

The road lay between a narrow mill race on the left and a some what protecting hill side on the right. A gate which crossed the road was open or off its hinges, but the huge locust posts stood solid in their places. The excited horses were hard to keep straight in the middle of the road, and in going through the gate way the first gun veered a little and fastened itself upon the locust post just between the wheel and the gun. The straining horses made the hold only the tighter, and the captain [W. T. Poague] taking in the situation, called for men to volunteer to cut down the post. Several at once offered themselves, but one strong man named Witt, accustomed to handle an axe, was selected, and jerking one from the caisson soon began to make the chips fly from the solid post.[10] The drivers were struggling with the frightened horses, while the men of the battery and those of the long column behind us, by order, jumped the little race and lay close down behind its protecting embankment. At each lick the axe-man grunted, as if playing an accompaniment to the music of his axe. The captain sat still and unmoved upon his horse and eager faces watched the axe-man to see what would happen when the post should fall. I became fascinated with looking at it and without thinking what I was doing I got up, crossed the race again and stood in the road watching the axe and flying chips. Suddenly, a strong rough hand caught me by the neck of my jacket and threw me back over the race, saying "Lay down, you damn fool." I fell with my nose in a bunch of mint and recovering my full sense of danger I lay as flat as a snake, wondering if when the call came I could ever get up again, or if any of the long column lying down behind the race would rise at the command and march forward into the hell that seemed to be pouring down upon us. Well, presently the last lick was struck and the post fell and the straining, struggling horses sprang forward with the gun while the cool headed captain called out above the din "Corporal Witt from this hour." And Private Witt was happy at his promotion for gallantry on the field of battle.

All along the line voices sung out "Fall in men," and without hesitation every man sprang to his place and I wondered why I had ever feared that I or any other soldier would not rather go to death than show a lack of courage.

The battery and the column following it moved forward like clock work. Some careless guide had made a mistake and led us beyond the place assigned us, directing us so badly that we came fully under range of the fire of the enemy's infantry and expected a volley every moment. But for some unaccountable reason the fire did not come and the commanding officer countermarched the battery as if on parade, and while the hostile infantry looked on amazed. we moved out of range and back to the place assigned to us. All of this occupied not many more moments than it takes to write it.

As we moved back to our proper positions, we passed the dead and wounded of our battery, and there lay Bob McKim dead, his fine and happy face stained with blood and his forehead crushed in by a bullet or fragment of a shell. By his side lay another man of the battery whose name was called on the roll just before mine, and he too had fallen dead at his post.[11]

By the time we got to our proper place two other batteries had come up. We then found that our 1st section had followed closely the infantry who had captured the hill and had taken their place on it and opened fire. The enemy falling back had placed their batteries on the hill just above Mrs. Carr's house and other batteries had been located by then at the south end of Washington Street and also on the lot where the Catholic Cemetery now is, and with their many guns they had concentrated their fire on our two guns on the hill near the old Williams Factory. It was this tremendous firing that had silenced our two guns, killing the men I mentioned and driving the others away from the guns and down the slope of the hill where we were at last were directed to, and which firing had extended to us along the Turnpike and to the other moving portions of our command, seeking their places for the fight.

Here we were directed to lie down for shelter while the guns of the three batteries were placed in line so that we could all advance together to the top of the hill again, the men of the first section taking their places on our left to go back with us and recover their guns. Lying in the grass awaiting this formation, an officer of the next battery [Cutshaw's], engaged in getting his guns in place, almost rode over me with his nearly frantic horse.

[Memoir of Robert T. Barton]

Marshall was tall (over six feet), with black curling hair and a black moustache, a very handsome man. I thought he looked splendid as he rode up on his grey mare, turning and giving commands to his gunners, under that awful fire, as cool as on dress parade.[12]

[Battle account of Robert T. Barton]

Recognizing him as my oldest brother, some eight or ten years older than me, I called out "Don't ride over a fellow," and he, looking down almost pityingly, said "Are you here boy?" But before I could make any answer, we all ran to our places, and the fourteen guns moved up abreast and got in line with the two abandoned guns, and at once the sixteen opened their throats and sought the range of batteries opposite them.

From the hill I could see by the smoke, and tell by the sound of the guns and rifles, the two opposing lines stretching from the extreme left, where we were, down beyond the place where the water pump now is.[13]

Besides the volumes of smoke there was a heavy mist which lifted as the sun rose in the sky, but in a little while the smoke of battle obscured everything. We kept up this firing for two solid hours. It was Sunday morning and in the midst of the din I heard a church bell in the town, and then I saw the smoke and flame rolling up where the enemy had set fire to the warehouses on the northern end of Market Street, which contained their stores, and the cry ran along the line, "They are burning the town."

Meantime we were working our guns as fast as we could load and fire them. About equi-distant between the enemy's batteries and ours was a heavy stone fence and behind it a line of Federal infantry had been located, whose good shooting was responsible mainly for the killing and wounding of some twenty-five men of our battery.

Towards the end of two hours, Gen. Jackson and a member of his staff rode up and took their places at the left of our guns. Soon Gen. Dick Taylor rode up with his staff and I was close enough to hear the brief conversation between the two generals.[14] The substance of it was, that Gen. Taylor should bring up his brigade and prepare, with our infantry supporting us, to charge the men behind the stone fence and on to the batteries in the distance.

Turning to the ravine behind us, I saw a column of infantry already on the march towards us, and this was Gen. Taylor's brigade, which was following him to the top of the hill. It passed under a large walnut tree, among the branches of which the shells were bursting, and small branches, with their fresh green leaves, were falling down upon the column and stuck on a number of the bayoneted guns. It is curious how little things happening in the midst of such danger and commotion impress themselves upon you.

About this time I was called for to help a gun which had lost its needed number of men, and hastening to it I came behind a Mr. [Kinloch] Nelson, afterwards a professor in the Theological Seminary at Alexandria. Our guns were all muzzle loaders and he was driving home a shell, which would complete the loading of the gun. I stood behind him to see what I was to do, and as he stepped back with the ram rod in his hand, he almost knocked me down. At that very moment the wheel of the gun in front of which he had been standing and which he had just avoided by stepping back on me, was carried away by a shell or solid shot from the enemy. If he had been two seconds slower, he would have been cut in two, and possibly I would have shared his fate. While we hurried to the caisson to get another wheel and brought it back and put it on, Gen. Taylor's brigade formed behind our batteries and our infantry rose to join them. Just then there was a terrific pouring of shells from the enemy's batteries and three men of one company of the infantry not far from me, were blown to pieces just as they rose up from the ground to fall in with the charging line.[15]

We ceased firing, and the infantry advanced through our guns, yelling and cheering at the tops of their voices. Many of our gunners, out of mere excitement, followed in the charge until they were called back to their places. The Federal infantry at once got up from behind the stone fence and took flight, and the batteries of the enemy seeming only to have waited for this movement also ceased firing and limbered up their guns. Way down along the lines the same thing was happening. The enemy were turning by columns into the roads and hastening on towards Winchester, while our men still in line, yelled and cheered and fired and ran forward as if they expected to capture the whole of Banks' army.

Just then, one of the officers of my company rode along calling me by name. I answered, and he told me that my brother [Marshall], whose battery had immediately adjoined ours in the fight, had been seriously wounded, and to leave the gun and go to see about him. My other brother [David], in the battery with me, joined me at the same time and urged me to go.

I went down at once to where his guns were getting ready to move with ours, and was told of his serious wound and that he had been carried down the hill. I went on, tracing him by those who had seen him, and found he had been

James E. Taylor's view of the Frederick County Court House, with Confederate prisoners from the 3rd Battle of Winchester confined within the fence, a scene often replicated—sometimes with Union prisoners—in the course of the war. The Barton and Williams law office was across from the Court House, on Lawyer's Row (left).
(Western Reserve Historical Society)

carried into the house which Mrs. Hack now lives in.[16] As I passed into the yard I found it full of wounded men and surgeons operating or furnishing first aid assistance as the cases seemed to require it. I went up on the porch and found the house closed and all its windows shut. I opened the front door and felt the pleasant coolness of the house after the heat of out of doors, and the intense fatigue that I had been undergoing. The parlor door was open and near the fire place was a horsehair sofa. On it lay my brother, his clothes saturated with blood, for the same shell had cut both his jugular vein and femoral artery and he had almost instantly bled to death. I was standing by him when Mrs. Hollingsworth entered the room and said to me, "Did you know him?", and I replied, "He was my brother." She instantly fell down upon her knees and put her arms around him and wept, as if he was her brother instead of mine. There was nothing there for me to do, so I left the house and went out upon the road, joining some of the infantry who had been in the skirmishing line all the night before, and we hurried along to get to the town so as to go in with the army.

The greater part of the troops, however, had preceded us, filling Market Street and Braddock Street with their onward rush. Many of the enemy had been killed or captured in the town.

. . . When the wind up was made we had 3500 prisoners in the Court House yard and the Court House and the office building adjoining, and it is said that the capture of material filled five miles of wagons. This was the prosaic end of this little battle, and the next day we buried our dead; one from my father's house.

Robby's battle account concludes here, but his memoir continued.

[MEMOIR OF ROBERT T. BARTON]

. . . I hurried on to Winchester, reaching there to be in the melee of the fighting through the streets; to see the women rush out heedless of the shots and embrace their brothers and friends and all the people wild with enthusiasm and almost crazy with excitement.

Among the jubilant who turned out on Market Street to greet the victorious army were the Bartons and the elder Mrs. Jones, Mrs. Lee, Miss Laura Lee, and their nieces, Lute and Lal Burwell. Mrs. Jones "was caught in town, unable to leave it the night before, because of Banks' retreating army. Consequently, was in hearing of the whole, & from the upper part of Mr. [William L.] Clark's house. I was with Sue, could see the smoke. . . . Our men passed in numbers before me in hot pursuit, & I could not help cheering them as they went. I soon discovered that Gen. Jackson was the commander, & how it fared with my own, I did not know, yet did not feel as if anything had happened. One of the soldiers in passing caught sight of me, called to me to say, 'Bev Jones is safe.'[17] Was it not kind? David [Barton] passed also. I could not hear what he said. . . ."[18] Miss Lee realized later that "it was a very hazardous thing we did in staying out there, but then we were so excited we had no sensation of fear."

[DIARY OF LAURA LEE]

. . . [Gen. Jackson had] ordered all on in pursuit, even the artillery were allowed to unhitch the horses and mount and follow. By this time a rumor reached us that Marshall Barton was killed. David rode up on an artillery horse, and said all were safe but Marshall who he told his mother was badly wounded but that they must send to him at once, but he whispered to Lute that he was already dead. . . . Mr. Barton went out to the battlefield at once. . . . Mrs. Barton has borne it nobly, she says she gave her sons to her country, and must not murmur at the sacrifice. She stayed down stairs all day Sunday, feeding the starving soldiers as they came back from the pursuit. . . . Marshall's funeral took place on Monday afternoon from the church, his Company (he was 1st Lieut of a Battery) attended and a long train of citizens.[19]

Robbie, bone-tired, was oblivious to all but his family's loss.

[MEMOIR OF ROBERT T. BARTON]

Worn out completely I turned into my father's house and, sinking down on the floor, in spite of the bitter grief of my mother and sisters about my brother's death, I fell asleep on the floor. Not long after my father, who had heard of my brother's death and had gone out to see about him, came in and greeted us striving in vain to keep back the tears that would come over his first born son.[20]

In that fight almost side by side were four of us, Marshall, David, Strother, and I. Rannie had been taken prisoner at Kernstown and was at Fort Delaware. In the fight I escaped without a wound, but two horses which I was tying together by their bridles were killed while I had hold of them, and a shell, at another time, striking at my feet, cut out a piece of sod which filled my mouth. At one time, there was a little flinching among some of the men under the heavy fire, and the Captain called loudly to the men to stand steady. My brother David who was a short distance off, ran towards me and seeing that I was at my post, said something about being glad that I was all right to which I remember, I gave quite an independent reply, as if he had any right to doubt me.

My brother Marshall was buried with military pomp, his saddled horse being led behind the hearse which was preceded by a band of music. My father and I walked close behind the horse, the dear old gentleman sitting at every stop, but holding his tearful face bravely up to that bright May sun. My brother lies in Mt. Hebron cemetery where you will often see his grave when perchance my boy, you go to see that mine is kept in order.

My sister Martha with her two children had come down from Staunton as soon as the way was clear. The Marshall children were at my father's and my sister Fannie had come home from Cecil Co. Md.[21]

I remember that week that I remained at home how she told me of her trip and how she dwelt upon the love and admiration she felt for Katie Knight with whom she had formed such a close friendship. She showed me her photograph and told me of her beauty and sweet girlish attractions, and how she would dearly love if I should survive the war and go over there some day and make her my wife. And I laughed at all that as if it was a pleasant story to beguile the time.

While the army went on to the Potomac River in pursuit of Banks' routed army, I was at home recruiting from the exhaustion of the long marches and bad food, hunger, cold, wet, & c. This occupied just a week and the Saturday night succeeding the Sunday of May 25 the Stonewall brigade marched through Winchester and to its bivouac five miles further South, making the unequalled march of 37 miles (from Bolivar Heights) in one day.[22] As the Cavalry force was still north of the town, a number of us ventured to remain at home that Saturday night.

Let me here remark two things. First, I am writing this memoir from time to time as my engagements permit and therefore I put down just what occurs to me at the moment. Now and then after I have passed the period at which certain things happened that it is of interest to record I recall them and hence events are not narrated in their exact order. Second, I do not pretend to give you an exact picture of the effect and results of the general events which I am recording for you. How could I portray to you the state of mind in our own and other families at that time. My oldest brother just killed in battle almost at our very door. My younger brother in a Federal prison. My father's farms overrun and laid waste, and all income from his law practice stopped; his slaves, including most of his house servants (who were then quite numerous) fugitives, and set at liberty by the Federal troops; a large family of young children thrown upon him for support by the death of my sister Maria, the absence of their father [Tom Marshall] in the army, and also by the death of Dr. John M. Baldwin, his widow and two children coming back also to be supported.[23] Then the retreat of the army south again, and the departure with constant danger and hardship of the three remaining sons and of Col. Thos. Marshall who was like a son: Words will not suffice to enable me to give you a picture of this misery, nor can I tell you in words how bravely and cheerfully it was all borne.

Nor must you judge by what I tell you of my experience, of the liberty allowed to the average Confederate soldier. It was well known how very delicate I was and that only by great indulgences could I remain at all in the service. The surgeons and other officers were my friends and acquaintances and I could always get their friendly aid and sympathy, without waiting the red tape of ordinary routine.

I recall here that when I got back to Winchester on May 25 I found that my

Robert T. Barton, late May 1862.
(Edith Barton Sheerin)

mother and sisters had made me a handsome new artillery uniform and in some way had gotten me a new felt hat. I put them on and went to a photographer's (then called a daguerrean gallery) and had my picture taken. It is this that I intend to have enlarged and will keep for my boy so that when he grows up he may see his father as a soldier boy of nineteen years.

Once again Jackson lacked the numbers to hold Winchester, and reinforcements sent to Banks threatened his line of retreat. The Confederate Army, with its precious wealth—200 wagons—of captured supplies furnished by "Commissary Banks," hastened south.

[Memoir of Robert T. Barton]

Before daylight that Sunday morning [June 1], my brother Strother, my cousin Willie Barton, and I think one other Winchester boy left Winchester on foot to catch up to the army.[24] In the night, the Confederate cavalry north of Winchester had been withdrawn, so that there was nothing between us and the enemy. The Stonewall brigade had left its bivuac about as early as we had left Winchester, so it had about five miles the start of us. That was the rear of the army except the cavalry. Fearing a dash of the enemies cavalry and our capture if we kept to the main turnpike we left the turnpike and made a cut across the country so familiar to us all. We made the eleven miles march to Vaucluse in time for breakfast, which eating in a great hurry there we reached Cedar Creek just as the Confederate cavalry was about to burn the bridge across it. Crossing it we were in comparative safety from capture, as we supposed, but soon we learned that the enemy [under Gen. Fremont] was approaching Strasburg from the west by the way of the village of Cottontown and from the east from the direction of Front Royal, and soon the booming of the guns in both directions told us that Gen. Jackson was holding them in check to let his tired old brigade march through.[25] We passed Strasburg nearly worn out and without food since morning. The cavalry hurried us up, saying that they could keep back the enemy no longer and we must push on to the main body of the army. Several hundred stragglers had gathered by that time, so we formed something of a disorderly body in ourselves, and would have given a cavalry attack a right good fight.

It was near dark when we reached Fishers Hill and thinking we were at last out of danger forty or fifty of us sought shelter from the then pouring rain in a barn some distance east of the road. Climbing into a bin full of wheat and huddling together for warmth, we were soon asleep. Only three or four of us however were in the bin, the others lying on the straw and hay piled about. Late in the night we were waked by a great noise, a rush of men and horses and trampling and shouting round the barn. The Yankee cavalry had driven in our pickets and surrounded the barn and were taking prisoners of all they could find. We lay perfectly still, and altho the Yankees searched, called and threatened, they did not find us. Before daylight we left the building cautiously and marching as fast as we could, we caught up to the army a mile or two north of Woodstock just in time to take part in a sharp skirmish caused by the enemies cavalry dashing upon our rear and scattering our cavalry, so that the artillery and infantry had to fight them back, which we did in fine style.

. . . To show you how pleasant were the relations between officers and privates in the Confederate Army, who knew each other to be gentlemen, I will tell you of what occurred between Gen. Turner Ashby and myself. Just after leaving Woodstock, the section of the battery to which I belonged was posted on the side of a hill where we were to receive and to return the fire of the enemy and thus to cover the leisurely retreat of our army. This position had been selected for us by Gen. Ashby. Looking towards the enemy we could see them in full view locating their batteries just on the hill back of where the B. & 0. R.R. depot now stands. Their guns were much more numerous and of greatly better range than ours. We knew therefore that we would soon be worsted should they open fire. I insisted that I would tell Gen. Ashby of it and ask him to remove us. The boys dared me to do it. Presently the General rode up and I pointed out to him the objections to the situation. He at once assented to it and to the relief of us all he ordered the battery forward. Our bold position however had retarded the enemy so much that our troops had gotten well on ahead and we followed after. This was the last time I saw or talked with Ashby.

I had known him quite well in the army and as a boy used to see him very frequently in Fauquier. I greatly admired his horsemanship and especially his riding at tournaments. He was a gallant fellow, but a man of few accomplishments and not much capacity as an officer. The day after the event I have narrated he was killed in a skirmish which took place west of the turnpike about a mile or two north of Harrisonburg.

That next day [June 5], expecting a fight near Harrisonburg, we stored our knapsacks in the town, but the fight did not take place and we went through the town without being allowed to get our baggage. It all fell into the hands of the enemy and I believe they destroyed it. It was not much to any of us, but the loss of it was a serious inconvenience. Our knapsacks usually contained a single change of underclothes, a tooth brush, & a New Testament. As we had to carry it on our backs we could not afford to have much. But when we lost that change of clothing, we could only get clean clothes by standing naked by a stream until we could wash and dry what we had on. To this extremity we were very frequently reduced.

Leaving Harrisonburg about one or two o'clock P.M. I remember that our battery halted about half a mile beyond the town. Our marching orders were to keep closed up all the time. On this occasion Bob Lee (son of Gen. R. E. Lee) was riding a lead horse to a gun and I the rear horse. This we often did to rest, as it was also a rest to the drivers sometimes to walk. When we halted, we found that we could not close up to the caison in front of us because Gen. Jackson stood with his horse partly turned in the road but close to the left side of it where there was a little bank. Either Lee or I proposed to close up and push the General down the bank. This was readily assented to and the shoulders of our lead horse gently shoved the General's horse out of the road and down the bank. He at once turned to see what was the matter and as in halting I came immediately by his side and above him, I touched my hat and said that we had strict orders to keep closed up all the time. The General touched his hat and smiled, and soon rode off to some point where he was needed.

Our battery which had been so long sustaining the rear next to the enemy was now sent forward and we commenced our weary march through the deep mud of the road leading from Harrisonburg to Port Republic. In this way we missed the skirmish in which Ashby was killed; for otherwise we would have taken part in it.[26]

All that afternoon and most of the night we toiled through the mud__ wet, tired, and hungry. The next day we went into camp on the right (west) bank of the Shenandoah river not far from Port Republic but shut off from a view of the river by a hill. It was not long after we went into camp that an ambulance with a cavalry escort came by bearing the body of Gen. Turner Ashby. The men stood along the road with uncovered heads and all were greatly grieved at the death of that gallant officer.

Two Federal armies, under Generals Fremont and Shields, were pressing to converge on Jackson's small force. Taking advantage of the Shenandoah River, swollen from recent rains, Jackson took on each army separately, defeating Fremont at Cross Keys on Sunday, June 8. The next day, Jackson crossed the river, burned the bridges so that Fremont could not follow, and defeated Shields at Port Republic.

[MEMOIR OF ROBERT T. BARTON]

Sunday morning early a number of us went down to the river to bathe and wash our only suits of under clothes. We had accomplished this and had just returned to our camp and lay down in the woods hoping for a peaceful quiet Sunday and some rest from our great fatigue. I had hardly lain down however when I was startled by the rush of a shell from over the hill in front of us and its explosion among some infantry just behind us. One man was instantly killed and, I think, some one else wounded. Soon a perfect shower of shells began to fall in the field in front of us where our horses were quietly grazing. We were ordered at once to catch the horses and hitch up the guns, but we supposed that the firing was from one of our own guns which was with the wagon camp over the hill beyond Port Republic, and which we concluded was emptying its guns after the wet and rain of the past few days. On this theory some very uncomplimentary things were said about the carelessness of the officer in command.

Confederate Artillery depicted on the C.S.A. ten-dollar bill. (Ann Dudley Field Lalley)

In a few minutes however Gen. Jackson and some of his staff rode up hastily and saying that the enemy had the bridge between us and our wagon trains, ordered our guns to the hill in front of us as rapidly as we could go. I had been helping to catch the horses amid the falling shells in the field, and had just brought in some when Gen. Jackson appeared. I did not belong to the section which went forward first and hence I was not a witness to that famous scene in which Capt. Poague refused at first to fire at the troops on the bridge believing them to be Confederates. Then it was that Gen. Jackson rode forward and ordered the troops on the bridge to "limber up," which order they answered with a shot. Capt. Poague immediately ordered his guns to fire and at the first shot which fell under the enemy's guns on the bridge, they ran away leaving their guns which we captured. The rest of our battery coming up rapidly, we ranged, with some other batteries, along the west bank of the river on the hill commanding it and we poured a deadly fire into the line of the enemy retreating along the east bank. They had no artillery and no position for it if they had it, and we were out of range of their rifles. So we had it all our own way and we did tremendous execution. So fast was our firing that we had to cool our guns by pouring water down them from our canteens. Gen. Jackson sat like a Statue immediately by the gun I was assisting to work, and he seemed quite to enjoy the firing.

The ultimate retreat of the enemy out of our range put a stop to our firing. Later in the day we heard heavy fighting in our rear and not far from us. That told us that the sharp fight of Cross Keys, on the ground we had come over on our muddy march, was in progress, and from time to time during the day we would hear by couriers how the battle went on. Shields army was in our front across the river and it was a part of his command that we had driven back early that morning. We were left, with a considerable body of infantry, to hold that position so as to keep Shields army from again advancing and cutting off our wagon train or attacking the rear of our army that was fighting with Fremont at Cross Keys.

That night our battery crossed the river at Port Republic and camped just beyond the village which itself is in the forks of the two rivers, or rather two branches of the same river.

I had been sick all day, but able to be with the guns, as we did not move about much. That night, I stood guard over the battery's corn pile, and by morning I was quite used up.

In a newspaper article in later years Robby wrote about that night.

[ARTICLE OF ROBERT T. BARTON]

There was no getting out of it, but the kind-hearted sergeant promised me duty at the corn post and a loud call from the guard when he should bring out the relief. Even this amounted at least to a chance to sit down and may-be a nap in the night; contrary, of course, to all military rule, but one of those concessions sometimes made in the army to the overtaxed demands on human endurance in such a campaign as we had just passed through.

I remember that the night was bright and pleasant, and as from my post I looked up at the stars and then down at the scattered smouldering fires and the sleeping figures that covered the plain, the thoughts of a nineteen-year-old boy, far away from home and cut off from all communication with his people and expecting a fierce battle in the morning, can readily be imagined.

Availing myself of the friendly promises of the sergeant, I had sat down on a bag of corn, and I suppose I must have dropped to sleep when I was aroused by a queer noise close to me. I sprang up at once and taking by the hilt the sabre which had rested across my knees, I started for the direction from which the noise came. It turned out to be the surgeon's horse, a noted forager, which had gotten loose from its picket, and was making a fine meal with its head far down in a quarter-filled barrel of flour.

The hard breathing of the horse and his greedy efforts to get at the flour sent a little volcano of white dust out of the barrel and around the horse's head. This received a notable accession when I struck the horse a sharp lick with the flat side of the sabre, and with a loud snort he extricated his head from the barrel. The same noise must have awakened the surgeon, for he came up just as I had walloped his horse and sharply resented such treatment for his foraging steed.

I was on my second turn of duty for the night and there were signs of the coming of the dawn. Here and there men were rising up and preparation had begun to be made to feed the horses, cook rations and move the wagon train, for the order had been given the night before that we were to march at five o'clock.

I had spent a sick day and a sicker night when in the morning I was relieved from duty, I went at once to my friend, the surgeon, for some medicine. Resenting perhaps the horse incident, I got no sympathy and but scant politeness from him, and he ordered me to go back to the wagon train. This was an order, however, the refusal to obey, which, when a fight was on hand, no military rule ever punished, so I did not regard it.

By five o'clock we were on the march, the infantry and artillerists crossing the south fork of the Shenandoah on a bridge of wagons constructed in the night. The surgeon seeing my poor condition, relented enough to let me ride in the ambulance close behind the battery. We had but a few miles to go before we came under the fire of the enemy's artillery, and when it became pretty fierce, the ambulance driver, wheeling directly around, commenced rapidly to retreat.

I was lying down at the time on the floor of the ambulance and had to roll out quickly from the rear. I then took my place with the guns, and the excitement of being under fire, seemed, until the fight was over, to be better medicine for me than any surgeon could have prescribed. . . .

Our battery had changed positions several times under heavy fire, seeking each time to get a better place from which we could do more damage to the enemy. Then crossing a muddy field of corn stubble, I was ordered by the captain to run ahead of the guns and ask the colonel of an infantry regiment lying behind the shelter of a small hill in front of us to move out and let our battery take position there.

I ran ahead and when I reached there I found that the regiment was the Twenty-seventh of our brigade, the Stonewall, with Colonel [Andrew J.] Grigsby in command. The colonel soon had his men up, fronted them and put them through a few turns of the manual, to keep them cool, I suppose, because of the heavy fire of shells that they were under. In fine order they moved off a little distance to the left and gave room for the battery to take their place. While waiting for the guns to come up, I walked off by the side of the colonel's horse, and the regiment halted and he dismounted, I stood talking with him with my arm over his horse's shoulder.

He was commending the qualities of his fine little animal and I felt for him truly when later that day I saw him marching along with a rifle on his shoulder and only about twenty of his regiment behind. The entire language of his reply when he told me that his horse had been killed in the fight can readily be imagined by those who knew Colonel Grigsby.[27]

In Robby's memoir he described his return to his battery.

[MEMOIR OF ROBERT T. BARTON]

It was a noisy and dangerous promenade for me among the bursting shells, and no better after I got there. Once a shell tore the wheel from a caison by which I was standing, and we had to go to a rail fence, under very heavy fire, and get rails to pry up the caison and put on the fifth wheel which we always carried on the caison in case of such calamities. To have to do things of this sort is a great deal harder to a soldier than actual fighting is.

Well——— of my incident. Our battery was in a wheat field and the ripening wheat was rich and heavy. It had rained hard for some days and the hot sun made it dreadful on men and horses to work the guns or move them in the mud and heavy wheat. Besides that I was sick, so weak that I had to ride to the field, as I told you, in an ambulance. We were firing rapidly at a large body of Federal infantry that was bravely advancing to charge us, and we were loosing men and horses by their rifles. The artillery of the enemy with which we had been contending for most of the day, was now directing its fire to our right wing which was advancing upon them. Just at this point, some of our own brigade and some of Gen. Richard Taylor's Louisiana brigade charged the enemy that was advancing upon us and were repulsed with heavy loss and fell back through our guns, thus stopping our fire for the time. Quickly the enemy was upon us and we were ordered to limber up and fall back. But the horses of my gun were killed, seeing which the officer in command, a gallant fellow named Cole Davis, now dead, ordered us to stand and fire in their faces.[28] I slung my blanket and oil cloth from my shoulders and on to a passing caison where luckily it clung and where I afterwards found it.

We could almost tell the colors of the eyes of the enemy before we were ordered to cease firing and fall back, leaving the gun to its fate. Lt. Cole Davis lay wounded on the ground, others of the men of the gun were killed or wounded: the whole field just there was thick with dead and wounded, and under other circumstances the screams of pain would have been more than I could stand. The enemys infantry was firing its shot into us and the bullets whistled in a weird way as they cut through the wheat or sounded with a dull thud as they hit some retreating Confederate. Sick, worn out, in the mud and wheat, I could not even run, so I took to the shelter of an apple tree not far from where the battery stood and lying down, tried to protect myself behind it. Soon two other men got behind me, but presently saying they would be killed there got up and attempted to run. One of them was instantly killed, and in the confusion, I did not see what became of the other. Shot after shot struck the tree. (I counted seven bullet holes in it afterwards) and I felt quite sure that I could not stay there; altho the only alternative to me seemed to be capture. Observing a ditch some yards in front of me towards the enemy, I jumped for it, hoping to tumble in and escape the dreadful fire. My foot caught in a dewberry bush and I tumbled head long into the ditch, which proved to be nearly full of cold water, accumulated by the recent rains. You can imagine the shock it gave me, for the heat of the day, the heavy exercise, and my extreme weakness, had put me in a great perspiration. But to stay in that water was my only chance for escape, so there I stayed with my body under the water and only my face above, while the heavy fire of bullets and of our gun which they had turned on the fugitives, swept over me. All that I have told you did not take many minutes, for when the retreating infantry and artillery men had all been killed, wounded or escaped, there was nothing else for the enemy to shoot at, and they did not pursue us beyond the wheat field, for while we were being driven back on the left, our right wing had forced the enemy back and had captured his artillery.[29]

As soon as the firing ceased I crawled out of the water as wet as a rat and as weak as a kitten. I took off my grey artillery jacket, which was covered with mud. Beneath it was a blue flannel shirt and that too, and my pants, were disfigured with mud. I was absolutely dazed and confused, but presently seeing a line of infantry resting in the field in the direction of where the enemy had been, and which had a Virginia flag over it, I went towards it, expecting to find out something about the whereabouts of my command. When very close to the infantry, I was called off by the dreadful entreaties of a wounded man for water and help. As I turned to go to him I was ordered in a very peremptory tone by one of the infantry officers to come to him. I refused, in a tone equally as peremptory, and went on to the wounded man. When I reached him, I found him fatally wounded. both arms broken and the ball had gone through both lungs from side to side. I gave him some water and he begged me to lift him up. This I did, but he died in my arms.

I was occupied some minutes in this when I became aware of shells passing over my head and exploding around me. I did not know whether they came from friend or foe, but no matter what the source they were equally dangerous to me. I sought shelter from them in a kind of ravine or track which ran across the field, and this I pursued for some distance. Finally I emerged from it just in time to confront some infantry which I found to be a part of the 5th regiment, Stonewall brigade, under the command of Major Williams of Augusta Co. Va.[30] He was as much surprised to see me as I was to see him and in response to my enquiry, said he was going to dislodge some Yankee infantry in the field just ahead. I told him he was greatly mistaken and begged him not to fire into them as they were our troops, for I had passed by them, spoken with them, and seen them bearing the Virginia flag. At this Maj Williams, leaving his command behind a vine grown fence, went forward by himself, but soon returned and laughing at me for my mistake, told me I had been in the hands of a Yankee

West Va. regiment. At that time they claimed to be the only true Virginians and they carried the Virginia flag. My wet and muddy condition and my blue under-shirt deceived them as to colours. . . .

Maj. Williams soon scattered the Yankee infantry and joined in the general pursuit of them which followed our success on the right wing. The gun we lost was recaptured but much damaged. We took one of the Yankee guns instead. The shells which came over me, and from which I escaped in the ravine, were fired by Fremont's army from the opposite bank of the river, who did not hesi-tate to shell the battle field where then only dead and wounded men and hospi-tals were. . . .

When Maj. Williams moved in with his command, I hastened to seek my battery, stopping long enough by a fire where some wounded men lay in dread-ful suffering, to dry my wet clothes.

I toiled along through the fields and rough roads through bivouacs of troops and hospitals of wounded men. My shoes were worn out and my feet almost on the ground, so when I came to a Yankee with a good pair of shoes on and whom I supposed to be dead, I started to pull off his shoes. But he turned over and groaned so that I desisted. Thinking he would die slowly I sat down by a tree to wait until I could get his shoes. I went to sleep and when, after some time, I woke I found my Yankee dead, but some one else had gotten his shoes.

My command had gone on in the pursuit and meanwhile a picket line had been established as the outpost of the army. When I reached that, the com-manding officer, a Louisiana Colonel, not without some reason taking me for a straggler and not fully believing the impatient explanation which I gave him of my movements, to my inexpressible rage put me in the guard house, which meant under the guard of a sentinel posted near a fence corner. I had not long to wither under this disgrace when, to my great joy, Capt Poague road up at the head of the battery returning from the pursuit. Seeing me in the fence corner, and having understood that I had been killed or captured—for he had left me with the gun to fire into the faces of the enemy some hours before—he jumped from his horse and taking me by both hands almost embraced me in his plea-sure at seeing me again. This was followed by like manifestations from other members of the command, and, as you may understand, from my brother David, who feared that I had been lost. Fortunately all this occurred in the presence of the Colonel who had put me in the guard house and at whom I had not ceased to scowl as I sat in the fence corner. The Colonel was a gentleman and a gallant fellow and seeing that I was all right came forward, asked my pardon and offered his hand, which I heartily shook. Then the Captain, finding that I could scarcely walk, mounted me on a caison, where to my great joy, I found my blanket and oil cloth.

Riding thus along the road, I was overtaken by Dr. R. F. Baldwin . . . who was my family physician at home and a very near friend. He was a brother of Dr. John M. Baldwin and had married my first cousin Cary M. Barton.[31] Dr. Baldwin, seeing my bad physical condition, took me on his horse behind him, gave me some food from his haversack and some medicine, and carried me a considerable distance up the mountain, on top of which we camped that night.

I waited along the road for the battery to come and when it reached me I joined it on its toilsome march. My sickness, aggravated by the shock of the plunge I had taken in the water that morning and the dreadful fatigue of the day had almost used me up. I could only whisper my words and drag myself along. Reaching the top of the mountain about midnight I lay down on our oil cloths and blankets with a row of men and covered ourselves with a tarpaulin which was generally used for the cannon. But it was raining hard now, and human lives, for the time, were more important than the guns. I covered my face with my big felt hat which I had brought from home after our fight with Banks, but in the night I was waked by the rain and found some one had stolen my hat from off my face. A little blue Yankee cap did me service until I procured a better one.

The next morning I was only fit for the hospital, and was quite content to take my place in an ambulance to be driven down the mountain to Charlottesville . . . and the road to Charlottesville led not far from Hill and Dale where the Colstons lived. I turned in there and was received most hospitably. There I stayed some days until I was much improved and where I was treated with all the kindness it is possible any one could have shown me. What a change that was from camp and marches and war! That sweet peaceful neighbourhood where my school days for two years had been passed; the bright, pretty girls in the house, full of kindness to a soldier boy; and the nice good food and the comfortable bed. Only those who have experienced such sharp contrasts can understand them in all their force.[32]

Troops began passing in box cars and gondolas up towards Staunton . . . I mounted a box car with the other troops and had a rough ride to Waynesborough where my uncle Strother Jones was stationed as a Quarter Master, and from where I hoped to be able to reach my command. A few days at Waynesborough showed my unfitness to return to active service. . . .

After a five-day respite near Weyer's Cave, the Stonewall Brigade was hurriedly leaving the Valley to join General Lee's army in the defense of Richmond.

In the eight days after leaving Staunton May 7, Frank and the 2nd Virginia had marched and fought for 137 miles. The physical ordeal was telling on the men. The Barton boys' old friend and neighbor Powell Conrad, an engineer with the army, contracted typhoid and died May 24. Frank's condition limited him and he was not in action, following the army on its way north. This pressing march north, and his ill health, left Frank no time for his diary.

VI

Summer 1862

WINCHESTER REOCCUPIED
BATTLE OF GAINES' MILL

Winchester was in the Confederacy for a scant week before the Federal forces came back, continuing an occupation begun in March. Susan Jones had intended to live at Carysbrooke again, at least for the summer, but the swift return of the Yankees in early June caused her to reconsider. She remained at her father's house in Winchester, where her brother Peyton Clark and his family were living, but they were again besieged by Yankee attempts (perhaps official, perhaps not) to requisition the Clark house for use as a hospital. The officer's reasoning: its "elevated position, the air is pure about it."[1] Mary Jones somehow heard of this threat and immediately wrote to ask her sister-in-law to bring her family to Vaucluse, but Susan and Peyton between them prevailed and the Clark house was not taken over. (Mrs. Lee had previously remarked on "the timid, retiring women, such as Susan Jones, Mrs. Mary Jones & many others . . . who have kept off the Yankees, defended their property, & where depradations were committed have gone alone [for there are no men to go about with the women now] to Banks or Shields for redress.")[2] It was hard for anyone to tell which Federal general was in command where, and Mary had found a Provost Marshal who would issue passes without requiring the oath of allegiance, soon to become so burdensome for the people of Frederick County.

[LETTER OF MARY B. JONES TO SUSAN C. JONES]

Vaucluse   19th June 1862

My dearest Sue __ We were truly shocked to hear through *Mrs.* Davis that you had had added to your many trials that of leaving your home.[3] I have been in a fidget to get to you each day since, but we were not allowed to go on the road at all, two *companies* of Pickets were stationed between this & Newtown beside soldiers in the field, & the difficulties of the Pass, but I ascertained that Gen [Franz] Segill [Sigel] was to be in Middletown yesterday & went to see him to get a Pass & there found the Provost-Marshall had the power & will too to give it. So I hasten to avail myself of it to beg you to come at once to stay with us until this tyranny has past, & Frank dear Frank can stay at home.

Now, I want you to come just as you would have me come to you if your home seemed safer than mine. Bring all you can that you value, we can store them away safely, & just what servants you choose. I can employ any number & I reckon they are safer with you. We have plenty of meat & bread & pure air, & can do without luxuries for the present. It will be a great pleasure to us all to have you with us these trying days, & Annie is wild with delight at Louisa's coming.[4] They all had a party on Frank's birth-day [June 14] & Annie kept a plate of cake for her, but I'm afraid they have dwindled down before this.

My plan is—for you to let some of your things & Children come this evening with Mama [Mrs. Jones] to Miss Hatty's place & she can bring some in her Brother's carriage tomorrow & I will go in for you & the remainder the same day & continue to bring out gradually all you want as I am afraid to send the carriage empty or wagon at all. There is no difficulty now about a Pass—our Provost Marshall cut off all pledges & seems only anxious to protect the people from the present outrages & condemns Banks' course thoroughly.[5] He says he has nothing to do with this part of the valley now. We are under Gen. [John C.] Fremont I have always had a horror of him, but this Provost Marshall is very courteous, of-

Mary E. Barton Jones, Mrs. W. Strother Jones. (Jeffrey B. Potter)

fered me any guard I would call for & written protection & when I wrote him of his men breaking again into the Barn came over after 10 last night to enquire into it—Etc—but did not pay for it.

I do trust you can tell us something of our dear ones—we have not heard one word since they left . . . Mr. Jones health keeps me tremblingly anxious & I have to keep busy[6]—& the fall of ones so near takes from the secure feeling I had but it ought not when we think of our large family exposed it is wonderful we should not have more harmed. . . . We were able to move much of the furniture. Hoping to see you tomorrow & that now you will have no more to annoy & distress you & that you & yours will be contented to stay quietly with us. Believe me most aff—Your sister

Mary

It was certainly not clear to the people of Winchester what was going on south of them in the Valley, but the distinctly audible sound of cannon made them continually apprehensive and fearful for their loved ones. News was fragmentary and as often false as true. Jackson had been running the Federal forces ragged. The Battles of Cross Keys and Port Republic on June 9 had allowed the Confederate wagon train to escape south and caused Union Generals Shields and Fremont to retreat into the northern Shenandoah. But the Confederacy had paid dearly in casualties. The Rebels rested for a week at Brown's Gap and Weyer's Cave.

In just six weeks, Frank and the 2nd Virginia's new chaplain, Abner C. Hopkins, had formed a "warm friendship." Hopkins recalled the men's camaraderie in the midst of a hard campaign, and this brief respite as particularly pleasant.

[MEMOIR OF ABNER C. HOPKINS]

Jackson had driven Milroy back to Franklin, and Banks from the Valley, had defeated Fremont at Cross Keys and Shields at Port Republic, and his army was enjoying a few days of rest near Weyers Cave. This day we were all sitting around the fire at H'd Qtrs talking over the hardship and glories of that campaign and in anticipating amusing ourselves as to what we should say "when this cruel war is over." Col. Botts said "wont we have a heap to tell our wives about it all? And, Jones, when you come to see me we'll talk Mrs Botts off to bed. Presently she'll come to the head of the steps and call me but we'll talk on and on into the small hours: and after awhile she'll come again and tell me, do let

Major Jones go to bed; but still we'll talk." Major Jones replied "Yes and you'll come to see me and the same thing will happen at my house. Mrs Jones will call and call, and finally will ask, 'do you mean to keep Col Botts up all night? It is long past midnight!!' "[7]

Although Frank would have had time for his journal, perhaps he felt too unwell to have any inclination to write; he did not resume until June 22. In mid-June, Jackson debated with Gen. Robert E. Lee their possible next actions. Although Jackson wanted to move on Winchester, the needed reinforcements were not available—and Lee, now in command at Richmond, needed him there. On the seventeenth Jackson's army began a long march east to defend their capital from McClellan's advance. Frank's next entry was written along the way, from the Piedmont where he had encountered some cousins.

[DIARY OF FRANK B. JONES]

Sunday 22nd June   Camp near Gordonsville
We reached here yesterday after a long, hot & very dusty march. We camped the night before on J. C. R. Taylor's land. He came over to see me & begged me to go over & spend the night. I declined, however, but went in the morning to breakfast. He was very kind. As I rode on to join the Regt. I passed Edge Hill & rode up & introduced myself to the family. I was kindly received & claimed as a relative. Regretted not to see Col. [T. J.] Randolph.[8] We are halting here preparatory, one supposes, to take the cars tomorrow for Richmond, or near there. A great battle is impending in which we are to take part. May the Lord give me cheerful courage to do my whole duty, sad & disagreeable as it may be, & shd I fall, may He receive me, a most unworthy servant truly but as one blessed & pardoned through Faith in the blood of my dear Saviour. Mr. Hopkins preached today & the Sabbath is being spent I hope as it shd be.

Jackson's army continued to Mechanicsville, northeast of the Confederate capital, where Lee's army was engaged in a struggle to repulse the Federal forces from "the gates of Richmond." These were known as the Seven Days' Battles, and were costly for both sides. Ultimately the Confederates prevailed and the Federal forces withdrew. On the twenty-seventh, the 2nd Virginia was engaged in the Battle of Gaines' Mill. Too weak from diarrhea to participate in the attack on foot, Frank Jones joined it on horseback. "Instantly Major Jones seemed to forget his ailments, dashed to the front waving his broad brim hat and cheering

most lustily," recalled Abner Hopkins. "Officers and men engaged in the charge
testified to the gallantry of [Col. James W.] Allen and Jones and in respect to
Major Jones that his conduct was an inspiration."9 In the charge on McGehee's
Hill, he was struck by a canister at almost the same time that his old friend Col.
Allen and the regiment's Lt. Col. Raleigh T. Colston were hit—the former
mortally wounded.10 Col. William S. H. Baylor, 5th Virginia Infantry, described
the charge.

[LETTER OF COL. WILLIAM S. H. BAYLOR]

For three quarters of a mile a shower of shell fell around us but our boys
kept up gallantly through the thick woods and miry swamps until we reached an
open and wide field, which gradually ascended into a commanding hill, where
the enemy was posted already receiving us with his artillery and now with his
small arms. Our lines were thinned by many having fallen by exhaustion in the
terrible effort to keep up at the rate we were going, and I do not think the brigade numbered over 800 now. It was already small. Our lines were formed by a
[*illegible*] of intuition and with a yell that must have frightened the souls of our
adversaries. We moved on in line of battle, my regiment the extreme left, the
2nd next on my right, and so on. We stopped but once, and that when poor
Allen and the beloved Jones fell. The 2nd stopped and as I was ordered to keep
in line I put myself into action with my trusty mountain marksmen. It was now
quite dark, and the 2nd only hesitated a moment, and then their yell told me to
charge, and in two minutes more my boys had taken the guns, but did not stop
to triumph until they had pressed the reluctant Yankees a hundred and fifty
yards beyond. The entire hill was gained, and gained I may say by a handful of
men against a much superior force. . . . If there ever lived a pure man, he was
Frank Jones. With almost everything that could be desired to make him a
friend, he possessed that unpretending and yet ever noticeable piety which is
the brightest and rarest of soldierly qualities, together with so much good sense
and gentleness of manner that his influence was felt wherever he went and
extended even beyond the circle of his immediate acquaintance. His loss will be
long felt by many friends, but who can repair the loss to the bereaved companion of his life and the dear little ones now fatherless!11

Frank spent the night on the battlefield and his leg was amputated at a field
hospital the next day. Mr. Hopkins, the chaplain, spent the night on the field
with him.

[MEMOIR OF ABNER C. HOPKINS]

. . . When the Surgeon J. A. Straith and I reached the field over which they had charged these two officers were lying on the field.[12]

The Major suffered accutely from the moment of his wounding and his sufferings grew more and more accute till his nervous system gave way. Some time after night he asked me to give him some water to drink. I brought it but so nervous was he that when I came near him he exclaimed "Oh don't come to me" and it was some time before he could receive the water.

He was taken back to the Cold Harbor house and put into a bed. The next day he asked me to go into Richmond and, if possible make arrangements for him to be cared for at Mr Haxall's, this I did and also arranged for a comfortable ambulance to be sent for him early the next morning.[13]

In Richmond, one of the doctors attending Frank was Dr. Howard T. Barton, Strother Jones's brother-in-law, and a surgeon at the army hospital at Chimborazo.

[LETTER OF HOWARD T. BARTON TO W. STROTHER JONES]

Richmond July 5th 1862
4½ a.m.—

My dear Strother—

I received your letter yesterday & hasten to reply, though with great distress that I cannot give you a better account of poor Frank. He was wounded severely in or near his right knee, the thigh badly fractured & after a consultation the next morning, Saturday 28th, his limb had to be sacrificed. The shock has been very great. We heard here, that he had been killed _ but after James [Jones] & I had most diligently enquired, we learned, that he was being brought by Dr. Davis from the battlefield in a field infirmary to Mrs. Hardgrove's S.W. corner of Grace & 28th Sts (& got there Sunday afternoon just after he did) where he has remained in a delightful room, & with every attention, from ladies & gentlemen.[14]

He did not stand the trip here well, though very cheerful & for some days he was doing well, but for several days he has been showing very decided Typhoid symptoms & now for two or three days has been delirious, & the pulse weak. We all feel exceedingly anxious about him. He has Dr. Davis with him constantly, when not at the Hospital, as he occupies his room, or has exchanged with the lady of the house, the use of her parlor, the very nicest & finest room, fine healthy position—every comfort & attention. Wm Clark & [*smear*] are with James, and Dr Robert [F.] Baldwin also [*tear*] the house, where Dr Davis has been boarding, & [*tear*] him constantly. Miss Mary Sherrard, Mr. Walker & others assisting to add to his comfort.[15] I have been so busy, I have not been able to stay but two nights. I see him though very often. Dr Davis is not at all hopeful of his recovery. I am very anxious about him, but hope his case is not desperate. We will do all we can, you may be sure—& he enjoys every advantage & greater than he could have at home—except the comfort of his family's presence. This now he could not fully appreciate.

I am grieved to hear of your being sick, as I know you would desire of all things to come. I will telegraph you at Charlottesville care of Dr J. S. Davis if Frank should not live, & there can be no use in your coming on—as both his other brothers are here—but I should be very glad to see you—& if you are well enough, think this will reach you in time for you to come even if our worst fears are realized. As I said I am hopeful—his stump looks pretty well . . . yrs very devotedly

Howard[16]

Frank died July 9. With the cruel uncertainties of wartime communications, especially to occupied Winchester, Susan Jones did not learn that Frank had been badly wounded until July 13, after her brother Peyton Clark had read it in a Maryland paper.[17] She and Frank's mother immediately set off, with little Ran, to go to him. They went as far as Middletown, where they chanced to meet a Newtown neighbor, Mr. Allemong, who told them that Frank was dead. (As had been the case with John Baldwin's death, false reports, nourishing unfounded hopes, continued to come in.)[18] Frank's mother's first opportunity to write her Florida cousins, the Parkhills, about the summer's dreadful events did not occur until Winchester was again part of the Confederacy in the fall.

[LETTER OF ANN C. R. JONES TO LUCY R. PARKHILL]

Winchester, October 15, 1862

Where to begin, or how to go on, in reply to your dear letter, my beloved friend, is difficult for me to determine, I feel almost overwhelmed by the many things I should like to say, & the impossibility there is for condensing them in the limits of this paper.[19] . . . Untill your letter reached me I had not heard a word of your heavy bereavement.[20] I had been trying to find out something about your son in all the trouble that was falling around, but had failed to do so.

Oh! how I rejoice in his conversion, God be praised for all his mercies! & may the blessing of our Heavenly Father rest upon the widow, the fatherless, & all the bereaved ones of his dear family. . . .

I have not been able to go to Fauquier since last February, twelve months, the Yankees were terribly bad in that neighborhood during the spring & summer. Families either forsook their homes, or remained for their protection, the last plan was deemed best for us, & *so* it proved to be, our dwelling would have been desolated, *left* to their tender mercies. Mary & myself were both brave showed no fear whatever, & in the kindness of Providence, we had to deal with a better set than those that infested Fauquier, a letter of protection was given us, & when that was disregarded, a Guard was allowed. We lost corn & hay & 22 sheep, but fared *very well* as times went, two only of Strother's own servants are lost, & none of mine—mine are women & children & not able to rough it in the way that freedom would have imposed upon them.

My son, Strother, was taken sick on the night of the twenty-fifth of May, that was the day you know of, the battle of Winchester. . . . Marshall's Captain [W. E. Cutshaw] was very badly wounded, & Mr. Barton & Fanny brought him to their house, where he staid untill his Mother could take him home. I suppose he was there fully two months.[21] The shock of Marshall's death brought Diarhea upon Strother [Jones]. He went home *very sick*, & has never been well since. We were free from our enemies but one week. Strother had scarcely been out of bed two days, when *all* my Precious ones, he amongst the rest, had to leave. Consequently, he could not have the care & the comforts of home. Strother Barton had a *sharp* attack of Typhoid fever, & I am very sure suffered for nothing that Strother could do for him.[22] . . . He came home in despite of the Yankees.[23] . . . Strother's health seems shaken beyond ever attaining its former position. Yet his recovery *this* far was exceedingly doubtful at one time, & we do not now know God's will concerning him. Oh! *may* he be spared!

It was on the first day of June I parted with them on their retreat, & I never heard one word from, or of, my two Younger children [Frank and Bev] untill the 13th of July. On that day I went to church in New Town. On my return, I found a travelling trunk in our Porch. I enquired immediately. It was Susan's. She had heard *that* morning that our hearts' best earthly treasure had received a wound, she set off to go to him, & I, of course, with her. I was then informed for the first time of the wound. It had been kept from me. We had not proceeded far beyond Middletown when we met an acquaintance just from Richmond, & by dint of enquiries, learned what had happened. I ordered that the carriage turn around, & we got home the best way we could.

I have been supported beyond what I could have believed. God has been most merciful to me. What I have lost, it would take time for me to tell, & why should I tell it. He was my chief earthly joy. . . . It might not be for *me* to say *all* he was, but I know that he is in Heaven. . . . He was most thoroughly ready, & had no regret but that of not seeing his Wife, his Mother & his Children. Our getting to him was impossible. Therefore our ignorance was fortunate. His last letter to his Wife came afterwards, & the sweet Piety that breathed in it was so precious. The last notice in his Diary, written five days before the battle, was a great joy to my heart, showing his Christian feelings, & readiness to meet his end. He was wounded in the battle at Gaines Mill on the 27th June. An amputation above the knee was necessary. Beverley heard of the wound, sought him out & was detailed as Nurse, so he never left him. Dr. Davis our Neighbour, is Surgeon in Richmond, has a high position there, heard of the wound, went himself & brought him with great care to his boarding house. He had a delightful airy room given him, every care, every attention, every necessary, every Luxury, was accorded him. He wanted for nothing . . . Mr. [Cornelius] Walker says he literally fell asleep. No trouble to him in his departure, from what I can learn. . . . The shock on his System of so terrible a wound & the amputation succeeding it, he never rallied from, & could not have lived as long as he did, but for the extraordinary care taken of him. His Colonel was killed, the Lieutenant Colonel received a wound in another battle afterwards, which caused his death.[24] & my Boy was the Major, *all are gone.*[25]

When the Federal armies returned to Winchester in June, it was with renewed determination to secure the area, in ways which made life burdensome for the secessionist inhabitants. It was important to be able to go to the farms outside town to oversee them and to supplement the meager daily supplies usually available, but there were travel restrictions. "Dr. R. T. Baldwin went out to camp to the Provost, for a pass to go in the country; he was refused, & the Dr. shook his fist in the Provost's face, & cursed him; he was ordered to the guard house, but he insisted on seeing [Gen. A. S. Piatt], who released him but without the pass."[26] The Federals strengthened the fortifications and regularly showed their might by firing over town. The missiles may have been wood, but as Mrs. Lee remarked, they would kill anyone they hit, and it was certainly alarming to have the enemy taking the town's range. They began to act, although irregularly, on their previously stated requirements regarding the oath of allegiance. It was particularly important to them to exact this from the leading citizens in hopes of setting an example, or from anyone else whom they considered suspect or influ-

ential. Within the southern citizenry it was a terribly divisive issue, the more extreme secessionists vowing they would refuse the oath when offered. When Gen. Julius White took command in late July, he was expected to be more lenient. But Mr. Barton and Mr. Burwell went to camp to get passes and found that the oath was now a condition of being granted one, and arrest the alternative. Although they were not detained, it was said that soon those who refused the oath would be imprisoned or sent from their homes to Confederate territory—"sent through the lines." At the same time, General White attempted to ingratiate himself with the more moderate local leaders to achieve his ends. David Barton and Philip Williams—attorneys in an age when their function was more that of mediation than confrontation and whose métier was compromise and negotiation—attempted to work with different Federal commanders to find ways to ease the life of the civilians. With General White, they arrived at a way to modify the oath "to suit their elastic consciences," acerbically wrote Mrs. Lee. "This war develops new friendships, &, I fear, may destroy old ones."[27] For their pains, Barton and Williams were scorned and vilified by some of their more extreme neighbors. Mrs. Lee enumerated those of her mind who viewed the modified oath as a "Yankee trap"—the Baldwins, the Conrads, Dr. Holliday, John Bell, and the remaining bankers—as opposed to the moderate party that included Mayor John B. T. Reed and other ministers. She was worried that Peyton Clark was wavering, because he had been under house arrest on accusation of spying on the Yankee fortifications from the Clark rooftop. After a wave of arrests (which proved to be inconsequential) and the recall of passes, the issuance of passes again became a more random thing. In late August, Anna Jones managed to obtain a pass and went out of town hoping to see her brother Marshall whom she had heard was in the vicinity. Lizzie Sherrard and Helen Holliday (both twenty-one and daughters of bank officers who had probably refugeed with the Farmers' Bank) tried to get a pass to go in search of Lizzie's father, said to be nearby. They were refused, so attempted to sneak through the lines. In crawling through a ravine, not only were Lizzie's knees "excoriated" but she was seen and thwarted by Federal pickets.[28] The oath as an issue passed from significance as the Confederate Army in eastern Virginia gathered themselves for a new offensive and put pressure on the forces occupying Winchester.

In March, the Kernstown prisoners had half expected to be sent to a colder climate, but went instead to a fort just twenty-five miles from Rannie's older sister's home in Maryland. Until Winchester was occupied by Federal forces in March, Jane and her family had been cut off and largely out of communication with their families in Virginia. Now with Winchester, however temporarily, part of the Union, the family could write and visit—as did Jane's parents and sisters. Maryland, a border state, was firmly under Union control, but not quiescent, and the Sheilds, in Cecil County, found many Southern sentiments, which were doubtless reinforced by visitors from the Confederacy. In this atmosphere, the Sheilds carried on their own quiet rebellion: apparently the Reverend Sheild stopped—or never started—or in any case, "habitually omitted to use the Prayer for the President." Some parishioners protested to the Bishop, who wrote him about the "allegation" in October 1861. Receiving no satisfactory answer, the Bishop and the Committee nevertheless "unanimously" decided to overlook this breach, deciding that "ecclesiastical trials in the present temper of the community cannot be expected to conduce either to edification or to peace."[29] It can be presumed that the Reverend Sheild carried on his own protest for the duration, while the Sheild family gave "aid and comfort" when the opportunity arose less than six months later, with Rannie and the other Winchester boys at Fort Delaware.

[MEMOIR OF RANDOLPH BARTON]

On the 30th or 31st of March . . . we marched through nasty snow, rain and mud down Calvert Street, past my present office to Baltimore Street, to Lombard to the wharf of the Ericsson Line, and thence we went to Fort Delaware. There we remained until August 5, 1862, suffering many discomforts. . . .[30]

Our particular group, when in Fort Delaware, consisted of Robert Burwell, George Burwell, Bushrod Washington, George Washington, Willie Barton, E. P. C. Lewis and others, whom now I cannot recall.[31]

One of the military companies in charge was a volunteer company made up largely of young gentlemen from Philadelphia. When they learned that Willie Barton and myself were receiving presents (as we did most bountifully, of choice eatables and clothes) from the Ettings, Moncure Robinsons and others most favorably known in Philadelphia, their native civility seemed to increase, and we at least had nothing to complain of so far as discipline was concerned.[32] Major Gibson, a regular army officer, was in command of the fort, and permitted my father and mother, visiting [the Sheilds] in Cecil County, Maryland, to come to see me.[33]

Some unknown friend in Philadelphia asked permission of the Major for the army tailor to take my measure for a suit of clothes and soon I received from that intensely Union city a splendid gray uniform perhaps the only Rebel uniform ever made in that city. Who the donor was I have never discovered, peace to his or her ashes.

The prisoners were allowed to receive mail but not to send any.[34] *Rannie saved a tiny note from a Baltimore lady who did much to help Confederate prisoners. Mrs. John Hanson Thomas's husband had been imprisoned after voting for Maryland's secession, and her elder son was with the Confederate Army near Winchester.*

[LETTER OF ANN C. THOMAS TO RANDOLPH BARTON]

Baltimore June 10th

My dear cousin,

I tried very hard to visit you and your friends when you were staying in Baltimore but could not get permission. We sent you clothing and food however, which I hope made you at least comfortable.

I have sent on a box containing some little comforts for you, your cousin, Mr. Barton, Mr. Burwell & Mr. Washington.

I hope you will write me, if there is anything you or your friends desire. Have no feeling about the matter, for I have the deepest sympathy for all prisoners, and particularly those from my own State.

My husband was a political prisoner for $5\frac{1}{2}$ months which makes me wonderfully sympathetic to all who have lost their liberty. I am thankful you are under the charge of Capt. Gibson who is represented as being so kind and humane.

My own dear son is in the Army near Winchester and I am glad to know he is near your Father and Mother who will minister to him if he should be sick or wounded.[35]

Will you remember me kindly to them when you write?

God bless you my dear young friend.

Yours most affect'ly

Annie C. Thomas

P.S. Should you desire anything write to

Mrs. Jno Hanson Thomas
Baltimore

Rannie and the Kernstown captives had languished at Fort Delaware as winter turned to spring and eventually to hot and humid summer. They were extraor-

dinarily fortunate in being the first prisoners sent to Fort Delaware, as it was not yet in the overcrowded, disease-ridden state that brought it later notoriety. Built on swampy Pea Patch Island about a mile from shore in Delaware Bay, it was unhealthy in several ways, at all seasons. In addition, food was inadequate and often spoiled and the water often polluted. Imprisonment was debilitating at best, and the men required varying periods of "recruiting" when released. In midsummer, the Kernstown prisoners and perhaps a thousand others were exchanged from Fort Delaware and after a week by ship arrived within Confederate territory near Richmond.

[MEMOIR OF RANDOLPH BARTON]

On the 5th we embarked on the old steamer Merrimac, formerly of the Collins Line, and on August 12, 1862, having sailed up the James in river boats which we took at Fortress Monroe passing on our way McClellan's Army, cowering on the banks of the river at Harrison's Landing, under the protection of gunboats. We landed at Aiken's Landing about twelve miles below Richmond.[36] . . . I remember most vividly the scenes of the disembarkment—the intense eagerness with which the wan and bleached Confederates left the boats and almost kissed the soil of old Virginia. I remember the splendid stream of sparkling water pouring from the pump as the almost famished Confederates surrounded the well. The want of pure water would have killed half of us if we had stayed at Fort Delaware a few months longer; old barrels regardless of former contents, were filled at Brandywine Creek, I think, loaded on river craft, brought under a blazing sun to Fort Delaware and, warm and putrid, was doled out to us. The Aiken's Landing water was nectar. Leaving Aiken's, the crowd, some twelve hundred, started on foot up the river road to Richmond. When we reached a point within six miles of the city, and safely within Confederate lines, we sank exhausted on the ground and slept profoundly.

Early the next morning we entered the city, and my group went to the American Hotel, Main Street, afterwards in the conflagration of 1865, destroyed and never rebuilt . . . but well recalled by me as our final resting-place after months of severe trial. Willie Barton, Bob Burwell and one or two others of my "clique" entered the hotel looking like the "Dusty Roads" and the "Weary Willies" of these days. We were, with manifest doubts in the face of the hotel clerk, assigned to attic rooms, from which we emerged later, clad in clean underclothes and I, particularly, well dressed in my handsome Confederate suit. . . .

My pay had accumulated to something over two hundred dollars. I drew it from cousin John Ambler, paymaster, and promptly lost it by leaving it under my pillow in a hotel in Lynchburg, where we spent the night en route, a few days later to Nelson County, Virginia.37

After recuperating there for some three weeks we proceeded to join our army. By rail I went to Gordonsville, and from there, on foot, and bare feet at that, for my boots, a Fort Delaware acquisition, I could not wear, I walked to Berryville, via Culpepper Court House, Fauquier White Sulphur Springs, Warrenton, Upperville, the Pot-House and Leesburg.38 From Berryville we went to Winchester in a hired wagon.

On August 1, Dr. Robert F. Baldwin had been transferred to the hospital at Lovingston, Nelson County, so perhaps that is why his young brother-in-law Willie and Rannie went there to recuperate. Willie in fact was so spent he entered the hospital for two weeks for "debilitas," probably scurvy. Most of the family was out of action in August, but David Barton was in the midst of the fray. As the Stonewall Brigade, with the Army of Northern Virginia, moved on to the offensive, battles were fought again on familiar ground in northern Virginia. His commander's official reports were sparse, but in latter years, Captain Poague remembered that at Cedar Mountain on August 9, "at one time we were on the edge of a serious disaster . . . from [a] rear attack, my guns were rendered useless, being surrounded by our infantry. . . . In the melee the most conspicuous persons, as I remember it, were General Jackson, General W. B. Taliaferro and David Barton."39 In mid-August, David was transferred from the Rockbridge Artillery to Cutshaw's Battery (formerly the Newtown Artillery), and was elected Lieutenant on August 19, in his brother Marshall's place. Bev Jones related,"Their Co wished to elect an officer . . . & it rested between me, & David Barton, & as one of the men told me afterwards that they concluded that they had tried one Barton (afterwards killed) & thought they would try another."40 David was in action at the Second Battle of Manassas August 29; there he commanded a battery of five guns placed at the focus of an attack at Sudley Ford, which was repelled in the course of the Confederate victory.41

The glove and dispatch bag belonged to Barton soldiers. (Edith Barton Sheerin, John Schwartz photo)

As for the rest of the family: Tom

Marshall had been appointed major in the reorganization of the 7th Virginia
Cavalry following Ashby's death. In a skirmish at Orange Court House on Au-
gust 2, he was surrounded, unhorsed by a sabre cut on the head, and captured;
a week later he found himself in Capitol Prison in Washington. Fortunately he
was exchanged in little more than a month. Strother Barton had contracted
typhoid fever, probably in Winchester, and was out of service for most of the
summer.[42] *Robby, recuperating from the arduous Valley Campaign, was well*
enough by late June to seek out his elder brother to nurse him. They too made
their way to the Lovingston Hospital.

[MEMOIR OF ROBERT T. BARTON]

At Waynesborough, I learned of the serious illness at some place near
Staunton, of my brother Strother. I set out at once to find him and take care of
him.

I had no money and did not like to ask my uncle [Strother Jones] for it, even
if he had it himself, which I doubt. . . .

Wandering along the street and wondering whether I might venture to ask
some of my acquaintances in Staunton for a loan, I met Col. John B. Baldwin,
that able and distinguished lawyer and most excellent gentleman, and he asked
me, after some general conversation, if I had *any engagement* for the evening. I
replied that I had not and he asked me to come to his house to tea. To this too,
I readily assented. So I went there to tea and enjoyed it very much and almost
equally as much the society of his pretty sisters-in-law, Miss [Jennie] and Miss
Nely Peyton, whom I already knew, and whose subsequent lives, I believe, have
not been very happy.[43] I think it was subsequently (not, I am sure, on that
occasion) that I formed a sort of marriage engagement with one of the young
ladies, which one I do not now remember, but it was all in fun and never came
to anything, as I never expected it would. When we parted however it was with
promises of daily letters and pledges of undying affection. No letters were ever
written by either of us, but when we met again which was some years afterwards in a train of cars, the young lady sighing heavily said to me, "How could I
have survived our long and cruel separation, had it not been for your daily letters?" These evanescent love affairs were not uncommon during the war but
many of them were more serious and not so harmless as this one of mine. . . .

I rose very early and started into the country on foot. I had no breakfast and
only a general idea of the locality in which my brother had been left. Resting by
the roadside a man came by leading one horse and riding the other. He offered

me a seat on his led horse which I accepted and this carried me not far from my destination, which was the house of a Mrs. Moorman about six miles from Staunton.[44]

There I found my brother Strother very ill with typhoid fever and I took his care in hand. Nothing could have been kinder than the Moormans were, and eventually he got well and he and I went together to Nelson Co. Va., he to go to a private house to board until he could get entirely well and where he met my brother Rannie and Willie Barton, both just exchanged from prison and trying to get well enough to join their commands.[45] I stayed in the hospital and was well enough to act as the Clerk, and this continued for perhaps a month.

While I was at Mrs. Moorman's the great [Seven Days] battles around Richmond had taken place and my uncle Frank Jones had been killed. . . .[46]

While I was in Nelson County, the second battle of Manassas took place [August 29–30] and the movement of Lee's army into Maryland cleared the Valley and left Winchester free once more. This made it proper to remove the general equipment of the Nelson hospital and I gladly got a transfer to Winchester.[47] I do not now recall how I got to Winchester, but suppose that it was via Staunton and thence down the Valley by stage. But I was very glad to be there once more in my much loved home. I continued to do some hospital work while at Winchester. . . .

VII

$\mathscr{S}eptember - \mathscr{D}ecember$
1862

WINCHESTER RETURNED TO THE CONFEDERACY
FREDERICKSBURG CAMPAIGN

Lee's first invasion of the North brought pressure to bear on the suddenly out-numbered Federal forces in Winchester. The approaching Confederate force sent a flag of truce allowing time for a peaceful evacuation. The Yankees with-drew September 2 in the middle of the night, blowing up their powder maga-zine. The enormous explosion blew in windows and doors in town and was felt as far away as Berryville and Capon Springs, and, Mrs. Lee was told, shook the house at Vaucluse.[1] They fired the public depot and many warehouses on Mar-ket Street in the center of town. The terrified populace was sure the Yankees were burning the town, as had often been threatened, and frantically readied themselves to leave their homes. Providentially this proved to be unnecessary. Lee's advance culminated in the Battle of Sharpsburg—Antietam, the Federals called it, for the creek—in western Maryland. The battle did not produce a clearcut victory, and Lee's vastly outnumbered army retreated across the Potomac. That day, September 17, remains the bloodiest day in American his-tory. Strother and Willie did not cross to Maryland; the 2nd Virginia was on provost guard duty near Martinsburg. David was in the thick of the battle as was the Rockbridge Artillery.

One wounded Rockbridge gunner, Ned Moore, found a haven with the Bartons in Winchester. "David Barton, a former member of our company, but now in command of Cutshaw's battery, kindly sent his ambulance, with instruc-tions that I be taken to his father's house in Winchester, which place, in com-pany with a wounded man of his battery, I reached on the following day. At Mr.

Barton's I found my cousin and theirs, Robert Barton, of Rockbridge, on sick leave, and a Doctor Grammer, who dressed my wound; and although unable to leave my bed, I intensely enjoyed the rest and kindness received in that hospitable home, which was repeatedly made desolate by the deaths of its gallant sons who fell in battle."[2]

Winchester was overwhelmed with wounded Confederates; of those, the fortunate ones were those who were taken into homes rather than accommodated in the inadequate medical facilities thrown together on short notice. Mrs. Lee and other women fell to again, and organized nursing and donations of money, food, and clothing to attempt to provide for those in the impromptu hospitals. Nevertheless, the citizens tried to carry on a normal life, and fall meant the beginning of the school year. Bolling had received an appointment to the VMI when it reopened in January 1862, and had for some reason (possibly his father's finances) not taken it up at the time. In spite of his evident unwillingness, his parents' plans for his education and their desire to have him in a relatively safe place prevailed. By late September, Ned Moore was sufficiently improved to travel south with Bolling and another Winchester boy, Theodore W. Reed: "After a sojourn of a few days, leave to go home was given me by the department surgeon, and at four o'clock in the morning, with young Bolling, Barton and Reid serving as my crutches (on their way to the Virginia Military Institute), I was put in the stage-coach at the front door."[3]

David W. Barton, whose flourishing law practice had been disrupted by the war, endeavored to find other revenues necessitated by the continuing pressure of his late brother's debts, which he and his brother Robert had guaranteed. He concluded that he must sell some of his properties and may have decided to sell the Shady Elm woolen factory among the first. He had a ready buyer: its manager, John C. Gaver, who had probably been contemplating the purchase for some time. Selling the mill at this time may have been a bad decision; business was thriving due to the demands of the military. The mill's active business included a new contract with the VMI, which of course could no longer obtain cadet cloth from its Northern sources. Barton corresponded in October with Gen. F. H. Smith, the institute's superintendent, expressing his preference for being paid in Confederate or Virginia bonds, Confederate currency being of little use in Winchester.

After Sharpsburg, the Confederates had withdrawn to northern Virginia, completing this movement September 23. Jackson established his headquarters at Bunker Hill a few days later. For most of the fall, the Stonewall Brigade occupied various camps east of Winchester, the hometown of many of its members. Rannie had recuperated from his months as a prisoner of war and *returned to the army at Bunker Hill on October 1. He enlisted as second lieuten-ant in Company K, 2nd Virginia Infantry, and was in time for some action at Kearneysville October 17.*

Doubtless remembering the homesickness of his year at the institute, Rannie was one of the first to write to Bolling. The following is the earliest of the sur-viving letters so carefully saved by the young VMI cadet.

[LETTER OF RANDOLPH BARTON TO BOLLING W. BARTON]

Winchester Oct 4th

Dear Boly,

I commenced a letter to you some days ago but was so lazy that I did not fin-ish it. Knowing how pleasant a letter from home is I have resolved to write. First I will let you know what I am doing here. I reported to my regt and entered upon my duties some 10 days since, the same day an election was or-dered to fill the vacancies in the army. I was recommended by the officers of the 2nd for a 3rd Lieut in Capt Stewarts comp. and am now awaiting the rank. Brother D[avid] is here on business he expects to be Junior 1st Lieut in Carpen-ters battery, composed of Carpenters & Cutshaws joined. Brother Tom [Marshall] has joined his Regt.[4] Brother S[trother] is acting adjutant of 2nd. I have been out to Vaucluse lately, took a little hunt, killed one squirrel & 2 par-tridges. The latter are abundant. It is two dry and the weeds are two high to hunt. Don does his duty however, that spotted Slut Dons pup stands beauti-fully.[5] Shot is scarce as hens-teeth. Uncle Strother is doing well. Robby is clerk in the Hospital. Johnny B[aldwin] left for Staunton and Lexington yesterday, you will no doubt see him. How is Bengy.[6] The corn at Springdale is very fine. Pa is very much interested in farming. Lud Baldwin is going to Hampden Sydney. Johnny has *joined the church.*[7] [Cousin] Robert was here a few days ago, sick; he has recovered and has joined his regt. Lew Fitch is courier to Jack-son.[8] Ma sends her love to you, as all do. . . . Give my love to Cousins G & M, remember me to all my friends.[9] I expect you find homesickness the hardest of your troubles, but recollect what you are gaining and study hard. Can you pos-sibly get me a pair of No 8 shoes. Send them by Johnny Baldwin also some shot and caps. Write soon to

your

devoted bro

R.J. Barton

P.S. Aunt Silla says she is much obliged to you for seeing her sister; she misses you very much. Sukey sends her love and wants to send you a box of eatables.[10]

Robby Barton, acknowledging finally that he was not fit for the rigors of the "foot cavalry," set about obtaining a medical discharge and transfer to another branch of the service. At a meeting of the Medical Examining Board, October 31, he was discharged because of "phthisis"—consumption.

[MEMOIR OF ROBERT T. BARTON]

My parents and friends now insisted that I had experimented enough to demonstrate the fact that I could not continue in active service, so I consented to give up all idea of returning to the field. I was offered a place under my uncle James F. Jones who held a Commission in the ordinance department, having in special charge the manufacture of nitre, so essential to war and yet so scarce in the Confederacy.[11] I was to be entitled to the pay, horses, and general rank of Captain, but no commission was then to be issued to me. My duties required me to have in charge about 150 men detailed from the army, as unfit for active service, and to occupy them in various points in Rockbridge, Augusta, Rockingham and Shenandoah Counties in gathering the dry earth from caves and from under old houses and extracting the nitre from it. My headquarters were at Staunton where I had to report each month. . . .

The Bartons must have been relieved to have two sons relatively safe. David W. Barton, overseeing the harvest at Springdale, evidently had not known the exact time of his youngest son's departure. Two weeks later he wrote Bolling the news from home. He left space for a note from his wife, with messages from Sukey, the cook.

[LETTER OF DAVID W. BARTON TO BOLLING W. BARTON, WITH POSTSCRIPT OF FANNIE L. BARTON]

Winchester

Dear Bolling

I was very sorry that I missed seeing you as you passed Springdale & especially as I saw the stage passing & might have overhaulled it if I had known you were there. I got up at day light that morning———had walked up to see Tim Bryan go work in the lane near the orchard & was standing within 100 yards of the Pike when the stage passed.

You express the hope that I have done threshing & have finished the ricks near the Barn but nothing more. Have my corn to cut up which is now about me, seeding to do which I can now begin as we had a fine rain last night, the

The gristmill at Bartonsville. (Edith Barton Sheerin)

first for many weeks. I have secured a fine supply of Winter apples, probably 100 Bushels. They are in great demand, readily bring $2 per Bushel.

But every article here has got to be extravagantly high——————potatoes $4 & $5 pr Bushel. Flour $12 per bl. Oats $1.25 & corn $2. Hay $25–$30 per ton, wood $10 pr ton & hard to get atall. Luckily the weather has been warm & the winter has kept off.

Your brothers have been a good deal with us, Robert has an office in the Hospital here. David & Ranny got leave to stay here some time. Strother is busy in camp at Bunkers Hill. Every thing seems quiet now in the Army but we expect a movement soon. Each Army is on its own side of the river & since the Battle of Sharpsburg little has been done but to gather in stragglers & drill the troops. Our men seem to be in fine spirits & speak hopefully of the future. They are certainly not scared. The straggling soldiers going up & down the road have been very troublesome & have done us a good deal of harm. They are more troublesome than the Yankees, because they go any where without fear.

Would it not be as well in these scarce times to have your pigeons killed & eaten. We killed a few the other day; they helped out very much.

I fear Genl Smith will be disapointed in his cloth the Army having impressed it as Mr. Gaver was making it. Gaver has no doubt written to the General explaining all. Mr. Russell gave one big promise to get the wool & I hope has attended to it.

I have more now to do than ever, the office business having revived & the former still requiring attention.

I leave a little room for your mother to write. I hope you will study hard and try to make up for last term.

Remember me to Theo. Reed & believe me

Yrs affectionately D.W. Barton

My darling Child

I only write a few lines to say how much I miss you and to explain why I do not send a box of eatables to you. We have no sugar for cakes and indeed scarce any thing that would be nice to send.

Suckey [desires?] much love and [wishes?] she had butter and some of her good bread every day for you. Write as often as you can and strive to be cheerful and studious.

God bless you my beloved child, and make you his own.

yr devoted Mother
FLB__

His parents' letter, and his grandmother's to her cousin Lucy, reflect the inflation and shortages that beset Winchester whether in Yankee or Rebel hands. Grandmother Jones was in town staying at the Clark house with her widowed daughter-in-law Susan, awaiting the birth of the Joneses' fourth child, and took the occasion to write her cousins in Florida. She gave news of Sue's and Rebecca's stay at Vaucluse; Bec, too, had left their own farm, as she could not manage in Bev's absence. Bev had been reassigned as Hospital Steward in the 33rd Virginia; Robby and Marshall Jones, both discharged by medical boards, transferred to "other employment connected with the army." Son James "has tried the Cavalry service" but "is not able to bear as much as Strother could. . . ." Mrs. Jones lamented the numbers of sick and wounded, both in Winchester and going south in the Valley, "the ladies are doing & giving but the Prices of everything exceed belief, and the Stores are nearly empty. I cannot get a dress & a servants shoes cost 8 dollars a pair. . . ."[12]

A week later Mrs. Jones wrote Lucy's daughter Harriet to convey the bittersweet news of the safe birth of Susan and Frank's fourth child. The continuing flux and uncertainty of wartime Frederick County and the constant puzzle of troop movements to civilians can be discerned in the note added just before sending.

[LETTER OF ANN C. R. JONES TO HARRIET PARKHILL]

[note in upper corner]
numbers of soldiers going through town this morning 29th of October
October 23d, 1862

When I shall reach the end of this sheet, Dearest Harriet, I cannot tell, but I thought I would make a beginning & be guided by circumstances. To tell you that I sympathize with you in this sad bereavement, seems *so cold*. What shall I say? May God bless & comfort you, my Child. Your Brother's conversion is a cause for such *deep joy*, the hope of being with him forever & ever in those heavenly mansions is an unspeakable support.[13] . . .

My long letter to your dear Mother left here, I forget how many days ago, but this will follow it with the intelligence of our Baby's arrival, precious little fatherless one! I had somehow been *certain* it was a Boy, & I had earnestly desired to have my son represented, but to Sue's *great* disappointment it is a Girl. *I* am now extremely satisfied, & sure that it is much better as it is. A Widow can manage Girls better than Boys, & then they need not leave her so early. The Child was born on Sunday the 19th. I had been nearly 4 weeks waiting for it. . . .

You could scarcely believe the number of the wounded that have passed through & remained in Winchester since the Sharpsburg battle. *Many*, *Many* sick are dying here, I fear to say how many were buried today. The Ladies are active in doing what they can. . . . My darling Bev is in town & has a miserable cold, but is not laid up. His location is not yet decided on.[14] He will report to the proper person the day after tomorrow I expect, & then I shall know where he will be & what he will have to do, dear Boy! the last of my younger children, & my heart is unspeakably anxious about him. Pray for him, my precious Child & for your old Cousin too, pray that I may be benefitted by sorrow, & more ready for my Heavenly Home.

How I wish I could see you all & wish I could write you a more respectable letter. This war & its miserable consequences are too absorbing for almost anything else to be written about. My Boy Randolph came to see me today.[15] He is a fine looking young soldier, so tall & stout tho' not deemed handsome you may remember. Our Army has been & is so near that occasionally my Grandchildren can come in. They are all three Lieutenants now. Tom Marshall is a Major, & is spoken of as Lieutenant Colonel, *he* belongs to the Cavalry.

The subject of evacuation & consequent return of the enemy is often conversed, & by many rather expected. I *trust* it may not be so, how I dread seeing those unclean birds flying round & round, & showing their audacious impudence as they have done. My spirit generally rose as they approached me, & I faced them with a feerless look & manner, but I may be helpless now, & I would be so glad if they did not come————a Portion of our Army passed through today, & are going to Berryville about 12 miles from here, Randolph goes in the morning, & then the other Boys have gone or will go directly. Gen. Jackson passed through today on his way there. The supposition is that he is only changing his Camp, but few pretend to know positively what he is about, untill there can be no concealment. Our army is a very large one. That number is now being removed to Berryville, I am not aware, but I imagine a small portion. If the Yankees *should* return, Poor Sue will have no Male protector—her Father *cannot* remain, & *none* of her Brothers either—her eldest Brother was here before, but is already gone & will not be able to come back.[16] However I hope the creatures stay away. . . .

Dr. Davis & family are warm Southerners.[17] Mrs Davis *surprises* me by the quantity of good she does in *every* way. Susy comes into town, every Wednesday I believe, to aid at the Cooking establishment where nice things are made for the sick. The ladies of the town who can, attend on different days, all the time, even on Sunday. . . . Fanny Barton is well. Her daughter Fanny & her son Robert are delicate, I am afraid very much so.[18] . . . May God bless you my Child,

Your truly fond Cousin, A.C.R. Jones

It was always preferable to send a letter with someone going in the right direction. Bolling's father availed himself of one such opportunity to reinforce and repeat his injunctions about Bolling's studies and his soul. Joining the evangelical Episcopal church was a matter of individual timing and conscience, and his family was increasingly concerned that Bolling had not yet committed himself. It is not hard to tell which was thought to be more important; local news takes third place.

[LETTER OF DAVID W. BARTON TO BOLLING W. BARTON]

Winchester Oct. 26, '62

My dear Bolling:

As Mr. Beverly will call on his way back from Camp to-morrow, I cannot miss so good an opportunity to write to you. It gives us great pleasure to hear from him that you are looking well, and I have every confidence that you are behaving well and studying faithfully. Now is the time my son to make up for many wasted months, and it is your last and only chance to acquire a respectable stock of knowledge before you take your start in life. I am glad to find you attend the prayer meetings, and hope you will never miss them or any other means of acquiring religious instruction. The good example of all your brothers and sisters will not I am sure be lost on you. Remember that you are the only member of the family out of the church. Do not let light and frivolous companions drive serious thoughts from your mind, but whilst I desire you to be cheerful and companionable, do not think of neglecting "the one thing needful." General Smith will take pleasure in directing your religious reading and in the absence of a minister of our own church, do not hesitate [to talk] freely with Dr. White or any other good man of any denomination.[19] All teach the same essential and vital doctrines and whilst greatly preferring our own forms and peculiar views, there is enough for salvation in our common creed.

This morning we were greatly surprised by a visit from David & Strother, who came up from Camp to pay us a short visit. They left all quiet in camp, the Federals having all retired to the Maryland side except a small force at Harper's Ferry. Last week we had a severe skirmish near Kearneysville, in which all the boys were engaged, but escaped unhurt. One of your Brother David's men was wounded but none killed, all escaped unhurt in the 2nd Regiment. The 5th Regiment lost in killed and wounded about 25 men. The enemy were in much larger force than we, but finally retired across the river pursued to the shore by our troops. Since then all has remained quiet. Jackson's Division is encamped at Bunker Hill. Genl. Lee with the bulk of the Army is near Jolliffe. Hood's Division is on Cedar Creek near Cupp's Mill and Walker's Division is near Millwood.[20]

We have a considerable force here in town and every thing in the shape of provisions is very scarce. Wood is selling in town at $10. a load (less than a cord), meat at 15 to 25c, butter $1., apples $2. to $3. per basket, &c. I have secured a respectable quantity of keeping apples, although the soldiers took their share. I am going to put up walnuts, hickory nuts &c for our winter amusements. The crop of walnuts is enormously large and I am advising all the poor to secure all they can. The weather has continued until to-day, warm and clear. . . .

The drought has delayed us, but if November is mild and moist, all will be well. I was at Lost Brook on Friday and found everything doing well, except that seeding was delayed there as elsewhere by dry weather. Your Uncle

Strother rode with me to Lost Brook and spent the whole day riding and walking, so you see how much he is improved.[21] Old Don amused us by his exploits in starting rabbits and partridges. He seemed quite at home at Lost Brook. . . .[22]

I hope General Smith's vigorous and persevering efforts to secure the cloth will prove successful. He appealed to General Lee and his sergeant told me yesterday he expected to take back with him a load of cloth. My factory men are under military rule and cannot sell any except to old customers.

By the way, I have sold the Factory and Barleywood at $15,000 to Mr. Gaver, I may sell Lost Brook if I can get my price $40. per acre.[23] These sales will enable me to improve Springdale and pay my debts.

All here join in love to you.

Yours affectionately,
D.W. Barton

The cadet cloth ordered by General Smith had been requisitioned by the army, but General Lee intervened on behalf of VMI and directed that Barton's factory be freed from its commitment to the army to fill the institute's order.[24]

[LETTER OF DAVID W. BARTON TO GEN. FRANCIS H. SMITH]

Genl Francis H. Smith   Winchester
Supt V.M.I.   Oct 31. 62

My Dear Sir

Before this reaches you I hope your Sergeant will have safely arrived at the Institute with his load of clothes. Mr. Gaver having bought the Factory has given me an order for the amount (being $1188.19 as you will see from the subjoined copy of his bill. Will you do me the favour to procure for me $1200 in Confederate 8 percent Bonds varying in size from $100 to $500 as soon as advised that you have them for me. I will inclose to you the order of Gaver &c & my receipt. The small fraction over $1188.19/100 I will adjust with you in the future bills.

Our army is moving towards the counties of Loudoun, Fauquier & Rapahannock, Eastward & southward, Jacksons Corps being the only part now remaining in the Valley. The Enemy is advancing from the Potomac toward the Rappahanock & a fight may be looked for shortly. Your son was well a few days ago.[25] Please say to Bolling we are all well at home & that his Brothers have been with us to take leave.

(85 yds Cadet cloth $6	$510.00	Most respectfully
88¾ suit lining $5	$443.75	
85¼ mix satinet $2.75	$234.44	D.W. Barton
total	$1188.19)	

Robby had set his transfer in motion with a medical examination and he included the report with his request to Col. J. Thompson Brown on October 19. A few days later he obtained a Certificate of Disability from his commanding officer, Capt. William T. Poague, and the examining doctor. At Poague's summons, he went before Dr. J. A. Straith and the Corps Medical Board and was adjudged as unfit for service. With these formalities taken care of, he was free to take up his duties with the Nitre and Mining Bureau in November.[26] *About the same time, portions of the Army of Northern Virginia began moving east in response to Union General Burnside's advance with the Army of the Potomac toward the Rappahannock, in the vicinity of Fredericksburg. Bolling's sister Fanny was aware of the troop movements, and had heard current rumors such as that of the arrival of English Commissioners, which would presage a hoped-for alliance with the Confederacy.*

[LETTER OF FANNY J. BARTON TO BOLLING W. BARTON]

Sunday night
Nov. 2nd

Your letter to [Cousin] Anna to day reminded me darling Bolling that I had owed you one for some time & I could fill a page with apologies, but I know you would rather have something more agreeable. First I must give you a scolding for being so dismal. You must cheer up & be brighter, & keep very busy & study hard. You will be repaid by seeing the pleasure it would give mama & papa. I feel sure you will be all else that they could wish. Well here is an end of the lecture. You must forgive your *old Sister* for this presumption & remember that her love for you has prompted this. I am so sorry if you should find the Institute so disagreeable but I hope you will become more accustomed to it after awhile. I hope we can send you a box of good things before very long. . . .

Anna & I have just returned from Vaucluse where we have been for the last week enjoying this charming autumn weather & the pure country air. . . . Our Army is gradually moving from between us & the Yankees & I fear that before long we may be left to their tender mercies. Longstreets Corps has moved towards Front Royal & Jacksons towards Berryville. We had a slight

Robert T. Barton's certificate of disability, signed by Capt. William T. Poague and surgeon J. A. Straith. (Edith Barton Sheerin)

skirmish over in Loudoun a few days ago in which Gen Stuart captured 300 prisoners.

Day before yesterday some of the Yankee Cavalry came as near to us as "Pewtown" & burnt two of our wagons full of empty flour barrels.[27]

That was in imitation of Gen Stuarts raid into Pensylvania I suppose.[28] There are rumours afloat that we have been recognized by England & that Comissions are in Washington. A surgeon on Gen Longstreets staff told me he had seen the Baltimore papers which mentioned it but I think it like the "cry of fox" & am not much affected by it. . . .

Next time you write dear Bolling I will thank you not to send your love *especially* to . . . the servants—& omit sending any to your sister. I dont suppose I do deserve much but I am very jealous of that little that I have. . . . All the household are in the *"land of Nod"* or you could have *lots of love* sent you. Good night. God bless you.

Your attached sister
Fan

His grandmother, although still in town helping Sue, found time to write Bolling in early November. Her reference to teaching him suggests that he spent periods of time with her when quite young, as Rannie may have also. A conspicuous, early, and ongoing shortage in the Confederacy was that of writing materials. Mrs. Jones was already using one of the spoils of war—Yankee paper—but she had cut a hole in it to eliminate Northern sentiments.

[LETTER OF ANN C. R. JONES TO BOLLING W. BARTON]

[the paper has an engraving of George Washington in the upper left corner]

Winchester Nov. 5th 1862

You do not know how glad I was to get your letter my darling Boy & you must not feel insulted these hard times at my writing upon captured Yankee Paper, I have cut out the objectionable words & Gen Washingtons face must always be a passport. I dined yesterday with your Mother she was of course as busy as a Bee, she had moved into the Library the day before, & had not completed her arrangements. It took me back a good many years in memory to see her in it as a [bed]chamber both Randolph & yourself were born there, perhaps you knew.[29] The Period at which I was teaching you my Child was a happier one than I may ever look forward to again in this world not that I mean to complain however of any thing for I am most mercifully dealt bye. You were a *very* good Child, & I remember *no* trouble with you. . . .

Fanny has written & I suppose has told you all Winchester News, the return of the Yankees is still a subject much talked of, but I hope & trust they will never again be Located here. The movements of an army is to me one of the most mysterious things in the world. I cannot divine what they are about & only pray that all things may end well for our Country, & ourselves. Our boys are not far off & can I reckon occasionally give us a Peep. Randolph was in Town last night & your Uncle Bev also. . . . Keep a good heart, & get through your time in Lexington like a man, May God bless you in Time, & in Eternity

your very fondly attached Grand mother A.C.R. Jones

Illustrated London News *war correspondent Frank Vizitelly, who was Mrs. H. H. Lee's paying guest when in town, drew this sketch of the Confederate Army near Winchester in the fall of 1862.* (Houghton Library, Harvard University)

Apprehension about the army's movements was beginning to manifest itself, although Jackson's army was still in the Winchester area. Rannie wrote to Bolly the same day as their grandmother, and was obviously enjoying the benefits of being in camp near home. He could not, however, get new shoes.

[LETTER OF RANDOLPH BARTON TO BOLLING W. BARTON]

Winchester Nov 5th 1862

Dear Boly

I went out to Spring-dale this morning intending to take a hunt, but you may imagine how shocked I was on the way out to hear of poor Don's death. He was killed day before yesterday by a tree falling upon him. Clayton Williams hunted with him some days ago when he hunted finely.[30] . . . I am very sorry but you know such accidents will happen. . . .

Things look like evacuating this county, I hope the[y] will not do so. If ever you want money write to one of us as as we generally have plenty. Can you procure me a pair of No 7½ *shoes* at any price.[31] Brother Tom [Marshall] is Lieut Col of the 7th Cavalry.[32] You know we are all Lieuts. Robby has gone off with Uncle James [F. Jones]. Uncle Strother [Jones] is getting much better. Study hard, dont get any demerits, and you will forget all these troubles, never leave the Institute while the War lasts. We were in a little skirmish at Kearneysville some time ago, none hurt, in the 2nd.

your dev bro   R.J. Barton
Co K 2nd Va Infantry—Stonewall Brig

Within the week, Rannie wrote again to his younger brother, responding to what must have been a very homesick letter, enlivening it with some army gossip and family news.

[LETTER OF RANDOLPH BARTON TO BOLLING W. BARTON]

Winchester Nov 12th 1862

Dear Boly

I have just read what you call your gloomy letter; I can sympathize with you in all your troubles. I know how painful it is to be cut off from home. . . . Frank Paxton of Lexington is our Brigadier. It will no doubt cause dissatisfaction, and cause the resignation of Cols. Grigsby & Ronald.[33]

Brother S[trother] is still act adjutant but I fear will not retain the place as Bob Hunter is expected to return. Brother S and myself bought a horse from F[rank] Clark we gave $400.00 for him, a big price, but a splendid horse.[34] I told you about poor old Dons death. We are saving two of his pups. Brother D[avid] is here . . . Marshall [Jones] is here. Uncle Bev [Jones] is Hospital Steward of the 33rd. Johnny B[aldwin] is Sergt Maj. The hogs in town one of which belongs to you, are in fine order, and will weigh on an average 250 lbs each.[35] George Ash is up the valley with old Charley and the grey colt, he went to haul sick when we expected to evacuate.[36] He probably has returned. Pa is very busy. Ma says she will write when she has an opportunity. Answer my letters, Sukey has a little boy a few days old, she is getting better. All would send love if they knew I was writing.

Your devoted bro
R J Barton

P.S. Pa says your report says no standing assigned, habits health and conduct good
R J Barton

Winchester was still part of the Confederacy, but the mails were uncertain, so Bolling's mother again took the opportunity of sending a letter with a cadet's father going to Lexington.

[LETTER OF FANNIE L. BARTON TO BOLLING W. BARTON]

Friday Evening [November 14]

My own precious Son

I have only time to write a few lines by Mr. Reed I need to encourage you in this endeavour to strive on and do your duty. I am well aware of the sorrows of your position . . . Mr R's son is sick and his Mother will not be contented that he should remain longer at the V M I—because he is not *contented* there.[37] Now if he returns the next step will be his enlistment in the Army such are the times that of the two evils the Institute is the least.

We think of you all the time and especially early in the morning, my darling, when your *rooster* regularly crows just under my window, & you know that I now sleep in the library, and the two chickens air themselves in the alley about day break, poor Suckey has been *very ill*, but she was highly pleased at your letter, she has another little *boy*, very little indeed could almost be put in a quart pot—she sends a quantity of love, and says this tiny boy shall be your dining room servant by and bye.

Now as for the Yankees I doubt not they return after a season, at present Jacksons army keeps us free, I hear to day that they are certainly in Charlestown. . . .

I am often very wretched, I dwell on all the dear ones gone, and then agonize over all of you, but it calms my spirit when I remember the great mercy of God how he has protected us all through these awful trials. . . .[38]

I send you a jar of jelly, I could not make a cake — not being able to get an egg and sugar is like grains of gold with us now. . . .

Your devoted Mother
FLB

Rannie and the other brothers of the brigade continued on duty but near home. Even his beloved grandmother had been in town this fall, and it seems that she only returned to Vaucluse, about ten miles away, on this day; with her was another grandson Marshall Jones, Anna's brother (who was more or less part of the Jones household), and two of the Vaucluse slaves. Rannie, though the youngest of the serving brothers, seemed more interested in army hierarchy and politics than the others (perhaps appropriate for the future AAG).

[LETTER OF RANDOLPH BARTON TO BOLLING W. BARTON]

Winchester Nov 18th 1862

Dear Boly

I read your letter to grandma a few minutes ago. She has just gone out to Vaucluse with Marshall [Jones], Uncle William & aunt Mary Braxton.[39] . . . This is a wet disagreable day in camp, I have to return this evening. They

intended to kill hogs at Springdale today, but the weather is so bad that I
suppose they will not do so. . . .

As I predicted Col Grigsby has resigned and it is rumored Col. Ronalds has
also. I have changed my opinion about Genl Paxton, I think he will make a fine
officer. . . . I can see no signs of evacuation. By order of Genl Lee we sent back
for surplus baggage left at Gordonsville and Jefferson a little town in Culpeper
Co. Sukey's last child died, she is getting better. . . .

*Perhaps Rannie was unsettled in detecting signs of movement, for although he
"saw no signs," Jackson did indeed evacuate the Winchester area three days
later, leaving only a cavalry screen. Cousin Anna conveyed that news and her
alarm to Bolling the next week.*

[LETTER OF ANNA M. JONES TO BOLLING W. BARTON]

Winchester Nov 24th 1862

. . . we have all been in such a confused state that to collect my thoughts sufficiently to indite a respectable letter would have been impossible and now I am so
much afraid that we will soon be in the hands of the Yankees that if I do not take
advantage of this opportunity I may not be able to do so again until next spring. . . .

We have still the "Maryland Line," and a Brigade of Cavalry with us but we
do not know how long they will be allowed to remain.[40] Also it makes my head
ache to think of the Yankees—[Gen. John White] Geary and his men will have
no compassion on us and we may make up our minds for the worst if we are
again left to their tender mercies. We have however great confidence in Gen
Jones who is I hear a splendid officer and we trust that he will have picquets
posted on all the roads so as to give notice of the approach of the enemy. The
Marylanders have such a dread of being surprised and taken prisoners.

Jackson's old division left here on Thursday and A P Hill's on Friday—it was
sad, sad in the extreme I felt like crying my eyes out but I had to control my self so
as to keep the boys up. I gave away once when I was telling *a friend* of mine
goodbye but he seemed to be so much distressed that I had to stop.[41] Dont let anybody see this letter but your self—tear it up as soon as you have finished it. . . .

Sukey has been very sick but she is better now she sends much love. Bolly is
growing very fast.[42] Dont make your self uneasy about us we will get on as well
as other people. . . . God bless you my darling Bolling. Write soon to

Your affectionate sister[43]

Anna M. Jones

Not wanting to alarm her younger brother, Fanny wrote him a playful, teasing letter.

[LETTER OF FANNY J. BARTON TO BOLLING W. BARTON]

Winchester Nov 27th

I have waited in vain dear Bolling, for an answer to my last letter but I fear that my *severe scolding* has deterred you from writing to me any more. . . .

We are all getting along very comfortably with the exception of any occasional panic or a *stirring* rumor. To day it is reported that there is an insurrection in Washington & that Burnside has been recalled with his forces to quell it; I cannot *vouch* for the truth of it however.

. . . I suppose you heard an exaggerated account of the skirmish with our Pickets the other night which caused such a panic in town. We have heard a true statement of it at last. Their were about 200 Yankees who attacked our 5 pickets but our men fired into them very bravely killing two & wounding one, they then returned to *Newtown* & fired again into the enemy who soon afterward retired.

We are all getting Confederate dresses.[44] You dont know how pretty they are. I belong to the infantry as mine is grey, trimmed with black. Anna's is grey flannel trimmed with red she is in the artillery service. Wont we make brave soldiers! We do miss the boys so dreadfully—and so often wish for you too. Dont be home sick Bolly it is worth while being away from home for a long time just for the pleasure you feel in getting back.

Suckey has been right sick but we hope that she is getting better. She was very proud of your little note & wants me to answer it for her which I will do very soon. . . .

your devoted sister

Fan

His grandmother's loving letters, giving news of all the family, as well as the local war news and rumors, were often the fullest report Bolling received. She had nothing good to say for the Yankees, and was "unwilling to believe that those miscreants will ever locate themselves in Winchester again [although] they may run in & out doing mischief. . . ."[45] *A few days later, Mrs. Jones was writing to her young Florida cousin while she still could, before, as she feared, the lines might change due to the return of Federal forces as a result of a battle all felt to be impending.*

Vaucluse December 4th 1862

Our communication is about to be closed again dearest Harriet & with the hope of this being carried up the Valley & mailed *some where*, I write in answer to your welcome letter, my Child, I had *thought* of writing to your dear Mother after my return from Winchester, but I think this is your due, miserable production as I prophesy it is to be, & *she* will hear from me at the same time. Our Army has again retreated, & we are just awaiting the reappearance of our enemy in Winchester at any moment. They are within a few miles of the place. . . . The Yankees behave dreadfully in some places, but I trust we shall escape as well as we did before. Strother has decided upon staying at home May God preserve him! If they take him prisoner, the confinement, the fare, & anxiety will, I fear, put an end to his most valuable life, but I will hope to the last moment.

Rebecca with her little children are in Town. They have no servant but an old man belonging to Bev, who cuts wood, & a free girl Bec hires as a nurse to her Children. Cooking & cleaning devolves upon them—the Ladies I mean—fortunately they are willing, industrious, & energetic. . . . Rebecca promised to return here if the difficulties were found strong, she *would* leave, because she thought it best, & I really think she seems brighter & happier where she is, uniting with her Sisters. . . . My darling Bev is engaged as Hospital Steward in the field, he must therefore be with the regiment. His pay is small, does not admit of his helping the family a great deal. But as yet they have money, & he makes more than a Private. When I saw him last, he had lost his cough & seemed well. . . .

Fanny & Mr. Barton have but one Child at home—Precious little Fan—but the return of the Yankees will enable Mattie Baldwin to come home from Maryland where she & her two children with Barton Marshall have been on a visit to Jane Cary [Sheild]. . . . Dear Maria's children [the four younger Marshalls] are with [the Bartons]. . . .

The Refugees from Winchester are I suppose all gone, & the inhabitants remaining are just waiting for the enemy to enter it. How long it will be before our Yard & house is to be polluted by their footsteps, the event must show, I trust I shall feel *no* fear, if they will let Strother alone, but a hand upon him will put me out of my judgement, I have such a dread of his being confined, believing it will shatter his measure of health so lately acquired. We are very much cut off from my son James's family. His business lies in Staunton &

in his trips to see his wife & children his capture has been close at hand.[46] The last time he was there he felt quite safe, but the day he was here on his way back we heard the enemy were again in Fauquier & not many miles from his home. . . .

Marshall Jones (my Grandson, you know, has been again discharged from the army on account of his health which is too delicate to bear the hardships of a camp life) is here, ready packed up to get out of the way at the last moment. He is unwilling to go until compelled.[47] Robert Barton, my grandson, is employed with James, *his* health was too bad also for him to remain in Camp. The Boys have both been in hard fought battles & must rest satisfied with that—— they cannot help it. . . .

I am writing to you as I would to your Mother, whether I shall ever perpetrate a scrawl pleasant to a young lady again, I cannot tell. I have entered my 67th year, & you must not be extreme to mark the oft repeated deficiency, but love me, as I love you, & you will burn my letters that they will never rise up in judgement against me . . . Sue's Baby is a lovely child, & *Randolph* —I scarcely ever look at him, that my precious, too precious Frank, is not brought more vividly before me, not his face, but his person, his ways, his character, Oh! God grant he may make as Holy a Man![48] . . . Sue looks *intensely* sad sometimes, but tries to bear the weight upon her now must be increased. Her Father's health she thinks is very precarious, & she is much devoted to him, he is so very kind & watchful of her. . . .

I want to enclose to your Mother an extract from a letter of Mr. Charles Moncure to my son Strother. I thought it so true, she would like to read it. I wish she could see my Child's Diary, particularly the last notice, written 5 days before that (to him) fatal battle.[49] News has just come saying that the Yankees are in Winchester & commanded by that wretch Garry [Geary], I do not know how to spell his name. God Bless you, my dear. I saw all my grandchildren on their way past, my Precious Randolph did not look well but said he was.

Your fondly attached cousin

A. C. R. Jones.

Please burn my letter. It will be difficult for you to comprehend it, but I cannot write another. Do not think I am frightened by the approach of the vandals. I am not yet *at all*. May God preserve you all from invasion I pray.

A Randolph family connection, Charles Moncure, had recently written Strother Jones his condolences on Frank's death.

[LETTER OF CHARLES MONCURE TO W. STROTHER JONES]

. . . no one has fallen, in this cruel struggle, so much valued, by my wife and self, as he was. He was *the* true type of that class, known, in their time, as *"the Virginia gentleman"*—the pink of honour—modest, brave, pious—genial, yet dignified—warm heart- & sincere attachments. Give my love to his wife. I shall never forget her countenance, when I saw her parting with Frank, in Winchester. . . .[50]

The Confederates evacuated Winchester on December 4, but left a cavalry screen. Mrs. Jones was apprehensive about Federal occupation, but General Geary sent only a reconnaissance in to town on the fifth. For once the news Rannie saw in the papers was correct. The Confederates were back in town soon after the Federal withdrawal.

[LETTER OF RANDOLPH BARTON TO BOLLING W. BARTON]

[written on a torn piece of paper]

Camp near Guinea Station
Dec 8th 1862

Dear Boly,

I suppose you know of course where we are, and what made it necessary for us to come hear. It was quite a dissappointment to us all to leave the valley. We have been in the neighborhood of Fredericksburg some 8 or 10 days and think we will stay here for some time. You see by the papers that the Yanks have been in Winchester but retired in a short time. If they make any serious demonstration in the Valley *I think* we will go back. I dont think they did any harm during their visit. Brother D[avid] has rec one letter from home since we left, all were well. Pa very busy at the farm. Uncle S[trother] intended to move his servants to Stanardsville if the Yanks approached, no doubt he has carried out his intentions.[51] You have a pair of shoes for me I think. Keep them until you have a good opportunity to send them, no doubt some of the Mo[o]re's will be returning soon.[52] I suppose you visit our cousins [the Bartons] frequently, remember me most affectionately to them. If you are cut off from home dont dispair or give up to *the blues*—write to brother David whenever you wish advice, he will be sure to advise you as to what is right. The 2nd numbers some 450 present— Hunter is adjutant but I think brother S[trother] will get the position yet. We are living on beef slap-jack and a species of fluid called *slide* from the friendly way in which it assists you to slip slap-jack.

I dined with brother D sunday last, he is well. Willie myself and brother S occupy an A tent with a stove in it which keeps us very comfortable.

when you write Direct to-

lst Va Brigade Jackson

Corps 2nd Regt Va.Inf

Brother David you know belongs to the same brigade Carpenters battery. It is quite dull in camp but but eating reading and sleeping we manage to get along. Excuse this paper and my obliging you to pay the postage.

Your devoted bro

RJ Barton

Lt Comp K

Rannie's ever optimistic nature showed in this letter. He was always ready to believe things were not so bad in Winchester. And sister Fanny hoped for the best despite one Yankee incursion. The 1st Maryland Cavalry and other regiments that had screened Jackson's departure withdrew on the thirteenth. On December 11 Federal forces had occupied Fredericksburg. Although worried about her brothers in what was taking shape as a major battle, Fanny's first attention was claimed by sad affairs at home.

[LETTER OF FANNY J. BARTON TO BOLLING W. BARTON]

Winchester Dec 13th

I fear this will be my last letter my darling Bolling for a long time as our defenders the "Maryland battalion" has left us. At present the enemy is no where near us & I trust they will not pay us another visit. You must not be dispirited by this news—brighter days I think are in store for us & wont we enjoy them together after all of our sorrows & troubles. God grant that we may be better for them.

I enclose a letter to you from Suckey which I think is very touching. Poor thing she has been badly afflicted. Both of her little children dead: It is so sad to see the two little graves in the garden covered with snow. But I believe Suckey is a true Christian & she bears it beautifully. She is *right smart* now & is going about again.

We have heard today some account of the battle at Fredericksburg. We feel so anxious about the boys. They were not in the first days fight but I *fear* very much they were fighting afterwards. It is great comfort to think that they are prepared for any thing, that having God on thier side if they fall they fall gloriously as soldiers not only of the Confederacy but of the Cross of Christ. . . .

Brother Tom [Marshall] just left us he has been stationed near here for several weeks but has now followed his regiment towards Front Royal. . . .

I suppose you have heard of the short visit we had from the Yankees? We were most agreeably supprised when they went off at a double quick after staying two or three hours. I expect we will have quite a lonely time now; the town looks like the "deserted village. . . ."

Papa has sold Shady Oak & the farm near Dr. Davis'es.[53] I expect there will be a right pleasant little neighborhood there but how we will miss dear brother Marshall & Uncle Frank. . . .

All the household I know would send love did they know I were writing. Grandma is in town to day but I have not seen her yet. May God bless you my darling brother.

Ever your loving sister
Fan

The following letter from Sukey to Bolling was probably the one enclosed in Fan's letter. The extremely faded, spider-fine handwriting is not that of any other known writer. Sukey signed her name to it.

[LETTER OF SUKEY TO BOLLING W. BARTON]

Winchester, 7th December 1862

My dear young master. As Miss Fanny has just been up here I am almost ready to say D—of the flesh and the spirit too and this morning I felt like one just raised from the dead by good nursing and attention but let us not always trust to drs or nurses but to the grace of God. My dear little baby died three weeks ago but he has gone to a better home, and I will not murmur. My little Bolling has also left me to go to heaven. He was taken Monday at four oclock with a fit after having been well all day sunday and busy looking at our Confederate army passing. You know I never was a Yankee. He died the same day. He was buried on Tuesday evening in the garden by his little brother. Oh I miss him very much. This trial is very hard to bear. The children throw flowers on his grave every morning and evening. I am very sorry I cannot write you a more cheering letter but I have had so much trouble lately, that it is hard to write cheerfully. But I am thankful to say with them of old for the days of my sorrow

I sought the Lord and he has never forsaken me. Blessed be his holy name forever. Oh my dear young master as you grow in years may you grow in grace.

Remember now thy Creator in the days of thy youth while the evil days come not nor the years draw nigh when thou shalt say I have no pleasure in them. Poor Phil is dreadfully distressed.[54] He told me to give his love to you & say he has had a heap of trouble since you was here last. He thinks of you all the time please write us something you think will comfort and cheer us. This is what comforts me in all my troubles.

> God moves in a mysterious way
> His wonders to perform . . .[55]

[here follow six stanzas of this hymn]

Goodbye my dear young master. I hope I may have greater pleasure in unpacking your trunk than packing. God only know my troubles the. I must say I owe my recovery thus far to my God and to my white friends for my mistress and master were more than masters.

> Believe me your
> affectionate nurse Sucky

P.S. I hope me you will excuse this peace of ignorance and teach me better.

> Suckey

Bolling's father, writing a day after Fan, was worried about three sons in battle at Fredericksburg, and was clearly rather dejected about damage done to the Springdale farm and the prospect of more. The continuing cares of his late brother Richard's debts, shared in part with his late brother Robert R. Barton's estate, were never out of his mind. Nevertheless, the annual ice cutting and hog killing went on, Bolling's profit on his pig being "banked" for him by his father, and Sukey's pork probably preserved for her own use.

[LETTER OF DAVID W. BARTON TO BOLLING W. BARTON]

> Winchester
> Dec 14 62

My Dear Bolling

We have all just returned from prayer meeting & whilst the girls & their Beaus are chatting in the sitting room I have retired to the chamber (the

Library) to write you a short letter. We are very dull here today in consequence of our troops having all left us. After the grand Army departed in November there remained here as a sort of Frontier guard about 2000 men under Genl. [William E.] Jones.

About a week ago the reported approach of Genl Geary with 6000 men induced our smaller Army to leave. Geary came into town but remained only an hour on his retiring our troops came back. But yesterday they moved again—for what reasons we know not. A great fight is said to be in progress at Fredericksburg & that may have something to do with it. Our Boys no doubt have again been in danger. God grant that their lives have been spared. Our suspense for several days will be dreadful.

I have had 3 Regiments of Cavalry on Springdale Farm for a week including that Cold spell.[56] The havoc in my barn will tell the tale for many a day—— but we must all bear our share of the burden.

On Wednesday & Thursday the ice on the dam [at the Bartonsville mill pond] was 4 inches thick, & many persons were cutting it up. We got nine wagon Loads in the Springdale Ice house. Probably we shall have other freezes as the winter is just begun. We availed ourselves of the last cold spell to kill & pack our pork. Our hogs were in good order. The 3 in the pen at home were very nice & weighed about 140 each so that for yours I owe you $25 which I will keep for you until you want it. Suckey salted up her hog. Poor Suckey I suppose you have heard of her double affliction—1st her miscarriage & serious illness & then the death of poor little Bolling. He had a fit & died in a few hours. I hope Phill will continue to live with us as he is very polite & obliging & suits me very well. I have not yet determined how to arrange my affairs at Springdale for next year, possibly I will carry on as usual—though my force so reduced & fences so much broken that I have not much encouragement to do much. My last crop of wheat, which was heavy in straw, is but indifferent in yield but high prices pay for all the labour it cost. Wheat sells at $2 corn at $12 & $15 per Barrel Hay at $25 & $30 per ton. . . .

Your brother Tom [Marshall] & his troops passed through town last night & have gone towards Front Royal. I suppose you have had the pleasure of seeing Robby last week, as he talked of going to Rockbridge in the pursuit of his business.

I have written to your cousin Virginia twice lately on a matter of business, but have no reply. I have forgotten who is Doctor Bartons ad.[ministrator] ascertain & let me know that I may open the correspondence with him. I find the Doctor & myself are jointly bound as securitors of your uncle Richard and will both have to pay pretty freely. My object in writing to Virginia was to apprise her of the fact & through her the administrator. I fear my Letter miscarried.

All join in much love & many good wishes. Do not neglect the one thing needful.

yrs affectionately

D W Barton

Rannie and the 2nd Virginia had left Winchester November 22, marching with the Stonewall Brigade through the Luray Gap in the Blue Ridge and the Wilderness to Fredericksburg.

[MEMOIR OF RANDOLPH BARTON]

We went into bivouac near Hamilton's Crossing (a railroad crossing some six miles out from Fredericksburg), and, on the night of December 11, 1862, my brother David came over to our brigade, from his battery (Cutshaw's), of which he was Lieutenant, taking the place of my brother Marshall, who had been killed at Winchester, May 25, 1862, and asked my brother Strother and myself to come over that night and hear Rev. Dr. Stiles, a distinguished Presbyterian preacher from Savannah.[57] We accordingly went over, and all three sat together on a mess-chest. On the morning of the 13th he was killed in the battle of that day. Our brigade was not much engaged in that battle. We had some casualties. Willie Colston was badly wounded very near me, and my cousin, Willie Barton, was grazed on the neck by a bullet, which striking a band on his musket, glanced and struck him slightly.[58] My brother Strother, obtaining leave when matters had quieted somewhat, to do so, went to look after my brother David. He had been shot by a Yankee skirmisher through the head, dying instantly. His intimate friend, Randolph Fairfax, a beautiful youth, was killed nearby and almost at the same time. My brother's body was taken back, wrapped in a blanket and buried near Hamilton's Crossing. We never recovered it.[59]

On the night of the 13th our brigade was moved down to the front line, and took position in the ditch on the side of the railroad running from Fredericksburg to Richmond. The weather was very cold and my bed consisted of two fence rails placed across the ditch. To lift one's head above the level of the rails was dangerous, as occasionally a ball from the Federal sharpshooters would strike the rails. The next morning it was discovered that the enemy had recrossed the Rappahannock River.[60]

Since Winchester was between the lines, news was often unreliable. Robby was the first to hear about his brother's death. His assignment with Nitre and Mining kept him on the move, usually in the central part of the Valley, and gave him a good deal of freedom, which he used at this time of family distress. In mid-December he was about twenty-five miles south of Winchester when he encountered some troops he knew. Johnny Williams, his old schoolmate, and his brother Clayton were among them.

[MEMOIR OF ROBERT T. BARTON]

A day or two after [the battle] I was riding along the Valley Turnpike not far from Woodstock when I met Chew's Battery of Artillery, many of the members of which I knew quite well.[61] I talked with them and we spoke of the great victory and of the hope it excited. I observed something strange in the face of one of my friends who drawing me aside, with infinite tenderness told me of the death of my brother David. I resolved to go to Winchester at once and tell my father of it.[62]

Chew's Battery and the cavalry which accompanied it was the entire Confederate force which at that time lay below Woodstock and when it withdrew there was nothing between me and the enemy which, it was said, had come in to Strasburgh. To get to Vaucluse that night and avoid the enemy I left the turnpike and followed what is known as the back road, west of the turnpike and not far from the mountains. All that country had become entirely familiar to me and I was not at all at a loss when night came on. I crossed Cedar Creek some time after dark and fearing to come upon the Yankees at any time, I rode as cautiously and quietly as I could, avoiding the broader roads and sometimes taking to the fields. About ten o'clock I reached the home of a Mr. Crisman who was one of my father's tenants at the "Lost Brook" farm. There I stayed all night and learning from him that the Yankees had been in that neighbourhood that day, I left my horse at his house and the next morning walked over to Vaucluse, which was about three miles distant. I there learned that the Federal troops had been there the afternoon before, but had not come from Winchester and it was supposed that Winchester was wholly unoccupied.

Bearing the burden of my dreadful news, I determined that I would risk a visit home. I think I went back for my horse and rode into Winchester, getting there in the night. You can imagine my reception and the sorrow which my coming brought. They had not yet heard of my brother David's death.

Fanny wrote immediately, although briefly, to Bolling.

[LETTER OF FANNY J. BARTON TO BOLLING W. BARTON]

[undated]

My precious Bolling

I cannot bear to tell you of the pain & heavy sorrow which has just befallen us but you must know it & I know you would rather hear it from one at home. Our dear noble brother David fell on Sunday. He was killed instantly & we know how well prepared he was for the change.

In anguish of heart we are still ready to exclaim "how merciful are the ways of God." Mama & Papa are wonderfully supported under it and I trust my darling that all of us will be brought near *very near* to Him who is ready to welcome the weary & heavy laden. How very precious His promises are to us now Oh! what else could enable us to bear it.—May God bless you my darling brother & show you where to seek comfort.

Brother David was buried in a private graveyard. He suffered little or no pain as he died instantly. The other boys were safe & well when we heard.

I cannot write more now but will soon

Your loving sister
Fan

Both Mrs. Lee and Cornelia McDonald, another Winchester lady who kept a diary, went to that week's prayer meeting, which happened to be at the Bartons'. Mrs. Lee had heard that David was killed instantly by a Minié ball; "Mr. Barton [was] utterly crushed & like a child in his grief . . . David had been in sixteen battles." The sensitive Mrs. McDonald was very moved:

[DIARY OF CORNELIA MCDONALD]

Mr. Barton himself prayed, and though his voice trembled and often ceased altogether from stifled sobbing, he uttered words of comfort and hope . . . standing by the hearth where all his life his boy used to sit and laugh and chat with his brothers and sister in the pleasant firelight. How his face and form must have been present to his mind, and how his sad thoughts must have wandered away to the silent traveler who was then on his way home.[63]

Robby's uncertain journey was followed by a brief family visit. It was untimely, as the Yankees entered town December 23 and occupied it the next day. After a hazardous escape from Winchester, he took a long way around to return safely to Rebel-held territory.

[MEMOIR OF ROBERT T. BARTON]

I found the family living in one room, where they sat and ate and mainly cooked———all to save fuel and expenses. The next day, my father sent to his Springdale farm for a horse for me, as the one I rode was very inefficient. I spent the day quietly with my mother and father and with a few friends to whom my presence there had been whispered. The enemy were not in town, but they were in all directions around the town, but it was hoped that I might escape before they came. To have it generally known that I was there might have led however to my betrayal. The servants who yet remained were, of course, aware of my presence at home but we trusted them and they proved faithful as long as they remained with my parents. The temptation to be free was too much for them, and before the war ended all of them left.[64]

The second morning of my stay at home, I was wakened quietly by my father who told me to get up and look cautiously out of the window. This I did and saw the horse of a Federal cavalryman fastened to the hitching post in front of the house. The soldier himself was in the kitchen getting something to eat. The servants had been out and discovered that the town was full of Yankees, the army of Gen. Milroy having come in in the night down the western turnpike.

The question then was how was I to escape. My new horse was in the Stable and we feared that he might be discovered and taken even if the house should not be searched. But neither trouble occurred. I determined that I would, when night came, mount my horse and boldly ride through the streets, trusting to audacity and darkness to hide my identity and conceal my Confederate uniform. What I feared most was the picket posts at the ends of the streets where the different roads entered town. To enable me to avoid them, Mr. Philip Williams (my father's law partner) and my father went up to the Cemetery and broke places in the fences so that I could get through to the lots and fields beyond and thus get between the picket posts. As there was a great deal of movement among the troops, it was deemed wisest to defer my departure until very early the next morning.

Between 3 and 4 o'clock I was ready: my mother gave me my breakfast and something to put in my pockets to eat, and I went to the Stable which was on

Kent Street back of the Market Street house. After examining my horse a little and reflecting that I had never been on his back and knew nothing about him, I feared to take the Cemetery route, lest, if I should be pursued, I could not manage my horse amongst the grave stones and might be captured. I therefore sent the servant man down the road then known as "Quillens road" and which runs east from town at the east end of Cork Street.[65] I waited at the Stable and he was to return and tell me if there was a picket on that road, for if there was not I had determined to try that route. Meanwhile I waited in the cold dark morning at the Stable. In about an hour he came back and said that while pickets were in sight north and south of the road, that is on the Berryville and Front Royal roads, the enemy had neglected to picket the "Quillens road." This seemed a very fortunate circumstance to me so parting with the friendly servant, I rode boldly down Kent Street, passing Federal soldiers on the way and with a sentinel in full view as I turned to the left at the street just north of the one that leads to the Cemetery and then passed along East Lane until I turned to the left again into the Quillens road.

In full sight and hearing was the picket on the Berryville road. They were dismounted and standing around a bright fire laughing and talking. The light showed them very plainly to me while I was moving cautiously in the dark. If I had had one or two companions, I could have killed or captured the crowd and yet made good my escape. As it was the boot was on the other leg and I feared every minute that the loud step of my horse on the frozen ground would attract their attention to me and that they would cut across the unfenced lots and capture me. Then too, I was in constant fear there might be a picket on my road with prudence enough not to have a bright fire. But no such misfortune befell me and when I was safely beyond the picket line that I could see, I spurred up my horse and let him go at rapid speed for a mile or two. . . .

Robby continued east to Fauquier County, then in Confederate hands, spending the night with Marshall relatives.

[MEMOIR OF ROBERT T. BARTON]

Early the next morning I went on my way, crossing the mountain at Linden Gap and from there directing my route to Strasburg. So I approached Strasburg, when just opposite the mouth of what is known as "The Fort" or "Powell's Fort Valley," I met some Confederates hastily fleeing from Strasburg where they said the enemy had come again and taken possession.[66] Joining

Lewiston, near Port Republic. (Lewis Fisher)

these Confederates I went with them up the Fort Valley and spent the night with an old farmer in that secluded and comparatively well protected place. The next morning I crossed the Massanutten Mountain and arriving at Woodstock, found myself well within the Confederate lines.

I think the next day was Xmas, but where I spent it I do not remember, but certainly not in either pleasure or comfort in those sad days.

This brings me near to the end of the year 1862 . . . but I cannot pass away from this year without telling you of a little visit I paid in the fall. . . .

In my duties in connection with the nitre department, I had frequently to visit the neighbourhood of Weyers Cave, near to which I had some men engaged in getting dirt out of a cave and extracting the nitre from it. A few miles from there was [Lewiston] the home of Gen. [Samuel Hance] Lewis. His mother or grandmother was a sister of my great great grandmother Mrs. Gabriel Jones, both of whom were Misses Strother and formerly from Culpepper Co. Va. I had often heard my parents speak of Gen. Lewis and I determined to pay him a visit.

On one of my trips to the Cave I went to the house of Gen. Lewis and was most cordially received by him. The General and all his family were strong Union people, altho one of his sons was in the Confederate Army. This however did not interfere with the kindly treatment which I received and I enjoyed the visit very much.

Now the house of Gen. Lewis was a very conspicuous feature on the battle field of Port Republic. I observed it during the fight and was in the yard in the afternoon after the battle. The General showed me where a shell from one of our batteries had penetrated the wall of his house and exploding in his china closet, had utterly destroyed his stock of porcelain ware. From the direction from which the shot came, it was very probable that it was fired by my own battery and I told the General so, but that only furnished a theme for jokes at the table that night and he seemed to feel no anger about it. We walked together over the battle field where the hogs had rooted up the dead, and bones and skulls lay thick around. It was then I found again my friendly apple tree and counted the seven bullet holes in it. The next day I rode round the Country with Gen. Lewis, crossing the river to visit the grave and former home of my ancestor Gabriel Jones and his wife.[67] . . .

VIII

January—May 1863

WINTER QUARTERS
LETTERS FROM OCCUPIED WINCHESTER AND THE FIELD
CHANCELLORSVILLE

Having decisively fended off the latest Yankee thrust toward Richmond, Lee's army settled into winter quarters around Fredericksburg. Perhaps uneasy at first, they soon made the best permanent camp they could; the Stonewall Brigade was near Moss Neck, about twelve miles east of Fredericksburg, naming their camp for their late commander. The winter was an unusually cold and snowy one for Virginia, and the men were short of clothing. Strother, for four months commanding his company, requisitioned shoes for his men on January 21, saying "the men were barefoot." Over the next month he placed several orders: "The men actualy kneeded the clothing."[1] (Rannie may have had little faith in requisitions; in any event, he began writing again to Bolling to send him shoes.) At Camp Winder, the Bartons of the 2nd Virginia—Rannie, Strother, and Willie—and Bev Jones were able to spend some time together. In letters to Bolling, both Rannie and Strother succumbed to the common error of misdating the new year.

[LETTER OF RANDOLPH BARTON TO BOLLING W. BARTON]

Camp Winder Jan. 18th 1862

Dear Boly

I rec your letter of the 11th several days ago, it is a great pleasure to rec them and they are generally read by us three and Uncle Bev [Jones]. I flatter myself that you enjoy mine as much as we do yours, not because they are *highly inter-*

esting but merely because they are letters. You don't hear from home now I suppose, but you see Robby often and he sympathizes with you in all our troubles. . . .

Cunningham was returned yesterday from a week's picket on the Rappahannock, the 2nd 5th and 27th were held as a reserve to the 4th and 33rd and were employed in fortyfying the heights along the river. I commanded a squad of 50 men engaged in the work and we made a right good cannon-stand. Our position is almost impregnable, and if the Yankees advance here (things look like they did intend to) we will slaughter them. I think it has been since last writing, that Uncle Bev, Willie, Bro S[trother] and myself all got horses and visited Fredericksburg and vicinity. We rode all over the town and battlefield, visited Mr. Barton's house. The river at that point is just like the North river a half mile above the bridge, same in size, width, bluffs, etc. We rode to the banks, saw plenty of Yankees, pitching quoits, riding, lounging, smoking and everything else a man who has nothing else to do, would do. Our men on this side doing pretty much the same thing. No firing was the order, which accounts for our boldness in going so close. Mr. Bartons house had only one shell through the main building, the Yankee soldiers however had torn everything like books, pictures and china to pieces.[2] The destruction as represented in the papers is not exaggerated, almost every house in each end of the town has been pierced by some half dozen shots of shell. We then visited cousin Charles Marshall, Major on Genl Lees staff, saw the Genl, and had a pleasant chat with cousin C, you reccollect him, cousin Lillys brother.[3] About sundown we started to return, Willie who was on a hard horse, after we had ridden about 8 miles got very sore and vexed, we had a good deal of fun out of him. Altogether we had an agreeable visit. . . .

Dear Boly although that passage of scripture may well apply to me, "Take the mote out of thine own eye, before seeking to pluck it out of thy brothers, trust in God and you can fear nothing." Direct as before. Get the shoes, even if they cost as high as $25.00 remember tight No. 8, please get them as soon as possible. Love to cousins J and M.[4] God willing, I pray we may meet again.

your devoted bro R.J. Barton

"Well done Master Bolling! Stick to it" was the message of Strother's little note enclosed in Rannie's letter. For Robby's new duties with Nitre and Mining he was based in Staunton, but his work took him all over the Valley and sometimes to the other side of the Blue Ridge, to Lynchburg. He frequently saw Tom Marshall, with the 7th Virginia Cavalry, as for most of the winter Gen. W. E. Jones's cavalry command was camped near Edinburg, about thirty-three miles

south of Winchester in the Valley. Robby's job was to supervise the collection of
nitre (produced from the decomposition of excrement), which when combined
with potash became saltpeter, an ingredient of gunpowder.

[MEMOIR OF ROBERT T. BARTON]

The opening of the year 1863 found me actively engaged in the duties of my
office, the needs of the army requiring that the manufacture of nitre should be
greatly increased and at the same time that only men should be employed in it
who were not fit for service in the field, for powder and soldiers to use it were
the crying demands of the hour. I was energetic in increasing the product per
man and quite successful in devising newer and better means of extracting it,
and I had also learned by experience where I could procure the richer earth.
We relied to some extent on caves, but the more valuable deposits were under
old houses which had no foundation. Generally the owners did not object to our
excavating under the houses, but sometimes they did and then we had to do it
by force, for those were rough times and the public need was regarded as superior to private rights. I had even a harder time about the men. Many of them
were feigning sickness or inability to serve, sometimes because they were cowards, and sometimes because their families and home affairs made it to the last
degree hard that they should be drafted into the service. But I had no right to
consider these things and when I found an able bodied man I was obliged to
give his name to the conscripting officer, and if he did not then voluntarily
report for service a file of soldiers was sent for him, and a sad scene ensued.

Sometimes the men fearing that they would be sent into service, deserted
and took to the mountains. Once I had some soldiers sent for two men who had
left in this way and the soldiers found them fortified in a little house. A sharp
exchange of rifle shots took place and they were only finally dislodged by firing
the building. Continuing still to fight, both of them were killed by the soldiers.

The great body of the Confederate soldiers were volunteers and no finer
troops ever lived. These I have told you about were the exceptions, but the
necessities of the army, as the war went on, required the draft to be very closely
applied and much poor material was turned into soldiers.

My communication with home was very uncertain and only by such people
as could from time to time pass through the lines. I knew how sad it was to all
at home and the cruel control of Gen. Milroy, who ruled at Winchester, made
life hard indeed to all who were compelled to stay there. . . .

Union Brig. Gen. Robert H. Milroy's command had entered Winchester at Christmas 1862, and his occupation was generally agreed to be the most onerous of the war. The occupying army was rougher and less disciplined this year, with all kinds of intrusions and thievery. They stole food from home gardens and tore down fences for their campfires, adding to the disorder and confusion of having an army present, and leading to frequent confrontations. "Dr. Baldwin's garden looked like a gypsy encampment," Mrs. Lee lamented to her diary; when Lute saw the troops starting to pull down the fence between her and the Bartons, she "ran to tell [Mr. Barton], he was very mad & was very near knocking the man down."[5] Milroy was an active abolitionist, and this exacerbated the towns-

General Robert H. Milroy.
(Massachusetts Commandery, MOLLUS, U.S. Army Military History Institute)

people's grievances. A week later, more fence burning precipitated another incident, and the redoubtable Mrs. Portia Baldwin went to complain. She later regaled Mrs. Lee with the account of her visit to Milroy.

[DIARY OF MARY GREENHOW LEE]

I found, this morning, that the Yankee negroes left to take care of the horses in Dr. [R. T.] Baldwin's stable, had been burning our fence again, so I went over to see the result of Mrs. B's last visit to Milroy, & Dickens himself could not have pictured a richer scene. She told him John Brown was the cause of the war; he said it was a lie; she drew up close to him & looked, as only Mrs. B. can look & said in a vicious tone, "don't you say I lie" whereupon he got into such a

Fanny J. Barton's watercolor copy of Cornelia McDonald's valentine. "Out, you damned rebel," cries the General. "Jackson will avenge us!" retorts the departing lady.
(Ann Dudley Field Lalley)

rage, that he danced about the room & ordered her out in the most insolent manner. She slowly retreated keeping her eye on him. She acted the whole scene.[6]

Mrs. Baldwin told the story around town, and a few days later Mrs. Cornelia McDonald wrote:

[DIARY OF CORNELIA MCDONALD]

Last Saturday I was in company with some girls, cousins and friends, at Cousin Mick [Millicent] Tidball's. One of them proposed to send Milroy a valentine. He had been rude to Mrs. Baldwin, ordering her from his room, and at the same time asking two coloured, and gorgeously dressed ladies to be seated. They entreated me to paint them one to send him. So I made a grey headed officer in uniform seated in a chair, and inviting two negro women to take seats, while with a frown he was repelling a handsome young lady (not Mrs. Baldwin) dressed in stripes of red and white, with grey muff and tippet. I heard he received it, and he might have done so, for he ordered a search and prosecution immediately.[7]

Among those at the Tidballs', and contributing her own sense of mischief, was Fanny Barton; she made a copy of Mrs. McDonald's watercolor for Mrs. Baldwin to keep. The general may have been amused as well as enraged, for he kept the sly caricature for the rest of his life. Apparently there were no reprisals, but his regime continued to be severe. Hoping to starve out the secessionists, he forbade produce for man or beast to be brought into town. The back garden had assumed added importance, but the destruction of fences ensured the escape of any pigs or chickens that had not already been stolen. Milroy's sway was high-handed and arbitrary: he conscripted private houses almost at whim, sometimes turning out the inhabitants. In one notorious instance, Milroy coveted the fine house of Lloyd Logan, a well-to-do tobacco merchant. Shortly after his arrival in Winchester, he moved in and made it his headquarters. Three months later, when Mrs. Milroy was expected, and despite the fact that two of the Logan ladies were very ill, he dispossessed the family and sent them through the lines. Elsewhere, officers were quartered in "secesh" houses, and in spite of Mr. Barton's attempted intervention and her own efforts, Mrs. Lee found herself with unwelcome Yankee guests in the back wing.[8] But under Yankee noses, she continued to play her dangerous games, collecting greenbacks from Southern sympathizers in the North, and spending them with lenient sutlers to obtain supplies she could hoard or send to the Rebels.[9] Milroy paid town servants to spy on their households, vigorously censored the mail, and exiled citizens who criticized him. Mrs. Eichelberger's school was closed by his order when a young teacher's note criticizing Milroy was intercepted; the teacher was sent through the lines six or eight miles out of town "and there left by the roadside to find friends and shelter as she may."[10] On January 1 the Emancipation Proclamation had become law, and it freed the slaves in all the rebelling states; many of the Yankee soldiery took it upon themselves to help freedom along, by direct action or by terrorizing slaves with rumors of what would happen to them on the return of the Confederates. Groups of Northern abolitionists appeared in the occupied territory and encouraged slaves to flee. Many left their owners with no destination and became camp followers or destitute refugees. As well as the hardships of military rule, the occupying army's large addition to the population of the town caused severe stress on its rudimentary sanitation system. Diseases reappeared in epidemic form, especially with the approach of warmer weather. In the spring of 1863, both of Robby's parents were seriously ill, his mother with typhoid fever and perhaps his father also. Robby may have suspected that his father's poor health was due to other causes as well.

However, the Federal occupation did allow for the renewal of communication with the North. For the Bartons it meant links with Jane's family in Maryland, and the return of sister Martha and the children from their prolonged visit there. But now they were largely cut off from their family members in the Confederacy. Vaucluse, ten miles south, was outside Yankee lines, and Bolling's grandmother found a way to send a letter to him. She was mourning David: "He had passed unhurt through such a number of battles that I felt as if he would never be touched. . . ." But she was confident that he was "clothed in that White Robe" and took comfort from that certainty. On an earthly plane, she missed being able to visit her loved ones in Winchester, especially Mattie and the children shortly due back from Maryland. The latest difficulties for those in Union-occupied territory were the effects of the Emancipation Proclamation and the required oath of allegiance.[11]

Apparently his grandmother's letter was the only one that Bolling received from Frederick County during this Federal occupation, although mail was regularly smuggled in and out. Bolly and Lud Baldwin, at Hampden-Sydney College, were also corresponding. Lud had seen his brother when he wrote on January 16: "Johnnie got here on Thursday looking very well, he only had 15 days furlough, he says he has a powerful boring time in Camp, that they go to bed between the hours of 8 and 2 and rise at 9 and dine at 4 fashionable hours for Rebels."[12]

Bolly's brothers, cousin, and brother-in-law furnished regular reports of life in winter quarters and whatever news or rumors from home they had to relay. Rannie's preoccupation this winter was new shoes; Robby's, the snafu in his transfer. They did not expect a Yankee advance after General Burnside's January 22 attempt had been bogged down in the mud. Rannie must have sent the following letter to Robby to be mailed in Staunton.

[LETTER OF RANDOLPH BARTON TO BOLLING W. BARTON, WITH ENCLOSURE OF ROBERT T. BARTON]

Camp Winder Feb 2nd 63

Dear Boly

Your letter and one from Robby, was received by bro S[trother] and myself with much pleasure. You cant imagine what pleasure it gives us to see them; we always read them over twice and then pass them to uncle Bev and Willie. I have been very much bored lately, by the monotony of a camp life, but the elegant news from Charleston and the west revived me greatly.[13] . . . Robby writes that the horse had arrived in safety—No doubt you will see, if so take a short ride on him. He belongs to bro S[trother] according to some arrangement made between him and dear bro David. Bro S would not have him injured for any consideration, as he hopes peace is so near he may preserve him for his riding horse. We sometimes picture to ourselves, the life we would live at old Spring dale with sister Mat. The picture is so delightful we dare not dream it. I see no signs of a battle for a long time, since Burnside *stick in the mud* we have had no evidence of a desire on their part to cross the river. Various rumours are in circulation about the lst Brigade going to the Valley under J.E.B. Stuart on a *plundering* and *rail*-road destroying expedition, we credit none of them, but would be delighted to do so. We are well and all send love. Give mine to all inquiring friends. Persevere in a course which I pray you have begun.

Your devoted bro

R J Barton

P.S. Enclosed is $20.00 for shoes. Robby has some idea of coming down, send them as soon as possible, and by a *safe* opportunity.

RJB

[on outside of self-envelope, within the fold]

Staunton Feb 7th/63

Dear Bolly,

    I intercepted this letter, read it and took out the money, this is a species of high-way robbery, but you must excuse the liberty. God bless you my dear Bolly

Yr affec bro

RT Barton

Early in January, Robby had learned to his dismay that his transfer from the Rockbridge Artillery had never been officially processed by the young but already full-blown Confederate bureaucracy. He wrote to the doctors on his Medical Examining Board and also must have asked Strother to talk to Dr. J. A. Straith, who had presided and was Assistant Surgeon of the 2nd Virginia. "On account of the great formality with which things are now conducted," Strother explained, much paperwork was required. Finally, at the end of February, the transfer became official. As for Strother, he was intent upon getting his horse (formerly David's) out of harm's way to Robby, and probably sent it to Staunton with someone going on furlough. In return he wanted Robby to send him "a bundle of the best segars in the town. I am a confirmed smoker," he confessed. He passed on Rannie's message to "forward by the first safe opportunity" the long-awaited pair of shoes.[14]

It was the season for furloughs, which apparently were freely given in the winter months, and for letter writing. The 1st Virginia Cavalry was encamped to the southeast of Camp Winder, and the relative inactivity of winter moved Bolling's cousin Robert Barton to answer his letter.

[LETTER OF ROBERT R. BARTON TO BOLLING W. BARTON]

Camp King William Co. Feb 5th

Dear Boley

I got your letter some days ago but havent been able to answer it until now. Although we have been in camp ever since I wrote we have so many roll calls drills & other duties that we have hardly had time to turn around. I commenced a letter to you two or three days ago but became so disgusted with the first half page that I concluded to wait until I felt more like writing which time I fear hasn't yet arrived (as you can easyly perceive—but the *Divil fly away with all such blarney*, the weather set in tremendously this morning—in the snowing line I mean—it has turned to sleet now it is just giving it to the horses. We are to march somewhere in three or four days—we have a dozen different reports as to where. I think it will be Culpepper & some where in that county— possibly the neighborhood of Winchester. I hope it may be so.

We very seldom get the papers here & dont know what is going on in the world—I wish we might wake up some morning & find that peace had been declared without ever having heard of the prospect.

The morrals of the men are improving very fast—we had only six horse blankets one oven & one pistol stolen out of our company last night—the pistol was found in the possession of a negro belonging to the company he was put down on his hands & knees & had his behind strapped with a stirrup leather for about an half hour—I hope it will do him good. I am very glad indeed to hear that you got through your examinations so well—I hope it may always be so.

I havent seen Ned Moore since I left but I have heard from him once since.[15] We have a fellow in the mess that we are continualy worrying two

Robert R. Barton's cartoon of his mess-mate.
(Mrs. C. Marshall Barton, Jr.)

fellows one scuffing with him now which with the want of paper to write oblige me to stop—I have endeavored to give you some idea of his phiz. I hope you may be able to read this however I may doubt it. Believe me yours most truly

R Barton

Since it was difficult, if not impossible, to write to the families in Winchester, Bolling received more letters than usual—even from Uncle Bev. Bev was never quite satisfied with his lot, which was now as Hospital Steward. The following letter and Rannie's of the same date were sent in one envelope. Their writing coincided with a visit from Robby, fresh from Staunton, delivering Rannie's long-awaited new shoes, procured by Bolly, and a "care package" from Willie's mother, Aunt Caroline.

[LETTER OF BEVERLEY R. JONES TO BOLLING W. BARTON]

Camp Winder
Feb 13/63

Dear Bolly,

I have just read your last letter to Ranny & will add a few lines & enclose them, in his missive to you. I suppose you know that I have an appointment as Med Steward & have been assigned to the 33rd Va Reg (Stonewall Brigade). I do not altogether like the position, I am anxious to get a situation with brother James. . . .

My Reg went on picket this morning & much to my joy Niep Baldwin did not require that I should accompany them.[16] I spent a week there about a month ago & was quite well satisfied. The whole Brigade does not go now (as it did then) but picket by Reg—which requires us to stay only 2 days at a time. . . .

I trust that God will soon bless us again with peace, This war has cost us dear enough but our lives being ordered by him who orders all things for the best, it is our duty willingly to submit. . . . God grant my dear Bolly that I may soon hear that you (now the last of your family not of the church) have united

yourself with it & chosen the side of the Lord. I am a poor hand to write letters. . . . Burn this little note and write soon to your

Affectionate uncle

Bev. R. Jones

[LETTER OF RANDOLPH BARTON TO BOLLING W. BARTON]

Camp Winder Feb 13th 63.

Dear Boly

Your letter has just reached us and we hasten to answer it. Robby arrived
here Wednesday; and of course was rec by us with great joy. He brings a box to
Willie, which we have not received yet, as he left it at the depot expecting to
send next day for it, we had no opportunity—however and hope it lays there
yet, we will walk down to-morrow with Robby and try to get it. It will be a sad
dissappointment to us if we lose it for *boxes are boxes* in the army.

Robby also brought my elegant pair of shoes, which suited and fitted me to a
perfection, many thanks to you for getting them. We were on pickett last Monday and Tuesday on the Rappahannock. My post was within a few feet of the
river out of which we washed and drank. The Yanks opposite do the same.[17] we
had some conversation with them, but as it was contrary to orders they were not
very talkative. We sent the last "Illustrated News" across on a rail, they in return
sent the Boston Journal. Uncle Bev and myself have put in for fifteen days furlough, which we hope will be granted, if so, and if impossible to get to *Vaucluse*
I will pay you a short visit. I hope it will go through as I am anxious to rove a
little. . . . The 33rd & 27th went on picket this morning, to be relieved tomorrow. Uncle Bev & bro S[trother] are playing back-gammon now on a homemade box. . . . Excuse a short letter. Dont expect me certainly. . . .

your devoted bro RJ Barton

*Despite heavy snows February 17, the Federals were moving, and two divisions
of Longstreet's corps moved on the eighteenth to the east of Richmond to protect
it from that direction. This activity did not seem to concern Strother Barton;
perhaps he knew the Yankees would be defeated again by the mud. His duties
this winter included sitting on court-martial cases. In mid-February he wrote
his youngest brother an unusually serious letter; as with the rest of the family,
he felt responsible for the state of Bolly's soul and joined in urging Bolly on in
his religious progress. He passed along army news and struck a tragicomic note
in describing the fate of Aunt Caroline's package.*

[LETTER OF W. STROTHER BARTON TO BOLLING W. BARTON]

Camp Winder
Feby 18th 1863

Dear Bolling

I am now about to fulfill my promise of writing. I could have written before but I have been much engaged in taking care of my important command and on court-marshaling runaways and cowards that I have not before this time, had a convenient opportunity. We are still at our old encampment about twelve miles east of Fredericksburg, on the Rappahannock. I would not be supprized at any time to receive orders to pack and be ready to move at a moments warning. The Yankeys from the other side have all disapeared. No one but Genl Lee, seems to know where they have gone to. A considerable portion of our army has already moved, and are still moving. The rain is now pattering upon the roof of our tent and I cant help thinking about what a "good time" Mr. Hookers yanks must be having trudging it through the mud.[18] Robby paid us a visit last week, he seemed to enjoy his visit. We certainly did. . . .

You do not know how rejoiced I was to see from your letter evidence of the working of Grace in your heart. . . . I know the difficulties to which one in your condition has to contend, and truely do I sympathize with you, amongst the wild boys that you meet at the institute, perhaps no one to give you counsel or advice or to extend their sympathies. I do not wonder if your heart sometimes sinks within you when you keep in view the prize, Is it not worth the trouble? Do you remember that I am now your oldest living brother, as such you know that I stand next to your parents. You can not doubt the interest and take in the important decision which I feel that you are now called upon to make. . . . Decide to enlist under the banner of Christ. I know well the time when I was called upon to make the same decision, can you think that I ever regretted the decision then made? My only regret is that I have not been a more zealous worker in the cause of the Lord. . . .

We received a letter from brother Tom [Marshall] the other day. He is still in the valley with Genl Jones. . . . I suppose that you have heard the rumor of Grigsby superseeding Jones. I can not tell whether there is any truth in it or not. Grigsby was here the other day and I think he is evidently fishing for it.[19]

The boys experienced a great disappointment the other day, in this wise. Aunt Caroline sent a box to Willie by Robby who brought it as far as Guineas Station, the station nearest to our camp, and placed it in the hands of the agent for receiving private boxes. He then came on to our camp intending to send for it, but, not finding an opportunity, we went down a day or two afterwards to the Station to try and contrive it up—You may well imagine our disappointment at finding that some fiend in human form had fourged an order and carried off the box—Poor Ranny was almost broken hearted—he has looked hungry ever since. Ranny has applied for a furlough. I think that he will get it. . . . Jim Garnett was promoted to Captain in the Ordnance department the other day "bully" position, you will say—perfectly bullet proof.[20] . . . that God may give you strength to decide properly is the prayer of your devoted brother

W.S. Barton

P.S. the boys send love.

In Winchester they were probably saying that David Barton would negotiate with the devil. He was one of the few who succeeded in gaining any sort of concession from General Milroy. Perhaps the Federal commander saw how very unwell he was and experienced a rare moment of humanity. Barton's persuasive letter—it might almost be called a brief—was well received; Milroy penned his approval on the back and returned it.

[LETTER OF DAVID W. BARTON TO GEN. ROBERT H. MILROY]

General R. H. Milroy

Winchester
February 24/ 63

Dear Sir—

As Spring is close at hand, it is high time our farmers should be making preparation for cropping. I find however in conversing with them a general indisposition to incur the labors & costs of putting in crops, which they may never be permitted to gather or enjoy & I fear that much of our Land in this section will for that reason remain uncultivated. As no good can result to anybody, but much harm every way, from such a condition of things, I take the liberty of suggesting to you very respectfully, that, by some general order or proclamation, you give to our people some encouragement to cultivate their Lands by an assurance that the crops will not be disturbed or molested by the Federal Authorities. In the Spring of last year General Banks then in command here adopted that plan to allay the fears & encourage the industry of our farming community, & the result was a very respectable crop of grain Hay & other necessary food for men & Beast. Our population quietly remaining at their homes, should certainly be encouraged to make timely provision for their actual wants; & if more should be raised than we need, your services have at least an equal chance with the Southern, to get the surplus.

My Farm 5½ miles south of Winchester on the Strasburg road, ought to have at least 100 acres in corn this Spring & my slaves having gone I shall have to rely on the small Farmers round me who work for themselves, to crop upon my land.[21]

This they are willing to do if they can be protected & secured in the fruits of their labour. It is for you, General, to give them this protection & assurance & to set them to work. Will you authorize me to give them such assurance?

Your endorsements of this letter would be a sufficient guarantee; for in the probable event of your promotion & removal to a wider field of services I am confident your order would be respected by all who may succeed you.

> Respectfully yrs
> D.W. Barton

Mr. Barton can proceed to cultivate & crop his Lands as he proposes & the protecting order which he already holds shall extend to any crops he may raise on his Lands through his tenants or otherwise.

> R.H. Milroy
> Feby 26 1863 Brig. Genl.
> U.S.A.

The approach of spring also meant the resumption of active campaigning. As he had expected, cousin Robert Barton and the 1st Virginia Cavalry had moved camp to the vicinity of Culpeper, where the forage was usually good. His letter was written on return from a scout from Centreville to Falmouth.

[LETTER OF ROBERT R. BARTON TO BOLLING W. BARTON]

> Camp near Culpeper C.H.
> Feb 27th 1863

Dear Boley

I found your letter here yesterday evening when we got off a scout which we had been on for the last three days.

We (our Brigade—part of it) crowsed the river at Kelleys foard & proceeded down the river (Rappahannock) eight or ten mls where we encamped for the night.

In the morning we went on to the U.S. foard near wich we encountered the Enemys pickets which we captured without any resistance on their part. We had only two squadrons of the first out (lst & 4th) & we were in front—from the hill where we captured the pickets we could see for two miles—where we came out of the woods we saw a yankee regiment march down the hill for three or four hundred yds & draw up in line as if to make or receive a charge—we were ordered to charge them & away we went at a slapping pace for over a mile but as soon as the *gentlemen* saw that we were going to pitch in to them they broke & ran in every direction firing behind them occasionaly—I noticed two fellows off to the left & pitched off after them yelling to them to surrender & throw down their arms—which they did in a hurry—they were armed simply with carbines & sabres having either thrown away their pistols or never having had any.

While we were disarming them I noticed a fellow in the woods dismount & behind a tree I rode up & took him—while I was fooling with him—two fellows rode off with my two prisoners & so I lost my horses & trappings—the horses would have to have been given up anyway.

We formed again & waited for them to come back which they did in about an hour—one or two companies from the lst were thrown out as sharpshooters & skirmished with them for a while until the yankees attempted a charge with a *sickley yell*—the 3rd regiment was ordered to charge them—which they did in very pretty style scattering the yankees to the four winds. We concluded then that we had *cleaned them out* pretty effectively & I supposed Gen Fits [Fitz Lee] had found out all he wanted to know so we turned tail & came to camp. I dont think they followed us at all. our regiment was in the rear & we didnt hear any thing of them—we took between one hundred fifty to two hundred prisoners & nearly as many horses arms & c. It is reported that Genl Stuart was to have crowsed at the United States foard where we would have joined him—but perhaps the river was too high to crowse—some of the prisoners said that he had crowsed before we got there if he did I suppose we will here from him before long.

The march was tremendous on our horses. Shep stood it pretty well however. I hope you will soon have an opportunity to ride him—the war being over and I being along with you on another.

It is still reported that it is likely we will go to the Valley. I would like very much to charge into Winchester down/up Market Street especialy. . . . Do you

ever hear from Winchester or from Strother Ran Rob & Willie? When you next
write to either give them my best love

I am very especialy yours
Robt Barton

*Rannie and Bev were both granted furloughs in late February, since there was
no military activity, and decided, since a visit to Winchester was impossible, to
attempt to reach Vaucluse to see some of the family and learn news of the others.
Vaucluse was about six miles outside the Union lines, and was subjected to frequent Yankee cavalry patrols, so such excursions were forbidden to individual
Confederate soldiers.*

*Unbeknownst to Rannie and Bev, on the night of February 25, pickets from
the 1st Maryland Cavalry had surprised their Federal counterparts at
Kernstown. The Steele children of Newtown saw all the war traffic on the Valley Turnpike: "This morning at five o'clock a squad of our men came through
town. They came on the pike at the toll gate and captured seven Yankees and
seventeen horses. At eight o'clock five hundred Yankees followed them up about
six miles above Strasburg. There they met Gen. Jones with three or four hundred men. The Yanks fired a few shots and ran. Our men after them, killing and
wounding them as they ran. Our men followed them as far as McLeod's Hill,
near town. Some of the Yanks were without hats, some were leading horses with
empty saddles. They were covered with mud. some threw away their overcoats,
some their guns. . . ."22 The Federal cavalry pursuit was almost to Woodstock,
even as the two truants were working their way north, and they witnessed the
Rebel counterattack, which chased the enemy all the way back to Middletown.*

*Stopping in Staunton on his way back to camp, Rannie wrote Bolly about his
frustrating furlough, using letterhead paper purloined from Robby's or his
Uncle James's supplies.*

[LETTER OF RANDOLPH BARTON TO BOLLING W. BARTON]

Confederate States of America
War Department
Nitre and Mining Bureau
Staunton March 3, 1863

Dear Boly,

You no doubt have heard that I was up on furlough. It commenced the 20th
of last month and ends the 7th of this. We, Uncle Bev and myself, spent the

21st in Richmond. We then came to Staunton and stayed one day, and then started down the Valley. We got to Edinburg on Wednesday, dined with bro. Tom [Marshall] and went on to Woodstock that evening.

Next day we started for Vaucluse, intending to *flank* Jones's picketts, and had gotten within 6 miles of Strasburg, when we met our Cavalry picketts just driven in. We immediately left the road, and started back marching along parrallel with the turnpike and about half a mile from it. After retreating about 2 miles thinking we were in a safe place we stopped to get dinner after which we started out towards the turnpike, upon reaching which we were informed the Yanks had been up opposite the house we were eating dinner in. Our Cavalry came charging down the turnpike, the 12th first, then the 7th bro Tom's. We got in an ambulance and followed in their rear. We succeeded in getting two miles below Strasburg when we met our cavalry returning from the chase. As soon as Genl Jones saw us, he turned on back and would have put us under guard but Holmes Conrad vouched for us, and we only gave him our word not to go farther.[23] We got on captured horses and returned to Woodstock.

You have heard the result of the chase. Some 200 prisoners, same no. horses and arms, pistols, sabres, etc. Col. Funsten did good service, bro Tom's stirrups broke and he consequently killed no one. Col. Dulaney killed two.[24] The prisoners were direct from Winchester, one Lieut. told me the Court House had been gutted. I don't believe Winchester is in as bad condition as some report.

Sukey has gone at last, Wm. Peterson demanded his 3 children. I don't know whether Nancy has gone or not.[25] I heard the above through a letter from cousin Anna to bro Tom, she heard lately from Pa.[26] I return day after to morrow to Richmond next day to camp. I had hoped to be able to visit you, but my stay down the Valley was longer than I expected. . . . Bro S[trother] will be up on furlough soon I expect. When he hears the result of my trip down the Valley, he will probably be up to see you. Robby is in Lynchburg, be back tomorrow. Uncle James is funny as ever. Pa has sold Shady Oak and Buena Vista.[27] Answer my letter to camp, excuse miserable writing.

Your devoted bro
R.J. Barton

Bolling must have been particularly distressed to hear that Sukey had left the family—many of the Winchester slaves had succumbed to Yankee blandishments. Practically in the same mail he must have received and been amused by Tom Marshall's account of Rannie and Bev's escapade.

[LETTER OF THOMAS MARSHALL TO BOLLING W. BARTON]

Head Quarters 7th Va Cavy
Near Edinburgh
March 8th 1863

Dear Bolly,

Your last letter in reply to one written by me reached me in due course of mail. I am very much pleased at having you as a correspondent, as we are both cut off from those we hold so dear, we must try to "bear one another's burdens", & so in the blessed language of the Gospel "fulfil the laws of Christ". Your letters give me unfeigned pleasure. I know how gratifying they would be to your dear parents.

You have, perhaps, seen some account in the papers of the nice threshing we gave the Yankees the other day. The eleventh Regiment under Lt Col. Funsten, & ours (the 7th) threshed them, pursued them beyond Middletown, killing & wounding some & taking from 150 to 200 prisoners.

I got in sight of dear old Vaucluse & sent a letter & paper there. *"Ran"* & *"Bev"* had just been to see me the day before, & had left me intending to try & flank the pickets & get to uncle Strothers. Our column passed them the next day on the road. I gave a cheer for the *"Old Stonewall"*, as we galloped by—but on my return in the evening found them at Strasburg. They had been in the mean time overhauled by *Genl Jones* in person, who made them give their word of honor not to try to return, so that they were effectually *bagged*. I got horses for them to ride & they returned with me as far as Woodstock that night, & the next day came to our Camp, and remained with me until Sunday evening, at which time they walked over to Mt Jackson, so as to be in place to take the stage the next day for Staunton. Poor fellows, they were no doubt sorely disappointed, consoling them selves however with the idea that they might have been caught by the Yankees at Vaucluse, if they had succeeded in reaching there.

I was sorry to see "Ran" looking badly. He has been suffering from the use of bad water. I thought I could see an improvement in him in the day or two he was with me, & urged him to try & get a sick furlough at once if he did not find himself very much better before his return to his Brigade. "Bev" was looking as well as I ever saw him. They were canvassing the idea of endeavouring to obtain transfers from the infantry to join our Regiment, which would of course be very pleasant to me—but I did not think it right for Strother & Ran to lose their commissions. None of us know how long the war may last, nor what events may betide ere its termination. It would be hardly right for them to throw away a promotion, which they have providentially received. If there were any mode by which they could join us and retain the same rank or obtain higher, I would be delighted at it, but I do not now see any such opening.[28] I am sorry they did not get to see you. I begin to look forward to another visit from Robby soon. They are a great treat to me. I think he seems to enjoy himself, when he is with us. Colonel Dulaney is a very pleasant gentleman & companion. I have been very much favoured by a kind Providence with respect to my associates . . . excellent Christians—so that we have nothing to mar pleasant intercourse.

I have heard only indirectly of our dear ones in Winchester . . . Anna & Marshall [Jones] had both favored me with letters. . . . Marshall is at Vaucluse & writes to ask my advice as a friend as to the course he ought to pursue in regard to the army[29] . . . Every one at last must be the judge in his own case. I should dislike very much, if I were in his place, to be in danger of being under Yankee rule. . . .

And now my dear brother, I must bid you Goodbye. Press on in the Heavenward path & may God bless, preserve, & keep you,

Your affectionate brother,
Thomas Marshall

It seems that Tom must have said how poorly Rannie was looking, in the letter he mentioned sending on to Vaucluse. That report produced an anxious letter from Fanny to Rannie. Sent under flag of truce, the letter was full of veiled references, including what appears to be an allusion to Fan's part in the "Milroy valentine." The letter must have passed through the hands of the Magruders in Woodstock, as Mrs. Magruder added a note about some Northern goods headed south.

[LETTER OF FANNY J. BARTON TO RANDOLPH BARTON AND ROBERT T. BARTON]

[written across the top in pencil]

I have some handkerchiefs & gloves for Mrs. Neill, let me know what to do with them   Hastily   Mrs. Magruder[30]

Winchester
March 5th

We have felt *very* anxious about you my darling brother since we heard that you were looking so badly & I take advantage of the permission given the citizens to send letters through the lines (provided they contain nothing *trea-sonable*) to write & *beg* that you will try to get a discharge from the army. Papa & Mamma both wish it & it would be such a relief to us all to feel that you were no longer exposed to all of the dreadful weather & I think you ought to be satisfied with the long & hard service you have already seen. Dont think your Sister very *unpatriotic* dear Ran but I do long to have you where your health will not be endangered. I fear that you have heard very exagerated accounts of our sufferings here & that your anxiety about us has had something to do with your sickness.

Please dont feel uneasy about us for we get on wonderfully. Gen. Milroy has been particularly kind to papa & he has been allowed to go to Springdale whenever he chooses. As for the servants going off *we are charmed now* that they are gone. Their places are all filled by much more capable ones & we work ourselves very little more than we ever did. I make the most beautiful bread you ever saw & I assure you I am very proud of the accomplishment. . . .

We heard from sister J[ane] a short time ago. She is living among the kindest people you ever heard of truly her lines have fallen in pleasant places. God has been very good to us in many ways & we are too apt to forget these mercies while brooding over our *heavy sorrow*. I do so long to get a letter from dear little Bolling the last news we had of him made us so happy. I trust the last of our family has been taken into the fold of the Good Shepherd. May God bless & keep him. . . .

I know dear Ran you will think my letter stupid & dull but you must remember how I am restricted. I have so much I want to talk to you & brother S_ about & so much to tell you. I still hope for peace & the time when you all will be once more at home. I want to write a few lines to Robby on this sheet so I will stop with my warmest love for yourself & brother S— & the heart felt prayer for your safety & speedy return to us. I advise you not to try *my feelings* any more. I fear it in us in that way you took cold.[31] Ever your loving sister

F———

Dear Robby I inclose to you this letter for Ranny. Please forward it to him as soon as possible & do try to send us word or letter to let us know how he is.[32] We were glad to hear through Anna that you were well. We have never heard from you—except once since the eventful morning on which you left us. Ran's letter will tell you all the news I am allowed to send. I have been drawing & painting a good deal lately & have some pretty pictures I want to show you when you are home.[33] . . . You all must not believe half the reports you hear about us because they are dreadfully exagerated. Good bye. May God bless you all my precious brothers

Cousin Robert, still in camp near Culpeper, was anticipating spring and even thinking of his boyhood summers in Lexington.

[Letter of Robert R. Barton to Bolling W. Barton]

Culpepper C.H. March 9th

Dear Boley

This is a regular spring day and I realy begin to feel spring feverish already—I am so lazy that I can hardly drag the pencil over the paper. Your letter came to hand very promptly this time, I hope it may always be so in future.

I think the Confederacy is about up in the horsefeed line—we havent gotten anything for our horses for two weeks except wheat in the sheaf—I hope they will soon conclude that they cant feed us and will send us home—I suppose though that they will be after puting us in the infantry when it comes to that. *Jeb* Stuart is amongst us again. I expect we will be moving out of this shortly. I am going to try very hard to get a furlough in a month or two on what grounds I dont know.

I suppose you look forward with pleasure to July when your session will be over—the months to come I think will be much more pleasantly passed for you than the months already passed—you can wander about & enjoy the sunshine or shade & when it gets warmer you can bathe and fish. I would like mightily to wander along the old Cliffs back of the Institute & along the river bank up to Cave Springs—I have had some bulley times up there.

The Company were out on picket last week (I didnt go) they amused themselves by shooting at the ducks & gees on the river with their pistols. I believe they *didnt kill many* I hope that the *nex* time we go there may be nothing wuse to shoot—I have made my arrangements to take a wash (*bodily*) I hope therefore you will excuse me for the present you know it is a necessary little performance—if you dont *I do*—so goodbye

Yours R Barton

Robert was not sent home. He was in battle at Kelly's Ford eight days later, when Fitz Lee's brigade repelled a Federal cavalry probe in what might be described as a series of bloody skirmishes. Rannie, guiltily aware of disappoint-

ing Bolly by not visiting him, wrote an apologetic letter when he returned from his furlough. He was full of explanations but proffered the legitimate excuse of concern about the family at home, especially their father who, he heard, "was looking much better than he had been." Rannie, though still in poor health, was excited: "For the past week I have been Act Asst Adjt Genl for Genl Paxton, the appointment however is not permanent."[34] His new duties, which in battle would require carrying orders and dispatches, necessitated his having one or two horses, which he would be obliged to supply himself.

[MEMOIR OF RANDOLPH BARTON]

After a short furlough . . . I returned to the army [on March 7], and one day was surprised to receive an order calling me to brigade headquarters. Upon reporting at that place, General Paxton told me he had detailed me to act as Assistant Adjutant General of the brigade. This was flattering—to be selected from so many officers, and at the age of not quite twenty. The position was one of responsibility and dignity, giving me the rank of Captain of Cavalry.[35] . . . Paxton was confirmed by Congress as a Brigadier General, and, without telling me that he was going to retain me permanently, he told me he thought I had better get a horse. I considered this significant, but did not ask him "what his intentions were."

I proceeded to get an animal called by courtesy a horse, very raw-boned and very foolish—good "crow-bait" and nothing more. Towards the latter part of April came the news that "[U.S. Gen. Henry W.] Slocum had crossed the river near Chancellorsville." We knew that great events were at hand, and our command moved up in the neighborhood of Hamilton's Crossing to confront Sedgwick, who had crossed at or a little below Fredericksburg. It will be found upon examining the war histories that General Jackson had expressed an opinion in favor of attacking Sedgwick, and that General Lee, while not approving the measure, had authorized it, if General Jackson, upon full consideration, still favored it. I remember that on the afternoon of the 29th or 30th of April, the latter day, I think, by some combination of circumstances, which I have never been able to recall, I found myself, on the miserable apology for a horse that I had procured, near General Jackson, who, on foot, with his arms folded, was from the elevation looking over the plain which interposed between us and the enemy. A very unexpected shell from the enemy came over and burst not very far above us. My horse commenced to prance and in spite of spurs would go backwards instead of forwards, and as luck would have it backed immediately upon General Jackson, who nimbly stepped aside out of the way, saying noth-ing, but giving me a glance as he did so.

General Jackson determined that General Lee's judgment against the attack was sound, and abandoned the plan. How much my hammer-headed horse contributed to this conclusion, I do not know, but I am satisfied that the great soldier was at that moment pondering the subject, which was full of tre-mendous possibilities. The incident I have mentioned is trivial, but we read today, with keen interest, every little circumstance attending the campaigns of Napoleon, and so I have thought thus to preserve the circumstance of my inter-rupting the thoughts of a great soldier planning the destruction of the enemy.

How wonderfully different is the Jackson of 1860 from the historic character we now read of! When he was a professor no one recalls a smile, a humorous speech, anything from him while at the barracks. He was not sullen, nor gloomy, nor particularly dull. He was simply a silent, unobtrusive man, doing his duty in an unentertaining way—merely an automaton. And yet the cadets held him in high estimation. . . . The writer turns to a "scrap book" kept by a cadet [Charles Marshall Barton] at the Institute in 1855, and finds this doggerel:

> "HICKORY, ALIAS MAJOR T. J. JACKSON."
> "Like some rude brute that ranged the forest wild,
> So rude, uncouth, so purely Nature's child,
> Is 'Hickory,' and yet me thinks I see
> The stamp of genius on his brow,
> And he, with his wild glance and keen but quiet eye,
> Can draw forth from the secret recesses where they lie
> Those thoughts and feelings of the human heart.
> Most virtuous, good and free from guilty art,
> There is something in his very mode of life
> So accurate, steady, void of care or strife,
> That fills my heart with love for him who bears his honors meekly,
> And who wears the laurels of a hero."

And this about expressed the sentiments of the entire corps.[36] . . .

His older brothers just did not seem to find time to visit Bolling, either on busi-ness or on leave. All of them wanted home news, and all seem to have been particularly worried about their father. Robby understood Bolly's concerns about Sukey and Springdale. "You saw Marshall [Jones] I suppose and he gave you all the news from home, poor Sukey how deluded she was to leave such a comfortable home, to go off among strangers who cared nothing for her." Uncle Strother Jones arrived to report that "the Yankees have taken nothing from Springdale but as nearly all the servants are gone of course there can be very little done on the farm. Pa goes out there nearly every day."[37] *Robby and Strother felt responsible for Bolly in various ways, and both offered or sent him money. Rannie's appointment as A.A.G. was requested by General Paxton on March 28 and he was elated at the prospect of a promotion and pay raise. His financial offers to Bolly were vague at best (he seems to have been habitually short himself), but he always was most concerned about Bolling's soul.*

[LETTER OF RANDOLPH BARTON TO BOLLING W. BARTON]

Camp Winder March 29th 1863

I rec your letter, dear Boly, a few days ago and you are perfectly excusable in sending two letters in one envelope, I am only glad to receive them in any form. I read over Uncle Bevs part of the letter, and although I knew of your interest on the subject of religion, I was truly gratified to see that it still is alive within you. Dear Boly strive ernestly in your efforts to please God and seek for a new life. . . . You spoke in one of your letters of having no place where you could read alone, When I was there the Chapel was always very comfortable and nearly always vacant. How often when overcome with home-sickness, have I visited that room, and found consolation in prayer and in reading the Bible. If you are under the same circumstances why not use it also.

You know I have been Act. Asst. Adjt. Gen. for Genl. Paxton since my return from furlough. Yesterday he proposed to me to bring my blankets over and mess with him, and also to get a horse, now it would be very inconsiderate in him to tell me to trouble me with getting a horse, unless he meant for me to retain it, consequently I have some hopes of promotion. I have written to Robby to send me a horse. I hope he will send me brother Strothers, as he has given me permission to keep him if Robby choses to give him up. I can expect nothing until in one battle at least I have shown my ability to carry orders etc. God granting me protection, I will do it to my utmost capacity.

We are all well and enjoying excellent health, and spirits.

I heard yesterday that Winchester had been evacuated by the Yankees. I cant believe it, although in a Military point of view, I think it probable.[38]

We have been having a series of meetings [of] late, a large Chapel being always crowded.

As I wish to attend Bible Class I must end, will write oftener when I draw a *Captain's* pay and can spend more in stamps.

Your attached bro

R J Barton

Direct as before—Love to all—Army in splendid condition—Extra baggage sent to rear

Strother, just back from his furlough, also continued to encourage his youngest brother, and described the many religious meetings in camp that winter. On Fast Day, "we had preaching in Chapel three times during the day. Altogether the day presented the appearence of a sabbath day in peace times, that is as much so as the white tents will admit of." Recognizing a fifteen-year-old's temporal needs, he enclosed ten dollars for Bolly, and offered more. The army was "looking forward to being lead against Mr. Hooker," he said, "as soon as the mud dries up."39

On March 30, also anticipating the spring campaign, cousin Robert wrote Bolling, "yesterday was one of the most disagreeable days we have had for a month—today though looks a little more like spring. I think the Campaign will commence in a few days. We got orders this morning to send back all of the unnecessary bagage & various other orders peparatory to a march."

Furloughs, freely given when the army was inactive in winter quarters, would be available only "in very urgent cases—what urgent cases are is the difficulty—I hope that a broken down horse will be considered as such."40 If cousin Robert's horse broke down, he would probably have to go home to get another; Confederate cavalrymen were responsible for supplying their own mounts. Robert had heard bad reports from Winchester, but the Bartons seemed not to have any complaints about the Milroy regime, and Rannie had some lighthearted stories to pass on to his young brother. Mrs. Baldwin, the mother of Johnny and Lud, was well known to the Barton boys who could especially relish the story of her confrontation with General Milroy, which precipitated the "valentine." Rannie was clearly very excited about his promotion and nagged all his brothers about his need for a horse.

[LETTER OF RANDOLPH BARTON TO BOLLING W. BARTON]

Camp Winder April 8 1863

Your letter, dear Boly, was rec this evening and you cant tell how much gratified we were by the ernest way in which you spoke on the subject of religion. I have been comforted or encouraged by it, when away from home and friends. . . . I have written a prayer which I will use before going into battle, and if it please God in his providence, that I should fall, I fall with my spirit commended to God, my heart in him and our blessed Saviour.

O that we all could go to battle armed with the "sword of the Spirit" having the "breast plate of righteousness, and the helmet of Salvation" what an army we would have. . . .

Willie got a letter from Staunton today. Milroy's HdQtrs are in Berryville, Winchester is garrisoned by some two or three Regiments; I am confident things are in a better state there than reported, sister Mat wrote . . . by Dr. Magruder . . . in very good spirits, not tired of working and all was well at home. I have heard that Pa said Milroy was the most gentlemanly commander (Yankee) ever been in Winchester, and if he did, why they are at least comfortable.[41] . . .

Mrs. Baldwin went to Milroy complaining about horses being picketed in her yard; Milroy—Is your husband loyal; Mrs. B.—Yes, loyal to the South. M. commenced accusing our people of bringing on the war. Mrs. B.—It commenced at the John Brown raid. Milroy—Madam you are a lion, sergeant take this woman off. Mrs. B.—Sir, I refuse to go till I am ready; she sat down and continued sitting for some time, she then arose, I am ready to go now, and off she went. Just like Mrs. Baldwin.

We are all in fine condition here, and when we get at the Yanks, calculate on a great victory. The old Stonewall is larger than it has ever been, since last April when reorganized.[42] I am still Act A A Genl and my chances of getting the place are pretty good, judging from appearances. Genl Paxton asked me some time ago to come and mess with him and also to get a horse. The former I have been doing for some time, the latter I tried to do immediately, by enclosing in a letter to Capt Airs from Genl P[axton] one to Robby, to send me a horse; brother S_ left the choice to Robby, I asked R_ to send Brother Strothers as he was much better fitted for the service I would put him to than the other, write to Robby and persuade him to do so, and that immediately, as it is all important to me, that I should have a horse directly. The 2nd returned from picket this evening, the pickets converse freely, send over letters, papers etc and are quite sociable. I send, for a specimen, a note sent over by one of them on a little boat, *chartered* for the purpose.

                    . . . Pray on dear Boly. Your devoted bro R.J. Barton

Strother wrote Bolling a week later, rejoicing that now "an entire family [was] enlisted in the army of the Lord." His relief and thankfulness at Bolling's spiritual progress was paramount, but he gave a lively commentary on the state of the army and President Lincoln's reported balloon ascent. Observation balloons had been used for the first time by the Federals during the Peninsula Campaign the previous year, and there had been many unfounded reports of Lincoln's ascents.

[LETTER OF W. STROTHER BARTON TO BOLLING W. BARTON]

Camp Winder
April 15, 1863

. . . Two balloons were up yesterday, we see them almost every day. It is reported that old Abe went up the other day in "suo persona," that is correct latin isnt it?

If the old kangaroo had fallen out and broken his neck what a howl the yankey dogs would have set up. No One can conjecture what move will be made when we do move. The Yankeys seem to be inclined to chainge their base a little. . . .

Our troops are in fine state of drill and discipline. I think the 2nd Regt in drill would put the "cadet corps" to the blush. We have one of the most beautiful drill grounds you ever saw. It is a perfect level of about one thousand acres surrounded by high hills, from the top of these hills you can see every evening six or seven thousands troops drilling, truely a beautiful sight. The Yankeys have a full view of us from Stafford Hills. I do not think however they divine much pleasure from the sight. I saw an entire brigade charge across the open plains at a double quick, yelling like demons—it looked really grand. . . .

On April 29, the Union spring offensive began with Sedgwick's corps crossing the Rappahannock west of Fredericksburg while the main force under Hooker crossed upstream at Kelly's and U.S. fords and moved into the Wilderness. Lee's army began moving westward in response, and the Stonewall Brigade received orders to proceed to Hamilton's Crossing near Fredericksburg, about twelve miles from Camp Winder, in the late afternoon.

[LETTER OF RANDOLPH BARTON TO BOLLING W. BARTON]

Camp Winder 29 April

Dear Boly,

Your letter was received a day or so ago to gether with one from Robby blowing me up about asking so often for bro S[trother's] horse. You asked me to write a few letters back to you just before going into battle; their has been heavy firing at Fredericksburg this morning, both infantry and artillery, we have heard the result of the fight, but are under orders to hold ourselves in readiness to move. I cant think it any thing more than a demonstration on the part of the Yankees, they would hardly dare to cross at that point. We are all prepared to meet them, and I trust and pray, prepared to die if God wills it. Dear Boly your conversion is a source of joy to us we pray that we may all hold firm to our profession. Pray for us dear Boly that God in his infinite mercy may protect us or if it be his will that we should fall, to receive us in heaven. Your devoted brother

RJ Barton

[on a separate paper]

Brother S sent you $10.00 in a letter did you receive it, I would do likewise if I had it on hand to spare possibly.

Robby may be able to get you clothes, let us know if he cant, we will write to cousin John Ambler who may be able to do so.[43]

On April 30 and May 1, the Stonewall Brigade moved west. On May 2, because of Jackson's famous march they successfully surprised and outflanked Hooker west of Chancellorsville. The brigade did not participate in the late-afternoon attack, having been positioned at the crossroads of the Plank and Brock roads in order to guard against a southerly enemy thrust. Jackson was severely wounded that night, in a reconnaissance in the dark woods. On the third the brigade was heavily engaged as the Confederate force punished Hooker from three sides and caused his retreat on the night of the fifth. Rannie, on Paxton's staff, was bound to be in the thick of it.

[MEMOIR OF RANDOLPH BARTON]

We were now upon the eve of Chancellorsville, the most brilliant movement of the war; indeed a movement which in audacity and success will compare favorably with any tactical military operation ever recorded. I cannot pretend to give details. . . . Suffice it to say that I was with our troops on the long and trying march of the 2nd of May, while flanking Hooker. I last saw General Jackson in conference with General Paxton, on whose staff I was serving, about 3 P.M., at the intersection of the plank road and Brock road. Our brigade, while not much engaged that afternoon, was under some hot fire of shells.[44]

After various vexing changes of position, about midnight our brigade took its line on the left of the road, the plank road from Orange Court House to

Fredericksburg, not very far from the point where the simple, but impressive, monument to Jackson now stands. I was required to connect the left of our line with the troops next on our left. I reached the end of the brigade line and then cautiously and noiselessly walked through the gloomy woods. Every sound had subsided, although within a radius of a mile one hundred thousand armed men slept or rested, awaiting the break of day to begin the work of destruction. I could not see twenty feet ahead of me and feared I would lose my course and wander into the lines of the enemy, which were very near. Stopping for a moment in this absolute death-like, midnight silence to catch some sound by which to continue my search, a whip-poor-will burst out with its shrill cry just over me. It alarmed me at first and somehow made a deep and lasting impression. I have somewhat curiously noted the allusion by many participants in the battles fought in the Wilderness to the disturbing cry of the whip-poor-will. The bird seems to love that gloomy region and its plaintive and far-reaching cry seems to have found an echo in the thoughts of every soldier whose duty placed him on guard in the melancholy hours which preceded a bloody battle.

I at last thought I saw on the ground something like men, and, carefully looking, I discovered the troops I was searching for, buried in slumber with no watch on post. I arranged the connection between the lines and returned to General Paxton.

H. Kyd Douglas [also on Paxton's staff] tells me, that when the brigade had finally been posted for the night, General Paxton said to him that he felt that he would be killed in the morning. He told Douglas where his will was to be found, and after some sober conversation sought some much-needed rest.

Paxton had been a rather profane and godless man, but the dangers of battle, and the example of General Jackson caused a change, and for months before Chancellorsville he had become a new man. I recall distinctly his efforts to read his Bible by the first ray of light on the morning of the next eventful day. Placing his book (a gilt-edged Bible) in a pocket just over his heart, with a face full of resolution, he awaited orders.

Early in the morning of the 3rd we were launched into the midst of a dreadful battle. In a short time General Paxton was shot dead within two feet of me. I called up men to carry him off. As he stiffened his arms to lift himself from the ground, I placed my arm under him, when he muttered, "Tie up my arm," and died. He was not shot in the arm, but through the heart. I reported his death to Colonel Nadenbousch, commanding the Second Virginia Infantry, of our brigade. . . .

I cannot say what time elapsed before I was struck myself. I was walking up the line to the left when a ball from the enemy struck me on the right shoulder blade, breaking or crushing the bone (scapula I will call it on a venture) and burying itself, burrowed its way across my back under the skin all the way to my left shoulder blade, where it stopped, carrying with it a small piece of bone. I was knocked flat; my change from a vertical to a horizontal posture was literally instantaneous. My first sensation was that of suffocation or uncomfortable restriction around my chest, and until the ball was removed my breathing was short and labored. Several men came to my rescue, lifted me up and my strength returning, I made my way to the rear. . . . If the ball had gone in its course the twentieth part of an inch deeper, instant death would have followed.[45]

[It] was an hour afterwards extracted by Dr. William Walls, surgeon of our brigade. I still have the ball.[46]

Before being wounded, however, I determined to take a shot at the enemy, and, picking up a dead man's musket, I carefully rested it against a tree and fired at a line of men not a great distance away. Whether I struck my man, I do not know, but I do know that I aimed as deliberately as if I was aiming at a squirrel. . . .

The battle continued at Chancellorsville until May 5, when the Federals began to withdraw. A simultaneous effort at Fredericksburg succeeded briefly but was thwarted at Salem Church. The Union Army fell back across the Rappahannock, and Richmond was saved again. Rannie was evacuated to the city by train.

[MEMOIR OF RANDOLPH BARTON]

Thus wounded, I went to Richmond, landed at Broad Street, which was then the terminus of the Richmond, Fredericksburg and Potomac Railroad, and, suffering and weak I staggered up Franklin Street to the residence of Mr. [J. T. B.] Dorsey, who had married Miss Kate Mason, daughter of Hon. James M. Mason, of Winchester.[47] By the Dorseys I was most hospitably received, and a day or so later went around to Mrs. [James M.] Mason's who then lived on the corner of Grace and Fouche Streets, and by whom I was treated as if I had been her son. While there cousin Barton Haxall visited me and was most affectionate in his manner.[48]

Judge W. S. Barton then in the Adjutant General's Department, also called to see me, and asking casually with what command I was serving, and learning that I was Acting Assistant Adjutant General on General Paxton's staff, asked if

I had been commissioned.[49] It had never occurred to me that General Paxton had gone so far as to recommend me for the position. I thought he was "trying" me, and with his death I had supposed that I would go back to my company, and so I told Major Barton. He said that upon his return to the office he would examine the records and let me hear from him, and sure enough that day, a copy of my commission as Captain and Assistant Adjutant-General, which had been forwarded through the usual channels, was sent up to me.[50] I was greatly rejoiced and very proud, and immediately sent my best coat to the tailor with instructions to add the insignia of my rank. . . .

Randolph J. Barton, recovering from his Chancellorsville wound and with his new captain's rank, in Richmond, May 1863. (Colin J. S. Thomas, Jr.)

Robby, learning that the Barton boys had come safely out of the battle, again took the risky trip into hostile territory to relay the news to an anxious family, and probably sent word to Bolling as well. Rannie and Willie, together in so many things, were wounded and went on to Staunton to convalesce at the same time. Willie's sister Cary Baldwin and her children had refugeed to Staunton that winter and, at least at first, were living with Dr. Baldwin's cousins, the A. H. H. Stuarts. Rannie and Willie were surely taken in by the Stuarts because of this connection. When Rannie could, he wrote to Bolly, and for the first and only time, sounded shaken. He had been badly wounded and had lost some friends.

[LETTER OF RANDOLPH BARTON TO BOLLING W. BARTON]

Staunton May 21st 63

Dear Boly

I arrived hear yesterday evening pretty stiff and sore from the unusual exercise of the day, but after a good nights rest and my wound being dressed I feel quite comfortable. God in his infinite mercy has been pleased to spare my life and that of our dear brother, it seems as if my every wish has been gratified. A week after I was wounded, I arrived at Richmond went to the Masons where I met with the greatest kindness, visited the Bartons from Fredericksburg also the Haxalls, rec every where with great kindness. The ball entered just behind my right shoulder and passed across to the left, a shot from a flanking party; Dr. B. considers it a severe wound, which will keep me some 4 weeks from the army. I am Captain now in the Adjt Genls Dept, my commission in my pocket, rank as Capt of Cavalry.

I am staying now at Mr. Alex H. H. Stuarts, expect to get a furlough of 30 days, when able to ride in the stage wish to visit you. Rec a letter from Robby yesterday, was at Vaucluse late as 17th, all well, sent word to Winchester to let them know of our fate.[51] Ma was quite sick, no doubt, from anxiety. Pa had recovered. God has been merciful to us. Also rec letters from Grandma, which bro S[trother] will send to you when he has seen them. Miller R my roommate was killed in the late battle, Downing wounded; Capt Chew is a prisoner.[52] I wish to see you badly.

your devoted bro
R.J. Barton

The A. H. H. Stuart house. A large wing at left, hidden by trees, harbored many wounded Confederates, including Rannie and Willie Barton. (Virginia State Library)

Rannie and Robby were able to see each other during Rannie's recovery in Staunton, as Robby was back and forth between there and his duties at the caves near Keezletown. The news from Winchester was sketchy; otherwise the boys would have known that their mother was ill not just from worry but with a bad case of typhoid fever. Rannie recovered his optimism before his good health, and managed to enjoy his recuperation.

[MEMOIR OF RANDOLPH BARTON]

From Richmond I went to Staunton, under an invitation to visit the house of Hon. Alex. H. H. Stuart, at one time Secretary of the Interior in the Cabinet of President Fillmore.[53] His house was beautiful and luxurious. He was a courtly and hospitable gentleman. His wife and daughters were all that refinement and loveliness can make of women. I was assigned to the best chamber, where every possible comfort awaited me, I was cut off from home, but a new home was made for me at Mr. Stuart's. I recall the beautiful chamber at this moment. Its quaint old furniture, the spaciousness of the room, the spotless linen, the glass bell on the table at the side of my bed, the gift of some of Mr. Stuart's "Bell

and Everett" admirers, the quiet reposeful look and feeling of everything in the room, and, above all, the motherliness of Mrs. Stuart and the sisterliness of Miss Augusta [25], Miss Fanny [21] and Miss Mary [19], the latter afterwards the wife of the distinguished surgeon, Dr. Hunter McGuire, of Richmond, Virginia. Mrs. McGuire lived to develop in her maturer years all the beautiful traits of which as a girl she gave full promise.

It was about this time of my life that my very great fondness

Mary Stuart, Mrs. Hunter H. McGuire, in an 1890 portrait. (Hunter McGuire, Jr.)

for the society of "ladies," as I was taught deferentially to call them, not "women" as is the style of this day, began to show itself. Before I left Winchester for Lexington it had begun to bud, but some frost nipped it and my days at Lexington and absence in the army threw it back. Now it was to come out in full bloom and from that time to this it has never withered. It has gotten me at times into a good deal of trouble, but take it all in all it has added greatly to the pleasure of my life, and I most heartily commend to my boys the cultivation of a like disposition. It was a tradition in our family that my grandfather, William Strother Jones, told his boys that if he ever caught them "out" of love he would thrash them. I believe in the beneficial influences of fondness for the society of females and I again commend it to my sons.

Among the charming ladies I met while at Mr. Stuart's were Miss Jennie and Miss Cornelia Peyton, sisters of Mrs. John B. Baldwin.[54] Both were exceedingly pretty, lively and kind. And so, my wound healing, my health good, my accommodations eminently satisfactory, no responsibility, fine weather, and lovely girls all around, I led a happy, careless convalescence, which was only too short.

IX

May–July 1863

MORE LETTERS UNDER OCCUPATION

SECOND BATTLE OF WINCHESTER

LIBERATION AND FAMILY REUNITED

The Confederates' decisive victory at Chancellorsville was marred by the terrible loss of Jackson. The Union armies fell back, and it was clear that Lee would soon take the offensive. But the Federal presence in the Valley became, if anything, more frightening and oppressive. The danger of Robby's clandestine visits to Vaucluse can be appreciated from the letters his grandmother Jones wrote, soon after his visit, to her Parkhill cousins in Florida. Sudden nocturnal searches were not unusual. At Vaucluse, the Yankees were hunting for Strother Jones, suspected of some sort of "espionage." When Strother was at home, the slave Uncle Alec kept a horse saddled and hidden down the hill near the house, ready for his master's escape when the Yankee troops neared.[1] The Federals also were looking for slaves to free, or they would settle for the silver. The slave William Braxton, who had already left Vaucluse, sent the soldiers to free his wife, Mary, and their children.

[LETTER OF ANN C. R. JONES TO LUCY R. PARKHILL]

Vaucluse, May 18th 1863

I cannot recollect, dearest Lucy, when I last wrote my second letter upon Foolscap Paper, nor do I know whether you have ever received it, but yours commenced on the 31st of March reached me not long ago, & altho' our enemy still retain possession of Winchester, I have hope of being able to have this mailed somewhere up the Valley sooner or later. . . . You have already heard of our glorious Victory, blessed be God for his merciful support of our arms! & I know you are anxious now about my dear Ones. . . . My Precious Randolph was wounded, but I am assured only a flesh wound, the Ball entered in the shoulder & was cut out at the backbone. He was able to walk about & wrote a Note himself. I hear he is in Staunton where he will meet with every attention. His Cousin, Willie Barton was also wounded in the arm, the Ball struck a Button on his Coat & glanced disabling his arm but it is considered a slight wound, dear Strother was not touched, praised be the Lord! Willie I hear is in Staunton where his Mother & Sister both are. My son James has taken his whole family to that town, so Ran will not be without relatives.[2] My Grandson Robert came down with the happy tidings of their safety, so anxious to relieve his Parents minds, tho' perhaps at his own risk, but he reached here in safety! & I trust has returned without seeing a Yankee, he used every precaution. . . .

Winchester is in such a terrible state that it has become very unhealthy. The Yankees are now cleaning the streets, but a man who hauls wood there told me yesterday that he thought turning the filth made the matter worse, however I should *suppose* it was better in the end to have it purified. . . . It is 5 months today since I was in Winchester, & *when* I can go again is a matter upon which I cannot even conjecture.

Are you not sorry for Gen. Jackson's death? Oh! I am *grieved*! He is such a loss to the Confederacy, but I have heard it suggested that it is a lesson to us to rest upon our blessed Creator & not look to man. He was truly an *able* Gen., made so for our benefit, he has fulfilled his Mission & entered into rest, he was truly a Pious praying Man, & wonderfully successful for he trusted in a higher power. I feel for his poor wife—his infant daughter cannot miss him. He died of pneumonia, not of his wounds, altho' he lost an arm.

Strother's health is greatly improved, & he is now able to stay at home, & is at present busy with his corn crop. Barton Jones has been very sick with dyphtheria, had a terrible throat, but is getting quite well, tho' does not leave his room yet.[3] I humbly hope it will be the last case, it was the sixth, the other 5 amongst the servants, two of whom (perhaps I told) died, Sue's dining room servant & my Boy, Tom.

It is a fortnight today, the 4th of the present month, since William Braxton sent the Yankees here for his family. Mary packed up rapidly, & went off. They told Strother they were to go by for Flora & her other children, who are living in the neighbourhood with as kind people as possible, but it was so late they did not call for her, she is still there, tho' I do not at all calculate upon her as ever serving me & sincerely hope I may never see a member of that family again, I wish them well most heartily, & pray that I may meet them in Heaven.[4]

So far I have done remarkably well without any servant but Kitty, who is in her 71st year & very *unable*. I have hired a poor girl living upon the Farm to wash for me & to aid in cleaning my room. Strother & Mary were very much worried at my refusing to allow my work to be put upon their servants, but I *insisted* that I must be let alone to make my *own* arrangements, & that one suits me far better. Kitty helps me make my bed, cleans my Candle stick & Basin, also the Hearth & the Girl I speak of sweeps, dusts the room, & wipes it over with a wet cloth (the floor is oiled) so that it comes light to everybody. I have starched my Caps, darned my stockings, & find it very easy to do, & maybe can come across some person to sew for me when I need it at *far* less expense than my servants cost me. I trust Flora will take her freedom, I never wish to own a servant again. Mary continued humble, attentive & kind to the last, she was an *excellent servant*, & has been a long, long, comfort to me, & I rested upon her, but I am glad she has gone. I hope her freedom may be a benefit to her.

Robert Barton brought me a letter from my Darling Child [Bev], his Brother [James] has sent him to Keezletown to establish some Gover't works, over which he makes him superintendent, his Pay is $76 a month, with Rations for himself & horse, a situation better I suppose than that of riding so constantly as Robert & Marshall Jones have to do, who are also in James's employment.[5] Robert went to Keezletown with his uncle Bev & is to remain with him untill the 1st of June. Their arrangements are pretty rough at present, but Bev was having a room built for himself & will be sufficiently comfortable. The business they are all engaged in is making Salt Petre. My Paper says stop. Our united love to you & your household. I trust that Scarlet fever has left all I love. I am going to write to Harriet & fear it will be a prosy production. Farewell, dearest friend.

Fondly yours, A.C.R. Jones

[LETTER OF ANN C. R. JONES TO HARRIET PARKHILL]

May 18th, 1863, Vaucluse

I must commence a letter to you dearest Harriet, in return for yours written last month, which I cordially thank you for. I hope the fair you speak of has answered admirably, & that you all may perfectly succeed in every effort for the benefit of our Soldiers & Refugees, I was lost in amazement, if not in shame, upon hearing how entirely your Mother had gone before me in the knitting line,

Vaucluse, c. 1890. The main floor had long windows with shutters that gave access to the encircling "platform." (Eleanor J. Burleson)

I used to count up my socks with a strong desire to compliment myself, & be complimented for my enterprise, but alas! I hide my diminished head & feel how triflingly lazy I have been, & beg you will never insult me by an expressed wish to know what number of socks I have perpetrated, for in order to preserve my character I must decline in answering. . . .

The continued rain, with sufficient warmth during the day, has made old Vaucluse look most beautifully, my interest in my yard & garden come with the returning spring, & altho' my fixtures are necessarily humble, I have been amused in working amongst my flowers & rearranging some of them. Were I ever to leave this place . . . how I should love to carry with me my dear flower friends. I pet & name some of them & should wish some of them greatly to accompany me. My attachment to the Valley is very strong, but with my children & grandchildren, I could go *anywhere* to spend the remnant of my days. . . .

I do not think I told your Mother of a night visit we had from the Yankees, & Oh! I was so glad that Strother was not here at home. I was lying if not *wide* awake, in that light dosing that makes it difficult for me to know, when I heard someone at the Front door.[6] I went to my chamber door, & asked who it was. Me, was the answer in a voice I had never heard, Who *is* me, was my reply, nothing was said. I flew upstairs to Mary's room, aroused her, waited untill she could put some clothes on, they in the meantime thundering *tremendously* at the door; they had forced open my blind, one of the dining room shutters, & going to the third, succeeded in rousing the young servants, & commanding them to open the window, they obeyed, so that when Mary reached the dining room she found it, as she thought, *full* of men, there *were* a great many I had retreated to my chamber to dress myself, fastened [nine-year-old] Ann Cary's clothes, who had been awakened by the noise whilst I was upstairs, & expecting them every moment to come in, feeling besides completely dumfoundered.

Mary had to bear the brunt alone. Her courage rose with the call for it, she was perfectly composed, they said they had come for that man Strother Jones, she told them he had not been here for weeks. They demanded the keys, she refused to give them, but said she would open any door they pleased. They rushed upstairs. She asked them not to go where her children were sleeping, for fear of alarming them. They said they would not hurt the children & passed on. They had lighted several candles of their own, she procured a light in my room, followed them around & found [twelve-year-old] Barton entirely calm, conversing with them, putting down his bed clothes to show there was no one concealed. Six of them flew into a Young Lady's room, who was sleeping up stairs, looked into her closet, went up to the servant Girl, who still slept, looked at her, & pretending they had just discovered there was someone in the bed, went out, leaving the door open, so that poor Miss Hattie had not the chance to shut it immediately, so many men were passing backward & forward in the passage.[7]

They went into another room which was unoccupied, in the Garret, in the Cellar, in the Parlour, had all the Closets unlocked, & never came into my room at all. How thankful, how grateful I am for the omission. I then went out, asked them why they came at that hour? One of them impertinently remarked—to make a visit. The others remained silent. They took the chance to steal my silver Fork—such a Pet it was—my napkin Ring too. Mary held the silver cup I used in her hand. They insisted upon the sideboard being opened, looking for spirits. There was part of a bottle of whiskey, which Mary took in her hand, told them it was for medicine, & they should not have it. They did not *dare* to touch it, & her composed & fearless manner & undaunted spirit kept them under. They did not presume to take what she *saw*, but they took their chance to deprive us of nearly all our knives, 9 out of 12 Forks, besides mine, & big & small spoons, but they were Pewter, the silver ones were locked up. Mary's *silver* Butter knife they took, & Strother's Ink-stands, pouring the *ink* upon the Table. They finally departed & now we have a protection.[8]

I have spun such a long yarn, dearest H I must stop. . . . God bless you, my child.

Your truly fond cousin, A. C. R. Jones

In a page added to Lucy's letter the next day, Mrs. Jones conveyed the frustration of having little news of her large and far-flung Randolph family, but gathering up what she could, including some of relatives in Iowa who were in their own way defying Federal authority. She, as well as the Barton boys, was dreadfully worried that Mr. Barton was suffering from something more grave: "O dear Lucy my heart fails me about Mr. Barton's health & I am anxious about dear Fanny." At home:

[LETTER OF ANN C. R. JONES TO LUCY R. PARKHILL]

Mary is not well & looks badly has not recovered from loss of sleep & anxiety about dear Barton he is "very smart" now & sleeps well. . . . Strother talks very boldly sometimes of leaving this place but whether it will *end* in talk or not I cannot tell. He is devoted to Vaucluse, very naturally, but the abolitionist measures make this a large place to cultivate & may *compel* a change. What I shall do will be governed by circumstances & not being troubled with the darkie question, shall dispose of myself agreeably to what I individually think best. . . .

Mrs. Barton was still bedridden when the girls did the spring housecleaning and took up the rugs for the summer. Mrs. Lee learned that "when the parlour carpet was removed, the spots of blood from Marshal[l]'s bleeding body, as it was brought in from the battlefield [the previous May] had to be scraped off."[9] At about the same time, not long after Robby's furtive trip to Vaucluse, Mrs. Strother Jones, his aunt, wrote to him, glad to report that his parents and other family in town were recovering from the typhoid epidemic, which everyone believed to be caused by bad air. Mary also described more recent Yankee visitations—apparently they were still hunting Strother Jones.

[LETTER OF MARY B. JONES TO ROBERT T. BARTON]

4th June 1863

My dear Robert—I hope you have heard before this of the improvement of your dear Mothers health & that you have reached your present home in safety. We have been anxiously hoping to hear from you.

Your Father has never failed I believe but once since you heard of him to go to his farm [Springdale] twice a week or oftener & I hope continues to regain his strength. I have never been able to see him altho' I have been several times to call. He expected to bring the little Marshall's [his grandchildren] out to Springdale Thursday or Friday to stay on account of fresh air & we went over Thursday to get them to come home with us but they did not come out, & yesterday we could not get a horse early (you know we are dependant on borrowed ones) & then we were guarded by about twenty yankees from ten o'clock until dark.

About two weeks ago in much larger number they came & & we were not allowed or any person or servant who came to the house to leave it all day or night & we had several to stay. Your uncle [Strother] they fear has communication with our people, & gives information.

All of your family are doing well now—none have been ill—but all more or less affected by the Typhoid fever. Your Mother is going about the house, & none of the others confined to their rooms. Plenty of medicines & whiskey have been sent to W—— now for the sick & the people are allowed to have it freely, & few have died tho no house is exempt your Father says from sick.[10] Rebecca's sisters have been sick, tell Bev with my love but his family are well. We would be so delighted to get all our dear people out of the Town. But it is impossible without their taking the oath.[11] The threats of the wretched people are awful about their burning the place [Winchester] if forced to leave it, & they seem more determined about it, than before, but I hope our people can manage that . . . we have been for two weeks hoping daily we were to be relieved from this fearful bondage. But are cut off from all news except of our glorious success at Vicksburg[12]—rarely see our papers. . . .

always yrs most aff MEBJ
[Mary E. Barton Jones]

The inveterate letter writer, Grandmother Jones, must have seized any unclaimed piece of paper to write her dear ones far away—soon again to her cousin Lucy. She was fully aware of Yankee threats to burn Winchester and worried about her family in town as well as those in the army. She wrote of the recent visit from the Yankees that Mary had described to Robby.

[LETTER OF ANN C. R. JONES TO LUCY R. PARKHILL]

June 6th, 1863 Vaucluse
It is not long, dearest friend, since I put a letter in motion for you, and one for Harriet, how they will speed in their journey south, or whether they will

ever reach you, remain to be told somewhat later. It might seem strange that I should be driving the Pen in such a hurry again with apparently little to say, but my eye fell upon this long sheet of Paper this morning and the desire arose *at least* to *begin* a letter and finish it as I could. . . .

We are singularly situated here at Vaucluse, tho' wonderfully cared for & blessed. A week ago Thursday, a party of Yankees came here, they kept guard at different points, would not allow persons belonging to the place to pass from the house (for a time), detained a lady & gentlemen all night, who happened to be here, and went away themselves before dark. Yesterday they were here again from morning untill nearly dark keeping guard, watching at different places, one of the Men from the Farm came to his dinner, and was not allowed to return to his work. They were however very civil, and I believe enjoyed the grass & shade. . . . They are watching for Rebels who they think might happen to come here, and keep those of us who are here from passing out lest they should give information. This morning they were back again, & searched the Barn for Arms. They prowl about any where, & I believe are hid in the woods still watching, but except for stealing the Butter from the Spring house & some eggs from one of the servants, & a portion of the milk, they have not meddled farther. It is not always the *same* party, they come as they are ordered by their commanders. I shall be glad enough when this kind of spying is over. I cannot help feeling a little uneasy sometimes about the Office, so many of the Carysbrooke affairs are there, when I did it I had *no* fear, & preferred having them there, now it would be difficult to remove them, & [the Yankees] could search the dwelling house as well. Sue's box of silver & my Darling [Frank]'s Gun are hidden, but not in the Office, & I have all of Bev's silver (not much) under my care.[13] I trust they may never find those articles. You do not know however how calm I am, how much supported, how little fear,—they have *very* seldom been here this year, untill the times I have mentioned, & I hope this cannot last.

I sometimes try to *hope* that the Winchester troops may be needed to reinforce the army of the Potomac, & that case we shall be left free. There was a Flag of Truce in Middletown today, the Purport of Gen. Lee's despatch we have not learned—there was one there some days ago beside, & I understand they laughed & talked together (the enemy & ourselves, I mean), shook hands, & drank with one another, & bragged in style, tho' not giving offense.

Here the writer was interrupted, and did not return to this letter for twelve days. In the meantime she wrote to Bolling, having gone to meet her granddaughter Martha who was visiting Joseph Barton's family with her father. Mr.

Ann Cary Randolph Jones in later years.
(Eleanor J. Burleson)

Barton had Milroy's permission to visit Springdale, and Joe's house, Hanover Lodge, was on the way. There, "between the lines," Mat intended to write a letter that could go south to Bolling. But Mattie spent her visit talking instead of writing, so gave the precious paper to Mrs. Jones, who conveyed to Bolling that his mother was "decidedly better" and that his father said he was. As for herself, she told Bolling she was "well, but looking old & wrinkled beyond expression."[14]

The Confederate victory at Chancellorsville had raised morale and stirred hopes for the recapture of northern Virginia. Their advance north occasioned a cavalry clash at Brandy Station on June 9. Rannie, hearing the news of the battle and troop movements, wrote to Bolly with excited anticipation about going home soon; he may have felt well enough to consider rejoining his unit.

Rannie's expectations were fulfilled. On June 10, Lt. Gen. Richard S. Ewell's Second Corps left Culpeper with orders to clear the Shenandoah and lead an advance into Maryland. General A. G. Jenkins's cavalry brigade and accompanying infantry forced the Federals out of Berryville on the twelfth. Robbie headed north, in the hopes that he might soon be able to see the family. He reached the Confederate advance guard, part of Maj. Gen. Jubal Early's division, the night of the thirteenth, and next day those forces moved north past Springdale and Joe Barton's farm and Kernstown. Winchester was struck from three sides on the fourteenth. Milroy retreated on the fifteenth.

[MEMOIR OF ROBERT T. BARTON]

Towards June when I was in Shenandoah [County] attending to duties, I learned of the movement of Gen. Early's army which promised to free Winchester from Milroy. I hastened down to join the army, and at the request of

Col. [James R.] Herbert of Maryland who was in command of the advance infantry force I acted as a sort of guide, or as he kindly put it, as his volunteer aide. Reaching Middletown we lay in line all night, and altho it was June the night was cold and it was anything but comfortable in the dewey grass. About day light we advanced and I took advantage of the opportunity to ride off to the left and in advance of the line, to Vaucluse. I reached there before sun rise when everybody was asleep and in utter ignorance of the approach of the Confederates. I hailed them from my horse, and soon the windows were thrown open and I had a joyful welcome. After reconnoitering to see if none of the enemy were in the neighbourhood I went back to the house and had a hasty breakfast, rejoining the column which by the time I got to it, had marched beyond Springdale and its skirmish line spread across the fields just in front of where my cousin Joseph Barton now lives. But a little way beyond, about where the B. & O. Station now is, the Federal Cavalry picket stood apparently and, as it proved in fact, unaware that an army was present in force. We had a small squad of cavalry between our skirmish line and the Federal picket, and looking toward it I saw a familiar looking carriage approach and stop at our picket. I rode up at once and found it was my father, but so changed that I would hardly have known him. His health was such that Milroy had given him a pass to go out from time to time and visit his farms, and in entire ignorance (as he said all in Winchester were) of our approach he had come out that morning.

I rode with him back to Springdale, the road and fields were so full of our advancing troops that it was most difficult to work his carriage through, I riding ahead and persuading the soldiers to give room. I had soon to return to the line. . . .

Going again to the front I made myself as useful as I could, barely escaping death from a shell fired from the Federal fort . . . which passed very close to me while riding across a field beyond the toll gate on the Valley turnpike. I witnessed about night fall the splendid display made by seventy pieces of our artillery playing at once upon the Federal forts and the return fire of their guns. I enjoyed this all the more because I was out of danger and the shells did not seem to fall in the town, as in fact they did not except in a few instances. The firing ceased at the forts after dark, but meanwhile quite a sharp fight of infantry took place through Mt. Hebron cemetery and to this day you may see the marks of the balls on some of the tomb stones.

I rode back to Joseph Barton's and spent the night. About day break I was on horseback again and riding to Winchester was happy to enter it with the troops, the main body of the army having in the night marched around the town and succeeded after a hot fight near Jordans Springs, in capturing the greater part of Milroy's army, the arch villain himself, however, escaping.

It was a day of great rejoicing in the town, not marred by the death or wounds of any very near us. But when my father came back home, and the excitement having subsided, I was shocked and grieved beyond measure to see how ill he looked and was.

The army passed on and made its great but somewhat disastrous campaign into Maryland and Pennsylvania, culminating in the battle of Gettysburg.

Rannie, galvanized by the news from Winchester, wrote Bolly a hurried note and rode north as soon as possible. The young cadet immediately wrote home for permission to leave the VMI after examinations but before the July 4 graduation.

[LETTER OF BOLLING W. BARTON TO DAVID W. BARTON]

V.M.I. June 17th

Dear Pa,

I heard the news of the capture of *the remains* of Winchester this morning and wishing very much to see them as well as you all I write you this to get your permission. My examination will come off in a few days and I will loose nothing by being absent from here.

There are several reasons which makes it almost necessary for me to come (of course there would be). Please write to Gen Smith and give him your consent to let me have a furlough and I think he will give it to me. Ranny has left for home by this time. I havent time to write more. That God may bless us all and let us meet again if not in this world in the one to come is the prayer of your Devoted son

B. Barton

In great jubilation, Grandmother Jones resumed her June 6 letter to Lucy Parkhill.

[LETTER OF ANN C. R. JONES TO LUCY R. PARKHILL]

This was laid bye from the 6th to the 18th & now WE ARE FREE. Now you will rejoice with me I know. You will have heard of the Battle of Winchester long before this letter will reach you, but old as part of it is, I will send it, you can see how it *has been* with us, & know the happiness of the community here.

Our enemy were not aware I believe of the near approach of the Confederate. Our troops came on in number & at points that surrounded the town or the
roads leading from it, the battle began seriously on Sunday; about twelve
o'clock the firing increased *decidedly*, about six or later it raged more fiercely
untill dark put an end to it. I knew it would begin again by light on Monday
morning, which it did, & after a terrible cannonading, all was quiet, I felt perfectly *sure* that our troops had taken the Fort which was strong, & of course
possession of Winchester, but I could learn nothing until evening.

Mr. Barton was with us & *could not* return, which was very fortunate, the
excitement in town was so great. I had intended to come home with him & *stick
it out* here, & Monday evening *free! free*, delightful thought! him & I set off,
heard the *best* news before we had proceeded a Mile & a ¼, & came on in fine
spirits, our dear ones are *all* safe, none taken that we had cause to mourn for.
When Mr. Barton left town *he* did not know, or the Yankees either how matters
stood. We had heard all the *rumours*, & were earnestly hoping for a speedy release, but in these times "waiting work" is generally allotted us.

Many Darkies were captured, amongst them the Braxton family except the
head of it, vile old William, I *do* hope for his own sake, as well as ours, he will
yet be caught.[15] The Yankees lost *everything*—the Confederates have gained in
a worldly view *considerably*, General Milroy escaped, a rumour yesterday,
announced his capture, but we never know what to believe. Another rumour
proclaims the taking of a large portion of Hooker's army, & our troops are some
of them now in Pennsylvania, & we expect to enter Maryland also, & it is said
that Gen Lee with his army will pass here on his route.

Oh! dearest Lucy, what joy to have all these wretches driven from the soil of
Virginia, torn & *worn* & desolated as she is, rejoicing will come up from *every
place*, when they are *gone*, but we must *wait* yet—a return of the Yankees to
this town is even spoken of but is *too* bad to look at, & I trust in our Heavenly
Father, *that* will never come.

I found my Children & Grandchildren all either well or getting so, &
delighted to see me. I walk from one to the other. . . . Sally Braxton [the slave]
is here now untill Strother can make the arrangements about them, & Lavinia,
a good little girl [11], Flora's daughter, who told me she never wanted to go. I
shall leave her with Susan. Sally I *think* ought to be sold, she is unhumbled.
Mary Braxton is with Fanny, in the depths of penetential sorrow, when it is all
arranged about them, I will let you know. They have lost everything but the
clothes on their backs, & in the effort to get to the Fort for protection, I wonder
they had not been killed. William [Braxton] galloped off & left Mary to shift for

herself, & she *seems* thoroughly disgusted with him, & only desires to get home.
I have not seen her, I do not allow her to come near me, & before I knew all her
sorrow, had requested Strother to do exactly with the servants what he thought
best, without a *question* being put to me. I must now abide with his decision,
but Fanny Barton is her fast friend, dear Fanny has been dangerously ill, was
entirely convalescent, tho! *excessively* weak, when this terribly trying time came
on, she suffered great agony, but fortunately did not know that Strother B- was
in the battle.

Randolph's wound kept him out. Oh! he is such a gallant fellow, he is Adjutant General to that portion of the army to which he belongs. I never *can* know
all their terms, & he was 19 the 24th of last April, how my heart rejoices in his
modesty, Piety & bravery, dear child May God bless him *always*. My son
Strother's health is greatly improved, such a state of pleasure & excitement at
our release, he *would* be near our army, & poor Mary [Jones] was miserable
about him, I became uneasy when he did not return Monday morning, altho' I
had been cheering her, but all was well praised be the Lord! . . .

I hope to see my Darling Bev before very long, & also my precious
Randolph, the way is now clear—*what a joy*! & today I can put this letter in
the Post Office only to think of that. You may imagine the happiness of
the people here to be relieved from the arrogant Tyranny of those wretches,
but they will never forget the bravery of the Southern women. I am told
they have threatened vengeance if they ever get back again. If our troops
had not come in time to prevent it, Anna Jones & many others were to have
been sent off next Saturday, Dr. & Mrs. Baldwin were at Vaucluse on their
way out, the old Dr. too in such wretched health.[16] Dear Mr. Barton looks
dreadfully but is better & I have hope for him now. Strother B could stay
but a little time, he took leave of us the day after the battle. Willie Barton
is very well & untouched. I am so thankful for that, he could not see his mother,
however, she is at Staunton. Joseph has not a servant left upon his place,
& 4 small children, the difficulty of procuring servants you cannot imagine.
Rebecca has two little girls just now, one is *quite* efficient, but *any day* she
expects her Master to come for her. She was brought to town by the Yankees,
left at some Negro's house that was acquainted with Rebecca, & he sent her
to her. . . .

Mary Barton, Jones I mean, was here on Tuesday, Strother went on to
Martinsburg & I have not seen him since. Mary does not look well. Tom
Marshall is away somewhere with the army. I have not seen him for a long time,

but he escaped in the battle [Brandy Station] where he was, thank Heaven! . . .
I shall have to stop, nothing farther can I think of. God bless you, my darling.

Yours fondly, A. C. R. Jones

*Willie Barton's wound received at Chancellorsville had healed and both he and
Strother Barton, with the 2nd Virginia, had participated in Winchester's new
liberation. Strother had been detailed to act as General Early's aide during the
battle—just as Robby had been utilized—for his intimate knowledge of the terrain.*[17] *The men paused briefly to enjoy the victory at home and moved north;
by June 19 they were near Hagerstown, Maryland, on their way to Pennsylvania. By now, the whole family was terribly worried about Mr. Barton, whose ill
health was apparent in his looks. (Mrs. Lee had apprehensively confided to her
diary a few weeks earlier that "he is the shadow of a shade & some of his symptoms so closely resemble those, which I know to be incurable, that I shudder to
hear him describe them."*[18]*) The years of attrition of the fortune and lands he
had amassed for his children, the recent deaths of two sons and a daughter, and
the threats to others, and the heavy responsibilities he felt for his community in
these harrowing times had taken a dreadful toll on him. But methodically, he
noted on the outside of Strother's letter that it was received on June 23.*

[LETTER OF W. STROTHER BARTON TO DAVID W. BARTON]

Maryland
Camp 1st Va. Brigade
June 19th 1863

Dear Pa

We crossed the river yesterday near Butlers Mills & are now bivouaced on
the Maryland side in the sight of Shepherdstown. Nothing has happened of any
importance since we left Winchester. We have not once heard the crack of the
enemies gun although our cavelry have had some skirmishing near Sharpsburg,
with the cavelry of the enemy. Jenkins with his cavelry command, is reported by
the northern papers of Tuesday to be in Chambersburg. From all the information we can gather we conclude that our entire army is advancing upon Maryland both on this & the other side of the blue ridge.

The entire north seems to be in a state of excitement at the prospect of invasion. Lincoln has issued a proclamation calling upon the states to protect themselves stating that Genl Hookers army was unable to defend them. The

Govenor of Pensylvania complains of the feble response which is made to his call for fifty thousand troops. Vallindgham has been nominated by acclamation for goviner of Ohio.[19] I do not see any immediate prospect of a fight. Our army will probably concentrate, that is our corps; in the neighborhood of Hagerstown. This is mearly conjecture, the whole move is wraped in impenetrable mistery. Our division camped for two or three days very near to shepherdstown. The colonel [J. Q. A. Nadenbousch] was so kind as to permit me to spend most of the time in Shepherdstown. I staid at Dr. Andrew's house.[20] They were kind as possible and did a great deal towards lightning the disappointment I felt at not seeing more of home. Tell Fanny I saw all of her friends the[y] enquired very particularly after her. The colonel is waiting for his writing desk so I must close. Please do not feel any anxiety about me God who has so graciously protected me hereto fore will still extend his protection toward me; That God may bless you all dear Pa & restore you to health is the prayer of your devoted son

W.S. Barton

Write as soon & as often as possible, you will find me a faithfull correspondent. Tell Fanny not to let her housekeeping prevent her from writing. Confederate paper. excuse bad writing[21]

WSB

Returning quickly to his duties at Keezletown in Rockingham County, Robby carried precious cargo: Mrs. Lee's journal, which he forwarded to her friend.[22] He also took care of some business for his father, including letters to General Smith, Superintendent of the institute, and to Bolly to see if he needed money for traveling. Martha and the whole family were excited at the prospect of having both her younger brothers at home soon, and promised to "save up & try to posh" them.

[LETTER OF MARTHA B. BALDWIN TO BOLLING W. BARTON]

June 26th

. . . We are once more free from the Yankey tyranny & you may well imagine—enjoying our freedom but cannot help dreading their return—although the men all assure us they never will be in this part of Va again. God grant it may be so. Ma is not yet able to use her hands well enough to write or would send you a letter from herself. It has given us infinite pleasure my darling Bolling to read your recent letters & see that the Holy Spirit has changed your heart & you are determined by God's help to be his child & renew the vow so early made for you. . . .

Pa's health is my fear, to-day is one of his bad days. You will be shocked to see how badly he looks, it seems so strange for him now to appear cheerful. He goes often to Spring Dale but never goes to the Office although too many see him on business at home. We are hoping he will be able to go to the Orkney Springs before long.

We have hear from Strother since he reached Md., his Regt is near enough to Shepherdstown to enable him to visit *Miss Lila* & the young ladies of the town.[23] Ranny has not yet reached us—his wound & other obstacles detain him. Robby was with us a short time & looks better than I ever saw him. Some soldiers have just had their supper here & tell us of a sure engagement near Ashbys gap—Stuarts Cavalry was principally engaged in it, the loss was heavy.[24] Brother [Tom]s Regt was prominent in it—as far as we can hear he is safe. Most earnestly do we pray that he may be spared to his children & to us all.

. . . any movement is kept so quiet that we do not know what is going on . . .

from your devoted Sister

Mattie Baldwin

Tom Marshall and most of Stuart's cavalry were by this time on a circuitous and daring route to Maryland and Pennsylvania. Generals W. E. Jones and Beverly H. Robertson with their cavalry brigades were left to guard the Blue Ridge passes and function as a rear guard as Lee moved into Maryland. So Cousin Robert, with the 1st Virginia Cavalry, passed through Winchester on his way north—time for a brief visit with the family. He wrote Bolling that he was "rejoiced and saddened" to be there again, and tried to prepare Bolling for his father's condition.[25]

The Bartons at home had much to agonize about: Strother and cousin Willie, cousin Robert, and Tom Marshall all converging on a battlefield near Gettysburg. In the three-day battle, the Stonewall Brigade was on the extreme left. The brigade as a whole suffered badly, but the 2nd Virginia did not participate in the bloody attack on Culp's Hill. They were skirmishing to the left to protect the flank against Yankee cavalry, and suffered just twenty-four casualties. By July 5 or 6, the news of the terrible losses of Gettysburg had reached Winchester. The townspeople were told to expect the arrival of 5,000 wounded—more than the town's prewar population.[26] Because of his father's failing health, Robby returned to Winchester as fast as he could.

[MEMOIR OF ROBERT T. BARTON]

I made a rapid trip up the Valley to see after my duties, but full of apprehension about my father, I returned in about a week. He had evidently become worse, altho he was still going about. He talked to me about his approaching death as calmly as if it was some trip of great importance which he was to take to a foreign land. He told me of all his business affairs, and advised me earnestly about my own future. . . . Finally, on July 7 1863 he became so weak that he did not get out of his bed, and that night quietly went to sleep and died. During the day, he had been visited by Bishop Wilmer of Louisiana who was here with the troops, and I heard him express to the bishop his absolute faith in his religion and his sure confidence in a future State, believing that the Great God Who put us here would forgive the sins and weaknesses which belong to our natures.[27]

Fortunately, Rannie had been able to reach Winchester by early July. David W. Barton was mourned by his church and his profession. The Bench and Bar of Frederick County paid tribute and went into mourning.

[MEMORIAL OF BENCH AND BAR OF FREDERICK COUNTY]

Amidst the calamities, which it has pleased the Divine Will, of late, to inflict upon our Community and Country, we cannot fail to mark as one of the most durable and afflictive, the death of our brother, late the Senior member of this bar, David W. Barton. Courteous and liberal at the bar, diligent and laborious in business, public spirited and hospitable in society, his memory and example as an influential public man, a kind friend, and Christian gentleman, will long remain to us. . . .

As Lee's maimed and daunted army retreated across the Potomac and the enormity of the defeat began to be understood, the elder Mrs. Jones wrote to her Florida cousin focusing on the family's particular loss.

[LETTER OF ANN C. R. JONES TO LUCY R. PARKHILL]

Winchester July 13th 1863

I am so glad to hear from you dearest friend, & so thankful for your kind, warm interest. Your feeling heart will again be pained by the sad intelligence of our dear Mr. Barton's death. One we have been in the habit of looking up to always . I came in to Winchester with him in his carriage, & little thought altho' he was, & had been for a long time looking *wretchedly* how very soon he was to go, his disease was of the Stomach, & altho' he regained strength to ride to Spring Dale three times a week, & occasionally came to Vaucluse, yet his wasted form & hollow cheeks were calculated to strike fear into our hearts, & poor Fanny hoped to the last day of his life. She had been *ill,* utterly prostrated, but was entirely convalescent when I came here, yet too weak to get across the room without difficulty. However she strengthened daily & when he was taken sick, went downstairs & devoted herself to him night & day——it was astonishing to see the power of will & devotion over her weakened frame. He lived eleven days, she wanted me to stay here which I did, & she is still so unwilling for me to leave her, that I can not yet do it.

It will be a week tomorrow night since his death, which occurred on the 7th. She bears it wonderfully, but Oh! do you not know that a few months show more deeply the desolation? She will struggle hard I know, & there are so many young people to look up to her, that she will have a strong earthly motive for exertion, beside the duty she feels towards her blessed Master. Randolph, Robert & Bolling are with her, but poor Bolling did not arrive in time, dear Strother Barton is with the army still, but safe to our best knowledge, & we feel that it is so thus far. . . . Mattie Baldwin is with her mother, & a perfect treasure in anybody's house, precious little Fan, Anna Jones, & Ellen Barton, poor Marshall's widow, & myself are with her. Marshall's little girl is the express image of himself. . . .

The anniversary of [Frank's] death was the one on which our dear Mr. Barton was laid in his grave, *how* little did I look for *that*, he has been such a healthy hearty man. I have usually fled from the death scene of those I loved, but I did not leave Mr. Barton untill I *thought* he was gone, tho' he lived longer, during all his sickness he had the most beautifully serene countenance you ever beheld, *nothing* seemed to disturb him, no noise even startled him, & throughout the *whole* time I never heard him say but once that he wanted quiet. He said to the Ministers he had no fear. How much he will be missed in the Church, in the Town & in his devoted family.

Randolph's wound is not yet healed, & he is troubled by boils but keeps about & has a furlough untill further orders. . . . Mary Jones was at Church yesterday & dined here, & for the first time, Poor Thing, acknowledged another child was to be expected at Vaucluse. I do not mean to say she ever denied her situation, but *never* spoke of it, & altho' I saw it, I would not speak of it first. The middle of next month her trial comes. She expects her parents the day after tomorrow. I earnestly hope they may come, she has seen them but once

since the war broke out, & only for a few days. Mary looks badly & I have often
noticed her appearance, but was wholly unconscious for a long while of the
cause of it. . . .

Our army, I hear, is in good spirits, what will eventually be done, I do not
know, a great many prisoners have been taken, & are being brought on at times.
Reinforcements from Richmond are near Winchester now, on their way to
General Lee. A little while ago someone came with News from Tom Marshall.
He is perfectly safe, but a third horse has been shot under him since the war
began.[28] . . . I have written so fast, & amongst others sometimes speaking, &
getting up, that my scrawl is worth nothing_ God bless you . . . with the truest
love, I am,

Yours, A.C.R. Jones

*The family learned of their loved ones little by little—Strother and Tom
Marshall safe, no news yet of cousin Willie, who may have been missing or captured, and nothing of cousin Robert.[29] The family's loss of patriarch David W.
Barton, a civilian but in a way a casualty of war, occurred at a time when one
more death was barely noticed among the many.*

X

July–September 1863

WINCHESTER BETWEEN THE LINES

In mid-July it became apparent that Confederate forces would withdraw from Winchester as a result of the Battle of Gettysburg. Many who were unwilling to endure another Yankee occupation comparable to the Milroy regime fled with the retreating armies. Cornelia McDonald said, "The whole town seemed to be trying to get away." She took her children south, destination unknown, with their belongings in one borrowed wagon and one captured by one of the McDonald boys at Gettysburg. Dr. Wilmer took two of her daughters and Julia Clark in his carriage. All made their way amidst segments of their army, their wounded, and other refugees.[1] General Ewell's forces were the last to leave, on the twenty-third, and the town was left open, subject to repeated cavalry forays by both armies. As well, Confederate guerrilla forces were active, and added to the hardships of the people. This continuing and dangerous uncertainty, together with the desire for a change after Mr. Barton's death, convinced his widow to move to Springdale. It would be easier there to provide for the numerous family if they could grow some of their own food—even the children could help. At the end of the summer, Mrs. Barton and her household moved to the country. The Market Street house was rented to Mrs. Tuley, a refugee who had been a wartime neighbor on Market Street. Robby, back at his post in Keezletown, took over some of the managing of his father's affairs. He wrote the VMI again, unsure that his youngest brother would be able to return through the lines to school. However, the Yankees did not, this time, occupy Winchester, although their cavalry, ranging from Martinsburg, were in and out of town

*frequently for the rest of the summer. In August, Robby arranged to resign from
his post in Nitre and Mining, reasoning that he should take on family responsibilities since he was not in active service and because he was most familiar with
his father's business.*

[MEMOIR OF ROBERT T. BARTON]

My father was dead now, and, altho not the oldest living son, yet I felt that
the burden and responsibility of his affairs and of the family fell on me. My
friends all urged upon me the necessity for my leaving the army entirely and as
it looked as if the "seat of war" was about to be transferred away from the Valley
there seemed to be no reason why I could not, as a private citizen be allowed to
remain quietly at home. With this view I again went back to my district, put all
of its affairs in the best order I could and then resigned my position and secured
also from the medical officers certificates of my exemption from military
service.

I returned speedily to Winchester which was now on neutral ground, but
subject constantly to incursions of cavalry from both sides. These were generally scouting parties or else in search of cattle and provisions, the latter generally being Confederates. The Confederates paid for what they took in such
money as they had, and it was seldom that any of the inhabitants withheld from
their demand anything they had that would feed the army, whether it was paid
for or not. . . .

*Winchester, Union or Confederate, was still full of disease, and Grandmother
Jones, during her celebratory visit, contracted typhoid fever and was laid up for
the best part of July. She had been staying at the Bartons' Market Street house,
but as soon as she could was removed to be with Sue, at the Clarks' house,
which was on one of Winchester's many hills. She was convinced the air would
be healthier there.*

[LETTER OF ANN C. R. JONES TO LUCY R. PARKHILL]

Winchester August 7th 1863

I wrote to you dearest Lucy, soon after dear Mr. Barton's death which
occurred exactly one month ago today. I have been flat on my back with fever,
a slight Typhoid they say, but it has taken a good deal of the starch out of me, &
left me somewhat slack twisted, altho' when you consider my *age* most surpris-

ingly strong. I asked Bolling to bring me to Sue the day before yesterday in a Buggy, I thought the change would do me some good, & I wanted to stay with her a while before I went home, the Ride, short as it was, fatigued me terribly, & quite put at fault my immediate arrangements for my leaving town, but I have rallied so much since, & believing now, my best chance for recovering strength is to use all I have, that when they come again to see me, I shall be able to say what day the carriage can come, altho' I feel tolerably *unable* to do anything at present, I have reason to hope, I shall be better & better every day. Our enemy all went off the day before yesterday, & this morning Sue's brother came in to see about her, he cannot of course *stay,* but must return to his Post, when the Yankees will come back I cannot tell, they may return as mysteriously as they disappeared, but I greatly hope they will never again hold this place as they have done.[2]

Mrs. Thomas Barton has been prevented from coming to Mary, but I ardently hope the departure of our enemy will enable her to come yet. I dread the period of Mary's trial without her Mother.[3] She knows all her little ways & necessities, & what to do for her without asking, during the nursing time besides, which would be to me a great relief, as I earnestly desire Mary's comfort in every way.

Poor Fanny [Barton] is excessively anxious to leave town & live at Spring Dale a very fine farm six or 7 miles from Vaucluse, whether she can *yet* bring the matter to bear or not I do not know. Typhoid fever has appeared there, it is *feared* & besides she must make a proper disposition of her present dwelling before she could leave it. I shall be delighted if they can go, it brings them so much nearer to me, & the ability to see them oftener will be increased. Fanny & dear Mattie, indeed all, were so kind in nursing me whilst I was with them.

The return of the Yankees sent our boys off, Ran I saw plainly was *utterly unfit* for service, & he *found* he *must* go back to Staunton, & be attended to longer. Oh! that there could be peace, blessed peace, & those that are left could go back to a more congenial occupation. . . . If these unwelcome human beings stay away any reasonable time the mail difficulty will I hope end. . . . You never saw such a place as Winchester has become, so many persons anxious to leave it, selling their houses & even old inhabitants, & some young, keen for going away, I have become disgusted with the town. . . . Sue is the best satisfied, hers is an airy, high situation, & I breathe here more as if I was in the country, the bad smells are so distressing———between us———in the lower part of the town, & whilst I had the fever, altho' perfectly in my senses, I felt as if I had such an *amount* if breathing to do, & the air sometimes laden with typhoid.

We live in a period for rumours, story telling, extortion, etc., Oh! how I long to *belong* to a nation serving God, but that will never be, except in Heaven. Yesterday every now & then we would hear the Yankees were coming—*just* on the edge of town.

Monday, 10th.—They have not arrived yet, & Oh! how thankful I should be if they *never* come. . . . Farewell, dearest Lucy, excuse this miserable production. I could not undertake anything better just now, it will serve to show you are never forgotten.

Love to all my relatives, with the fondest of love, I am

As ever yours, A. C. R. Jones.

. . . Sue a wonder to scuffle on as she does . . . [her] life is one of exertion & loss of sleep. . . .

Bolling spent the summer in Winchester, but left in late August to return to the institute. His mother wrote him soon after he left. The family had not yet moved to Springdale; the house, after being closed for about two years, needed to be cleaned and readied.

[LETTER OF FANNIE L. BARTON TO BOLLING W. BARTON]

Winchester Aug 26th

My darling child

You can never understand my anguish at parting with you, I know you suffered even as much as I did, my only consolation is in prayer. . . . How I missed you every where, especially at night. I longed to hear your flute once more, Madge [Marshall] has not the heart to play much. I was out at the farm to day, and was much pleased to find so much done. Hardy has painted the parlour and will paper it day after tomorrow, Drake has finished the garret, nicely whitewashed and indeed it looks very sweet, Mr. Rogers house is also nearly finished, one day more will do all that is necessary.[4] I shall begin to move in earnest next week, and hope by the last of Sept, to be well fixed.

You must not forget to write often and tell all your wishes as to your hares and pigeons. Barton [Marshall] will attend most faithfully I am sure to them.

A rumour to day has made us a little uneasy, 'tis said that Millroy is to be sent back here with ten thousand men, I do not believe it, but still hate to hear such reports.

We are all well, I feel as usual, my life must ever hereafter be but one of sorrow and suffering my children and these dear little ones are all that makes life desirable. I long to be at rest . . . excuse this sad letter, good night my child may God help you.

Yr devoted Mother
F L Barton

Fannie L. Barton, Mrs. David W. Barton, a few years after the war.
(Mrs. C. Marshall Barton, Jr.)

During the previous school year, Bolling and his boyhood friend Lud Baldwin (who had also been sent south to school, to Hampden-Sydney) had conducted a sporadic correspondence. They had spent time together again during the summer, although it was a sad one for both of them, with Bolling's father's death, and Lud's father, as he feared, dying. Even before Dr. Robert T. Baldwin became so ill, the family had decided to dispose of the house and move south. Both of Lud's parents, outspoken Confederates, did not wish to remain vulnerable to Federal domination. (Mrs. Lee, losing her neighbors on both sides, lamented the associations of twenty years that were gone.) Lud was still at home for a while after Bolly returned to school. He, too, had heard rumors of Milroy's return.

[LETTER OF W. LUDWELL BALDWIN TO BOLLING W. BARTON]

Winchester August 26th 1863

My Dear Friend,

. . . There is very little news of any kind about here; it is rumored that *dear* Mr. Milroy is in Martinsburg with a large force coming on here, the Union people are charmed at it. I hope he wont *hurry up the cakes.* I dread the idea of going away from here to live but I think we will come back next spring if all is well with us, if the rest dont come I will if nothing prevents. I have had kind invitations to stay all around with different persons but I will miss the old house and yard which we and so many other boys have played in but even that has been a long time.

What sort of boys have you up there, you must write and let me know as I will be here for three weeks yet, if it is according to gods will we will leave the dear old *homestead*. You dont know Dear Bowly how much I miss you and Barton and Tom. . . . Barton drives Mr. Hardy out to SpringDale every morning, starts by six oclock and returns about the same time. He is papering and painting the house I think. Barton and all miss you very much. . . . The town is very quiet as you know, the boys go out and shoot bull bats every evening I have no gun or else I would go. We went up to Mr. Reeds last night . . . and there was a large *ball* in Fagans house just on the other corner, they had a band and were dancing at a great rate. That was the first excitement of that sort I had seen in this town for a long time or rather—since the war. I did not know there were that many men in town, the *Conscript officers* ought to have gotten in that crowd, *really* I did not know there were that many men in the town but there are a plenty of them hiding about when the *Rebels* appear.[5] I dont suppose the ball broke up before one oclock, it had no signs of it when I was at Mr. Reeds which was nearly 11 o'clock.

They say the Yankees will be here on Sunday with a large force. Tell Sandy [Stuart] if you know him that I will write to him on Monday thinking he would like to hear a little gas from this part of the country. I have not seen your *sweetheart Lucy* since you left, I suppose she is grieving for you. Pa is better this morning but still very weak and poorly, I thought he would die last night but it was not gods will. . . . Tell me all about your *conversion* which I will do in my next. . . .

Your dear friend
W.L. Baldwin

Lucy says you are her beau, you must write to her which I expect you will do to keep up the love. . . . Excuse all mistakes and bad spelling.

Everyone was particularly fond of the youngest Barton, and missed him after having him at home for the summer. Once again Fanny expressed her affection by teasing him—this time about his "summer romance," Miss Lucy.

[LETTER OF FANNY J. BARTON TO BOLLING W. BARTON]

Winchester Aug 31st

Dear Bolling

I have just written to Ran but I could not put down my pen until I had written you a letter too. what sort it will be, *time only will divulge*. First I will touch upon the subject *nearest your heart*. Miss Lucy had turned out quite a *pedestrian* since your absence. She walked out to Mr. Robert Glasses & stayed several days & then walked back again & last night I saw her looking quite *robust* notwithstanding this extraordinary exertion.[6]

I have been missing you *very much* (like a bad tooth ache) since you left especially the soothing influence of the music of your *flute*. I have wanted you too, about my flowers which I have been taking up ready to move to Springdale. Much to our joy Robby has come & we keep the poor fellow *very busy*. The *drawing room* is finished at Spring dale & looks very sweet mama says, I have not seen it yet. I hope you can come down at Christmas. You must keep up your spirits until then tho mighty hard to do I know Bolly but every sorrow small & great is sent to us for some good. We could not bear them did we not feel sure of this. We heard from sister Jane yesterday & from brother S[trother] to day both are well & I should not be much supprised if both were with us before long.[7] The children started to school this morning. . . . Marshall Jones is here looking very well.[8] My hand is so cramped that I cannot write more now. May God bless you dear Bolly. Mama is at S———d——— or she would send some message. I believe she wrote to you not long ago. do write very soon to your devoted sister

Fanny

All summer, Winchester, an "open city," tempted Confederate soldiers to venture into town. Marshall Jones was in and out several times in August, as was Frank Clark.[9] But these visits were interspersed with those of Yankees, sometimes disguised as Rebel troops. On August 5, Mrs. Lee and the girls "were sitting on the porch & two soldiers passed & made some remarks on the 'Secesh;' they returned to the porch & asked if Mrs. Lee lived here; my first thought was they were two of the Jessie scouts, who have been going about town to-day, but in a moment afterwards we gave a joyous greeting to Shippey & Marshal[l] Jones, the first Confederates who have ventured in town, since the army left. It was quite refreshing to see persons from Dixie."[10] Cavalry raids were so common that Mrs. Lee affected to be blasé. She wrote only a day later: "The first sound I heard this morning was the clanking of sabres & dash of Cavalry; so accustomed have I become to border warfare that I did not get up to see whether they were Confederates or Yankees, but completed my morning nap . . . by dinner time, all had vamosed."[11] It is hard to believe Mrs. Lee had no fears, and this prolonged period of uncertainty was perhaps Winchester's most difficult and stressful. It was impossible to know what to expect. Frank Clark, meeting his sister Susan Jones near Middletown (which should have been relatively safe), was almost captured in a Yankee cavalry foray. He escaped but his fine horse was lost to the enemy.[12] *The Steele children were "badly frightened" when the Yankees searched their house one morning in August, in one of a number of raids on Newtown for horses, "Rebels, whiskey, and tobacco."*[13] *Confederate conscript officers and guerrillas were active, and any approaching party of horsemen was a potential threat, a menace. Relatively safe as a civilian again, Robby Barton returned home and took up residence in late August. The family moved to Springdale in stages over the next few weeks.*[14] *The household consisted of Mrs. Barton, Martha and her children, the Marshall children, Fanny, Robby, and, much of the time, "sister" Anna Jones.*

[MEMOIR OF ROBERT T. BARTON]

I put on citizens dress; let my discharge from the army be generally known so as to prevent, if possible, the few evil minded in the Community from doing me harm. There was not much trouble on this score, for if I did not wish the Union men to put the Yankees on me, so they were even more solicitous that I should extend protection to them against any vengeance the Confederates might inflict for harm done the citizens by the Yankees. Hence there was a sort of "armed neutrality" among us.

I took charge of the farm and was very diligent and industrious in my duties as a farmer. I rose very early and after seeing that the stock was fed and the hands started to the fields I would come in and before breakfast teach my nephew and niece Barton and Madge their Latin lessons. The days were spent in active supervision of the farm and my father's other landed estates; in as far as possible settling up his affairs, and not a little time in visiting among the neighbours.

Rannie had gone south with the army in July but could not yet sustain the demands of that life. Soon recognizing this (as his grandmother had wisely perceived), he diverged from the brigade as they were about to cross the Blue Ridge toward eastern Virginia. He continued south through the Luray valley to Staunton, where as always he received a warm welcome.

[MEMOIR OF RANDOLPH BARTON]

As the army returned from Pennsylvania, I joined it, reporting to General James A. Walker, who had succeeded General Paxton in command of the "Stonewall" Brigade, but about Front Royal my wound gave me so much trouble that I again left the army, going with my two horses, "Mary Stuart" and

Staunton in the mid-1850s. The train station is in the foreground; the A. H. H. Stuart house is the large building at the far left. (Library of Congress)

"Priam" by way of Luray. Both animals were very handsome and my colored boy, "George," was an excellent groom. I know how I selected the name of the first horse, but upon what classical knowledge I drew for the second has always been a conundrum to me. Both horses were beautiful bays and their coats, under George's care, shown like satin. "Priam" eventually broke down, and "Mary Stuart," after carrying me safely through several battles, in one of which Hatcher's Run, February 6th, 1865, was wounded, and then to Appomattox and back to Winchester, came to an untimely end by overeating green corn. How unromantic! . . .

I worked my way back to Staunton, drawn to that haven of rest than to any other in Virginia, by Miss Mary Stuart, or Miss Jennie Peyton, or Miss Cornelia Peyton, I have never been able clearly to decide. To have yielded to the attracting powers of any one of them would have been to my credit. To have successfully resisted the combination would have been to my infinite discredit. In perhaps six weeks, my wound having healed, as I thought (for later, after I had rejoined the army, a small piece of bone worked its way out), I again set out for the army.

Robby remembered this rather differently, and took some credit for treating Rannie's wound.

[LETTER OF ROBERT T. BARTON TO RANDOLPH BARTON]

I think you went back to Camp and suffered so much from pain in your healed wound that you came away and then visited Mr Stuarts. You must remember that I stayed there with you one night and while we were dressing to go see the Peyton girls you asked me to look at your wound which was hurting you very much. I looked at it and saw what I took to be a small splinter protruding from it. Without consulting you I took hold of it with a small pair of tweezers which I had in pocket and gave a sharp jirk. The 'splinter' proved to be the point of an arrow shaped piece of bone and as it came out, with its widening shape, it made a sharp gash on the healed over but inflamed surface and a good deal of blood followed. I remember how I had to dodge the blows you aimed at me until I had time to show you the bone and to demonstrate my skill as a surgeon. After that you went back to Camp and your wound healed all right.[15]

Soon after, Rannie set off for the army again, with a pleasant detour. His father's cousins Barton and Bolling Haxall each had plantations near Gordonsville.

[MEMOIR OF RANDOLPH BARTON]

I was in fine plight, and my horses, equipment, manservant and all, made me quite "distingue." I struck out for Gordonsville, and then for Rocklands, cousin Barton Haxall's exquisite estate, about three miles from the village, the army being near Orange Court House.

I reached Rocklands about mid-day. I had never met any of the family except cousin Barton before, for when I reached the house, dismounted and ascended the steps with clanking sword and spurs, I was greeted by cousins Octavia, Mary, Lottie, Fanny and Rosalie, at first as a stranger, but, upon introducing myself, immediately we had known each other all our lives. The hospitality, brightness and beauty of the family captivated me. Just as the wind sometimes veers with suddenness from one quarter to the other, so my thoughts turned from the girls I had left behind me, to the girls I had around me. Mary, as the eldest, I suppose, enlisted my most marked attention. She and her sisters, differing one from the other in details, were all most attractive. True, Fanny and Rosalie were then quite young, but their incipient loveliness was unmistakable to my penetrating eye. I yielded with alacrity to the pressing invitation to spend the night, and the next morning, either at the breakfast table or just when breakfast was announced, the servant said, "Miss Lou" was outside.[16] I did not know who "Miss Lou" was, but it was hardly necessary for cousin Octavia to suggest that I should go out and be introduced to her as a new cousin.

A September morning in that exquisite country could not have been more beautiful. The outlook from the front porch elevation was over a rich and well-

Louisa Triplett Haxall in a carte de visite *taken in Lausanne, Switzerland, in 1868, where she was visiting her brother Bolling in school.*
(John Triplet Harrison, Jr.)

cultivated country, shaded here and there by noble forests, and bounded in the distance by the Blue Ridge Mountains, the entire landscape smoothed and softened by the haze of the season, through which the sun came in streams of gold.

With nature in its most beautiful form as a frame work to the picture, I found handsomely mounted, near the front door, "Cousin Lou." To say that she was radiantly beautiful is only to speak the verdict of all who knew her. She was then about sixteen, and her home for the summer was "Springfield," some five or six miles distant. With a faithful servant she had galloped over to Rocklands for "before-breakfast" exercise. I was duly introduced to her as a cousin, and that marked the beginning of a friendship which the lapse of many years only served to intensify. I only caught that morning a glimpse of her, for, after asking after the welfare of all, she bade us a gentle good-bye and galloped off, my cousin Octavia no doubt reading in my eyes the fatal effects of the vision, remarking to me as we turned to go into the house, "Now, don't fall in love with your pretty cousin," an injunction which no man should have obeyed, even at the risk of his life.

I went on to the army the next morning, which I found encamped in Orange County. . . . My proximity to the Barton Haxalls enabled me to visit them often. The army was undergoing rigid reorganization. There it was that I saw nine men and boys shot for desertion—the most horrible sight I ever witnessed but their desertion was of the most aggravated kind, and even General Lee could find no extenuation.[17]

Lee's army was having increasing difficulty with desertion from the ranks, and Rannie was back by September 5, in time to witness this severe measure. Those bent on deserting after this often fled to the enemy. From camp, Rannie wrote telling his younger brother the army news, as well as some from home. Bolling may have received the letter on his way to class—his algebra notes were scrawled on the last page.

[LETTER OF RANDOLPH BARTON TO BOLLING W. BARTON]

Brigade Hdqtrs
Near Mortons ford
Sept 23rd 1863

Dear Boly,

We have been here at this point the last four days—waiting patiently for the enemy to cross but, [Union Gen. George G.] Meade shows his sense and keeps clear, until at last disgusted with his delay, we have gone into regular camp. We have an elegant position, some seven miles southeast of Culpepper C.H. and just on the banks of the Rapidan river. We overlook the north side, see Cul C.H. in the distance, Mount Pony, Stephensburg, Slaughter mountain, and other interesting objects. We are behind first rate earthworks and really wish for the enemy to come.

Brother Strother got back day before yesterday; he was in and about Winchester five days.[18] All were well. Brother S[trother] rec a letter from cousin Anna [Jones], just now, written from Springdale; the family have moved out permanently; I am delighted with the change; If we live to get back, it will be delightful to walk across the country, and in the evenings, about the barnyard amongst the cows and horses.

My mare is in elegant order, also Old Priam. I am saving every dollar to pay my absolutely necessary debts. I have just rec a letter from Miss Gussy Stuart, she and *Miss Mary* are charming ladies. . . . You no doubt have heard of the death of Old Dr. Robt Baldwin.[19] . . . Ben Holladay was taken prisoner in the Cav fight a few days ago, brother Tom [Marshall] had a horse shot under him.[20] Three men deserted from our brigade yesterday, to the enemy, they had been whipped last winter and no doubt had intended it all the time. You know I succeeded in getting a boy from Maj. [Beverley] Randolph, he proves himself to be an excellent valet-de-chambre.[21] Dr. Straith has just come in, and brings a report of the capture of J.E.B. Stuart. I hope it is false. We receive the first news from the west with anxiety; God grant it may prove favorable.[22] God bless you my dear brother

yours affectionately
RJ Barton

Rannie's next letter does not mention the deserters, but speaks volumes about life in Winchester at this time: cavalry forays after church; raiders delivering letters, which must immediately be hidden rather than read; constant problems with the informal "requisitions" by the enemy. Rannie may have been feckless about money, but he also had the expenses of his rank, as he spelled out in this letter. He apparently had talked Bolling out of a watch when they were both at home that summer.

[LETTER OF RANDOLPH BARTON TO BOLLING W. BARTON]

Brigade HdQrs
Sept 30 1863
Camp near Rapi[dan]

Dear Boly,

I have just received your letter of the 19. inst and as it is interesting I propose answering in the same strain. Brother Strother ret some days ago from Springdale. He was in Winchester several times at home five days. The family have moved out permanently to the farm and drive in to town as naturally as if it were an old arrangement.

The other day I received a letter from sister Fan, she says "We went in to town to hear Mr. Suter preach but were disappointed and had to put up with Mr. Graham; after service on coming out from the church, we found ourselves in the midst of a skirmish; about that time some one dashed up and handed me your letter which I commenced reading but someone cautioned me to put it up.[23] It was amusing to see Robby strutting about, as if he had never done them harm; The Yankees took one of the horses from him which Mr. Rogers hopes to recover." She goes on, plaguing me about my love affairs and writes in good spirits.

By the way, did I tell you about it. On my way down I dined at cousin Barton Haxalls where I was received very cordially by his family, especially I fancied, by cousin Mary, his daughter. She is just seventeen years old, black wavy hair and eyes, bright complexion and the sweetest mouth you ever saw she is charming. I'll go to see her next winter as sure as you are born.

Well, about smoking. Before the death of our dear father, he told brother Strother, he saw no reason why a soldier should not smoke; the V.M.I. is equal as far as fair is concerned, any day, to the army; consequently, I see no objection, except expense, to your smoking, provided you use tobacco moderately. I wish I could send you pocket money, but every cent is taken up paying for horses, mess-bill, blanket, negro boy's hire. Please, state, as a favor, when, exactly, you will want the $60.00 I owe you, as I can raise it in a few weeks. The watch I find is a very good one, and indispensable to my comfort and convenience.

The mare is in *beautiful* order, and as for "Priam" you would'nt know him. A Quartermaster asked me yesterday, if I would sell him? I asked, what is he worth? he said $1000.00. I value him at $200.00 more than that and am going to hold on to him. He dog-trots delightfully. He is much superior to the mare as far as spirit and activity is concerned. . . . I am delighted that you have such a good set of fellows, I hope and know they will appreciate you. Remember your devoted brother in your prayers.

R.J. Barton
A.A.G.

XI

October—December 1863

THE FAMILY AT SPRINGDALE
CAMPAIGNING IN THE WILDERNESS

In the fall, Federal Gen. William W. Averell's forces threatened and raided the southern part of the Valley from West Virginia, and the commander of the Rockbridge Home Guard felt sufficiently pressed to call out the VMI cadets (including Bolling) three times in November and December. In three forays, each of about five days, the ill-equipped corps did not see action—only the hardship of severe weather.

It had been wrenching for the Bartons, particularly Mrs. Barton, to leave their home on Market Street. Of course they all came into town regularly, and from time to time, Mrs. Barton went to the old house, now rented to Mrs. Tuley, for things she had left behind in August. Mrs. Lee was with her on October 27. "It was a painful scene; she rushed over the house in an uncontrollable agony of grief; finding various articles belonging to her dead husband & sons." Mrs. Barton had worries as well as grief. Mrs. Lee continued, "Fanny came back to dinner with us & Mrs. Barton went to Dr. Conrads. Poor Mrs. Barton, I am so sorry for her; she has just heard that Jane's lungs have been examined & that both are affected—& Fan has a constant cough. Her estate is involved to the amount of $85,000."[1]

Daily life was difficult in town and country, although there was mercifully little military activity in Frederick County. Yankee foraging and raiding—often with looting and destruction—continued sporadically in and near Winchester. On November 9, Mrs. Lee said, "They took Mrs. Barton's corn & burned her *fences" and took a horse, which Robby had managed to get back.*[2] *The town's situation was still fluid and undefined, but its people hoped that the worst was over for them, that the Yankees would not come again, in force. The lines of communication, though uncertain, were open to the North and to the South, and Grandmother Jones found solace in writing to her Florida cousin Lucy Parkhill.*

[LETTER OF ANN C. R. JONES TO LUCY R. PARKHILL]

Vaucluse October 5th 1863

Your last letter dearest friend reached me the day after it was a full month old, yet it was cordially welcomed & I trust it may not be long before I hear again. I think I receive all you write, I am not willing to believe that any are lost, tho sometimes they *tarry* on the way. . . . Are you not cheered by the success of our arms? Yet we must wait untill our Heavenly Father shows more clearly his blessed will. Freedom in the end, I have *no* doubt is ours but the time *he* will judge of & that time is best, *how* thankful I should be if it was *now*, but Patience patience, I feel sometimes sinfully weary of this terrible struggle. Trouble comes out of the army as well as in it, & I have sorrowed for the death of my friend & relative Innes Randolph. . . .[3]

Mary Jones is unusually well for her predicament, yet her face & complexion show the want of fresh air. Next Friday her confinement will be over, if the weather allows her venturing out, we have had a great many lovely days for a long time, with one day of [close?] pouring rain which I suppose was beneficial to the Farmers. The Baby is an uncommonly fine, hearty, healthy one, it is Marys *tenth* child.[4] . . .

Fanny I am sure I have said, is established at Spring Dale, I dined with her on Saturday, she looks very sad, but, is still attending to her household, she is gifted with untiring energy & a *will* to carry her on, in what she thinks she ought to do, her family consists of 12 persons, & comfort usually reigns in her dwelling.[5] Mattie Baldwin is a rare person, & a great support to her Mother, she, with Anna Jones & Mats two children are going this week to Staunton . . . [she] made many friends during the period of her residence in Staunton, her Husband [Dr. John M. Baldwin] was greatly beloved there, & had many relations in the place, he was a bright Christian, & a first rate Man, *very* useful, *very* intellectual, & elegant looking. . . . those two young people were perfectly devoted to each other, it was surely a love match, as Sue and my hearts darling [Frank] you know was. Both are broken up, but we must not doubt the wisdom & love that decreed it, Mattie bears up *wonderfully*.

Poor Sue! cannot always. She looks so intensely sad sometimes, you would grieve to look at her. Her Fathers house the spot on earth she loves has been sold, she cannot *yet* go to her own home, this winter must be filled with *unrest*, & sad forbodings.[6] I shall stay much with her. In the spring she expects to return to Carysbrooke, & altho her sufferings must be often *bitter*, when she misses him there, which she must do every moment, I trust she will *after a while* be *better* there, than any where. . . . I know she has always looked forward to going there as her home, but not yet. She felt it a duty to minister to her Fathers comfort, & whilst the Yankees were near, she *feared* to live in the country yet her Father never stays when the Yankees *are* near & now, it has become right for him to part with the Property. My darling [Frank] thought her & his children better protected in town, & would not have been willing for her to stay at Carysbrooke, but I trust the Yankee reign will be over here, before the Spring. Oh how ardently I *do* hope that you & yours will wholly escape the Tyranny of these wicked Yankees, & their hideous allies. . . .

The last day of this month I complete my 69th year, thereby entering the 70th. Is it not horrible to look back upon, so many years of sin, & Illness in the Lords Vine yard. God help me, for I need it. I know Mary & Strother would wish much love sent you, & Rebecca too, as well as darling Bev. Oh! when shall I see my child again except by snatches, I bless the Lord he is not in active service, he has to lead a Rough life & religion where he is located is unfortunately in error. . . .

God Bless you dearest friend my love makes me an imposition sometimes but I *trust* you————yours ever A.C.R. Jones

After Gettysburg, Lee had withdrawn to the south bank of the Rapidan near Orange Court House, while General Meade encamped on the Rappahannock. Longstreet and his First Corps were detached to Tennessee. After the Southern victory at Chickamauga, Meade dispatched heavy reinforcements there, providing Lee with an opportunity to attack. The Confederate movement began October 9, but despite brilliant maneuvering and success on the part of Stuart's cavalry, the Rebel infantry was repulsed at Bristoe Station. They retired across the Rapidan by the end of October. Rannie had returned to the brigade in September and was appointed Assistant Adjutant General to Gen. James A. Walker, its commanding general since Paxton's death.

[MEMOIR OF RANDOLPH BARTON]

In the latter part of October, or early November, General Lee determined to bring Meade to battle, and so, crossing the Rapidan, some miles above the railroad crossing . . . he sought to get around on the flank of Meade. But that officer was wary and backed from the Rapidan until he had reached Centreville. At Bristoe Station Warren's Federal Corps dealt A. P. Hill's Corps an ugly blow [October 14]. Our army moved up within a mile or so of Broad Run, which crosses the Orange and Alexandria Railroad, a short distance east of Bristoe Station, and there we encountered a tremendous rain. General Stuart, with his cavalry, had crossed the run towards Manassas, and as it rapidly rose, General Ewell and a group of General officers in council became much concerned about General Stuart's safety.[7] General Walker took part in the consultation, and, as his Adjutant, I sat on my fine horse, "Priam," near by. It was determined to send word of the situation to General Lee, who was a mile or two back. For some unknown reason, unless it was my fine horse, I was selected to carry the message. I left the group in a fast gallop, which I kept up over streams, ditches and all obstructions, and finally reached General Lee's headquarters. I found his tent and dismounting, hung my rein over my arm and knocked upon the tent pole for admission. He bade me come in and I found him with his feet resting on a box, the floor of the tent (the sod) being saturated with water.

I knew the Broad Run was rising every minute, and that the difficulty of securing the safe return of General Stuart was momentarily increasing, and so the importance of my mission, the rapidity of my ride, and the noble presence of General Lee probably caused me to deliver my message with some excitement of manner.

I was quite crest-fallen when, after reflecting a moment, General Lee said, in a slow and measured manner, "Go back and tell General Ewell if he thinks it better to recall General Stuart he can do so." I returned quite rapidly, delivered General Lee's instructions and General Stuart was safely recalled.

That night our brigade slept on a wet flat without blankets, food or shelter; but General Walker, who was bold in battle and everywhere else, sent an orderly back a mile or two to our headquarters' wagon, directing that our tents should be set and supper cooked. After seeing that the men were as comfortable as the case permitted, we stole back to our tents, where we had an excellent supper and a splendid night's rest. By daylight we were at the front, and when General Walker met General [Edward] Johnson, our Division Commander, his first words were "Well, General, we had a rough time last night." Johnson was never the wiser.

Mail from the Bartons' soldiers reached Springdale only irregularly, but Rannie's account of the Bristoe Station Campaign got through.

[LETTER OF RANDOLPH BARTON TO ROBERT T. BARTON]

HdQrs. Stonewall Brigade
19 Oct 1863

Dear Robby,

Your very interesting letter of the 4th inst. was received yesterday and I wrote an answer to it last night but was prevented from sending it by unavoidable circumstances. I suppose our campaign, from which we have just returned, will entertain you most, so I will give a brief account. October 8th we attempted to flank Meades Army by Madison C.H. and Warrenton. Meade fell back rapidly and in good order. Several cavalry fights took place, in which we always wounded the enemy, taking in all 1500 prisoners, killing probably 60, losing ourselves some 30 men killed and wounded. It seems that Genl Lee wished to avoid a general engagement, for he laid at Warrenton half a day, and at other places he loitered considerably.

About the 13th we left Warrenton and two Divisions of our "Corps" came up with the enemys rear guard (Warren's Corps) and after some skirmishing started them again on the run; our "corps" followed leasurely. At Bristoe Station O&A RRoad 4 miles above Manassas Junction Hills Corps on our left came up with the enemy, and there we received a miserable, disgraceful vexatious repulse. Heth's (the unlucky) Division attacked the enemy strongly posted behind the railroad and on the hills around, with two Brigades in line with a very weak support. The two front Brigades (Cooks and Kirklands) advanced gallantly within 30 yards of the railroad, when the enemy poured a destructive fire into our men. Cooks brigade, on the right broke, leaving Kirklands exposed to a terrible flank fire which also broke running back in great confusion, passing a battery of five guns, which having its horses killed was unable to get back, the enemy advancing his skirmishes rapidly actually took the battery pulling of the pieces "by hand." Summary. Brigadiers Generals Cook, Posey and Kirkland wounded, one hundred and twenty-five killed outright, 540 wounded. This fight will not make any difference in the issue of the war, but neither will Kernstown. It has no effect either way upon the spirits of the army, but is so

Bettie Colston, later Mrs. Basil Gildersleeve.
(Virginia Historical Society)

provoking. It is rumored that Hill is under arrest.[8]

After the fight the enemy retreated; we then tore up the railroad track back to Rappahannock river (20 miles) destroying bridges, culverts etc. Having accomplished (as far as we could discover) the object of our trip, destruction of the road, delaying the advance of the enemy and thus enabling us to reinforce Bragg; all this latter is conjecture you must know. I think *we* (our Corps) are done campaigning and fighting. Maybe Hills Corps will go West. We go into a permanent camp tomorrow. Capt. [W. E.] Cutshaw has just come in, hunting for his Quarters, but as I know the difficulties of such a thing I have insisted upon his staying with me, which he has agreed to do. On the campaign I got soaking wet once by carrying a dispatch from Genl Ewell to Genl Lee and thus swimming on horseback, or nearly so, a swollen stream, and to day I got a good ducking in a severe rain.

You want our opinions of "Bettie."[9] Well *I* think she is a fascinating little thing, *very* pretty, agreeable, sensible and with all this not near equal to Miss Mary Stuart. You know I saw her the night of the day you left Staunton.

Capt. Cutshaw sends his kindest regards to all.[10] Brother Strother is perfectly well, and in first rate spirits. I am going to write to Col Holliday tomorrow about my regular army appointment. My being a minor prevents my getting anything higher at present than a Cadetship.[11] . . . I would like very much to have the gum coat I gave you, as I have no overcoat. Give my love to all and tell dear Ma I will write soon to her. . . .

Your devoted bro
R.J. Barton
A.A.G.

Winchester remained between the lines during October and November, the military focus in Virginia being on the Rapidan. The Federals contented them-

*selves with guarding the Baltimore & Ohio Railroad near Martinsburg, while
Confederate cavalry remained well south of town. Both forces continued to send
cavalry reconnaissances through Winchester, unsettling the anxious inhabitants
in town and country. Robby had taken charge of the Springdale farm and the
family. Sister Fanny was at Springdale, and Mrs. Lee's nieces, who missed having the Bartons next door, came to visit, perhaps when Martha and her children
and cousin Anna were away.*[12] *Cousin Cary Baldwin, aunt Caroline Barton,
and uncle James Jones and families were living in Staunton, and Martha had
friends to visit from her years there.*

*From the army, Tom Marshall wrote Robby with, naturally, particular inter-
est in his children's well-being. He also apprised Robby of the reorganization of
the Confederate cavalry, in process since Gettysburg. J. E. B. Stuart and
"Grumble" Jones (Tom's brigadier) had continued their feud, culminating in
Jones being court-martialed for insubordination. Although he was found guilty,
Lee did not want to lose him, and Jones was reassigned. Lee promoted a favorite of Stuart's, Col. Thomas L. Rosser, to Jones's former command—not initially
a popular appointment with the brigade. Tom also described the October 19
cavalry engagement, known as the "Buckland races," when Stuart, covering the
Confederate retreat from Bristoe Station, routed the Federal cavalry.*

[LETTER OF THOMAS MARSHALL TO ROBERT T. BARTON]

HeadQrs 7th V.C. Nov. 3rd 1863

My dear Robert,

. . . Your letter gave me sincere pleasure, your account of the children & the
arrangements made for their improvement was truly *gratifying*. The task of
teaching will (if you are like myself) call forth *your patience* or *impatience*——
which? It is with you & all, I know, a *labour of love*. May you receive a *present
reward* in *the rapid improvement* of those in your charge, & the *future one* in
the "Well done, good & faithful servant" thou hast been faithful in a few things
&C &C! You see notwithstanding my soldier-life, I have not forgotten how to
preach; but perhaps you may ask "have you forgotten how to practice?"

All of you speak of promised letters from Mattie & Anna from *Staunton*.
None such have reached me. I would enjoy them very much. You can easily call
to mind how a letter from *home* or *home-friends* brightens the path of the soldier separated from all those ties, which endear one so to this world. *Bolling* has
abandoned me as a correspondent, but I believe the fault rests with myself as I
have owed him a letter a long-time. His communication with you all at

Thomas Marshall as a major, probably photographed in Winchester in the fall of 1862.
(T. Marshall Duer, Jr.)

Springdale, being now so much more open than last winter, makes him feel less dependent upon others for sympathy. I was glad to hear through a letter from *Ran* that he [Bolling] has a set of *choice companions* in his room.

You are, perhaps, aware that our Brigade has recently changed its *name* & style being now *Rosser's* Brigade. We belong to [Wade] *Hampton's Division.* Our New Brigade-Commander, though making his entree under a cloud of *prejudice* against him has by *wise* & *cool conduct* on the *field,* his *pleasant manners* in *official intercourse* dispelled it to a great degree. There were some ugly rumours about his *private character,* which have not been altogether cleared up.[13]

Genl [W. E.] Jones (who was no particular pet of yours) has been assigned to duty in Southwestern Virginia, & has also, I understand, been recommended as Major Gen of Cavalry by Genl Sam Jones—We shall lose the agreeable Society of Capt [John D.] Richardson (now Major, QrMs), who will go to Genl Jones, our New General desiring to have his own friends. This is to us the most *grievous loss* we will sustain.

You are pleased to allude to the flattering notice of me in a late [Richmond] Enquirer. It was shown to me by Lieut [McKim H.] Wells, Co E. Upon reading it I found that it was conceived in error & bestows upon me *thunder* robbed from "Lt. Col. T. B. Massie" whom you know, I believe. The part acted by our Regiment in that fight was somewhat similar but not so *successful.*[14]

While fighting Buford in *front,* Kilpatrick got in our *rear* had nearly succeeded in cutting off our way of retreat to the *Rapidan.* Col. [Oliver R.] Funsten (commanding our Brigade) was ordered to the rear to check this movement of the enemy. He succeeded in reaching a commanding point with the *artillery* just as Kilpatrick seized the road in *our rear.*

As we reached the vicinity of this point a large column of ours in front of our

Regiment (or rather about 2 squadrons of the 7th) seemed to break to the *right* & *left* in a good deal of confusion—the enemy's sharpshooters firing over the hill. Some one on the crest of the hill (I think it was Capt [M. Gilbert] Martin, our Adjt Genl) called to me (by name) to charge.

Thinking the enemy (who were hidden by the hill in front) were about to charge Our artillery in order to take it we started at a round pace, passed the crest of the hill, & then had to go a considerable distance on the other side before reaching the *foe,* who were *dismounted* in a heavy piece of timber, & were peppering us as we came down the pike. When nearly up to them, I found the column very much strung out & only a few men near me, & seeing it would prove a failure I turned by the left into a thick piece of pines, in order to gather up & rally the men. While rallying them Genl Stuart rode up & urged another charge, which being led off by Capt Magruder who was near him, resulted in the immediate death of that gallant young officer.[15] I was about one hundred yards from him when he received the *fatal wound.* We succeeded in bringing off his body.

The 11th & 12th followed in charges, which proved *successful.* I think however, we are entitled to the credit of having *broken* thrice for them.

I have given you quite a dish of *military matters*—more than I should have done except for the mistake before alluded to. . . . Give much love to all for me. Kisses to my darling children.

Yr affectionate brother
Thomas Marshall

Rannie's next letter to Robby was a mixture of military news, mild homesickness, and talk about girls.

[LETTER OF RANDOLPH BARTON TO ROBERT T. BARTON]

Headquarters Stonewall Brigade
19 Nov 1863

Dear Robby,

I have just received a letter from dear Boly, written in his sweet and affectionate way; and he talks so much about dear old Springdale and you all that I can't help writing myself, to supply the place of my thoughts. . . .

I think we are gradually working our way down to Fredericksburg. Major Genl Hampton did a handsome thing night before last, as brother Toms regiment (Rossers Brigade) is in that Div maybe it was engaged, I don't know. Crossing the Rapidan river at Mortons ford, in *our* front, he attacked the enemy, in camp, somewhere near Culpepper C.H. killing and wounding a good many, taking 50 prisoners, 200 horses, 8 wagons and 2 ambulances, besides collecting a large number of small arms, and returning in safety. Genl Early is now commanding our Corps, in the absence of Genl Ewell, whose wound compels him to leave for a time.

Write soon and tell us all about affairs at Springdale. Didn't I give you my opinion about cousin Bettie [Colston]. If it was not for cousin Mary Haxall, I believe you would have a rival. Give much love to all and try to win cousin Bettie; you know old fellow, you are getting old. We will all meet again at the right time. Love to all the little ones. Why don't you "regale" them sometimes with wild ducks.

Your devoted brother
R.J. Barton

After the Bristoe Station Campaign, Lee prepared to go into winter quarters, only to discover on November 26 that Meade was launching an offensive on the lower Rapidan in an attempt to turn Lee's flank. Lee marched north and met the Federals the next day at Mine Run, in the Wilderness. The battle, also known as Payne's Farm, continued on the twenty-eighth and twenty-ninth and was a major one. The heaviest fighting took place November 27 on Lee's left flank, where Johnson's division held off the Federal advance at odds of six to one.[16] Union delays and strong Confederate entrenchments finally thwarted Meade's plans. Rannie was on Walker's staff with the Stonewall Brigade.

[MEMOIR OF RANDOLPH BARTON]

Later in the season we moved beyond Orange Court House, well down on the Rapidan River, near Morton's Ford. While in that part of the State the battle of Mine Run occurred. Meade was making a formidable demonstration and General Lee, burning with a desire to obliterate Gettysburg, was maneuvering to get him to attack him. The two armies were marching on parallel lines southward, when French, commanding a corps in Meade's army, took the wrong road, and most unexpectedly to him and to us, brushed up against our (Johnson) division. A very sharp fight occurred. Our brigade instantly faced from the road on which it was marching to the direction from which the unexpected bullets came, and charged through the woods, encountering the enemy and driving them back. This was my first experience under fire with General Walker, and so, when he boldly dashed into the open field, leading his line forward, I perforce, followed him, as if I liked it. The line discreetly stopped at the fence. Later in the action, our relative, Raleigh T. Colston, Lieutenant-Colonel of the Second Virginia, was badly wounded, and the regiment having no Major, the command devolved upon one of the Captains who was untrustworthy. General Walker quietly said to me, "Go to the regiment (it was on the left flank of the brigade) and take command of it; do not let Captain— know of this order, but take command."[17] I did so, but there was not much fighting afterwards. Either before this or afterwards, I was sitting on my horse near my brother, Strother, who was on foot, when I heard a ball strike, and he fell to the ground. I immediately saw the blood welling out on his trousers just above his left knee, and asked him to extend his leg, to see if it was broken; he did so, and said he did not think it was broken, and I called up some men and had him carried to the rear. About dark, the enemy having retired, we returned to the road on which we were marching and resumed our course. We were quite soon in line of battle, and I went in search of my brother, whose wound I had learned had necessitated amputation of his leg above the knee. I found him in an old church crowded with wounded, deathly pale, suffering intensely, with his head lying in the lap of Mr. Hopkins, Chaplain of the Regiment (and an excellent and brave man). I consoled him as well as I could, saying, among other things, that he was now out of the war and could honorably go back to Springdale and take charge of the farm. He told me afterwards that the remark had a most happy effect upon him, inspiring him with courage to stand the pain from which he was suffering and opening a brighter future to him. . . .

Strother's captain, James B. Burgess, immediately wrote Mrs. Barton, even though he himself had been wounded at Mine Run. He tried to reassure her that Strother was doing well and was in good spirits and in good hands, those of Dr. R. F. Baldwin. In later years, Rannie attempted to learn what had happened to Strother after he was wounded, and so he corresponded with the 2nd Virginia's "Fighting Chaplain," Abner Crump Hopkins, who was before and after the war the Presbyterian minister in Charles Town.

[LETTER OF ABNER C. HOPKINS TO RANDOLPH BARTON]

Charles Town W. Va. Dec 23rd 1897

My dear Friend,

I was truly grateful to you for your kind letter recently received. It revived so many recollections of 27th Nov. '63 especially those connected with your brother . . . that noble gallant brother, yet gentle & refined as a woman.

Capt. James B. Burgess's letter to Mrs. David W. Barton. (Edith Barton Sheerin)

The 2nd Regt. had been fighting nearly all day against French's Corps, & in the afternoon the Brigade came to us. After hours of fighting there was somewhat a cessation of the firing. Genl. Walker was sitting quietly on his bay horse in the road & at the gate that led from wood to field, & a number of us was standing around him talking over events. Your brother Strother was standing by the left side of Genl W. stroking the Generals horse's neck, but somewhat facing the field. I heard suddenly a sharp crack like an old fashioned black wagon whip. At that instant Strother began to reel around & then fell. We learned instantly that he was shot in the leg just below the knee. I think now that it was the *left* knee which was wounded, but my recollection is not positive about this. He was soon sent back to the field hospital. You say it was a church; my recollection is that it was a farm dwelling house some 2 or 3 miles to the rear but nearer to Mine Run than our position that day was. I did not leave the line of battle till night closed the fight. . . .

I set out in search of the hospital, which it seemed to me my weary limbs would never reach. There I found Strother & Col Colston. Soon they were upon the bench & Dr Straith & others at work with knife & saw, & I was as usual administering the chloroform.[18] There is often the wit of surprize at most serious moments. So when Dr. S. began to saw Strother's bone he, Strother, exclaimed, as if in playful surprize, "Hello! Jack Straith, that's *my bone* you are sawing there!" When the operation was completed he told me that he knew & felt everything the surgeons did but that he suffered no sense of pain. The next morning (Saturday) our wounded were sent through a chill rain to Orange C. H. . . . We reached Orange C. H. about dark; but the R.R. train did not arrive for some time, & was composed of one or two passenger coaches & a number of freight cars, all filthy & some very damp. We got the last of our wounded on about 1 o'clock that night. The train moved off. Most of them I have never seen since & your brother was one of this number. That was the last time I had the privilege of seeing him. . . .

With highest esteem, & bright memories of your coolness & dauntlessness on many a field, particularly Payne's Farm, I am

Yours truly,
A.C. Hopkins

Strother had been wounded on the twenty-seventh, spent the next day in a painful fifteen-mile journey to the railroad at Orange Court House, and after an eight-mile train ride arrived sometime on the twenty-ninth at Gordonsville. He was fortunate in having family fairly close by. Martha, in Staunton, learned

Strother Barton carried this kit during his service with the 2nd Virginia. It is lined with green silk and contains crystal jars with silver tops, horn brushes, and bone-handled writing and shaving implements. (Edith Barton Sheerin, John Schwartz photo)

very quickly of her brother's wound and was soon on her way to him. The next day she sent the family at Springdale a letter she evidently started at Gordonsville and finished in Staunton. The letter was written, urgently and rather crudely, in pencil.

[LETTER OF MARTHA B. BALDWIN TO ROBERT T. BARTON]

Gordonsville Nov. 30th

You will no doubt be surprised dear Robby to see the date of my letter & at the same time feel relieved to think I could so soon come to dear Strother whom we find doing so well & as bright as he always is.[19]

The first news of the fight reached us yesterday (Sunday) morning about 9 o'clock though a telegram from Holmes Boyd saying that Strother was wounded in the knee & Ranny safe.[20] I could not feel the usual relief I generally experienced when I heard of the boys being wounded & waited with anxiety for another dispatch stating something more definite. The next was a telegram from Strother himself saying, "I am at Gordonsville wounded." Aunt C[aroline] & I went down to Aunt Nannie [Jones]s [illegible] thinking it probable he would come in the cars. In the mean time Uncle J[ames F. Jones] & Dr. [R. F.] B[aldwin] went over to the depot & not finding S. dispatched to Mr. [Ingram?] at G[ordonsville] who immediately returned an answer that Lt. Barton had had his leg amputated. This I did not hear until after church when Cary [Baldwin] broke it to me as gently & affectionately as was possible.

Dr. B. Uncle J. & I decided directly to come down to day & we find S— so well that we are now on our way back: in the baggage car comfortably fixed & Strother as bright as a bird, Dr. B. says I must give all his best love & say that S is doing *very well*. Ma must not be uneasy—we have so much to be thankful for & if Ranny was only as safe my mind would be at rest. Betsy Catlett came directly to claim S. as her guest & Uncle J. was right mad because all agreed in thinking Mr. C.'s the best place for him.[21] Dr. B was afraid of the noise on the street & that there was not room for me to stay at night with the children. Of course we have insisted on Betsy's taking pay.

Tuesday morning—Strother bore the ride very well, had an excellent night & is quite smart this morning. In half an hour he moves up to Mr. Catlett's. The dressing of the wound is the most painful part now but every thing is favourable. My present plan is for Fanny to come up with you (if you can be spared); the change will be of service to Fanny & Aunt Nannie will be glad to have her here when she is not with S. Then too there is a much greater probability of her getting whiskey here.[22] I am sure the Stuarts would send her a bottle, but I dont like to *hint* about it—but a*t any rate* she shall have some if it is $75 a gallon. Cary B has secured a quart bottle of oil for Fanny & I am sure the change will do her good.

Anna will go down with Dr & Mrs. Baldwin. & take Maria, unless some other arrangement is made before they leave.[23] I thought at first Ma might wish to come but as there is no necessity & the weather getting so cold, she had better not attempt it. Ask Ma to have some coffee prepared & sent up with some of the blackberry wine. Betsy has no coffee & Cary has divided her tea & sugar with S. Oh I cant tell you how kind every body is, as for the Stuarts they are outstanding for their attentions, but with all details I have not given the particulars of Strothers wound. He had been in the fight but left to ask Gen Walker to send more ammunition to his regt & while talking to Ranny & the General, he was struck above the cap of the knee by a minnie ball. His first exclamation was "I have lost a leg." . . .

Dr. B. will be with S. constantly & do every thing to make him comfortable. I fortunately have clothing suitable for him & a dressing gown which he seems to enjoy. Col. Raleigh Colston lost his leg also & Capt. Burgess a finger. All of our other friends are safe so far but they were fighting yesterday. I shall write frequently. . . . Best love to all in which Strother unites—he is just about taking a nice dose of *oil* dont you envy him?

Your Mattie

A few weeks later, the Springdale family received Rannie's brief account of the battle that had cost Strother so dearly.

[LETTER OF RANDOLPH BARTON TO ROBERT T. BARTON]

Camp of the "Stonewall Brig."
15th Dec. 1863

Dear Robby,

It has been a long time since I have written and since I heard from you, and I eagerly seize this opportunity to write. You know we have been engaged in a brisk little battle since I last saw you, and again it has pleased Almighty God to protect us and spare our lives. Brother Strother was wounded severely; resulting in the amputation of his leg. I received a letter from him day before yesterday and if his spirits are really what his letters represent, his are better than ever during this war.

Please let me hear from you all whenever you can. I am so deeply interested in the welfare of you all. Tell me please the condition of every thing relating to Springdale. We are very quietly encamped near Morton's Ford with the prospect of being undisturbed during the winter. About February, I expect to get 25 days furlough which I will spend part of in Richmond (enjoying Miss Mary Haxall's company) and partly in Staunton, enjoying the company of brother Strother and others.

I am very pleasantly situated as A.A.G. of this brigade; I fancy I can fill the office to Gen. Walker's satisfaction. He thus winds up his official report of the operations of this brigade during the late action, "to my personal staff and especially to Captain Barton, A.A.G., I am indebted for much and valuable assistance."[24] I feel very proud of the mention, in the first place as coming from Genl. Walker, secondly, specifying me more particularly than his other aids. . . . Genl. Walker is soon going on furlough when I will be subject to the orders of the illustrious "Stover Think" senior Col.[25] . . .

Never be discouraged in regard to our national affairs. A just God will lead a brave nation safely through all perils. Give all love to our precious mother and sister Fan, cousin Anna, and the little children; also to dear Grandma when you see her.

P.S. I hear you are paying particular attention to Miss [Susie] Davis. what of it. I heard from Boly a few days ago. He is very well and has been made Corporal.[26] When brother Strother comes down to Springdale to live, you two ought to do first rate. . . .

> Your devoted brother,
> Ran J. Barton
> A.A.G.

Both armies went in to winter quarters after Meade fell back on December 1, and remained relatively inactive until late February.

[MEMOIR OF RANDOLPH BARTON]

General Lee so strongly entrenched his army [at Mine Run] that although Meade had ordered on the next day a general attack, Warren, one of his corps commanders, declined to make it, and General Meade approving his course, his entire army retired for winter quarters to the neighborhood of Culpepper Court House, while the Confederate Army retired to the Orange Court House neighborhood. . . . I remember that a day or two before Christmas our brigade was detailed on picket duty at Morton's Ford relieving Stuarts's Brigade.[27] Our headquarters were at Gibson's House, not very far from the river, and the day before Christmas General Walker and his staff rode down the river to the ford below Morton's, where, finding a comfortable-looking farmer's house we engaged dinner the next day. My recollection is that the day was raw and bleak, but at the appointed time we found a very substantial dinner prepared for us. At that point the [Rapidan] river is very narrow—I would say not more than two hundred feet wide. On both sides a bluff . . . rises precipitously from the water, and while we ate our dinner in comfort, on the opposite bluff sat a Yankee sentry on his horse. He could have shot any one of us as we entered the yard, but a tacit truce existed between the pickets and no shooting was engaged in.

Late in the afternoon we raced back to our headquarters and made a bucketful of vile stuff, which we called egg-nogg, and which sent me to bed with my boots on, so the General and his staff charged, although I remember calling my boy to pull them off, and he did so. The next morning a splitting headache reminded me of the frolic of the night before, but a sunrise gallop in the frosty air soon made me all right.

XII

January—June 1864

BATTLES OF THE WILDERNESS AND SPOTSYLVANIA
BATTLE OF NEW MARKET

Christmas 1863 was spent by other members of the family in places and ways they had not anticipated. Anna went home to Springdale, but Martha stayed in Staunton to look after Strother. Strother's Christmas circumstances were certainly new to him, but he had a little diversion from his pain and suffering from the Stuart girls, and fixed his affections on Mary. Martha had no lack of holiday invitations, but wanted to be at home with the family at Springdale, and fretted about the sporadic mail.

[LETTER OF MARTHA B. BALDWIN TO ROBERT T. BARTON]

Dec 24th

What in the world has become of you all dear Robby that we dont hear a word from home. My heart is sick from hope deferred. I suppose the raids have interrupted the mails but we hear of so many persons receiving letters & see so many who have come up the Valley that I am at a loss how to account for your silence. . . .

Strother is still doing finely. Tomorrow he will celebrate by going into the parlor. His close confinement has brought on his old dyspepsia & he is looking a good deal paler & not with much appetite, but very well in any other respect. I do want so much to be at home now this moment & help you all through Christmas indeed if I dont get there soon I shall die of home sickness of the most malignant form. Strother is thinking of going over to the Hospital &

boarding until he is well enough for some occupation. It is much the best place
in point of fare & many other respects, but just as soon as he begins to wait on
himself you will see me at Spring Dale. I am so much afraid of some of
the bridges being burnt & the stages stop coming. Will it be at all inconvenient
for you to send for me at Woodstock if I can let you know the day I could
get there?[1]

Do try & send Strother his overcoat & the flannel drawers if there is a pair at
Spring Dale. S. says I must tell you he wants to see you *powerful* & that he is
doing "bully." Expects to ascend *"Pisgah Heights"* before long—which means
Stuarts Hill I suppose—as he is considerably *struck* in that quarter. Mary &
Gussy [Stuart] come quite frequently to see him, & M. says she would come
every day if *people didnt talk so much.* There are to be several handsome parties in town during Christmas week . . . Cousin Raleigh Colston is better.[2] . . .

I hope you have had a visit from brother [Tom]. I hear the brigade is in the
Valley & if Early has gone down far enough he may be able to get a furlough.[3] I
have promised to take my Christmas dinner at Dr. Striblings.[4] . . . Stuart is well,
Maria right complaining from cold & begging all the time to go back to 'Ping
Dale'.[5] Give quantities of love to all, & let me hear from some of you soon——
Ever your devoted sister

MB

*The Springdale family spent part of the Christmas holidays visiting in town. In
spite of the circumstances, there were parties, no doubt on a greatly reduced
scale. It was hard to plan many festivities because of the constant passage and
expected return of the Yankees, but the Lutheran church held a Christmas fete
and magic lantern show for the whole town, with carols and gifts for the children.[6] The oldest Marshall child, Barton, fourteen, missed the absent family
members, particularly Bolling, who was only four years older and close enough
to share some interests. Barton wrote Bolling at the VMI about Christmastime,
and Miss Lucy, Bolling's summer romance.*

[LETTER OF D. BARTON MARSHALL TO BOLLING W. BARTON]

SpringDale Jan 3rd 1864

Dear Uncle Bolling—

I thought that I would set down and give you an account of the way we spent
our Christmas. Mrs. Willia[ms] asked us to come and spend it with her. We
went in Town on Xmas eve and stayed their until the following Wednesday. We

had four parties while we were in Town. Two of which were at Mrs. W's. I
spoke of you quite often while I was in town to Miss Lucie. I had the pleasure
of dancing with Miss Gertie and of escorting her home every night. Mrs. Averit
gave me this paper on which I am writing to you.[7] Uncle Bolly you do not know
how much I want to see you. I am whishing for summer to come so that I can
see you again. You and myself raising chickens together. Our pigeons are increasing and I expect that by the time you come back I will have a very pretty
set. Dear Uncle Bolly think that we are commencing another year and little do
we know what will hapen before it is ended. Maybe *you* and *I* may be *dead* and
buried. Their is consolation that we may be in a better world. My main study
now is about my soul. I hope that if this misfortune should be [[8]
we shall meet in heaven above. A [

   As my stock of news is out [

Your most Devoted Nephew
D.B. Marshall

*Winchester experienced eight cavalry raids in January and seven the next
month, and there was frequent troop movement up and down the Valley Turnpike. Despite so many other concerns, Robby's fancy turned to the young lady
up the pike.*

[MEMOIR OF ROBERT T. BARTON]

   About a mile from Springdale in the house on the west side of the turnpike
and just north of Newtown . . . lived the family of Dr. Wm. A. Davis, then consisting of his wife, his young son Charlie and his daughter Susie; the doctor himself being absent in the Confederate service as a Surgeon.[9]
   Miss Susie Davis is the same person who is now Mrs. Dr. Daniel B. Conrad.
She was pretty and intelligent and had read a great deal. I enjoyed her society
and as she was the only young lady in the neighbourhood I fell in love with her,
or at least I certainly thought I did. The consequence was that in February 1864
I addressed her, but she kindly and as pleasantly as a girl could do a thing of
that sort, declined to accept me. Not sure that we quite understood each other
I shortly after repeated my proposition. There was then no more room for mis-
understanding, altho she was no less gentle than before. Like a boy I demanded
reasons, and among others she gave the slight difference in our ages. As I was
nineteen months her senior I could not well comprehend that reason, but I
lived to know that the young lady's penchant for much older men was no fancy,

and she has demonstrated the reality of this feeling in her subsequent marriage. Well she has now a fine daughter, and as there is only a few years difference between her daughter's age and that of your mother, I can not complain of those who have fancies about much older men.[10]

During that winter of 1863–64 as there was no permanent occupation of this section of the Country by the Federal troops, many of our poor fellows stole the opportunity of coming home and many a narrow escape they made from capture by raiding parties who would scour the Country at night. . . .

In January and February 1864 Colonel Marshall and my cousin Marshall Jones returned to Springdale on a visit.[11] The Davises spent the evening there and as a consequence the parlour, all the windows of which are plainly visible from the road, was brightly lighted up, scarce as lighting material was at that time.

About 10 o'clock that night Marshall Jones and I accompanied the Davises to their home, I, of course, walking with Miss Susie. When we reached the hill just south of Springdale on the turnpike, on our way back home, we were startled by the sound of horses' hoofs on the bridge just below and at once a troop of Federal Cavalry came trotting up the hill. Marshall Jones promptly climbed the stone fence on the east side of the turnpike and lay flat on the ground behind it. The troopers rode up to me and insisted that another man was with me. This I urged must have been my shadow, as the moon was shining. They took this view of the case, but proceeded to interrogate me at great length as to "rebel camps" and movements of "rebel" troops, and also about the "rebel" who was supposed to have been recently at the Springdale house. I refused to give any information, altho I was much alarmed at their intimations of what had taken place at Springdale, for I feared that they had captured Col. Marshall and were concealing the fact from me. Finally they released me and went on up the road while I hastened to the house. Then I learned what had occurred in my absence.

All had gone to bed, leaving the house open and the lights burning for Marshall Jones and me. This troop of cavalry had come along on a mid night raid and attracted by the bright lights had sent in a squad to see if any captures could be made. The party that came in belonged to what was known as the "Jesse Scouts" and wore a grey uniform which was a close imitation of that of the Confederates. Old Scylla [Priscilla Piper] the nurse of the Marshall children and the slave of their father Col. Marshall, one of the best of women, and who would have died rather than betray her master, came down stairs for something just as the squad of Yankees dressed in grey walked into the house. They, entirely at random, asked her where "the Colonel" was, and she supposing they were Confederates and perhaps a part of Col. Marshall's command, answered promptly that he was up stairs. Meanwhile my mother and sisters had heard the unmistakable tramp of the horses' feet on the turnpike and attracted by the sound of voices down stairs, had come out of their rooms and with the quickness of wit and action, begotten of living constantly in danger and in the midst of alarms, divided their forces. One went to the head of the steps to entreat the soldiers to delay until they could dress. Another quietly informed Col. Marshall of his danger and then with the others except my mother who was parleying with and delaying the troopers, went into a room which had only one means of ingress which was a door leading from another room and with the strength which danger sometimes gives, pushed a wardrobe over the door of the room, leaving only a small space through which Col. Marshall was to creep. Immediately upon the alarm Col. Marshall seized his clothes and his accoutrements and hurried across the hall and while only a few feet from the soldiers who were in the stair way he dropped his pistol making a great clatter. Seizing it again he hurried in and slipped through the narrow space left for him, and the wardrobe was pushed over it.

The soldiers, startled by the sound of the dropping pistol, now ran up the steps and searched (as they supposed) every niche and corner of the house, but they searched in vain for they did not suspect the existence of a room behind the wardrobe.[12] Of course they were told that no one was there: that the noise they heard was some sound other than it was in fact; that "the Col." had been at the house but had gone away, the old nurse not having been informed that he had left, & c.: all of these deceits being justified by the maxim that "all is fair in war" and that it is no lie to deceive your enemy. Finally the squad, unable to discover anybody, left the house and joined the rest of the command which was waiting for them at the gate. It was just then that I met them coming up the hill when they were still in hopes of catching "the Colonel."

The rather amusing sequel to that night's adventure was, that, fearing a return of the Cavalry, Col. Marshall left the house, as soon as they were out of sight, and took to the back fields and woods. Marshall Jones too, as soon as the troopers moved on, left his hiding place and scampered in the same direction. Coming over a hill from different directions the two men got very close before either saw the other, and in the misty moonlight each taking the other for a Yankee promptly drew his pistol. Quickly recognizing each other however, they rejoiced over their escape. We sent them out provisions in the night and before morning they were many miles away.

It was not always that these marauding parties did so little harm.[13] Sometimes a whole regiment would come and camp all night in the field, yard or barn yard. They would then demand food, break into the smoke house and carry off the meat and steal the horses. Sometimes our Union friends would aid us to recover these things, and generally the officer in command would put a guard at the house to prevent violence there.

It was another cold winter in Virginia, and Rannie was in winter quarters at Camp Stonewall Jackson on the Rapidan. His expenses as an officer were heavy, and he was short of everything, especially money; he wrote Bolling again deferring payment of his debt. The letter was written on coarse, thin paper in ink now faded almost to illegibility.

[LETTER OF RANDOLPH BARTON TO BOLLING W. BARTON]

Hd. Qrs. Stonewall Brigade,
15th Jan 64

Dear Bolly,

Your letter of the 11th has just been received. I am so pinched to meet my expenses incurred by clothing, hiring a boy and my mess bill that I have been totally unable to pay you a cent of the $60.00 I owe you for your watch. This month my mess bill will be small, and with $30.00 owing me for a pair of pants I sold Nepe Baldwin [Dr. Cornelius Baldwin] I am confident I can pay you at least $20.00. Can you wait until about the last of this month. You were quite right in asking for money, never hesitate to do it, and I will honor your requests as often as possible. Unless rations are issued to officers of which I think there is a strong probability, I will have to sell one of my horses. That I would hate to do, not only on account of the uncertain condition in which it would place me for doing duty, but because consulting all aims, Priam would have to go. I am terribly sorry that you do not come up to the mark in your studies, strive on dear Bolly and never neglect them. I am writing by a [*illegible*] candle.

good bye
your devoted brother
Ranny

Rannie made equally generous but insubstantial financial offers to Robby, who as head of the family at home was trying to arrange for Bolling to continue at the institute. The mails were erratic at best; Rannie had not received Robby's recent "long letter."

[LETTER OF RANDOLPH BARTON TO ROBERT T. BARTON]

Headquarters, Stonewall Brigade
25 Jan. 1864

Dear Robby,

Your answer to my letter was received a few days ago. It was the first time I had heard from home for some time. . . .

Your dispositions are no doubt the very best, as I have forsaken the idea of farming, I would not pretend to criticise or find fault. I would like very much to see your pretty colts. I did not know before that you had rented the farm from Ma.

A few nights ago I asked Genl. Walker for a furlough, he declined granting it at present, saying "he could not spare me at present" but in a week or so I expect to go. However much I would like to visit you all, it would be impossible, the shortness of my leave and besides Genl. Lee requires a pledge from all not to go beyond our lines.

I most cordially second you in your arrangements about Bolly, it will be a great pleasure to me to sacrifice anything to promote his welfare. Call on me whenever you want to and I will endeavor to honor your drafts always.

I don't intend to contradict any report about your attentions to Miss Davis. I think she is worthy of you, and to be candid, vice versa. I always did admire her, but never ventured as she is too "larned" for me. Now don't humble yourself to the dust, and ask me to deny the report any more "for the young ladies sake etc." You are a great flirt, have you forgotten cousin Bettie [Colston]. Pecuniary circumstances may deter any matrimonial alliances for a time no doubt but next summer let me welcome "sister Susie." Write long and often to,

Your devoted brother
R.J. Barton
A.A.G.

As Martha had intended, Fanny soon went to Staunton to visit cousin Cary Baldwin and care for Strother. She wrote a lively, gossipy letter home, obviously enjoying her stay in a town that had not yet known invasion and occupation. Her plan was to go on to Lexington with Strother, by now recovered enough to take a "desk" job at the arsenal.

[LETTER OF FANNY J. BARTON TO ROBERT T. BARTON]

Staunton March 15th

. . . Cary & I are busy getting ready for our trip to Lexington, we go on Thursday. Brother Strother has accepted the position of Adjutant of the post there & will go up with us, to remain. I got a very kind letter from Aunt Sally urging us to come. . . . My cough has been so much better for several days that Dr. Baldwin says there will be no objection to my going if the weather is good. Brother Strother says Aunt Sally is a *famous housekeeper* & as kind as possible, she promises in her letter to do all in her power to make our time pleasant. I wish she would send us up to the Natural Bridge.[14] I dont think I should enjoy any thing more than that.

Brother Strother Nanny [Mrs. James F. Jones] & myself & Willie Gardiner spent the day at Mrs. Catletts on Saturday. We had a real *Peace dinner* & a most delightful day. . . . Tell sister Mat I dont need any more money at all. She forgets how rich I am with my $40 extra. I am trying to have it all changed into the new currency or rather into five dollar notes as I cannot get the new currency until the first of April.[15] I have scarcely spent any thing since I have been here so I do not need any more money.

Is there any truth in the report that Miss Ann Sherrard's lover has left her? I heard that some other young lady who had similar claim upon him sued him for breach of promise & that Miss Ann consequently resigned. is it so? I should be glad to contradict it if it is a slander. I am afraid the *"waiting—many"* of Winchester will have their prospects ruined for life if such reports get in circulation about many more of them. . . .

I wish you could have seen a beau who came to see us last night. He came hobbling in the room all enjured & brused from a street fight. Cary & I thought we would investigate the affair so Cary asked why it was that he used a cane. I inquired anxiously if there had been a battle lately? when he entered into all the particulars admitting however that it was exceedingly vulgar & ungentlemanly, but in his case it was a necessity. He is the enrolling officer here & although not a gentleman by any account he is highly educated & very agreable man. . . .

I cannot appreciate the Staunton beaux even the Poet Laureate of Staunton, to be sure he has not honoured us with a visit yet but I do not think his appearance prepossessing. I like Cary's Artillery friend, Carter Berkely better than any of them *when he is sober* he is very gentlemanly & agreable. John Opie is Handsome but conceited & not smart. . . . Frank Clark has been very kind & attentive.[16] He is much struck with Miss Jinnie [*illegible*] The Miss Peytons have returned & have been to see me but I was out.[17] I want to see them very much. But I know this is boring you to death. . . .

I have not said anything about coming home because I can tell better about it when I come from Lexington. I have written to Lal & we will probably come down together.[18] . . . I have got "Jean Valjean" to bring home with me. Marshall [Jones] gave it to me before he left.[19]

I suppose brother Strother will settle affairs on *the Hill* before he leaves. He *seemed* to be doubtful as to the result & is in a very tremulous state now. Much love to everybody, Mrs. Davis & Susie particularly.

Ever yr attached sister Fanny

None of the Staunton beaux appealed to Fanny because she had fixed her affections elsewhere. Her visit to Staunton did nothing to distract her from him; nor, alas, did the change of scene improve her fragile health or slow the dreadful course of her illness. Bright, young, merry, full of life, Fanny had however been consumptive for years, and wartime conditions made recovery virtually impossible. As for Strother, he was not of the fickle temperament of Rannie; he had fallen in love with Mary Stuart, and felt the parting acutely when he went to Lexington. He confided to Robby why he had not spoken to Mary, and passed off his feelings with his usual wry humor.

[LETTER OF W. STROTHER BARTON TO ROBERT T. BARTON]

Lexington March 30th 1864

Dear Roby

Your letter of the 12th inst. has been recd and also two others of more recent date for all of which recieve my warmest thanks. . . .

Imagine a youth of some twenty odd summers with one wheel removed by the common accidents of war seated in a comfortable room, near a good fire, on a chair by a table, opposite two inches of tallow candle about a hundred & twenty yards from the graves of the lamented Jackson & Paxton. The youth is the subscriber the room &C including the two inches of tallow candle aforesaid belong to his Aunt Sally. Now let me tell you how I got here. When in Lexington a few weeks ago I went to see Col. McDonald & family.[20] he told me that the position of adjutant of the post under him was vacant and offered it to me yea! even pressed it upon me, which by the by, he might have dispensed with as I was anxious to get it any how. But dont you say my going to see him was *"malice prepense"* for indeed I only went to see him for the love of dear old

W. Strother Barton, on a visit to Baltimore after the war. (Mrs. C. Marshall Barton, Jr.)

Winchester. However he offered me the position & I took it, and when the girls [Fanny and Cary] came up to pay Bolly & Aunt Sally a visit I came up with them. Aunt Sally offered me board & lodging *"free gratis for nothing"* and really seemed so anxious for me to come, that I consented. I have not yet recd my assignment to duty from the Secty War, notwithstanding I am doing duty. The office pays well. My salary as Lieutenant is $80.00 two dollars extra for acting adjutant $30.00 commutation for two rooms fifty dollars commutation for two cords of wood. . . .

I think I deserve some credit for bearing myself away from Staunton. It was like tearing the gizzard out of a youthful *"pullet."* And so you want to know why I dont *"culminate."* If you will answer one question satisfactorily for me I will know my fate as soon after the answer is recd as possible. When the Honerable leangthy leged Gentleman steps up to your diminutive brother Strau & and says in tones of thunder *Wal* Mr. Barton what means have you for supporting a wife?[21] I suppose I will have to say as that fellow in Louden [county], Wal' sir hasnt she enough for us both? But you asked the question with so much seriousness that I must answer it accordingly. Do not think that it would be *unwise* in me, without an *education,* without an *occupation* without an *expectation* to burden myself and family with a wife? Now! do not think because I am this practical, and don't go it *blind,* that I am not a victim to that tender sentiment I may decieve myself and think I am, whilst I am not, but surely a subject which fills ones thoughts by day and dreams by night must be one of more than ordinary interest. Ranny, I think is out of dainger. His affection is but as the morning due- or more properly "Like the early grass appeareth for a little while and is nipped by an ass."

I approve highly of all you have done in the farming line . . . I am somewhat afraid you cannot attend properly the quantity of land you propose putting in corn. I heard the other day that the Buena Vista farm had been sold, is it so? . . .

I confess that I was surprised at the advice given by Mr. Williams &
concured in by your self with regard to my running for the office of C of C.Ct.
Now whilst I dislike exceedingly to do any thing contrary to Mr Williams'
advice, for his kindness to us all and his intimate association with my father
causes him almost to take *his* place in my affections: I have gone so far in this
thing and have given my friends so much concern about it, besides having committed myself to Joe Sherrard, whose state of health is exagerated, that I cannot
with-draw.[22] That is my own decision I do not know what my friends would say
to it. If I find that the office of CC is an empty honour Of course I will not
retain it, and then I will have to look out for some other way of making a living.

My candle is burnt out so I must close for to night

                                                                        March 31st 64

How short sighted is man? Last night just before going to bed in a fit of
abstraction I forgot all about my lost leg, and put out my leg that wasnt there to
walk Of course I came down on the stump and hurt myself severely. The blood
flowed freely for a while so much so that I feared a hemorrhage. I finally succeeded in stopping it. My candle being nearly burnt out I was about to be left
in total darkness, I succeeded by knocking on the floor in waking Aunt Sally
who brought me a candle and assisting me to fix up. I thought that I would be
"hors de combat" for some time but about eleven oclock this morning I succeeded in getting up and dressing. I fear that I shall be thrown back five or six
weeks by the accident, as you may imagine I feel as blue as indigo. I think I will
rally soon however. I don't generally stay down long. Brother Tom [Marshall]
has just passed with his regiment.[23] He looks as well as usual_ The money you
sent Capt [William L.] Clark was recd; He wrote to me the other day asking
what disposition he should make of it, at the same time stating that he had
failed in all his efforts to change it into five dollar notes. I asked him to purchase
the new issue with it at the discount which I suppose he will do as soon as pos-
sible_ I spend most of my time reading, occasionally I meet the girls, but oh!
how incipid and uninteresting they seem when I think of _____.

At the advise of my friend Tommy Hood I am about to read the following
books, viz__ Kosciusko on the Right of the Poles to stick up for themselves;
Rules for Punctuation, by a thorough bred Pointer; John Knox on "death's
door"; On Sore throat Throat and the Migration of the Swallow; Barrow on the
common Weal and &C very interesting works and highly recommended by
good judges. Boly is well and doing well. I will enclose the estimate of his
expences. I have written a long letter surely though I can't answer for its being
an interesting. Give oceans of love to Ma, sister Mat, Anna & all. If this war last

much longer I shall feel very much like coming home and giving up to the Yanks. I get terribly home Sick sometimes. . . .

Pay me in kind for this letter.

Very truly your affectionate bro
W. Strother Barton

P.S. This letter is strictly Private.

Friday night

Bolling has come up without the estimate so I will close, and send it another time, Frank Clark and Bolly are with me to night. Dont mention my having hurt myself.

Winchester remained open to the incursions of both forces. The Federal troops were in town April 3, and seized three of the town leaders as hostages for Union men captured by Rebel raiders, taking Philip Williams, the Rev. A. H. H. Boyd, and Robert Y. Conrad to the military prison at Wheeling.[24] Mrs. Williams wrote a frantic but factual letter to her son Johnny about his father's arrest. "Our men do but little good when they make arrests of Union people of no standing and thereby cause to be taken as hostages for them, the men on the Border who are battling slowly and enduring heavy burdens for the sake of the South . . . the Yankees have so often threatened to take him, have spoken so much of his influence here, have watched him so closely, that even one of their own number warned him secretly, have cursed the house in passing, all these things make me uneasy."[25] Only a few days later, Mrs. Lee viewed a brisk cavalry fight from the top of the Clarks' house, and was pleased to see Clayton Williams and Holmes Conrad with captured Yankees—some return, she thought, for the Yankees' carrying off their fathers.[26] Mrs. Williams wished "Mildred [Lee] . . . could have seen Phip [the Williamses' daughter Philippa] that Friday (as we say) when Capt Calamise dashed through after the Ys and brought them back as prisoners . . . Clate was one of the heroes, I was a proud mother, but a sorrowing wife. Phip usually quiet was not composed for days, said she thought she would join the army if we could always have such blood-less victories."[27]

All too soon, a Union Army was back in strength. On May 1, Gen. Franz Sigel took Winchester; a week later he moved south toward Staunton. Federal armies took on fresh force and determination with the appointment of Gen. U. S. Grant, who after his Vicksburg and western successes had been reassigned to command in the east. Massing hitherto unseen numbers and materiel, Grant crossed the Rapidan on May 4 and advanced on Richmond, the inevitable and unvarying Union target. By rapid movement, Lee managed to position his forces to catch Grant in the Wilderness east of Fredericksburg, where the difficult terrain helped him compensate for vastly inferior numbers. Rannie, on General Walker's staff, and Willie, Sergeant in the 2nd Virginia Infantry, were expecting a difficult campaign.

[MEMOIR OF RANDOLPH BARTON]

With the opening of spring (1864) began the famous Wilderness Campaign. Our command was in the battles of the 5th and 6th of May, 1864, and on the 5th General Walker and myself had an exceedingly narrow escape from being captured or killed. The brigade on our right had fallen back in some confusion, the woods being extremely dense, and quite a gap existed, which General Walker was anxious to fill. Accordingly, leaving the right of our line we (mounted) threaded our way through the woods. We had not gone a hundred yards when the General observed a wounded Confederate some little distance ahead of us, sitting with his back to a tree and holding up his hand as if signaling to us; at the same moment, peering through the trees, we saw a group of Yankees just ahead of us, apparently not fifty yards away and leveling their guns at us. As quick as thought we spurred our horses and, turning, sped through the woods. I do not remember whether they shot at us or not, but ten steps more and we would probably have received in our faces a murderous volley.

General Walker has since told me that after the war he met the wounded man who had warned us off. He had fallen at that spot and his line retreating had left him where he fell. As the Yankee line approached through the woods, he peered through the trees to see what was happening in the direction of his friends, when he saw the General and myself approaching and gave us the signal of danger. He said the Yankees were very angry with him and some of them wanted to kill him, but their officers restrained them. I would like to meet that man. He most assuredly saved our lives.

From the morning of the 5th until the night of the 12th, with the exception of a half-hour one afternoon, my saddle was never removed from the back of my horse (Priam). I do not remember that a day passed during that week that we were not at some time under fire. On the afternoon of the 10th a determined charge was made upon our line, which was strengthened by field fortifications, and [Brig. Gen. George Pierce] Dole's Brigade, immediately upon our left, was broken and the enemy got through. The left of our brigade, probably to the length of a regiment, was "refused," or rather fell back at right angles

with its former position, and in that position poured into the enemy, as they
rushed through the break made by the repulse of Dole's Brigade, a heavy fire.
Troops came up from various directions and the line was finally restored, the
enemy being driven back with severe loss. I remember quite well when the
enemy broke through, General Walker sending me to General [Edward]
Johnson, who commanded the division, and who was some three hundred yards
to the right of us, for reinforcements. I found General Johnson anxiously looking out for an attack upon the angle in our line, subsequently baptized the
"bloody angle" [at Spotsylvania]. He asked me when I delivered my message
what troops he could send, and knowing that [Gen. George Hume] Steuart's
Brigade held the right of our division, which was "refused" at that point, I suggested that if Steuart's Brigade was faced about and marched back of the rest of
the division on a line of battle at right angles with it, it would come face to face
with the enemy who were coming up the left of our line. General Johnson said,
"But if Steuart leaves his lines the enemy will break through at that point." Why
I said it I do not know, but I impetuously replied, "No they won't!" and he
authorized me to deliver the order to General Steuart.

I did so. His line faced about and assisted in repulsing the enemy, after
which it returned to its position.

Burnside, it seems, commanded the Federal line in front of Steuart, and
Grant, in his book, somewhat blames him for not attacking the line in front of
him (Steuart).

Johnson's apprehension, therefore, was right, but I blundered into a good
suggestion, not so bad for a youngster of twenty. . . . The lines having been
restored, we were all much elated. The attack was a well-organized one, and
consisted of twelve selected regiments, with powerful supports, the twelve regiments being placed under the immediate command of General Emory Upton,
who was wounded in the assault and was promoted to Brigadier on the field by
General Grant. The assault failed because of the bad action of the supports
under General [Gershom] Mott, so says Grant but also because of the good
action of the Rebels under General Lee, so says Barton. The Yankee dead were
thickly strewn over the narrow field or clearing over which they charged as they

Randolph Barton's sword, acquired near the Bloody Angle at Spotsylvania in May 1864.
(Colin J. S. Thomas, Jr.)

approached our works. Many were dead immediately outside of our fortifications, and as I walked along looking over at them I observed a dead officer's infantry sabre, metal scabbard. I asked one of our men to hand it to me, which he did, and this sword I wore to the end of the war, brought it home with me and "Ran" subsequently used it in his cavalry drill.[28] I have felt curious to know who it belonged to, and perhaps could have ascertained, but never followed it up. Many of the Yankee dead and wounded were within our lines and I recall one poor fellow, particularly, who was shot through the body and was suffering terribly. With one or two others I went to his relief, but cold water poured on his wound only intensified his pain, and we could literally do nothing for him. His groans were agonizing and we could only listen to them as they grew more and more feeble, until finally some time during the night he died. When the enemy fell back and disappeared in the woods, immediately their bands began the most stirring music and kept it up for some time. This was the only occasion during the war that I recall an incident of the kind. But their line was probably a quarter to a half mile from us, and they were comparatively safe. Our musicians were all too busy with their wounded or their guns. Our "tooters" had become "shooters," as General D. H. Hill once endorsed on an application for furlough by a brass band, "respectfully returned disapproved, 'shooters' before 'tooters.' "

May 11th passed without much fighting. Mott, on the Yankee side, made something of a forced reconnaissance in front of our division. Our skirmishers were somewhat sharply engaged and balls flew around for a while, but the advance was feeble and was soon repulsed. I remember General Walker saying with elation to General Terry, when the enemy retired, "If this be war, may it be eternal."[29] I really think General Walker enjoyed the thrilling excitement of battle. He was nervously constituted and could not help dodging bullets, but he was a splendid soldier and leader.

Mott's advance, however, on the 11th, disclosed to the Yankees the salient or advanced point, or angle in our line of field works, in which, on the next morning, the 12th, was fought perhaps, the most desperate battle of the war.

As well as I can remember, the weather on the 11th was dark and rainy; it certainly rained on the night of the 11th, for General Walker and myself considered ourselves very fortunate in securing a "fly" or "dog" tent, consisting of a single canvass sheet, about six feet by five in size, and rigging this over us in the shape of a roof at a point back about two hundred feet from the centre of our brigade, we crept in and went to sleep. About dusk our Generals had determined to send out a select body of about two hundred men, under Colonel

Terry (afterwards General Terry) of the Fourth Virginia ("Stonewall" Brigade) to "feel" the enemy. I stood very near when the arrangement was being made and recall Terry's serious expression as he received his instructions. He was to take his command over the breastworks and through the abattis, pass the skirmish line and advance until resistance became too strong, if resistance was developed, and ascertain whether the Yankees were still in force in front of us. If he had done so he would very soon have encountered the thirty thousand men [Gen. W. S.] Hancock was massing in front of our division for the daybreak assault upon the salient. General Lee was kept constantly on the alert for fear Grant would slip by our right flank. The order for Terry was revoked, however, to his great relief. He would have performed the duty well. The artillery also guarding the salient was removed. The massing of the enemy in our front was evidently mistaken for the passing by on a flank movement of a large column. The condition of the atmosphere made the conversation of thirty thousand men, no matter how subdued, quite audible, but we could not tell whether it was a moving mass or an assembling mass. Our brigade was in the breastworks, guns loaded and guards detailed for the night watch. General Walker and myself slept side by side, profoundly. Just about daybreak one of our men rushed down to our tent and called, "General, they are coming!" From the profoundest slumber we jumped to our feet wide awake, Walker calling in a voice that could have been heard half a mile, "Fall in!" We rushed up to the breastworks and heard the cheers of the advancing enemy. A heavy mist overhung everything and through it we could hardly see one hundred yards. But succeeding the cheers, we, little by little, perceived the advancing line, rather a broken line, but still an ugly rush. Our men opened a vigorous fire, and all along the line from our left and centre, up to the right, where the fatal salient stood, some three hundred yards distant, the crack of musketry kept up; two or three shots were fired from the one or two cannons that had remained in the salient or angle and added to the din and uproar, their smoke still further enveloping every thing in the almost impenetrable mist. I remember being depressingly struck by the deliberateness with which the enemy tore away the abattis obstructing their advance, and recall quite vividly the motions of one particular Yankee, who, having his side turned to our line, was shot evidently in the thigh. The immediate change from his bold advance to a turn and rapid limp to the rear, with his hand slapped upon the wound, amused me then, or, at any rate, the recalling of the incident amuses me now. The attack was irresistible and very soon the enemy were over the works on our right and had captured a portion of Stafford's Brigade, and all of Jones' and Steuart's, and also Generals Johnson and Steuart. The angle was the objective point of the charge, and our brigade being on the left flank of the division was little off from the line of rush but we were from the time the first gun was fired under deadly volleys. The enemy swept down the line towards us. I soon lost sight of General Walker, whose elbow joint having been penetrated by a ball, was carried to the rear. By this time our men were confronting the enemy advancing upon them, not so much in front as from the right and inside of the breastworks. At distances of about forty feet along the line of breastworks, shorter works (logs) about twenty feet long had been placed at right angles with the main line of defense, called "traverses," intended to protect the men from a flank fire. The battle was raging from traverse to traverse, our men standing boldly to their duty, when I felt a numbing blow on my left arm, between the elbow joint and shoulder, and was at once conscious that I was wounded. I yielded to the first impulse and moved to the rear, getting out of the range of fire as quickly as I could. I do not recall just now how violent the blow was or whether I thought my arm was broken or not. Perhaps if I had been high in command I should have and would have remained on the field, but I am under the impression that I felt justified in leaving. However that may be, I left. On my way back I met General Lee and his staff going towards the thickest of the fight. He was perfectly composed, superb in all respects. It was a little while afterwards that he prepared to lead the reinforcements into battle, and when General Gordon protested that he should go back and the men promised if he would go back they would go forward. The battle raged at that point, the bloody angle, all day and extended far into the night of the 12th. The enemy retained the angle, but that was all; they did not gain another. I trudged along with the stream of wounded to the nearest field hospital and among the first sights I saw was General Walker lying on a table, just falling under the influence of chloroform, preparatory to having his shattered elbow joint cut out. The operation was entirely successful and today he uses his arm, thus mutilated, with almost the freedom of his other arm. I proceeded to take off my jacket, or rather I think the surgeon slit my coat sleeve to my shoulder, and laying bare my arm, found that a ball had gone clear through it, grazing the bone and making a beautiful temporary-disabling furlough wound. It was washed, bathed and bandaged. A support was provided, my jacket was pinned or tied or sewed over it, my large army cloak was thrown over me, and my faithful boy, George, getting my clothes, together we mounted our horses, Mary Stuart and Priam, and started through a drenching rain to Louisa Court House, on the then Virginia Central Railroad, some twenty-five miles distant. The rain, the dreary, lonely country, the booming of the cannon, the discomfort of my wound, and the uncertainty as to how the battle was going, and who of my friends were falling, made the ride intolerably dismal. About four o'clock I reached Louisa Court House, a small hamlet on the railroad, which looked gray, desolate and deserted. I went at once to the most pretentious house, quite a large one, and was at once hospitably received.[30] My boy and horses were well taken care of; I got some dinner and was shown to a comfortable room. Then, after having my wounded arm dressed, I retired to bed, to which comfort I had been a stranger for a week. The unceasing strain of that week, the change from the dangers and turmoil of the front line of battle prepared me for profound slumber, and so I passed a luxurious night.

The Battle of Spotsylvania flared again a week later, but was inconclusive except for the terrible casualties on both sides. The Stonewall Brigade had suffered such losses—it was reduced to about 200 men—that it was shortly thereafter consolidated with other diminished brigades.

In contrast to other Union commanders, Grant did not fall back after this campaign, but began moving, in a slow and bloody progress, inexorably south and east, eventually laying siege to Petersburg.

The family at home surely knew that Rannie and Willie were in battle near Richmond, and eventually word came that both had been wounded—that Rannie's wound was "slight" but that Willie's was "severe."[31] For once the first reports were correct. Willie could not return to active service. It must have come as a tremendous shock to learn that Bolly, with the VMI cadets, had been hastily marched from their supposed sanctuary to do battle with the Valley's latest invaders. Union General Sigel was moving south with an army that greatly outnumbered the available Confederate forces. Maj. Gen. John C. Breckenridge called out the Home Guards and put the VMI cadet corps on alert. On May 11, 261 cadets, including Cpl. Bolling Barton, left school.[32] They were in Staunton for a festive evening, May 12, and perhaps Bolling was able to see his older brother Strother who had been transferred to the post there by late May.[33] The cadet corps joined the main Confederate force next morning. Two days later, a mile north of New Market, battle was joined. Breckenridge, loath to send in the cadets, held them in reserve until a gap opened in his line. Joining the final charge, they advanced in memorable order under direct fire across an open field against a strong Federal position. (Bolly recalled that, in the rank in front of him, Pvt. Preston Cocke's gun was "shot to pieces.") Reaching a fence,

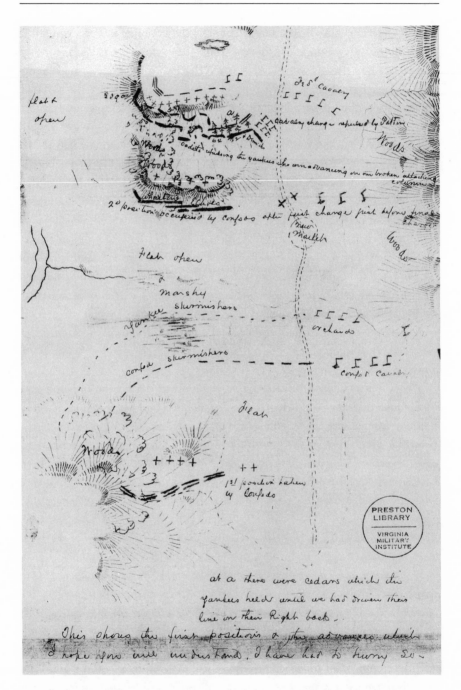

Benjamin A. Colonna, a New Market cadet who later served with Bolling Barton in the First Foreign Battalion, drew this battle map from his memory of the fray.
(Virginia Military Institute Archives)

they helped fend off a Yankee attack as the Southern line rallied, then charged, capturing a gun. The Union attack disintegrated, and Sigel went north in disorder and disgrace. He was relieved May 19.

The cadet corps had suffered—ten dead and forty-seven wounded. Bolly spent the night on the field with the mortally wounded cadet Thomas G. Jefferson.[34] The corps left New Market on the eighteenth. (Many by this time were barefoot, like real veterans.) They returned to Staunton and then went by train to Richmond to be honored by their president, the government, and the city on May 24.

The Yankees recovered from the New Market debacle with unprecedented speed. Gen. David Hunter took over Sigel's command on May 21, and five days later, greatly reinforced, his army moved south from Cedar Creek. In Staunton, the Post Commander evacuated supplies and tried to rally all available men. Local militia units were called out, including John Opie commanding a cavalry reserve, and Bev Jones as Captain of the 1st Local Defense Troops of Rockingham County.[35] Maj. James F. Jones activated the men in his widespread Nitre and Mining District, and in a few days they gathered in Staunton and formed two companies commanded by brothers Capt. Will Clark and Capt. Frank Clark, marching to join other Confederate forces at Mount Crawford. On June 5, the armies met near Piedmont, the Federal advance having been briefly retarded by Lt. Carter Berkeley's battery, with the support of Opie's cavalry. After initial Confederate success, the battle went against the Rebels. Gen. "Grumble" (William E.) Jones was killed, and the fall of Staunton next day was assured. Many townspeople and the small garrison fled, and those remaining had their first direct experience of the war. General Hunter met with prominent citizens including Dr. Stribling and A. H. H. Stuart to announce his plans for destruction and confiscation of Confederate property.[36] Public buildings were put to the torch and there was much indiscriminate destruction and theft of personal property.

The Union armies marched on Lexington June 10, a day after the Cadet Corps had returned to the institute. The town could not be defended, and preparations were made to evacuate. Ned Moore, recently wounded in battle near Richmond, had just come home to recuperate. He was in time to help his family bury the silver in the backyard, and then he fled into the mountains. His sister-in-law remembered tying the silver forks and spoons underneath hoop skirts.[37] The cadets retreated into the mountains and then by the canal to Lynchburg.[38] The staff of the arsenal scattered. Col. Angus McDonald was overtaken near Natural Bridge; he put up a fight but was captured and taken to Wheeling prison.[39] The buildings of the institute and the arsenal were looted

*and then burned; the library of Washington College was vandalized. Looting
and stealing were extensive. Hunter then turned on Lynchburg, and on June 13
Gen. Jubal Early's Second Corps was sent to its defense. They moved by train
from Richmond, finding Carter Berkeley's small force endeavoring to hold
the last bridge.*[40] *They joined the local militia and the VMI cadets in the
trenches defending the town on June 17. Hunter was overextended and could
not prevail. On June 19, he beat a retreat to the Union fastnesses of West Virginia, hotly pursued by Confederate cavalry. Early then turned north to clear
Federal forces from the Shenandoah. The Barton family in Winchester was torn
between anxiety for their young men on new battlefronts and anticipation that
Early might lead them home again. Their immediate concern was the illness of
both Fanny and Robby at Springdale.*

[MEMOIR OF ROBERT T. BARTON]

My health, which had improved at first after I reached home, began to fail,
and as I could get neither proper medicines, food or medical advice I became
more and more unwell. At first my lungs gave me no trouble but about April I
contracted a cold which, added to my other malady, greatly debilitated me. But
worse than my own sickness was the ill health of my sister Fannie. She had
never been quite well since her return the previous year and altho she was very
bright, and being the most unselfish of creatures, did all in her power to conceal
her sickness from us, yet at last it dawned on us that she had a serious pulmonary affliction and in the condition of our surroundings there was but little that
we could do to retard the progress of her disease. I bought her a riding horse,
but that exercise soon became too much for her. Late in the month of May she
went, for a change, to Vaucluse and we hoped, as people always do under similar circumstances, that she would come back much improved. In a day or two
however we were greatly startled by a message that my mother must come to
her at once as she was extremely ill. It was early in the morning and having a
buggy without a top I started to drive my mother to Vaucluse, and this is what
befell us on the way.

Some few weeks prior the Federal army under Gen. Hunter had passed up
the Valley doing no special harm at Springdale but in revenge for the death of
some of their troopers caught in Newtown and hanged on the spot for some vile
acts of vandalism, Hunter burned several houses in that village.[41] He had gone
on his marauding way up the Valley until he was finally met and scattered
between Lexington and Lynchburg and was obliged to divide his beaten army

and retreat in several directions. Either a part of his wagon train with the troops guarding it was retreating down the Valley, or else the Federals were trying to establish communication with Hunter up the Valley.[42] I don't remember which, but so it was the train and troops was attacked by Col. Mosby's command a little south of Newtown, and most, if not all, of it was captured and either carried off or turned over in the road.[43] The fight was over before I reached the scene of it, and the participants had all vanished. I was first apprised of it by my horse shying in the road and looking down I found it was a dead Federal Cavalryman. Then we came to the debris of the overturned wagon train. Most of the things of value had been carried off, but under one wagon was a pile of brown sugar which, I suppose, had escaped from a barrel broken in the melee. This was a prize worth taking possession of, for "coffee" made of burnt rye and drunk without sugar was our most common beverage. I took the sugar up with my hands, and having no other receptacle I filled the buggy under the seat and packed it in as closely as I could get it.

We did not realize how ill my sister really was, but in those sad times sickness and death were the commonest of events and neither ever deterred anybody from making such provision as we could for the living.

When we reached Vaucluse we found that my sister had had a dreadful hemorrhage and was in a very weak and low condition; but I can see her bright and cheerful face as she fondly greeted me, and the pain it seemed to give her when she witnessed my great distress. For herself she was all happiness, and never have I seen or heard of any body who seemed to be going so delightedly to what she believed to be a most glorious consummation of all the hopes her religion held out to her. Thus she lingered for several days, and then she died exultingly, seeming to see the very light of Heaven and to hear the music of its choirs. We buried her at Vaucluse in the old family grave yard there, and there she still rests, the loveliest, and most loving and gentle being I ever knew.

Mrs. Lee and her family heard of Fanny's death the next afternoon (May 29) and planned to go to the funeral, despite the difficulties of finding transport and encountering armies on their way; they finally managed to appropriate an army ambulance.

[DIARY OF MARY GREENHOW LEE]

It [Sunday] was particularly sad this evening from the news of dear Fannie Barton's death, dear child, how I envy her her heavenly rest; I can imagine her reunited to her father, sister & her brothers; her patriot brothers, who have died fighting for their country—but above all, she is with her Saviour. We have made arrangements by which some of us will be able to go to Vaucluse to-morrow, to her funeral. What a terrible fatality attends that family; years of uninterrupted prosperity followed by blow after blow. May God have mercy on those who are left & enable them to see God's Hand in these afflictions.

Monday night [May 30]

... I thought it best for Lal [Burwell] to go (she being Fan's age & intimate friend) I had given up my seat to her ... they sent word they could make room for me & I joined them; our party consisted of Dr. B. & the two girls, Mrs. Magill, A. Sherrard, Mr. Maury & ourselves.[44] The day was exquisite & the country so beautiful, that I enjoyed the ride; the absence of fences made the fields look like parks & one might imagine they were driving through the grounds of some princely estate. Four miles from town there was a cry of Yankees ahead; first a few, then a large squad of Cavalry; then over the rise of the hill the glistening of bayonets heralded the approach of Infantry. I was somewhat apprehensive lest the five horses to our wagon might prove an irresistible temptation, but as they belonged to the driver, a negro, I hoped they might not be taken. As we approached we found it was the advance guard of a double wagon train—about 200 wagons & an escort of 500 men. We turned aside & stopped & they passed us without a word or, strange to say, a rude look. They looked very subdued and timid. Having escaped so well, we drove rapidly to Newtown, passed the houses Hunter had burned last week, & then saw some horsemen ahead of us; I saw at a glance they were Confederates & when we got to the inn where they were collected, we stopped to talk to them; several dashing, fine looking soldiers came up & told us Gilmore had captured the whole train that has passed through yesterday evening & that Col. Mosby ... had had a skirmish with the rear guard of the train we had passed, & driven them out of Newtown. He also said we had whipped Grant again & driven him to the river. He pointed to a Yankee prisoner & said they were about to hang him as he had been caught in the act of firing a house. This was a startling announcement. As we passed out of Newtown, we drove by 16 wagons, burning on the road; several dead horses &, to my infinite horror the bodies of two dead Yankees who had been shot this morning; involuntarily I covered my eyes that the sight might be excluded. The Yankees were preparing to burn Newtown today, when Mosby sent word to Hunter that for every Rebel house he burned, he would hang ten of their men, &, as he has prisoners, he can carry out his threat. ...

But to return to the order of the day; we got to Vaucluse about 11 o'clock & found them in dire confusion. The fight yesterday evening had prevented the necessary arrangements being made & the grave was not dug; expecting Vaucluse would be burned before night; Mrs. Jones had been packing up some few valuables & the hall was filled with trunks. Dear Fan was the only peaceful one, in this scene of turmoil. She lay in her coffin, covered with flowers, so calm, so heavenly that it was rest to look at her. Mr. Avirett had (most improperly) been asked to conduct the services . . . it was a fulsome eulogy which would have shocked dear Fan's shrinking, humble spirit.[45] Finding the ambulance could not go over the road to the grave yard, Lal & I went in a rockaway with Mrs. Crawford; there had been some delay in making this arrangement & when we moved off, we could not see the procession & drove two miles without finding it.[46]

Robby made record of Fanny and Tom Marshall's devotion. Mrs. Barton had opposed any idea of their marriage because Tom had been married to Fanny's sister Maria.

[MEMOIR OF ROBERT T. BARTON]

Let me tell it to you here, as it is a part of our family history. Col. Thomas Marshall and my sister Fannie had an unacknowledged, but none the less real—I was about to call it—engagement of marriage. It was not a real engagement however, because devotedly attached as they were to each other, Fannie was willing to sacrifice herself to my mother's unyielding prejudice against such a marriage. I do not doubt however that had they both lived, after the war ended they would have been married, and my mother would have yielded, as she did years after in exactly a similar case. But in less than six months after Fannie's death Col. Marshall was filling a soldier's grave, and thus that unfinished romance takes its place too among the many real things which are so much stranger than fiction.

In midsummer, Tom Marshall answered Robbie's letter describing Fanny's death. Tom and the 7th Virginia Cavalry had been in central Virginia since the May battles, and Tom had lost another horse in a victory against Custer's cavalry June 11 at Trevilians. General Rosser was wounded in the battle and Col. R. H. Dulany took over command of the brigade, leaving Tom in command of the regiment.

[LETTER OF THOMAS MARSHALL TO ROBERT T. BARTON]

Hd Qrs 7th V.C.

Aug. 2nd 1864

Dear Robert,

Perhaps you will consider me dilatory in answering your kind & affectionate letter. I should have written about the time I wrote to your mother, but for the condition of your health, which I understood was *uncertain*. . . .

Your letter & Mattie's recording the history of the "dying moments of our *"darling Fan"* are to me most precious & shall ever be preserved as such. Was there ever anything more exquisitely beautiful? While enjoying her delightful society, her *bright sparkling wit* & *humour,* it would occasionally flash across my mind that perhaps there was too much *lightness* for the *solemn time* through which we are all passing, though I confess I generally joined in with full zest (for I was *never happier* than when in her presence).

But I am *fully* satisfied now, as I was partially then, that "the *joy* of the *Lord* was *her* strength" Would God it were so with me to the same extent! Creatures as we are of *sense,* how hard it is for us to *realize* the land of spirits, the mortal remains of those so *dearly loved* & highly prized are laid in the *dark cold grave*. Their spirits go to God who gave them—& *we are left alone.* No more for us does the *bright eye* sparkle, or do we hear the *tones* of the much-loved voice or feel the pressure of the *gentle hand*. No more does the *ringing laugh* resound to the *passing jest* or the lively "bon Mot." . . .

I call to mind now on one occasion when talking with darling F. about *"death"* her saying that it might be sometimes *selfish* to wish to *die*. And this is doubtless true. But yet how many are there, even of experienced Christians, who look upon death, only with something of *horror,* who *shrink* from it, not realizing that it is the passage to a "Heavenly Canaan," the blessed means of bringing us to "Our Heavenly Father," "Our Divine Saviour", "Our Holy Sacrifice" & the spirits of the "just made perfect", & the blessed society & renewed intercourse with our dearest earthly friends, who have departed in *the faith.* I am persuaded that these things ought *not* so to be, that we are falling short of *duty* or *not living* up to *our privileges* to continue in such a state. . . . But, perhaps, I have dwelt *too long* upon *this theme*. Replying to your letter written about our *precious one* has led me into this strain.

My children have been doubtless, a good deal disappointed at not seeing me this summer as our army has again been in your midst, but I see no prospect as yet for any change in this respect. . . .

I hope my children continue to be a source of light & happiness to the household. To you, my dear Robert, am I deeply indebted for the trouble & pains you have taken about them. To your dear mother & Mattie it would be needless to say anything on this respect, I can only *mourn* over my inability to be of any service to them. But such for the *present,* & *perhaps, forever* seems to be the Will of my Lord. I am truly sorry that what I can save from my salary, should be worth so little owing to the general depreciation of our currency, so that, the "onus" of their livelihood falls upon you all. Some future day, perchance, they may be able to make some return for the kindness extended them. . . . Much love to all

Tell my children to hug & kiss each other for me. Kind regards to the servants especially, "Scilla" & "Nancy."[47] . . .

> Yours truly & devotedly
> Thomas Marshall

Robby's health took a turn for the worse during the summer.

[MEMOIR OF ROBERT T. BARTON]

After my sister's death I was miserably despondent for I was truly devoted to her. I had witnessed her delighted death, altho I was not present at the actual moment of dissolution, and in comparison with her blessed peace, the wretched conditions of my surroundings greatly aggravated by my extreme ill health made me feel that death would be a blessed exchange, and I contemplated its apparent approach with at least indifference, if not indeed with unaffected pleasure. My cough became much worse, and at last as I rose one morning from what had been a very restless sleep I spit quite a quantity of blood from my lungs.[48] This new calamity seemed to overcome my mother and sisters [Martha and cousin Anna] and while I was put to bed in a most exhausted condition, either their distress or the love of life which seems to come sometimes when death threatens, or perhaps both considerations, greatly changed my mental condition, and instead of my theretofore great depression my spirits became lighter, and I was a much happier man. In spite of the probabilities that I would die I did not believe it, and I thought that a crisis in my life had arrived when the turn would be for better things. . . . When my illness became so serious as at least to make it probable that I could not again take charge of affairs [Strother] was sent for and came at once to Springdale.[49] He and my sister

Martha whom we all called Sister Mat, were both of very bright and happy dispositions. This combination added greatly to remove the sadness of the house. My cousin Anna Jones too, was a member of our household, and being both pretty and witty the Springdale fireside was not wanting in elements of brightness, however sombre the outlook was otherwise.

In the previous winter, among our soldier visitors who ventured visits on that dangerous ground, was Col. W. E. Cutshaw. Col. Cutshaw was the Captain of the Battery of which my brother Marshall (and afterwards my brother David) was the First Lieutenant. The same shell which killed my brother Marshall on May 25 1862 had badly wounded Capt. Cutshaw in the knee and he had been brought to my father's house. As he could not be removed when the Army fell back a week after, he was left there to be cared for and nursed by our household. Anna Jones, auburn haired, pretty and petite, and always ready for a flirtation, was quite a constant companion of the wounded Captain when he had so far recovered as to be dressed. It was not to be wondered at that he fell in love with her, or that after his complete recovery, having been exchanged, entered service again and been promoted to be Colonel he had not forgotten the pretty Anna. Well his visit to Springdale in the winter had been to tell her so, and all that that implied. We had but one sitting room with fire: the Colonel's time was very limited and none of us suspected his errand, so if he might tell his love, he had to do it then and there, under very grievous disadvantages. He beguiled Anna off to the piano which in that long parlour, with her skillful drumming gave a whisperer some chance of telling a secret. But he did not speak quite low enough to escape the quick ears of the rest of the party, and I remember my infinite amusement, when one of those at the fire, repeated aloud at the very moment that Anna was shaking her pretty head to his entreaties:

> Tis sweet to love but oh how bitter,
> To love a girl and then not *git her.*

And this too as if it had no relation at all to the interesting occasion.

The Colonel fell back that very night in confusion, and did not renew his solicitations afterwards. He was a most gallant soldier and excellent man. Subsequently he lost his leg in battle but survived the war and is at this writing the very efficient Chief Engineer of Richmond City.[50] As for Anna she might have smiled on the Colonel if her heart had not been captured by another soldier. She was not engaged to be married at the time, but she, no doubt, knew pretty well what she intended to do with herself. . . .

XIII

July–September 1864

EARLY'S VALLEY CAMPAIGN
THIRD BATTLE OF WINCHESTER

After being wounded in the Battle of the Wilderness, Rannie almost instinctively headed for Staunton. But this refuge soon was threatened, and he escorted some ladies in flight, pausing at a plantation that furnished an enduring memory.

[MEMOIR OF RANDOLPH BARTON]

Next day [May 13 or 14], dispatching my boy and horses by way of Gordonsville and Charlottesville, to Staunton, I took the first passenger train for the same place, reaching there that night. As I recall the fact that from this wound I suffered more than any other I ever received, my qualms at not having returned to the line from the field hospital are quieted. I remained in Staunton, enjoying all the hospitalities of that place, for some weeks, my wound gradually healing, when the town was alarmed by the advance of the Yankees [under Gen. David Hunter] up the Valley. This determined Mrs. [John B.] Baldwin to "refugee" with her two very pretty sisters, Miss Jennie and Miss Cornelia, to her half-brother, Colonel William Peyton, in the highlands of the southern part of Albemarle [County].[1] I was invited to join the party, which I did with the alacrity to be expected of a young man who had fast fallen under the influence of two winsome young girls. I remember that our caravan consisted of the carriage, a baggage wagon and my outfit, a boy and three very fine horses, for my uncle [James F. Jones] had committed to me for safe-keeping his noble Morgan

Pharselia, the Massie plantation, near Massie's Mills. (M. B. Colt)

horse. The first night we bivouacked about twenty-five miles from Staunton and spent a very delightful night.

The next night, crossing the Blue Ridge at a gap called Tye River, we descended the eastern slope, and at the base came to the plantation of Colonel Massie. This establishment was typical of southern life. It had never been visited by either army. It was a beautiful farm just at the foot of the mountain, which rose with some grandeur back of it or to the west, protecting it from the cold blasts of winter. . . . The little Tye River, with its banks heavily fringed by large trees, traced its course as the northern boundary of the estate. The mansion house was large, irregular and with all the numerous out-buildings in a condition which betokened the care of a prosperous and intelligent Southern farmer. The negroes were around in the usual large numbers, docile and attentive. . . . on all sides were evidences of peace and plenty. And to crown all was the unbounded hospitality of Colonel and Mrs. Massie and their family, the chief ornament of which was their pretty daughter, Miss Florence.[2] Think of a tiresome day's journey crowned by such a reception . . . I remember so well the beauty of the next morning. Dew, sunlight, shadows, sparkling water, a full feeling of refreshment, safety, an incomparable breakfast and three exceedingly pretty girls all to myself; and the enjoyment of all justified by a painlessly-healing, honorable wound! I record these incidents to show that the dark clouds of war sometimes lifted and we basked once in a while in glorious sunlight.

We resumed our travels, Miss Florence accompanying us for several miles on her handsome riding horse, which she managed with the skill of a Virginia girl. Here, again, I was in Elysium. It was the month of June in the highlands of Albemarle, a portion of the country, so far, never desecrated by the enemy and almost free from wandering Confederates. Colonel Peyton's house was large, and all the surroundings, the collections of fifty years, were the results of prosperous ease and here I spent happy days of convalescence, tortured somewhat by the coquetry first of one of the young girls, and then of the other. I remember so well one bright Sunday morning my ride with Miss Cornelia (for whose pleasure Priam was brought up by George shining like silk, while I mounted the noble Morgan horse) over to the Episcopal Church. . . . The road, a type of a semi-mountainous Virginia road, led through woods and valleys, up hill and down. All was peaceful; the day was bracing; Miss Cornelia was beautiful and I was susceptible. A specially romantic dell was too much for me, and quiet insinuations, as I rode side by side with the pretty girl, warmed into unmistakable expressions, which were abruptly checked by my companion giving her horse a sharp cut and galloping ahead of me until I reached the church. . . .

An alloy to my pleasure now began to be felt. I became conscious that my wound was healing rapidly, and this meant that a much longer absence from the army was a dishonor. Soldiers in our army applied this test to their absenteeism: "Am I in proper condition to return?" and, in the main, irrespective of the surgeon's views, it was honorably respected. And so in a little while my conscience bade me go, and with much regret I turned my back upon Colonel Peyton's and started for Staunton, to which place I learned General Early's army, which, including our division, had been detached by General Lee to pursue Hunter, was going. . . .

After relieving Lynchburg and pursuing Hunter to West Virginia, Early turned to move north to Staunton, arriving June 26. While Rannie had been enjoying some semblance of peacetime pleasures, Winchester and Frederick County were the scenes of constant military activity, albeit on a small scale. With the prospect of a bumper crop of grain, the Valley again became an important military focus. Early's army was to spend the summer attempting to emulate Stonewall Jackson's diversionary activities in the Valley and draw Federal attention and support away from Richmond. The family at Springdale was struggling to make ends meet, but troop movements often destroyed farming efforts, although at least the Confederates paid the Bartons for forage.[3] The shortage of ordinary commodities was acute. Robby became more and more disabled by consumption, and there was no medicine to be had.

Union artist James E. Taylor portrayed Springdale (across the road) and Bartonsville and himself from a vantage point upstream above the gristmill. On the near side of the turnpike, by the bridge, is a farm building which was burned out in the skirmish on the night of May 24, 1862. (Western Reserve Historical Society)

[MEMOIR OF ROBERT T. BARTON]

The summer of 1864 was one of most active military operations in the lower Valley and the Country was occupied most of the time by the Confederate troops. About all this you must read in history, for I would like my boy to know all that concerned our civil war so that he may learn what a slander it is to call those who fought for the highest motives of patriotism and to sustain our Constitutional rights, rebels; and to learn also that no army ever marched or fought, in all the world's history, that was composed of braver men than the armies of the Confederacy.

As for myself, to everybody else I seemed to grow worse and worse. I had many more hemorrhages—sixteen in three months—and very many indications of hopeless consumption. I weighed only ninety-two pounds, and while I could walk around the house and drive even to Vaucluse and Winchester, yet I was so weak that I could not hold up a book to read. But my desire for reading was inordinate and irrepressible. My brother Strother, to enable me to be gratified, made me a frame on which I could rest my book and thus read without so much fatigue. I was repeatedly informed that I could not live more than a few weeks. I did not in my heart believe this, but I always cheerfully replied that I had prepared for such an emergency, and I did in fact always endeavour to so hold myself that I could play the man in such a solemn and trying hour. But death then was so much more familiar to us all than it is in time of peace and I had learned to confront it so often before, that to die quietly in my bed did not then seem such a strange or awful thing after all. You can form some idea of how pressed we were for what is considered the commonest necessities of life, when I tell you that we did not even have mustard out of which to make a plaster, and I had to use horse radish leaves instead.

Rannie returned to duty late in June as A.A.G. to Gen. William R. Terry, former Colonel of the 4th Virginia Infantry. Following the wounding of General Walker and the severe losses in the May battles, the Stonewall Brigade had been combined with two other units into a small brigade under Terry's command. The army continued north from Staunton, passing through Winchester on July 2 on their way to Maryland. They began crossing the Potomac on July 5.

[MEMOIR OF RANDOLPH BARTON]

Up and down the Valley we went that summer, pursuing one day, pursued the next, and finally we went to the Potomac. . . . We crossed towards Monocacy Bridge, and there had a stiff battle [July 9] with the enemy under General Lew Wallace. . . .

Upon the forming of our line, knowing that we would soon be under a heavy fire, and being mounted upon my pet mare, Mary Stuart, I looked around for a change. Observing three farm horses grazing in the meadow, I selected the best, a large, strong sorrel, covered with mud from wallowing, which, having dried, had cracked all over him in squares, reminded me of the hide of a rhinocerus. Changing my bridle and sending Mary Stuart to the rear, I mounted this horse and joined our advancing line of battle. As we rose over the crest of the hill we were received by a murderous volley from the Yankee line, lying behind a fence not very many yards away, which we returned with interest. In a little while I felt a blow upon my sword belt; a blow which as I now recall it was severe, but not painful, evidently made by a glancing ball. I record this as one of the times I was "struck" in battle, but not as a wound. A moment later the thud of a ball, and the wincing of my horse, who was behaving splendidly, assured me that he was wounded. Perhaps he staggered, for I immediately spurred him so as to get slightly under cover, the enemy having by that

Araby, the Thomases' farm on Monocacy Creek. (Enoch Pratt Free Library)

time broken away from the fence in retreat, and save my saddle and bridle. After galloping a short distance I felt him reeling, and, jumping off, the poor animal fell, rolling over on his side and laid mortally wounded.

In the year 1867 or 1868 in Baltimore I met Miss Thomas, from whom I learned that she was from the neighborhood of Frederick, Maryland. In the course of our conversation I easily located her home on the battle-field, and the horse [Old Davy] I had taken up and succeeded in getting killed as having belonged to her father. She enthusiastically repudiated any claim against me and expressed her satisfaction at being able to contribute in any way to the Southern cause.[4] . . .

I think it was on this trip into Maryland that somewhere near Harper's Ferry . . . We were on a road, to the east of which arose a range of very high hills covered with woods, branches, no doubt, of the rather singular formation at that point terminating in Maryland and Loudoun Heights. The Yankees were feeling, from the crown of Maryland Heights, the line of our march indicated, notwithstanding the intervening but somewhat lower elevations by the cloud of dust rising from our marching column. The troops had stopped a little while and had flung themselves as usual on the grass bordering the road. An interval of perhaps one hundred yards existed between the head of our brigade and the one next in advance, and the only man in that interval was a straggler who was marching along, taking advantage of this rest, to catch up with his command. I was standing with the reins of my bridle thrown over my arm when, hearing the distant report of a cannon off to the right towards Maryland Heights, I casually glanced along the tops of the trees covering the crest of the ridge when I saw a speck, which I at first took to be a bird, but in an instant the shrill sound of an approaching cannon ball struck my ear, and in a moment it had descended, and as the unfortunate straggler stepped out the ball knocked off his left leg. A cloud of dust, a scream of pain and terror, a rush of soldiers to lift the stricken man, and the incident was over. Strange to say, not long afterwards I saw that man in an ambulance, in high spirits, going to the rear.

. . . After the battle of Monocacy we made for Washington, getting as far as Silver Spring, the country residence of old man Frank Blair. . . .[5]

After the victory at the Monocacy, the Rebels came within sight of Washington, even shelling Fort Stevens on the outskirts. They retreated under pressure on July 12, having accomplished their purpose of scaring the Federal government, and additionally had negotiated the release of certain hostages, including Messrs. Williams and Boyd.[6] The Confederates were back in the Valley on July 16, and on July 24 Early routed a Federal force under General Crook in what is called the Second Battle of Kernstown. A week later he sent cavalry forces to raid Maryland and Pennsylvania, and on July 30 they occupied Chambersburg. Their demands for reparations for Hunter's destruction in the Valley were not met (as they had been elsewhere), and the viciousness of the conflict escalated yet again as the Confederates burned the town. Skirmishing continued in late July along the Potomac and more occasionally throughout August, Winchester changing hands several times. The Confederates were back among old friends and familiar surroundings. Jed Hotchkiss again visited the Joneses at Vaucluse. Rannie, Will and Frank Clark, Joe Sherrard, and the Burwell boys had opportunities to see their families and to visit Mrs. Lee and other friends in town. Holmes Conrad took time to get married, to Mary Magruder, sister of the Woodstock doctor.[7] Bolling came home for the summer as the VMI cadets had been furloughed June 27. When and where they would reconvene, after the destruction of the institute, was not known. Tom Marshall, with the 7th Virginia Cavalry near Petersburg for most of the summer, was badly wounded in an attack near Reams's Station in late August. After about a week in the hospital, he, too, came home to Springdale on medical leave. While the army was in the vicinity, Rannie was attached as A.A.G. to Gen. Zebulon York of Louisiana, presumably due to his familiarity with the region. That summer seems to have been one of the pleasant periods of the war for him, but that changed with the season. U.S. Gen. Philip Sheridan had assumed command of the Army of the

Shenandoah on August 6, with orders to drive the Confederates south and to render the riches of the Valley useless to them.

[MEMOIR OF RANDOLPH BARTON]

Gradually we drifted through the summer, and September came. Being much around Winchester and Springdale (to which place my mother had moved after my father's death, in the summer of 1863) I saw a good deal of my family, as General York, commanding the Louisiana Brigade, and on whose staff I was temporarily serving, was very indulgent. On Friday, September 16, Bob Burwell and myself made preparations for an old-time, ante-bellum partridge hunt, and so on the next day we went out to the neighborhood of Neil's Dam, about three miles northwest of Springdale, and just to the rear of the battlefield of Kernstown, and there, on a glorious day, away from every hostile sight and sound, we wandered as in our boyish days over the grounds which so delighted us, and especially over the very ground upon which, in March, 1862, both of us had been taken prisoners. But on this Saturday nothing disturbed us. All was peaceful. The day was in September, but war to us was as remote as if the hostile armies were in Russia, and we reveled in the irresponsibility of the hour, while enjoying the sport of which we were both so fond. Sunday, we spent in Winchester, going peacefully to church, little dreaming of the great events of the next day. Our old home being closed, I spent the night with Bob.[8] About daybreak, awakening, I heard some musketry firing down the Berryville road. After a while I aroused Bob, and we both concluded it was a cavalry affair, as we knew our infantry was well down towards Martinsburg, whither General Early, against the protest of General Fitz Lee, as he told me himself, had gone on Saturday.

Bob and myself agreed to get up, ride down the road, capture, perhaps, saddles and bridles, which we both needed, and return to breakfast. When we had gone out of town about a mile and a half we found General Fitz Lee deploying his cavalry and, mounting a hill, to our dismay, observed a column of Yankee infantry forming in line of battle on the left-hand side of the road.[9] General Lee being near us, we could in decency do nothing less than tender our services to him, and shortly afterwards Bob started off on a message from the General. He had not gone far when a ball struck him on the left hip, ranged around somewhat spirally under his leg and came out near his knee. Bob bolted for home, and in the course of an hour, as things seemed to have quieted down and the enemy appearing to be merely taking up a position, I rode leisurely back to town. I had heard of Bob's wound, and that, although disabling, it was not serious—that is, dangerous. I was disposed to chaff him about that saddle and bridle. When I dismounted at the door of the annex to Mrs. Lee's house, always called the office, and entered the room, there lay Bob, comfortably helpless. His good aunts and sisters had put him to bed; everything looked clean and cozy, and I recall especially an ingenious arrangement had been rigged up over his wounded leg, from which the water dropped continuously upon it.[10]

His helplessness amused me very much when I remembered with what "brashness" he had sallied out of the room two hours before, and so I burst out laughing and asked him, "How about that saddle?" He took it good-naturedly, only remarking, as he brushed away a fly, "Never mind, you'll be in here yourself after a while."

I breakfasted and then started down the Martinsburg road from which direction Early was returning at top speed, with his little army of eight thousand infantry to meet Sheridan's formidable advance with twenty-five thousand.[11] Early spoke the truth when he said that instead of the North making a hero of Sheridan for the results of that day, he ought to have been cashiered for not capturing his [Early's] entire command.

As I rode along I had an opportunity to reflect upon my surroundings. A brilliant late September day, far off to the East trended the beautiful Blue Ridge. The heights of Harper's Ferry to the north were in full view. . . . I was reminded of war by an occasional shot in the distance, but the hour was the lull before the storm. . . . A holiday of two days, and such a holiday, spent in the fields and woods of my boyhood, had softened me. Riding by myself I had crowded upon me the awful changes of three years. Two of my brothers and my uncle Frank dead upon the field of battle, one brother maimed for life, my father dead, my brother Robert dying, as we all thought, of consumption, my mother prostrate, and standing upon the brink of a terrible battle, with its countless dangers, staring me in the face. "Oh, for a lodge in some vast wilderness!" I felt like exclaiming. Some relief from this dread suspense!

But these thoughts were speedily driven away, as I met our column, dust-covered and panting, hurrying up the road. I rejoined General York until I could find General [William] Terry, to whom it had been arranged I should return that day, and in a little while left the road, somewhere between Stevenson's Station and the town, striving by the most direct route across the fields to throw ourselves across Sheridan's path, between the railroad and the Berryville road. As we approached we became aware that the engagement had commenced, and as we neared the scene the distressing intelligence reached us that General [Robert E.] Rodes had been killed. The hours of the morning had been consumed in the march, and in getting into position, but as soon as we connected with Rodes' Division, which had preceded us, swinging into line of battle, we faced to the left, advanced upon the advancing enemy and were soon in the midst of a heavy fire. This was at a point about three miles northeast of Winchester. The ground was entirely open and we drove the enemy in confusion for probably a half a mile when coming upon their reserves, our line fell back in some disorder. It rallied after crossing the crest of the hill and the officers busied themselves in reforming the ranks. I was directed by General Terry to go back a few hundred yards and bring up quite a group of men who had assembled behind the hill. I went back, and while engaged in stirring up the men, I heard far down on our left, towards the Myer's place, a shout and firing, and looking in the direction from which it came, I saw the long line of Merritt's Yankee Cavalry charge, attacking our left flank.[12]

I knew we were in for a desperate fight and rode rapidly back to our brigade, which I found in line of battle in the open field, with no earthworks, and not in as good a condition, so I thought, in "morale" or numbers as I would have liked. I remember quite well the bad impression made upon me when a half hour before, in assisting to rally the men, I found officers, whom I had never seen flinch before, walking to the rear with their swords under their arms as if they had had enough.[13] As I approached our line firing had commenced; not heavy firing, but most dangerous and disagreeable, and just as I was about on the line I felt a violent and painful blow upon my left thigh, and my horse staggering at the same time. I instantly realized that I had been pretty badly wounded, and that the force of the ball, after piercing my leg, had been so great in striking my hide-bound McClellan army saddle as to stagger my horse. I at once turned, and my first impulse was to stand in my stirrups to see if any bone was broken. To my great relief it seemed to be all right, and just then meeting a surgeon I asked him to ascertain. He grasped my leg forcibly and giving it a wrench, pronounced the bone all right, and I resumed my course back to Winchester. The pain in my leg increasing and feeling somewhat enfeebled from loss of blood, I checked my horse (Mary Stuart) to a walk, and, later on, for relief, I lifted my foot over the pommel of my saddle and rode on in that way. I passed by Mr. George Baker's over-familiar ground, especially marked in my memory as the place where, with my mischievous but bosom friend, John Baldwin, I once stealthily resorted to smoke my first cigar, with a result the very recollection of which sickens me, and neared the toll-gate on the Berryville road.[14]

By that time I had become faint, and could only proceed in a slow walk. Just then a column of our cavalry was moving rapidly between me and the town to our left flank, and the enemy, with a battery down the Berryville road, was pounding away at it. I soon found that I was in the line of fire, but I could do nothing. My weakness had increased so much that I could hardly sit upon my horse and I concluded that I would have to take the chances. Looking towards the battery, I saw the puff of white smoke and, being in line with it, saw the ball approaching as I thought immediately towards me. Fortunately it struck the ground some hundred yards or so short of me and buried itself. I rode down Piccadilly Street, an occasional shell bursting above me, and reaching Mrs. Lee's tumbled exhausted from my horse into the hands of some men there standing.[15]

I was taken in and laid alongside of Bob Burwell, who, as soon as he found that my wound was not dangerous, greeted me with repeated grunts which can be uttered but not expressed; they can be imitated, but not written. They were aggravatingly expressive, and in this instance had a "what-did-I-tell-you-this-morning" sound about them. A surgeon soon reached my wound and found that the ball had pierced my thigh between the thigh bone and the femoral artery. The bone was not injured, so he said, after meeting his two forefingers through the wound, although the call was exceedingly close.

So, sure enough, here I was with Bob, having lived with him for several days, and finally having been wounded with him, the same day, and almost in the identical place. General Fitz Lee, later in the day, was also wounded in the left thigh, just as Bob and myself had been. Some six weeks later we all met in Richmond on crutches; perhaps Bob had discarded his, and was walking with a cane, as his recovery was more rapid than General Lee's or mine.

In the course of an hour the indications were that our army must fall back. The noise of the battle was distinctly heard in our room and the town was in great confusion. Wagons, ambulances and wounded men were hurrying along the streets, and we became alarmed about our safety. Fortunately, Frank Clark stopped at the door to ask after us, and inform us of the outlook. We urged him to get an ambulance and, in a little while, meeting an empty ambulance of the Louisiana Brigade, he turned it around and brought it to our door.[16] The driver hesitated to take us, but I asserted my authority and telling him I would take all responsibility he backed up to the door; a mattress and some covers were thrown in, and Bob and myself being carefully carried to the vehicle, we started off.

*Mrs. Lee's other guests, including Mrs. John B. Gordon, the general's wife, and
Bob's brother Lewis, hurriedly made their departures amid screaming shells.
The Confederates all seemed particularly loath to leave Winchester for what
they may have sensed was their last departure. Both Henry Kyd Douglas and
Jim Garnett made their social rounds along the way to say their goodbyes,
despite Yankee skirmishers at the next corner. Douglas "amused himself bowing
to them while they were shooting at [him]," and vowed he would not shave
again until his return to the "beloved town"—a promise he soon regretted. On
the retreat, Garnett paused to see the Bartons as he passed Springdale.[17] The
confused and massive exodus made it difficult for Rannie and Bob's ambulance
to make headway on the Valley Turnpike. Late in the afternoon they reached
Springdale and paused briefly to assure the family and Grandmother Jones,
who happened to be there, that they were all right. At about the same time, both
Tom Marshall and Bolling must have recognized the danger and left Springdale
in the midst of the retreating army. Bob and Rannie were on the road three days
and nights to Staunton.*

[MEMOIR OF RANDOLPH BARTON]

Both Bob and myself suffered on this long trip. I cannot say that we suffered
severely, as our bed was easy, and the road was good. Still, our wounds were
severe and the jolting of ninety miles tended to inflame and irritate them. We
were extremely lucky, however, in getting out of Winchester, and in having an
ambulance to ourselves. I have never learned how the driver fared after returning to the army. I suppose he excused himself as having gone under the duress
of my very positive manner.

*Robby, in his enfeebled condition, and the wounded Colonel Marshall had
driven to town with sister Martha on the day of the battle.*

[MEMOIR OF ROBERT T. BARTON]

On the morning of September 19 1864, in entire ignorance that a great
battle would be fought that day my sister Mat drove Col. Tom Marshall who
disabled by a wound through his shoulder, had come back to Springdale, and
myself wholly disabled by sickness and weakness, into Winchester. [I had to be
lifted out of the carriage & Col Marshall had his arm in a sling.][18] We were resting at Mr. Philip Williams' when the sound of cannon and musketry startlingly

The Rebels retreat toward Winchester, September 19, 1864. The ambulance (center) carries the body of Gen. Robert E. Rodes. (James E. Taylor sketchbook, Western Reserve Historical Society)

near, excited our attention and we were soon informed that the battle had commenced within a mile from and north and north-east of Winchester. [We did not leave however until about the middle of the day. At that time one of our batteries was working in full sight at the east end of Piccadilly street.] We now hurried into the carriage and found the streets alive with many wagons, troops, and scattered soldiers. For some reason (perhaps the crowds on other streets) we went round by Market Street. Just as we reached the corner of Market and Picadilly Streets a shell struck the roof of the house on the north east corner [George Baker's] at the same time an ambulance containing the dead body of the Confederate General Rhodes came up.[19] From the corner of Picadilly Street down Market [from the Baldwins corner to Mrs. Lees] for a hundred yards the wounded and those who had died from their wounds after being brought from the field, lay thick and close side by side on the pavement on such blankets, coverlids, & c. as the already much despoiled people stripped their homes of. [Bob Burwell had been in for a long time, and we knew of his wound.] And the Winchester ladies were there, heedless of the bursting shells and undismayed by the blood and agonizing wounds, trying to comfort the dying and doing all they could to ease the pain and save the lives of the wounded.

The horse [old bay Charlie] my sister was driving was a miserable poor creature which she could hardly force along. I remember that, anxious to escape the danger of the bursting shells and get her two disabled charges safely out of danger, she called on a cavalryman who was riding by and he, with the flat side of his sabre, beat the old horse into an active trot.

We were just in time to get ahead of the great wagon trains [about Hahn's mills, which were turning in from the fields to start up the pike] and extra artillery which was filing into the road. [We could see our cavalry being pressed back on the hills on the Front Royal road and the shells were thick in that direction.] The battle too was a defeat for Early and we had not long reached Springdale before the beaten and tired army came marching by. There was not a little confusion and disorder and many ambulances and wagons of wounded men, but no panic nor any apparent apprehension but that at a more advantageous place Early would turn his veterans round to confront his foes.

As the army moved many men out there dropped back and many of them were captured, while many were concealed by friends and ultimately reached the Confederate lines. Many badly wounded had to be left at friendly houses. I remember that one dying [North Carolinian] man was taken out at Springdale and put on the porch. He was too desperately wounded to be further moved, so a mattress was slipped under him, and there he lay just under the parlour window groaning far into the night, until at last death came to his relief. . . . Col. Marshall whose arm was tied to his body for a severe wound in the shoulder mounted my horse and rode off, after giving me such a parting as I never experienced with any other human being. He believed that I would only live a few weeks and that he would never see me again. But there was no gush or sentimentality between us. Earnest and serious as we both were, with a smile and a wring of my hand he went away, never to meet again. . . .[20]

Later in the night we heard the clanging sabres and the loud tramp of the horses of the rear guard of Early's army as it sullenly retired, the great wagon trains and the wearied host of infantry and artillery having long before swept out of sight and hearing, altho some miles south of Springdale the army had gone into camp and the light of their fires could be seen reflected against the dark sky. You can imagine that there was but little sleep at Springdale that night, but much distress and apprehension.

My room was on the first floor with two of the windows opening on the porch. The floor of this—the back porch—was at one end on a level with the ground By my bedside was a small table on which were numerous bottles of medicine, and the light, which had been extinguished by some member of the family when they left me to myself late in the night. I had fallen into a troubled sleep when suddenly, towards daylight I was aroused by the loud tramp of a horse's hoofs on the back porch, followed immediately by heavy blows of a sabre on the back door which was soon burst in by kicks and knocks. In a moment my room door was opened and a rude, swearing, loud talking Federal Cavalryman entered and approached my bed. Almost at the same time my mother ran into the room in her night dress with her grey hair streaming down her back and pitifully entreated the soldier to leave the room, pointing to me lying weak and ill in bed, and telling the man that she feared such excitement would kill me. To which that cowardly creature replied, "Yes, I know all about you. We have sent two of your damned sons to Hell and I am going to send this other one now," indicating by his movements that he would carry out his threat.

I did not much fear that he would kill me but I was enraged beyond expression at his barbarous conduct, my feeling being the more intense because of my absolute helplessness. Meanwhile my Sisters had come in, half clothed and stood around my bed as if to protect me from that inhuman brute. Just at this juncture a Federal officer entered and speaking with great kindness to my mother and sisters and to me, ordered the soldier out of the room and made him remove his horse from the porch, threatening him at the same time with dire punishment for his outrageous conduct. Of course, I do not know if it was ever inflicted. The officer put a guard over the house and he managed to protect it and its inmates from actual violence during that dreadful day.

The crop of wheat cut that summer had been a splendid one, but my brother Strother who was then managing the farm, had been unable to have it threshed. Gen. Early however, who wanted the wheat for his army, had, the day before the battle, sent a lot of men and a machine to thresh it. I suppose there were in the stacks not less than 1500 bushels, and the General knowing the necessities of our household and the great sacrifices the family had made in the war, had offered to pay for the wheat at the rate of $2.00 per bushel in United States money. Situated as the family was this would have indeed been a Godsend to them. Well, quiet had hardly been restored after the scene in my room when attracted by a curious noise towards the barn I looked through the window in that direction and saw the flames rising from the wheat stacks, only a small portion of which had been threshed the day before. . . .

The wheat was all consumed except the few bushels which had been put in the grainary, but the barn and buildings were saved with great effort. . . .

While these scenes were being enacted the Federal hosts were pushing their way up the road in three solid and seemingly innumerable columns, but a small portion of which had been engaged in the great battle of the day before. One column marched in the turnpike, and one east and one west of the road, those in the fields destroying everything before them. Hogs, sheep, cattle, & c. were shot down and left to rot and horses were taken and carried away, whether needed by the army or not. Springdale was left like a wilderness, almost every living animal on the place either being driven off or else killed and left in sheer deviltry and wickedness.

Rannie and Bob Burwell had reached Staunton about September 22. Early's army had retreated south and took a stand at Fisher's Hill from which they were routed on that day. (It was probably there that cousin Robert Barton was wounded, shot through the lungs, and of necessity left behind when the Confederates retreated. Somehow, one of his sisters managed to reach him and nurse him.)21 The Federal pursuit continued as far as Port Republic, and was expected to reach Staunton just a few days after Rannie and Bob had.

[MEMOIR OF RANDOLPH BARTON]

Alarmed by the reports which reached Staunton, all the wounded who could move were placed in a burden (nowadays called freight) train and started for Charlottesville and Richmond. By the time we had crossed the Blue Ridge I was suffering a good deal, and so began to think of what I should do. Fortunately I remembered that my cousin, Raleigh Colston, lived near Charlottesville, and that Ivy Depot was the nearest point to his place, "Hill-and-Dale," and so I determined to communicate to Bob Burwell my intention not to go on to Richmond.22 The noise of the cars was so great that I could not talk to him, he being some ten feet away from me, both of us lying on the floor of the car, or on cots. I therefore took from my pocket the little testament Miss Netta Lee had given me, and as I now hold it in my hand I can trace very rudely written these words, "I think I will stop at Ivy Depot," and passed it from man to man to Bob, who at once understood and assented. . . .

Arriving at Ivy Depot I was removed from the car on a cot, placed near the station and the train went on. I had no difficulty in sending word to the Colston's of my whereabouts, and in due time an old-fashioned two-horse carriage, with C. springs, I think, driven by an old-fashioned "Uncle-Remus"-looking darkey, with cousin Raleigh inside, reached the railroad. My kind relatives had provided pillows for my comfort, and so I made the two or three miles to Hill-and-Dale with comparative comfort. A welcome such as only that family

Hill-and-Dale, near Ivy Depot. (M. B. Colt)

could give awaited me. Mrs. Colston (cousin Gertrude), Bettie . . . Annie . . . and Jeannie . . . were ready for me. . . .

And here I was again. The wounded Confederate soldier, a guest at the old-fashioned home in that beautiful country of Albemarle, of relatives. And such relatives! . . . Mr. and Mrs. Colston were the best types of everything which has embalmed the attractiveness of the Virginia country gentleman and his wife in the memories of the fast-dying generation which knew them in their ante-bellum glory. Of the three girls I have named I cannot say too much. Exceedingly pretty and unusually attractive, I associate them with all that was beautiful in nature in that lovely country at that best of seasons when departing summer is shaking hands with approaching autumn. At their hands I received the care prompted by the consideration that I was a guest, a cousin and a Confederate soldier. Imagination must do the rest. . . .

This life I led for a month at least, and finally accepting the cordial invitation of Mrs. Alexander Taliaferro, I visited her family at the University of Virginia.[23] Still on crutches, after a week's stay with the Taliaferro's, I went to Richmond, going to the place where I was ever welcome, cousin Barton Haxall's, and from there, as probably in November, I gradually recovered, I returned to the army, still in the Valley.[24]

XIV

October 1864–
April 1865

Last Battles in the Valley
Final Campaign in Eastern Virginia

After the Third Battle of Winchester, Sheridan's pursuit of the demoralized Confederates continued until, overextended, he fell back to lines at Cedar Creek. Rannie admired Early's spirit.

[Memoir of Randolph Barton]

Early had been badly defeated and his army was rallied and reorganized with difficulty at Fisher's Hill, and then from there back up the Valley. It had enough grit left in it, however, to make, on the morning of October 19, just one month after the Winchester battle, a bold attack upon Sheridan's army at Cedar Creek, which came near being an overwhelming success. Want of discipline and undue discretion on Early's part, suddenly converted the success into a disastrous retreat. It was on this occasion that Sheridan added greatly to his fame by his dashing ride from Winchester to Belle Grove, and his impetuous attack upon Early.[1]

Early had ceased his advance about noon to assess his progress, and lost his momentum. His men were desperate enough for supplies to jeopardize and annul their victory in their preoccupation with plunder, especially shoes—forgetting "their honor as soldiers in the mad hunt for Yankee gimcracks," a Richmond lady sourly observed.[2] In fact, many of the Rebels were barefoot and certainly all were undernourished. This pause gave Sheridan enough time to make the ten-mile ride to Middletown and rally his troops.

After the Battle of Cedar Creek, the immense Yankee occupying armies engulfed Springdale and the surrounding farms, and what had seemed hardship the previous year must have looked like plenty in retrospect. The Barton family was desperate enough to accept rations from the occupying Federal forces and for Robby, virtually at death's door, to leave the Confederacy.

[MEMOIR OF ROBERT T. BARTON]

... Sheridan's army had its main front near Middletown, but like some great beast, while its mouth lay at that distance its great body and tail stretched all the way back to Winchester. Springdale was in its very track and glad to save the house and have the protection of a guard the beautiful farm was per force surrendered to absolute devastation. The fences, stone and plank were destroyed; the pretty woods cut down; and the fields were marked and crossed with miry roads.[3] In the general destruction one old horse, an old carriage and one or two cows alone escaped. These cows and the horse would have perished of hunger (for there was nothing left to feed them with) but for the kindness of some Federal officers who supplied the family with provender. Before the battle at Winchester a beef had been killed, and after being cut up in the hall upstairs the meat had been salted and stored away in different parts of the house, and the few bushels of wheat which had escaped the fire were put in bags under the beds in our sleeping rooms. This provision, with such small supplies of salt, sugar & c. as had from time to time been gathered from various sources and economically used, served to keep

Gen. William Dwight.
(Massachusetts Commandery, MOLLUS, U.S. Army Military History Institute)

Robert T. Barton's pass. (Edith Barton Sheerin)

away actual starvation until at last the supply being exhausted, the family had to beg rations from the Federal Army.

About this time a Gen. Dwight from Boston took the house at Springdale for his headquarters, leaving a part of it for the family. He was a gentleman and a very kind and humane man.[4] To him was mainly due the fact that the family got food sufficient for them and to him and some kind people in the North who were influenced by his representations my mother and sisters were indebted for supplies, including many things which then were absolute luxuries, and to many thoughtful acts of kindness besides, which seemed to relieve the horrors of that dreadful winter.

For myself, in my exceedingly delicate condition of health, the want of food which I could eat and the entire deprivation of medicine, seemed to leave the number of my days as a matter of short computation. It was therefore determined by my friends to make an effort to have me sent to my sister (Mrs. C. H. Sheild) on the eastern shore of Maryland. For some time I was refused permission by the authorities to go north of their lines. Then they proposed that if I would forswear the Confederacy and take the oath of Allegiance to the United States, I might go. This, of course, was not even considered by my friends. At last I was taken into Winchester in the hopes that a personal interview and the proof which a sight of my wretched condition would give the authorities, of my entire incapacity to hurt the United States, would persuade them to let me go through their lines. I stayed at Mr. [Philip] Williams' house and as soon as I was able I crept down to the office of the Provost Marshall, which was then in the brick building on the north east corner of Main and Water Streets. The Provost [G. L. Montague] was a rough but not unkindly man. I told him frankly of my views as to my allegiance to the State and the Confederacy with which it had cast its lot, and that I never could give up my duty or forswear my obligation there: that it was only my ill health which kept me out of the Confederate army: and I narrated fully my family history and its connection with the Southern cause. I then asked that he would treat me as a prisoner of war and put me on parole, and urged that even if I was disposed to break my word, in my condition the U. S. Government did not have much to fear from me. After many objections urged by him and many persuasions used to turn me to what he regarded as my patriotic duty, he finally took my view of the case and roughly (but really not unkindly) telling me that I could live but a few weeks at the best, gave me a pass to go through to Baltimore.[5] Thus the principal obstacle was removed. The money question was settled by an order from a gentleman to whom I had some time before sold a flock of sheep for which he had not paid, or some one indebted to him in Baltimore, to pay me there in United States currency. How I got the money to pay my expenses to Baltimore I do not now remember.

The railroad from Winchester to Harpers Ferry had been torn up and Martinsburg was the nearest railroad point. Between this and there, in spite of the great army south of Winchester the Confederates hovered like hawks and darted down on any wagon train that was not too heavily guarded and on any conveyance which communicated between those points. As none but Federal troops and their people now had a conveyance, every horse and vehicle was proper prey to the Confederates.

I could therefore only travel with a guarded Federal wagon train.[6] Mr. Williams secured for me a seat in the carriage of a Union man, and that started off in a long line of wagons, all heavily guarded by cavalry with scouts out in every direction. With the train was also quite a number of Confederate prisoners. . . . These, of course, marched on foot. Several times during the day there were alarms of attacks, but the train was never really attacked. The apprehensions of the Federals and especially of the Union citizens with the train were quite amusing to me. . . .

The next day I took the train at Martinsburg and got to Baltimore at night quite wearied with my trip. I went at once to the house of Dr. P. C. Williams . . . where almost immediately I had a severe hemorrhage.[7] Dr. Williams was sent for and then and for a month more he and his family attended me with a degree of kindness that it is impossible for me to make you fully understand. In Baltimore I collected the order given me for the sheep, which was, I think, about $70.00. A very kind friend then gave me a handsome suit of clothes and as I could otherwise supply myself by purchases, I put aside my coarse and worn garments, and looked quite respectable. I got a great deal better with these advantages of proper food, medicine and treatment, and enjoyed the lionizing which I got as a disabled Confederate, for you know Baltimore was a very Southern city in its sentiments.

On November 11 Rev. Mr. Sheild came to Baltimore for me and on the next day I went with him to Elkton . . . and I was driven rapidly down to the parsonage [in Earleville] two or three miles from Cecilton in Cecil Co. Maryland.

My sister Jane, the wife of Rev. C. H. Sheild, was in exceedingly delicate health, but you can imagine she was overjoyed to see me. Anna Jones too was on a visit there, but I do not remember exactly at what time she left Springdale.

A short time after we heard the sad news of the death of Col. Thomas Marshall which occurred [November 12th] in a Cavalry fight not far from the place known as Old Forge in Frederick Co.

Robby left home a few days before the Battle of Cedar Creek on October 19, and Tom Marshall returned to the army and command of the 7th Virginia Cavalry a few days thereafter. Following that battle, the Confederates withdrew south. A month later they rallied to the attack again. In Robby's memoir of the colonel, he described more fully the circumstances of Marshall's death. At that time, the Confederate lines ran northwest-southeast through Vaucluse and the Yankee lines were parallel, with camps at Bartonsville and Kernstown.

[MEMOIR OF THOMAS MARSHALL BY ROBERT T. BARTON]

. . . Gen. Early, having determined upon another advance down the Valley, ordered Gen. Rosser, now acting as Division commander, to move his force of cavalry down the back road towards Winchester, while he with the main army advanced down the turnpike. Crossing Cedar Creek, Gen. Rosser repulsed a portion of the enemy's cavalry, and drove them back on the main force. The whole body then moved against Gen. Rosser, and owing to the rough and hilly condition of the ground, he was compelled to meet them by detached regiments. Lieut.-Col. Marshall, in command of the Seventh, had made a successful attack; but his regiment had become somewhat scattered; and from the advanced position he had gained, he with two of his men was watching the movements of a column of the enemy from behind a vacant house. Engrossed in this occupation, he had not observed that the greater portion of the regiment had retired before a flanking troop of Yankees, and he with his two men was left in an isolated position. The enemy were within a few yards of him when he first saw them, and he had immediately to put spurs to his horse, while a shower of balls whistled round him. As they rode off, he remarked to one of his companions, in a laughing manner, "it would be *hard* to be shot in the back." The words had scarcely passed his lips, before he was observed to turn pale; and young Rector, who rode at his side, said, "Colonel, you are wounded!" "Yes," he said; and as he began to lose the firmness of his seat in the saddle, he was seized on one side by Rector, and on the other by Charlie Davis, a gallant, noble boy who not long after yielded up his own young life, and leaves behind to this day saddened, sorrowing hearts.[8]

Soon Col. Marshall faintly said, "Put me down, boys; I am dying; save yourselves." Thoughtful, tender, forgetful of self, his last words on earth were for the good of others. These two soldiers, unselfish in their affection, would not put him down, but rode on by his side, holding the lifeless body upon the madly running horse. Crossing a stream and leaping up a steep bank, they lost their hold upon the body, and it fell to the ground. Seizing it again rapidly, they hurried on; but soon the enemy pressed so closely, that it was impossible to ride this death-charge longer; so, placing the now flexible yielding body at the foot of a locust-tree, these devoted guardians of a loved commander had barely time to escape the shots and clutches of their pursuers. In about two hours the tables of the fight were turned; and seeking the spot where they had last laid the body, they found it stripped of everything except a pair of pants and a flannel shirt; and even the pockets of these were turned inside out.[9]

Tom died near the house of E. P. Hancock, northeast of Old Forge. He could not be buried at Oak Hill with his wife, as it was then in the hands of the enemy, so he was interred at the University of Virginia. Rannie, too, had treasured memories of Tom Marshall.

[MEMOIR OF RANDOLPH BARTON]

    . . . He entered active service as a volunteer aide on General Jackson's staff, and served with him in that capacity at First Manassas. I am under the impression that he went into that battle with a linen "duster" on which, of course, made him very conspicuous. When I was wounded he was very near me on his favorite horse, "Mont-joy," killed very soon after. . . . In a skirmish not far from Vaucluse, received his mortal wound. . . . His death was most bitterly deplored by an unusually wide circle of relatives and friends. In the army his profound piety and splendid bearing as a soldier caused him to be trusted and beloved by all. In his domestic relations he was a model. I can even now hear his ringing, cheery laugh, so hearty, so infectious. I have known the Lees, our next-door neighbors in Winchester, to leave their table and come running over to our ever-open house to enjoy the fun which the pealing laugh of Colonel Marshall assured them was going on. . . . It is highly creditable to General Sheridan to relate that when he heard of Colonel Marshall's death he sent a detail of his men to endeavor to recover his body, not knowing that it had been rescued by our own men.

The foray in which Tom Marshall had been killed was the Confederates' last effort near Winchester. Rannie, with Terry's brigade, left the Valley December 6 for Richmond and Petersburg, arriving three days later. He had time between trains to visit the Bolling Haxall family before continuing, with the two regiments in his charge, to the besieged Petersburg.

[MEMOIR OF RANDOLPH BARTON]

    We took the train for Petersburg, and upon arriving at Dunlop's Station, four or five miles out of the city, we were embarrassed by finding no orders or directions as to our further movements. I think the conductor and myself are responsible for the indiscretion of ordering the train on to the city. No train had been so far for several months and our appearance was the signal for a tremendous bombardment from the enemy. The novelty of a train had drawn a crowd to the depot, particularly of Negroes, and as the well-directed shells from the enemy began to burst about us a general scattering followed. . . . The disembarkation of the two regiments from that train was perhaps the quickest piece of work of this kind ever recorded in militay annals, and, strange to say, no one was hurt, and the train backed out from this dangerous forbidden ground without injury.

We found the rest of the brigade quite far down on the right of our line about six miles from Petersburg, and there, in a position to reinforce any part of our line, we went into winter quarters.

During the fall of 1864, Vaucluse was in a no-man's land, desolated by the traffic and ravages of both armies. The Yankees had taken Frederick County with invincible numbers, and with the determination to destroy anything that could be of use to the populace or the Confederacy—the policy of devastation that Sherman was implementing in Georgia—the first application in North America of the concept of "total war." Crops, livestock, barns, and farm equipment were systematically destroyed. Columns of flame and smoke rose all over the northern part of the Valley. Confederate raiders continued to operate, enraged by the destruction and attacking anything that moved. Their acts by this time were little more than harassment to the immense Federal forces and sometimes provoked them to more extreme measures. The war escalated in destructiveness and brutality. Somehow, perhaps through James, Mrs. Jones got a letter out to Lucy Parkhill in Florida.

[LETTER OF ANN C. R. JONES TO LUCY R. PARKHILL]

30th of November 1864, Vaucluse

To tell you all that has happened since June, my own dear Cousin, would take long to write & long to read, but I will give you many items, along with the assurance that we have, in comparison with others, been truly blessed, God has cared for us & we adore His Holy Name. I would like you to see how beautifully my Son Strother & his Wife bear the loss of more thousands than I know of. . . .

On the 12th of this month, in a skirmish near Newtown, our dear, dear Tom Marshall was killed, Oh! Lucy such a loss to his five motherless children, such a bitter grief to poor Fanny, I loved him dearly, & he was to me another Grandchild. . . . My darling Randolph was wounded in the battle near Winchester on the 19th of September. . . . I was at Spring Dale when our Army retreated & could just see him for a few moments in the ambulance as he went up the Valley. . . .

On the 19th of October you know our troops made an effort to retrieve their lost battle just a month before, altho' that battle was *nobly* fought, but we were out numbered. We surprised the enemy & were going on victoriously; right through our Meadow the Federals were retreating, Waggons, Ambulances, &c. &c., the Yankee soldiers & Officers in our yard, upon the Platform, & we had every reason to expect a battle *close* upon us, when we saw a stand amongst the enemy, then they turned & went all back again, the day was *lost* to us, the terrific sound of musketry I had never imagined untill that day, cannon I have heard over & over, but not the musquetry so near us.[10] We *took* in the beginning of the day *many* prisoners & they we retained, but altogether it was a sad affair, & much worse at Fishers Hill afterwards. On the 11th of this month our troops came down again, [Gen. Joseph B.] Kershaw's division encamped on our farm, the camp fires looked beautifully, & we felt glad to see our people once more, but alas! the loss to us was heavy, the timber & rails suffered, the last, more from the fire accidentally spreading, than their being taken; the next day they retreated again, & we are still in the hands of the enemy with this difference that for a long time we were in their lines. Sheridan's headquarters were at Belle Grove on the other side of Middletown, where Mrs. Hite used to live, but they broke up & moved near Newtown before Early came down.[11] He it seems came with a view to stop them, & prevent reinforcements being sent to Grant.

Now their whole Army consisting of three Corps is encamped on the other side of Newtown, stretching along I am sure I could not undertake to say where, but in good portions, fortifying themselves, taking stone fencing, Rails, planks, tearing down unhabited houses whenever it suits them, & using *everything* they need, the whole neighborhood nearly seems turned out of doors, enclosures torn down, & the appearance of things *sad indeed*. Houses are searched, things stolen, food taken, but they are strangly kind in giving guards often. My not being in their lines prevents my going to poor Fanny, Sheridan was appealed to for a pass, but positively refused me, & I cannot see them, nor can I go to Winchester, they are not allowed to go from Dr. Davis' to Spring Dale. General Dwight is in Fanny's house, Gen. Wright in Joseph Barton's, Gen. Emery near Mr. Crawford's just in sight of Carysbrooke, Gen. Sheridan at Mahaneys, about three miles this side of Winchester.[12] I am told there is not a rail to be seen at Carysbrooke, I do not *know* how it is on the other side of the Farm but if wanted, they have used; some of their men wanted to board in the house, the Man to whom it is rented declined taking them for want of room & said Mrs. Jones' things were stored in the only room upstairs.[13] They immediately said they would put them all out of doors—it was then raining. But most fortunately they had a guard, & they were prevented. Joseph Barton has had almost everything about him destroyed, has five little children & not a servant except when he can hire one which is not always the case. . . .

Such a time as we had for 5 days [in August], when our troops returned, & the enemy schedadled. They broke into the smoke house, taking nearly all our meat, three pieces of poor little Sue's allowance, they went all over the house, where they chose to go, *my* room was locked, & fortunately they did not insist upon having it opened. One of them seized a Packet from Mary in which she had jewelry, bruised her arm to make her let it go, & carried it off, one of the *kind* ones alluded to, followed him & brought back her Mothers Picture set in gold, & an elegant bracelet Strother had given her when they were married. They shot the fowls, shot the Pigs, & carried them away in Bags, killed altogether *every hog* Strother had for his next year's support, & many shoats, nine or ten Shoats which we succeeded in putting out of the way were all that was left. They found out where the corn had been secreted took almost *every bit*, carried off green corn, took quantities of Hay. . . .

Many persons have suffered far more than we have, poor things!! Our gentlemen are arrested & carried off, old Dr. Stuart Baldwin was twice taken up, & is so feeble they let him go, twice they have been after *poor old Mr. [W. L.] Clark*, but could do nothing with him, Mr. Conrad is now in Prison, I do not know how many have been arrested, some released, & they have never taken my dear Strother, thank Heaven![14] Our enemy *say* they will remain the winter, if so, I cannot see my children. . . . Our minister, however, had to fly to avoid arrest, & I am ignorant of his where abouts, I cannot even *think* of going to Church, & have heard but few sermons since the War began.[15] . . .

They are fearfully desolating every place, they tear down houses, & some poor families have to live on Rations principally that they obtain from the Yankees, others go north.[16] Their Generals are very polite, guards are given continually, & we must yet a while live on hope. . . . One thing has distressed me much, My Darling [Frank]'s Camp Chest was broken open, Clothes taken, his Pistols, his Fine comb, I do not know what else, his shirts I had looked to for [his son] Randolph, we could not buy a piece of cotton to save our lives. Susan's Boxes of glass, china, & books burst open, the outer door of my closet demolished nearly, the next door forced open & the lock broken, both the other doors forced open, they stole from one box 12 silver fruit knives that poor Sue valued so much, & every knife for the table that she had, a beautiful gift cup, & really I do not *know* what else, the dear Child loses every way, but she is in God's hands, & he means it for her good. They took Marshall Jones' shirts & vest, I standing by & remonstrating with them. I succeeded in getting away from a Boy Strother's flannel shirt & it would have been hard to replace it. . . .

A few weeks ago Sarah Ann went off taking her eight children with her, one was in our dining room, one nursed Mary's Baby, & another was in the crop & a 4th becoming useful, but they are gone. Mary has hired a servant, & has a white girl to hold the child, you do not know how bright they all are, the children lend a helping hand where they are able, & you would not believe how cheerfully all is borne. We have had quite a comfort in a crop of Sorgham, delightful Molasses we have, at least we enjoy it very much.[17]

And now dear Lucy, I must tell you of my Precious Bev, the Yankees reached his works, he packed up his things before they got there, & started his Waggon, then rode off himself, but they captured the Waggon, & with it all his clothes, he has nothing but those on his back.[18] I am utterly unable to help him, I can buy nothing, money would lay helpless in my Purse, & *did* untill I lent it out, but he insists on it he will get along, I trust so, but *how*, he thinks he can draw clothes in Staunton. I hope he may, it is so hard to buy anything. Poor Child! he is beginning his work again at another place. May God bless him!

. . . I have not time or space to say all I might think of, dear Fanny, Oh! how I sorrow for her, she is so much grieved, dear dear Tom, he was a gallant fellow as ever stepped, & never spared the risk to his precious life. . . . God bless you all, dear friends. I am obliged to leave other things unsaid. With the truest affection, I am Your friend & Cousin

A.C.R. Jones

Having experienced more than once the Yankee horde's invasion of their home and destruction of much of their farm and its animals, the Jones children at Vaucluse were in a "constant state of panic." Their greatest fear was losing their remaining pet, their pony, but the Jones boys were determined to save it. Fourteen-year-old Barton Jones probably concocted the scheme: They led the pony to the top floor of the house and secreted him in a huge mahogany wardrobe, to which they faithfully carried hay and grass for the duration of the threat.[19]

For the Marshall children at Springdale, all frivolity and merriment had vanished with their father's death. The Union officers living there tried to make Christmas a little brighter by sending to Baltimore for presents for the children, but at the same time, Mrs. Barton needed to order mourning clothes for little Fan. The family sent a joint letter, all on one sheet, to Robby; since it went through Yankee hands, names were abbreviated. Fifteen-year-old Barton Marshall led off, followed by Strother and Martha.

[LETTER OF D. BARTON MARSHALL, W. STROTHER BARTON, AND
MARTHA B. BALDWIN TO ROBERT T. BARTON]

SpringDale Dec 2nd 1864

Dear Uncle Robby

Aunt Mat just received your letter. And one from Cousin [Marshall, crossed
out] J[ones], he says that he is very well, and that *all* is *well*. Dear Uncle Robby
I cannot express my thanks to you, & Uncle S. I love you both a hundred times
more than I ever did, and hope that you will forget all my impertinent speaches
to you. I know the love that my dear Pa had for you, and you for him. But I cannot believe that he is gone from us, and I cannot keep down the feeling of,
Filius patris sui mortem vindicabit![20] Oh Uncle Robby if my tongue could
express my gratitude to you I would do it but I cannot.

C[harlie] D[avis] is very well—we heard from him not long since, he is a
brave as a Lion all ways in front of the battle. Miss S[usie Davis] & her mother
are quite well. . . . We have been very fortunate in getting a gentleman [Gen.
Dwight] to stay with us, he is very kind to us all. He says that when ever Cousin
A[nna] J[ones] wishes to come home, that if Grandma [Barton] will let him
know it that he will contrive a way for her to come. . . .

I hope you will have a pleasant Xmas, but we dont look forward to ours with
much pleasure. I hope my dear Uncle that ere long I will be an open soldier of
our Lord and Saviour Jesus Christ, sometimes I almost trample Satan under my
feet, and then again he throws me down like he did Christian and jared his
sword of faith out of his hand, but he regained it again, and so I believe it will
be with me.[21] Dont think dear Uncle that I am not thinking of what I say but I
mean it. Remember me when I am a good ways from you that the love of the
father has fallen upon the sun. Love to all I must close, your most devoted
nephew

B

Dear Roby

I would like to write but really can not bring my self down to it. We were
very thankful to hear that you all were getting along so well. Don't be uneasy
about us. We are doing well. Give my best love to Sister Jane, Anna, Mr. Shield
and all the children. How I long to see them. Kiss little F[anny] & S[ally] and
tell them it is my Xmas gift to them. I suppose that Charly would be insulted if
I sent him a kiss.[22] Sister Mat will give you all the news.

Your affectionate brother
W. Strother Barton

DEC. 23RD

This is a formidable looking page dear Robby & with my clouded brain it is rather an imposition upon you to attempt to fill it—but I always think home details of any character contain some interest. . . .

I cant tell you dear Robby how delighted we all are at the improvement in your own health & your cheery accounts of dear Sister Jane. I always thought if your mind could be in a *measure* relieved of anxiety you would soon improve, & not for all the help & assistance you have afforded by your presence, would we have you here again under such trying circumstances. I often wish S[trother] was at his comfortable post in S[taunton] & Ma & I battling it out alone hard as it would be to do so.[23] We are more than gratified by your offers of assistance & do appreciate Mr. S[heild]'s generous wishes with regard to the dear children but you know brothers wishes about T[om] & B[arton] & Ma would not give up the girls, little Fan we hope to get to Sister J. some time.[24] I do not see much of the *Sunnysiders* [the Davises] as the sight of them is only obtained by my walking up there a feat I do not often perform these windy days & with the crowded state of the *streets* between ourselves & them but S[usie Davis] & I carry on a brisk note exchange. . . .

Ma would be very much obliged to you if you could send Fanny a black dress of some kind & a little black ribbon to trim her hat. She particularly desires the dress to be cheap, which no doubt will be hard to find.[25] Tell Sister J. we have a beautiful offspring of Cora [the dog]'s for her if she desires it—the colour is not pretty but it is beautifully formed & playful. Associations connected with its parentage are its chief recommendations.

I am not surprised at your favourable opinion of our friends in Ce[cil County]—I shall never forget their kindness & affections as for Dr. [P. C.] W[illiams] & his wife I never expect to thank them enough for their attention to you

M

Despite the family's grief and straitened circumstances, there were some funny moments at Christmas—in some measure due to the Yankees. The family must have regaled Rannie with the stories, which he retold.

[MEMOIR OF RANDOLPH BARTON]

During the winter of 1864–1865, General Dwight, of Sheridan's army . . . occupied Springdale as headquarters, and when Christmas, 1864, was approaching the two Generals sent to Baltimore and filled quite a large box with presents for Colonel Marshall's five orphan children, then at Springdale.[26] It may be amusing to recall one of the incidents of the Christmas dinner of 1864 at Springdale.

General Dwight very civilly asked my mother if he could borrow her best china, for the occasion, and would she superintend the preparation of the dinner, to which Sheridan and his staff were to be invited. As this presented the only opportunity to the family to get anything outside of a very poor meal, she gladly assented and a beautiful dinner at the cost of the Yankees was prepared. The climax of the banquet was to be reached when an old-time Virginia plum pudding, wreathed in a purple flame of burning brandy, was to be carried in. The moment had arrived, the pudding was just going in, when "horribile dictu" the sauce-pan was upset and its toothsome contents went spreading in a thin and pasty stream over the much-used kitchen rag carpet! The ladies in the kitchen were aghast for a moment, but my ever-ready sister "Mat" exclaimed, "Oh, they are nothing but Yankees!" and, proceeding to scrape up the sauce, soon filled the sauce-bowl and the pudding went in. Funny to relate, when the officers had left the room and the family went in to dine on the leavings, they forgot all about the rag-carpet flavor given to the sauce, and enjoyed the plum pudding to their hearts' content.

While these Northern invaders were thus thrusting themselves into my home, I was eating my poor Christmas dinner in the swamps of Dinwiddie County, Virginia. Sweet reflections these reminiscences bring up!

The Union Army built winter quarters near Bartonsville in late 1864.
(James E. Taylor sketchbook, Western Reserve Historical Society)

The Federal Army was encamped over a large area encompassing the Bartonsville farms, well north through Kernstown with many forces in Winchester. General Sheridan's headquarters were in the Logan house on Piccadilly Street. "The Adjutant General has his office in Mr. [Philip] Williams parlour. The Signal Corps Officer has taken possession of the parlour & a chamber at Dr. S. Baldwin's," wrote Mrs. Lee.[27] The town was overwhelmed by the army, and the people were forced to ask the Federal forces for many necessities. The Joseph Bartons had a baby, William, and no fodder for the milk cows they relied on, so Joe wrote the commanding general.

[LETTER OF JOSEPH M. BARTON TO GEN. PHILIP SHERIDAN]

Jan. 9 65
Hanover Lodge

Maj. Genl. Sheridan
General

    The undersigned living in the House recently occupied by Genls Wright & [George] Crook as HeadQuarters has five children under seven years of age The youngest an infant _entirely_ dependent on cows milk. I have two cows but not one thing to feed them on and take the liberty of applying to you for feed for them. I have no means of sending for feed but my House is not five miles from Winchester this side of the Calvary Pickits, & if General you can send feed to me it will relieve from suffering five children & one of them apparent starvation as it is too young to take any thing but milk & this I cannot longer have without feed

Respectfully
yr Obdt svt
Jos. M. Barton

Sheridan did not respond to Joe's plea—despite General Crook's good reference—and the baby died.[28] Not long after, the general attempted to requisition rations for some of the more destitute inhabitants. But Sheridan also took a firmer line with some of the more obstreperous secessionists—Mrs. Lee was finally called to account. The published charge was giving "constant annoyance"—little did the Federals know, seemingly, of the extent of Mrs. Lee's offenses. Aside from her open disdain and hostility, her covert activities included continuous espionage and smuggling of letters, and she had done all boldness and ingenuity could to provide the Confederates with purloined and contraband Yankee supplies. *The Lee family and the hard-pressed but defiant Sherrard ladies were sent through the lines February 25, despite the protests of many in the town. Sheridan's General Dwight had been willing to receive the Christmas package that Robby had sent from Maryland for the family. It eventually elicited a joint thank-you letter from Fanny Marshall, ten, and her younger cousin Stuart Baldwin. Stuart's mother, Martha, appended the local news, the most important being the exiling of the Lees and the Sherrards.*

[LETTER OF FANNY B. MARSHALL, A. STUART BALDWIN, AND MARTHA B. BALDWIN TO ROBERT T. BARTON]

Springdale Feb 24

My dear Uncle Robby

I have been wanting to write to you for a long time. Grandma has been unwell for some weeks. Aunt Mattie has been very busy that she could not well attend to me you dont know how much oblidged to you I am for all the nice things you sent me. I have finished heming my handkerchiefs to day. I have just as many as grand ma. [tear] gets well that she will go to [tear] all. Stuart is going to wite to you and thank you for the nice cravat you send him. I think of you evry night give my best love to Aunt Jane and Sallie Fanny Chaley tell Cousin Anna that Ria is so fat.[29]

Your devoted niece
Fanny Marshall

My dear Uncle Robby:

I must write you a little note to thank you for the pretty cravat you sent me I put it on every Sunday and feel like a man if I dont look like one. I am right well again and fat as a pig. Ma has some hens left that are laying now.

I hope we will have some little chickens this Summer. Give my Best love to Aunt Jane thank her for her nice present. And Cousin Anna too love to uncle Charles and Charley Fanny and Sallie.

your affectionate
nephew Stuart

Feb. 26th

I send you dear Robby in their original forms, dirt & all, Fanny & Stuart's communications. You will certainly have to consider the motive & overlook deficiencies. . . . Each bright day makes me hope for an early start for Ma &

Fan [to Maryland]. There is so much dampness in the air! Ma is not strong enough yet to travel. I have proposed to her to take Fan with her as an escort back since we hope to see Anna before that time. We have not mentioned it to F. as the house could not contain her if we did. And Ma I think has her heart set upon it & as she will only count *half price* we will try to carry out the plan. . . .

We were not a little surprised and dismayed at seeing the Lees and Sherrards *sent through* yesterday. Their train presented quite a surprising spectacle—first an escort then two ambulances then another squad & a four mule wagon containing baggage. They were fortunate in being permitted to carry so much. Various charges brought against them—one was trying to gain *notoriety* by communicating contraband intelligence &c &c. The society of W. is quite reduced & shall miss them a great deal. All join in love———I feel really like a lady with the beautiful handkerchiefs & shall be tempted to [illegible] as a cold in my head to shew them off. The blots are the childrens work. from your attached

M.B.

The Lee-Sherrard party was put down by the Federal troops outside Newtown, and they narrowly escaped having their baggage searched for contraband goods, which Mrs. Lee was carrying in plenty. In Newtown that night, an exhausted Mrs. Lee scribbled in her journal:

[DIARY OF MARY GREENHOW LEE]

We stopped a moment at Springdale. Mattie was dumbfounded. . . . We drove into Newtown & the first thing met Strother & Mrs. Jones. It was delightful to us to see them, knowing he would help us about getting conveyances. . . .

The Joneses took the younger women to Vaucluse that night and the others were "kindly entertained" in Newtown. Next day the exiles went on to Woodstock. "The country is a barren waste. Sheridan—Sheridan, what demon of destruction has possessed you? . . . Barton Jones had his carriage with three of our party. . . . He is the dearest little fellow I ever saw & has more manliness than many men I know."[30] The wanderers spent almost two weeks in Mount Jackson. While there, they were unwitting witnesses to part of the cavalry action in which Charlie Davis was killed.[31] All along the way they were helped by friends and acquaintances who knew of Mrs. Lee's war activities. They arrived in

Staunton on March 14 and immediately found themselves among friends: "Bob Baldwin" and Cary and her mother, Caroline Barton, "Major (alias Jim) Jones," the Catletts, the Striblings, and others who vied to take them in or entertain them.[32]

Robby was benefiting from the peace and tranquillity, as well as decent nourishment and medicine in Maryland, and his mother must have been thankful to see his improvement when she was able to visit. In later years, he attributed his recovery to cod liver oil and sleeping outdoors, but it seems clear that the best tonic was falling in love.

[MEMOIR OF ROBERT T. BARTON]

And now I must tell you of the beginning of an acquaintance that had so much to do with my future life.

Both my sister and Anna did not cease to speak with the utmost enthusiasm of "Katie Knight," of whom my sister Fannie used to talk, and they held out to me as one of my chief pleasures in the future an acquaintance with that young lady.

A few days after my arrival I ventured one afternoon, to mount a little bay pony which belonged to Mr. Sheild, and rode down the road. After going about a mile I passed an open gate and looking up a broad avenue of fine old trees, I saw at the end of it a handsome brick house and on the lawn in front of it several young girls amusing themselves. They seemed to be principally diverted at the pranks of another girl in riding habit and hat, mounted on a fine horse, and who was making him perform in various ways—galloping around the circle, jumping, pretending to ride over the other girls, & c. I walked my horse slowly and watched with much interest the pretty scene. Observing presently that the mounted young lady had turned her horse down the avenue, I rode on, but when I noticed her emerge from the gate and turn her horse's head in the direction from which I had come, I turned back and rode after her. I rode very slowly, while she at first went in a gallop, but happening to look back and see me, she slackened the pace of her horse until I nearly caught up, and then off she went again. This happened several times in the course of the ride to the parsonage, so I had only an opportunity to observe what a trim, well built slender figure she had and how gracefully she sat her horse. I rather guessed who it was, and when she turned in at the parsonage gate I felt sure that I had guessed right. To prevent an embarrassing meeting on horseback, I did not follow her in at the gate, but rode on until the church cut off the sight of her. Then delaying a little I turned back and was glad to find her horse hitched in the yard and the young lady safely in the house. I dismounted at the back door and went at once to the dining room where my sister and Anna Jones were. As I entered the door, my sister said, "Come in Robbie, here is Katie Knight," and thus was the simple introduction so full of momentous consequences to me.

From a little hassock near the fire rose up quickly the sweet figure of a young girl with the rosiest of cheeks and lips, a deep dimple in either cheek, and laughing blue grey eyes. She gave me her hand in cordial salutation, and there, to remain as long as I live, was that pretty picture impressed upon my mind and heart. Ah me, little boy, the sweetest, tenderest and most heavenly of all the things that happen to us in this world, are in happy human loves. They are the only things that do not wear or waste with time and in the keen enjoyment and recollection of which there is no sting or bitter taste. Beyond the fate of most men I have been blessed with two such loves, and he who tells you that loyalty to and love of the living involves forgetfulness of the dead, never did love with all his heart, and mind and soul.

The little prejudice which the oft-repeated praises of this sweet girl had excited in me against her, vanished in that meeting, and from that moment I believe I was wholly the slave of those tender expressive eyes. If I should tell you now that acquaintance grew and ripened into love I should be but telling you the same old old story, which I trust you will read back in your own happy experience. Certain it is that as I write these lines, full as my heart is of you and your loving girlish mother, my eyes fill and my thoughts go quickly back to those days when the sun seemed to shine brighter and the air to be pure and life to put away its care and be full of zest and hope and love when I was where I could see her smile and listen to the murmur of her gentle voice.

My life in Cecil Co. Md., while it was all the time under the shadow of care about those at home and about my brothers Rannie and Bolling who were in the army—the two remaining of six soldier brothers—and while the fear that the Southern cause was on the wane pressed heavily upon me, yet there were two happy causes operating to keep up my spirits and to make me very glad indeed. One was the gradual but very apparent restoration of my health, and the other was my love for that sweet girl. . . .

A great deal of my time I spent in reading, both law and miscellaneous books, and after so many years of hardship, danger, deprivation and sickness, those winter days were joyous times of rest to me. My mother, deeply concerned about both my sister and myself, managed to get permission and paid us a visit at the rectory in January or February, 1865.[33] She was, of course, delighted to find us both doing well and me so much improved as to surprise her. Anna, who was restive to get within communication with her lover [Dr. Cornelius Baldwin] in the army, went back with my mother, and I accompanied them to Baltimore, where I spent a week with the McKims, the family of Bob McKim.[34]

Leaving Springdale in the wake of the Confederate retreat in September, Bolling made his way to Richmond where the VMI reopened in early October for military duties. (The institute later relocated to the Richmond Almshouse and attempted to resume an academic schedule.) In October, he and some other cadets were assigned to a new unit, the 1st Foreign (Irish) Battalion, and were made officers.[35] The battalion was called "foreign" because it consisted of Federal prisoners of war, principally Irish immigrants, who "volunteered" to serve the Confederacy in order to get out of prisoner of war camps. The unit, envisioned primarily as doing provost guard and engineer duty, was raised in South Carolina and thither the young officers went in early November. They found their battalion in Columbia, encamped in a field next to Mrs. James Chesnut's house. The local populace was apprehensive about the 1,100 troops, thinking them "traitors" and "renegades"; but the officers, "splendid young fellows," were frequently entertained by Mary Chesnut and others.[36] By Christmas, the war, personified by Gen. William Tecumseh Sherman, was fast approaching Columbia. On December 23, the young officers petitioned the Confederate War Department to reassign the battalion to Texas so that the men would not be exposed to more "risks than ordinarily fall to the lot of a Soldier."[37] The department was not swayed by the fact that these turncoats would be shot if captured by their former comrades-in-arms. The petition was turned down January 19, but the battalion had left Columbia several days before to join Gen. Joseph E. Johnston's army.

To most Southerners, it was apparent that the Confederacy could not last much

Bolling W. Barton's carte de visite *was taken in New York in July 1865, a few days before his departure for Europe.*
(Edith Barton Sheerin)

longer. Men, equipment, and morale were exhausted. Rannie in the trenches at Petersburg knew it, although with a mixture of denial and unquenchable optimism, he applied for a cadetship in the Confederate Army.

[MEMOIR OF RANDOLPH BARTON]

Our life in camp during the winter of 1864 and 1865 occurs to me now to have been unusually dull, dreary and monotonous. I think the spirit of the people at home had begun to break. So many had been killed, so many widows and orphans peopled the land. Food was so hard to get. The locusts of Egypt seemed small in number compared to the ever-enlarging Yankee army, and I think I can now trace the fatal despondency of our people step by step. We drilled, reorganized, preached, prayed, sang and played cards, and so whiled away the gloomy waiting for the bloody springtime. I remember one night riding up with General Terry to pay a friendly visit to General Lee. We found him occupying a house outside of Petersburg, and his reception and entertainment of us was as natural, dignified and interesting as if we had been seated under the roof of his beloved Arlington. About this time I was invited, or if not invited, my inclinations were ascertained relative to my accepting a position upon the staff of General [William] Mahone. I took the matter under consideration and among others consulted my cousin, Colonel Charles Marshall, aide-de-camp to General Lee, who even before his great kindness to me as a young lawyer, I regarded as an adviser, counsellor and friend. The result of my inquiries was a refusal to consider the change, although it meant promotion. January passed and Grant's impatience began to show itself. On the morning of the 6th of February, 1865, the alarming long-roll called our command to arms and we hastened down the road about a mile to Hatcher's Run. The alarm proved to be false and we slowly returned to camp.

About three o'clock the alarm again rang out. . . . We again turned down to Hatcher's Run, and found that the enemy was advancing in force. We quickly went into line of battle and advancing, soon were engaged in sharp action. . . . Riding to the right, [I] was told that the enemy was flanking us in that direction; continuing my course to ascertain the facts, I suddenly found myself face to face with the blue Yankee line of battle at a distance which I hardly think could have exceeded fifty feet. Intervening pines and cedars probably saved me from capture or death, but before I could retreat I was fired upon, and I felt the ball ripping through my leg. I whirled my horse [Mary Stuart] around and, upon my own responsibility directing the men to fall back (General Terry being then, I think, on the left of the line, and not knowing the condition of affairs on the right), I started back. I soon found myself near a stream, the banks of which were covered with tangled boughs, making the approach even on foot very difficult. I had no time to go either up or down the stream, for our line was fast falling back before the rapidly pursuing enemy. My horse seemed to appreciate the difficulty, and when I touched her with my spur, she rose nobly to the occasion, and crawling and climbing, surmounted the obstructions and gallantly leaping the stream landed in safety on the other side. The pursuit stopped at about that point, and in a little while I was able to examine the extent of my wound. I found the ball had cut through a track about six inches in length and almost exactly parallel with and a few inches below the wound of September preceding.

The ball did not tear the flesh as severely as the September ball, and I at once saw that, barring the absolute inability to walk and the increasing inability to ride, and the inevitable soreness and stiffness, I was again in for an agreeable furlough. With considerable satisfaction, therefore, I rode back to camp with Dr. Cornelius Baldwin, a surgeon in our brigade, retired to my tent, had my wound carefully dressed and bandaged, ate some supper and went to sleep. . . .

The Battle of Hatcher's Run marked a Federal advance, increasing the Confederates' difficulties in defending the lengthy Petersburg-Richmond perimeter. Rannie's difficulties were momentarily reduced to choosing between invitations for his next convalescence.

[MEMOIR OF RANDOLPH BARTON]

The next morning I went up to Petersburg in an ambulance. . . . Taking the train for Richmond, I was seriously embarrassed where to go. The Barton and Bolling Haxalls, and the family of Mr. Thomas Barton, had all affectionately exacted from me when I had last been in Richmond a promise the next time I was wounded to stay with them. Weighing the various promises, I concluded that I would go to the Barton's, and was in an ambulance with directions to the driver to go to their house, when I observed Jimmy Thompson (gallant Jimmy Thompson, Major of Chew's Battalion of artillery, and killed the April following at High Bridge) hurrying down to the depot.[38] Hailing him, he said he was just on the lookout for me, with a peremptory requirement that I should come straight to cousin Bolling's, and thither I went, reaching the house just as Lou turned in at the gate.[39] The welcome I received was inexpressibly cordial. Two or three gathered around me and I hobbled and limped on one foot into the

The Bolling W. Haxall house on Franklin Street. Built in 1858, its fashionable Italianate style must have made the Barton boys feel like country cousins.
(Cook Collection, Valentine Museum)

house, upstairs, and from the bleak discomforts of camp a few hours before, I was ushered into the luxuries of the "blue room."

The person who has never seen Niagara, has never seen a cataract, and the person who did not have an opportunity to enjoy the hospitality of cousin Bolling's family as I did, has never enjoyed unbounded kindness. I was disabled, fairly, honorably, thoroughly. I could with difficulty get from my bed to a luxurious chair by an open fire. For some time I could not bear to have my leg suspended even, and could not use crutches. But I had no severe suffering. . . . Kindness of all sorts streamed upon me. My room was frequently filled with visitors, of both sexes, and particularly do I remember the pranks of Bolling Haxall, who then quite a boy [14], would by the hour stretch himself upon the rug and detail his daily doings. . . . Lou and her friends . . . would sit with me, and beguile what were supposed to be my weary hours. Among other visitors I remember Mrs. John B. Baldwin, who cautioned me against the "danger" of my position, and John M. Robinson, who, using a military metaphor, spoke of the fairness of the field for an engagement. As I gradually recovered and resumed the use of crutches I would go to early morning Lenten services and would, with many other in like plight, hobble up the aisle of crowded St. Paul's Church. . . .

Before returning to the army I made a very brief visit to Staunton, and then, with some melancholy, set out for Petersburg. It was on the occasion of this stay in Richmond that I suddenly and impulsively determined to study law if I survived the war. I must candidly admit that having heard the mother of a charming girl, both of whom I desired to propitiate, say that she liked lawyers, my resolution was then and there formed. The ruse failed to work, but I never for a moment faltered in my purpose afterward.

But to have two irons in the fire, I sought and obtained a cadetship in the regular army of the Confederate States, and on the 24th of April, 1865, the day on which I reached the age of twenty-one, I had an engagement to go to Richmond for the purpose of standing an examination for a Lieutenancy in the regular army.[40] Circumstances, as will be seen, prevented. Suppose I had gone and the Confederacy had succeeded? "There is a Providence that shapes our ends, rough hew them as we may." . . .

I found our command had moved up to the line of the northeast of Petersburg when I returned, and was occupying that portion known as the "crater," from the desperate sortie made by the Yankees in July previous.

Capt. Randolph J. Barton in a carte de visite *taken in Richmond in 1865; it was probably burned in later years by his cigar.*
(Ann L. Barton Brown)

Our brigade stretched along the brink of the chasm made by the explosion of eight thousand pounds of powder when Grant had undermined that point, and looking down into the great funnel-shaped abyss, I fancied I could see fragments of the miserable Yankees and negroes buried in that horrible charnel-house made by the gentlemanly, unfortunate, pretentious and incompetent Burnside. The picket lines were very close together, seeming not more than one hundred yards. One of my duties was to go along these lines every morning; a tacit understanding prevailing that neither side would open fire in the day time without notice, I did so in safety and sometimes exchanged with the Yankees the ordinary morning salutations. But any moment we were liable to the warning to "look out," and so trenches five or six feet deep had been cut in the ground behind our breastworks in every direction, for safe communication from point to point. We also had bomb-proofs into which we would rush when the periodical shelling and mortar firing occurred. . . .

On the morning of the 25th of March, an hour or so before daybreak, we made an assault upon the Yankee fort "Steadman" or Hare's Hill, under General Gordon, to whom General Lee had sent about half the army. . . . The place of attack was selected because the picket lines were exceedingly close at that point, and although the lines were fortified by earthworks of a most formidable kind, and in addition by sharpened fence rails, the points elevated about four feet from the ground and the other ends fastened securely in the ground, it was hoped that by a sudden rush we could overcome the pickets, cut away this "chevaux-de-frise," break into the enemy's line and, turning right and left, effect a lodgment with a strong force at this most important point of Grant's line, and thus by threatening his line of communication with City Point, relieve our sorely pressed right flank. The surprise of the enemy was perfect as on that grey, cold and gloomy morning about four o'clock we stole out of our lines, stealthily crossing the open plateau, and preceded by axemen who cut away the obstructions, burst upon the sleeping and unsuspecting foe. I remember we very soon had many prisoners, among them Brigadier-General McLaughlin, who I think I relieved of his sword, not to use, but simply to perfect his capture.[41] He was the sourest and maddest man I ever saw but he was helpless. Not all the Yankees were asleep, for I was told at the time that some of our men coming upon a bomb-proof and looking through the single pane of glass which gave it day-light, surprised four officers who had spent the night at cards by firing into their midst. The attack had been very successful up to that point, but just then our guides lost their way and our men, instead of developing right and left, crowded into a confined space, upon which the Yankees began to concentrate a hail of shot and shell. Before long the order came to regain our own lines, and here the greatest danger followed. From long occupation of the ground the Yankees had every point reduced to a science, and so the open field over which we had come, and over which we had to return, became a most dangerous gauntlet. An unfortunately large number of our men preferred the ills they had, stormed as they were in the hostile works, to risking the return. I suggested to General Terry to precede me and, arriving in our lines, be ready to rally the returning men. Possibly I wanted to see how the experiment of his crossing the field would work before I tried it. He got across but suffered considerably from a wound by concussion. Just as I approached the breastworks, from the inside of the Yankee fort over which I had to climb before making the run across the field, a shell struck the very place I had intended to climb and threw a column of earth into the air. A moment later I climbed over and then marbles could have been played upon the skirts of my coat. On my way over I received a blow on my right hip. It did not break the skin: indeed, it did not even tear my clothes, but it was a decided blow, either from a piece of shell, or a glancing or spent bullet, but sufficiently decided to justify me in counting it as the seventh time I had been struck in battle. I however regained our line, and busied myself in aiding in reforming the men. This, I think, was the last effort of any importance made by the Army of Northern Virginia of an aggressive kind. Grant angrily bombarded us a good deal that day, and then we settled down into the usual routine of the siege. I remember going into Petersburg about that time, one Sunday night, to St. Paul's. . . . I doubt whether such a scene was ever presented in the history of the world. The church was crowded, pews, galleries and possibly the aisles, with citizens, men and women, and particularly with soldiers. The beautiful Episcopal service was rendered as if in profound peace; the eloquent preacher was equal to the unexampled situation; and yet, in the death-like silence which prevailed, as effectively and solemnly he would occasionally pause, we could hear around the city the pattering of musketry and the occasional angry boom of a cannon.

About this time I received a letter from General Evans, commanding our Division, which, as it came spontaneously from him, I have carefully preserved, and here give a copy:

"Private."

Petersburg, Va., March 30, 1865

"Captain:—I have thought of seeing you personally during the last three days, but various causes have prevented me.

Private

Petersburg Va
Mar 30, 1865 —

Captain

I have thought of seeing you personally, during the last two or three days, but various causes have prevented me:—

I have been so much impressed with your gallant bearing and zeal in the Cause that I desire to recommend your promotion either on the General Staff or to some Command. I do not know who Genl Terry has selected for the field officers of his new Regiments, or whether he has selected them at all. If he has not I think you ought to have a field office in one of them; If he has, then I shall forward a recommendation for your promotion on the Staff & my object in writing to you, is to ask you to lay aside delicacy for a moment, and tell me, whether you have any preferences, or in what direction your wishes lead you; — Let me hear from you as early as practicable =

Sincerely yours
C. A. Evans

Gen. C. A. Evans's letter to Capt. R. J. Barton. (Randolph Barton, Jr.)

I have been so much impressed with your gallant bearing and zeal in the cause that I desire to recommend your promotion either on the general staff or to some command. I do not know who General Terry has selected for the field officers of his new regiments, or whether he has selected them at all. If he has not, I think you ought to have a field office in one of them; if he has, then I shall forward a recommendation for your promotion on the staff, and my object in writing to you is to ask you to lay aside delicacy for a moment, and tell me, whether you have any preferences or in what direction your wishes lead you.

Let me hear from you as early as practicable.

Sincerely yours, etc.,
C. A. EVANS

The address is "Confidential."
"Captain Barton, A. A. G. Terry's Brigade."[42]

As I have written these recollections, I have occasionally feared that some reader of a skeptical disposition might suspect me at times of blowing my own horn a little loud, and so I offer this documentary evidence for what it is worth.

About the same time that I received this letter, my old General [James A.] Walker, who had been placed in command of a Division, sent for me, and after some little conversation, said, "Barton how would you like to have a star on the collar of your jacket?" which, although a round-about way of putting it, meant how would I like to be a major.[43] Of course I expressed the pleasure it would give me, and he then and there appointed me, subject to confirmation by the authorities, Assistant Adjutant and Inspector-General of his Division. I immediately joined him and remained with him until the surrender at Appomattox.

On Sunday night, April 2, 1865, the pressure upon General Lee's line became unbearable, and the evacuation of Petersburg having been determined upon, the movement began, at nine o'clock. For the first time since the morning of May 5, 1864, when the Wilderness campaign opened did the army of Northern Virginia turn its back to the enemy. But the end was at hand. Silently and gloomily the army in long columns marched out from the breastworks, and marched through the desolate streets of Petersburg. We had little to say, the intuition of every man told him that Richmond was about to fall, and we all wondered, what next. We marched all night, and on the way encountering General Evans I rode with him for some miles, availing myself of the opportunity to thank him for his cordial letter, the purposes of which seem to have been anticipated by General Walker's action.

I recall few incidents of great interest on the retreat. I know the weather was in keeping with our spirits; that we were most scantily fed; that I checked my hunger for some time with parched corn; that we trudged through mud and rain, from time to time repelling the enemy and that we had little sleep or rest. One of the Federal Cavalry Generals, [Bvt. Brig. Gen. William M.] Gregg, (there being two of them) on the way was rewarded for his temerity in attacking us, by being captured. He was put in charge of our brigade and I rode at his side for some time. He was profoundedly disgusted with his luck. The idea of having his brigade hovering upon our flanks and he a captive as liable to be shot by his own men as we were. At Sailors [Saylers] Creek the enemy came upon our rear in great force, and a "sauve qui-peut" engagement ensued. Many of our troops and wagons were captured. I recall very distinctly the condition of affairs as I approached the only bridge across the narrow but deep stream. . . . Every one was crowding to this only crossing, and as bad luck would have it a caisson, or wagon broke down just on the bridge. Upon observing this disaster I turned away and rode down the stream, which although as I have said was narrow, had precipitous banks, cut prone down through the soil of the meadow bottom, looking for some place to cross. Every thing was in flight and the enemy closely pursuing, and I had not much time to deliberate or much choice as to what I should do. Desperately I ran my mare, "Mary Stuart," at the stream and taking a flying leap she reached the opposite bank with her feet well up and struggling to the top I thus escaped capture as beyond the stream our men again reformed.

Near Farmville the Yankees again pressed us with insolent closeness and our men savagely turned upon them and boldly drove them back. I remember with very great satisfaction that on this, the last action in which I was exposed, I happened to be on the line on horse-back and have still the pleasant thrill of being with a successful charge. As the enemy retreated and I rode back of our line I encountered General Lee, who seeing from what point I had come and having observed the good behavior of our men, said to me "Go back and tell my men that is the way I like to see them act, not to let those people run over them." I observed on the march some "discretion" shown by very, very brave men, but in the main all did well.

On the night of the 8th we knew at headquarters that the "jig was up" and having come up with our wagon I exchanged my worst suit of clothes for my best and so after the restless, uneasy night I appeared on the morning of the 9th, the day of the great catastrophe, well mounted and well dressed. As soon as it was light enough to see, every one was up; we knew something final would be reached that day. Firing commenced in all directions, front and rear, be-

Union artist Alfred Waud was with Gen. George A. Custer when he received the white towel from Maj. Robert M. Sims at Appomattox. (Library of Congress)

tween our skirmishers and those of the enemy, and after a while I found myself with General Walker in the village of Appomattox Court House, a hamlet of only a few houses. The enemy had succeeded in throwing a large force across our path, as we struggled to reach Lynchburg, and although the last action of our men was to drive back this force and capture a battery, their ever increasing numbers made further effort useless.

A group of officers had assembled in the road, General Gordon in their midst, when an officer galloped up, whom I now know to have been Major R. M. Sims, with orders to General Gordon to cease hostilities and send out a flag of truce requesting the enemy to do the same.[44] General Gordon directed Major Sims to carry this request to the nearest commanding Federal officer, and ordered me and some one else who I think was Willie Myers of Richmond (quite satisfactorily identified as the husband of the lovely Mattie Paul of Petersburg) a Major, to accompany Major Sims. We dashed off, passing soon through our enfeebled line of battle and then through our amazed and wondering skirmishers and approached the Yankee line of sharp shooters, who not at first understanding our mission, directed their dangerous shots at us. I suggested to Myers (if he was the third officer) or Sims to wave a white flag of some kind, whereupon rooting in his haversack he produced a towel and upon exhibiting it, the shots at us ceased and we soon entered the Yankee lines, with the cold chill that sudden and horrid transition would naturally bring. Meeting a Lieutenant Colonel, he turned and rode with us to General Custer, who upon ascertaining our errand, replied excitedly and testily, "Tell your commanding officer that I will hear of nothing but an unconditional surrender, that I will be into his trains at once."

Feeling like strangling him, we turned to go back. While the interview was being held, one of Custer's officers secured the towel as a memento, and since Custer's death at the hands of the Indians, I have observed its production at a banquet of the survivors of his command. A portion of the towel is among the Custer relics in the Hall of History of the National Museum, Washington, D.C.[45]

We reported our interview to General Gordon, and were immediately dispatched in another direction to stop the advance of General Ord. We reached his splendid line of battle and rode along its front for some distance, the eager Yankee soldiers asking me as I followed behind Major Sims, "Is that Lee? Is that Lee?", to which inquiries I preserved a contemptuous silence. The line of battle was halted. The concentrating folds of the great Federal army were arrested, and the war was over.

The details of the paroling of officers and the final arrangements for the dispersion of our army are too well told by Taylor, Long and Lee for me to repeat them. Our division at the time appointed marched in front of a Yankee division, which presented arms as we filed by, the officers saluting and we returning the salute, halted, faced to the front, "ordered" and "stacked" arms, broke ranks at the command and the transition from soldiers of four years, to civilians, was complete.

Partings touching and pathetic followed. Forming a party of a dozen we started for the James River; crossing it upon a raft, we rode many miles down the tow path of the canal, now a railroad, and passing through Nelson and Albemarle and riding through the long [Virginia Central] railroad tunnel under the Blue Ridge we reached Staunton.

News of the surrender traveled slowly to Winchester and Staunton. Mrs. Lee heard, and refused to believe, the first reports received April 11, and the many contradictory rumors kept hope afloat until the fourteenth. Rannie, Bob Burwell, and other Winchester boys arrived by Easter, the sixteenth, and supplied the mournful details. "We have been seated around the fire in our parlour to-night with our home boys, Bob, Ranny, Dr. [R. F.] Baldwin, Willie Barton &

Appomattox Court House, Va.

April 10th, 1865.

THE BEARER, *Capt R. D. Barton* of Co. *A. Q.* Regt. of *Early's Div*, a Paroled Prisoner of the Army of Northern Virginia, has permission to go to his home, and there remain undisturbed. *He is entitled to take with him two (2) private horses.*

J. G. Walker
Brig Gen Comdg Div

Rannie's signature on his parole demonstrates why he was listed in the Appomattox roster as "R. D. Barton." (Ann L. Barton Brown)

Marshal[l] Jones. Bob & Ranny are staying with us."[46] At Appomattox the roster of the 2nd Virginia Infantry listed sixty-two men (of whom thirty-one were in line of battle), and the 33rd Virginia listed only fifteen (of whom six were in line of battle). Aside from Rannie, the following "home boys" were among those who surrendered at Appomattox: Assistant Surgeon Cornelius ("Nepe") Baldwin, 33rd Virginia Infantry; Second Lt. John ("Johnny") H. Baldwin, Company A, 1st Virginia Battalion Infantry; Pvt. W. Ludwell ("Lud") Baldwin, Rockbridge Artillery; First Lt. E. Holmes Boyd, Ordnance Officer, Terry's Brigade. Rannie and some of the others continued north a few days later.

[MEMOIR OF RANDOLPH BARTON]

Within a day or two I was at Springdale and my sword was turned into a pruning hook, and may this transformation be perpetual.

Thus I have reviewed a period of my life filled with excitement, sorrow, danger and delight in quick alternations. The God Mars and Goddess Venus condescended to give me some samples of their attributes, dealing with me on the whole with reasonable consideration, for which I tender my grateful and respectful acknowledgments I wish unaffectedly to disclaim having evinced any special courage in battle or any marked faithfulness to my duty. Many men were as much exposed as I was and stuck to their posts as faithfully as I did and yet escaped unscathed. I, however, believe that a staff officer of a brigade is more exposed than anyone else in battle. Field officers of regiments invariably dismounted in our war, and staff officers of divisions and corps were one degree further removed from the line of fire. To my position on the staff I attribute the frequency with which I was struck. But then I see men who occupied exactly

my position and escaped harmless. Providence took care of me and I might
have turned the life that was spared to me to better account, but I fear that as
danger disappeared, callousness measurably took its place. In one respect I
believe my experience was unique. I doubt whether any soldier in either army
had this combination—excellent health, a creditable post, frequent disabling
wounds, kind friends, luxurious retreats and exceptionally attractive acquaintances of the female persuasion. Is it surprising that the war period is not
remembered as one of unmixed evil, but that its darkness is dotted over with
spots of brightness upon which the sun seems to have concentrated all of its
rays? As a choice, I would not wish to repeat the four years, but if war comes to
this land again and my boys are called into it, I only hope that as with me its
ruggedness was so often softened, so with them their lines may as often fall in
pleasant places.[47]

XV

The Devastated Valley at Peace

THE FAMILY DISPERSED

When reports of Lee's surrender were verified in Winchester, Gen. Winfield S. Hancock, in command of the town, ordered a great illumination in honor of the victory. Many citizens refused to comply, and the celebration that night was abruptly cut short by the shocking news of Lincoln's assassination. The bands were stilled and the lights were extinguished.

Gradually the soldiers made their way home. General Hancock sent out cavalry groups to parole returning Confederates at different points in the Valley. Bev Jones and Willie Barton were paroled in Winchester April 23, and Willie returned to his brother Joe's to farm. Strother Barton's war had been over for some time, and his mind was on the spring planting, the fine grass, and a horse he had bought instead of a courting coat. He duly reported on their joint interests to Robby in Maryland.

Upon the news of peace, Robby's first thought was to go home. In late April, he left Katie Knight with an "understanding" perhaps, but not with an engagement.

As soon they could, those divided by wartime circumstances were reunited, Jane Sheild visiting Springdale early in the summer. Bolly had been paroled in Burksville, Virginia, April 23, on his way home from the Carolinas, and apparently paused in Richmond to renew his acquaintance with the Bolling Haxall family. They were quite taken with their young cousin, and Bolling Haxall, his fortune relatively unimpaired, assumed responsibility for the education of his cousin David's youngest son. Bolly had decided to study medicine, and it was

determined to send him to Europe to be
educated, along with the Haxalls' sons
William and Bolling. In the immediate aftermath of the war, conditions were unsettled, and for the period of the Haxall
men's absence, Rannie agreed to prolong a
visit to their Orange County plantation,
Springfield, to provide protection for the
ladies. This surely was a pleasurable duty
as he was still enchanted by Louisa Haxall,
daughter of the house, whom he had met in
1863. Bolly made his rendezvous with the
Haxalls in New York before sailing to
France, and was thrilled with his brief visit.

Bolling Walker Haxall.
(Bolling W. Haxall)

[LETTER OF BOLLING W. BARTON TO RANDOLPH J. BARTON]

We have been a good deal over this greatest of cities and I am almost dumbfounded with the extent and the magnificence of the buildings, I won't attempt
to describe. . . . I expect to visit this evening the Central Park, Greenwood
Cemetery and other places of interest.[1] Cousin Bolling has supplied us with
very nice clothing of every description. We are staying at the York Hotel but
take our meals at the different restaurants in the city, some of which are magnificent. We visited Taylors confectionery establishment this morning. I never
imagined anything so grand. . . .

I have had my cartes de visite taken today and will get them tomorrow, some
of them I will send to you to take home or dispose of them as you like, *of course
all want one.*[2] . . .

*Rannie stayed at Springfield until mid-August. On his return to Winchester
from his prolonged visit, he acted on his earlier decision, and began reading law
with Judge Richard Parker. He and Johnny Williams were both admitted to the
bar in Frederick County in June 1866, but the dislocation of the Reconstruction
years and the desolation of the Valley must have prompted Rannie's decision to
leave Winchester. Later that year, he decided to try his fortunes in Baltimore,
drawn as were many Virginians to the only Southern city unscathed by the war
and familiar from the past. It was not too far from home, familiar if only by connections and reputation.*

Hard times had come to the Joneses at Vaucluse. Strother Jones had almost certainly put all his equity in Confederate bonds and money, and as Grandmother Jones had foreseen, "the abolitionist measures make this a large place to cultivate and may compel a change."[3] *As early as October 1865, they were forced to take a mortgage on the farm.*

Strother and Robby struggled to make the best of the remaining land and law practice inherited from their father.

[MEMOIR OF ROBERT T. BARTON]

You will read in the different books on the subject a better account than I can give you of the condition of affairs about Winchester, when the war closed, and what it was then, it was generally throughout the South.

The slaves had been set free and by all sorts of airs those who had not run away (with some admirable exceptions) and those who having run away had now returned when assured of their freedom, were with many airs and graces, asserting their equality with their late masters: the Freedmans Bureau, established by the Federal Government and supported by the military, officered by the very worst element of [illegible] who had drifted in the wake of the armies, under the guise of feeding, clothing and educating the darkies, was sustaining them in all their arrogant pretensions and encouraging them to make issues with the whites, all of which were sustained in favor of the negroes by the powers that were: no courts whatever were in existence at which even this form of justice could be secured to a white Southerner.

The fences and woods were wholly destroyed, the stock and farming implements all gone, no crops in the ground, many of the houses and barns destroyed or decreped from long want of repairs, and as camps were still in all parts of the Country, the fields and yards were as common and as much used by the public as the highways. The presence of near ten thousand troops in the neighbourhood of Winchester put in circulation some currency and, as now peace was restored, they needed many things which now this exhausted Country could begin to supply.[4] Aid societies were formed in Baltimore which sent farming implements, seeds, etc., to the farmers, and the young men coming home from the army with their horses, and eager and willing to work themselves, right speedily something of a corn and potatoe crop was put out in the unfenced fields. The land having lain fallow and the season being good, responded promptly to the plow and when the fall came there was at least some provision for the winter. I recall how earnestly all this interested me at Springdale, and how I stimulated my brother Strother, who had the farm in charge, to greater and greater efforts to make a crop.

The military took all things political in charge and pretended to restore civil government. In May, shortly after my return, the officials ordained a popular election (so called) for officers of the county, but confined the candidates and voters to those who could swear that not since January 1, 1865 had they given aid and comfort to the Confederacy. As I had been in Maryland during that time and on parole not to give aid or comfort and in fact had given none, it was decided by my friends that I could and ought to take the oath, and I did so. Thereupon I was nominated by the Southern element for the office of County Clerk which was then regarded as quite a lucrative office, as indeed it is yet. Other persons similarly situated were nominated for the other offices and the Anti-Southern element also put their ticket in the field. The election was held by the military and in spite of the very restricted suffrage our ticket polled a decided majority. But that did not avail, for the military arbitrarily threw out all votes, the sincerity of whose oaths they assumed to doubt, and failing thus to overcome the majority for me at length excluded me on the ground that having once taken an oath of allegiance to the Confederate States (which in fact I had never done) I was an alien and not being a citizen was not eligible to election. So they installed my opponent Mr. C. W. Gibbens who had been a tailor in Winchester, and a persistent "Union Man" and hater of the Southern people.

I was greatly chagrined, of course, but I was powerless and had to submit. The blow was harder because I saw in the rewards of that office a comfortable support and I hoped a speedy realization of the constant dreams I had about returning in triumph to Maryland and bringing home my sweetheart.

What I regarded as a dreadful blow was really a blessing to me. It would have been a great misfortune to me in after life, had I put myself in the tread-mill of that office instead of relying on my own resources and carving out my place and name at the bar.

That election business over I devoted myself eagerly to studying law. I was still very delicate and in the fall of 1865 I had two slight hemorrhages, but I gradually improved and having strong faith in my ultimate recovery I was not much discouraged by even these serious setbacks.

In the latter part of August I was examined by Judge [Richard] Parker at Winchester and Judge [Lucas P.] Thompson at Staunton and given a license to practice law. I was admitted to the bar by the County Court at its September term, 1865, and I opened an office in the same room which had been occupied by my father and which is the room I still occupy at the time of this writing.[5]

Of my little personal property at Springdale all that was left was a cow and two Colts, which were preserved through the kindness of the officers who occupied the Springdale house. The colts had grown into good horses. One of them my brother Strother rode to Staunton in September and it was stolen from him, so I lost that. The other horse I used to ride in and out from Springdale each day, until finding the exercise too much for me I sold the horse and determined to stay in town. . . .

Robby took a room in town with Mr. W. C. Meredith, the Episcopal minister, visiting his family frequently. Doubtless Robby and Strother were both caught up in the complications of their father's estate—not only the debts inherited from their uncle Richard but also the unfinished legal business that could never be resolved due to the economic upheaval of the war. Particularly the failure of the Valley Bank in Winchester after it had refugeed to Farmville "so impaired [David W. Barton's] assets which would otherwise have been amply sufficient to pay all of his debts, that his estate is insolvent and some part at least of his debts will go unpaid."[6] *Robby was involved in litigation relating to his father's estate off and on for thirty years.*

During 1866, Robby had little communication with Katie as there was no formal relationship between them, but he did not cease to think of her.

[MEMOIR OF ROBERT T. BARTON]

During this time I had no letters from my sweetheart, for she felt that she had no right to write to me, but I managed now and then to send her a letter by a friendly hand, and I was delighted to hear of the pleasure which they gave her. The beginning of the practice of law is a slow and most discouraging thing, and my experience was like that of most young men. But commencing to practice, as I did, just after the upheaval and at the restoration which succeeded the war, and full of zeal and energy, I had something of the advantage of a man commencing in a wholly new Country. I got first one piece of business and then another, and attending to each faithfully I got more business until I began to establish quite a practice. I made more than a support the first year and I was so far successful that in August, 1866 at the sale of my father's law office I bought it for the sum of $750.00, paying $250.00 down, and as I remember I anticipated the deferred payments. No purchase or acquirement of property which I have made since, has made me half so happy as the pleasure which the sense of ownership of this office gave me, both because it was my own and because it had been my father's.

Among other matters of business which were entrusted to me was the affairs of my cousin Anna Jones at New Orleans. The war and mismanagement had greatly confused the condition of her father's estate and it became necessary for some one to go there to set things right, and I was selected to do it.

In March 1866, Robby met Marshall Jones in New Orleans where the latter had gone for a prolonged stay when the war was over. Robby managed to retrieve and separate Anna's affairs from her brother's, having observed that Marshall was running with a "hard crowd" involved in "all sorts of dissipation," and that his life was one of "idleness and self-indulgence."[7] Robby returned by way of Richmond, where he visited the Barton Haxall family.

[MEMOIR OF ROBERT T. BARTON]

From Richmond I came back to Winchester, bringing with me a good deal of money for Anna Jones and a very satisfactory settlement of her affairs. She was only waiting for this to marry Dr. Cornelius Baldwin, and in a short time after my return they were married [in April 1866]. A year of apparent happiness and then death in childbirth ended the cares of this bright young girl. Marshall Baldwin, now of Kansas City, Mo., was the child.[8]

The spring and summer of 1866 was spent by me in diligent studying and reading, for I greatly felt the lack of education which was due to the interruptions of the war. Indeed this is a lack which I have never ceased to endeavour to supply, both as to my professional and general education. The stimulus of my knowledge of what I lacked has made me a much better student than I would otherwise have been, and has led me to find relief in books from all the cares of life.

During this time I used to enjoy frequent trips at night to Springdale and I not unfrequently spent my Sundays there after the morning service.

Among my associates in Winchester at this time were E. Holmes Boyd, Holmes Conrad, R[obert] W[aterman] Hunter, John J. Williams, and H. Kyd Douglas. . . . Hunter and Douglas were already at the bar when I qualified to practice, for they are six or eight years older than me & were admitted, I believe, before the war. The others too were older than me, but the war (in which they were all gallant soldiers) interfered with their studies, so that they did not qualify until about a year after I did. The oldest lawyers there were Philip Williams and Robert Y. Conrad. . . .

The younger members of the bar and other young men of the town formed a debating society which afforded to us and to the public considerable entertainment, and considering the lack of wealth in the community, there was a good deal of gaiety in society and many small sociable entertainments.

Among the many pretty girls at Winchester the prettiest by far was Lily Dandridge. I do not think I ever saw a prettier girl, and in all other respects she seemed equally attractive. She had many lovers, but of them all she preferred E. Holmes Boyd and they were married in October 1866. I did not attend the wedding because a few days before my uncle James F. Jones who lived at Woodside near Oak Hill, was brutally murdered by a man named Bailey, who escaped and fled the country.

Terrible legacies of the war were to exist and claim lives for years to come. One of the first for this family was the murder of James F. Jones by "a man he was denouncing for cowardice in keeping out of danger during the war."[9] *Nannie Jones was left widowed with seven children, ranging in age from twenty to six. Financially, she was better off than others in her family: her neighboring brother and sister eventually had to sell their portions of the old Marshall estate due to wartime losses, "just debts," and postwar tax obligations. Nannie was able to stay at Woodside, and for a while harbored her brother Fielding Lewis Marshall's family.*[10] *Tom Marshall's Oak Hill, the original Marshall house, which had suffered from occupation and vandalism by Federal troops, passed out of the hands of the family at this time. Strother was Tom's executor and guardian of his children, but it fell to Robby to preside over this melancholy business.*

[MEMOIR OF ROBERT T. BARTON]

The settlement of the estate of Col Thomas Marshall was in the hands of my brother Strother, but his health had become bad and in the fall of 1866 I had to take the matter wholly in charge. A decree of Court for the sale of Oak Hill had been obtained and the sale was set for the latter part of the month of October. About the same time the body of Col Marshall was removed from its place of burial at the University of Virginia and on the day of the dedication of the "Stonewall Cemetery" at Winchester, it was buried where it now rests.[11]

The Stonewall Cemetery was established largely owing to the efforts of Mrs. Philip Williams and her sister-in-law, Mrs. A. H. H. Boyd. The remains of about 2,500 Confederate soldiers were gathered from battlefields in the northern Valley

and reinterred there. Thomas Marshall was buried in the front rank of the Con-
federate dead, next to the Ashby brothers. At his sister Sue's request, Frank
Clark undertook the "sad duty of exhuming Major [Frank] Jones' body" in Rich-
mond. In May 1868, it was reinterred near that of his dear friend Tom Marshall.[12]

The South was, in certain respects, returning to normal. Once again visitors
flocked to the Virginia springs, some for the curative mineral waters but most
for the social scene. In 1867, a young lady of Baltimore, Agnes Kirkland,
embarked on a round of the Virginia spas with her father, aunt, and cousin.
Their first visit was at White Sulphur Springs—so nearly the victim of Hunter's
torch in 1864—in the new state of West Virginia.

[LETTER OF AGNES P. KIRKLAND]

White Sulphur Springs
August 5th 1867

My dear Janet

It is a shame that I have not shown my appreciation of your letter before but want of time has been my only excuse. We left home two weeks ago today and arrived here on last Thursday week. It is truly a lovely place and pronounced by good judges to be the most charming watering place either here or in Europe except Baden. The grounds are beautiful and the society delightful. The water is the only thing that is not agreeable. It is horrid and I am happy to say is too strong for me. So I am spared the infliction of drinking it four times a day. It is such a sociable free and easy kind of place, and we don't have to be dressing all

the time. We rise here generally the early ones at six and the late about seven walk to the spring take a glass of the water walk around take breakfast. After breakfast make calls (nearly all live in cottages who can and it is quite the thing to call) or play tenpins. Drink another glass of the water dine at two after dinner chat in the parlor for an hour and then nap until halfpast five or six o'clock dress for tea at ½ after six walk a while after tea then go to the ball room to dance until half past ten or

Agnes P. Kirkland, photographed in Rome, spring
1868. (Mrs. C. Marshall Barton, Jr.)

eleven drink a final glass which is generally brought to your cottage or room and retire. There are about 500 people here, the majority Baltimoreans.

Gen. Lee his wife, daughter Agnes & son Gen. Custis are here, and of course the lions of the place.[13] They are great favorites, but there is no toadyism at all as a letter here published in the Balto Gazette falsely asserts. He gave Cousin Mary a lovely little bouquet of flowers yesterday and she has pressed it. Mrs. Lee is a very pleasant lady but great invalid. Miss Agnes is a nice girl but not exceedingly attractive. Gen. Custis is very nice & generally polite and agreeable but exceedingly diffident. We had some tableaux last week and when Aunt Mary told him she wanted him to be in them his face & neck became a reddish purple with a white streak across his nose.[14] The old general is the handsomest best nicest most agreeable and polite man I have ever met. I believe him to be a perfect Christian. He won't allow us girls to talk of "the Yankees" for he says there are no "Yankees" now. . . .

With love your friend
Agnes P. Kirkland

The rest of Agnes's letter is full of the inconsequential girlish chatter General Lee so enjoyed. Agnes became part of the group that clustered around him at White Sulphur, and she and her relatives formed a friendship with the Lee family that continued when, in due course, both parties moved on to the Sweet Springs.

Rannie's early months in Baltimore were difficult, but he had some professional assistance and moral support from Col. Charles Marshall, who had returned to the legal profession in Baltimore. Rannie learned that another year of law study was required for admission to the Bar in Maryland, and he spent it clerking for Cousin Charley. Rannie was not as lonely as most strangers in a new town. Many Winchester people had migrated there. There were familiar faces, and neighborhood ties were reestablished. He saw Frank Clark, Johnny Baldwin, and others. The indomitable Mrs. H. H. Lee, who was not allowed to return to Winchester, with the Misses Lee made their new home at 806 St. Paul Street, and Rannie became one of about a dozen lodgers there. His customary optimism was flagging that September; he was mortified at having to write home to Strother for a loan but was behind on his rent to Mrs. Lee.

The family at home was having difficulties, too. Strother's health was weakening, and perhaps farming was proving too strenuous for him. The Davises, still their neighbors, were particularly fond of Strother. Susie recalled, "Strother Barton, the oldest living son . . . was an unsung hero. His right leg was shattered in battle, the amputation on the field was imperfect, and every day he 'calmly

*broke in twain the fiery shafts of pain.' A constant sufferer, he tried with cheer-
ful patience to manage the large farm and make a living for so many helpless
ones."*[15] *Rannie thought Strother should consider a railroad job; on the new line
there was to be a station stop just up the creek near the woolen factory. The family
was trying a variety of schemes to bring in money. Barton Marshall, eighteen,
started a school for neighboring children, including the Reverend Mr. Crawford's,
at Springdale. In the summer, the Bartons had taken in paying guests, and
Rannie had been able to direct a number of Baltimoreans to Springdale. By late
fall, his spirits seemed to have improved, and he was full of advice and optimism. By then he must have known he would soon be admitted to the Bar.*

[LETTER OF RANDOLPH J. BARTON]

Baltimore Nov 13.67

Dear brother Strother,

. . . Sister M speaks of you as "systematically independent" and recollecting
your indifference here, as to your health, I fear it is too true; I earnestly beg you
to be more careful and seek to restore your health by judicious care of yourself.

If the RR is built, and a station established I see no reason why you should
not take the position; I presume it would have a salary attached to it, and it
would put you in a position to be an agent both for sellers there and buyers here
of produce.[16] Every thing, every rock, has money under it, if it is only properly
overturned. . . .

All are well at Mrs. Lee's. . . . Miss Nelly blushes most unaccountably when
your name is mentioned. . . .

"In time of peace, prepare for war"; what about next summer? is not Spring
Dale again to be the scene of gaiety and hilarity as of last summer? if the cheifs
sister Mat and Ma (or reverse) say we have time enough for that, well enough. I
know I can send more and as agreable persons as I sent last year.

*Among those Rannie had sent to Springdale as summer visitors were members
of the Duer family, whose acquaintance he had probably made by handling
some legal matters for John Duer's large hardware business.*

*By December 1866, Robby felt well enough established in his chosen career
to return to Maryland—overtly to visit the Sheilds for Christmas, but primarily to
ask Katie Knight to marry him. They were betrothed, with her father's grudging
assent. A long engagement followed before Robby and Katie were married by
Rev. Charles Sheild at her parents' home in Cecil County. Sister Martha was*

A gathering of family and paying guests (including some Duers) on the Springdale steps, summer 1868. Framed in the doorway are Bolling W. Barton, just back from France, Martha Barton Baldwin, and Jane Barton Sheild, visiting from Maryland. Mrs. David W. Barton, seated in front of Martha, is the apex of the pyramid of Sheild, Baldwin, and Marshall grandchildren, with Mammy Priscilla Piper as its firm foundation. Seated to Mrs. Barton's left is Madge Marshall holding Cora the dog. Barton Marshall, interrupted at croquet, is at far left. (Mrs. C. Marshall Barton, Jr.)

visiting the Sheilds, and Strother and Rannie came for the small wedding February 19, 1868.

Everyone was in reduced circumstances and trying to make the best of it, partly by living under the same roof with old friends and neighbors. Robby took a room for himself and Katie at Mrs. Sherrard's house, and among the other boarders were some of the Boyd family—Holmes Boyd and his wife, Lily, and his recently widowed mother. Perhaps this was when Robby became well acquainted with Holmes Boyd, and a year or so later, in October 1869, they became law partners, a relationship that endured for forty years. The younger Barton brothers, both working to establish themselves in their professions, did what they could for the family at Springdale, but Strother's health made leasing the farm a necessary consideration.

In spite of their new happiness, 1868 brought Robby and Katie some painful losses. Robby's aunt Mary Barton Jones died in childbirth in January, and her eleventh child, a daughter, did not survive and was buried with her.

[MEMOIR OF ROBERT T. BARTON]

In April 1868 I had been greatly shocked and disturbed at the sudden death at Woodstock, while in the midst of the trial of a case, of Mr. Philip Williams.[17] He had been my father's law partner and friend from the time when they were both young men up to my fathers death, and after that he had continued his friendship and almost fatherly care to me. No better, truer man ever lived, and few better lawyers ever practiced in Virginia.

In the Spring of 1868 a sadness was hanging over my otherwise great happiness in the ill health of my brother Strother. He had become so delicate that he had to give up farming at Springdale and now it was very evident that his days were numbered. Katie and I often rode out to Springdale at night to see him and between Strother and herself a very warm attachment had sprung up. [He was of an especially vivacious & witty disposition & mind. Altho a very brave soldier, his tastes were for music & books & the joys of peace.][18] . . . life seemed to have many attractions for him. He had lost his leg at the battle of Mine Run and the attempts to wear the then very clumsily made artificial legs had served greatly to aggravate the weakness which had resulted from a very bad cold, until at last he fell into consumption and rapidly declined. The immediate cause of his death, however, was pneumonia, which he had contracted the day before by sitting in a draught in an open carriage in which he had driven into Winchester. He died on the 28th day of July 1868 and is buried in Mt. Hebron Cemetery.

Bolly returned from Europe in 1868, planning to continue his medical studies at the University of Maryland. That summer, he and others of the family gathered at Springdale—Jane and her children visiting from Maryland. In late 1868, the Sheilds moved to a parish in Washington, D.C., and perhaps the move was hard on Jane. She was probably still grieving for her young daughter Sally, who had died the previous year, and her own health, frail for so long, declined still further. In March 1869, she succumbed to her long struggle with consumption. She was thirty-six years old.

In the spring of 1869, Agnes Kirkland had been abroad with her father, on what was probably a business trip for him, for the family import-export firm. Soon after her return she received an irresistible invitation from Mrs. Robert E. Lee, through her cousin Mary. In the excitement, Mary sent the letter on to Agnes, jotting her own note at the end.

[LETTER OF MARY CUSTIS LEE]

Tuesday, 15th June, 1869

I heard last night from one of the students my dear Mary that Agnes Kirkland had returned & would probably come on here to commencement & I write to say that if you young people do not mind a little crowding, we shall be very glad if she will come with you here. I thought she was still in Europe.[19] . . . the mails are so uncertain in these parts that I determined to lose no time in writing to you. We write in love to you and your Mamma.

Believe me, ever yrs truly,

Mary C. Lee

Dear Agnes, put your things in your trunk & go with us tomorrow morning at day break. We will have a nice time all together.

in haste

Cousin Mary

Dear Cousin Mary,

Pa says I can go if I can get ready in time which I will try to do, but I don't suppo[se] I will need very much.

In haste,

Agnes

Family legend has it that Agnes Kirkland and Randolph Barton were intro-
duced by none other than General Lee. The occasion could have been Agnes's
visit to the Lees in Lexington in June 1869, when Rannie might have been
there to visit VMI again. (Agnes apparently already knew who he was: "When
he came to Baltimore in 1866 with numerous other young Confederates he was
always pointed out as the most gallant of them all, always in the thickest of the
fight, wounded in every battle he was in."20) If this was indeed their first meet-
ing, it must have been a whirlwind courtship. Rannie's mother and sister
Martha were visiting the bereaved Sheild family in Washington in late October
when they received word of Rannie's engagement to Agnes. They were to be
married at the Kirkland home a few days after Christmas. Mrs. Barton did not
plan to attend. She had suffered too many losses to bear a celebration.

[LETTER OF FANNIE L. BARTON TO AGNES P. KIRKLAND]

Wash City Dec 13th 69

My dear Agnes

Your kind note arrived during my absence from the City, which will account
for my not answering sooner. My heart will be fully with you on that most
eventful day of your life and my most earnest prayers for your happiness both
temporal, and eternal.

My life for some years past has been a repetition of singularly severe affliction. While I feel it necessary to cultivate a serene and cheerful demeanour in
the social circle, I am aware of a shattered nervous system that would be unable
to maintain even the appearance of calmness in a festive scene. I look forward
with bright anticipation to your promised visit here, and shall after that accept
with pleasure your invitation to become acquainted with your family.

Most affectionately yrs

FL Barton

From Lexington came warm wishes from the Lees, and a pair of gold cufflinks
for the groom.

[LETTER OF MARY CUSTIS LEE TO AGNES P. KIRKLAND]

Lexington 22d. December '69

Though I have no costly gifts to send you dear Agnes on this most important
event of your life, yet I will offer you my blessings & prayers for your happiness
in which I deeply sympathize. You must not forget us in Lexington for you are

half a Virginian now, & many here have a most pleasant remembrance of you & we should be delighted to welcome you here again. The Genl unites with me in all I have written & says he considers Mr. Barton a most fortunate man.

> Ever dear Agnes yrs
> most faithfully
> Mary Custis Lee

The girls regretted so much they could not be present at your wedding & send love.

At first the young couple lived with her family, but when babies started arriving they set up their own establishment at 1316 Bolton Street. Bolly, studying at the University of Maryland, was living nearby. Skipwith Wilmer, the bishop's son, whom Rannie had known only slightly during the war, had settled in Baltimore after a sojourn in Europe and law school in Louisiana, and he and Rannie became friendly. In 1870 they formed a partnership that lasted until Wilmer's death, and a law firm that still bears their names.

Strother Barton's death had left the Springdale family bereft in many ways. There was no one to run the farm, and the dwindling family was without a protector. The sad little group grew smaller when a Marshall family connection, Mrs. Susanna Lees, appeared and assumed responsibility for the younger Marshall children's education and a new start in life.

By 1870, the Springdale household was reduced to Mrs. Barton, Mattie and her children, young Tom Marshall, and the faithful Priscilla Piper. Charles Sheild and Martha, perhaps in their mutual loneliness, decided to marry. They overcame Mrs. Barton's initial resistance and were married at Springdale in October, uniting their two families and soon starting another.

The indestructible Mrs. Jones was keeping house for the widowed Strother Jones at Vaucluse. Strother was fighting a losing battle to keep the farm; about this time, he sold off almost half of the original acreage.

[LETTER OF ANN C. R. JONES TO HARRIET PARKHILL]

We have not yet learned how to manage farms deprived of the labour we have been accustomed to, but I insist that something can be gained, and will be, when our new lesson has been learned. Those who have no profession and no trade, and have the land, are compelled to try, tho' success does not often reward the effort.[21]

Mrs. Jones, still the tireless reporter, detailed to her Florida cousins the virtual diaspora of the Jones children. Several were in schools in Baltimore under the auspices of their mother's sister Emily. Three were taken to New York by Mrs. Lees, the Marshall children's benefactor. Young Strother Jones won a scholarship to St. Paul's School, in New Hampshire; Mrs. Jones had a few misgivings about "that school which is said to be an admirable one. I am an old fogie, you know, and hope to die one, but is a High Church school, and located in the North."[22] Barton, and later Howard, Jones found work on the new line the B.&O. was constructing from Winchester to Strasburg.

Mrs. Jones wrote to Rannie and Agnes, with messages for Bolly and Martha, then living in Baltimore. Bolly had completed a period of clinical instruction similar to internship and was about to establish his own practice.

[LETTER OF ANN C. R. JONES TO AGNES K. BARTON]

. . . Bolling is too happy to remember his promise given last summer that I should be informed whenever there was any thing pleasant to communicate respecting his future but I suppose he *concludes* I am not ignorant of matters & things in general where he is concerned. Give him my warmest love, with hearty congratulations upon his bright prospects. I wrote a long letter to Mattie yesterday, but intending to write to you, *believe*, that I sent you no message. Tell me whether there is any failure of health in her, or whether the uncomfortable feelings belonging to her condition, is all that assails her, I have no *reason* to fear any thing else, but want to know certainly, I did not allude to her situation at all having only heard it from others when I wrote.[23]

Mattie's baby was born while the Sheilds were in Baltimore. Not much later, Mrs. Jones wrote again to the Baltimore Bartons, acknowledging the receipt of some hand-me-downs the Bartons had sent to Bev Jones's family, who always seemed to have a hard time making ends meet. The house Bev and Bec had been building in 1861 had been burned in the war, and they had bought a farm they called the Willows, about two miles up the Opequon from Springdale. Mrs. Jones had recently bid a sad farewell to Martha. The Sheilds were moving to Kentucky, where Charles Sheild had been called to St. Andrew's Church in Louisville. They were leaving their sons Stuart Baldwin and Charley Sheild at school in Baltimore, and taking the girls and their new baby boy.

[LETTER OF ANN C. R. JONES TO AGNES AND RANDOLPH BARTON]

I went last Saturday to Spring Dale, hoping to meet Mattie__ the last time I probably should ever see her. I was not disappointed, herself, & her three children came, Fanny sent for them, but they could not remain all night, & I staid with your Mother untill Sunday evening.[24]

Fanny still talks of a visit to you this winter, altho she seems to think a trip to Fauquier will come first. I hope she may be able to carry out all her different plans, & spend a pleasant season instead of a lonely one at Spring Dale.[25]

Bolly decided to practice medicine in Baltimore and opened an office on Madison Street. Not far from his rooming house lived the twice-widowed Mrs. McKenzie, and Bolly met and fell in love with her daughter Ella.[26] They were married November 26, 1872, and traveled south for their wedding trip.

Mrs. Barton was by this time almost alone at Springdale, and visits did little to alleviate her solitude or solve the problem of running the large farm. Robby had prospered sufficiently to begin building a fine house on South Washington Street, and it was out of the question for him to assume the responsibilities of Springdale. With reluctance no doubt, the Bartons agreed it was time to sell the farm. It was planned for Mrs. Barton to live with Rannie and Agnes in Baltimore. In the summer of 1873, Rannie and Bolly, their wives, their nieces Madge and Fan Marshall, their nephew Stuart Baldwin, and even baby Ran, Jr., went to Springdale. They had a photograph made to commemorate what was probably their last visit. Mrs. Barton stayed on until after the sale was concluded in September.

[LETTER OF FANNIE L. BARTON TO BOLLING W. BARTON]

Winchester Sept 30th 73

. . . I left Springdale yesterday after the sale and shall remain here until my affairs are put in some shape, Robert is much engaged in arranging for me, and I feel most grateful for his services which I believe have been skilfully managed, you may suppose that my new condition is somewhat bewildering.[27] Change so entire is hard to realize but I look forward to the future with more pleasure than I have ever felt since your dear Fathers death. Agnes is to me more like what I know my precious Fan would have been, than any other human being alive, and I feel sure that Randolph will be an able councellor in every time of need. . . .

A month later, Mrs. Barton was staying with Robby.

[LETTER OF FANNIE L. BARTON TO BOLLING W. BARTON]

. . . Spring Dale is now being beautifully repaired by its present owner and bids fair to be far more attractive than it ever was.

Mr. Harrison intends making it a dairy farm. Robert has reserved a portion of the money paid for S.D. to put up a little cottage on the other part, to make it saleable.

All our friends are well, Marshall [Jones] gone to teaching at last, I hope for a change in him, poor fellow. He has at last come to the very end of the rope.[28]

Marshall Jones, always in ill health, had run out of money and options. He went to live in nearby Berryville, where he was a teacher for some years. Robby lost touch with him, but remembered that he had been a "bright, happy, intelligent boy," had wasted his fortune in a "sensual, dissipated life," and was "afflicted with disease," later becoming a recluse and a "victim to opium."[29] When Marshall died in 1893, Robby had not seen him in many years. Cousin Robert Barton had somehow survived the grievous wound suffered the last winter of the war, and took up farming near Natural Bridge in Rockbridge County. He married ten years after the war, fathered six children, and lived to the ripe old age of seventy-six in Pulaski County.

Grandmother Jones stayed on at Vaucluse keeping house for her stepson Strother until the children had all left home. To her Florida cousins she continued to relate good news and bad. Susie Davis had married Dr. Daniel B. Conrad and had a new baby. "Willie Barton, dear Willie" had died in the spring of 1874, about ten years after being badly wounded at Spotsylvania, an injury from which he evidently never fully recovered.[30] And of Vaucluse, dear Vaucluse:

[LETTER OF ANN C. R. JONES TO LUCY R. PARKHILL]

. . . in the last year . . . the property had then passed on to other hands but the wish was that my son should retain it, by paying the tax, untill a sale could be effected. On the 13th of [May] it was publicly sold and bought by a neighbor [John M. Miller] who could not bear that Strother and myself should leave the place. . . . Poor Strother has suffered dreadfully at the thought of my leaving here, as well as going himself. I have sold all that I could to show him how willing I was to take my departure. . . . This is a lovely place, and I may never again be strictly, as comfortable in body, as here, but oh! the changes that have taken place here. There are only three persons left on the farm amongst the crowd of white and black that I found upon my arrival. My joyous happy husband, affectionate children, where are they? Strother, a little boy not quite eight, is one of the above mentioned three, the other two are servants, and one of them lies upon her death bed now, I am very sure. Strother will have a gay time with an 80 years old woman. . . .[31]

Strother continued for several years to try to make a go of it, taking in summer boarders in an attempt to supplement the meager farm income. In her last years Mrs. Jones joined her son Bev's household at the Willows, with frequent long visits to her daughter-in-law Susan and family. She was pleased that the two families were close enough that she could "vibrate between them," but she missed Vaucluse.[32]

[LETTER OF ANN C. R. JONES TO HARRIET PARKHILL]

. . . You would be sad to see Vaucluse as it is, I daresay, there is but one house on the place inhabited, all others desolate, and when I look back 50 years ago and bring before me the condition of the place then and now, it ought to teach me what this life is. One change I rejoice in, however, is the abolition of slavery, for myself the loss of servants has fallen lightly but I sorrow for those who cannot obtain help, when much needed. The slave has not been free long enough to know the value of a good character except in some instances, and they are triffling as to give great trouble instead of relief. Altho' I would prefer anybody that would take the coarser part of the work off my hands, *if* I had it to do, but my old life is easy, the general feeling seeming to be that my strength must not be tried.[33]

Ann Cary Randolph Jones died January 20, 1877, and was buried near Mary Jones and Fanny Barton in the secluded family graveyard at Vaucluse, not far from her beloved garden. Her son Bev Jones lived out his days near Winchester, somehow raising eight children while trying ineffectually to farm, and dabbling in genealogy.

Her daughter-in-law Susan Jones raised several families of children, her own four and successively those of her widowed brothers Peyton and Will. For some years after the war she lived at Buffalo Marsh, the house and school Peyton had built near Middletown. At times her household numbered twenty people. The school's enrollment shrank in the mid-1870s, and Peyton reluctantly left the Valley, accepting a teaching position in Rockville, Maryland. Will remained in Winchester, as one its leading citizens. Eventually, Sue was able to return to her beloved Carysbrooke, where she lived almost to the end of her long life in 1907. Her last few years were spent with her daughter Frankie (born after her father's death), who had married their neighbor, the widowed Joe Barton, the family's only noncombatant.

By about 1880, Strother Jones had given up the struggle to stay at Vaucluse, and spent his latter years with Marshall relatives in Warren County, with prolonged visits to his children in New York, New Jersey, and Baltimore.

His sister Fannie Barton lived for at least ten years with Rannie and Agnes's family.

[MEMOIR OF ROBERT T. BARTON]

The last few years of her life . . . were spent at her grandson's, D. Barton Marshall, not far from my brother Randolph's and there she died [in January 1890]. She was first sent to her grandson's because in her failing condition the noise of my brother's children distracted her, and the item of her monthly board was of decided advantage to her grandson, his circumstances being quite narrow. In the last few years of her life, her mental faculties almost entirely failed and for some months just previous to her death she could recognize no one. The disasters, alarms and losses of the war: the death of her children and then of my father, and the change in the pecuniary circumstances greatly affected my mother's naturally bouyant disposition. But up to the time that her faculties began to fail she was one of the wittiest and brightest persons I ever knew. Indeed, for a long time after her memory failed and her mind had become perceptibly dimmed, her sense of humour and her power of quick repartee remained.[34]

Martha, valiant sister Mat, lived in Louisville until her husband's health declined; in about 1883 they returned to the more congenial climate of Staunton. Martha died just a few months after her mother, in May 1890, at only fifty-six. Her son Stuart Baldwin had gone to seek his fortune in San Francisco in the 1880s, where he founded a family; her daughter Maria had moved to Staunton with the Sheilds, and married there.

By mid-1890, only three brothers survived of the numerous Barton family. They were in close touch, visiting each other for holidays, Bolly living part of the time in Baltimore and part in Loudoun County. Rannie and Agnes went to Winchester every summer, and the Robert Bartons visited Baltimore for her shopping and his business.

Rannie and Agnes produced nine children. In 1884, he built a fine house he named Vaucluse, near Pikesville, and thereafter commuted by trolley or train to

Randolph, Bolling, and Robert posed with David and Robert Jr. in Winchester in 1892.
(Edith Barton Sheerin)

his law offices in the city. Two of his seven sons eventually became lawyers, one joining his own firm. Rannie developed a large and successful practice, and, with his partner Skipwith Wilmer, was a leader of the Baltimore Bar. "He arrived at his office at nine promptly, and at once took up vigorously the work of the day, being actively occupied with clients, or in court, until he went home by train in the late afternoon. On reaching home he usually took a short nap before supper, and afterwards spent the hours up to bed time in his study, working on his cases, or reading his law books. . . . The home life of the Bartons was serene and beautiful . . . between the parents and the children there existed a complete understanding, making evidence of discipline invisible. . . ."[35] *At Vaucluse, the Bartons' extended family at times included his mother, her father and grandmother, his brother Bolly, various Marshall, Baldwin, and other nephews, and her widowed sister-in-law Leah. Rannie's niece Madge Marshall had married one of the Duers (as would one of his daughters) and lived nearby, and her children thought of Vaucluse as a second home, especially after their father's death in 1891. The lovely Louisa Haxall had married a Baltimorean and moved to Pikesville.*

Robby and Katie's marriage, though childless, was a happy one. In his spare time, and as a method of self-education, he began to write a book that became a guide to legal practice. "Defective though that book is, yet it seemed to meet a want, & was quite favorably received by the bar in Virginia."[36] *When published in 1877,* Barton's Law Practice *quickly became a success and a standard in Virginia, even going into another edition. Later he published* Barton's Chancery Practice, *and the additional income enabled him to enlarge their house, and to travel. Robby's growing success led to modest political ambitions; he served in the Virginia House of Delegates in the 1884–85 session. Any continuing political career was curtailed by Katie's ill health. In 1884 she had an accident that, while not serious in itself, seemed to bring on a decline that resulted in her untimely death at forty-three in 1887. Robby, cast into deep depression, went on a lengthy trip to Europe with Bolly. The two brothers did the grand tour for five months in 1888, and on their return, Robby found a new life beginning with young Gertrude Baker. They were married in 1890, and little more than a year later Robby was somewhat bemused and delighted at becoming, at forty-eight, a new father. Three years later, Robert junior's little sister Gertrude was born. Robby took on other new responsibilities: He was elected president of the Virginia Bar Association in 1892, but was disappointed in his aspirations to the Bench, which were thwarted by "political log-rolling." By 1902, he characterized his work as "a multitude & rather strange combination of duties—Lawyer,*

Mayor, Commander, Banker, Farmer, Prest. of Telephone Co."[37] *When his old friend Johnny Williams died, Robby had succeeded him both as mayor, and as commander of the local Turner Ashby Camp of the Confederate Veterans. He served as mayor of Winchester from 1898 to 1902. He was a founder and first president of the Farmers and Merchants National Bank from 1901 to 1917. Despite a busy legal practice including much traveling, he produced another book, a legal history,* Virginia Colonial Decisions, *published in 1909. Like his father before him, it was his pleasure to own and visit a farm, north of town on Apple Pie Ridge, and he was among the first to plant the commercial apple orchards that for so long sustained Winchester's agricultural economy.*

Bolly's marriage had been brief, and had ended with Ella's death, probably in childbirth, in 1880. Apparently disheartened, he left the practice of medicine. He spent the next twenty years teaching botany, physics, and geology at several Baltimore schools and at Johns Hopkins University, and living when in Baltimore with the Randolph Bartons. He gradually gravitated back to Virginia, acquiring a farm near Middleburg and the young Bolling Haxalls, and spending his summers there. He and Bolling had become fast friends while students in Europe, and in his latter years he took up residence with that family. For some years he kept company with Lily Baker, Gertrude's older sister. People talked, but Bolly had settled comfortably into his role as bachelor uncle. He taught nephews and nieces and young Haxalls (and later their offspring) the fine points of fishing, hunting, making dog whistles and gunpowder for toy cannons, and occasionally treating them to a baseball game—a benign presence on holidays and at parties in Baltimore and Middleburg, cycling with the Haxall girls over to Winchester to visit Robby and family.

As the only remaining Winchester Barton, Robby may have been particularly aware of old ties and obligations, although some had fallen away with years and circumstances. His associates were men and women he had grown up with and grew old with, no matter what their position in life. He kept a benevolent eye on the family's former slaves and occasionally lent a hand. Flora Braxton Turner, who had belonged to Vaucluse, still lived near Newtown.

[LETTER OF FLORA BRAXTON TURNER TO ROBERT T. BARTON]

March 14 1895

Mr. R.T. Barton

I write to acknowledge the receipt of your letter and check received last week and to express my great thank and appreciation. It is so kind and nice of you all to think of me so kindly. Please thank Mr. Ranny and Mr. Bolling for me. I certainly will drink to your health and wish that you have good luck and that the Lord may stand by you always. I appreciate your kindness toward me more than I did the money. but the money is certainly *very* acceptable. It just reminds me how I use to walk after you up at Vaucluse and give you your supper under the old oak trees. How perticular you were about little slices of bread and drink out of your little silver mug.

Tell Mr. Ranny and Mr. Bolling I am making some real nice work that I send to their house. I am coming in to Winchester soon and I will bring it in I don't know Mr. Ranny and Mr. Bolling's address.

I am very much oblige to you for writing to my "white children" for me.

Please excuse me for being so childish but I feel like I am in the house with you all like old times.

Thanking you all again I remain your humble servant

Flora Turner

Those of the Barton brothers' years and experience had arrived at the age of retrospect. There were anniversaries to be marked, reunions to be attended, and in the occasional solitude of their offices or studies they put down their memories. Bolly, whose mother had remarked his "intense aversion to writing" did honor his experience by attending the fiftieth anniversary of the Battle of New Market, and accompanied Rannie to at least one of his battlefields, Manassas.[38] *It was not Rannie's first return to that field.*

[MEMOIR OF RANDOLPH J. BARTON]

On the fiftieth anniversary of the battle (July 21, 1911), I went over the very ground on which the batteries of Ricketts and Griffin were posted, and where the Thirty-third Virginia made its timely and famous charge. I must have been on the very spot where I was wounded, and around me I could see in memory the one hundred and eighty dead and wounded of the little battalion. But under what different conditions! Then I was seated in a most comfortable carriage, drawn by two fine horses, the reins held by a good driver and having as my companion Mr. James M. Garnett, who had gone through the battle as a member of the Rockbridge Battery, and my brother, Dr. Bolling W. Barton, while stowed away for future use was an abundant lunch, bottles of tea, and a large block of ice.[39]

Bolling Barton, with Col. Scott Shipp and Pembroke Thompson on the battlefield at the fiftieth anniversary New Market celebration. (Mrs. C. Marshall Barton, Jr.)

Rannie had visited Manassas fifteen years earlier. For a few moments, "I was absolutely alone . . . I believe I even lowered my walking stick into a charge of bayonets. I barely repressed the stirring yell."[40] In early 1897, Rannie completed a first draft of his Recollections and sent it to Robby for his comments.

[LETTER OF ROBERT T. BARTON TO RANDOLPH BARTON]

MAY 26TH 1897

Dear Rannie:

It was something of a coincidence that your mss narrative should have come to me on May 25th, the 35th anniversary of the battle here with Banks—the day of the death of brother Marshall and of the happening of so many pathetic incidents which then, and for years after, seemed, in the crowd of similar incidents to have been too common place to deserve a special mark in memory. The day and its events were however continually before me yesterday—ancient history as it was with its 35th birth day.

This sort of environment however added the especially receptive mind to the natural interest with which I read your narrative. I read it almost at a single sitting and was sorry when I was done. It is strange how vivid my recollections of

Leaving for the Mexican Border campaign, Robert T. Barton, Jr., and his militia unit parade down Loudoun Street past the Taylor Hotel. (Edith Barton Sheerin)

all those events remains. You did wisely to write it and my children will claim pride in your military record only next to your own. . . .

I have no sort of criticism to make of your story either as to matter or style, and surely you do not violate any rule of modesty. But there are a few slight inaccuracies which do not affect the substance but may as well be set right. . . .[41]

To Robby's great delight, his son Robert intended to go into his law office. Robert's militia duties intervened, taking him to the Mexican Border in 1916, with his father's "full approval but inexpressible grief." Robby's last entry in his journal, June 27, 1916, noted sadly, "Fifty-five years ago I was the eager soldier boy and my mother and father the sorrowing parents. I had not thought that any war would ever come to change conditions for me."[42] Less than six months later, Robby wrote a long and thoughtful letter to Rannie, expressing a number of mixed feelings.

[LETTER OF ROBERT T. BARTON TO RANDOLPH BARTON]

. . . I believe we deserve your congratulations on Little G[ertrude]s engagement. Arthur [Field], as we call him now, is a young man of twenty five, modest, educated and a gentleman. He has the quality of efficiency in all that he undertakes, and in his office here has made himself very popular.[43]. . . . But I never thought that I would cheerfully give my daughter to a man born and raised in the northern part of New York. But the over fifty years since have elapsed since 1865 have made many *great* changes in our way of looking at things.

Robert delighted and surprised us by walking in on Saturday night after nearly six months absence on the border. (He has a furlough of thirty days, near one half of which (with his long trip home) have expired. In the hope and expectation that his regiment will be ordered home before Feb 5, I have induced him to apply for an extension of 30 days, which will save him the very long Journey back and home again to Brownsville [Texas]. His experiences in Army service have been good for him, *even* to his health, as he has gained twenty pounds in weight.

The National Guard system is known as an expensive imposition upon the few to the advantage . . . of the many, and I look with strong approval to its abolition, *so* far as Federal service is concerned, *and the adoption of universal service*. If the compulsory feature is made the *law*, I believe there will be no difficulty in recruiting *voluntarily*, as large a standing army as we engage to have. Patriotism is becoming an article that has to be made to order—it does not grow naturally as it used to do, in this Country. But still the Country must be saved. Hence the need for compulsion.[44]

Robby did not live to see America drawn into the European war he dreaded for his son; he died in January 1917, from a recurrence of pulmonary trouble that everyone had thought would carry him off over fifty years earlier. He was the last Confederate soldier at the Winchester Bar. His son, Robert T. Barton, Jr., returned from the Border, and then went to France where he served as a captain with the 313th Field Artillery.

Rannie sent three children to war: David W. Barton in the 110th Field Artillery Regiment, 29th Infantry Division, and Alexander K. Barton, his youngest, in the 149th Field Artillery Regiment, 42nd Infantry Division, and Katie Knight Barton with the Red Cross at a Hospital Hut in France. He joined the war effort himself, serving as chairman of the Baltimore City draft board. He and Agnes celebrated their fiftieth wedding anniversary in 1919, surrounded by children, grandchildren, and numerous friends. It was thought that Rannie's strenuous war work, followed by the task of chairing a committee to prepare a new charter for Baltimore County, weakened his robust health. He died in March 1921 after an "illness of several weeks due to a general breakdown."[45] Those who eulogized him at memorial services before the Supreme Bench of the Baltimore

Bar remarked on his "poise, sense of proportion, willingness to give and take, [and] humane disposition"; that he was "unconquerable, honorable . . . with unswerving fidelity to duty." They said that "his erect and stalwart figure was a true index of his character", that he was "as straight in the conduct of his life as he was in his figure"; and finally spoke of his "white simplicity."[46]

Bolly, the youngest and last, died during a visit with Agnes at Vaucluse, after a week's illness, in February 1924. He was buried in Middleburg, where he had spent so many happy years.

Both Robert and Randolph taught their children to be patriotic Americans while cherishing their Southern loyalty. Although their Confederate past was alive in them and they gloried in it, they did not feel a conflict, as time went on, in their ties and obligations to the reunited country. Rannie spoke eloquently of what he termed the "Appomattox contract" one Confederate Memorial Day in Winchester.

[ADDRESS BY RANDOLPH BARTON]

. . . . But the end had come. Human beings could do no more than our army had done, and then and there at Appomattox the scene changed. An over-riding Providence so decreed. Common honesty then and there required that we should give our whole souled allegiance to the United States, or quit the country. This was the contract and I recognize no qualification to it. And so from that day to this I have kept the faith. From that day to this I have sought to incorporate myself and my children into the body politic of the United States as if I had never had toward it a hostile feeling.

And yet I do not feel bound to say that I am glad the war ended as it did. If I applied to the case, cold, callous, commercial reasoning, perhaps I would find occasion for such congratulations. But I am not bound to settle the question by educating myself into such gladness.

And again I must confess that the unfolding of the Stars and Stripes does not thrill me with patriotic feeling. I saw it advance upon my people for the first time in my life, at Manassas. I saw in it then the emblem of all that I hated. I can forgive it all but simple truth requires me to declare that I cannot forget it.

But I inculcate in my children, love of country. What was burned ineffaceably into me, need not, must not be burned into them. I can be as true a citizen as the best man North of the Susquehanna River. I uphold this country as firmly as any of them. I can teach my children to sustain it right or wrong in preference to any other country. But if patriotism means that I must forget my Confederate people living and dead, then I am not a patriot.

Still every inch a soldier, Randolph Barton, chairman of the Baltimore City draft board, marches with World War I recruits to the station. (Randolph Barton)

But a generous North does not require us to do this. It does not expect us to do it. The true Northern patriot looks with suspicion upon the man who has blotted from his memory the country we did once much love, and overflows with love for the country we did once much hate.

There is no difficulty in pursuing an honest life in our relations to the past and the present. There is no difficulty in keeping the Appomattox contract; all that is necessary is to be a true Confederate. . . .

My friends, I love to dwell upon the events which I have brought up before you this evening. That they are tinged with melancholy is unavoidable, but we are not here as on a festive occasion. This one day in the year we devote to laying our tributes at the feet of those we love to honor. Let not the custom decline. As long as your mountains stand over these graves as silent sentinels, so long may it be that your people make their pilgrimage to this lovely spot and add to its historic riches the emblems of their love for those who have gone before.[47]

SERVICE RECORDS

BOLLING WALKER BARTON
(November 24, 1845–February 19, 1924)
1862 Appointed to V.M.I. for Jan. term. Matriculated Sept. 25.
1863 July 4: Promoted 4th Corporal, Co. B., V.M.I. Nov.–Dec.: Cadets called out for three expeditions against Gen. Averill.
1864 May 15: Battle of New Market: 279 cadets engaged; 10 killed, & 47 wounded. June 9: Corps returned to Institute; June 10: Gen. Hunter's campaign forced flight to Lynchburg. Mid-June: Cadets in trenches at Lynchburg helped stave off Hunter. Oct.: Returned to V.M.I., relocated in Richmond. Nov. 7: Appointed 1st Lt., Co. D., Tucker's Regt. (formed as the 1st Foreign or Irish Bn. of Confederate Inf.) also known as 1st Conf. Regt. P.A.C.S. Nov.–Jan.: Quartered at Columbia, S.C.
1865 Apr. 23: Paroled as "Cadet of Engineers, 1st Lt." at Burksville, Va.

CHARLES MARSHALL BARTON
(November 30, 1835–May 25, 1862)
1856 Graduated from V.M.I. after attending Episcopal High School, Alexandria.
1861 May: Raised a volunteer rifle company in Winchester. July: Enlisted and was appointed 1st Lt., Jackson Lt. Arty. of Winchester. Summer–fall: Inspector of fortifications at Winchester.
1862 Mar. 10: Appointed Lt. in Wilfred E. Cutshaw's battery when organized from the Jackson Lt. Arty. Joined unit in late March. Valley Campaign. May 25: First Battle of Winchester: mortally wounded on hill overlooking Winchester, about 1½ miles from his parents' house. All officers were wounded & 2 enlisted men, one mortally.

DAVID RITTENHOUSE BARTON
(November 27, 1837–December 13, 1862)
1856–58, 1859–61 Attended University of Virginia after attending Episcopal High School, Alexandria.
1861 Mid. Apr.: Joined Southern Guards, one of two U. Va. militia units, when ordered to Harper's Ferry; two weeks later, unit returned to U. Va. & was later disbanded. June 2: Enlisted as Pvt., 1st Rockbridge Arty. at Lexington. June 30: Battery mustered 4 officers & 81 men. July 2: Falling Waters: Battery fired the first cannon shots in defense of the Valley. July 21: First Battle of Manassas: Battery suffered 4 wounded. Nov. 10: At "Camp Stephenson," 4½ miles north of Winchester. Dec. 16: Expedition to Dam #5; battery losses 2 wounded. Dec. 21: Returned to Winchester vicinity.
1862 Jan. 1: Bath & Romney Campaign. 2 wounded at Bath, 4–5th.
Jan. 25: Returned to Winchester; various camps until Mar. 11.
Mar. 23: Battle of Kernstown: 3 killed, 8 wounded & 2 captured of 225 present. One gun & 2 caissons lost. Apr. 19: Battery reorganized & limited to 150 men. May: McDowell Campaign: skirmish at Franklin on the 11th. May 24: Skirmish at Newtown: 3 wounded, 2 horses killed. May 25: First Battle of Winchester. June 9: Battle of Port Republic: 6 wounded & 1 captured out of 71 engaged. June 27: Battle of Gaines' Mill: 1 wounded. July 1: Battle of Malvern Hill: 2 killed, 1 wounded. Aug. 9: Battle of Cedar Mountain: 2

wounded. Mentioned by Capt. Poague in his memoir as being "one of the most conspicuous persons." Mid Aug.: Battery assigned to the Stonewall Brigade. Aug. 19: Elected 1st Lt., Cutshaw's Battery, replacing brother Marshall, & assumed command in the absence of Cutshaw. Aug. 29: Second Battle of Manassas. Sept. 16: Battle of Sharpsburg/Antietam. Battery losses: 1 man and 1 horse killed. Sept. 23: Battery (100 men) amalgamated with Carpenter's. In various camps near Winchester until Nov. 21. Dec. 13: Battle of Fredericksburg: Killed in action. Buried by brother Strother near Hamilton's Crossing. His grave was never found. Battery losses: 2 killed; one missing; 24 wounded; 4 horses killed & 4 wounded. Memorialized in regimental history as "brave and true."

RANDOLPH JONES BARTON
(April 24, 1844–March 16, 1921)
1860 July: Matriculated at V.M.I.
1861 July 6: Appointed Sgt. Major, 33rd Va. Inf. at Winchester. July 15: Regt. joined the 1st Va. Bgde. July 21: First Battle of Manassas: wounded in the side charging Rickett's Battery. Brother-in-law Tom Marshall was nearby & uncle Frank Jones carried Randolph to the rear on his horse. Regt. suffered 52 killed and 84 wounded, the worst in the Bgde. & the most grievous of the war. July: Recuperated at home with brother Strother thru Aug. Sept.: Returned to duty either at Camp Harmon or Fairfax C.H. Nov. 12: At "Camp Stephenson," 4½ miles north of Winchester until expedition to Dam #5 (Dec. 17–21) & return to Winchester.
1862 Jan. 1: Bath and Romney Campaign. Jan. 25. Mar. 11: Winter quarters at "Camp Zollicoffer" near Pughtown (Gainsboro) 7 miles northeast of Winchester. Mar. 23: Battle of Kernstown: his pistol was shot from his hand and he was captured with cousin Willie Barton at Neil's Dam (about 2 miles from Springdale). Regt. losses: 18 killed, 2 wounded and 14 missing out of 275. Prisoners were taken to the Winchester jail. Mar. 25: Prisoners sent by train to Baltimore Jail. Mar. 29: By ship to Ft. Delaware, the first POWs there. Aug. 5: Exchanged at Richmond and went on leave in Nelson Cty. Returned to Winchester around Sept. 22. Oct. 1: Enlisted at Bunker Hill as Pvt., Co. K, 2nd Va. Inf., joining brother Strother and cousin Willie Barton in the Regt. Oct. 9: Appointed Lt.; in Winchester vicinity until departure for Fredericksburg Nov. 22. Dec. 13: Battle of Fredericksburg: Regt. briefly engaged, losing 4 killed and 13 wounded. Winter quarters at "Camp Winder," Moss Neck.
1863 Feb. 20: On leave with uncle Beverley Jones, attempted to visit Vaucluse (between the lines). Feb. 24: Dined with Tom Marshall, in camp near Edenburg. Feb. 25: Was nearly captured in Federal cavalry attack south of Strasburg and witnessed Marshall's counter-attack. Mar. 7: Returned from leave and was named acting AAG to Brig. Gen. E. Franklin Paxton, C. G. Stonewall Bgde. Became AAG, Mar. 23. Promotion to Capt. of Cavalry in the AG Corps approved May 18 with date of rank Mar. 28. May 3: Battle of Chancellorsville: Gen. Paxton was killed next to him and then Randolph was shot through both shoulders, in front of the log works near Plank Road. Was evacuated to Richmond. May 20: Went with cousin Willie, also wounded, to Staunton to recuperate in the home of Alexander H. H. Stuart. Late June: Returned to Winchester after its liberation. Mid July: Rejoined the Bgde. which was returning from Gettysburg, but his unhealed wound forced him to return to Staunton. Sept. 5: Had returned to duty at Morton's Ford and was appointed AAG to Brig. Gen. James A. Walker, the new Brigade commander. Oct.: Engagements at Warrenton 10/13 and Bristoe Station 10/14. Nov. 27:

Battle of Payne's Farm/Mine Run. Brother Strother wounded next to him. Dec. 2: Went in to winter quarters.

1864 Winter quarters at "Camp Stonewall Jackson" near Pisgah Church until May 4. Feb. 15: Confirmed as IG to Gen. Walker. May 12: Battle of Spotsylvania: he and Gen. Walker were each wounded in the arm during the breakout from the Bloody Angle. Recuperated in Staunton and Albemarle Cty. Late June: Returned as AAG to Gen. William Terry, in command of three amalgamated brigades (incl. the Stonewall). July 2: Marched through Winchester on the way to Maryland. July 9: Battle of Monocacy Bridge: was hit on the belt by a spent bullet and his borrowed horse was killed. Gen. Terry's command was reduced to 159. Aug. 17: Stationed near Winchester and temporarily assigned as AAG to Gen. York (Louisiana Bgde.). Sept. 19: Third Battle of Winchester began while Randolph was on brief leave with neighbor, Bob Burwell. They volunteered their services to Gen. Fitz Lee and both were wounded, Randolph in the left leg. Commandeered an ambulance and joined Confederate retreat from Winchester. Convalescence with Colstons at Ivy Depot. Nov. 4: Returned to duty in the Valley as AAG to Gen. Terry. Dec. 6: Brigade left the Shenandoah for the last time and entered winter quarters at Petersburg, a mile from Hatcher's Run.

1865 Jan.: Was offered promotion and position with Maj. Gen. William Mahone but declined after consulting Col. Charles Marshall, Gen. Lee's military secretary. Feb. 6: Battle of Hatcher's Run: was wounded again in the left leg and horse was wounded. Recuperated in Richmond with the Bolling Haxalls. Apr. 15: applied for Cadetship CSA (appointed Feb. 10 and approved Feb. 14) and scheduled exam for Lieutenancy CSA for Apr. 21 (his 21st birthday). Apr. 25: Battle of Ft. Stedman: received a blow on the right hip when near Gen. Terry, who was seriously wounded. Mar. 30: Was offered field or staff position by Maj. Gen. Clement A. Evans. Apr. 1: Was appointed Brevet Major and IG to Brig. Gen. Walker, CG of Early's Division. Apr. 9: Appomattox Court House: accompanied initial truce flag, which was received by Gen. Custer. Paroled Apr. 11.

ROBERT THOMAS BARTON
(November 24, 1842–January 17, 1917)
1859-61 Attended Bloomfield Academy near Charlottesville.
1861 June: Enlisted in Co. F., 2nd Va. Inf., joining brother Strother, was soon discharged for disability. Remained in Winchester.
1862 Mar. 7: Enlisted as Pvt., 1st Rockbridge Arty., joining brother David. Mar 21: Absent sick in Staunton at the home of brother-in-law, Dr. John M. Baldwin, thru Apr. 30 muster. May: Returned to duty at Staunton in time for McDowell Campaign. May 11: skirmish at Franklin. May 24: Skirmish at Newtown: 3 wounded and 2 horses killed. May 25: First Battle of Winchester: fought near brothers David, Marshall and Strother. A shell killed 2 horses he was tethering; another exploded at his feet. Found Marshall dead. Battery losses in 2 hours were: 3 killed and 18 wounded of 89 (the highest percentage among Confederate units), 4 horses killed and 5 wounded. June 9: Battle of Port Republic: was nearly hit numerous times, forced to abandon his gun, separated from unit and nearly captured. Battery losses: one gun, 6 wounded and 1 captured out of 71 engaged. June 12: "Sent to the rear" seriously weakened from exposure, and convalesced with the Colstons at Ivy Depot. Spent July near Staunton caring for brother Strother who had typhoid, and Aug. in Lovingston as hospital clerk. Early Sept.: was relocated with hospital to Winchester. Oct. 22: Discharged for phthisis. Oct. 23: Transferred to Nitre and Mining Bureau under uncle James F. Jones and posted to Staunton with rank of agent. Oct. 31: Paid in full for service in 1st Rockbridge Arty.

Nov. 13: Position in Nitre and Mining officially approved. Dec. 15: Rode north to inform family of brother David's death and escaped about Dec. 23 when Union troops came in to Winchester.

1863 Feb. 1: Paid as Asst. Supervisor effective that date. Feb. 4: Officially released from the Army. Early May: Rode to Vaucluse (between the lines) with news that his brothers were safe after Battle of Chancellorsville. June 13: Second Battle of Winchester: fell in with Confederate advance and was detailed to act as guide to Col. James R. Herbert, 2nd Maryland Inf. Aug. 26: Resigned from Nitre and Mining in order to assume family duties following the death of D. W. Barton. Paid in full.

1864 Sept. 19: Third Battle of Winchester: ill with consumption, visiting Winchester with convalescent Tom Marshall and sister Martha Baldwin when the battle began. Sister Martha drove them home in the midst of the Confederate retreat. Mid Oct.: Left the Confederacy for reasons of health and stayed in Baltimore and with sister's family in Cecil County, Md. until end of war.

WILLIAM STROTHER BARTON

(November 24, 1838–July 28, 1868)

1856-58 Attended Episcopal High School, Alexandria.

1861 May 1: Enlisted as Pvt., Winchester Rifles, under William L. Clark Jr., uncle Frank Jones's brother-in-law. May 11: Mustered as Co. F, 2nd Va. Inf. May 18. early June: to Shepherdstown and Williamsport to guard Potomac crossings. July 21: First Battle of Manassas: wounded in the knee. Regt. losses were the second highest of the war: 23 killed or mortally wounded; 53 wounded out of some 130. Recuperated at home with brother Randolph.

1862 Jan.: Returned to duty. Bath-Romney Campaign. Jan. 25–Mar. 11, winter quarters at "Camp Zollicoffer" at Pughtown (Gainsboro, 7 miles from Winchester.) Mar. 23: Battle of Kernstown: Regt. losses 6 dead, 31 wounded and 51 missing. Apr. 20: Appointed 2nd Lt. Valley Campaign. May 24-25: On approach to Winchester, led advance to right over Opequon at Springdale, outflanking Yankee skirmishers. May 25: First Battle of Winchester: fought with brothers David, Robert and Marshall. Regt. losses: 3 dead and 13 wounded. Early June: Contracted typhoid, was tended by brother Robert at Mrs. Moorman's near Staunton. Date of return to Army unknown. Sept. 17: Battle of Antietam, Regt. on provost duty in Shepherdstown. Stationed in the vicinity of Winchester until Nov. 21. Signed payrolls as Commanding Officer Nov. and Dec. Dec. 13: Battle of Fredericksburg: Regt. losses: 4 dead and 16 wounded. Buried brother David. Winter quarters at Moss Neck.

1863 May 3: Battle of Chancellorsville: Regt. lost 16 killed or mortally wounded; only 3 casualties in Co. F. June 14: Second Battle of Winchester: was detailed as guide to Gen. Early and commended for "efficient service." July 2: Battle of Gettysburg: Regt. lightly engaged: 4 killed or mortally wounded, 11 wounded and 9 captured. Nov. 27: Battle of Payne's Farm/Mine Run: while standing next to brother Randolph, he was wounded; his lower left leg was amputated. Co. F suffered 7 casualties out of 45 incl. Col. Raleigh T. Colston, friend and relative. Recuperated in Staunton, Dec. thru Mar. 16 and then in Lexington for some weeks.

1864 Jan.: Assigned to the Lexington Arsenal as Adjutant of Post under Col. Angus McDonald. Feb. 26: Officially appointed Major and IG. Was posted to Staunton and there by May 29. Summer: resigned to return home because of Robert's illness.

1865 Jan. 18: Officially retired to the Invalid Corps.

1868 July 28: Weakened by his wound, he died of pneumonia.

FRANCIS BUCKNER JONES

(June 14, 1828–July 9 1862)

1848 Graduated from V.M.I. after attending Episcopal High School, Alexandria.

1858 Appointed I.G., 16th Va. Militia Bgde.

1861 Apr. 18: To Harper's Ferry and was soon appointed AAG to Brig. Gen. J. H. Carson commanding the militia. May 2: Appointed AAG to Col. Thomas J. Jackson. July 21: First Battle of Manassas: rode with Gen. Jackson and witnessed charge of 33rd Va., then helped wounded nephew Randolph off the field on his horse. Aug. 26: Appointed Major, 2nd Va. Inf. but served as AAG to Jackson probably until Nov. Joined V. M. I. comrades Col. James Allen and Lt. Col. Lawson Botts in the Regt. Nov.: At "Camp Stephenson," 4½ miles north of Winchester Nov. 12–Dec. 31 except for Expedition to Dam #5 (Dec. 17–21). Late Dec: Commanded Regt. in absence of Allen and Botts.

1862 Jan 1: Bath-Romney Campaign. Jan. 25–Mar. 11: Winter quarters at "Camp Zollicoffer" at Pughtown (Gainsboro) 7 miles northwest of Winchester. Mar. 23: Battle of Kernstown. Was detailed as AAG to Gen. Jackson and commended. Battle was fought within two miles of his farm and he spent the night of 23–24 at the family home Vaucluse. Apr.: Elected Major (third in command). Mar.–June: Valley Campaign. June 9: Battle of Port Republic: Regt. losses: 1 killed and 25 wounded. June 27: Battle of Gaines' Mill. Weakened from diarrhea, he remained mounted during charge on McGehee's Hill; and was struck by canister on the leg. After a night on the field, his right leg was amputated. Evacuated to Richmond. July 29: succumbed to typhoid. Regt. losses were 10 killed or mortally wounded; 17 wounded and 1 captured incl. Col. Allen (dead) and Lt. Col. Colston (wounded).

THOMAS MARSHALL

(January 7, 1826–November 12, 1864)

1845–46 Attended University of Virginia after attending Episcopal High School, Alexandria.

1861 Apr. 17: To Harper's Ferry with the militia. Apr. 25–26: On Frank Jones's orders, stopped B.&O. train from Ohio and took Gen. W. S. Harney prisoner. May: Appointed "volunteer" aide to Gen. Jackson and honorary Capt. June 7: Appointed Captain. July 21: First Battle of Manassas: his horse was killed. Around Oct. 15: resigned after Gen. Jackson's promotion in order to facilitate staff selection; returned to Oak Hill for several weeks. Nov.: Appointed Capt. under Brig. Gen. J. H. Carson, CG of the Winchester militia; raised a cavalry company.

1862 Mar. 11: With his Co., joined friend and neighbor, Gen. Turner Ashby's 7th Va. Cav., and was appointed Capt. Mar.–June: Valley Campaign. June 20: Elected Col. of 12th Va. Cav. but Gen. Jackson refused to confirm all elections. Was appointed Maj., 7th Cav. in early July. Aug. 2: Skirmish at Orange Court House: received sabre cut on his head and was captured. Aug. 9: In Capitol Prison, Washington. Sept. 12: Exchanged; rejoined 7th Cav. at Berryville. Appointed Lt. Col. in Oct. (confirmed Oct. 30). Nov. 20–Dec. 13 (approx.): Regt. pastured at Springdale. Winter quarters near Edenburg.

1863 Feb. 24: Encountered Randolph Barton and Beverley Jones who were attempting to visit Vaucluse. Apr.: Raid into West Va. Assumed command when Col. Dulaney was wounded at Michael's Gap. June 9: Battle of Brandy Station: his horse may have been killed. July 3: Battle of Gettysburg: at Fairfield, lost 3rd horse, for which he was later reimbursed $500. Sept. 13: Skirmish at Culpeper Court House: horse killed, was later reimbursed $575. Oct. 19: "Buckland Races" near Bristoe Station.

1864 Jan.: While on furlough at Springdale (between the lines) was nearly captured by Federal raiding party. Winter: Col. Dulaney returned to command. June 11: Battle of Trevilian's Station: horse killed. Assumed command of the 7th following Dulaney's promotion. Aug. 27: Petersburg: wounded in left shoulder in the charge at Ream's Station. Recuperated with Bartons until Third Battle of Winchester forced Confederate evacuation Sept. 19; then stayed with sister Nannie M. Jones (Mrs. James F.) in Staunton and with sister Agnes M. Taliaferro (Mrs. A.G.) in Charlottesville. Oct. 21 (approximate): Returned to duty at Rude's Hill. Nov. 12: Skirmish at Marlboro/Cedar Creek: killed near home of Mr. E. P. Hancock, some 4 miles from Vaucluse and 7 miles from Springdale.

OCCUPATIONS OF WINCHESTER

Period	Status	Commander
March 12–May 25, 1862	Federal	Banks
May 25–May 31, 1862	Confederate	Jackson
May 31–June 3, 1862	Between the Lines	
June 4–Sept. 2, 1862	Federal	Sigel
Sept. 3–Nov. 21, 1862	Confederate	Jackson
Nov. 22–Dec. 13, 1862°	Confederate	Jones
Dec. 14–Dec. 23, 1862	Between the Lines	
Dec. 24–June 13, 1863	Federal	Milroy
June 14–July 23, 1863	Confederate	Ewell et al.
July 24–Apr. 31, 1864	Between the Lines	
May 1–July 1, 1864	Federal	Sigel
July 2–July 20, 1864	Confederate	Early
July 21–July 24, 1864	Federal	Averill and Crook
July 24–Aug. 11, 1864	Confederate	Early
Aug. 11–Aug. 17, 1864	Federal	Sheridan
Aug. 17–Sept. 19, 1864	Confederate	Early
Sept. 19–April 9, 1865	Federal	Sheridan et al.

° Dec. 5, 1862, Gen. Geary occupied the town for two hours.

	Confederate Control		Between the Lines		Federal Occupation	
	No. of Days	%	No. of Days	%	No. of Days	%
1861 (a)	265	100%	_	100%	—	—
1862	177	48	13	4	175	48%
1863	31	9	162	44	172	47
1864	96	26	121	33	148	41
1865 (b)	—	—	—	—	99	100
TOTAL	**569**	**39%**	**296**	**20%**	**594**	**41%**

(a) From April 10. (b) Thru April 9.

The information in this chart is derived largely from the diary of Julia Chase, as outlined by Lewis N. Barton in *W.–F.C.H.S. Papers,* Vol. 3, pp. 9–13.

NOTES

INTRODUCTION

1. His first wife, Katherine Knight, died in 1887. In 1890 he married Gertrude W. Baker, with whom he had two children.
2. Randolph built "Vaucluse" in 1884 near Pikesville, Maryland, and named it for his mother's family house in Frederick County, Virginia.
3. Springdale was deeded by the Heirs of David Brown to Richard Peters Barton on March 20, 1802. Frederick County Deed Book S.C. 4, p. 484. Possibly the Bartons were renting it earlier, as David is said to have been born at Springdale in 1801.
4. See "Occupations of Winchester" table in Appendix.
5. Mary Greenhow Lee, *Diary*, Apr. 1, 1862, transcript p. 47. Courtesy of the Winchester-Frederick County Historical Society, Handley Library Archives.
6. Ibid., May 9, 1862, transcript p. 99. Mrs. Lee refers to Mrs. David W. Barton's conduct.
7. Ibid., Apr. 1862, passim., transcript pp. 51, 78.

CHAPTER 1

1. Early schooling was at "dame schools" such as those run by Mrs. Tidball, Miss Holliday, and the Eichelbergers. Later the boys attended Winchester Academy; the older girls probably went to Winchester Institute although this was only one of several such in the town.
2. This corresponds to 126 North Cameron (then Market) Street. The house was from about 1888 to 1930 the Lutheran parsonage, but then was demolished.
3. The Williams house is still standing at 25 West Piccadilly.
4. John Peyton Clark was principal of the academy until the war began, when the building was taken for use as a hospital. He attempted to continue the school elsewhere in town, but it did not survive the war.
5. The first Mrs. Jones was Anna Maria Marshall, a daughter of Charles Marshall, a younger brother of Chief Justice John Marshall.
6. Charles Marshall Jones was the eldest son of this generation, but was compelled to leave Virginia after fighting a duel; he settled in New Orleans where his children were born.
7. The great Indian Valley road, which preceded the turnpike, ran east of Springdale and forded the Opequon. The turnpike, chartered in 1834, was laid out to bridge the Opequon on the west side of Springdale; the house entrance probably was reoriented then.
8. Richard W. Barton served five terms in the Virginia State Assembly in the 1820s and 1830s, and was elected as a Whig to the 27th Congress, 1841–43. He was involved in land speculations and property

development in western Virginia, and the Randolph County land was the only property listed in his will. A young neighbor of the 1850s recalled that "Mr. Barton had bought a tract of wild land in Randolph County, now West Virginia, and every spring a wagon train went from Springdale to develop it. Mrs. Barton had to have clothes and food prepared for the men to last all summer, a large undertaking. The scheme proved his financial ruin." Conrad, *Springdale*, p. 2.
9. Martha was listed as a communicant of Trinity P.E. Church, Staunton, in a list encompassing 1855 to 1857.
10. Springdale is about six miles south of Winchester, Vaucluse over three miles farther.
11. Charles Marshall Jones, a year younger than Robert, and his sister Anna, a year older, came to Frederick County to live with their relatives in the 1850s, presumably after their father's death and their mother's remarriage. It appears that Marshall lived mostly at Vaucluse and was W. Strother Jones's ward whereas Anna lived with the Bartons perhaps because she was about Fanny's age.
12. W. S. Jones (1857–1925) memoir of February 5, 1910. Courtesy C. Maury Jones.
13. Marshall may have been farming one of the family farms in the Bartonsville area from 1856 to 1859; Strother was probably at the Lost Brook farm, south of Middletown.
14. Francis B. Jones made a down payment on the farm he named Carysbrooke in 1848, and started building a house; he married Susan Peyton Clark in 1853. Beverley R. Jones married Rebecca Tidball in 1854, and appears to have taken up farming near Frank. Joseph M. Barton married Mary Neill in 1857. Joe farmed the Shady Oak farm for several years in the late 1850s (renting it from his uncle David) before buying the farm he named Hanover Lodge, a mile north of Bartonsville.
15. When she was born, all her great-grandmothers were living, and she was named for all of them.
16. The Marshalls lived at Shady Oak farm, near Bartonsville, until sometime in 1853. Three of their children were born there.
17. John was listed among the slaves in D. W. Barton's will, made June 1, 1861. Frederick County Will Book 24, p. 15. Powell and Holmes Conrad were two of eight children of the Robert Y. Conrads, Market Street neighbors.
18. Thomas Marshall was a grandson of Chief Justice John Marshall, and Oak Hill was the family plantation. It is situated between Delaplane and Marshall, then called respectively Piedmont Station and Salem.
19. Shady Oak was probably one of the farms rented by Richard P. Barton before he acquired Springdale. In 1838 his son Richard W. Barton bought Shady Oak, later, in 1845, conveying the house and 225 acres to his younger brother David W. Barton. The latter conveyed the same to Mr. and Mrs. Thomas

Marshall in late 1849, probably for the same $1 for which they sold it and the Buena Vista farm (227 acres) back to D. W. Barton in May 1853.

20. Tom Marshall's elder brother John's "liberal" life style brought him to the point of selling the family home in 1852, but the Thomas Marshalls did not move there until the next year. The Oak Hill farm comprised some 1,000 acres as late as 1884. Tom's siblings had shared in their father's estate; Tom's brother Fielding Lewis Marshall built a house, Ivanhoe, on his portion; sister Madge (Margaret), later Mrs. John Thomas Smith, built Ashleigh; Nannie (Anna Lewis) Jones's portion was Woodside, which she and James expanded. All these were on the original estate, almost in sight of each other, and the families signaled each other with flags. Marshall, *Recollections*, p. 75ff.

21. Susie's father, Dr. William A. Davis, owned a 127-acre tract on the northern edge of Newtown, called Mill Farm in Frederick County records, and also leased 844 acres of state land.

22. Conrad, *Springdale*, pp. 1–2.

23. Anna Maria Barton Marshall, Oak Hill, July [illegible], 1854, to Susan C. Jones.

24. The letter must date from winter 1856–57. Baby Randolph, the James F. Joneses' seventh child, was born August 24; February 10, 1857, Frank's mammy died. The baby died April 12, 1857.

25. Louisa Peyton Jones, the Frank Joneses' first child, born February 16, 1855.

26. February 23, 1860, letter to Susan C. Jones, visiting in Baltimore. Her brother William L. Clark, Jr., was active in the militia.

27. These were school nicknames for Col. Francis Henney Smith, Superintendent of the VMI, and Maj. William Gilham, Professor of French and Infantry Tactics, Commandant of Cadets. The latter had joined the VMI faculty in 1846. He wrote a *Manual of Instruction for Volunteers and Militia . . .* published in Philadelphia in 1861 and much used in the Civil War.

28. Six years later he not only found it interesting but also practical, as he worked on remodeling some of the old frontier forts for the defense of Winchester.

29. The subject of this bit of doggerel, Thomas J. Jackson, had been since 1851 the VMI Professor of Natural and Experimental Philosophy, and Instructor in Artillery.

30. The letter has no envelope but was with the Clark and related family papers, so can be assumed to be addressed to Franklin P. Clark, a brother of Susan C. Jones. Frank attended the university beginning with the 1857–58 session, when his "ticket" was Latin, modern languages, and natural philosophy.

31. The university's enrollment had more than tripled in the previous fifteen years, and Jefferson's ideal of a community of scholars living on the lawn was no longer possible. Mrs. Sidney S. Carr had for some time operated a boardinghouse on the hill, with "as many as fifty young men seated daily at each meal in her comfortable dining room." Archives, Alderman Library, University of Virginia [RG-31/7/1.832].

32. John T. B. Dorsey had married Katherine, a daughter of U.S. Sen. James M. Mason of Winchester.

33. David R. Barton, *Diary* 1858.

34. Samuel Marx letter to his nephew Joseph M. Barton,

March 12, 1856. Lewis N. Barton Papers, Handley Library Archives, WFCHS 485.

35. A William Bell was later mentioned as the R. T. Baldwins' servant by Mrs. H. H. Lee. *Diary*, July 17, 1862, transcript p. 181. Robert T. and Portia Baldwin were the parents of Bob, Johnny, and Lud.

36. The *Winchester Republican* of May 20, 1859, listed W. L. Goggin of Bedford County as a Whig candidate for governor and Alexander R. Boteler of Jefferson County as an independent running for Congress. Both were moderates, opposing secession. The issue of June 3 reported that the former lost, and the latter was elected to the 36th Congress. During the war, Boteler served as A.D.C. to two Virginia governors and on the staff of T. J. Jackson and then J. E. B. Stuart.

37. John Lipscomb Johnson, *The University Memorial*, Baltimore, Turnbull Bros., 1871, p. 293. John T. B. Dorsey had married Katherine, a daughter of U.S. Sen. James M. Mason of Winchester.

38. Richard W. Barton and his wife Caroline Marx Barton deeded the house and 610 acres, "mill & saw mill . . . several dwellings . . . overseers and tenants houses, etc" to David W. Barton on April 22, 1858. Frederick County Deed Book 11, p. 118. ". . . after all that he conveyed was credited at high prices, it still left Richard W. Barton my father's debtor for debts which he assumed or paid in about the sum of $80,000.00. This burden my father did not live to shake off. . . ." Robert Barton, writing in the 1890s, was still involved in litigation concerning his father's estate.

39. These two boys were the same age as Robert. McGuire, a brother of Hunter H. McGuire, served briefly in both Company F, 2nd Virginia Infantry, and the Rockbridge Artillery before joining the 11th Virginia Cavalry. He was badly wounded in the closing days of the war and died a month later. Williams served in the Rockbridge, then Chew's Battery, later joining the 11th Virginia Cavalry.

40. Raleigh Colston of Albemarle County was Mrs. Barton's second cousin through the Marshall family. His daughters Eliza (Bettie), Anne (or Anna), and Jane (Jeannie) were then about thirteen, ten, and nine. The house, previously and since called Woodstock Hall, is still standing.

41. Evening at this time usually meant afternoon.

42. Letter to Holmes Conrad, October 20, 1859 (transcript). Handley Library Archives, THL 1151.

43. Marshall, *Recollections*, pp. 75–77.

44. Randolph Barton, "Reminiscences of Major Randolph Barton . . .," Lawyers' Round Table. Baltimore, privately printed pamphlet, 1919, pp. 28–29. This is a curious story given the precautions others describe to prevent any attempt to free Brown; however, it is a matter of record that Brown received a number of visitors in jail. The verdict was handed down November 4. Maj. T. J. Jackson of the VMI commanded a company of cadets at Brown's hanging, December 2.

45. Rt. Rev. William Meade, Protestant Episcopal Bishop of Virginia, and presiding Bishop of the Church of the South.

46. David R. Barton attended J. P. Holcombe's lectures on constitutional law at the university that year, and his notes reflect Holcombe's extreme states' rights

interpretation of the Constitution. The notebook, a ledger of sueded stamped leather, is in the Virginia Historical Society.

47. William L. Yancey, virulent states' rights spokesman, was briefly in the U.S. Congress and later a Confederate senator.

48. Charles H. Sheild was Rector of Trinity Church, Piedmont Parish, from 1852 to December 1860 and eventually of three other churches in the vicinity, including the Marshalls' church, Emmanuel, built in 1859. His new parish, St. Stephen's, was at Earleville, near the head of Chesapeake Bay. The Sheilds had three children: Sallie, about six and a half, Fanny, five and a half, and Charles H., four, the latter two both born at the Marshalls' home, Oak Hill, according to Fauquier County records.

49. The Marshalls' sixth child, Bolling Walker, was born in early 1860 and evidently died in infancy.

50. On March 4, Lincoln was to take office.

51. Acelie Togno, a refugee from Santo Domingo, ran the Winchester Institute for girls ("a French school, with all the accomplishments") in the early 1840s. It seems likely that Maria, and possibly Jane and Martha, were her pupils. Quarles, *Story . . .*, pp. 66–67. Mrs. Togno was listed in the Charleston 1860 directory, with her daughters, Ascelie and Elize. She is mentioned in early 1862 by Mary Chesnut, and identified by C. Vann Woodward as head of the Barhamville Female Institute, just outside Columbia. Mary Boykin Miller Chesnut, *Mary Chesnut's Civil War,* edited by C. Vann Woodward. New Haven, Yale University Press, 1981, p. 274.

52. W. LeRoy Brown became a colonel in the Confederate Engineers Department and subsequently a professor at the University of Alabama.

53. Richard Thomas Barton was the eldest son of Richard W. Barton by his first marriage to Alcinda Gibson.

54. A hickory tree, so named because the guard tent was pitched under it during summer camp, stood on the edge of the parade ground. Apparently it was forbidden territory for "rats" (first year men), but there is no clearly documented record of this tradition.

55. Typescript of an address delivered June 20, 1912, to the graduating cadets at VMI.

56. Typescript of a speech written for a Confederate Memorial Day in Winchester, c. 1908.

57. This episode, known as the "Flag Pole Incident," and the resulting speeches, occurred April 13.

58. This is an abbreviation at best of the generally accepted version of this speech.

59. The Corps left for Richmond on April 21. Forty-seven cadets were in the detail left to act as drillmasters for local recruits; after gradual attrition among them, the last left July 2.

60. Holmes Conrad is listed in VMI records as a member of the class of 1858, with one year's attendance.

CHAPTER 2

1. It appears that Frank's brother Bev had also rushed to Harpers Ferry with the militia, but almost immediately became ill and went home.

2. He refers to the hasty Federal departure from Harpers Ferry on April 18, after they had fired the arsenal and works. The latter were saved.

3. Powell Conrad, letter to his mother, April 25, and to his father, April 26, 1861, transcripts. The latter is a very detailed account of the episode. Handley Library Archives, THL 1151.

4. Frank owned or was leasing the Catlett farm, 350 acres near the Front Royal Road, seven miles from Winchester and perhaps adjacent to Carysbrooke. Old Dick was most likely Henry Dick, fifty-nine, a day laborer living near Frank and Bev, but conceivably Edward J. Dick, fifty-six, a nearby farmer.

5. His son William Randolph Jones, then four.

6. Frank P. Clark, Frank Jones's brother-in-law, was apparently, like Tom Marshall, a volunteer off and on until July.

7. Conrad and James Marshall of Winchester opposed secession but had been elected to the Secession Convention in early 1861. They had voted against secession April 17. Both ran for the State Legislature later in the year and lost by large margins.

8. Kitten was Frank's pet name for his daughter Louisa, six.

9. James Mercer Garnett, *"Extracts from the Diary of Captain . . . ,"* S.H.S.P., Vol. 28, p. 59ff. Garnett enjoyed the Bartons' hospitality for several days in July when he returned to Winchester to enlist in Pendleton's battery.

10. The aforementioned notebook in the Virginia Historical Society, on page 37.

11. Robert Hall Chilton had been a career U.S. Army officer; he was at this time in the Adjutant and Inspector General's Office, and later Chief of Staff to Gen. R. E. Lee. Frederick W. M. Holliday, a Market Street neighbor, had read law with D. W. Barton and was Commonwealth Attorney before the war. He raised a unit that became part of the 33rd Virginia Infantry.

12. Letter to VMI, May 22, 1861, VMI Archives; letter from Colonel Holliday, May 26, 1861, cited in Reidenbaugh, *33rd Virginia Infantry,* p. 3.

13. Robert Sherman and several Newcombs were day laborers in Newtown.

14. Nathaniel B. Meade ran the *Winchester Republican* until Union troops destroyed the plant in 1862. Norris, *Lower Shenandoah,* p. 177.

15. Mrs. David W. Barton had three sons already in the army, and Mrs. Richard W. Barton's younger son Willie had joined the 2nd Virginia Infantry.

16. Susan Jones's father, William L. Clark, was president of Winchester & Potomac R.R., and had been James M. Mason's law partner. He also was principal of and teacher at the Winchester Academy, and had been instrumental in starting the Valley Telegraph and bringing a water pipe system to Winchester.

17. Frank Jones's brother-in-law recruited this unit, which became Company F, 2nd Virginia Infantry. On May 18, the regiment was sent to Shepherdstown and Williamsport to guard Potomac crossings, returning in two weeks.

18. His brother-in-law and nephew, both of the 2nd Virginia, had just returned from the expedition up the Potomac.

19. Southern sympathizers in northern Virginia were

already refugeeing to areas they thought would be less vulnerable.

20. His elder half brother William Strother Jones of Vaucluse.

21. James Innes Randolph, fifty-five, was his mother's third cousin, to whom she was particularly close. He and his family, including his sister Lucy, subsequently refugeed to Virginia, his three sons joining the C.S. Army.

22. Communications were obviously in chaos.

23. Gen. Winfield Scott, commander of the U.S. Army in the Mexican War, and initially of the Federal forces in the Civil War, oversaw the preparation of numerous manuals used by several branches of the U.S. forces for two generations. The first edition of *Infantry Tactics* was published in 1825 and went through many editions. Frank undoubtedly had studied it at the VMI. The book, three volumes, is usually found in broken sets, for the reason manifested here.

24. Letters to W. Strother Jones and to Susan C. Jones, June 10, 1861.

25. William Braxton was a Vaucluse slave.

26. Rebecca's fourth child, Edward McGuire, was born June 7. The attending doctor was Robert T. Baldwin, the Bartons' neighbor.

27. The Beverley R. Joneses were building a house, which was downstream from Carysbrooke, near Parkin's Mill. Apparently the family had been living in the kitchen outbuilding while the main house was under construction. There is no record of land ownership by Bev at this date, but there is mention in his obituary that a house was burned during the war.

28. Frank B. Jones to Susan C. Jones, May 6; David W. Barton to Francis H. Smith, June 29.

29. Original will of Francis B. Jones, dated July 2, 1861, on deposit in the Frederick County Court House.

30. Cummings commanded the 33rd Virginia Infantry; Rannie was appointed July 6.

31. Cousin Willie Barton was in the 2nd Virginia and cousin Marshall Jones joined the same regiment on June 15. Bev Jones, his health improved, enlisted in the Rockbridge Artillery July 3, following Frank's advice in late June: "It is time for every man to be up and doing, none can now hold back. The state needs every man, we have a great cause and I believe we are certain of victory in the end." Letter to Susan, June 24. No service record can be found on W. Strother Jones's quartermaster post, nor on the duties of Dr. John M. Baldwin.

32. There is no official record of Robert's brief service in the 2nd Virginia Infantry, but it must date in the latter part of June, as Gen. Joseph E. Johnston evacuated Harpers Ferry on June 14. Johnston claimed that 40 percent of his men were sick and he had insufficient forces to hold it.

33. This skirmish occurred July 2, when General Patterson pushed toward Martinsburg. The Rockbridge Artillery participated, though only one gun of the battery was engaged. It was fired by David E. Moore, Jr., of Lexington, and David R. Barton was one of the crew.

34. James Murray Mason had had a long congressional career, which included authoring the Fugitive Slave Act. He became the Confederate envoy to Great Britain where, after the Mason-Slidell affair, he spent most of the war. His Winchester house, Selma, was systematically destroyed by Federal troops in 1862.

35. S.H.S.P., Vol. 43, p. 10.

36. Randolph Barton's memory of the battle was refreshed by visits to the field in September 1896, and for the fiftieth anniversary, July 1911, and he read extensively about it. In June 1900, Barton addressed a reunion of the Stonewall Brigade in Louisville, Kentucky. His speech was published in the *Confederate Veteran* in 1900, pp. 481–85.

37. Brig. Gen. Pierre G. T. Beauregard was second in command to Gen. Joseph E. Johnston.

38. John T. L. Preston of Lexington was a founder of the VMI, and he and F. H. Smith had constituted the faculty in 1839. James W. Allen, VMI '49, had been a teacher and farmer, and was elected colonel of a militia regiment later incorporated into the 2nd Virginia. Arthur C. Cummings, VMI '44, had been a major in the Mexican War.

39. John Casler did not hesitate to name the cowardly adjutant, L. Jacquelin Smith, who was dismissed by Colonel Cummings when he reappeared a few days after the battle. Casler, *Four Years,* p. 47.

40. William Nelson of Millwood, Clarke County, had served in the Mexican War. He was a secession candidate in 1860 and went to Harpers Ferry with a company of infantry. At Manassas he was commanding the Hanover Artillery, serving with Pendleton's artillery, but received a disabling wound in the battle. Nevertheless, he served throughout the war; his silk top hat was famous.

41. Col. Nathan George Evans, commanding two regiments on the left, and Lt. Col. Barnard E. Bee, commanding a brigade of recruits.

42. Daniel B. Conrad, S.H.S.P., Vol. 19, p. 91. Rannie reported years later what Frank must have told him: "During that battle his staff officer, the writer's uncle ... despairingly remarked, 'General, I fear the day is against us,' and he almost angrily remarked, 'If you think so, you should not say it.'" Barton, S.H.S.P., Vol. 38, p. 274.

43. Arthur C. Cummings and W. F. Lee (VMI '53), both of the 33rd Virginia.

44. His brother-in-law J. Peyton Clark and brother James were then visiting camp. James F. Jones was not then in Confederate service and had apparently taken over running all the Marshall farms for his brothers-in-law, who had joined the C.S. Army.

45. In the Louisville speech, Randolph Barton said that the 33rd had about 450 men going into the charge and that 43 were killed and 140 wounded, a little over 40 percent casualties. *Confederate Veteran,* p. 484. Reidenbaugh, *33rd Virginia,* p. 102, cites Compiled Service Records listing 52 killed and 84 wounded. The Official Records list 1 officer and 44 enlisted men killed; 101 men wounded. By anyone's count, the understrength regiment suffered proportionately more than any other in the brigade. Its Lieutenant Colonel, William Fitzhugh Lee, was mortally wounded in the battle and died July 29.

46. J. E. B. Stuart with the 7th Virginia Cavalry and R. C. W. Radford with the 2nd Virginia Cavalry.

47. Conceivably this was Charles H. Padgit, listed as overseer of a farm in White Hall in the 1860 census.

48. Lloyd F. Powell, of Winchester and Company F, 2nd Virginia Infantry, was taken from the field by Dr. Hunter Holmes McGuire of Winchester. The latter was Jackson's medical director and personal physician, and later Medical Director of the Second Corps, A.N.V. Several of his brothers also served in the C.S.A.
49. Col. Francis John Thomas, West Point class of 1840, was until 1852 a career officer in the U.S. Army. He had commanded the Maryland Volunteers, and was Johnston's acting chief of ordnance. In the midst of the battle's confusion, he was ordered to lead leaderless Alabama troops in a charge, and was killed.
50. Robert Waterman Hunter, A.A.G. of the 2nd Virginia Infantry, was from Martinsburg as was Holmes A. Conrad, the latter one of the two sons of D. Holmes Conrad, who were both killed at Manassas.
51. Mary was his sister-in-law Mrs. W. S. Jones; Kitty, an elderly Vaucluse slave belonging to his mother.
52. Old spelling, referring to merchant named Manassa who lived at the gap.

CHAPTER 3

1. Gen. J. E. Johnston reported that he left "nearly 1700" sick men behind in Winchester, in care of the militia. *O.R.* Series I, Vol. 2, p. 473. Recruits generally came from isolated areas and had not been exposed to many diseases to which their urban peers had early developed immunities (although they may have acted as carriers). Therefore, the first "seasoning" of troops was more often sickness (measles, mumps, etc.) than company drill.
2. Edward Owen Burgess, Lloyd F. Powell, Peyton R. Harrison, Henry Tucker Conrad, and Holmes Addison Conrad (brothers), all of the 2nd Virginia Infantry. The Conrads were first cousins of the Winchester Conrads; Burgess was the son of a local farmer, James H. Burgess, and was about Robert's age. Winchester hospitality was already famous in the army: Mrs. Barton was said to have given breakfast to 180 soldiers one morning that June. Capt. J. J. White's letter of June 14, 1861, to his wife, cited in W. G. Bean, *The Liberty Hall Volunteers,* Charlottesville, University Press of Virginia, 1964, p. 25.
3. Rannie in September; Strother not until late in the year.
4. Vandiver, *Mighty Stonewall,* p. 170. Frank B. Jones to Susan C. Jones, August 6.
5. "Extracts from the Diary of Capt. James M. Garnett," S.H.S.P., Vol. 28, pp. 68–69.
6. Mary Anna Jackson, *Life and Letters of General Thomas J. Jackson.* New York, Harper & Bros., 1892, p. 179. Mrs. Jackson does not cite the date of the letter, but Robby annotated it in his copy of the book. Robert was to leave camp August 7, according to a letter Frank wrote to Sue the previous night to send with him.
7. Frank B. Jones to Susan C. Jones, August 15.
8. Letters to Susan B. Jones, August 16 and 27.
9. Frank B. Jones to Susan C. Jones, September 2.
10. Frank B. Jones to Ann C. R. Jones, August 22; and to Susan C. Jones, September 12 and 18.
11. Frank B. Jones to Susan C. Jones, August 15: "I

always thought you were the smartest as well as the best wife, how did you manage to sell Billy for such a sum! It beats all my financing. I hope he will prove valuable in the service of his country."
12. Jackson's official report of July 23 cited both Francis B. Jones and Thomas Marshall as "having rendered valuable service." *O. R.* Series I, Vol. 2, p. 482.
13. Frank had finally been paid on August 20—$444 for three months—but had immediately applied it to his debts.
14. Frank Clark, by now in the Quartermaster Department, could possibly employ Bev Jones if he could obtain a transfer or discharge from the Rockbridge Artillery.
15. Henry Kyd Douglas, in *I Rode with Stonewall,* p. 236, wrote that "an officer in his command" applied to Jackson for a brief leave under such circumstances, first in writing and then in person, and was denied in "cold and merciless tones." The latter can only be hearsay, as Douglas was not yet on the general's staff. Kenton Harper resigned in September.
16. James Innes Randolph, Mrs. Jones's cousin, had three sons in the Confederate Army: Innes, John B., and later Wilton.
17. Letter to Susan C. Jones, October 2.
18. Although there was constant skirmishing, most of the mortality was from disease rather than battle.
19. Rev. A. H. H. Boyd, Philip Williams, and Mrs. David W. Barton all had sons in the army. Personal packages and supplies were sent down to the army with some regularity, and Frank's letters were full of requests for everyday articles. The Meades lived at Mountain View, near Millwood, Clarke County, and the bishop's son, Philip A. Meade, fifty-one, gathered the neighborhood's contributions. The weekly wagon, which was sent fifty miles to the hospital at Fairfax Court House, bore "garments, brandy, wine, nice bread, biscuit, sponge cake, butter, fresh vegetables, fruit." McGuire, *Diary,* pp. 48–49. William R. Denny was a merchant tailor in Winchester.
20. William L. Clark's Company F, 2nd Virginia Infantry. Frank's nephew Marshall was in Winchester, assigned to rebuild the old colonial fortifications.
21. J. E. B. Stuart, commissioned Brigadier General, September 24.
22. Arlington House, the Custis mansion, was R. E. Lee's home.
23. Frank attended the Episcopal High School from 1839 to 1844. The Howard house (c. 1750) and tract of eighty acres adjoining the seminary were bought for the Episcopal High School in 1839. L. M. Blackford, *Mine Eyes Have Seen,* p. 251. At first it was called the High School at Howard. The school was used as a Federal military hospital for most of the war. Williams, *The High School,* p. 13.
24. Kentucky attempted to remain neutral but in September was invaded by both Union and Confederate armies.
25. "Indeed Bev is encamped only about a stones throw from my HdQrs. I am quite concerned about his affairs, no corn & no oats is very bad. I have borrowed on my own responsibility 112$ to pay his Carter int[erest]. I have tried to persuade him to look out for promotion in the Army, but he seems to

have no fancy for military life, he seems to think if he cd get a position in a Machine Factory he would prefer it, if he could succeed I would advise it. He certainly carrys out the Bible admonition 'take no thought for the morrow' while I on the other hand am filled with future anxieties." F. B. Jones letter to Ann C. R. Jones, August 22. On October 25, Bev Jones received a medical discharge from the Rockbridge Artillery, and on October 26, the hoped-for transfer to the Quartermaster Department in Frederick County. His three months' pay totaled $45.20, with another $25 for clothing.

26. Letter quoted in Peyton Clark's memoir of Jones, written for inclusion in Walker, *Memorial. Virginia Military Institute . . .,* p. 306. Clark's manuscript of the memoir is among the Jones/Clark papers.

27. This is from Frank B. Jones's October 10 letter, which continues below.

28. This was Payne's Church, on the Ox Road (Route 123), near Fairfax Station. Built 1766–68 as an Anglican church, it became in 1840 the Jerusalem Baptist Church. The building was destroyed by Federal troops in the winter of 1862–63, its brick used for their winter quarters. A new Jerusalem Baptist Church was built on the site in 1865. Martin Petersilia and Russell Wright, *Hope Park and the Hope Park Mill,* Fairfax, J. McGuire, 1978, pp. 17–22.

29. Furgusson was a British military observer.

30. This refers to the countless kinds of paper money being printed, by banks, municipalities, counties, states, and even businesses, as well as the new Confederate government. Their unknowable worth caused many to hold out for hard currency. Frank was apologizing for sending the letter "collect."

31. Frank B. Jones to Ann C. R. Jones, October 18.

32. The road (Route 672) was named for British general of the French and Indian War; it runs north of Winchester toward Pittsburgh. Here and elsewhere "evening" means afternoon.

33. F. B. Jones letter to W. L. Clark, June 11.

34. Barton's argument is the only detailed record known of this incident. The identity of Miller's attorney is unknown.

35. Chase, *Diary,* transcript pp. 22–23, Handley Library Archives. Jackson took command in the Valley on November 5, and must have been approached at that time. His friend Rev. James R. Graham wrote that he had asked Jackson for a pardon for Kerfoot and was refused. James Robert Graham, "Some Reminiscences of Stonewall Jackson," *Things and Thoughts,* Winchester, July–Aug. 1901, pp. 127–28. George W. Ward said it was General Johnston who was appealed to for pardon. W.F.C.H.S. *Papers.* Vol. 3, p. 15. Probably Jackson refused the first appeal, which was passed on to Johnston, then commander of the C.S. Army, in Richmond.

36. Frank B. Jones to Ann C. R. Jones, December 30, 1861.

CHAPTER 4

1. Lt. John Francis Neff, VMI '58, was elected Colonel on April 22, 1862. He was killed in the Second Battle of Manassas on August 28, 1862.

2. Camp Zollicoffer, which everyone disliked, on January 25.

3. Lawson Botts, VMI '44, and captain of the prewar militia company, the "Botts Greys," was at this time Lieutenant Colonel, 2nd Virginia Infantry. A Charles Town lawyer, he had been one of John Brown's defense attorneys.

4. Robert W. Hunter was A.A.G. of the 2nd Virginia. Gen. Richard B. Garnett was commanding the Stonewall Brigade.

5. Three Vaucluse slaves to whom Frank had sent small Christmas presents.

6. Letter to Ann C. R. Jones, Camp Zollicoffer, February 4, 1862.

7. In January, Tom raised a cavalry company that enlisted March 11 for the duration. When he returned to the army for the spring campaign, the Oak Hill house was closed. It was later occupied and damaged by Federal forces.

8. Jackson stayed in town at the houses of Col. Lewis T. Moore and later Rev. James R. Graham, both on North Braddock Street and only a few blocks from the Bartons.

9. Robert enlisted March 7 as Private, 1st Rockbridge Artillery, joining his brother David in the unit. Capt. William McLaughlin had replaced Capt. William N. Pendleton of Lexington.

10. Subsequent events proved otherwise: although Banks had detached two divisions from his command, Jackson was severely repulsed at Kernstown due to the enemy's superior numbers.

11. Francis B. Jones's *Diary* is in the Handley Library Archives, in the collections of the Winchester-Frederick County Historical Society. Excerpts appear in this chapter, with one later entry in chapter 6.

12. Lee, *Diary,* Mar. 13, transcript p. 8.

13. Ibid., transcript p. 5. Hugh Holmes Lee had died in October 1856.

14. Trinity Episcopal Church, Staunton, church records.

15. Sukey was one of the Barton slaves. Mrs. Lee's household included two sisters-in-law, one, Antoinette Lee, also forty-one.

16. George H. Stottlemeyer (variously Stottlemyer or Stottlemier), thirty-three, local merchant, constable, and farmer, was arrested the next day. Lee, *Diary,* transcript p. 81. Yorktown was then under siege in McClellan's advance up the peninsula.

17. Dr. and Mrs. Archibald S. Baldwin were John's parents. This family lived on Piccadilly Street between Loudoun and Braddock, and their household included their daughter-in-law "Cary," Mrs. Robert F. Baldwin (the David Bartons' niece), and her two young children. The Baldwins' daughter Sallie had been visiting John, Mattie, and other relatives in Staunton. Their youngest son, Cornelius, "Nepe," was Assistant Surgeon with the 2nd Virginia.

18. Lee, *Diary,* Apr. 26, transcript pp. 79–80.

19. Francis B. Jones to Ann C. R. Jones, March 19, 1862.

20. John M. Miller was a Middletown farmer.

21. The baby was Ann Cary Randolph Jones, fifteen months old.

22. Three of his slaves.

23. Three batteries of artillery.

24. *O.R.* Series I, Vol. 15, p. 383.

25. Sgt. Robert S. Burwell, Company F, 2nd Virginia Infantry, was one of Mrs. Lee's nephews who lived with her next door to the Bartons. Cousin Willie was also in the 2nd Virginia.

26. The mass of the army retreated past the Shady Elm factory to Bartonsville and the turnpike. C. D. Fishburne in S.H.S.P. 23, p. 133.

27. An outbuilding, used at different times as farm office or schoolhouse. His grandmother lived in the main house.

28. Despite the chaotic aftermath of battle and enemy control, Mrs. Barton and Mrs. Lee managed to visit their boys, after learning from a note received by Mary Jones (Mrs. W. S.) that Bob Burwell, Bob Bell, Willie, and Rannie were at the town jail. Lee, *Diary,* Mar. 25, transcript p. 31. The jail was at the corner of Cecil and Market (about four blocks from the Barton house), and the prisoners marched from it up Market to the train depot on March 24. Mr. Barton and Fannie were not in town; it seems that he had gone to bring her home from visiting Jane in Maryland. On their way "they passed the prisoners at Harper's Ferry, but it was dark and they could not recognize anyone," reported Miss Laura Lee, adding, "Mrs. Barton had in the battle 4 sons, 4 brothers, 1 son-in-law and 2 nephews. . . ." *History,* Mar. 24, p. 22.

29. Surely an overstatement.

30. In his *Recollections,* Barton reprinted lengthy articles from the Baltimore papers, which described the pro-Southern crowds lining the prisoners' route in Baltimore.

31. Colonel Cummings, 33rd Virginia Infantry, reported that casualties were 18 killed, 27 wounded, 14 missing; i.e., 59 out of a strength of 275 men. *O.R.* Series I, Vol. 15, p. 396.

32. Anne Tucker Magill, widow of Dr. Alfred T. Magill, was one of the militant secessionist ladies of Winchester.

33. Joe, who may have refugeed with his family there, had no way of knowing that his younger brother had been taken prisoner in the battle that had taken place on their farm.

34. This Thomas Marshall was a first cousin of Tom Marshall of Oak Hill. He was shortly to enlist in his brother Capt. James Marshall's company, 7th Virginia Cavalry (which became Company E, 12th Virginia Cavalry), and was killed in action at Brandy Station, October 12, 1863.

35. Sue's brother Peyton Clark noted in his diary that the mules had been taken from Austin at Carysbrooke. Clark, *Diary,* Mar. 28, transcript p. 11.

36. Marshall was probably nephew Marshall Barton, in Cutshaw's Battery, but possibly nephew Marshall Jones who had reenlisted in the 2nd Virginia Infantry on February 24.

37. This was the Battle of Shiloh or Pittsburg Landing, Tennessee, April 6–7. "Capt. S" was probably Capt. E. A. Shands, 7th Virginia Cavalry.

38. Union Gen. George B. McClellan and the Army of the Potomac had landed at Fort Monroe and were attempting to move up the Peninsula and attack Richmond. The C.S.A. line was at Yorktown. Gen. Joseph E. Johnston was commanding the defense of Richmond.

39. The guns at Fredericksburg could be heard in the Valley.

40. Probably a Dutch oven.

41. Mrs. R. W. Barton may have been in Nelson County with her son Joseph. In any event, she came through the lines to Winchester April 26. Lee, *Diary,* transcript p. 81.

42. Gen. Albert Sidney Johnston was mortally wounded while commanding at Pittsburg Landing.

43. Mrs. Lee wrote March 27, "I was very much gratified to find how much pleasure my letter had given, not only to the Col. [William S. H. Baylor] but to others; he read it to Genl. Jackson & Turner Ashby & the Genl. commended the spirit of our household. . . ." *Diary,* transcript p. 40. On the same day, she was writing that letters had been seized by the provost marshal, "an uncomfortable idea, for many reasons, one of which was, the possibility of being arrested for treasonable correspondence. I arranged to pack a trunk, to have ready for any emergency."

44. This may have been the onset of his illness.

45. Frank Clark was assigned to Jackson's command as Quartermaster. "Dr. M_" was almost certainly Dr. Hunter H. McGuire.

46. Edmund must have run off. Albert was a slave rented from his half brother James F. Jones.

47. Robert L. Dabney was chaplain of the 27th Virginia Infantry and future Jackson biographer.

48. Robert W. Baylor of Charles Town had raised Baylor's Light Horse, which became Company B, 12th Virginia Cavalry. He was severely wounded at McGaheysville and taken prisoner.

49. Capt. Elverton A. Shands, Company I, 7th Virginia Cavalry. His service record gives only his last appearance on the muster roll, April 22.

50. This occurred April 25 after Admiral Farragut ran the forts on the lower Mississippi.

51. Gabriel Jones (1724–1806), the "Valley Lawyer," and his farm, Bogota, near Port Republic on what is now Route 708.

52. Writer corrected from "1st" and "Thursday" to "2nd" and "Friday."

53. Samuel H. Lewis, of Lewiston near Port Republic, had served in the War of 1812 as an artillery captain, and subsequently became brigadier general in the militia. He was a connection of Frank Jones through the Marshall family. While remaining a staunch Union man through the war, he was hospitable to all; Jackson and his staff had spent the night of April 30 at Lewiston.

54. Mat's husband, John M. Baldwin, had died just three weeks before. Sally B_ was Sally Baldwin, John's sister.

55. Wednesday crossed out.

56. Strother Jones was with the Quartermaster Department at Waynesborough, according to Robert Barton. No service record can be found.

57. U.S. Gen. Robert H. Milroy.

58. Abner Crump Hopkins had recently joined the 2nd Virginia Infantry as its chaplain. A major's pay was $150 a month, a private's, $11.

CHAPTER 5

1. Parts of the army were in the vicinity of Staunton from May 5 to May 7; the battle occurred May 8.

2. This account, an original typescript, appears to have

been prepared for publication but never published. It is somewhat more detailed than that in the memoir, and has been substituted for it.

3. All the Broadus families listed in Luray in the 1860 census were mulatto. The only one with daughters was that of Eliza Broadus, thirty-seven, whose three eldest daughters ranged in age from ten to eight in 1860.

4. This is St. Thomas P.E. Chapel, on Church Street.

5. According to Lenoir Chambers, the cavalry with Jackson were unnerved by the hidden rifles, as was the 33rd Virginia, just behind them. They broke and "rushed to the rear," but the situation was retrieved by Winder who called up the 27th, the 2nd, "which he sent to the right of the road" [Springdale], and the 5th. *Stonewall Jackson,* Vol. 1, pp. 534–35.

6. William F. Rogers was listed as "overseer of farm" in the entry following C. M. Barton (then at Springdale) in the 1860 census. Mr. Rogers was mentioned in 1863–64 in a context to suggest he had continued in this capacity.

7. This mill was on the northeast side of Abram's Creek.

8. The Hillman toll gate was on the Valley Turnpike (Route 11), just north of its intersection with Cedar Creek Turnpike.

9. Robert E. Lee, Jr., attended the University of Virginia from 1860 to 1862, and enlisted in the Rockbridge Artillery in March. Robert B. McKim, a student at the University of Virginia when the war began, enlisted at Darkesville, July 6, 1861.

10. Algernon Sidney Whitt served from August 1861 to Appomattox.

11. Possibly Pvt. Jonathan Agner or Agnor of Lexington.

12. This description is from R. T. Barton, *Memoir,* p. 79.

13. The hill, about fifty to sixty feet high, provided a fine view of Winchester, about a mile and a half away.

14. Gen. Richard Taylor, Louisiana Brigade.

15. The 1st Rockbridge was engaged two hours and in that time had three men killed and eighteen wounded out of eighty-nine, the highest percentage of all C.S.A. units. Four horses were killed and five wounded.

16. "Willow Lawn" belonged to the mill owner, Isaac H. Hollingsworth, Jr. The house, on the Valley Turnpike, is no longer standing.

17. Her younger son, with the Rockbridge Artillery.

18. Ann C. R. Jones to Lucy Parkhill, October 15, 1862.

19. Laura Lee, *History,* May 27, pp. 55–57.

20. Randolph Barton, *Recollections,* p. 16: "My last ride with [Marshall] was to an elevation about half a mile south of the city near Hollingsworth's Mills. During the winter of 1861–2 he was appointed First Lieutenant of Cutshaw's Battery, which on the morning of May 25, 1862, in the pursuit of Banks, took position on that very hill. The last shell from the guns of the retreating enemy exploded almost in his face and, dreadfully mangled, he was carried to the nearby mills and very soon died. Later in the day his body was carried to my father's house in Winchester, where it was laid upon a cot in the parlor. Unconsciously to those around, the blood from his wounds fell upon the carpet, and left a stain which was never entirely effaced. In after years, when we removed to Springdale, and the same carpet was used, my mother would often wonder what the stain came from. We could not dispense with the carpet, but she ever remained in happy ignorance of the tragic cause."

21. Mrs. John M. Baldwin, widowed in April, Stuart, and Maria had been added to the household. Tom Marshall's five motherless children had gone to the Bartons when their father joined the army. Fanny had visited their sister Jane and family in April.

22. Due to the Union movement from Fredericksburg toward the Valley, which threatened to cut them off, the 2nd Virginia left Loudoun Heights the night of May 30 and reached Newtown at 10:00 P.M. on the thirty-first.

23. Mrs. Lee recorded that Mrs. Barton was "in the depths of despair, as Jim had gone" March 22, and two days later that "two" had gone. *Diary,* transcript pp. 26, 29.

24. Cousin Willie was then at Fort Delaware with Rannie.

25. Fremont was moving from Wardenville and Shields from Manassas.

26. Ashby was killed June 6, in rearguard action defending the retreat of the wagon train, two miles south of Harrisonburg.

27. *The Evening News-Item,* Winchester, Vol. 14, No. 175. Robert wrote a series of three articles, published in 1905.

28. Lt. James Cole Davis of Lexington served from April 1861 to Appomattox.

29. The losses were not as severe as might be expected: six wounded, one captured, one gun captured.

30. H. J. Williams as militia captain had been instrumental in recruiting the Southern Guards, which became Company D, 5th Virginia Infantry.

31. After a month at Fort Warren, Dr. Baldwin had been sent to Fortress Monroe, Virginia, to be exchanged for a Massachusetts colonel Lee, in early April. He had been commissioned Surgeon, C.S.A., May 6, and about this time was attached to the hospital at University, just west of Charlottesville.

32. Robert was listed on the June 30 muster roll as "absent sick sent to the rear June 12." The Colstons lived near Ivy Depot, west of Charlottesville.

CHAPTER 6

1. Clark, *Journal,* June 16–18, transcript pp. 30–33. There had been attempts to requisition or occupy the Clark house during the previous Federal occupation in April.

2. Lee, *Diary,* Apr. 5, transcript p. 54.

3. Mrs. William A. Davis, neighbor at Sunnyside, was about halfway between Vaucluse and Carysbrooke.

4. Mary's daughter Annie and Sue's daughter Louisa were both seven.

5. Evidently the Newtown provost marshal did not require the oath for a pass.

6. The elder Mrs. Jones wrote that her stepson was taken ill in late May, but it had been necessary for him to leave home when the Yankees returned; he was by this time probably in Waynesborough.

7. Memoir of Frank B. Jones by Abner Crump Hopkins written for Frank's son W. Randolph Jones, 1909.

8. Thomas Jefferson Randolph was a brother of C.S.A. Secretary of War George Wythe Randolph and a

first cousin of Frank's mother. His estate, Edgehill, was near Monticello. John Charles Randolph Taylor of Albemarle County was married to T. J. Randolph's daughter and doubly related to Frank Jones through his mother's family.

9. Hopkins, op. cit.

10. The guns on McGehee's Hill were those of Battery L/M, commanded by Lt. Horace J. Hayden, part of Capt. John Edwards's 3rd U.S. Artillery. The 2nd Virginia suffered grievously in its leadership in this battle; regimental losses were ten killed or mortally wounded, seventeen wounded, one captured.

11. Peyton Clark copied a portion of this letter and kept it in his diary, but the original may have been Baylor's August 7 letter to Mrs. H. H. Lee, who mentioned how "tenderly" the colonel wrote of Frank. Mrs. Lee was in frequent correspondence with Baylor and other C. S. Army leaders. Clark, *Diary,* additional page. Lee, *Diary,* Sept. 5, transcript p. 225.

12. John Alexander Straith served as assistant surgeon, 2nd Virginia Infantry, from May 1861 until Appomattox, frequently tending various Bartons and Joneses.

13. Hopkins, op. cit. Mr. Haxall was either Bolling W. or R. Barton Haxall of Richmond, first cousins of David W. Barton.

14. Dr. William A. Davis, the Joneses' neighbor, had been commissioned Surgeon at Chimborazo Hospital in Richmond November 13, 1861, and spent most of the war in Richmond. Mrs. Hardgrove's may have been a boardinghouse listed in the 1860 census as in charge of Nancy Eubank, in which William and Anne Hardgrove lived, with ten others.

15. Dr. Baldwin's assignment at this time was not indicated in his record, but other evidence suggests he was attached to the 5th Virginia Infantry until midsummer when, finding active service too strenuous, he was transferred to hospital duty at his own request. Mary Sherrard was a Winchester friend, probably visiting in Richmond. Dr. Cornelius Walker was Assistant Rector of St. Paul's Episcopal Church, Richmond, but had been at Christ Church in Winchester from 1847 to 1860; the Joneses were parishioners and friends.

16. Howard T. Barton, VMI '43 (Mary B. Jones's brother), was at Chimborazo Hospital for most of the war, having been commissioned November 13, 1861. In latter years, Dr. Barton lived in Lexington, was provisional surgeon at the VMI, and attended Gen. R. E. Lee.

17. Clark, *Diary,* July 14, transcript p. 36. *The Maryland News Sheet,* taken from the June 30 Richmond *Dispatch.*

18. Lee, *Diary,* July 12–July 15, passim., pp. 171–74.

19. Lucy Randolph Parkhill and Mrs. Jones were first cousins. Mrs. Jones wrote faithfully to her and her daughter Harriet, who both lived in Tallahassee, Florida.

20. Lucy's son (Harriet's brother), Capt. G. Washington Parkhill, a Tallahassee doctor, was killed in action during the Seven Days' Battles, leaving a young widow and two children.

21. Cutshaw's mother came to stay with the Bartons and nurse her son; Mrs. Lee mentioned her being there as late as August 5. *Diary,* transcript p. 196.

On August 8 Cutshaw was issued a pass, on his parole to stay within Federal lines until exchanged.

22. Winchester suffered an epidemic of typhoid as summer came on—many cases were mentioned in Mrs. Lee's journal, including Lal and other members of her own household and Madge Marshall, next door. It seems likely that Strother contracted it there.

23. He was home by August 8, when he wrote to Rev. William A. Crawford, pastor of the Old Opequon Church near Kernstown, that he could not leave his bed. W. S. Jones to W. A. Crawford, August 8.

24. Col. James W. Allen, also killed at Gaines' Mill, was succeeded by Frank's friend Lawson Botts who was mortally wounded at the Second Battle of Manassas, August 28.

25. This letter is continued in chapter 7.

26. Lee, *Diary,* July 24, transcript p. 184.

27. Ibid., Aug. 22 and 19, transcript pp. 211, 207.

28. Ibid., Aug. 20–22, transcript pp. 208–10.

29. Letter of Bishop William Rollinson Whittingham, quoted by Rev. William Pinkney, Secretary of Standing Committee of the Diocese of Maryland in Resolutions to the Bishop, December 15, 1861. The Archives of the Episcopal Diocese of Maryland.

30. According to the Baltimore papers, the prisoners arrived March 25 and left for Fort Delaware, March 29.

31. The first five named were of the 2nd Virginia Infantry. Over 250 Kernstown prisoners were sent to Fort Delaware.

32. The Ettings and Robinsons were related to Rannie's aunt Caroline M. Barton, Willie's mother.

33. Then-Capt. Augustus A. Gibson was in charge at Fort Delaware. The Sheilds lived in Earleville, about twenty-five miles from Delaware City, the town nearest the fort. Lee, *Diary,* Apr. 12, p. 63: "Jane Shields has been to Fort Delaware to see the boys & though it was positively against orders, Capt. Gibson allowed Ranny to see her; she says she will send him, Willie & Bob supplies every week." On June 28, Mrs. Lee wrote that Jane was so "delicate" that Mr. Sheild wanted her parents to come—and on June 30 that the Bartons left to go to Jane, returning July 8 (pp. 153, 161, 167). Since Martha left to visit Jane, July 15 (p. 172), perhaps she was able to see Rannie, too.

34. Ibid., May 2, p. 86.

35. Dr. John Hanson Thomas was Mrs. D. W. Barton's second cousin, through the Marshall family. He represented Baltimore in the 1861 State Legislature, which determined the secession issue. Although Maryland did not vote to secede, "Dr. Thomas and other leading citizens were arrested by military order, at midnight, and confined at Fortress Monroe and thence removed to Fort Lafayette." Paxton, *Marshall Family,* pp. 220–21. This occurred September 12, 1861, and the prisoners were sent to Fort Warren, according to Bradley T. Johnson, *Maryland,* Vol. 2, *Confederate Military History,* ed. Clement A. Evans, p. 61. Capt. John Hanson Thomas, Jr., Company H, 1st Maryland Infantry, was subsequently on General Loring's staff. (The Thomases' younger son Lt. Raleigh Colston Thomas later served in the 1st Maryland Cavalry and as aide to General Lomax.)

36. Rannie confused the date of his exchange at Aiken's Landing with that of his departure from Fort Delaware. His service record shows that the exchange took place at Aiken's on August 5.

37. On August 8, Rannie was paid $205.80 for his service from September 9, 1861, to July 1, 1862, and $25 for clothing by Maj. John Ambler, Quartermaster C.S.A. Ambler was a cousin through the Marshall family, and had married a daughter of Sen. James M. Mason.

38. As described, this would be about 120 miles. This seemingly illogical route may have been delineated by Rannie's attempts to reach the army, which was on September 4 at Leesburg before crossing into Maryland. Possibly the Upperville diversion was occasioned by a swing past Piedmont (Delaplane) to visit family or an attempt to find transport to his destination. "The Pot-House" was approximately at Leithtown.

39. Poague, *Gunner with Stonewall,* p. 33.

40. B. R. Jones letter to VMI, July 1, 1910.

41. *O.R.* Series I, Vol. 12, Part 2, p. 653.

42. There is no mention of Strother's absence or return in the regiment's muster roll; his grandmother's letter of October 15 is the only clue to the onset of his illness.

43. John B. Baldwin was a first cousin of Robert's late brother-in-law Dr. John M. Baldwin. Mrs. John B. Baldwin was the former Susan M. Peyton. The Peyton girls were daughters of Staunton lawyer John Howe Peyton: Jennie (Virginia F.), later Mrs. Joseph F. Kent, and Cornelia B., married three times.

44. A Moorman family was listed in Burke's Mills in the 1860 census. Mrs. M. S. Moorman was a widow with five children.

45. Willie was able to rejoin the 2nd Virginia Infantry September 1; Rannie was out of service until early October.

46. This reorganization, reducing the size of the unit, had occurred in late June; Marshall was appointed Major in early July.

47. Dr. Baldwin was at Lovingston until September 5. The hospital equipment and at least some personnel apparently were transferred to Winchester, where the newly organized facility was called the Lovington (or Lovingston) Hospital. (This accounts for Willie's service record showing that he was in "Lovingston Hospital, Winchester" in late August.) Robert was "an employee at Belmont and York Hospitals from Aug. 15th to Nov. 1st at 25 cts. per day."

CHAPTER 7

1. Lee, *Diary,* Sept. 3, transcript p. 222. Clark, *Diary,* Sept. 8, transcript p. 54.

2. Moore, *Cannoneer,* p. 161. David R. Barton was the only officer remaining in his unit. Robert R. Barton of Lexington, David W. Barton's nephew, had enlisted in Company C, 1st Virginia Cavalry at the beginning of the war. He had been absent in July and August, at home on sick leave. Ned Moore had seen Robert in Richmond when he was on his way there. Ibid., p. 95.

3. Ibid., p. 162. Their ninety-six-mile trip to Staunton took twenty-six hours by stage. After a stopover, they took another stage to Lexington, arriving to matriculate at the VMI, September 26, 1862, as members of the class of 1866.

4. Rannie's appointment as Second Lieutenant was confirmed October 9, 1862. Charles H. Stewart was in command of Company K, 2nd Virginia Infantry. W. E. Cutshaw and Joseph H. Carpenter had both been pupils of T. J. Jackson at VMI. The two units were amalgamated September 28 due to losses, including that of Carpenter, wounded August 7 at Cedar Run (a wound that killed him six months later). Cutshaw had been seriously wounded at Winchester May 25 and taken prisoner there when the Yankees returned. The boys' brother-in-law Thomas Marshall had been exchanged September 12, rejoining the 7th Virginia Cavalry at Berryville as Major.

5. Don was a Springdale-based hunting dog.

6. Robert had returned to Winchester with his hospital unit. Bengy may be Benjamin T. Holliday, who briefly attended VMI before going into Chew's Battery.

7. John Hopkins Baldwin was the second son of Dr. Robert T. Baldwin. Johnny and Rannie were the same age and boyhood friends and Johnny's younger brother Lud was Bolling's friend and schoolmate at Winchester Academy. Johnny served in Company F, 2nd Virginia Infantry, from June 1861 to Appomattox; his family had heard this happy news by letter July 31. Lee *Diary,* transcript p. 191.

8. Lewis H. Fitch, about sixteen, of the Hartman/Fitch family of Winchester.

9. Virginia (known as Jenny, Jinny, or Ginny) and Martha Barton, sisters of Robert, the Lexington cousins whom Rannie had doubtless come to know while at VMI.

10. Two slaves. Aunt Silla was Priscilla Piper, mammy of the Marshall children. Sukey had been the younger Barton boys' mammy and now was the cook.

11. James was then lieutenant in the Nitre and Mining Bureau; since July he had been based at Staunton.

12. Ann C. R. Jones to Lucy Parkhill, October 15. Marshall Jones had twice enlisted with the 2nd Virginia Infantry and had both times been discharged by the medical board. In September he had been detailed as a nurse in Winchester but on October 11 was again discharged. No record can be found of James's cavalry service. Perhaps he served with the militia in the emergency period of April–May 1861 and realized his limitations.

13. Harriet's brother, Capt. G. W. Parkhill, killed in July 1862.

14. Bev Jones, after service in the Rockbridge Artillery, and Quartermaster Department, was appointed hospital steward to 33rd Virginia Infantry on October 11.

15. Rannie Barton was perhaps her favorite grandson, with the special association owing to the name.

16. With the return of the Federal forces, all the men could be expected to leave again. Peyton Clark, after his summer experiences with the Federals, was moved to join the Confederate forces in some capacity, apparently connecting himself with Nitre

and Mining (as had William). Frank of course went with the army.

17. Though the Davises were from Massachusetts, Dr. Davis was serving as a surgeon and Charlie was later in the 7th Virginia Cavalry.

18. As so often, "delicate" is a euphemism for consumptive. Mrs. Lee recorded that Fanny had had a hemorrhage May 1. "She took cold on her journey home [from Maryland], & has had a troublesome cough ever since." *Diary,* transcript p. 86.

19. Rev. William S. White, of the Presbyterian church in Lexington.

20. William P. Cupp's mill was at the confluence of Cedar Creek and a small stream just downstream from Turkey Run.

21. Strother was recovering from his debilitating summer illness. Maj. Jed Hotchkiss had met him in Middletown on October 15 and at "Maj. Jones's" invitation, went on to spend the night at Vaucluse. Hotchkiss, *Make Me a Map,* p. 88.

22. Lost Brook farm was near Cedar Creek and Buffalo Marsh. Strother Barton had farmed it before the war.

23. The Shady Elm woolen factory, and an adjacent farm, at Bartonsville, were bought by the mill's manager.

24. Letter of Gen. R. E. Lee, in "Camp near Winchester," October 26, 1862, in the VMI Archives.

25. Smith's eldest son, Thomas Henderson Smith, VMI '62, was serving as a lieutenant in Alexander's battalion of artillery.

26. He was on the muster roll of the Rockbridge Artillery through October 31; November 13 he was officially approved as "agent" of Nitre and Mining.

27. Pughtown, now Gainesboro, was about seven miles northwest of Winchester, its name evidently a family or local joke.

28. The raid of October 10–12 around McClellan's army to Chambersburg was called "Stuart's second ride."

29. It was usually arranged for childbirth to take place in a downstairs room, and for an older female relative to visit for the period of birth and confinement. The Bartons' first three children had been born at Vaucluse, but the younger ones in Winchester, probably with Mrs. Jones in attendance. Now, perhaps to have room for other people (e.g., wounded soldiers), the parents took over that room for their own. In a December 14 letter, D. W. Barton referred to "the chamber (the Library)."

30. Thomas Clayton Williams, "Clate," was a son of their father's law partner. He was Rannie's age, and serving in Chew's Battery.

31. Serious inflation was afflicting the Confederacy that fall, and shoes had become not only expensive but also hard to obtain (price increases were 500 to 1,000 percent). *Political Science Quarterly,* Vol. 14, p. 287. That winter VMI established a shoe factory. Couper, *One Hundred Years,* Vol. 2, p. 166.

32. Promotion officially approved October 30.

33. Maj. Elisha Franklin Paxton was chosen to command the Stonewall Brigade, passing over Col. Charles A. Ronald and Col. Andrew J. Grigsby (4th and 27th Virginia Infantry respectively), both of whom had temporarily commanded the brigade, and the latter the division.

34. Lt. Robert W. Hunter had previously been regimental adjutant. Frank Clark was relieved of his duties with Jackson's command on October 1 and was assigned as paymaster at Winchester. As "agent" for the Quartermaster Department he was doing a little horse-trading.

35. Hogs would have been kept in the long back garden by the stable, and fed on the household's garbage. Evidently each of the boys and some of the slaves had a piglet to raise.

36. George Ash may have been a hired hand or the slave George listed in David W. Barton's will.

37. John B. T. Reed, sometime coppersmith and clergyman, served as mayor of Winchester for part of the war. He may have been going to Lexington to withdraw his son from VMI; school records indicate that Theodore, eighteen, attended only three months, later enlisting in the army.

38. Mrs. Barton had lost a son, a brother, and a son-in-law in 1862.

39. The Braxtons were Vaucluse slaves.

40. The Maryland Line consisted of a battalion of the 1st Maryland Cavalry and a battalion of the 2nd Maryland Infantry, both forming in Winchester and under strength.

41. The friend was perhaps her "intended," Dr. Cornelius Baldwin.

42. Bolly was Sukey's little boy.

43. Anna had lived with the Bartons for so long that the boys regarded her as a sister. She was listed as part of the household in the 1860 census.

44. Despite their favored status with Mr. Gaver, now owner of the woolen factory, this must have been a special occasion—any new dress was, in the Confederacy. The cloth was probably as coarse and sturdy as the uniforms.

45. Ann C. R. Jones to Bolling W. Barton, December 3.

46. Woodside was vulnerable to Yankee raids and incursions.

47. Although discharged for medical reasons from the Confederate Army, Marshall might have been liable to the Federal draft and of course would have had to take the oath.

48. Ranny was Frank Jones's son, then five and a half.

49. The diary is Francis B. Jones's diary of early 1862.

50. Charles P. Moncure was connected to the Randolph family. His October 22, 1862, letter to W. Strother Jones, written at "Horse Shoe," is among the Jones/Clark papers.

51. Strother Jones would have moved his slaves to Stanardsville, about seventy miles south, to avoid their possible emancipation.

52. Ned Moore, still recovering from his Antietam wound, did not return to the army until December 31. His brother John, also of the Rockbridge Artillery, had been discharged for ill health in July.

53. Both these farms were in the Bartonsville vicinity.

54. Phil presumably was her husband. He was not listed among the household slaves in D. W. Barton's will, and was mentioned in Barton's letter of December 14, 1862, as if he were a free man. Philip Wormley, a "domestic" in Isaac Hite's household at Cedar Creek, was one of only two Philips listed in the *Abstract of Free Negroes, 1860,* the other having a large family.

55. This appears in various editions of the *Hymnal*

of the Protestant Episcopal Church, Revised and Enlarged.

56. One regiment was Tom Marshall's, the 7th Virginia Cavalry.

57. Joseph C. Stiles, seventy-year-old chaplain of Ewell's division, actually a Virginian.

58. The 2nd Virginia Infantry suffered only four killed and sixteen wounded. William Brockenbrough Colston, Captain since September 17, had been wounded also at Kernstown. Apparently he did not recover sufficiently from this wound to return to active service, and was transferred to the Invalid Corps in May 1864. He was Col. Raleigh T. Colston's brother.

59. Robert T. Barton had "always understood that brother David was not killed by a skirmisher but was struck on the side of the head with a piece of shell. There is a man here in the employ of the B & O RR who recently sent me word that he was standing right by him when he was killed and it has been on my mind for quite some time to see him and get from him a detailed account of his death." Letter to Randolph Barton, May 26, 1897. Johnson, *Memorial*, p. 292, stated that Strother carried David to the rear, where he died fifteen minutes later. This appears to be impossible. U.S. War Department, *Atlas*, Plate 31 #4, shows positions on the morning of the thirteenth, with David's unit, Carpenter's Battery, at the left end of the C.S.A. line on the heights, a good mile to the left of the 2nd Virginia's position with Taliaferro's division. David had known Fairfax at Episcopal High School, the university and in the Southern Guards before they both served in the Rockbridge Artillery.

60. The Federals began to withdraw the night of the fourteenth.

61. Capt. Robert Preston Chew commanded a light horse-drawn battery, which was operating with General Jones's cavalry brigade in the Valley in December. Two of Philip Williams's sons, as well as other Winchester boys, were members.

62. Woodstock is about twenty-six miles from Winchester.

63. McDonald, *Diary*, Dec. 17, p. 115. Lee, *Diary*, Dec. 16, transcript p. 275. The ladies' journals agree on these dates, Mrs. Lee saying that the news came in a dispatch.

64. When the Federals occupied in force at Christmas, the provost marshal sent search parties to look for Rebels home for the holiday; often they were guided by the servants' information. Phillips, *Lower Shenandoah*, p. 294.

65. Robert's Quillen's Road unquestionably corresponds to the Senseney Road, but there is no record of its having this name at any time.

66. A narrow and secluded valley within the Massanutten mass, running on the same northeast/southwest axis for about twenty miles. Robby must have approached it from Waterlick. Its hidden northern entrance made it ideal for Confederate guerrillas later in the war.

67. Gabriel Jones (1724–1806), the "Valley Lawyer." The house in 1862 and now called Bogota is a later one, near the site of the original house. It is west of Lewiston (which was at what is now the intersection of Routes 340 and 708) and across the Shenandoah

River. The Lewises fled there from Lewiston when the battle was impending, and are said to have watched it from the upstairs porch of Bogota, which would have offered a splendid view. Mark W. Cowell et al., *The Family of John Lewis, Pioneer*, San Antonio, Fisher Publ., 1985, pp. 316–17.

CHAPTER 8

1. National Archives, Compiled Service Records. [#124] Special Requisitions #40, Jan. 21 and Feb. 14, 1863.

2. Mary Barton Jones's father, Thomas B. Barton. The house, at what is now 904 Princess Anne Street, had been used as a field hospital during the battle, but was sufficiently damaged and dangerous that the Bartons refugeed to Richmond. They returned in 1865 and there entertained Gen. R. E. Lee for a week in May 1869.

3. Marshall, Lee's military secretary from March 1862 through Appomattox, was a first cousin of Mrs. D. W. Barton.

4. Lexington cousins Jenny (Virginia) and Martha Barton, whom Bolling saw regularly.

5. Lee, *Diary*, Feb. 5, transcript p. 307, and Feb. 6, p. 308. Lute was one of Mrs. Lee's nieces, Louisa Burwell, about twenty-five.

6. Ibid., Feb. 13, p. 312.

7. McDonald, *Diary*, Feb. 19, p. 137.

8. Ibid., Mar. 30, transcript p. 330ff.

9. Ibid., Jan.–Mar., pp. 300–20 passim.

10. McDonald, *Diary*, Apr. 10, p. 153. The Steele children recorded a number of instances of people being sent through and coming into Newtown. Steele, "Diary," *W.-F.C.H.S. Papers*, Vol. 3.

11. Ann C. R. Jones to Bolling W. Barton, January 23.

12. W. L. Baldwin to Bolling W. Barton, January 16.

13. He refers to the successful attack by southern gunboats on Federal blockading ships—what was believed to be the lifting of the blockade at Charleston—and the failure of the first Federal gunboat attack on Vicksburg.

14. W. Strother Barton to Robert T. Barton, February 5.

15. His cousin Edward A. Moore, Rockbridge Artillery, was at home until the end of 1862 recuperating from his Antietam wound. Cousin Robert had probably been to Lexington on his furlough.

16. Dr. Cornelius Baldwin, "Nepe," was Bev's superior as Assistant Surgeon of the 33rd Virginia. Bev obtained a discharge and was appointed to Nitre and Mining on April 10, 1863.

17. Ignorance of sanitation, infection, and how disease spread was universal. Contaminated water and food were the most common causes of the chronic diarrhea Rannie suffered later, and Tom Marshall's comment on "bad water" shows that at least he suspected a cause.

18. Gen. Joseph F. Hooker had replaced Burnside as commander of the Army of the Potomac, January 25.

19. Brig. Gen. William E. "Grumble" Jones commanding a cavalry brigade and commander of the Valley District. Jones, who had feuded with his superior

J. E. B. Stuart since the beginning of the war, had been temporarily separated into an independent command. A. J. Grigsby, who had resigned in chagrin in the wake of Paxton's appointment, here continued to politick for a star.

20. James M. Garnett, David's friend from the university and the Rockbridge Artillery, had been made Ordnance Officer, Stonewall Brigade.

21. John and Sarah Steele of Newtown were ten and twelve in 1863. Together they kept a diary: "Sun. Feb. 8: Six Yankees came out at ten oclock. They left some of their men at Barton's [Springdale] to take their negroes. About three o'clock twenty-three abolitionists came to town. . . ." They mentioned many more roving abolitionists over the next month. Steele, "Diary," *W.-F. C. H. S. Papers*, Vol. 3, p. 63.

22. Ibid., Feb. 26, p. 65.

23. Maj. Holmes Conrad, the Bartons' neighbor and Powell's younger brother, was then serving as brigade adjutant. In spring 1864 on just such an escapade as Rannie's, he spent several days in occupied Winchester with H. Kyd Douglas, who was enamored of Conrad's sister Sallie. They were discovered and pursued by Federal cavalry. Douglas, *I Rode with Stonewall*, pp. 274–75.

24. Oliver R. Funsten was Colonel of the 17th Virginia Cavalry, and Richard H. Dulany, of the 7th.

25. This suggests that Sukey was one of the children of William Peterson, a free black who appears as such in Frederick County records in 1861 and after the war. He was a forty-eight-year-old day laborer, in a large household of free blacks living near the Episcopal church in Winchester. Nancy was another slave listed in D. W. Barton's will as being at the Winchester house.

26. Anna may have remained at Vaucluse rather than return to occupied Winchester; it was surely easier to get Southern mail and news to and from Vaucluse. Possibly she had gone on to Staunton.

27. Two aforementioned farms in the Bartonsville area, each about 225 acres. Shady Oak had been in the family since 1838, and had been sold to John H. Meade the previous December.

28. It was not uncommon for soldiers to transfer to the cavalry after a year or two of marching.

29. Marshall had been discharged for disability for the second time the previous October, and Mrs. Jones's letter of December 4 implies that he was consumptive. No official record can be found of Marshall's service in the Nitre and Mining Bureau, although there is a letter from James Jones, of August 10, 1863, telling him how to "secure the transfer" and giving details of the position. Other references suggest he was working there before appointed.

30. Dr. George Magruder and his wife, Catherine, of Woodstock, were named by Mrs. Lee as willing to receive letters for her. *Diary*, Sept. 15, 1864, transcript p. 682. Evidently they also passed on small articles that came through the lines from the North, such as the little luxuries for Mrs. Neill (probably Kate Neill of Clarke County, who had evidently refugeed south to be with her husband, Dr. S. S. Neill, army surgeon in Charlottesville).

31. Consumptive herself, she knew it ran in the family and was afraid for Rannie. However, he never developed the disease.

32. Possibly Robby did not send this letter to Rannie as Fan asked, as it was among his papers.

33. This appears to be a veiled allusion to Fanny's complicity in the "Milroy valentine."

34. Randolph J. Barton to Bolling W. Barton, March 15.

35. This appointment was at the suggestion of H. Kyd Douglas, according to Barton's letter of September 14, 1885, published in Paxton, *Memoir and Memorials*, p. 106. In fact, Rannie was six weeks short of nineteen.

36. Rannie evidently thought it discreet not to name his older brother as author of the verse, but he was so identified by H. Kyd Douglas, *I Rode with Stonewall*, p. 60. Marshall Barton's notebook is in the VMI archives. This passage, from "When he was a professor . . ." to this point, appears verbatim in Barton's review of Henderson's *Stonewall Jackson* first published in the *Conservative Review*, Feb. 1899, Vol. l, pp. 41–59, and later in S.H.S.P., Vol. 38, pp. 271–72.

37. Robert T. Barton to Bolling W. Barton, from Staunton, March 27.

38. And he's right, yet another rumor—but also because Winchester proved to be virtually indefensible.

39. Undated fragment, W. Strother Barton to Bolling W. Barton. Fast Day was March 27.

40. Robert R. Barton to Bolling W. Barton, from camp near Culpeper, March 30.

41. If this is so, Mr. Barton was the only "secesh" citizen who ever had a good word for Milroy.

42. After the First Conscription Act of April 16, 1862, at Swift Run Gap, the brigade attained its greatest strength.

43. Quartermaster, C.S.A.

44. Barton is referenced in Bigelow, *Chancellorsville*, p. 275, note 2, as having seen a Federal observation balloon when the brigade was near the Furnace. If this is so, the Federals either did not see the Rebs, did not communicate it, or the information received on the ground was disregarded. William W. Hassler, "The Rise of the Union Air Force," *Civil War Magazine*, Vol. 19, p. 25, says that Lowe's balloons were grounded by fog and high winds "most of the time."

45. This paragraph is taken from an article published in the Lexington *Evening News*, May 8, 1913, in which Rannie expanded on the account of his wounding.

46. Maj. John William Walls, twenty-four, was surgeon, 5th Virginia Infantry. He was a doctor in Newtown (as was his father of the same name).

47. The Dorsey family, with whom David Barton had spent a year as a tutor before the war, had refugeed to Richmond. Mrs. Dorsey's father was the Confederate representative in London courting a British alliance.

48. Richard Barton Haxall and Bolling Walker Haxall were David W. Barton's first cousins. Both families lived in Richmond but had plantations near Gordonsville. Their wealth derived from flour mills, cotton, real estate, railroads, and import-export.

49. William Stone Barton, a brother of Mrs. W. Strother Jones, Dr. Howard T. Barton, and Gen. Seth Barton. He was at this time Major in the A.I.G.O., and living with his parents, the Thomas B. Bartons, who had refugeed from Fredericksburg. After the war, he

was again a lawyer in Fredericksburg and then Circuit Court Judge.

50. The promotion was confirmed April 30, retroactive to March 28, and officially accepted May 18.

51. His family learned of Rannie's wound twelve days after the battle, and then that it was "slight." Lee, *Diary,* May 15, transcript p. 380ff. The first news of the victory had been received May 8. Ibid., p. 375. "Dr. B." was probably Dr. Robert F. Baldwin, cousin Cary's husband then assigned to the General Hospital in Staunton. But possibly Rannie had consulted Dr. Howard T. Barton, Mrs. Strother Jones's brother, at Chimborazo Hospital in Richmond.

52. These were two VMI friends, Randolph Russell Miller, '63, 10th Virginia Infantry, killed at Chancellorsville, and Capt. Samuel Downing, Jr., '62, 55th Virginia Infantry. Nothing in the record of Capt. R. Preston Chew, VMI '62, suggests that he was captured.

53. Stuart served in this capacity from 1850 to 1853 under Fillmore and Pierce. The Stuarts had five daughters and two sons, one of whom, A.H.H., Jr., "Sandy," seventeen, was a VMI cadet. Of the daughters, Augusta was by this time twenty-five, Frances twenty-one, and Mary nineteen.

54. Five of Susan Peyton Baldwin's brothers and sisters were living with the Baldwins in 1860. Virginia and Cornelia were by this time twenty-two and twenty.

CHAPTER 9

1. C. Maury Jones, *Memoir,* c. 1970, p. 2. Courtesy C. Maury Jones, Jr.

2. Mrs. Richard W. Barton, and Cary, Mrs. Robert F. Baldwin. The James F. Jones family left Fauquier County in late 1862 and spent the rest of the war in Staunton.

3. Thomas Barton Jones, Strother Jones's eldest child.

4. Flora, a Braxton daughter, about twenty-nine, was the wife of George Turner.

5. Keezletown is on the southwestern flank of Massanutten Mountain, an area rich in caves.

6. Mrs. Jones's room was on the main floor, which had tall, triple-sash windows also serving as doors to the balcony (or "platform") on three sides of the house.

7. Harriet Hardy, at this time about sixteen, was listed in the 1870 census as the Jones's governess.

8. A guard requested from the Union Army.

9. Lee, *Diary,* June 4, transcript p. 395.

10. Whisky was believed to be a remedy for almost everything.

11. Mary's sister-in-law Rebecca Jones was living with her Tidball sisters in town. The oath of allegiance was required by Federal forces for all comings and goings.

12. The Confederates continued to withstand Grant's siege.

13. It seems that Susan had availed herself of Mary's offer to store the Carysbrooke valuables when she closed the house in June 1862; some were secreted in the "office," an outbuilding near the main house.

14. Ann C. R. Jones to Bolling W. Barton, from Vaucluse, June 9.

15. Confederate forces overtook many of the departed slaves. Lavinia, Sally, Mary Braxton their mother, and others were returned to Vaucluse.

16. The Federals' retaliation for local agitation and defiance was to send citizens "through the lines" to the Confederacy, making them refugees. Dr. and Mrs. Robert T. Baldwin had just been "sent out." Dr. Baldwin (who suffered from a heart condition) had from the first refused to treat Federal soldiers, and Mrs. Baldwin was marked for her confrontational behavior. The particular incident precipitating this step, Milroy's insistence that the Baldwin servant Remus be paid (when the Baldwins had no money), was detailed by Mrs. Lee on June 10. *Diary,* transcript pp. 401–3. Possibly Anna Jones's offense was the wearing of a mourning badge for General Jackson, which Mrs. Lee described at some length on May 24, but there had probably been previous incidents. Ibid., May 23, transcript p. 386ff.

17. S.H.S.P., Vol. 3, p. 530; and Jubal A. Early, *War Memoirs,* edited and with an introduction by Frank E. Vandiver, Bloomington, Indiana University Press, 1960, p. 240.

18. Lee, *Diary,* May 24, p. 387.

19. Clement L. Vallandigham, leader of the "Copperheads," the peace party; he had already been banished to the Confederacy.

20. Charles W. Andrews, Episcopal minister.

21. The paper is extremely browned and mealy.

22. Lee, *Diary,* June 19, p. 419. Mrs. Lee continued to keep a journal.

23. Possibly Eliza A. Andrews, twenty-three, one of the minister's daughters.

24. In the June 21 Battle of Upperville, Federal Gen. Alfred Pleasonton's brigade pushed Stuart west toward the Blue Ridge.

25. Robert R. Barton to Bolling W. Barton, from Winchester, June 27.

26. Lee, *Diary,* July 6, transcript p. 430.

27. Joseph P. B. Wilmer had been ordained in the Protestant Episcopal Church in 1838. When the war began he left his parish in Philadelphia to return to his Virginia plantation. Traveling by ship, he and his family were detained at Fortress Monroe when it was discovered he was carrying contraband. In 1866 he was named bishop of Louisiana.

28. This horse was killed in a charge against the 6th U.S. Cavalry near Fairfield, Pennsylvania, ten miles southwest of Gettysburg, on July 3. Marshall was able to continue on a captured horse and again encountered the 6th U.S. Cavalry near Funkstown, July 7. *O. R.* Series I, Vol. 27, Part 2, pp. 756–62. He was later reimbursed $500 for the horse by the Confederate government.

29. Willie was listed as one of those killed, wounded, and missing from Early's division in this campaign. Since shortly before Gettysburg the Union had ceased to exchange prisoners, it follows that he was perhaps wounded or missing but not captured. He was detailed in the Ordnance Department from August 2 to January 2, 1864.

CHAPTER 10

1. McDonald, *Diary,* p. 178.

2. Frank Clark had been stationed in Winchester from

June 15 to July 1; by September he was back in Staunton.

3. Mrs. Strother Jones was expecting a baby, and her parents, living in Richmond since the Battle of Fredericksburg, were unlikely to come if there was any threat of Yankee occupation. Thomas B. Barton had been one of nineteen of Fredericksburg's leading citizens taken hostage by Federal forces in August 1862; he had been held for about six weeks in Capitol Prison in Washington, and was understandably reluctant to be in their power again. Silvanus J. Quinn, *The History of the City of Fredericksburg*, Richmond, Hermitage Press, 1908, p. 72.

4. Several Hardys were listed as craftsmen in the 1860 census; James Drake, sixty-two, and his son George, thirty-one, were both listed as "plaisterers" of Newtown; the Springdale overseer was William F. Rogers.

5. The Fagan family were stonecutters, whose "corner" was Loudoun and Cork streets. By this time the Confederacy so badly needed manpower that previously enacted conscription laws were being enforced. Lud had written Bolly on January 16 that several of his teachers, under forty-five, had to go. Julia Chase remarked that "several have been conscripted and some are already leaving town to get out of their clutches. Should this Act be carried out, there would be a general skedaddling on the part of the citizens here and there would not be 100 men left in the place." *Diary*, Aug. 20, transcript book 2, p. 16.

6. Robert J. Glass of Long Meadow, south of Opequon Village.

7. Jane Sheild, in Maryland. Winchester's unsettled and changeable situation meant that mail came from the North and South.

8. By this time he was with the Nitre and Mining Bureau, probably as one of its many civilian employees.

9. Lee, *Diary*, passim, August.

10. Ibid., Aug. 6, transcript p. 452.

11. Ibid., Aug. 7, transcript p. 454.

12. Ibid., Sept. 6, transcript p. 471.

13. Steele, op. cit., Aug. 1 and Nov. 8, pp. 81, 89.

14. Lee, *Diary*, Sept. 14, transcript p. 477.

15. Robert T. Barton letter of May 26, 1897, commenting on Rannie's manuscript. This incident would date before August 26, Robert's last day in Nitre and Mining.

16. The Rocklands ladies were Octavia, Mrs. Haxall; her daughters: Mary, seventeen; Charlotte, fifteen; Fannie, eleven; and Rosalie (or Lola), nine. Louisa Stone Triplett Haxall, sixteen, daughter of the Bolling W. Haxalls and summering at their plantation, was another of Rannie's second cousins.

17. General Lee had recommended "rigid enforcement of the death penalty" to discourage the increase in desertions. *O.R.* Series I, Vol. 29, Part 2, p. 650. In this instance a group of thirty men from the 1st and 3rd N.C. regiments (Steuart's brigade) had started for home, taking their arms; they fired on pursuing Confederate troops, killing an officer. The ten men caught were executed September 5 after being court-martialed. The incident was described at length in Casler, *Four Years*, pp. 188–90, where

he further stated that later deserters went to the enemy to avoid capture.

18. Mrs. Lee noted with pleasure brief visits by Strother and her nephew Bob Burwell, who were staying at Springdale, on September 10 and 11. Lee, *Diary*, transcript pp. 475–77.

19. Lud's father had died in the early hours of September 11. Lud was still at home with his mother.

20. Ben T. Holliday of Winchester was serving in Chew's Battery. This was apparently the fourth horse Tom Marshall lost, in a cavalry skirmish near Culpeper, September 19; it was also reimbursed by the C.S. Army.

21. Randolph, a nephew of Mrs. Jones, was then Ordnance Officer in Staunton.

22. Stuart's capture was another false rumor. The battles of Chickamauga and Chattanooga had been fought September 19 and 20.

23. Many Winchester Episcopalians took to attending the Kent Street Presbyterian Church, their minister having gone to the army and their church frequently in use by the Yankees. Rev. James A. Graham was the rector; Rev. Henderson Suter, of Grace P.E. Church in Berryville, had apparently been expected to preside that day.

CHAPTER 11

1. Lee, *Diary*, transcript pp. 502–3.

2. Ibid., transcript pp. 509–10.

3. Mrs. Jones's cousin, who had refugeed from Washington to Richmond, had died at age fifty-eight, leaving a young family.

4. Charles Marshall Barton Jones was born September 11, 1863.

5. Mrs. Barton, daughter Fanny, Robert, Martha and her two children, Anna Jones and the five Marshall children, ranging in age from fourteen to five.

6. William L. Clark's house had been sold on September 9 (and the furniture some six weeks later), but Susan continued to live in town, probably renting a house on Fort Hill. Many were available as so many inhabitants had refugeed south by this time.

7. This incident occurred October 18 while Stuart's cavalry was screening the retreat and was almost trapped near Auburn.

8. Generals John R. Cooke, W. W. Kirkland, and Carnot Posey. The latter's wound was severe, but he died of the ensuing infection on November 13. Losses were an estimated 1,900. Freeman, *Lee's Lieutenants*, Vol. 3, p. 246. Gen. A. P. Hill had hastily placed Heth's division in a position to be flanked, and it suffered heavy losses. Hill was rebuked but not arrested.

9. This suggests the revival of Robby's prewar flirtation with Bettie Colston, a cousin who lived near Charlottesville.

10. Cutshaw was well known to the family, having been nursed at the Bartons' for several months after the First Battle of Winchester. Due to a long convalescence and a stint as a prisoner at Fort McHenry, he was not fit to return to active duty until the fall. His service record indicated he was on detached duty at the post at Staunton, but VMI records suggest he was Asst. Commandant of cadets at this time.

11. Rannie was thinking of a career in the regular Confederate Army. Holliday, his first captain (in the 33rd Virginia Infantry), was by this time in the Confederate Congress. He had been invalided out of active service the previous winter following the loss of his right arm after being wounded at the Second Battle of Manassas.

12. Lee, *Diary,* Oct. 4, transcript p. 489.

13. Rosser missed his young wife and was known to have sought solace occasionally in drink. Freeman, *Lee's Lieutenants,* Vol. 3, p. 212ff.

14. Thomas B. Massie, 12th Virginia Cavalry.

15. Probably Capt. J. H. Magruder, Company B, 7th Virginia Cavalry, killed in Madison County. McDonald, *Laurel Brigade,* p. 388.

16. Graham, Martin F., and George F. Skoch, *Mine Run: A Campaign of Lost Opportunities,* Lynchburg, H. E. Howard, 1987, p. 57.

17. Raleigh Thomas Colston of Millwood, Clarke County, had commanded the regiment since August 1862, with this rank as of March 1863. He was a second cousin of Mrs. D. W. Barton. The unnamed captain must be Charles H. Stewart, a Captain in the 2nd Virginia and commanding the regiment in November and December. Frye, *2nd Virginia,* pp. 57–58, 134.

18. The ubiquitous J. A. Straith, surgeon, 2nd Virginia Infantry

19. Word apparently reached the Bartons (either from Martha or Captain Burgess) by December 4. Mrs. Lee "heard yesterday morning the sad news that Strother Barton had lost his leg at the battle near Germanna last Friday. He will bear it bravely, but it will be another bitter drop in Mrs. Barton's full cup of sorrow." *Diary,* Dec. 5, transcript p. 525.

20. Son of Rev. A. H. H. Boyd, in the Rockbridge Artillery, a friend of Robert's (and later, his law partner).

21. Betsy was the wife of Nathaniel P. Catlett of Staunton.

22. The cure-all, in this case for Fanny's consumption.

23. Mat's parents-in-law, Dr. and Mrs. A. S. Baldwin of Winchester, and her daughter Maria then age three.

24. This appears in *O.R.* Series I, Vol. 29, p. 850.

25. Dr. John Henry Stover Funk of Winchester had become colonel of the 5th Virginia Infantry the year before. Mortally wounded at the Third Battle of Winchester, September 19, 1864, he died at his father's house.

26. On July 4, 1863, at the graduation ceremonies he had been unable to escape, Bolling had been promoted to Fourth Corporal, Company B; apparently this had just been approved.

27. Morton's Ford is some seven miles east of Culpeper Court House, on the Rapidan.

CHAPTER 12

1. Cavalry activity of both armies was frequent and unpredictable. Martha had probably been home for some time when she visited the Williamses in Winchester in early February, and Mrs. Lee had a party for her. Lee, *Diary,* Feb. 5, transcript p. 550.

2. Col. Raleigh T. Colston of the 2nd Virginia Infantry had in fact died of his Mine Run wound on December 23, in Charlottesville.

3. Federal cavalry was ranging from Martinsburg, and Rosser from near New Market where the 7th Virginia Cavalry was camped in January. Tom did get a furlough that month.

4. Dr. Francis Taliaferro Stribling was Superintendent of the Western Lunatic Asylum from 1840 to 1874.

5. Her children: Stuart, five, and Maria, three.

6. Lee, *Diary,* Dec. 23, 1863, transcript p. 533.

7. Mrs. Philip Williams was the wife of their father's law partner. Their daughter Mary was married to Rev. James B. Avirett who had been chaplain of Ashby's brigade, but had resigned due to ill health and was by fall 1863 back in Winchester.

8. Brackets in these three lines represent a corner torn from the page.

9. The Davises lived south of Springdale at Sunnyside. Dr. Davis was in Richmond, but Charlie may still have been at home with his mother and sister. He enlisted June 4 in the 7th Virginia Cavalry, two months before his eighteenth birthday.

10. Dr. Conrad was about thirteen years older than Susie. Robert's second wife, Gertrude W. Baker, was born in 1871.

11. Tom Marshall had a furlough in January 1864; Marshall Jones, presumably still with Nitre and Mining, had some freedom to rove. Mrs. Lee mentioned to her diary that "Col. Marshall was at Spring Dale on Sunday [the 10th]." Lee, *Diary,* Jan. 12, transcript p. 543. Tom had returned to the regiment by February.

12. Rannie described this curious feature of the house referring to the 1873 photo: "It will be seen . . . that a wing of one story and an attic with a 'dormer' window appears on the left of the main central building. This attic room opens into a chamber adjoining in the main building." *Recollections,* p. 71.

13. Elsewhere Robert mentioned that Colonel Marshall had to take to the woods another time during this visit. Barton in Avirett, *Ashby,* pp. 308–9. Tom was exceedingly lucky. The Steele children witnessed another incident where the Jessie Scouts were more successful: "Jan 6th: . . . This evening at dark about four hundred Federals came to town. Some of them in gray. . . . They stopped [at Mary Nisewanger's] and asked for Confederate soldiers, and some children, thinking they were Rebels took them to Mrs. Nisewanger's back door. Capt. Blackford and Snodgrass had just gotten there and eaten supper. They ran out the back way, saw the Yanks coming. The Captain jumped the garden fence. Some of the Yanks ran after him. He shot one, and the same fellow shot him through the heart. He died in ten minutes." Steele, op. cit., p. 93.

14. Aunt Sally, Mrs. Robert R. Barton, lived in Lexington with her young children. The Natural Bridge was about fourteen miles south, and a popular excursion.

15. The Confederacy was to exchange old currency for new (at a complicated rate) in an effort to combat galloping inflation.

16. Carter Berkeley was a lieutenant in McClanahan's Battery. John N. Opie, VMI '64, 6th Virginia Cavalry,

had been badly wounded October 11 near Culpeper
Court House and was recuperating in Staunton.
Both were from Clarke County and may have been
known to the Bartons. Frank Clark's quartermaster
duties were at Staunton in early 1864.

17. Jennie (Virginia) and Nelly (Cornelia).

18. Her friend Laura Lee Burwell, Mrs. Lee's niece,
had left Winchester shortly after Christmas to visit
in the Confederacy, and was back by Easter. Lee,
Diary, Dec. 29 and Mar. 27, transcript pp. 535, 574.

19. "Jean Valjean" was one of five volumes of Victor
Hugo's *Les Misérables.* It had been recently trans-
lated and published in Richmond and was very
popular, giving rise to the nickname "Lee's
Miserables." Henry Kyd Douglas read it when a
prisoner of war in 1863, and Mrs. Lee mentioned on
February 20 that she was reading one part. Douglas,
I Rode with Stonewall, p. 257. Lee, *Diary,* transcript p. 559.

20. Col. Angus W. McDonald of Winchester had raised
the 7th Virginia Cavalry (which absorbed Ashby's
Mountain Rangers) in 1861 at the age of sixty-two.
In March 1862, he retired to command the home
guard at Winchester. His family refugeed to Lexington in July 1863, where he was appointed post
commander that November. His wife Cornelia's
diary is an important source for the war in Winchester and Lexington.

21. Mary's father, A. H. H. Stuart.

22. Their father's partner, Philip Williams, apparently
advised against Strother's running for Clerk of
County Court, but he must have had some agree-
ment with Joe. Joseph H. Sherrard, Jr., served in
Company D, 11th Virginia Cavalry and was by this
time Sergeant Major. He had been wounded several times and was absent with leave the first months
of 1864; he had been absent sick for most of 1863,
and that, coupled with Strother's remark, suggests
he was sick again. He returned to service April 1 and
was wounded again, badly, at Trevilians Station on
June 11.

23. Rosser's brigade was camped near Lexington in late
March.

24. Hale, *Four Years,* p. 341. In January, Dr. Boyd had
been arrested for the same reason, and taken to
Martinsburg, but was quickly released. Chase, *Diary,* Jan. 22, transcript p. 61.

25. Ann D. Williams to her son John J. Williams, April
18. Handley Library Archives, Philip Williams papers, 172 WFCHS.

26. Lee, *Diary,* Apr. 8, transcript pp. 578–79. Clayton
Williams was in Chew's artillery and Major Conrad
was Inspector General of Rosser's cavalry divison.

27. Ann D. Williams, op. cit. Maj. Fielding H. Calmes,
Company D, 23rd Virginia Cavalry, attacked about
200 Union troops with half their number, and took
32 prisoners. He was himself captured a few weeks
later and spent most of the rest of the war in Camp
Chase, Ohio.

28. R. J. Barton's second son, Randolph Barton, Jr.

29. Then Col. William Terry, his rank as brigadier
general dating from May 19, 1864.

30. Since the South had few hostelries and those only in
large towns, it was common to call upon strangers
when no cousins were available.

31. Mrs. Lee did not hear about the Barton boys until
she received a note from Dr. Nepe Baldwin on May
22. (Some of the rumors of the preceding week were
that one of the Williams boys had been killed; that
Mr. Sheild was dead in Maryland and Jane on her
way to the Bartons'; and that Fanny was "desperately ill at Vaucluse." Only the last of these was true.
Lee, *Diary,* May 13, transcript p. 599.) Willie was
admitted to a Richmond hospital on May 15; the
nature of his wound was such that he was not able to
return to the infantry. On September 12 he was
retired by a medical examining board, and later in
the year was detailed to the Invalid Corps for ordnance duty at Hanover Junction.

32. William C. Davis, *The Battle of New Market,* New
York, Doubleday & Co., 1975, pp. 196–97. At the
July 4, 1863 graduation, Bolling had been promoted
to Fourth Corporal, Company B.

33. Strother was posted in Staunton by May 29.

34. Couper, *New Market Cadets,* p. 18.

35. Certificate in Jones/Clark papers.

36. "Report of Capt. James F. Jones," *O.R.* Series I, Vol.
51 Supplement, pp. 1225–27; and Brice, *Conquest
of a Valley,* pp. 48–49, 96–101.

37. Moore, *Cannoneer,* p. 235ff. Mrs. John Moore,
Memoirs of a Long Life in Virginia, Lexington,
McClure, 1930, pp. 65–69, passim.

38. Wise, *End of an Era,* p. 313.

39. The sick old man was incarcerated at the military
prison at Wheeling until November 7. He died
three weeks after his release.

40. Address by Hon. John W. Daniel, Memorial of
General Jubal A. Early, S.H.S.P., Vol., 22, p. 296.

41. Mrs. Lee wrote May 25: "Anna Jones came in this
evening & gave us the correct account of the house
burning yesterday at Newtown. Hunter ordered
that three rebel houses should be burned, because
his wagon train had been fired into. [Maj. Timothy]
Quin[n, 1st N. Y. Cavalry] went to Mrs. [William A.]
Davis & told her to prepare to have hers fired; she
told him she could not & that he was mistaken if he
thought she would plead with him. He changed his
mind & burned those in Newtown." Lee, *Diary,*
transcript pp. 607–8. Five days later, the Union
troops sent by Hunter to burn the whole town
refused to do so.

42. This would have been part of Hunter's train going
south.

43. John S. Mosby organized his Partisan Rangers in
early 1863 and successfully harassed Federal forces
in northern Virginia from his base in Loudoun
County.

44. Dr. Stuart Baldwin, his daughters Sally, twenty-
eight, and Fannie, nineteen, Mrs. Anne T. Magill,
Ann Sherrard, the interim Episcopal minister
Thompson B. Maury, and the Lee/Burwell ladies.

45. In late 1863, the Rev. James B. Avirett had been
serving the Episcopalians during their minister's
absence with the army, apparently hoping for the
position at Christ Episcopal Church. Mrs. Lee frequently mentioned and deplored the possibility and
particularly disapproved after Mr. Maury had been
appointed. Lee, *Diary,* transcript pp. 488–611,
passim.

46. Ibid., May 29 and 30, transcript pp. 609–11. Mrs.

Crawford was the wife of Rev. William A. Crawford of the Old Opequon Church near Kernstown; they were near neighbors to Springdale and Carysbrooke, at Skirtwood Curve (now Hilandale). The Jones family graveyard is at some distance from Vaucluse, around a hill, and not visible from house or road.

47. Nancy was listed in David W. Barton's will as one of the slaves at the Market Street house.

48. On June 26, Mrs. Lee "was inexpressibly shocked . . . to hear Robbie Barton has had two hemorrhages." *Diary,* transcript p. 626.

49. Strother was certainly home in September, although he was still on the 2nd Virginia Infantry roster in October 1864 and his retirement from the Invalid Corps was not official until January.

50. Cutshaw ended the war as Inspector General and Lieutenant Colonel of Artillery, Second Corps. He was wounded April 6, 1865, at Sayler's Creek, and his leg was amputated the next day. He did not marry until 1876. *Confederate Veteran,* Feb. 1908, p. 84.

CHAPTER 13

1. On December 1, 1862, William M. Peyton and his wife acquired a tract of some 900 acres, known as Alta Vista, on Green Mountain in southern Albemarle County, about ten miles west of Scottsville. Albemarle County Court House, Deed Book 60, pp. 319–20.

2. Col. William Massie's plantation was Pharselia, near Massie's Mills, Nelson County. Colonel Massie had died in 1862, but his fourth wife, Maria, at this time forty-eight, was an able manager. Their daughter Florence was about sixteen.

3. C.S.A. Maj. Jno. B. Lady gave a voucher for sixteen cents per head per day for forage at Springdale in July 1864.

4. Alice Thomas was a daughter of Col. C. Keefer Thomas of the farm, Araby. She and her family had spent the hours of battle in the basement. Worthington, *Fighting for Time,* p. 104. In latter years, this incident had further amusing repercussions as Randolph Barton encountered Worthington, Commonwealth Attorney and later Judge of the Court of Appeals in Maryland. Worthington, six years old at the time of the battle, had watched it from the basement of his family's farm, adjacent to the Thomases'. His rendition differs in numerous details, including Barton's rank as colonel.

5. Early used the house as his headquarters July 11.

6. Mrs. Lee wrote that Mr. Williams was back from prison July 23 (transcript p. 650), and on August 6 Jed Hotchkiss mentioned that the return of Dr. Boyd had been negotiated for three weeks hence (p. 220); Julia Chase noted that Boyd got home September 11 (transcript p. 110).

7. Mrs. Lee mentioned seeing Rannie at least four times during this period and Frank Clark almost as often; and that Holmes Conrad was celebrating his marriage July 12. Lee, *Diary,* transcript pp. 634–68 passim.

8. Robert S. Burwell, one of Mrs. Lee's nephews, was

in the 2nd Virginia Infantry, and his need for a saddle suggests that he may have been serving in a staff position while near Winchester. Mrs. Lee recorded on September 18 that Rannie had come for dinner and spent the night, and then that he and Bob were off at 6:00 A.M. *Diary,* transcript pp. 684–85.

9. Elsewhere he described it as beyond "the turn of the turnpike at Burgess's." Randolph Barton, carbon copy of letter to Hon. Holmes Conrad, January 27, 1913.

10. The annex had been Hugh Holmes Lee's law office. Mrs. Lee, the Misses Lee, and Lal and Lute Burwell were all by this time experienced nurses. Mrs. Lee wrote that Rannie rode up wounded "after dinner." *Diary,* p. 685.

11. Estimates of total forces engaged are as many as 37,300 Federal troops versus 17,700 Confederates, of which 31,800 and 14,800 respectively are combined infantry and artillery. Stackpole, *Sheridan,* pp. 404–5.

12. William Myers's farm was north of Redbud Run, near what now is Route 661.

13. Soldiers on both sides shared the feeling that this battle was the worst that they had experienced. Wert, *From Winchester,* p. 102.

14. John H. Baldwin, "Johnny," was serving in the 2nd Virginia Infantry. The Bakers had a farm on the north side of the Berryville Pike, now commemorated as Baker's or Baker Lane. The tollgate was at Smithfield and National avenues.

15. Mrs. Lee identified one as Charlie Davenport, who was mortally wounded later in the day, dying September 25. Lee, *Diary,* Sept. 25, transcript p. 692.

16. Frank Clark, as a quartermaster officer, was in a position to commandeer a vehicle.

17. Lee, *Diary,* Sept. 19, transcript p. 686. Douglas, *I Rode with Stonewall,* p. 311, and Garnett, S.H.S.P., Vol. 27, pp. 6–7.

18. Brackets here and in the next three paragraphs represent interpolations from Robert's account in his 1897 letter. R. T. Barton to Randolph Barton, May 26, 1897.

19. Gen. Robert E. Rodes.

20. Marshall went to Staunton to convalesce with his sister Nannie Jones; then to Charlottesville to stay with his sister Agnes, Mrs. A. G. Taliaferro. R. T. Barton in Avirett, *Ashby,* p. 341.

21. Moore, *Cannoneer,* p. 162.

22. This Raleigh Colston was a first cousin of the colonel, and thirteen years older. His family of five children, ranging from about seventeen to nine, included Jeannie and Bettie. The house, which harbored many sick and wounded Confederates, still stands as Woodstock Hall. Bob Burwell may not have been able to return to active service; he was in Robertson Hospital in Richmond as late as November 1.

23. The disabled Gen. A. G. Taliaferro was in charge of the military post at Charlottesville. Paxton, *Marshall Family,* p. 197. Tom Marshall was probably there at the same time, recuperating from his August wound.

24. He was back by November 4 when he was assigned to Gen. William Terry's brigade.

CHAPTER 14

1. Belle Grove is just south of Middletown, in sight of Cedar Creek. The house was the headquarters of the Union command during the battle.
2. Putnam, *Richmond during the War,* p. 333.
3. The woods were not just "pretty," they were woodlots supplying firewood. None were left by the end of the war.
4. U.S. Gen. William Dwight commanded First Division, XIX Corps from that August until the following March.
5. The pass was dated October 16, 1864, and signed by G. L. Montague as "Lt. Col. & Pr. Mar." for Col. Oliver Edwards, post commander at Winchester and commanding the 3rd Brigade, First Division.
6. The wagon trains were often as many as 200 wagons, guarded by 1,000 infantry and 500 cavalry, due to the threat of the raiders. Tyler, *Recollections,* p. 293.
7. Dr. Philip C. Williams of Baltimore was the eldest son of Philip Williams by his first wife, Ann Hite.
8. Five Rectors appeared on the roster of Company A, 7th Virginia Cavalry. W. N. McDonald, *Laurel Brigade,* p. 386. Charles B. Davis, Susie's brother, was killed March 6, 1865.
9. R. T. Barton in Avirett, *Ashby and His Compeers,* pp. 314–15. "In 1865 I wrote a sketch of the life of Col. Marshall which was published . . . in a little book entitled 'Ashby & His Compeers.'" R. T. Barton, *Memoir,* p. 186.
10. Vaucluse was on a hill, which would have afforded some view of the action. The platform, a porch or balcony, can be seen in the photograph on page 251.
11. The Hite family had built, among others, Springdale, Shady Oak, and Belle Grove in the second half of the preceding century. Belle Grove was sold by the Hite heirs to the Cooley family in 1860. It now belongs to the National Trust for Historic Preservation.
12. The Davises lived on the northern outskirts of Newtown, less than a mile from Springdale. Maj. Gen. Horatio G. Wright, staying at Hanover Lodge, was commanding VI Corps. Gen. William H. Emory's army was encamped on the farm of Rev. William A. Crawford. (It is said that the general refrained from taking over the house itself because Mrs. Crawford was in confinement with baby Frank, born November 15, 1864.) Joseph J. Mahaney's residence in Kernstown had been used by occupying generals of both sides.
13. Susan Jones and her children continued to live in town. She had rented the farm to a tenant, storing many possessions there, although the more precious ones were in her mother-in-law's safekeeping. She apparently had a share in the Vaucluse produce.
14. U.S. Capt. Mason Tyler wrote to his brother from Winchester, October 27: "Yesterday and day before we arrested nearly one hundred citizens of disloyal tendencies, and at present have them confined. . . . Some old men sixty or seventy years of age and much broken down with the infirmities of old age are there." Tyler, *Recollections,* p. 302. Robert Y. Conrad endured another imprisonment, at first in Martinsburg in early November where his brother

D. Holmes Conrad was able to provide and negotiate some comforts for him. D. H. Conrad to Mrs. R. Y. Conrad, November 3. Handley Library Archives, THL 1151. From Martinsburg, R. Y. Conrad was taken to the military prison at Wheeling.
15. Rev. J. Thompson Maury, at Christ P.E. Church, was arrested twice for refusing to pray for the President of the United States. Hale, *Four Valiant Years,* p. 492.
16. Mrs. Lee lamented November 16: "Another blow has fallen on that doomed family at Spring Dale, Col. Tom Marshall was killed at Vaucluse on Saturday, in Rosser's fight, another family of helpless children left dependent on Mrs. Barton. Mat writes word Gen. Dwight has his Hd Qrs in their yard & also that Sheridan has ordered that their family shall be provided for. They have been robbed of almost everything." On December 2: "I am saved the degradation of receiving rations from the Yankees; Mrs. Barton & the Strother Joneses & Joseph Barton have to depend upon them; we may be reduced to it." Lee, *Diary,* transcript pp. 722, 730.
17. By this time the only sweetener available.
18. Bev was presumably still in Rockingham County with Nitre and Mining. This must refer to late September when Federal forces reached Harrisonburg and for two weeks waged a systematic campaign of destruction in that part of the Valley.
19. C. Maury Jones, op. cit., pp. 2–3.
20. "The father's son will avenge his death."
21. Barton had evidently been reading *Pilgrim's Progress* by John Bunyan.
22. The Sheild children were Sally, about eleven, Fanny, nine, and Charley, eight.
23. Strother had been posted in Staunton the previous spring, and presumably until he resigned. The official date of his "retirement" from the Invalid Corps was January 15, 1865, but he was home long before then.
24. Apparently the Sheilds had offered to take the Marshall children after their father's death.
25. Wartime inflation had affected all goods, and in the Confederacy even cheap calico had multiplied by about 18,000 percent.
26. Emma Riely, a Winchester girl, heard that the Union generals "at Christmas had a tree for them. . . . The next morning, besides the small things, such as candies, cakes, and fruits, there was a suit of clothes each for the boys and a dress and pair of shoes each for the girls, and they were made very happy." Macon, *Recollections,* pp. 105–6.
27. Lee, *Diary,* Dec. 26, 1864, transcript p. 748.
28. Letter of December 27, 1864, certifying Joseph M. Barton as a "good peacable citizen." Handley Library Archives, Lewis N. Barton Papers, WFCHS 485.
29. Her cousin Maria Baldwin, Stuart's sister, four.
30. Lee, *Diary,* Feb. 25 and 26, transcript pp. 789–90.
31. Ibid., Mar. 7, transcript p. 797. Charles B. Davis, Susie's brother, was killed in action at Rude's Hill, as the ladies learned that night. Laura Lee, *History,* Mar. 7, p. 120.
32. Ibid., Mar. 14, transcript p. 801ff.
33. It must have been March; at the time of Martha's February 25 letter, the trip was still in the planning stages.

34. Anna's "lover" was Nepe Baldwin, surgeon of the 33rd Virginia Infantry. Robby's friend killed at the First Battle of Winchester was the son of Robert McKim, "gentleman," of Baltimore.
35. Lt. Col. Julius G. Tucker was in command, and Bolling was first lieutenant in Company D, under Capt. Benjamin A. Colonna, another New Market cadet.
36. Mary Boykin Miller Chesnut, *Mary Chesnut's Civil War*, edited by C. Vann Woodward, New Haven, Yale University Press, 1981, pp. 661, 678, 683, 685.
37. National Archives, Compiled Service Records, Record Group 109, A.I.G.O. Letters Received.
38. James W. Thomson, VMI '64, was killed April 6.
39. The Haxall house still stands, as the Women's Club, at what is now 211 East Franklin Street. According to Louisa T. Haxall, later Mrs. Charles K. Harrison of Baltimore, "In our house, as in many in Richmond, one large room was devoted to the sick and wounded soldiers. The cots were arranged as in a hospital, and filled again as soon as emptied." Quoted in De Leon, *Belles, Beaux . . .*, p. 127.
40. The appointment was made February 10, 1865, and accepted four days later.
41. Napoleon Bonaparte McLauglen, Brevet Brigadier General, was in Libby Prison for the duration after his capture at Fort Stedman.
42. Clement Anselm Evans had been appointed Brigadier General the previous May, and had taken over Gordon's old brigade in September He was later a minister and editor of the twelve-volume *Confederate Military History*.
43. Walker had returned to duty not long after his Spotsylvania wound, but had not had a field command until he was given Gen. John Pegram's division following the latter's death at Hatcher's Run, February 6, 1865.
44. Capt. Robert Moorman Sims had been on Gen. A. P. Hill's staff, but since Hill's death on April 2 at Petersburg, had been serving as aide on Longstreet's staff.
45. Sims described this as a "crash towel" bought for "$20 or $40 in Richmond." R. M. Sims letter of May 22, 1886, in J. L. Smith, ed., *History of the 118th Pennsylvania Volunteers Corn Exchange Regiment*, Philadelphia, J. L. Smith, 1905, 2nd ed., p. 590. The towel is well traveled. For many years it was deposited at the Smithsonian with other Custer memorabilia belonging to Mrs. Custer. When the Custer Battlefield National Monument was established in Montana, the towel and the other Custer relics were removed there. It is now, appropriately, in the museum at Appomattox Court House National Historical Park. Perhaps understandably, official reports on the final actions were scanty. After writing this memoir, Barton must have come to doubt his impression that Myers was the other of Sims's escorts, and he endeavored to open correspondence with witnesses to the flag transaction, including U.S. Col. E. W. Whittaker, who was with Custer.
46. Lee, *Diary*, Apr. 11–17, transcript pp. 812–16.
47. Writer altered verbiage in original galleys to this from: "ruggedness will be softened, so that with them . . ."

CHAPTER 15

1. Greenwood Cemetery in Brooklyn was a tourist attraction because of its hundreds of acres of landscaped hills and vistas of the bay. Central Park, recently laid out, was still a novelty.
2. Bolling's carte de visite is reproduced on page 361.
3. Ann C. R. Jones to Lucy Parkhill, May 19, 1863.
4. According to some estimates, there were 20,000 Federal troops in Frederick County in May 1865. Hale, *Four Valiant Years*, p. 521.
5. Robert described the office as "immediately opposite the north side of the Court House facing the first two windows on that side." R. T. Barton, *Memoir*, p. 4.
6. Ibid., pp. 5–6.
7. Ibid., p. 182.
8. Nepe Baldwin never remarried; he and his son lived with his parents in Winchester.
9. Paxton, *Marshall Family*, p. 202, who gives October 9, 1866, as the date of the murder. James was buried at Emmanuel Church about a mile from Woodside.
10. The F. L. Marshall family was with Nannie in the early seventies.
11. The Stonewall Cemetery was dedicated on Turner Ashby's birthday, June 6, 1866, which became Confederate Memorial Day. The Ashby brothers were reinterred there on October 25, 1866. The nearby National Cemetery, dedicated April 8, 1866, contains the graves of over 4,400 Union soldiers killed in battle in the northern Valley.
12. Frank P. Clark to William L. Clark, Jr., April 30, 1868.
13. Robert E. Lee was then President of Washington College in Lexington; his son G. W. Custis Lee was a professor at VMI.
14. Aunt Mary appears to have been the wife of Andrew Keys, Agnes's eldest uncle.
15. Susan Davis Conrad, op. cit., p. 2.
16. The railroad in conjecture, the Winchester & Strasburg, was part of the B.&O. system. It was begun the following spring, and the small station established at the head of the mill pond was called Bartonsville.
17. Williams's health suffered during the war years and was probably destroyed by his imprisonment in 1864, as was that of the Rev. A. H. H. Boyd who had died December 16, 1865, at only fifty-three. On April 2, sixty-five-year-old Williams suffered a fatal attack of apoplexy in court at Woodstock.
18. R. T. Barton, *Memoir*, p. 20.
19. Agnes was in Paris in early April when General Lee visited Baltimore.
20. Agnes Kirkland Barton note in her copy of *Recollections*.
21. Ann C. R. Jones to Harriet Parkhill, March 22, 1875.
22. Ann C. R. Jones to Lucy Parkhill, June 23, 1874.
23. Ann C. R. Jones to Agnes K. Barton, May 17, 1871. The Sheilds were living in Baltimore, the Reverend being at St. John's Church in Mt. Washington. George Norton Sheild was born July 22, 1871.
24. Maria Baldwin, eleven, Fanny Sheild, sixteen, and the new baby.
25. Ann C. R. Jones to Agnes and Randolph Barton, November 23, 1871.

26. Ella J. Gibson was the daughter of Prof. William Gibson, M.D., of Newport, R.I.
27. The house and a portion of the farm was sold to R. F. Harrison, the deed of sale dated September 16, 1873. The contract had been made June 25.
28. Letters from Fannie L. Barton to Bolling W. Barton, September 30 and October 26, 1873.
29. R. T. Barton, *Memoir/Journal,* p. 303.
30. Ann C. R. Jones to Lucy Parkhill, June 22, 1874. Willie had died April 14.
31. Ibid.
32. Ann C. R. Jones to Lucy Parkhill, August 21, 1876.
33. Ann C. R. Jones to Harriet Parkhill, March 22, 1875.
34. R. T. Barton, *Memoir,* pp. 21–22, 17.
35. Redmond C. Stewart, at the memorial services. *Recollections,* 2nd ed., appendix, p. 6.
36. Robert T. Barton, *Memoir,* p. 228.
37. Robert T. Barton, *Memoir/Journal,* Vol. 3, p. 1.
38. Fannie L. Barton to Bolling W. Barton, October 26, 1873.
39. Garnett had become a professor and teacher of agriculture at various Baltimore schools, at St. John's College in Maryland, and at the University of Virginia.
40. *Confederate Veteran,* 1900, p. 483.
41. Some of these comments appear in earlier chapters.
42. R. T. Barton, *Memoir/Journal,* Vol. 3, p. 87.
43. Arthur M. Field was city manager of Winchester then and again in the 1930s.
44. Robert T. Barton to Randolph J. Barton, December 24, 1916.
45. Baltimore *Sun,* March 16, 1921.
46. Memorial services, op. cit.
47. Typescript of a speech written for delivery in Winchester on Confederate Memorial Day, c. 1908.

SOURCES

The most important papers of the Barton and Jones families, over 200 items, were found in private hands. The majority of them are published herein.

In transcribing the documents, the original spelling has been retained, but some contractions and abbreviations have been spelled out and punctuation and paragraphing modernized for the reader's ease. Portions of Randolph and Robert T. Barton's memoirs have been rearranged to fit the chronological presentation.

Previous transcriptions of some documents in the Handley Library Archives have been referred to, and the efforts of the late Charles Cochran, Lewis N. Barton, Garland R. Quarles, and others are gratefully acknowledged. Arthur M. Field, Jr.'s transcript of his grandfather Robert T. Barton's memoir/journal has been invaluable. In every case I have read and altered transcripts against the original documents, so any lingering errors are mine.

°Mrs. C. Marshall Barton, Jr.—Wartime letters to Bolling W. Barton; two typescript speeches by Randolph J. Barton; 1867 letters by Randolph J. Barton; letter by Mary Custis Lee, Dec. 1869; letters by Ann C. R. Jones to Agnes and Randolph Barton; letter by Acelie Togno; letter by Thomas Marshall to R. T. Barton, 1864.

°Eleanor J. Burleson—Papers and letters by, to, and about Francis Buckner Jones; letter by David R. Barton; letter by Maria Barton Marshall; letters by Frank P. Clark and J. Peyton Clark; letter by W. S. Jones; letter by Ann C. R. Jones, Oct. 1863; letter by Mary E. B. Jones, 1862; papers of Jones/Clark/Crawford families.

C. Maury Jones, Jr.—Memoirs by W. Strother Jones (1857–1925) and C. Maury Jones.

Edith Barton Sheerin—Robert T. Barton's memoir/journal and his account of the First Battle of Winchester; letters to Robert T. Barton from Thomas Marshall, W. Strother Barton, Martha Barton Baldwin (and children), Randolph J. Barton (1865), Frances J. Barton; correspondence and papers relating to Robert T. Barton's medical discharge and his passage to Maryland; 1858 diary by David R. Barton; letter by Bolling W. Barton to David W. Barton; "Argument for George W. Kerfoot" by David W. Barton; letter by David W. Barton to Gen. Robert H. Milroy; resolution of Bench and Bar of Frederick County, 1863; letter by James B. Burgess; J. B. Lady voucher received by Frances L. Barton; Jones family Bible.

Betty H. Stewart—Susan Davis Conrad, "Springdale," original typescript.

E. C. Teviotdale—Letter by Joseph M. Barton to Gen. Philip H. Sheridan.

Colin J. S. Thomas, Jr.—Letters from Randolph J. Barton to Robert T. Barton, 1863–64; letter by Anne C. Thomas; letter by Bolling W. Barton to Randolph J. Barton; letter by David W. Barton, October 26, 1862; letter by Agnes Kirkland; letter

by Mary Custis Lee, June 1869; letter by Frances L. Barton to Agnes Kirkland; letters by Frances L. Barton to Bolling W. Barton, 1873; letter by Abner C. Hopkins to Randolph J. Barton; letters by Robert T. Barton to Randolph J. Barton, 1897 and 1916.

Documents from the Handley Library Archives are published courtesy of the Handley Library and the Winchester-Frederick County Historical Society.

Handley Library—Letters by Ann Cary Randolph Jones to Lucy R. Parkhill and Harriet R. Parkhill, and to Francis B. Jones, 1861.

Conrad family papers (typescripts).

Julia Chase diary.

Winchester-Frederick County Historical Society—Francis Buckner Jones, 1862 diary, John Peyton Clark, 1862 diary.

Mary Greenhow Lee (Mrs. H. H.)—Diary 1862–65.

Also: Lewis N. Barton papers, Philip Williams papers, various wartime diaries.

County Clerk's Office, Frederick County Court House—Birth, death, marriage, land transfers, land taxes, will records.

Manuscript Division, Earl Gregg Swem Library, College of William and Mary, Williamsburg—Laura Lee, *A History of Our Captivity.*

U. S. Census Office, population schedules of the census of the United States 1850–1900. National Archives Microfilm Publications.

U.S. National Archives and Record Service—Compiled Service Records of Confederate Soldiers Who Served in Organizations from the State of Virginia.

Virginia Military Institute, Archives, Lexington—Letters by David W. Barton to Col. Francis H. Smith; letter by Charles Marshall Barton to Joseph Marx Barton; letter by Beverley R. Jones, 1910.

Virginia State Archives—Personal property tax records.

°These collections will be donated in 1994 to the Handley Library Archives, Winchester, Virginia, which includes the collections of the Winchester-Frederick County Historical Society.

SELECT BIBLIOGRAPHY

Books that have been of significant use, among the many which have been consulted, are listed below.

Ashby, Thomas A. *Life of Turner Ashby*. New York, Neale Publishing Co., 1914.

Atlas of Frederick County. Philadelphia, D. J. Lake & Co., 1885.

Avirett, James B., comp. *The Memoirs of General Turner Ashby and His Compeers*. Baltimore, Selby & Dulany, 1867.

Barton, Mary Neill. "Barton-Tidball-Thruston Families. Also a Little about the Ward, Holmes, and Allen Families." Privately printed pamphlet.

Barton, Randolph. *Recollections*. Baltimore, privately reprinted, 1949. 2nd edition.

Barton, Randolph. "Remarks of Major Randolph Barton." Lawyer's Round Table. Baltimore, 1919. Privately printed pamphlet.

Baylor, George. *Bull Run to Bull Run, or, Four Years in the Army of Northern Virginia . . . The Baylor Light Horse*. Richmond, B. F. Johnston, 1900.

Berkeley, Henry. *Four Years in the Confederate Artillery*. Edited by William H. Runge. Chapel Hill, University of North Carolina Press, 1966.

Beyer, Edward. *Description of the Album of Virginia or the Old Dominion*. Richmond, Enquirer Book and Job Printing, 1857. 3 volumes.

Bigelow, John. *The Campaign of Chancellorsville, a Strategic and Tactical Study*. New Haven, Yale University Press, 1910.

Blackford, Lancelot Minor. *Mine Eyes Have Seen the Glory. . . .* Cambridge, Harvard University Press, 1954.

Blackford, Susan Leigh, comp. *Letters from Lee's Army . . .* New York, Charles Scribner's Sons, 1947.

Blackford, William W. *War Years with Jeb Stuart*. New York, Charles Scribner's Sons, 1945.

Boatner, Mark M. III. *The Civil War Dictionary*. New York, David McKay Company, 1959.

Bond, Christiana. *Memories of General Robert E. Lee*. Baltimore, Norman Remington Co., 1926.

Brice, Marshall Moore. *Conquest of a Valley*. Charlottesville, University Press of Virginia, 1965.

Brock, R.A., ed. *The Appomattox Roster*. New York, Antiquarian Press Ltd., 1962.

Brooks, Stewart. *Civil War Medicine*. Springfield, Ill., Charles C. Thomas, 1966.

Brown, Stuart E., Jr., comp. *Rev. Thomas Barton and Some of His Descendants and Some of Their In-Laws*. Berryville, Virginia Book Co., 1988.

Cartmell, Thomas Kemp. *Shenandoah Valley Pioneers and Their Descendants. A History of Frederick County, Virginia*. Winchester, Eddy Press, 1909.

Casler, John O. *Four Years in the Stonewall Brigade*. Girard, Kansas, 1906. 2nd edition.

Chambers, Lenoir. *Stonewall Jackson*. New York, William Morrow & Co., 1959. 2 volumes.

Confederate Veterans magazine, Nashville. 1893–1932.

Couper, William. *One Hundred Years at V. M. I.* Richmond, Garrett and Massie, 1939.

Couper, William. *The V. M. I. New Market Cadets. Biographical Sketches. . . .* Charlottesville, Michie, 1933.

Cunningham, H. H. *Doctors in Gray*. Baton Rouge, Louisiana State University Press, 1960. 2nd edition.

Dabney, Robert Lewis. *Life and Campaigns of Lieutenant-General Thomas J. Jackson*. New York, Blelock & Co., 1866.

Davis, William C. *The Battle of New Market*. New York, Doubleday & Co., 1975.

De Leon, Thomas C. *Belles, Beaux and Brains of the 60's*. New York, G. W. Dillingham Co., 1909.

De Leon, Thomas C. *Four Years in Rebel Capitals*. Mobile, Gossip Printing Co., 1890.

Douglas, Henry Kyd. *I Rode with Stonewall*. Chapel Hill, University of North Carolina Press, 1940.

Driver, Robert J., Jr. *The 1st and 2nd Rockbridge Artillery*. Lynchburg, H. E. Howard, 1987.

Driver, Robert J., Jr. *The 1st Virginia Cavalry*. Lynchburg, H.E. Howard, 1991.

Duer, Thomas Marshall. *The Duer-Marshall Family*. Baltimore, privately printed, 1944.

DuPont, Henry Algernon. *The Campaign of 1864 in the Valley of Virginia and the Expedition to Lynchburg*. New York, National Americana Society, 1925.

Ebert, Rebecca A., and Teresa Lazazzera. *Frederick County Virginia. From the Frontier to the Future. A Pictorial History*. Norfolk, The Downing Co., 1988.

Evans, Clement A., ed. *Confederate Military History*. Atlanta, 1899. Vol. 2. *Maryland* by Brig. Gen. Bradley Johnson. *West Virginia* by Col. Robert White. Vol. 3. *Virginia* by Maj. Jed Hotchkiss. Extended editions.

Fonerden, C. A. *A Brief History of the Military Career of Carpenter's Battery*. New Market, Henkel & Co., 1911.

Freeman, Douglas Southall. *R. E. Lee: A Biography*. New York, Charles Scribner's Sons, 1934.

Freeman, Douglas Southall. *Lee's Lieutenants. A Study in Command*. New York, Charles Scribner's Sons, 1942–1944.

Frye, Dennis E. *2nd Virginia Infantry*. Lynchburg, H. E. Howard, 1984.

Gold, Thomas D. *History of Clarke County Virginia and Its Connection with the War Between the States*. Berryville, privately printed, 1914.

Goldsborough, W. W. *The Maryland Line in the Confederate States Army*. Baltimore, Kelly, Piet & Co., 1869.

Goolrick, John T. *Historic Fredericksburg. The Story of an Old Town*. Richmond, Whittet & Shepperson, 1922.

Gordon, John Brown. *Reminiscences of the Civil War*. New York, Charles Scribner's Sons, 1903.

Hale, Laura Virginia. *Four Valiant Years in the Lower*

Shenandoah Valley, 1861–1865. Front Royal, Hathaway Publishing, 1986. 4th edition.

Hotchkiss, Jedediah. *Make Me a Map of the Valley. The Civil War Journal of Stonewall Jackson's Topographer*. Edited by Archie P. McDonald. Dallas, Southern Methodist University, 1973.

Howard, McHenry. *Reminiscences of a Maryland Confederate Soldier and Staff Officer under Johnston, Jackson and Lee*. Baltimore, Williams & Wilkins, 1914.

Howe, Henry. *Historical Collections of Virginia, containing . . . biographical sketches, anecdotes &c relating to its history & antiquities, together with geographical and statistical descriptions. . . .* Charleston, S.C., 1856.

Jacob, Diane B., and Judith Moreland Arnold. *A Virginia Military Institute Album, 1839–1910*. Charlottesville, University Press of Virginia, 1982.

Johnston, Angus J., II. *Virginia Railroads in the Civil War*. Chapel Hill, University of North Carolina Press for the Virginia Historical Society, 1961.

Jones, Virgil Carrington. *Grey Ghosts and Rebel Raiders*. New York, Henry Holt and Co., 1956.

Keen, Nancy Travis. *"Confederate Prisoners of War at Fort Delaware."* Pamphlet, reprinted from Delaware History, vol. 13, no. 1 (April 1968) for the Fort Delaware Society.

Kellogg, Sanford C. *The Shenandoah Valley and Virginia, 1861–1865; a War Study*. New York, Neale Publishing Co., 1903.

Kercheval, Samuel. *A History of the Valley of Virginia*. Woodstock, J. Gatewood, 1850.

Krick, Robert K. *Lee's Colonels. A Biographical Register. . . .* Dayton, Press of Morningside Bookshop, 1979.

Krick, Robert K. *Roster of Confederate Dead in the Fredericksburg Confederate Cemetery*. Fredericksburg, 1974.

Long, E. B., and Barbara Long. *The Civil War Day by Day, An Almanac 1861–1865*. Garden City, Doubleday & Co., 1971.

Longstreet, James. *From Manassas to Appomattox, Memoirs of the Civil War in America*. Philadelphia, J. B. Lippincott Co., 1896.

Macon, Emma Cassandra Riely and Reuben Conway. *Reminiscences of the Civil War*. Cedar Rapids, privately printed, 1906.

Marshall, Fielding Lewis. *Recollections and Reflections of . . .* Compiled by Maria Newton Marshall. Orange, Va., privately printed, 1911. Privately reprinted, c. 1988.

McClellan, H. B. *The Life and Campaigns of Major General J. E. B. Stuart*. With an introduction and notes by Burke Davis. Bloomington, Indiana University Press, 1958.

McDonald, Cornelia. *A Diary with Reminiscences of the War and Refugee Life in the Shenandoah Valley, 1860–1865*. Nashville, Cellom & Glertner, 1934.

McDonald, William Naylor. *A History of the Laurel Brigade, originally The Ashby Cavalry of the Army of Northern Virginia, and Chew's Battery*. Edited by Bushrod C. Washington. Baltimore, privately printed, 1907.

McGuire, Judith White Brockenbrough. *Diary of a Southern Refugee*. Richmond, J. W. Randolph & English, 1889.

McKim, Randolph H. *A Soldier's Recollections*. New York, Longman's Green & Co., 1910.

Moore, Edward A. *The Story of a Cannoneer Under Stonewall Jackson*. New York, Neale Publishing Co., 1907.

Morton, Frederic. *The Story of Winchester in Virginia. The Oldest Town in the Shenandoah Valley*. Strasburg, Shenandoah Publishing House, 1925.

Neese, George M. *Three Years in the Confederate Horse Artillery by . . . a Gunner in Chew's Battery*. New York, Neale Publishing Co., 1911.

Norris, J.E. *History of the Lower Shenandoah Valley, Counties of Frederick, Berkeley, Jefferson and Clarke*. Chicago, A. Warner & Co., 1890.

Opie, John N. *A Rebel Cavalryman with Lee, Stuart and Jackson*. Chicago, W.B. Conkey Co., 1899.

Paxton, John Gallatin, ed. *Memoir and Memorials. Elisha Franklin Paxton, Brigadier General C.S.A. . . .* New York, privately printed, 1907.

Paxton, William McClung. *The Marshall Family, or a Genealogical Chart of the Descendants of John Marshall and Elizabeth Markham . . .* Cincinnati, R. Clarke & Co., 1885.

Phillips, Edward H. *The Lower Shenandoah Valley during the Civil War; the Impact of the War upon the Civilian Population, and upon Civil Institutions*. Ph.D. thesis. Chapel Hill, University of North Carolina, 1958.

Poague, William Thomas. *Gunner with Stonewall. Reminiscences of. . . .* A memoir written for his children. Edited by Monroe F. Cockrell. Jackson Tenn., McCowat Mercer, 1957.

Pond, George E. *The Shenandoah Valley in 1864*. New York, Charles Scribner's Sons, 1883.

Putnam, Sallie A. (Brock). *In Richmond during the War. Four Years of Personal Observation, by a Richmond Lady*. New York, G. W. Carleton, 1867.

Quarles, Garland R. *Occupied Winchester 1861–1865*. Winchester, Farmers and Merchants National Bank, 1976.

Quarles, Garland R. *Some Old Homes in Frederick County, Virginia*. Winchester, Farmers and Merchants National Bank, 1971.

Quarles, Garland R. *The Story of One Hundred Old Homes in Winchester, Virginia*. Winchester, Winchester-Frederick County Historical Society, 1993. Revised edition.

Reidenbaugh, Lowell. *33rd Virginia Infantry*. Lynchburg, H. E. Howard, 1987.

Robertson, James I., Jr., editor-in-chief. *An Index-Guide to the Southern Historical Society Papers. 1876–1959*. Millwood, N.Y., Kraus, c. 1980. 2 volumes.

Robertson, James I., Jr. *The Stonewall Brigade*. Baton Rouge, Louisiana State University Press, 1963.

Russell, William Greenway. *What I Know about Winchester. Recollections of . . . 1800–1891*. Reprinted from *The Winchester News* by The Winchester-Frederick County Historical Society. Winchester-Frederick County Historical Society Papers Vol. 2. Edited by Garland R. Quarles and Lewis Neill Barton. Winchester, 1953.

Scheel, Eugene M. Frederick County. City of Winchester. Commonwealth of Virginia. [MAP] Surveyed and Drawn by . . . for the Farmers and Merchants National Bank. Winchester, 1974.

Selby, John M. *The Stonewall Brigade*. Reading (England), Osprey Publ., 1971.

Selby, John M. *Stonewall Jackson as Military Commander*. Princeton, Van Nostrand, 1968.

Slaughter, Philip. *Memoir of the Life of Rt. Rev. William Meade, D.D.* . . . Cambridge, J. Wilson & Son, 1885.

Southern Historical Society. Papers. 1876–1959. 52 volumes.

Stackpole, Edward J. *Drama on the Rappahannock. The Fredericksburg Campaign*. Harrisburg, Military Service Publishing Co., 1957.

Stackpole, Edward J. *Sheridan in the Shenandoah. Jubal Early's Nemesis*. Harrisburg, The Stackpole Co., 1961.

Steiner, Paul E. *Disease in the Civil War. Natural Biological Warfare in 1861–1865*. Springfield, Ill., Charles C. Thomas, 1968.

Tanner, Robert Gaither. *Stonewall in the Valley, Thomas J. "Stonewall" Jackson's Shenandoah Valley Campaign, Spring, 1862*. Garden City, Doubleday & Co., 1976.

Taylor, James E. *With Sheridan up the Shenandoah*. Dayton, Western Reserve Historical Society, 1989.

Taylor, Richard. *Destruction and Reconstruction. Personal Experiences in the Late War*. New York, D. Appleton and Co., 1879.

Tyler, Mason Whiting. *Recollections of the Civil War*. New York, G. P. Putnam's Sons, 1902.

U.S. War Department. *Atlas to Accompany the Official Records of the War of the Rebellion*. Washington, D.C., 1891–95.

U.S. War Department. *List of Staff Officers of the Confederate States Army*. Washington, D.C., 1891.

U.S. War Department. *War of the Rebellion. A Compilation of the Official Records of the Union and Confederate Armies.* . . . Washington, D.C., 1864–1927. 128 volumes.

Vandiver, Frank E. *Jubal's Raid. General Early's Famous Attack on Washington in 1864*. New York, McGraw-Hill Book Co., 1960.

Vandiver, Frank E. *Mighty Stonewall*. New York, McGraw-Hill Book Co., 1957.

Virginia Military Institute. *Register of Former Cadets. Centennial Edition. Virginia Military Institute, Lexington, Va.* Roanoke, Roanoke Printing Co., 1939.

Walker, Charles D. *Memorial, Virginia Military Institute. Biographical Sketches of the Graduates and Eleves . . . Who Fell during the War between the States*. Philadelphia, J. B. Lippincott & Co., 1875.

Warner, Ezra J. *Generals in Gray*. Baton Rouge, Louisiana State University Press, 1959.

Wayland, John W. *Stonewall Jackson's Way: Route, Method, Achievement*. Staunton, McClure, 1940.

Wert, Jeffry D. *From Winchester to Cedar Creek. The Shenandoah Campaign of 1864*. Carlisle, South Mountain Press, 1987.

Williams, Richard Pardee. *The High School. A History of the Episcopal High School in Virginia at Alexandria*. Boston, Vincent-Curtis, 1964.

Winchester-Frederick County Historical Society. *Journal*. 1986–1992. Vols. 1–6.

Winchester-Frederick County Historical Society. Papers. Especially Vol. 3, 1955. "Diaries, Letters and Recollections of the War Between the States," edited by Garland R. Quarles.

Wise, John S. *The End of an Era*. Boston, Houghton Mifflin Co., 1899.

Wise, Jennings C. *The Long Arm of Lee, or the History of the Artillery of the Army of Northern Virginia.* . . . Lynchburg, J. P. Bell Co., 1915.

Wise, Jennings C. *The Military History of the Virginia Military Institute from 1839–1875*. Lynchburg, J. P. Bell Co., 1915.

Worthington, Glenn H. *Fighting for Time, . . . or, The Battle That Saved Washington*. Frederick, Frederick County Historical Society, 1932.

$\mathscr{Index}$